THE
MACMILLAN
VISUAL
DICTIONARY

THE
MACMILLAN
VISUAL
DICTIONARY

Unabridged Compact Edition

MACMILLAN • USA

Library of Congress Cataloging-in-Publication Data

The Macmillan visual dictionary / (compiled by) Jean-Claude Corbeil, Ariane Archambault.

   p.   cm.

   Includes index.

   ISBN 0-02-860814-3 -- ISBN 0-02-860810-0 (pbk.)

   1. Picture dictionaries, English. 2. Handbooks, vade-mecums, etc.
I. Corbeil, Jean-Claude. II. Archambault, Ariane.

PE1629. M34 1995

423'. 1--dc20   95-20838

                                                             CIP

Created and produced
by Québec/Amérique International
a division of
Éditions Québec/Amérique Inc.
425, rue Saint-Jean-Baptiste, Montréal, Québec H2Y 2Z7
Tel. : (514) 393-1450 Fax : (514) 866-2430

Copyright © 1995, by Éditions Québec/Amérique Inc.

Published under license in the United States by Macmillan General Reference, a division of Macmillan, Inc.
MACMILLAN

A Simon & Schuster Macmillan company

1633 Broadway

New York, NY 10019-6785

MACMILLAN is a registered trademark of Macmillan, Inc.

First American Paperback Edition , 10 9 8 7 6 5 4 3 2 1

Printed in U.S.A.

ENGLISH LANGUAGE UNABRIDGED COMPACT EDITION
Natalie Chapman - *Publisher*
John Michel - *Senior Editor*
Susan Joseph - *Production Director*
Matt Hannafin - *Production Editor*

EDITORIAL STAFF FOR THE ORIGINAL EDITION
Jacques Fortin - *Publisher*
Jean-Claude Corbeil - *Editor-in-chief*
Ariane Archambault - *Assistant Editor*
François Fortin - *Illustrations Editor*
Jean-Louis Martin - *Art Director*

COMPUTER GRAPHIC ARTISTS
Jacques Perrault
Anne Tremblay
Jocelyn Gardner
Christiane Beauregard
Michel Blais
Rielle Lévesque
Marc Lalumière
Stéphane Roy
Alice Comtois
Jean-Yves Ahern
Benoît Bourdeau

COMPUTER COPYEDITING
Yves Ferland

RESEARCH EDITOR
Serge D'Amico

PAGE SETUP
Pascal Goyette
Lucie Mc Brearty
Martin Langlois

PRODUCTION
François Fortin
Jean-Louis Martin
Tony O'Riley

GRAPHIC DESIGN
Emmanuel Blanc

ACKNOWLEDGMENTS

In preparing *The Macmillan Visual Dictionary*, we have benefited from the help of numerous groups, organizations and companies, which have provided us with up-to-date technical documents. We have also received judicious advice from various specialists, colleagues, terminologists and translators. We extend a special thank-you to our initial contributors, Édith Girard, René St-Pierre, Marielle Hébert, Christiane Vachon and Anik Lapointe. In addition, we wish to express our sincere gratitude to the following individuals and organizations:

A.C. Delco
Aérospatiale (France)
Aérospatiale Canada (ACI) Inc.
Air Canada (Linguistic Policy and Services)
Amity-Leather Products Company
Animat Inc.
Archambault Musique
International Association of Lighthouse Authorities (Marie-Hélène Grillet)
Association des groupes d'astronomes amateurs (Jean-Marc Richard)
Atlas Copco
Atomic Energy of Canada Ltd. (Pierre Giguère)
Bell Canada
Bell Helicopter Textron
Bellefontaine
Benoît, Richard
Beretta
Black & Decker
Bombardier Inc.
Boutique de harnais Pépin
British Hovercraft Corporation Ltd. (Division of Westland Aerospace)
C. Plath North American Division
Caloritech Inc.
Cambridge Instruments (Canada) Inc.
CAMIF (Direction relations extérieures)
Canada Billard & Bowling Inc. (Bernard Monsec)
Canadian National (Information and Linguistic Services)
Canadian Kenworth Company
Canadian Coleman Supply Inc.
Canadian Liquid Air Ltd.
Canadian Curling Association
Canadian Coast Guard
Canadian Broadcasting Corporation (Gilles Amyot, Pierre Beaucage, Claude L'Hérault, Pierre Laroche)
Carpentier, Jean-Marc
Casavant Frères Limitée (Gilbert Lemieux)
Centre de Tissage Leclerc Inc.
Chromalox Inc.
Clerc, Redjean
Club de tir à l'arc de Montréal
Club de planeur Champlain
Collège Jean de Brébeuf (Paul-Émile Tremblay)
Collège militaire royal de Saint-Jean
Communauté urbaine de Montréal (Bureau de transport métropolitain)
Complexe sportif Claude-Robillard
Control Data Canada Ltd.
Cycles Performance
David M. Stewart Museum (Philippe Butler)
Department of National Defence of Canada (Public Relations)
Detson
Direction des constructions navales (Programmes internationaux) (France)
Distributions TTI Inc.
Energy, Mines and Resources Canada (Canada Centre for Remote Sensing)
Environment Canada (Atmospheric Environment Service, Gilles Sanscartier)
FACOM
Fédération québécoise des échecs
Fédération québécoise de tennis
Fédération québécoise de luge et bobsleigh
Fédération québécoise de canot-camping
Fédération québécoise de boxe olympique
Fédération québécoise de badminton
Fédération québécoise d'haltérophilie

Fédération québécoise d'escrime
Fédération de patinage de vitesse du Québec
Festival des Montolfières du Haut-Richelieu
Fincantieri Naval Shipbuilding Division
Fisher Scientific Ltd.
Ford New-Holland Inc.
Gadbois, Alain
GAM Pro Plongée
G.E. Astro-Space Division
G.T.E. Sylvania Canada Ltd.
General Electric Canada Inc. (Dominion Engineering Works, Mony Schinasi)
General Motors of Canada Ltd.
GIAT Industries
Government of Canada Terminology Bank
Gym Plus
Harrison (1985) Inc.
Hewitt Equipment Ltd.
Hippodrome Blue Bonnets (Robert Perez)
Honeywell Ltd.
Hortipro
Hughes Aircraft Company
Hydro-Québec (Centre de documentation, Anne Crépeau)
IBM Canada Ltd.
Imperial Oil Ltd.
Institut de recherche d'Hydro-Québec (IREQ)
International Telecommunications Satellite Organization (Intelsat)
International Civil Aviation Organization (IATA)
Jardin Botanique de Montréal
John Deere Ltd.
Johnson & Johnson Inc.
La Maison Olympique (Sylvia Doucette)
La Cordée
Le Beau Voyage
Le Coz, Jean-Pierre
Lee Valley Tools Ltd.
Leica Camera
Les Manufacturiers Draco ltée
Les Instruments de Musique Twigg Inc.
Les Équipements Chalin ltée
Les Appareils orthopédiques BBG Inc.
Leviton Manufacturing of Canada Ltd.
Liebherr-Québec
Manac Inc.
Manutan
Marcoux, Jean-Marie
Marrazza Musique
MATRA S.A.
Matra Défense (Direction de la communication)
Mazda Canada
Médiatel
Mendes Inc. (François Caron)
Michelin
MIL Tracy (Henri Vacher)
Ministère des transports du Québec (Sécurité routière, Signalisation routière)
Monette Sport Inc.
Moto Internationale
National Oceanic and Atmospheric Administration (NOAA) — National Environmental Satellite and Information Service (Frank Lepore)
National Aeronautics and Space Administration (NASA)
Nikon Canada Inc.
Northern Telecom Canada Ltd.
Office de la langue française du Québec (Chantal Robinson)
Ogilvie Mills Ltd. (Michel Ladouceur)

Olivetti Systems and Networks Canada Ltd.
Ontario Hydro
Paterson Darkroom Necessities
Petro-Canada (Calgary)
Philips Electronics Ltd. (Philips Lighting)
Philips Electronics Ltd. (Scientific and Analytical Equipment)
Pierre-Olivier Decor
Planétarium Dow (Pierre Lacombe)
Plastimo
Port of Montreal (Public Affairs)
Pratt & Whitney Canada Inc.
Quincaillerie A.C.L. Inc.
Radio-Québec
Remington Products (Canada) Inc.
Russell Rinfret
Rodriguez Cantieri navali S.p.A.
S.A. Redoute Catalogue (Relations extérieures)
Samsonite
Secretary of State of Canada (Translation Bureau)
Shell Canada
SIAL Poterie
Smith-Corona (Canada) Ltd.
SNC Defence Products Ltd.
Société Nationale des Chemins de Fer français (S.N.C.F.) (Direction de la communication)
Société de transport de la Communauté urbaine de Montréal
Spalding Canada
Spar Aerospace Ltd. (Hélène Lapierre)
St. Lawrence Seaway Authority (Normand Dodier)
Sunbeam Corporation (Canada) Ltd.
Swimming Canada
Teleglobe Canada Inc. (Roger Leblanc)
Telesat Canada (Yves Comtois)
The Coal Association of Canada
The British Petroleum Company p.l.c. (Photographic Services)
Thibault
Tideland Signal Canada Ltd.
Transport Canada (Montreal Airports, Gilbert L'Espérance, Koos R. Van der Peijl)
Ultramar Canada Inc.
United States Department of Defense (Department of the Navy, Office of Information)
Université du Québec à Montréal (Module des arts, Michel Fournier)
Université du Québec (Institut national de la recherche scientifique, Benoît Jean)
Varin, Claude
Via Rail Canada Inc.
Viala L.R. Inc. (Jean Beaudin)
Ville de Montréal (Bureau du cinéma; Service de l'habitation et du développement urbain; Service de la prévention des incendies, Robert Gilbert, Réal Audet; Service des travaux publics)
Volcano Inc.
Volkswagen Canada Inc.
Volvo Canada Ltd.
Water Ski Canada
Weider
Wild Leitz Canada ltée
Xerox Canada Inc.
Yamaha Canada Music Ltd.

INTRODUCTION

The Macmillan Visual Dictionary is quite unlike other dictionaries with respect to both contents and presentation. Given its uniqueness, a few words of explanation will help you appreciate its usefulness and the quality of the information it contains. The following introduction explains how and why The Macmillan Visual Dictionary differs from language dictionaries and encyclopedias. For dictionary "fans" and professional lexicographers, we have included a brief description of the principles and methods that guided us in producing the dictionary.

A PICTURE/WORD DICTIONARY

The Macmillan Visual Dictionary closely links pictures and words.

The pictures describe and analyze today's world: the objects of everyday life, our physical environment, the animal and vegetable life that surrounds us, the communication and work techniques that are changing our lifestyles, the weapons that preoccupy us, the means of transportation that are breaking down geographical barriers, the sources of energy on which we depend, etc.

Illustrations play a specific role in our dictionary: they serve to define words, enabling dictionary users to "see" immediately the meaning of each term. Users can thus recognize the objects they are looking for and, at a single glance, find the corresponding vocabulary.

The Macmillan Visual Dictionary provides users with the words they need to accurately name the objects that make up the world around them.

The terms in the dictionary have been carefully selected from current documents written by experts in each area. In case of doubt, the vocabulary has been studied by specialists in the corresponding field and cross-checked in encyclopedias and language dictionaries. We have taken these precautions to ensure the accuracy of each word and a high level of standardization.

A DICTIONARY FOR ONE AND ALL

The Macmillan Visual Dictionary is aimed at all persons who participate in one way or another in contemporary civilization and, as a consequence, need to know and use a great number of technical terms from a wide range of fields.

It thus addresses the needs and curiosity of each and every one of us. It is not designed only for specialists.

The depth of analysis varies according to the subject. Rather than arbitrarily providing a uniform breakdown of each subject, the authors have acknowledged that people's degrees of knowledge differ from one field to another, and that the complexity of the topics dealt with varies widely. For example, more people are familiar with clothing and automobiles than with atomic energy or telecommunications satellites, and find the former subjects simpler than the latter. Another aspect of the same problem is that, in describing human anatomy, we are obliged to use medical terminology, even though the terms seem more complicated than those for fruits and vegetables. In addition, our world is changing: photographic vocabulary, for example, has become much more complicated due to camera automation. Similarly, although microcomputer fans are

familiar with computer terminology, the field remains a mystery for much of the rest of the population.

The Macmillan Visual Dictionary allows for these phenomena, and thus reflects the specialized vocabulary commonly used in each field.

AN EASY-TO-CONSULT DICTIONARY

People may use The Macmillan Visual Dictionary in several different ways, thanks to the List of Chapters (page xxxi), the detailed table of contents (page xv), and the index (page 833).

Users may consult the dictionary:

By going from an idea to a word, if they are familiar with an object and can clearly visualize it, but cannot find or do not know the name for it. The table of contents breaks down each subject according to an easy-to-consult, stratified classification system. The Macmillan Visual Dictionary is the only dictionary that allows users to find a word from its meaning.

By going from a word to an idea, if they want to check the meaning of a term. The index refers users to the illustrations, which provide the names for the individual features.

At a glance, by using the List of Chapters. The colored page edges help users find the chapters they are looking for.

For sheer pleasure, by flipping from one illustration to another, or from one word to another, for the sole purpose of enjoying the illustrations and enriching their knowledge.

A DICTIONARY WITH A DIFFERENCE

We are all familiar with several types of dictionaries and encyclopedias. It is not always easy, however, to grasp their distinguishing features. The following overview highlights the main differences between The Macmillan Visual Dictionary and other reference works.

a) Language dictionaries

These dictionaries describe the meanings given by speakers to the general vocabulary of their language.

They provide two major types of information: headwords (vocabulary), and a list of the meanings of each term (dictionary entries).

The vocabulary, which comprises all of the words covered by lexicographical descriptions, constitutes the framework of the dictionary. For consultation purposes, the headwords are arranged in alphabetical order. Generally speaking, the vocabulary includes common, contemporary language, archaic words useful for understanding the texts

or history of a civilization, and a certain number of widely used technical terms.

Each dictionary entry provides an itemized, semantic description of the corresponding headword. Generally, the entry indicates the part of speech for the headword, its etymology and its various meanings, as well as the word's social usage (familiar, colloquial, vulgar, etc.) according to criteria that, even today, remain somewhat "impressionistic."

In general, language dictionaries are classified according to their target users and the number of terms in the vocabulary, which, in addition to nouns, includes all other parts of speech (verbs, pronouns, adjectives, adverbs, prepositions, conjunctions, etc.). A 5,000-word dictionary is intended for children, one with 15,000 words is suitable for elementary schools and a 50,000-word dictionary covers the needs of the general public.

b) Encyclopedic dictionaries

In addition to the information included in language dictionaries, encyclopedic dictionaries provide details about the nature, functioning, and history of things, thus enabling laymen with solid general knowledge and specialists to understand the scope of a word. They devote much more space to technical terms, and reflect current scientific and technological developments. Generally speaking, pictures play an important role in illustrating the text. The size of encyclopedic dictionaries varies according to the breadth of the vocabulary, the length of the entries, the emphasis placed on proper nouns and the number of fields of specialization covered.

c) Encyclopedias

Unlike the preceding category of reference works, encyclopedias do not deal with language. They are devoted to providing scientific, technical, occasionally economic, historical and geographic descriptions. The arrangement of the entries varies, as all classification systems are valid: alphabetic, conceptual, chronological, by field of specialization, etc. The number of different encyclopedias is virtually unlimited, given the fragmentation of civilization into multiple categories. There is, however, a distinction between universal encyclopedias and specialized encyclopedias.

d) Specialized lexicons and vocabularies

These works usually address specific needs created by scientific and technological progress. They focus on ensuring efficient communication through precise, standardized terminology. They vary in all respects: the method of compilation, the authors' approach to the subject matter, the scope of the vocabulary, the number of languages, and the means of establishing equivalents in the various languages (i.e., by simple translation or by a comparison of unilingual terminologies). Specialized lexicography has become an area of intense activity. The number of works is multiplying in all sectors and in all language combinations.

e) The Macmillan Visual Dictionary

The Macmillan Visual Dictionary is a terminology-oriented dictionary. It is aimed at providing members of the general public with the specific terms they need to name the objects of daily life, and helping them grasp the meaning of words through illustrations. Grouped together in interlocking categories, the various elements are interdefined. The dictionary is thus organized according to chapters, subjects, specific objects, and features of these objects. Depending on a person's degree of familiarity with a given chapter, the terminology may seem simple or technical. The fundamental goal, however, is to provide non-specialists with a coherent analysis of useful, necessary vocabulary for each subject.

The Macmillan Visual Dictionary is not an encyclopedia, for at least two reasons: rather than describing objects, it names them; in addition, it avoids listing all the objects in a given category. For example, rather than enumerating the various types of trees, it focuses on a typical representative of the category, and examines its structure and individual parts.

It may even less be considered a language dictionary: like other terminological works, it contains no written definitions and covers only nouns and, in particular, noun phrases.

Nor may it be seen as a compendium of specialized vocabularies, as it avoids terminology used only by specialists, focusing instead on more widespread terms—at the risk of being considered simplistic by experts in specific fields.

The Macmillan Visual Dictionary is the first terminology-oriented dictionary to group together in a single volume the thousands of technical and not-so-technical terms most commonly used in our society, where science, technology, and their end products are part of everyday life.

This is the editorial policy that has guided us in creating this dictionary. Consequently, the number of words it contains does not have the same significance as for a language dictionary, for several reasons: in keeping with our editorial policy, we have deliberately chosen to limit the number of words; unlike conventional dictionaries, this work focuses exclusively on nouns, the most significant words in the language, to the exclusion of adjectives, verbs, prepositions, etc.; and finally no one is sure exactly how to count compound terms!

COMPUTER-PRODUCED ILLUSTRATIONS

The illustrations in The Macmillan Visual Dictionary have been created by computer from recent documents and original photographs.

The use of computers has given the illustrations a highly realistic, almost photographic look, while allowing us to highlight the essential features corresponding to the vocabulary. The graphic precision of The Macmillan Visual Dictionary is one of the main sources of its excellence as an encyclopedic and lexicographical reference tool.

In addition, thanks to computers, we have been able to improve the accuracy of the lines joining objects to their names, thus enhancing the clarity of the link between words and the things they describe.

CAREFULLY ESTABLISHED VOCABULARY

In creating The Macmillan Visual Dictionary, we have used the method of systematic and comparative terminological research, which is standard practice among professionals who prepare works of this type.

This method comprises several steps, which follow one another in a logical order. The following paragraphs provide a brief description of each of these steps.

Field delimitation

First of all, on the basis of our objectives, we defined the scope and contents of the proposed work.

We began by choosing the chapters we felt it necessary to cover. We then divided each chapter into fields and sub-fields, taking care to abide by our editorial policy and avoiding overspecialization and the temptation to cover all subjects in detail. This step resulted in a working table of contents, the dictionary framework, which guided our subsequent steps and was refined as the work progressed. The detailed table of contents is the end result of this process.

Documentary research

In keeping with our production plan, we assembled pertinent documents likely to provide us with the required information about words and concepts in each subject matter.

In order of reliability, our documentary sources were as follows:

• Articles and books by experts in the various fields, written in their native language, with an acceptable degree of specialization. Translations of such texts provide revealing information about vocabulary usage, but must be used with due caution;

• Technical documents, such as national standards or the guidelines of the International Standard Organization (ISO), product instructions, technical documents provided by manufacturers, official government publications, etc.;

• Catalogs, commercial texts, advertisements from specialized magazines and major newspapers;

• Encyclopedias, encyclopedic dictionaries, and unilingual language dictionaries;

• Unilingual, bilingual, and multilingual specialized vocabularies and dictionaries. The quality and reliability of these works, however, must be carefully assessed;

• Bilingual and multilingual language dictionaries.

In all, we consulted four to five thousand references. The selected bibliography included in the dictionary indicates only the general documentary sources consulted, and does not include specialized sources.

Sifting through the documents

A terminologist went through the documents for each subject, in search of specific concepts and the words used to express them by different authors and works. Gradually, a framework was established, as the terminologist noted the use of the same term for a given concept from one source to another, or, on the contrary, the use of several terms for the same idea. In the latter case, the terminologist continued his research until he was able to form a well-documented opinion of each competing term. All of this research was recorded, with reference notes.

Creation of terminological files

The preceding step enabled us to assemble all of the elements for our terminological files.

Each concept identified and defined by an illustration has been paired with the term most frequently used to describe it by the leading authors or in the most reliable sources. Where several competing terms were found in the reference material, following discussion and consensus between the terminologist and the scientific director, a single term was chosen.

Terminological variants

Frequently, several words may be used to designate virtually the same concept.

We dealt with such situations as follows:

• In some cases, a term was used by a single author or appeared only once in our documentary sources. We retained the most frequently used competing term.

• Technical terms are often compound words with or without a hyphen, or several-word expressions. This results in at least two types of terminological variants:

a) The compound technical term may be shortened by the deletion of one or more of its elements, especially where the meaning is clear in the context. The shortened expression may even become the normal term for the concept. In such cases, we retained the compound form, leaving users the freedom to abbreviate it according to the context.

b) An element of the compound term may itself have equivalents (most often synonyms from the commonly spoken language). We retained the most frequently used form.

Variants may stem from the evolution of the language, without terminological consequences. We therefore retained the most contemporary or well-known form.

TERMINOLOGICAL APPROACH

A few comments about the terminological approach, as compared to the lexicographical approach, are in order.

Language dictionaries have a long history. They are familiar reference works, used by most people since early school age, with a well-established, widely known and accepted tradition. We all know how to consult a dictionary and interpret the information it provides—or fails to provide.

Terminological dictionaries are either very recent or intended for a specialized public. There is no solid tradition to guide those who design and produce such works. Although specialists know how to interpret dictionaries pertaining to their own fields, given that they are familiar with the terminology, the same cannot be said for the layperson, who is confused by variants. Finally, whereas language dictionaries have to a certain extent established standard word usage among their users, specialized vocabularies are characterized by competing terms in new fields of specialization.

Users of a reference work such as *The Macmillan Visual Dictionary* should take into account these elements in assessing this new type of reference tool.

JEAN-CLAUDE CORBEIL
ARIANE ARCHAMBAULT

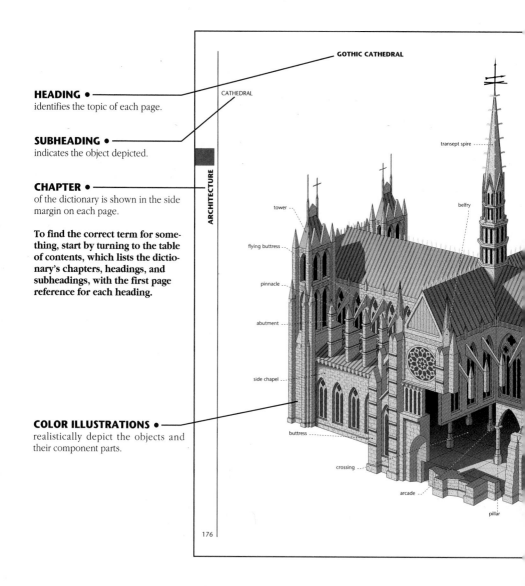

HEADING •
identifies the topic of each page.

SUBHEADING •
indicates the object depicted.

CHAPTER •
of the dictionary is shown in the side
margin on each page.

**To find the correct term for some-
thing, start by turning to the table
of contents, which lists the dictionary's chapters, headings, and
subheadings, with the first page
reference for each heading.**

COLOR ILLUSTRATIONS •
realistically depict the objects and
their component parts.

CATHEDRAL

GOTHIC CATHEDRAL

ARCHITECTURE

transept spire

tower

belfry

flying buttress

pinnacle

abutment

side chapel

buttress

crossing

arcade

pillar

176

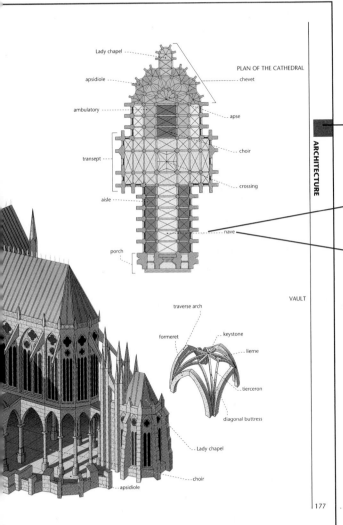

Lady chapel

apsidiole

ambulatory

transept

aisle

porch

PLAN OF THE CATHEDRAL

chevet

apse

choir

crossing

nave

ARCHITECTURE

• COLORED TAB
on the edge of the page corresponds
to the chapter as shown in the List of
Chapters. This color-coding allows
you to find, at a glance, the subject
you are looking for.

• DOTTED LINES
link the terms with the objects they
describe.

• TERMS
are included in the index, with references to all pages on
which they appear.

**To see an illustration depicting
a term that you know,
consult the index.**

VAULT

traverse arch

keystone

formeret

lierne

tierceron

diagonal buttress

Lady chapel

choir

apsidiole

177

DICTIONARIES

- *Gage Canadian Dictionary*. Toronto: Gage Publishing Limited, 1983, 1313 p.
- *The New Britannica/Webster Dictionary and Reference Guide*. Chicago, Toronto: Encyclopedia Britannica, 1981, 1505 p.
- *The Oxford English Dictionary*. Second edition. Oxford: Clarendon Press, 1989, 20 vol.
- *The Oxford Illustrated Dictionary*. Oxford: Clarendon Press, 1967, 974 p.
- *Oxford American Dictionary*. Eugene Ehrlich, et al. New York, Oxford: Oxford University Press, 1980, 816 p.
- *The Random House Dictionary of the English Language*. Second edition. New York: Random House 1983, 2059 p.
- *Webster's Encyclopedic Unabridged Dictionary of the English Language*. New York: Portland House, 1989, 2078 p.
- *Webster's Third New International Dictionary*. Springfield: Merriam-Webster, 1986, 2662 p.
- *Webster's Ninth New Collegiate Dictionary*. Springfield: Merriam-Webster, 1984, 1563 p.
- *Webster's New World Dictionary of American Language*. New York: The World Pub., 1953.

ENCYCLOPEDIAS

- *Academic American Encyclopedia*. Princeton: Arete Publishing Company, 1980, 21 vol.
- *Architectural Graphic Standards*. Eighth edition. New York: John Wiley & Sons, 1988, 854 p.
- *Chamber's Encyclopedia*. New rev. edition. London: International Learning System, 1989.
- *Collier's Encyclopedia*. New York: Macmillan Educational Company, 1984, 24 vol.
- *Compton's Encyclopedia*. Chicago: F.E. Compton Company, Division of Encyclopedia Britannica Inc., 1982, 26 vol.
- *Encyclopedia Americana*. International Edition, Danbury: Grolier, 1981, 30 vol.
- *How It Works, The Illustrated Science and Invention Encyclopedia*. New York: H.S. Stuttman, 1977, 21 vol.
- *McGraw-Hill Encyclopedia of Science & Technology*. New York: McGraw-Hill Book Company, 1982, 15 vol.
- *Merit Students Encyclopedia*. New York: Macmillan Educational Company, 1984, 20 vol.
- *New Encyclopedia Britannica*. Chicago, Toronto: Encyclopedia Britannica, 1985, 32 vol.
- *The Joy of Knowledge Encyclopedia*. London: Mitchell Beazley Encyclopedias, 1976, 7 vol.
- *The Random House Encyclopedia*. New York: Random House, 1977, 2 vol.
- *The World Book Encyclopedia*. Chicago: Field Enterprises Educational Corporation, 1973.

FRENCH AND ENGLISH DICTIONARIES

- Collins-Robert, *French-English, English-French Dictionary*, London, Glasgow, Cleveland, Toronto: Collins-Robert, 1978, 781 p.
- Dubois, Marguerite, *Dictionnaire moderne français-anglais*. Paris: Larousse, 1980, 752 p.
- Harrap's *New Standard French and English Dictionary*. Part one, French-English. London: Harrap's 1977, 2 vol. Part two, English-French. London: Harrap's 1983, 2 vol.
- Harrap's *Shorter French and English Dictionary*, London, Toronto, Willington, Sydney: Harrap's 1953, 940 p.

CONTENTS

ASTRONOMY

Earth coordinate system.. 3
celestial coordinate system... 3
solar system 4
    planets and moons, orbits of the planets
Sun... 6
    structure of the Sun
Moon 7
    phases of the Moon, lunar features
solar eclipse.. 8
lunar eclipse.. 8
seasons of the year... 8
comet... 9
galaxy... 9
    Hubble's classification
constellations of the northern hemisphere.. 10
constellations of the southern hemisphere 12
astronomical observatory... 14
    observatory, telescope
radio telescope 15
    altazimuth mounting
Hubble space telescope.. 16
planetarium 16

GEOGRAPHY

profile of the Earth's atmosphere... 19
configuration of the continents.. 20
structure of the Earth 22
section of the Earth's crust 22
earthquake 23
cave 24
volcano 25
glacier 26
mountain 27
ocean floor 28
    mid-ocean ridge, topographic features, abyssal plain, continental margin
wave 30
common coastal features.. 30
ecology.. 31
    structure of the biosphere, food chain, pollution of food on ground, pollution of
    food in water, atmospheric pollution, hydrologic cycle
precipitations.. 36
    stormy sky, classification of snow crystals
meteorology 38
    weather map, station model, wind
international weather symbols.. 39
    fronts, sky coverage, present weather
meteorological measuring instruments 40
    measure of sunshine, measure of rainfall, measure of temperature, measure of
    air pressure, measure of wind direction, measure of wind strength, measure of
    humidity, measure of snowfall, measure of cloud ceiling, instrument shelter
weather satellite 42
    geostationary satellite, polar-orbiting satellite, orbit of the satellites
clouds and meteorological symbols.. 44
    high clouds, middle clouds, low clouds, clouds of vertical development

CONTENTS

climates of the world.. 45
> tropical climates, continental climates, temperate climates, subtropical climates, polar climates, highland climates, subarctic climates

desert 46

cartography 47
> grid system, hemispheres, map projections, political map, physical map, urban map, road map

remote detection satellite 48
> Radarsat satellite

VEGETABLE KINGDOM

mushroom... 55
> structure of a mushroom, edible mushrooms, deadly poisonous mushroom, poisonous mushroom

leaf 56
> leaf margin, types of leaves, compound leaves, simple leaves

structure of a plant.. 57

conifer... 58
> branch, types of leaves

structure of a tree 59
> tree, cross section of a trunk, stump

structure of a flower.. 60
> types of inflorescences

grape... 61
> maturing steps, vine stock, grape leaf, bunch of grapes

fleshy fruits: berry fruits 62
> section of a berry, section of a raspberry, section of a strawberry, major types of berries

stone fleshy fruits... 63
> section of a stone fruit, major types of stone fruits

pome fleshy fruits... 64
> section of a pome fruit, major types of pome fruits

fleshy fruits: citrus fruits.. 65
> section of a citrus fruit, major types of citrus fruits

dry fruits: nuts 66
> section of a hazelnut, section of a walnut, major types of nuts, husk

various dry fruits 67
> section of a follicle, section of a legume, section of a silique, section of a capsule

tropical fruits 68
> major types of tropical fruits

vegetables 69
> fruit vegetables, inflorescent vegetables, bulb vegetables, tuber vegetables, root vegetables, stalk vegetables, seed vegetables, leaf vegetables

herbs 74

ANIMAL KINGDOM

insects and spider... 77

butterfly.. 78
> caterpillar, chrysalis, hind leg

honeybee... 80
> foreleg (outer surface), middle leg (outer surface), hind leg (inner surface), mouthparts, worker, queen, drone, honeycomb section, hive

gastropod 83
> snail, major edible gastropods

CONTENTS

amphibians 84
    frog, life cycle of the frog, eggs, tadpole, major amphibians
fish 86
    morphology, gills, anatomy
crustacean 90
    lobster, major edible crustaceans
mollusk 92
    oyster, major edible mollusks
univalve shell 94
bivalve shell 95
    dorsal view, left valve
reptile 96
    rattlesnake, venomous snake's head, turtle
types of jaws 98
    rodent's jaw, carnivore's jaw, herbivore's jaw
major types of horns 99
major types of tusks 99
types of hoofs 99
horse 100
    morphology, skeleton, gaits, horseshoe, hoof
deer family 105
    deer antlers, kinds of deer
dog 106
    morphology, dog's forepaw
cat 107
    cat's head, retracted claw, extended claw
bird 108
    morphology, head, egg, wing, contour feather, principal types of bills, principal types of feet
bat 112

HUMAN BEING
plant cell 115
animal cell 115
human body 116
muscles 120
    anterior view, posterior view
skeleton 122
    anterior view, posterior view
blood circulation 124
    schema of circulation, heart, principal veins and arteries
male genital organs 127
    spermatozoon
female genital organs 128
    egg
breast 129
respiratory system 130
digestive system 131
    large intestine, small intestine
urinary system 132
nervous system 133
    peripheral nervous system, central nervous system, lumbar vertebra, chain of neurons, sensory impulse
sense organs: touch 136
    skin, finger, hand

CONTENTS

sense organs: hearing 138
   parts of the ear, auditory ossicles, auricle
sense organs: sight 140
   eye, eyeball
sense organs: smell 141
   external nose, nasal fossae
senses of smell and taste 142
   mouth, dorsum of tongue, taste sensations
teeth 144
   human denture, cross section of a molar

FARMING
tractor 147
farmstead 148
farm animals 150
principal types of cereals 152
bread 153
steps for cultivating soil 154
   ribbing plow, manure spreader, tandem disk harrow, cultivator, seed drill, flail
   mower, rake, hay baler, combine harvester, forage harvester, forage blower

ARCHITECTURE
traditional houses 165
architectural styles 166
   ionic order, doric order, corinthian order
Greek temple 168
Roman house 170
mosque 172
arch 174
   semicircular arch, types of arches
gothic cathedral 175
Vauban fortification 178
castle 180
roofs 182
downtown 184
cross section of a street 186
city houses 187
theater 188
   stage
office building 190

HOUSE
blueprint reading 193
   elevation, site plan, mezzanine floor, second floor, first floor
exterior of a house 196
structure of a house 198
   frame, roof truss, foundations
wood flooring 200
   wood flooring on cement screed, wood flooring on wooden structure, wood
   flooring arrangements
stairs 201
door 202
   types of doors
window 203
   structure, types of windows

CONTENTS

heating 204
    fireplace, slow-burning stove, chimney, fire irons, forced warm-air system, elec-
    tric furnace, types of registers, forced hot-water system, column radiator, boil-
    er, oil burner, humidifier, hygrometer, electric baseboard radiator, convector,
    auxiliary heating, heat pump, room thermostat
air conditioning 214
    ceiling fan, room air conditioner
plumbing system 215
pedestal-type sump pump 216
septic tank 216

HOUSE FURNITURE
table 219
    types of tables
armchair 220
    principal types of armchairs
seats 222
side chair 223
    types of chairs
bed 224
    linen
storage furniture 225
    armoire
window accessories 228
    types of curtains, types of pleats, types of headings, curtain pole, curtain track,
    traverse rod, roller shade, Venetian blind
lights 232
    incandescent lamp, fluorescent tube, tungsten-halogen lamp, energy saving
    bulb, adjustable lamp, track lighting, chandelier
glassware 237
dinnerware 238
silverware 239
    principal types of knives, principal types of forks, principal types of spoons
kitchen utensils 242
    types of kitchen knives, for straining and draining, for grinding and grating, set
    of utensils, for opening, for measuring, baking utensils
coffee makers 247
    automatic drip coffee maker, vacuum coffee maker, percolator, plunger,
    Neapolitan coffee maker, espresso coffee maker
cooking utensils 248
    wok set, fish poacher, fondue set, pressure cooker
domestic appliances 250
    hand blender, beaters, blender, hand mixer, table mixer, food processor, citrus
    juicer, juicer, ice cream freezer, kettle, toaster, deep fryer, waffle iron,
    microwave oven, griddle, refrigerator, range hood, electric range, steam iron,
    coffee mill, can opener, dishwasher, washer, electric dryer, hand vacuum clean-
    er, canister vacuum cleaner

GARDENING
pleasure garden 263
tools and equipment 264
    impulse sprinkler, hose trolley, watering can, hedge trimmer, wheelbarrow,
    motorized earth auger, hand mower, edger, power mower, chainsaw, tiller

CONTENTS

DO-IT-YOURSELF

carpentry: tools 275
    nail, mallet, claw hammer, ball-peen hammer, screwdriver, spiral screwdriver,
    crescent wrench, hacksaw, plane, handsaw, slip joint pliers, rib joint pliers,
    locking pliers, washers, screw, bolt, nut, electric drill, hand drill, twist drill,
    brace, auger bit, C-clamp, vise, router, drill press, circular saw, table saw
building materials 286
    basic building materials, covering materials, insulating materials, wood, board,
    wood-based materials
lock 290
    mortise lock, tubular lock
masonry 291
    caulking gun, mason's trowel
plumbing: bathroom 292
    toilet
plumbing 294
    stem faucet, ball-type faucet, disc faucet, cartridge faucet, garbage disposal
    sink, gas water-heater tank
plumbing: examples of branching 298
    washer, dishwasher
plumbing 299
    plumbing tools, fittings, transition fittings
ladders and stepladders 302
    extension ladder, stepladder, platform ladder
painting upkeep 304
    spray paint gun, brush, scraper, paint roller
soldering and welding 305
    arc welding, soldering gun, cutting torch, welding torch, oxyacetylene welding,
    pressure regulator, butt welding, soldering torch, striker
soldering and welding: protective clothing 308
electricity 309
    American plug, lamp socket, European plug, electrician's tools, multimeter,
    voltage tester, drop light, multipurpose tool, lineman's pliers, fuse box, fuses

CLOTHING

elements of ancient costume 315
men's clothing 319
    raincoat, trench coat, duffle coat, overcoat, windbreaker, jacket, parka, dou-
    ble-breasted jacket, vest, single-breasted jacket, belt, pants, suspenders, shirt,
    necktie, athletic shirt, underwear, socks, briefs
sweaters 326
    V-neck cardigan
gloves 327
headgear 328
    felt hat
women's clothing 330
    types of coats, pea jacket, raglan, pelerine, suit, types of dresses, types of skirts,
    types of pleats, types of pants, types of blouses, jackets, vest and sweaters,
    types of pockets, types of sleeves, types of collars, necklines and necks, hose,
    underwear, bra, nightwear
children's clothing 349
    bathing wrap, plastic pants, blanket sleepers, high-back overalls, sleepers,
    grow sleepers, training set, crossover back straps overalls, snowsuit
sportswear 352
    running shoe, training suit, exercise wear

CONTENTS

shoes 354
    parts of a shoe, major types of shoes, accessories, shoeshine kit

PERSONAL ADORNMENT
jewelry 361
    earrings, necklaces, precious stones, semiprecious stones, cut for gemstones,
    brilliant cut facets, rings, bracelets, pins, charms
manicure 365
    manicure set, manicuring implements, nail clippers
makeup 366
    lip makeup, eye makeup, sponges
hairdressing 368
    lighted mirror, hairbrushes, styling brush, combs, haircutting scissors, notched
    single-edged thinning scissors, notched double-edged thinning scissors, hair
    roller, curling iron, hair dryer

PERSONAL ARTICLES
dental care 373
    toothbrush, oral hygiene center
razors 374
    straight razor, double-edge razor, electric razor, shaving brush
umbrella and stick 375
    umbrella, stick umbrella, telescopic umbrella
eyeglasses 376
    eyeglasses parts, bifocal lens, frames, major types of eyeglasses
leather goods 378
    attaché case, bottom-fold portfolio, briefcase, checkbook/secretary clutch, card
    case
handbags 380
    satchel bag, shoulder bag, accordion bag, drawstring bag
luggage 382
    garment bag, carry-on bag, vanity case, luggage carrier, weekender, pullman
    case, trunk
smoking accessories 384
    cigar, cigarette, cigarette pack, pipe, pipe tools, matchbook, gas lighter,
    matchbox, ashtray

COMMUNICATIONS
writing instruments 389
    fountain pen, ballpoint pen
photography 390
    cross section of a reflex camera, camera back, single-lens reflex (SLR) camera,
    lenses, electronic flash, tripod, still cameras, films, exposure meter, spotmeter,
    slide projector, projection screen, transparency slide, developing tank, enlarger,
    negative carrier, developing baths, print washer
sound reproducing system 400
    system components, loudspeaker, tuner, amplifier, cassette, cassette tape deck,
    record, turntable, compact disk, compact disk player
dynamic microphone 406
headphones 406
radio: studio and control room 407
portable sound systems 408
    personal radio cassette player, portable CD radio cassette recorder
video camera 409

CONTENTS

television... 410
    television set, picture tube, remote control, videocassette recorder, studio and
    control rooms, production control room, studio floor, camera
mobile unit.. 415
broadcast satellite communication 416
telecommunications by satellite... 417
telecommunication satellites.. 418
    examples of satellites, Eutelsat II, launching into orbit
communication by telephone.. 420
    telephone answering machine, telephone set, telex, facsimile machine, types of
    telephones, telecommunication terminal, pay phone

ROAD TRANSPORT
automobile.. 425
    types of bodies, body, bucket seat, rear seat, lights, door, dashboard, instru-
    ment panel, windshield wiper, disk brake, drum brake, wheel, tire, gasoline
    engine, turbo-compressor engine, radiator, exhaust system, battery, spark plug
types of engines.. 436
    four-stroke-cycle engine, two-stroke-cycle engine, diesel engine, rotary engine
trucking 440
    truck tractor, tandem tractor trailer, semitrailer, flatbed
motorcycle 442
    protective helmet, motorcycle dashboard
snowmobile 445
bicycle... 446
    power train, accessories
caravan 449
    trailer, motor home
road system 450
    cross section of a road, major types of interchanges, cloverleaf
service station 453
    gasoline pump, service station
fixed bridges... 454
    types of beam bridges, types of arch bridges, types of arches, suspension
    bridge, cable-stayed bridges
'movable bridges 457
    swing bridge, single-leaf bascule bridge, floating bridge, lift bridge, transporter
    bridge

RAIL TRANSPORT
high-speed train.. 458
types of passenger cars.. 460
    coach car, sleeping car, dining car
passenger station.. 462
railroad station.. 464
yard... 465
railroad track 466
    rail joint, rail section, remote-controlled switch, manually-operated switch
diesel-electric locomotive 468
car 470
    box car, container, coupler head
highway crossing... 471
types of freight cars 472
subway 474
    subway station, subway train, truck and track, passenger car

CONTENTS

MARITIME TRANSPORT
four-masted bark 478
    masting and rigging, sails
types of sails.. 482
types of rigs 482
anchor.. 483
    ship's anchor, types of anchors
navigation devices.. 484
    sextant, liquid compass, echo sounder, echo sounder probe
maritime signals.. 486
    lighthouse lantern, cylindrical buoy, lighthouse, high focal plane buoy
maritime buoyage system 488
    cardinal marks, buoyage regions, rhythm of marks by night, daymarks
harbor.. 490
canal lock 492
hovercraft 492
ferry 494
container ship 494
hydrofoil boat 495
passenger liner.. 496

AIR TRANSPORT
long-range jet 498
types of tail shapes... 498
types of wing shapes.. 499
flight deck... 500
turbofan engine 501
airport 502
    passenger terminal, runway, ground airport equipment
helicopter.. 508
rocket.. 509
space shuttle.. 510
    space shuttle at takeoff, space shuttle in orbit
spacesuit 512

OFFICE SUPPLIES
stationery.. 515
office furniture 520
calculator 523
    pocket calculator, printing calculator
electronic typewriter.. 524

OFFICE AUTOMATION
configuration of an office automation system 526
    input devices, communication devices, data storage devices, output devices
basic components 528
    personal computer, video monitor, floppy disk, mini-floppy disk, hard disk drive, keyboard, mouse, dot matrix printer
photocopier.. 532
    control panel

MUSIC
traditional musical instruments 535
    zither, balalaika, mandolin, lyre, banjo, accordion, bagpipes, Jew's harp

CONTENTS

musical notation 537
    staff, clefs, time signatures, scale, intervals, note symbols, rest symbols, accidentals, ornaments, chord, other signs
musical accessories.. 539
    tuning fork, quartz metronome, metronome, music stand
keyboard instruments 540
    upright piano, upright piano action
organ.. 542
    organ console, flue pipe, reed pipe, mechanism of the organ, production of sound
stringed instruments... 544
    violin, bow, violin family, harp, acoustic guitar, electric guitar
wind instruments... 548
    saxophone, woodwind family, reeds, trumpet, brass family
percussion instruments... 552
    drums, snare drum, kettledrum, xylophone, triangle, tambourine
electronic instruments 555
    synthesizer, electronic piano
symphony orchestra 556
examples of instrumental groups 558

CREATIVE LEISURE ACTIVITIES

sewing 561
    sewing machine, foot control, presser foot, needle, tension block, bobbin case, pin cushion, tracing wheel, scissors, underlying fabrics, pattern, fasteners, hook and eyes, fabric structure, zipper, snap, buckle
knitting 567
    knitting needles, stitch patterns, crochet hook
knitting machine.. 568
    needle bed and carriages, latch needle, tension block
bobbin lace.. 570
    pillow, bobbin
embroidery 571
    frame, hoop, cross stitches, flat stitches, couched stitches, knot stitches, loop stitches
weaving.. 572
    low warp loom, shuttle, heddles, high warp loom, warping frame, bobbin winder, ball winder, diagram of weaving principle, basic weaves, other techniques
fine bookbinding 577
    bound book, gathering, trimming, sawing-in, sewing, board cutter, sewing frame, backing, backing press, backing hammer, covering, bookbinding leather, pressing, standing press
printing.. 580
    relief printing, intaglio printing, lithographic printing
relief printing process.. 581
    inking slab, equipment, etching press
intaglio printing process 582
    equipment
lithography 583
    equipment, lithographic press, levigator
pottery.. 584
    turning, coiling, tools, slab building, turning wheel, electric kiln, firing
wood carving 586
    steps, accessories, types of tools, major types of blades

CONTENTS

painting and drawing 588
    major techniques, equipment, supports, airbrush, drafting table, utility liquids

TEAM GAMES
baseball 595
    catcher, batter, bat, fielder's glove, baseball, field
cricket 598
    cricket player, cricket ball, bat, wicket, field, pitch
soccer 600
    soccer player, soccer ball, playing field
football 602
    football player, protective equipment, football, offense, scrimmage, defense,
    playing field for American football, playing field for Canadian football, scrim-
    mage in Canadian football
rugby 606
    field, rugby ball
field hockey 607
    playing field, stick, hockey ball
ice hockey 608
    puck, rink, player's stick, goalkeeper, ice hockey player
basketball 610
    court, basket, basketball
netball 611
    netball, court
handball 612
    handball, court
volleyball 613
    court, net, volleyball
tennis 614
    court, net, tennis ball, tennis player, tennis racket
squash 616
    squash racket, international singles court, squash ball
racquetball 617
    racquetball racket, court, racquetball
badminton 618
    badminton racket, shuttlecock, court, net
table tennis 619
    table tennis paddle, table, types of grips
curling 620
    curling brooms, curling stone, rink

WATER SPORTS
swimming 621
    competitive course, starting block, front crawl stroke, breaststroke, butterfly
    stroke, backstroke, backstroke start
diving 624
    diving installations, starting positions, flights, entries, forward dive, twist dive,
    armstand dive, inward dive, backward dive, reverse dive
water polo 626
    playing area, goal, water polo ball
scuba diving 627
    scuba diver
sailing 628
    points of sailing, sailboat, upperworks, traveler
sailboard 631

CONTENTS

rowing and sculling 632
  rowing (one oar), sculling boats, rowing boats, sculling (two oars), types of oars
water skiing 633
  types of skis, twin skis, slalom ski, figure ski, types of handles

AERIAL SPORTS
ballooning 634
  balloon, basket
sky diving 635
  sky diver
paragliding 636
  canopy
hang gliding 637
  hang glider
gliding 638
  glider, cockpit

WINTER SPORTS
alpine skiing 640
  alpine skier, safety binding, ski boot
cross-country skiing 642
  cross-country skier, cross-country ski
luge 643
bobsled 643
skating 644
  figure skate, hockey skate, skate guard, speed skate
roller skate 645
snowshoe 645
  Michigan snowshoe

EQUESTRIAN SPORTS
riding 646
  competition ring, obstacles, rider, saddle, bridle
types of bits 650
  snaffle bit, curb bit
horse racing 651
  jockey, stand and track
harness racing 652
  standardbred pacer

ATHLETICS
track and field athletics 654
  arena, starting block, high jump, pole vault, throwings, hammer, discus, javelins, shot
gymnastics 659
  asymmetrical bars, balance beam, trampoline, vaulting horse, springboard, rings, horizontal bar, pommel horse, parallel bars
weightlifting 662
  weightlifter, two-hand snatch, two-hand clean and jerk
fitness equipment 663
  weight stack exercise unit, barbell, stationary bicycle, rower, climber, hand-grips, ankle/wrist weight, chest expander, jump rope, dumbbell, twist bar

COMBAT SPORTS
fencing 666
  piste, fencing weapons, parts of the weapon, fencer, positions, target areas

CONTENTS

judo 668
   judo suit, mat, examples of holds
boxing 669
   ring, boxing gloves, bandage, mouthpiece

LEISURE SPORTS
fishing 670
   fly rod, artificial fly, fly reel, spinning rod, open-face spinning reel, fishhook,
   spinner, fishing garment, accessories, terminal tackles
billiards 673
   carom billiards, English billiards, pool, snooker, table, bridge, billiards cue
golf 676
   course, golf ball, golf clubs, wood, iron, golf bag, electric golf cart, golf cart,
   head cover, golf glove, golf shoe
mountaineering 680
   mountaineer, descender, hammer ax, piton, carabiner, ice ax, tubular ice
   screw, chock
bowls and petanque 682
   green, delivery
bowling 683
   types of pins, setup, lane, bowling ball
archery 684
   target, arrow, archer, compound bow
camping 685
   two-person tent, family tent, pup tent, major types of tents, bed and mattress,
   sleeping bags, Swiss army knife, cooking set, cutlery set, two-burner camp stove,
   propane or butane accessories, single-burner camp stove, heater, lantern, tools
knots 691
cable 692
   shot splice, twisted rope, braided rope

INDOOR GAMES
card games 695
   symbols, standard poker hands
dominoes 695
chess 696
   chessboard, types of movements, men
backgammon 697
go 697
   board, major motions
game of darts 698
   dartboard, dart, playing area
video entertainment system 699
dice 699
roulette table 700
   American roulette wheel, American betting layout, French roulette wheel,
   French betting layout
slot machine 702

MEASURING DEVICES
measure of temperature 705
   thermometer, bimetallic thermometer, clinical thermometer, room thermostat
measure of time 706
   stopwatch, mechanical watch, digital watch, analog watch, sundial, grandfa-
   ther clock, weight-driven clock mechanism

CONTENTS

measure of weight.. 708
   beam balance, steelyard, Roberval's balance, spring balance, bathroom scale,
   electronic scales, analytical balance
measure of pressure... 710
   barometer/thermometer, tensiometer
measure of length 711
   tape measure
measure of distance.. 711
   pedometer
measure of thickness.. 711
   micrometer caliper
watt-hour meter.. 712
   exterior view, mechanism
measure of angles... 713
   bevel square, theodolite, protractor
measure of seismic waves... 714
   detection of seismic waves, amplification of seismic waves, transcription of seis-
   mic waves, visualization of seismic waves

OPTICAL INSTRUMENTS
electron microscope 717
   cross section of an electron microscope, electron microscope elements
binocular microscope.. 718
telescopic sight... 718
prism binoculars... 719
magnetic compass 719
reflecting telescope 720
refracting telescope 721
lenses... 722
   converging lenses, diverging lenses
radar 722

HEALTH AND SAFETY
first aid kit... 725
first aid equipment.. 726
   stethoscope, cot, stretcher, syringe
wheelchair... 727
walking aids 728
   forearm crutch, canes, underarm crutch
ear protection 729
   safety earmuff, ear plugs
eye protection.. 729
   safety goggles, safety glasses
head protection.. 729
   safety cap
respiratory system protection.. 730
   respirator, half-mask respirator
safety vest.. 730
feet protection 730

ENERGY
coal mine 733
   open-pit mine, strip mine, pithead, underground mine, jackleg drill, pneumatic
   hammer

CONTENTS

oil 737
    drilling rig, rotary system, production platform, offshore drilling, Christmas tree, crude-oil pipeline, fixed-roof tank, floating-roof tank, tank trailer, tanker, tank car, refinery products

electricity 746
    hydroelectric complex, cross section of hydroelectric power station, embankment dam, gravity dam, arch dam, buttress dam, tidal power plant, generator unit, Francis turbine, Kaplan turbine, Pelton turbine, steps in production of electricity, pylon, electricity transmission, overhead connection

nuclear energy 758
    nuclear generating station, carbon dioxide reactor, heavy-water reactor, pressurized-water reactor, boiling-water reactor, fuel handling sequence, fuel bundle, nuclear reactor, production of electricity from nuclear energy

solar energy 768
    solar cell, flat-plate solar collector, solar-cell system, solar furnace, production of electricity from solar energy, solar house, Trombe wall

wind energy 773
    windmill, post mill, horizontal-axis wind turbine, vertical-axis wind turbine

HEAVY MACHINERY

fire prevention 777
    fireman, helmet, hand lamp, ladder and hose strap

fire engine 778
    pumper, nozzle, fire hose, dividing breeching, fire hydrant wrench, aerial ladder truck, portable fire extinguisher, pike pole, percussion bar, hook ladder, fireman's hatchet

heavy vehicles 782
    wheel loader, bulldozer, scraper, grader, dump truck, hydraulic shovel

material handling 786
    tower crane, truck crane, gantry crane, forklift truck, hydraulic pallet truck, wing pallet, box pallet

WEAPONS

Stone Age weapons 791

weapons in the age of the Romans 791
    Gallic warrior, Roman legionary

armor 792
    armet

bows and crossbow 793
    modern bow, bow, arrow, crossbow

thrusting and cutting weapons 794

harquebus 795
    flintlock

submachine gun 795

automatic rifle 796

light machine gun 796

revolver 797

pistol 797

hunting weapons 798
    rifle (rifled bore), cartridge (rifle), shotgun (smooth-bore), cartridge (shotgun)

seventeenth century cannon 800
    muzzle loading, cross section of a muzzle loading, firing accessories, projectiles

modern howitzer 802

mortar 803
    seventeenth century mortar, modern mortar

CONTENTS

hand grenade.. 804
bazooka... 804
recoilless rifle 804
tank.. 805
submarine.. 806
frigate.. 808
aircraft carrier 810
combat aircraft 812
    in-flight refueling
missiles.. 814
    structure of a missile, major types of missiles

SYMBOLS
heraldry 817
    parts of a flag, flag shapes, shield divisions, examples of partitions, examples of ordinaries, examples of charges, examples of colors, examples of metals, examples of furs
signs of the zodiac.. 820
    fire signs, earth signs, air signs, water signs
safety symbols... 821
    dangerous materials, protection
common symbols 822
road signs 824
    major North American road signs, major international road signs
fabric care... 829
    washing, drying, ironing
common scientific symbols.. 830
    mathematics, geometry, biology, chemistry, miscellaneous symbols
diacritic symbols... 832
punctuation marks 832
examples of currency abbreviations 832

GENERAL INDEX 833

LIST OF CHAPTERS

1 **ASTRONOMY**

17 **GEOGRAPHY**

53 **VEGETABLE KINGDOM**

75 **ANIMAL KINGDOM**

113 **HUMAN BEING**

145 **FARMING**

163 **ARCHITECTURE**

191 **HOUSE**

217 **HOUSE FURNITURE**

261 **GARDENING**

273 **DO-IT-YOURSELF**

313 **CLOTHING**

359 **PERSONAL ADORNMENT**

371 **PERSONAL ARTICLES**

387 **COMMUNICATIONS**

423 **TRANSPORT**

513 **OFFICE SUPPLIES**

533 **MUSIC**

559 **CREATIVE LEISURE ACTIVITIES**

593 **SPORTS**

693 **INDOOR GAMES**

703 **MEASURING DEVICES**

715 **OPTICAL INSTRUMENTS**

723 **HEALTH AND SAFETY**

731 **ENERGY**

775 **HEAVY MACHINERY**

789 **WEAPONS**

815 **SYMBOLS**

833 **INDEX**

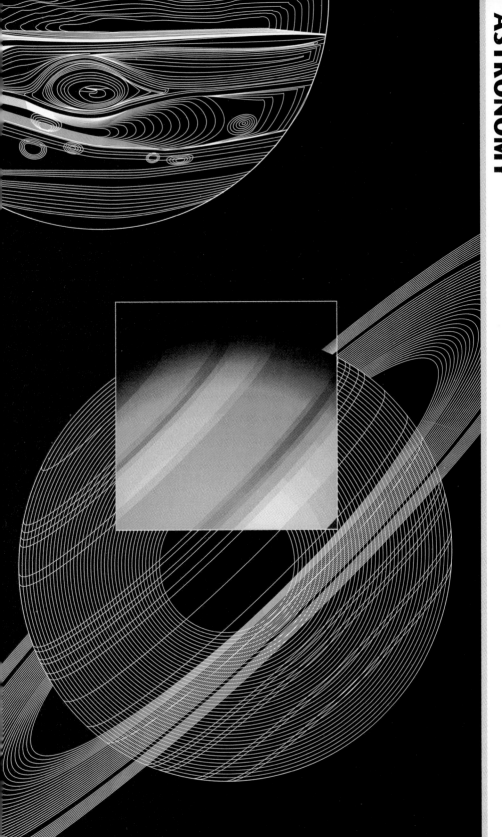

CONTENTS

CELESTIAL COORDINATE SYSTEM

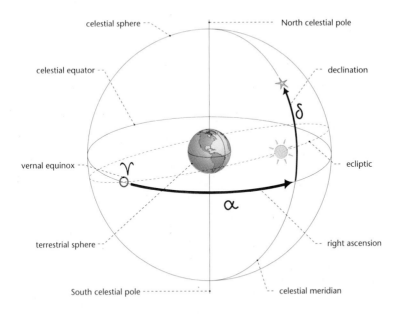

celestial sphere

North celestial pole

celestial equator

declination

vernal equinox

ecliptic

terrestrial sphere

right ascension

South celestial pole

celestial meridian

EARTH COORDINATE SYSTEM

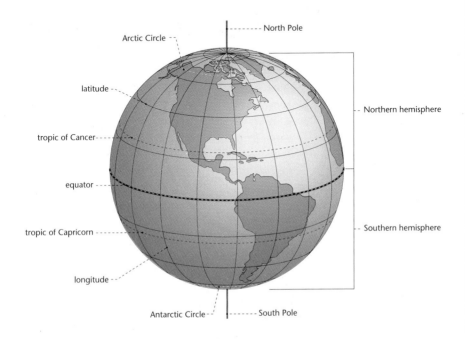

North Pole

Arctic Circle

latitude

Northern hemisphere

tropic of Cancer

equator

tropic of Capricorn

Southern hemisphere

longitude

Antarctic Circle

South Pole

SOLAR SYSTEM

PLANETS AND MOONS

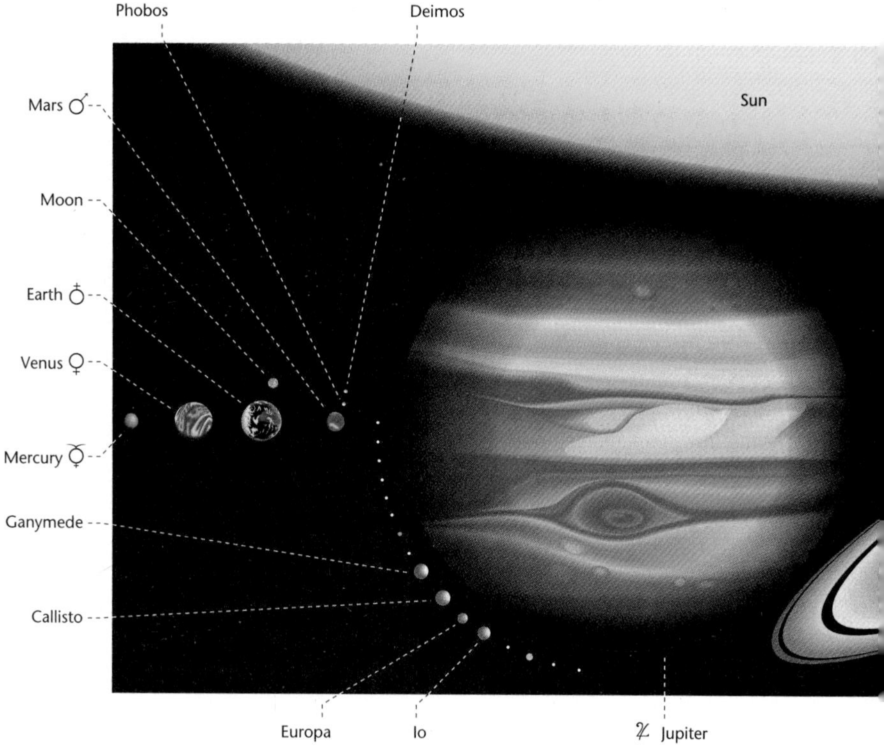
Phobos
Deimos
Mars ♂
Sun
Moon
Earth ♁
Venus ♀
Mercury ☿
Ganymede
Callisto
Europa
Io
♃ Jupiter

ORBITS OF THE PLANETS

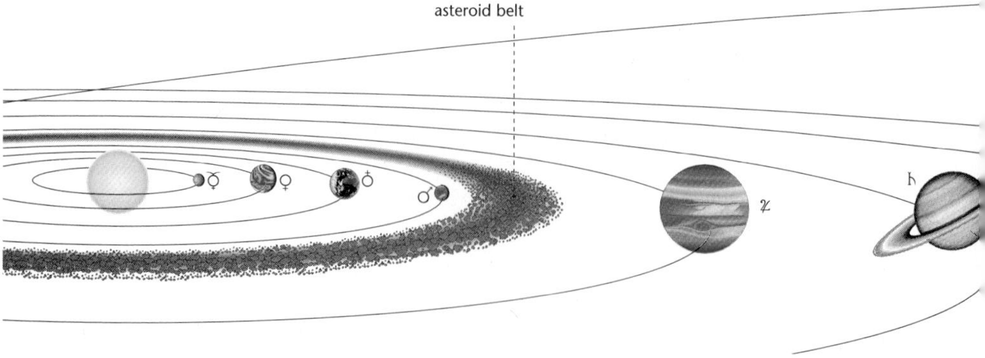
asteroid belt
☿
♀
♁
♂
♃
♄

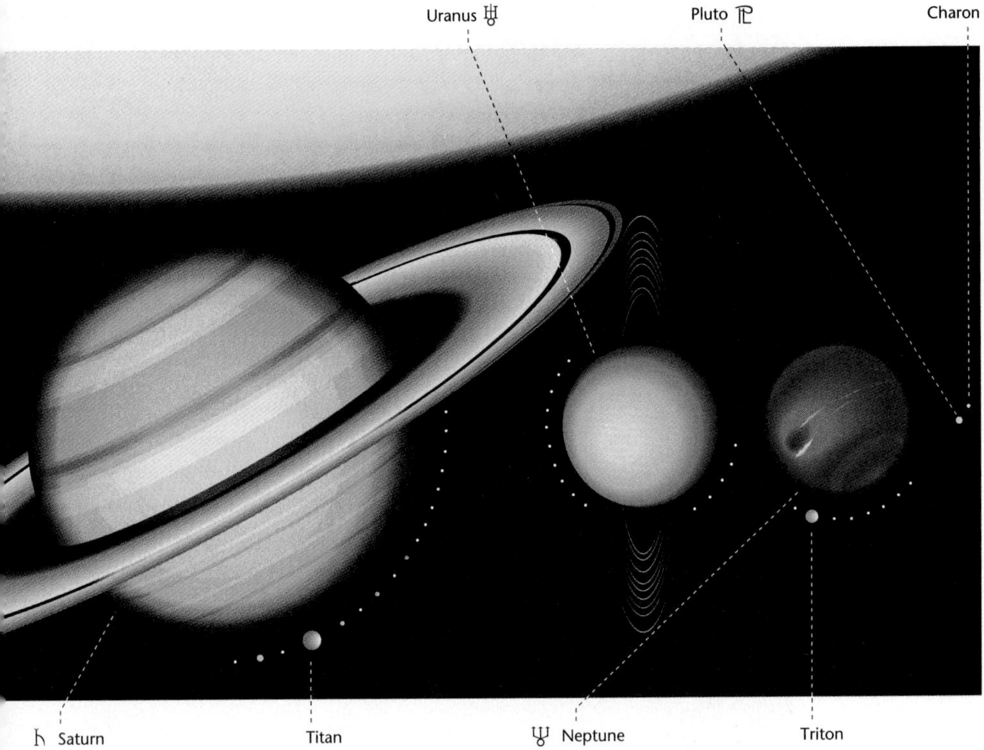
Uranus ♅
Pluto ♇
Charon
♄ Saturn
Titan
♆ Neptune
Triton

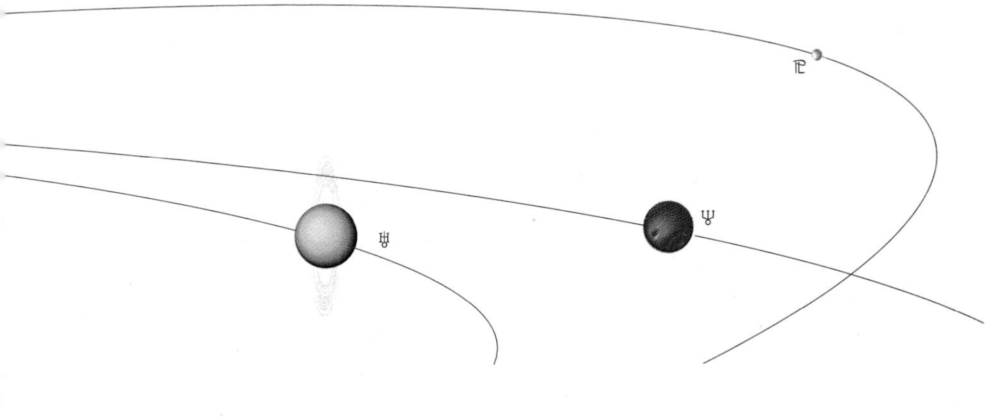
♇
♅
♆

STRUCTURE OF THE SUN

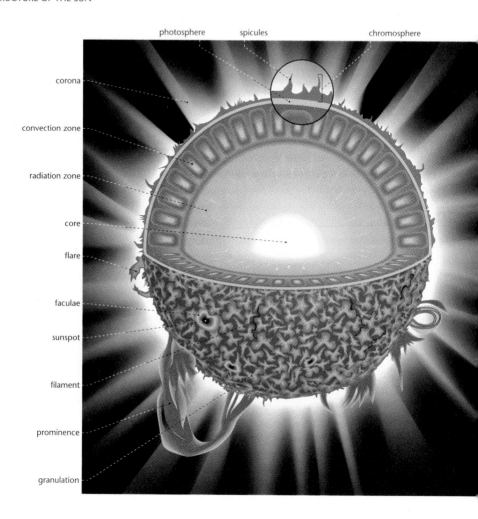

photosphere   spicules   chromosphere

corona

convection zone

radiation zone

core

flare

faculae

sunspot

filament

prominence

granulation

PHASES OF THE MOON

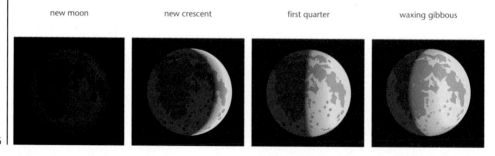

new moon   new crescent   first quarter   waxing gibbous

MOON

LUNAR FEATURES

bay
cliff
ocean
lake
sea
mountain range
crater
wall
cirque

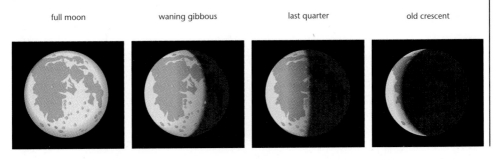

full moon

waning gibbous

last quarter

old crescent

SOLAR ECLIPSE

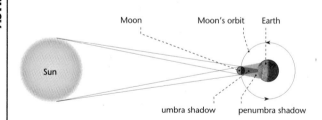

Moon   Moon's orbit   Earth

Sun

umbra shadow   penumbra shadow

TYPES OF ECLIPSES

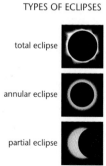

total eclipse

annular eclipse

partial eclipse

LUNAR ECLIPSE

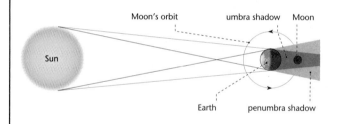

Moon's orbit   umbra shadow   Moon

Sun

Earth   penumbra shadow

TYPES OF ECLIPSES

partial eclipse

total eclipse

SEASONS OF THE YEAR

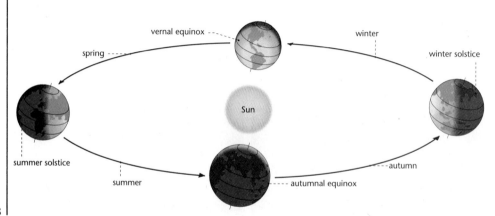

vernal equinox   winter

spring   winter solstice

Sun

summer solstice

summer   autumnal equinox   autumn

COMET

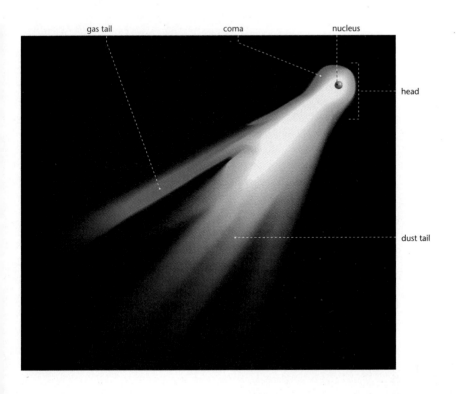

gas tail   coma   nucleus

head

dust tail

GALAXY

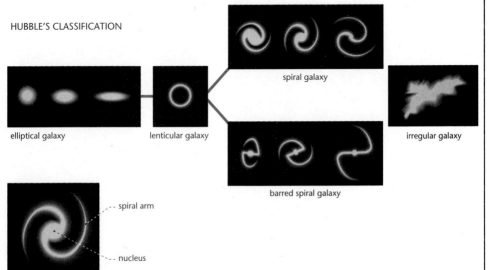

HUBBLE'S CLASSIFICATION

spiral galaxy

elliptical galaxy   lenticular galaxy

irregular galaxy

barred spiral galaxy

spiral arm

nucleus

9

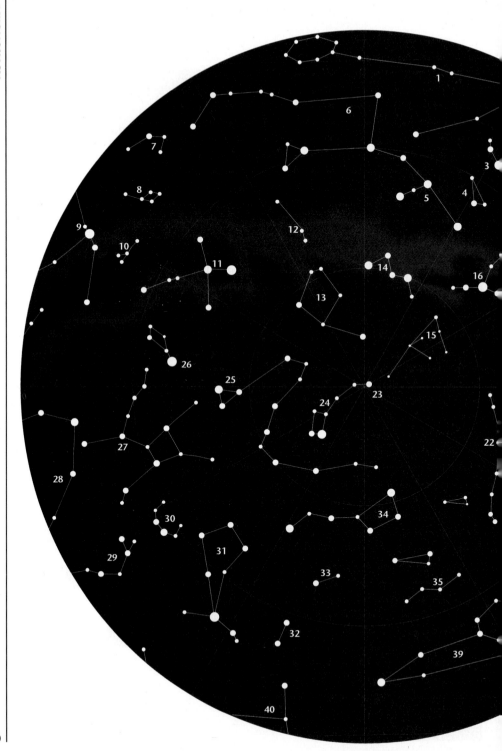

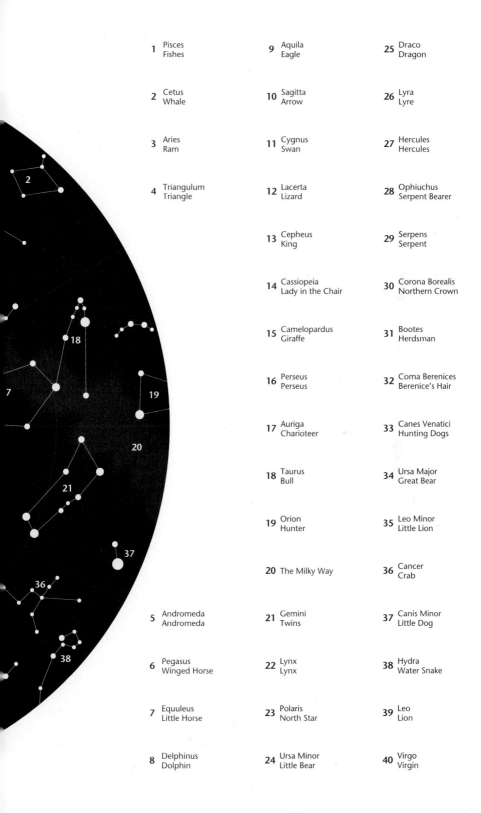

1 Pisces
Fishes

2 Cetus
Whale

3 Aries
Ram

4 Triangulum
Triangle

5 Andromeda
Andromeda

6 Pegasus
Winged Horse

7 Equuleus
Little Horse

8 Delphinus
Dolphin

9 Aquila
Eagle

10 Sagitta
Arrow

11 Cygnus
Swan

12 Lacerta
Lizard

13 Cepheus
King

14 Cassiopeia
Lady in the Chair

15 Camelopardus
Giraffe

16 Perseus
Perseus

17 Auriga
Charioteer

18 Taurus
Bull

19 Orion
Hunter

20 The Milky Way

21 Gemini
Twins

22 Lynx
Lynx

23 Polaris
North Star

24 Ursa Minor
Little Bear

25 Draco
Dragon

26 Lyra
Lyre

27 Hercules
Hercules

28 Ophiuchus
Serpent Bearer

29 Serpens
Serpent

30 Corona Borealis
Northern Crown

31 Bootes
Herdsman

32 Coma Berenices
Berenice's Hair

33 Canes Venatici
Hunting Dogs

34 Ursa Major
Great Bear

35 Leo Minor
Little Lion

36 Cancer
Crab

37 Canis Minor
Little Dog

38 Hydra
Water Snake

39 Leo
Lion

40 Virgo
Virgin

CONSTELLATIONS OF THE SOUTHERN HEMISPHERE

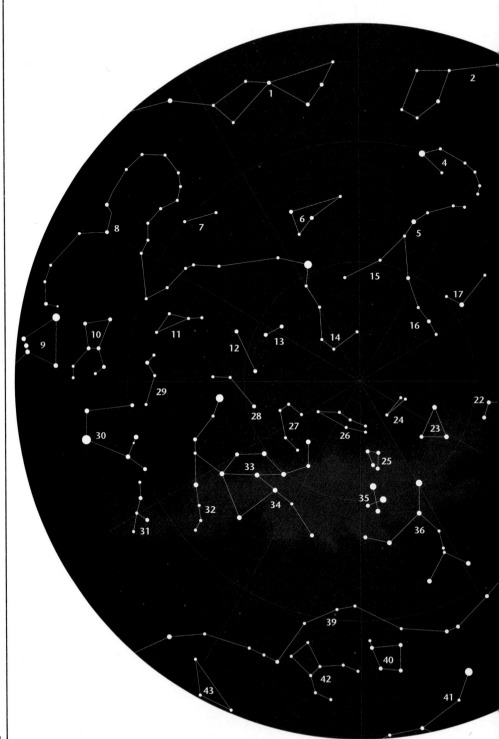

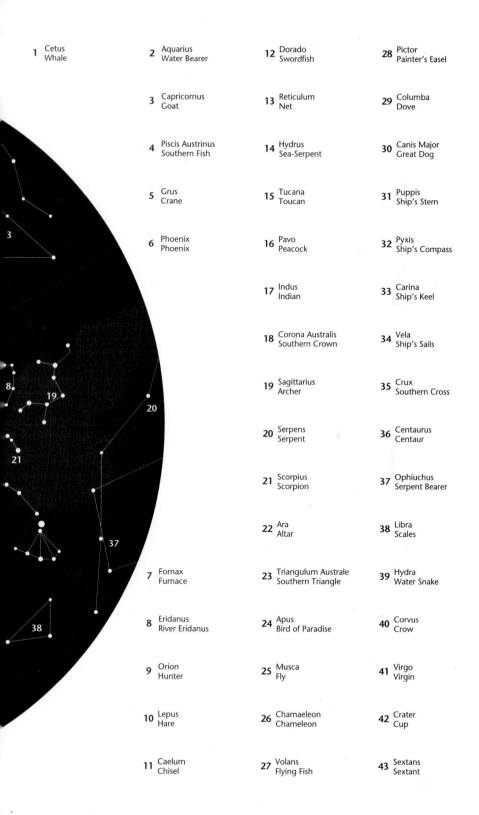

1 Cetus
Whale

2 Aquarius
Water Bearer

12 Dorado
Swordfish

28 Pictor
Painter's Easel

3 Capricornus
Goat

13 Reticulum
Net

29 Columba
Dove

4 Piscis Austrinus
Southern Fish

14 Hydrus
Sea-Serpent

30 Canis Major
Great Dog

5 Grus
Crane

15 Tucana
Toucan

31 Puppis
Ship's Stern

6 Phoenix
Phoenix

16 Pavo
Peacock

32 Pyxis
Ship's Compass

17 Indus
Indian

33 Carina
Ship's Keel

18 Corona Australis
Southern Crown

34 Vela
Ship's Sails

19 Sagittarius
Archer

35 Crux
Southern Cross

20 Serpens
Serpent

36 Centaurus
Centaur

21 Scorpius
Scorpion

37 Ophiuchus
Serpent Bearer

22 Ara
Altar

38 Libra
Scales

7 Fornax
Furnace

23 Triangulum Australe
Southern Triangle

39 Hydra
Water Snake

8 Eridanus
River Eridanus

24 Apus
Bird of Paradise

40 Corvus
Crow

9 Orion
Hunter

25 Musca
Fly

41 Virgo
Virgin

10 Lepus
Hare

26 Chamaeleon
Chamaeleon

42 Crater
Cup

11 Caelum
Chisel

27 Volans
Flying Fish

43 Sextans
Sextant

ASTRONOMICAL OBSERVATORY

TELESCOPE

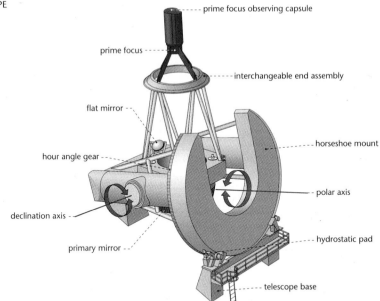

prime focus observing capsule

prime focus

interchangeable end assembly

flat mirror

horseshoe mount

hour angle gear

polar axis

declination axis

hydrostatic pad

primary mirror

telescope base

OBSERVATORY

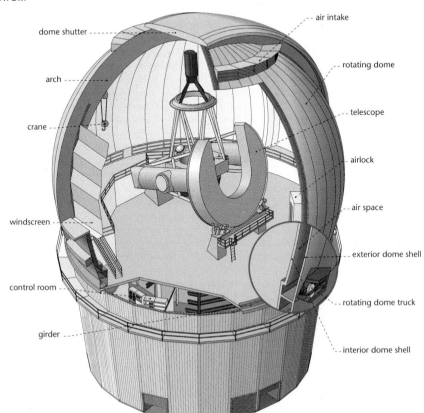

dome shutter

air intake

arch

rotating dome

crane

telescope

airlock

air space

windscreen

exterior dome shell

control room

rotating dome truck

girder

interior dome shell

RADIO TELESCOPE

ALTAZIMUTH MOUNTING

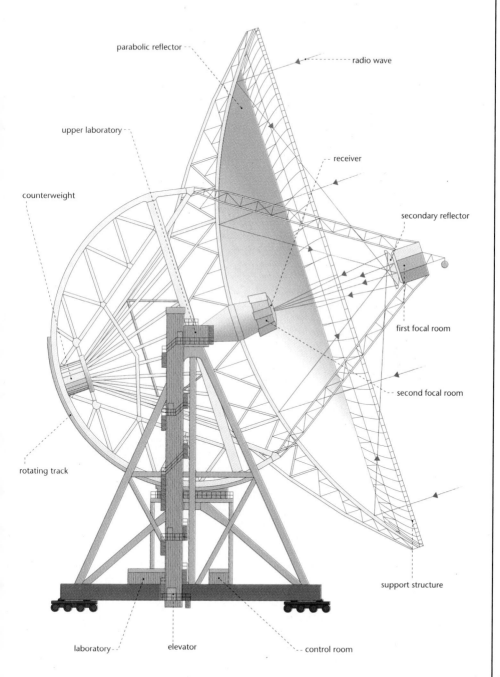

parabolic reflector

radio wave

upper laboratory

receiver

counterweight

secondary reflector

first focal room

second focal room

rotating track

support structure

laboratory

elevator

control room

HUBBLE SPACE TELESCOPE

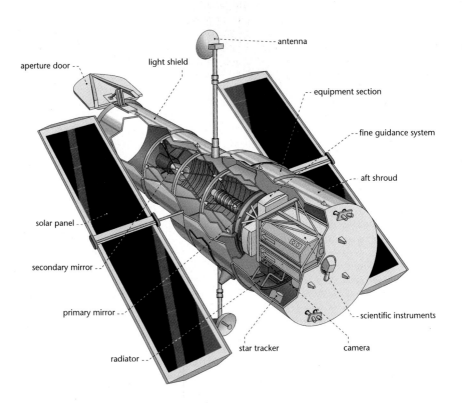

antenna

aperture door

light shield

equipment section

fine guidance system

aft shroud

solar panel

secondary mirror

scientific instruments

primary mirror

star tracker

camera

radiator

PLANETARIUM

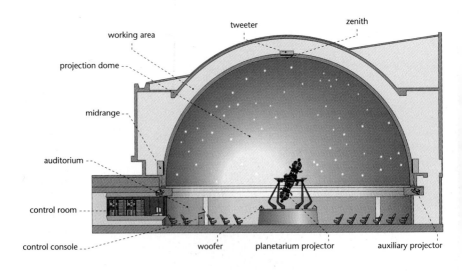

working area

tweeter

zenith

projection dome

midrange

auditorium

control room

control console

woofer

planetarium projector

auxiliary projector

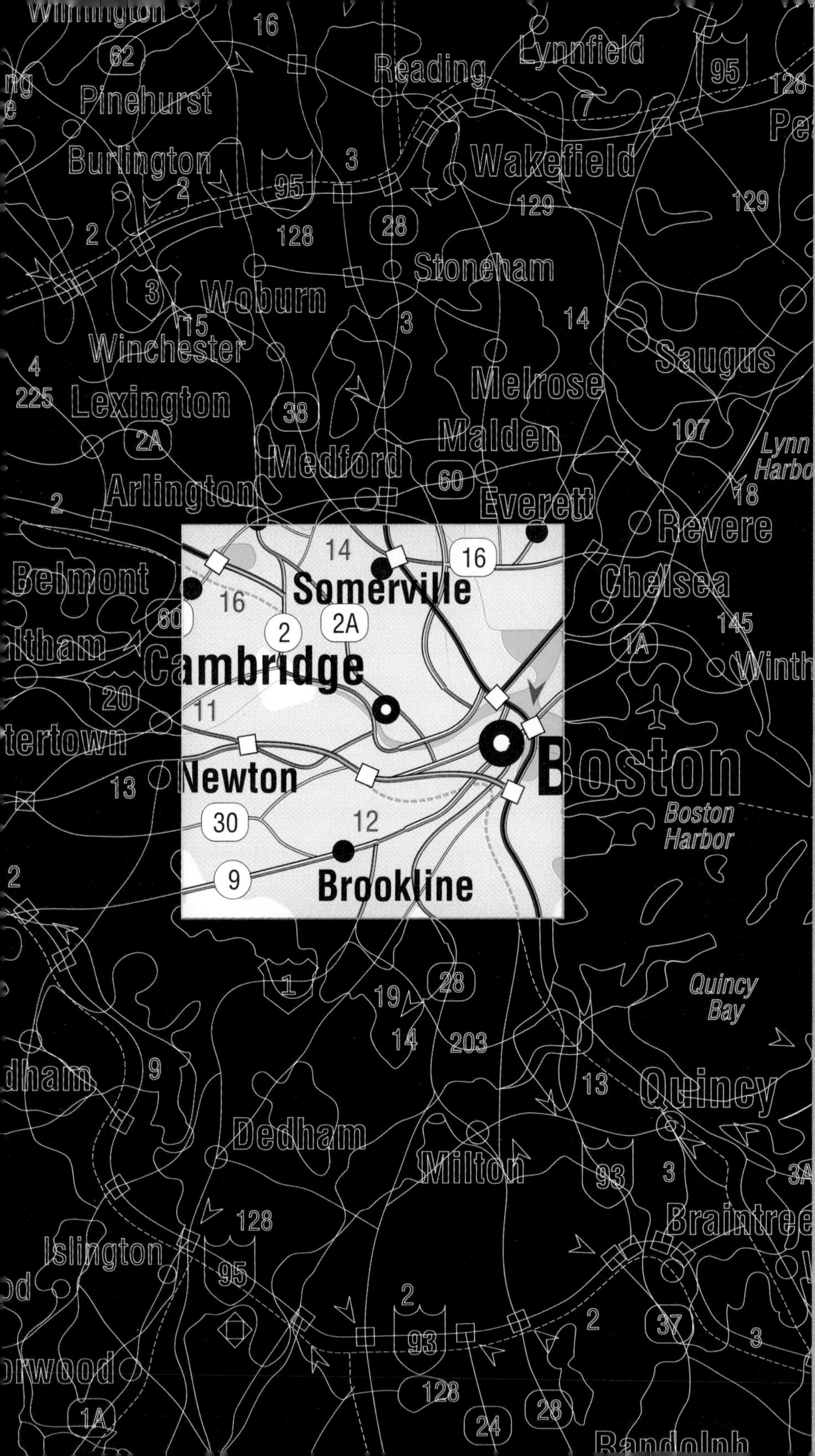
Reading
Lynnfield
Pinehurst
Burlington
Wakefield
Stoneham
Woburn
Winchester
Melrose
Saugus
Lexington
Malden
Medford
Arlington
Everett
Revere
Lynn Harbor
Belmont
Somerville
Chelsea
Cambridge
Newton
Boston
Boston Harbor
Brookline
Quincy Bay
Quincy
Dedham
Milton
Braintree
Islington

CONTENTS

PROFILE OF THE EARTH'S ATMOSPHERE

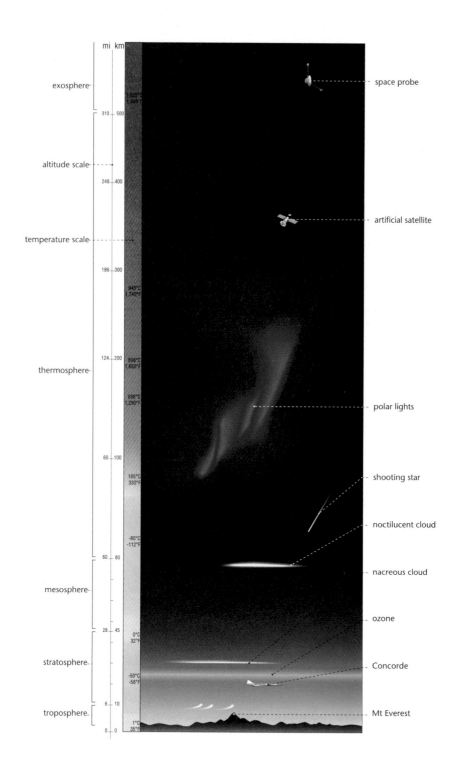

exosphere

altitude scale

temperature scale

thermosphere

mesosphere

stratosphere

troposphere

mi km

space probe

artificial satellite

polar lights

shooting star

noctilucent cloud

nacreous cloud

ozone

Concorde

Mt Everest

CONFIGURATION OF THE CONTINENTS

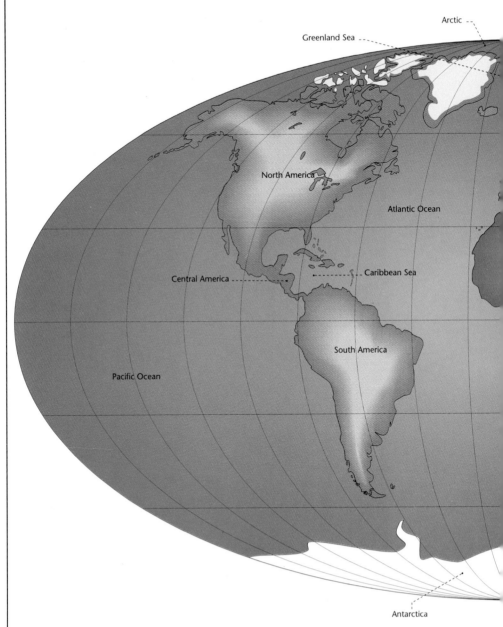

Arctic

Greenland Sea

North America

Atlantic Ocean

Central America

Caribbean Sea

South America

Pacific Ocean

Antarctica

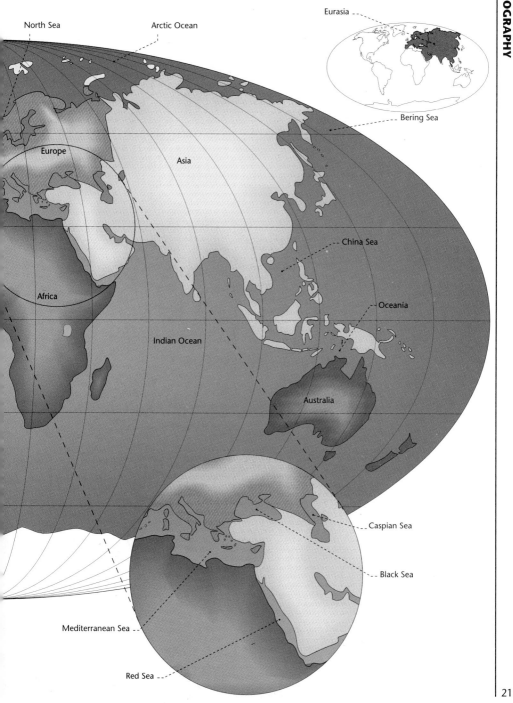

North Sea

Arctic Ocean

Eurasia

Bering Sea

Europe

Asia

China Sea

Africa

Oceania

Indian Ocean

Australia

Caspian Sea

Black Sea

Mediterranean Sea

Red Sea

STRUCTURE OF THE EARTH

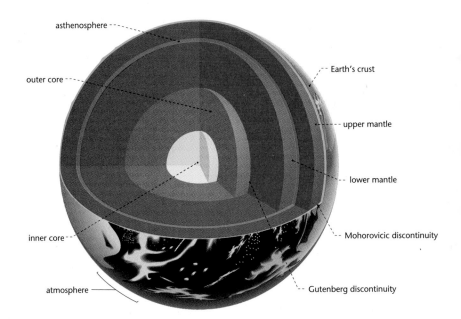

asthenosphere

Earth's crust

outer core

upper mantle

lower mantle

inner core

Mohorovicic discontinuity

atmosphere

Gutenberg discontinuity

SECTION OF THE EARTH'S CRUST

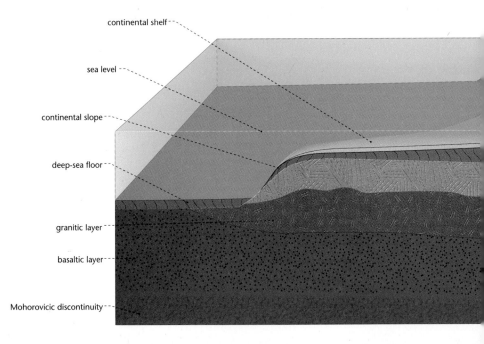

continental shelf

sea level

continental slope

deep-sea floor

granitic layer

basaltic layer

Mohorovicic discontinuity

EARTHQUAKE

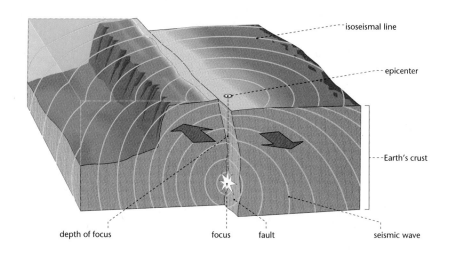

isoseismal line

epicenter

Earth's crust

depth of focus   focus   fault   seismic wave

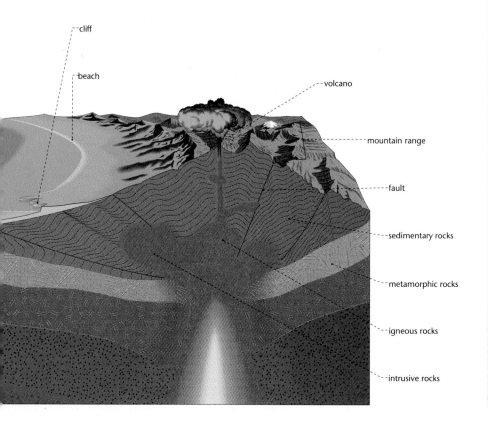

cliff

beach

volcano

mountain range

fault

sedimentary rocks

metamorphic rocks

igneous rocks

intrusive rocks

CAVE

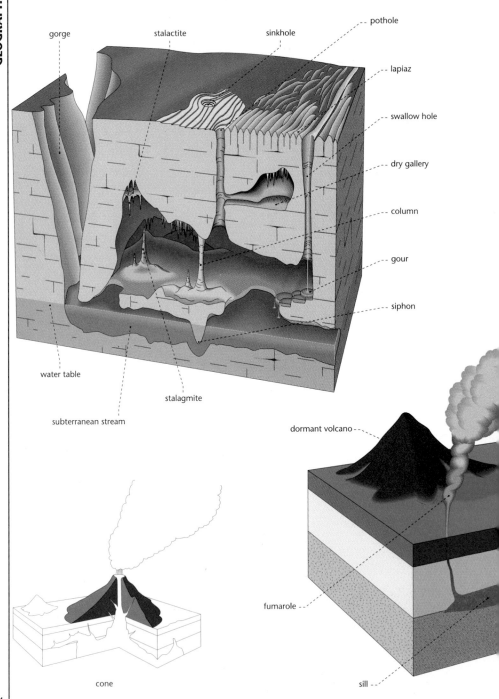

gorge

stalactite

sinkhole

pothole

lapiaz

swallow hole

dry gallery

column

gour

siphon

water table

subterranean stream

stalagmite

dormant volcano

fumarole

cone

sill

24

VOLCANO

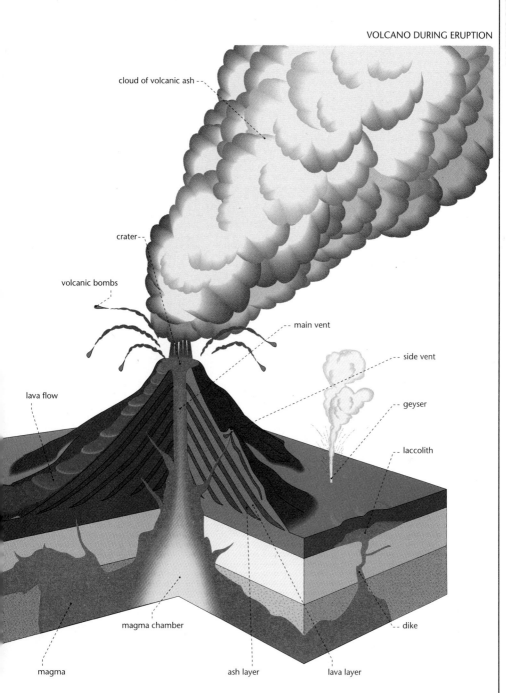

VOLCANO DURING ERUPTION

cloud of volcanic ash

crater

volcanic bombs

main vent

side vent

lava flow

geyser

laccolith

magma chamber

magma

ash layer

lava layer

dike

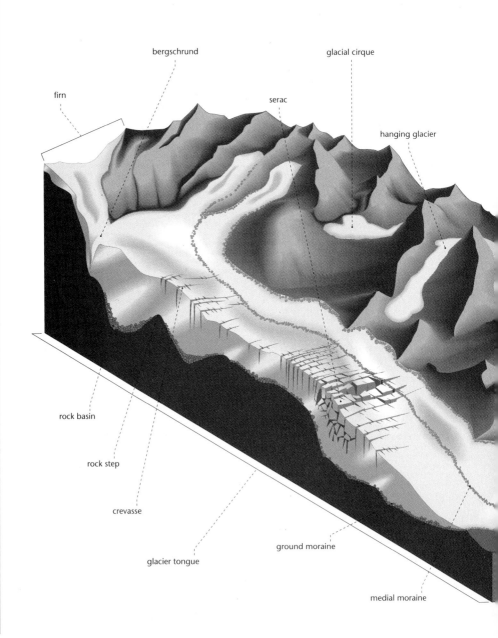

firn

bergschrund

glacial cirque

serac

hanging glacier

rock basin

rock step

crevasse

glacier tongue

ground moraine

medial moraine

MOUNTAIN

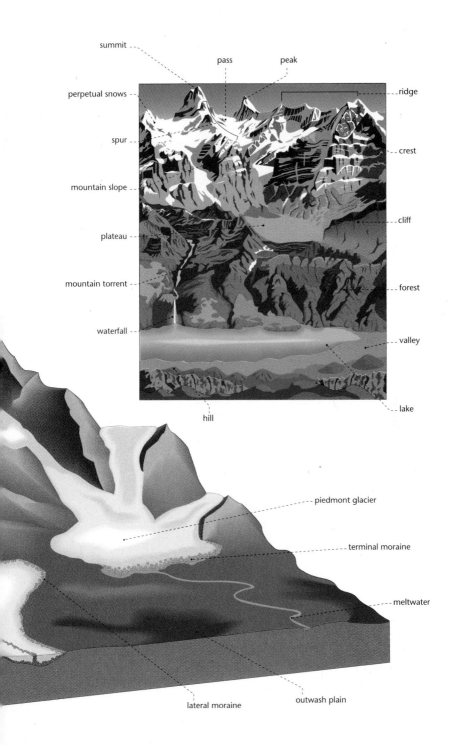

summit

pass   peak

perpetual snows

ridge

spur

crest

mountain slope

cliff

plateau

mountain torrent

forest

waterfall

valley

lake

hill

piedmont glacier

terminal moraine

meltwater

lateral moraine   outwash plain

MID-OCEAN RIDGE

TOPOGRAPHIC FEATURES

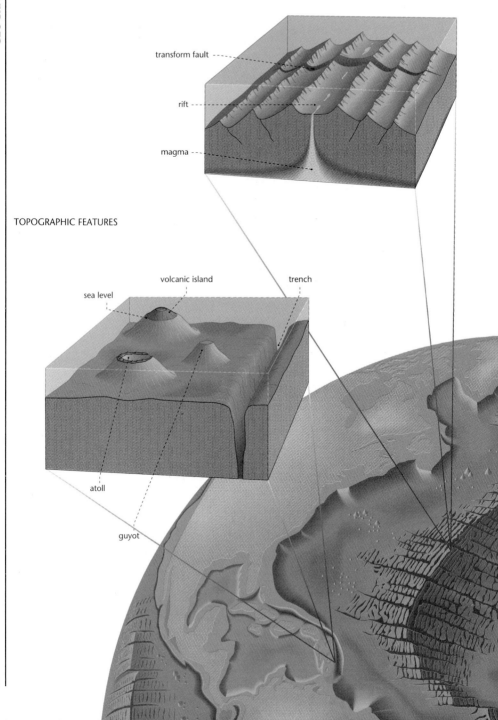

transform fault

rift

magma

volcanic island

trench

sea level

atoll

guyot

ABYSSAL PLAIN

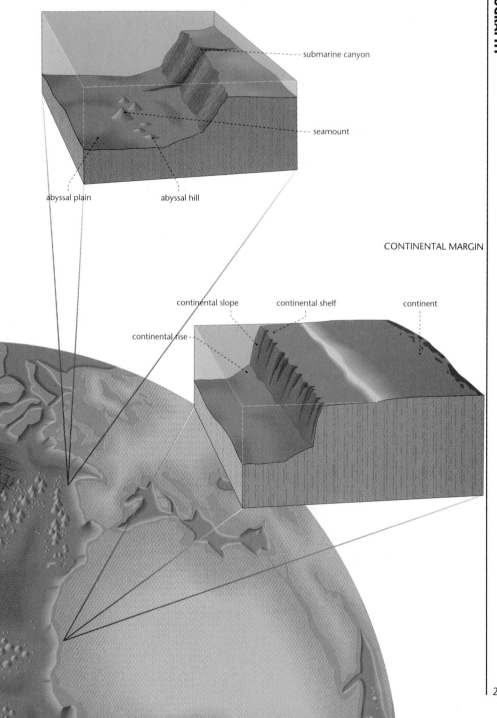

submarine canyon

seamount

abyssal plain

abyssal hill

CONTINENTAL MARGIN

continental slope

continental shelf

continent

continental rise

29

WAVE

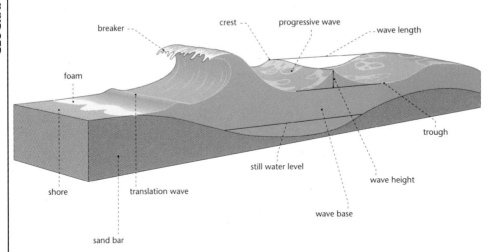

breaker

crest

progressive wave

wave length

foam

shore

translation wave

sand bar

still water level

wave base

wave height

trough

COMMON COASTAL FEATURES

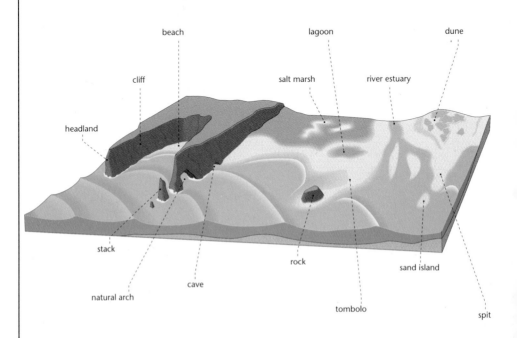

beach

lagoon

dune

cliff

salt marsh

river estuary

headland

stack

natural arch

cave

rock

tombolo

sand island

spit

STRUCTURE OF THE BIOSPHERE

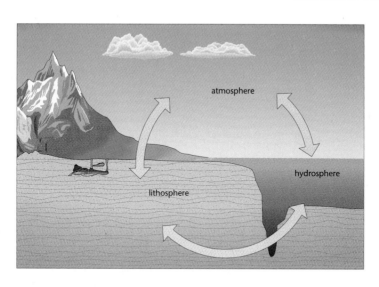

atmosphere

hydrosphere

lithosphere

FOOD CHAIN

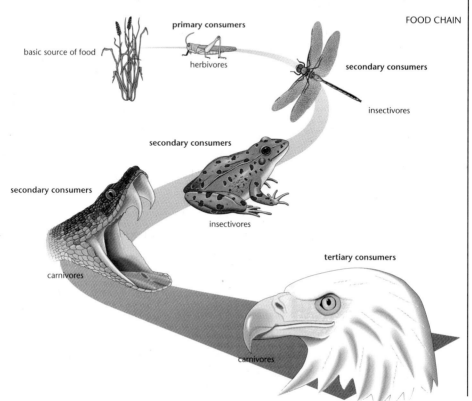

basic source of food

primary consumers

herbivores

secondary consumers

insectivores

secondary consumers

insectivores

secondary consumers

carnivores

tertiary consumers

carnivores

POLLUTION OF FOOD ON GROUND

POLLUTION OF FOOD IN WATER

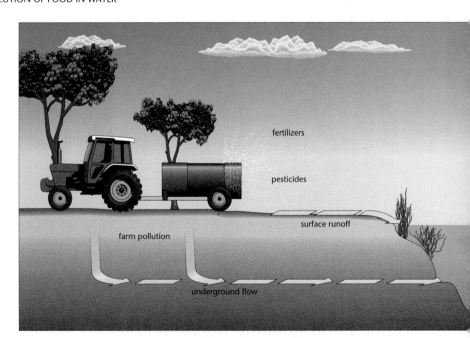

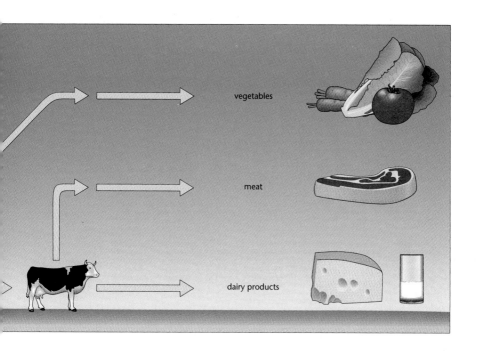

vegetables

meat

dairy products

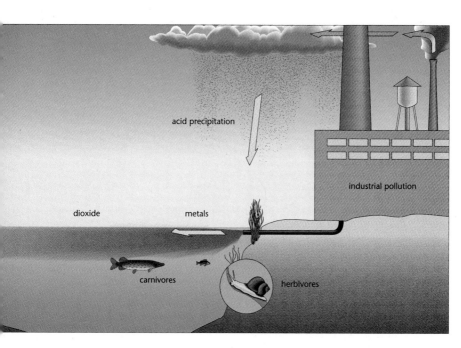

acid precipitation

industrial pollution

dioxide

metals

carnivores

herbivores

ATMOSPHERIC POLLUTION

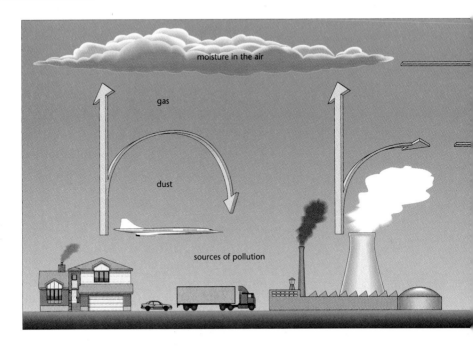

HYDROLOGIC CYCLE

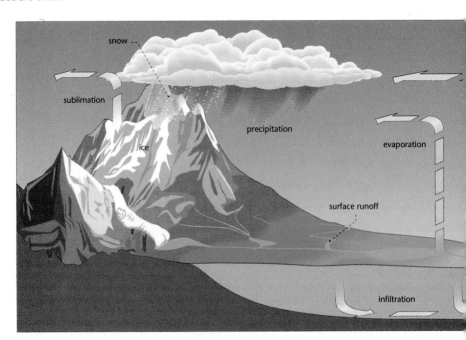

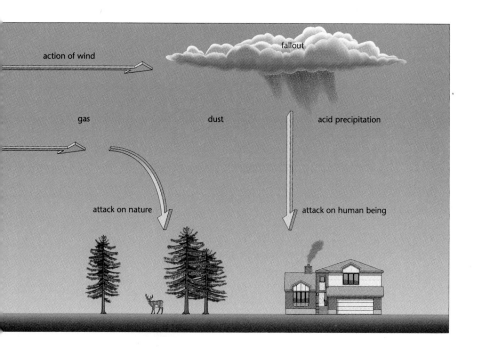

action of wind

fallout

gas

dust

acid precipitation

attack on nature

attack on human being

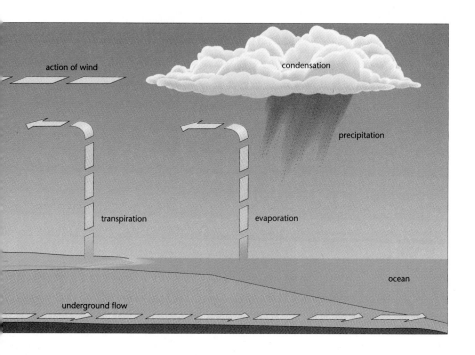

action of wind

condensation

precipitation

transpiration

evaporation

ocean

underground flow

35

STORMY SKY

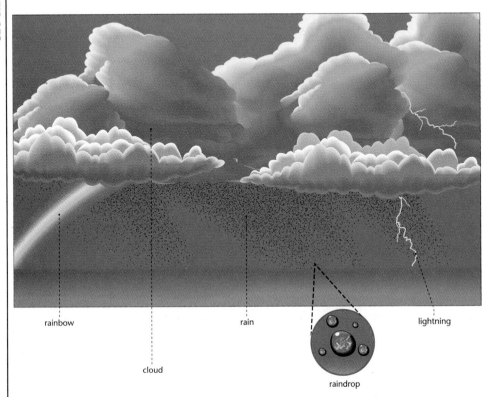

rainbow

rain

lightning

cloud

raindrop

CLASSIFICATION OF SNOW CRYSTALS

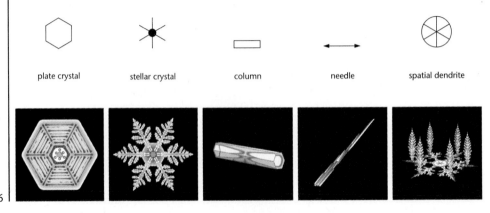

plate crystal

stellar crystal

column

needle

spatial dendrite

mist

fog

dew

frost

capped column

irregular crystal

snow pellet

sleet

hail

WEATHER MAP

wind direction and speed   barometric pressure   isobar

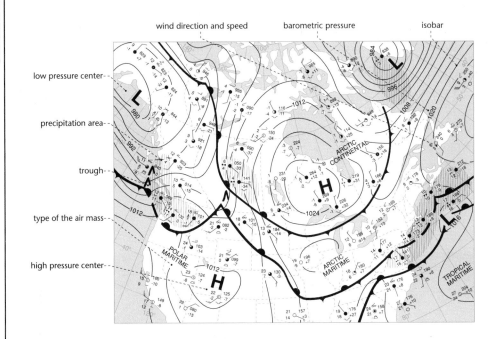

low pressure center

precipitation area

trough

type of the air mass

high pressure center

STATION MODEL

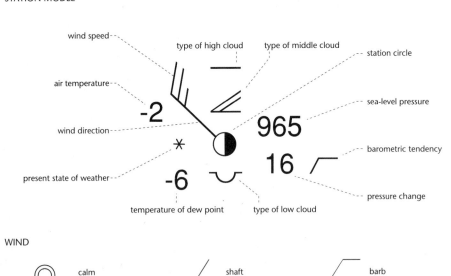

wind speed   type of high cloud   type of middle cloud   station circle

air temperature   sea-level pressure

wind direction   barometric tendency

present state of weather   pressure change

temperature of dew point   type of low cloud

WIND

calm   shaft   barb

wind arrow   half barb   pennant

INTERNATIONAL WEATHER SYMBOLS

FRONTS

surface cold front

surface warm front

occluded front

upper cold front

upper warm front

stationary front

SKY COVERAGE

clear sky

scattered sky

very cloudy sky

overcast sky

cloudy sky

slightly covered sky

obscured sky

PRESENT WEATHER

intermittent rain

snow shower

continuous rain

thunderstorm

sleet

intermittent drizzle

heavy thunderstorm

hail shower

continuous drizzle

sandstorm or dust storm

squall

intermittent snow

tropical storm

freezing rain

continuous snow

hurricane

smoke

rain shower

slight drifting snow low

mist

heavy drifting snow low

fog

METEOROLOGICAL MEASURING INSTRUMENTS

MEASURE OF SUNSHINE

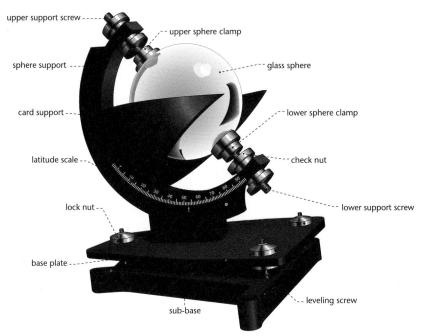

sunshine recorder

upper support screw

upper sphere clamp

sphere support

glass sphere

card support

lower sphere clamp

latitude scale

check nut

lock nut

lower support screw

base plate

leveling screw

sub-base

MEASURE OF RAINFALL

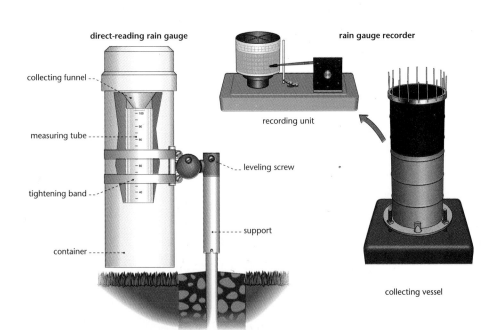

direct-reading rain gauge

rain gauge recorder

collecting funnel

measuring tube

leveling screw

tightening band

recording unit

support

container

collecting vessel

MEASURE OF TEMPERATURE

minimum thermometer

maximum thermometer

INSTRUMENT SHELTER

MEASURE OF AIR PRESSURE

barograph

mercury barometer

psychrometer

MEASURE OF WIND DIRECTION

wind vane

MEASURE OF WIND STRENGTH

anemometer

MEASURE OF HUMIDITY

hygrograph

MEASURE OF SNOWFALL

snow gauge

MEASURE OF CLOUD CEILING

theodolite

alidade

ceiling projector

41

GEOGRAPHY

GEOSTATIONARY SATELLITE

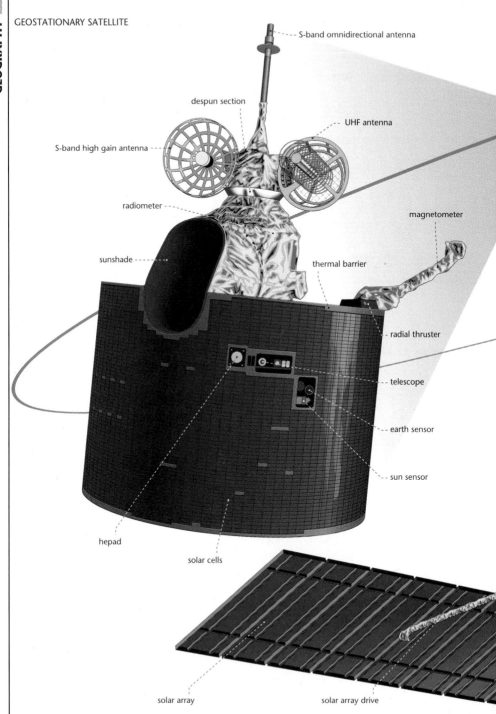

S-band omnidirectional antenna

despun section

UHF antenna

S-band high gain antenna

radiometer

magnetometer

sunshade

thermal barrier

radial thruster

telescope

earth sensor

sun sensor

hepad

solar cells

solar array

solar array drive

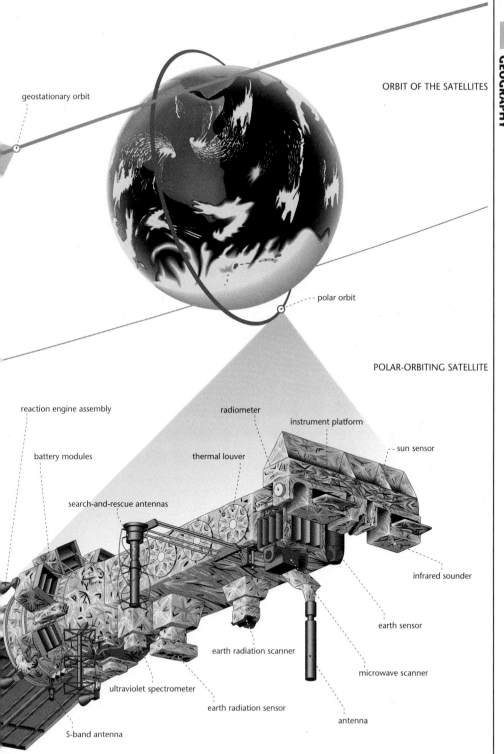

ORBIT OF THE SATELLITES

geostationary orbit

polar orbit

POLAR-ORBITING SATELLITE

reaction engine assembly

radiometer

instrument platform

sun sensor

battery modules

thermal louver

search-and-rescue antennas

infrared sounder

earth sensor

earth radiation scanner

microwave scanner

ultraviolet spectrometer

earth radiation sensor

antenna

S-band antenna

CLOUDS AND METEOROLOGICAL SYMBOLS

HIGH CLOUDS

CLOUDS OF VERTICAL DEVELOPMENT

cirrus

cirrocumulus

cirrostratus

cumulonimbus

MIDDLE CLOUDS

altostratus

altocumulus

stratocumulus

LOW CLOUDS

nimbostratus

stratus

cumulus

CLIMATES OF THE WORLD

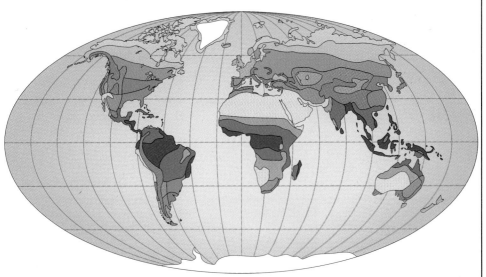

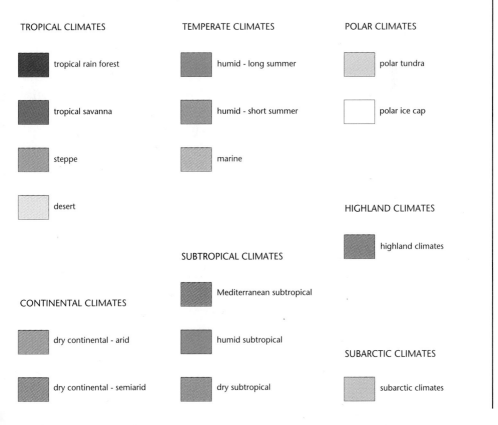

TROPICAL CLIMATES

- tropical rain forest
- tropical savanna
- steppe
- desert

TEMPERATE CLIMATES

- humid - long summer
- humid - short summer
- marine

POLAR CLIMATES

- polar tundra
- polar ice cap

HIGHLAND CLIMATES

- highland climates

SUBTROPICAL CLIMATES

- Mediterranean subtropical
- humid subtropical
- dry subtropical

CONTINENTAL CLIMATES

- dry continental - arid
- dry continental - semiarid

SUBARCTIC CLIMATES

- subarctic climates

DESERT

oasis   palm grove

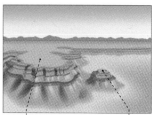

mesa   butte

rocky desert

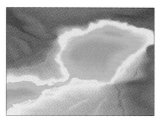

saline lake

sandy desert

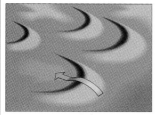

crescentic dune

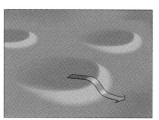

parabolic dune

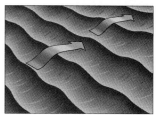

transverse dunes

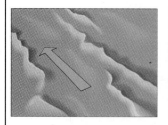

chain of dunes

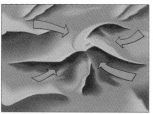

complex dune

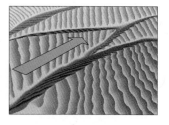

longitudinal dunes

CARTOGRAPHY

HEMISPHERES

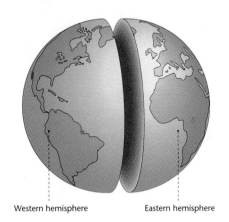

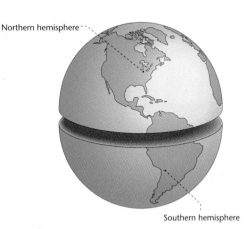

Northern hemisphere

Western hemisphere

Eastern hemisphere

Southern hemisphere

GRID SYSTEM

lines of latitude

lines of longitude

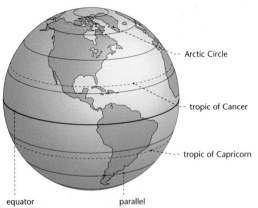

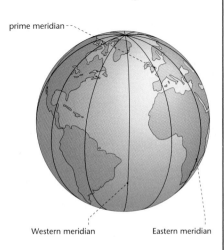

Arctic Circle

tropic of Cancer

tropic of Capricorn

equator

parallel

prime meridian

Western meridian

Eastern meridian

REMOTE DETECTION SATELLITE

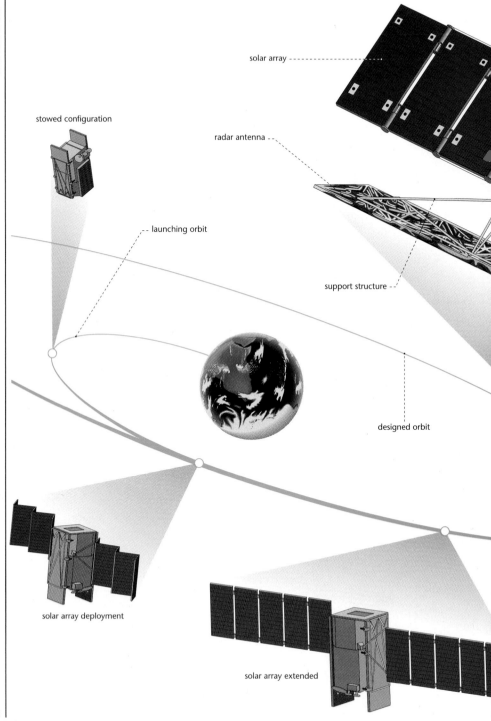

solar array

stowed configuration

radar antenna

launching orbit

support structure

designed orbit

solar array deployment

solar array extended

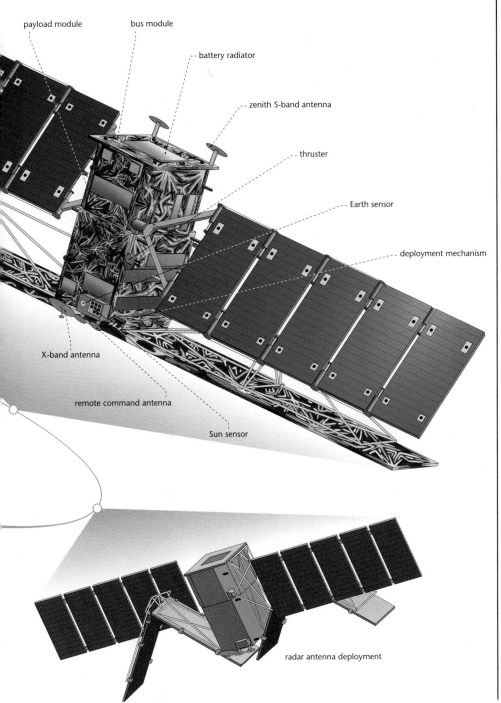

payload module

bus module

battery radiator

zenith S-band antenna

thruster

Earth sensor

deployment mechanism

X-band antenna

remote command antenna

Sun sensor

radar antenna deployment

MAP PROJECTIONS

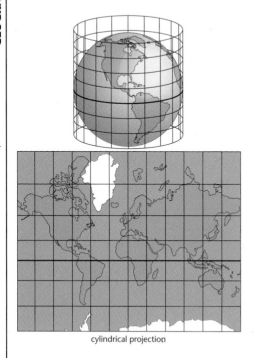

cylindrical projection

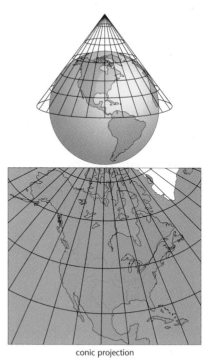

conic projection

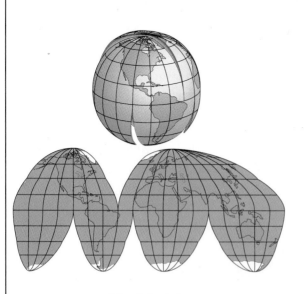

interrupted projection

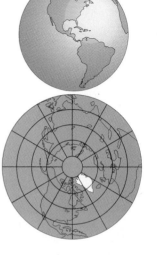

plane projection

POLITICAL MAP

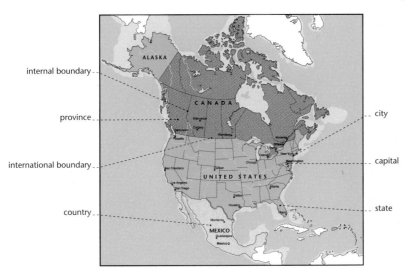

internal boundary

province

international boundary

country

ALASKA

CANADA

UNITED STATES

MEXICO

city

capital

state

PHYSICAL MAP

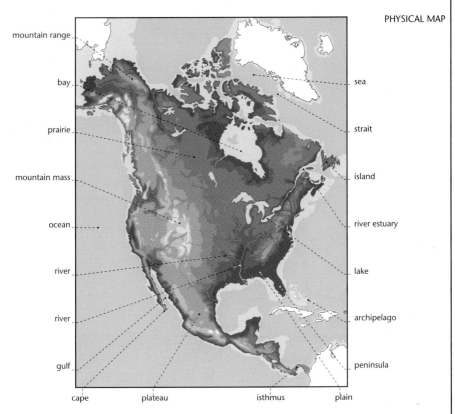

mountain range

bay

prairie

mountain mass

ocean

river

river

gulf

sea

strait

island

river estuary

lake

archipelago

peninsula

cape   plateau   isthmus   plain

51

URBAN MAP

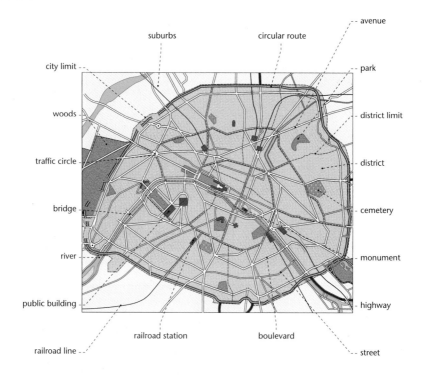

suburbs
circular route
avenue
city limit
park
woods
district limit
traffic circle
district
bridge
cemetery
river
monument
public building
highway
railroad station
boulevard
railroad line
street

ROAD MAP

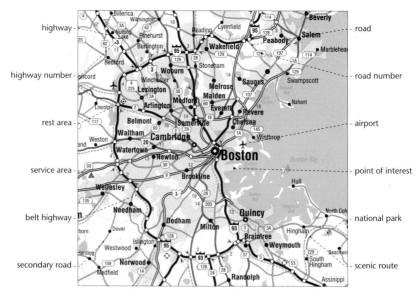

highway
road
highway number
road number
rest area
airport
service area
point of interest
belt highway
national park
secondary road
scenic route

VEGETABLE KINGDOM

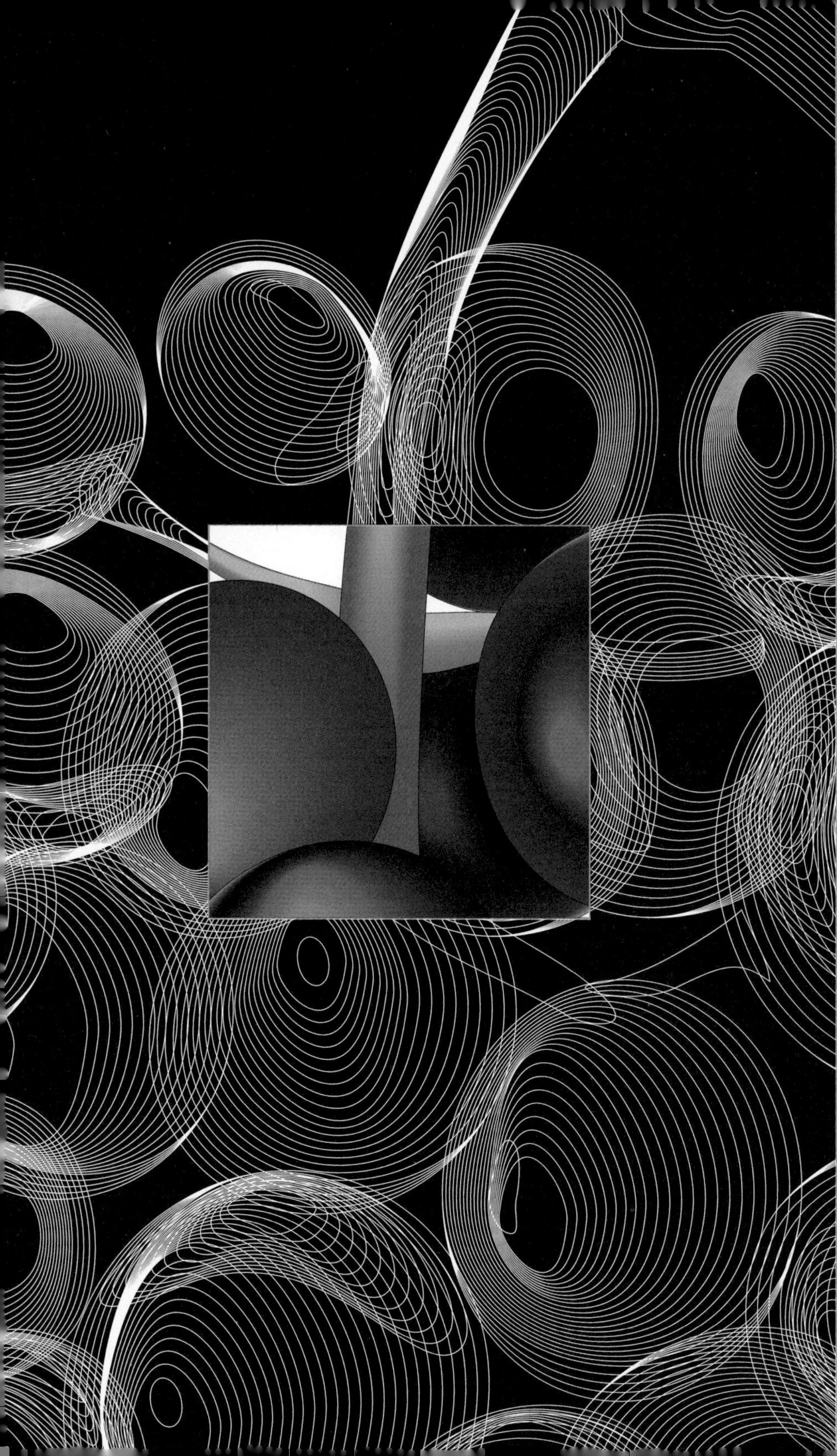

CONTENTS

MUSHROOM

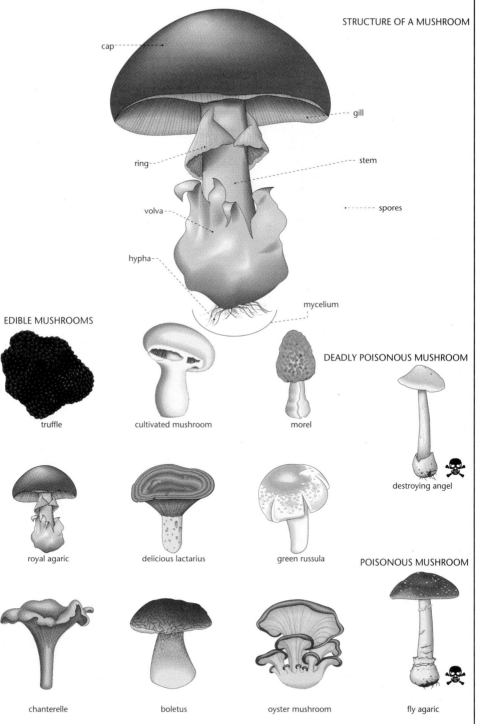

STRUCTURE OF A MUSHROOM

cap

gill

ring

stem

volva

spores

hypha

mycelium

EDIBLE MUSHROOMS

truffle

cultivated mushroom

morel

DEADLY POISONOUS MUSHROOM

royal agaric

delicious lactarius

green russula

destroying angel

POISONOUS MUSHROOM

chanterelle

boletus

oyster mushroom

fly agaric

TYPES OF LEAVES

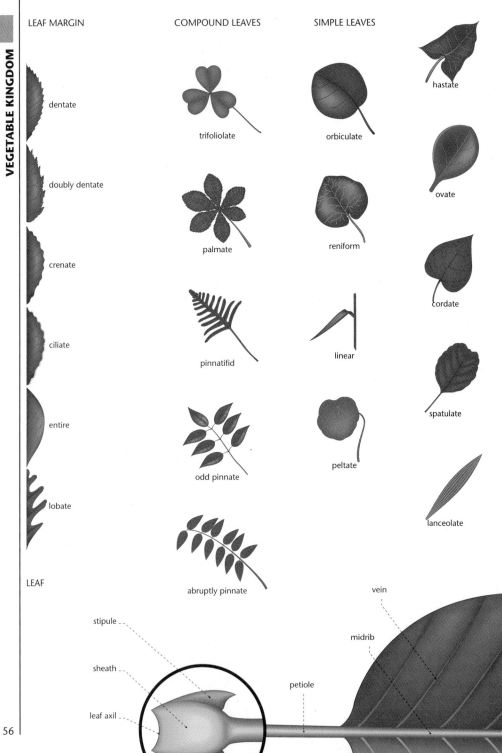

LEAF MARGIN

dentate

doubly dentate

crenate

ciliate

entire

lobate

LEAF

COMPOUND LEAVES

trifoliolate

palmate

pinnatifid

odd pinnate

abruptly pinnate

SIMPLE LEAVES

orbiculate

reniform

linear

peltate

hastate

ovate

cordate

spatulate

lanceolate

stipule

sheath

leaf axil

petiole

vein

midrib

STRUCTURE OF A PLANT

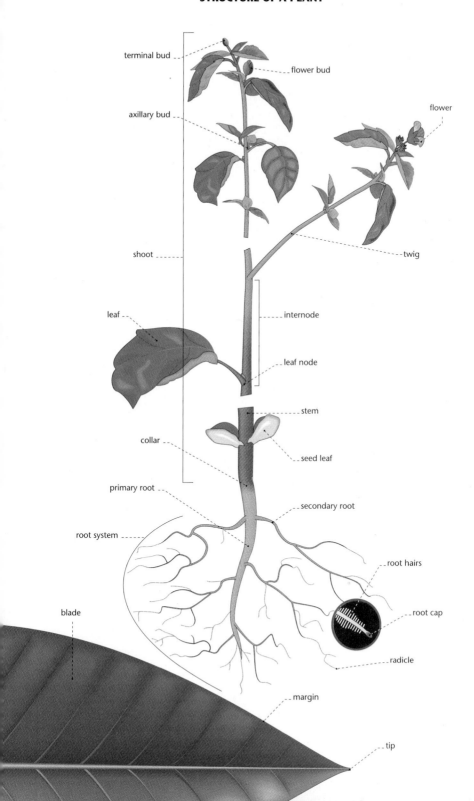

terminal bud

flower bud

axillary bud

flower

shoot

twig

leaf

internode

leaf node

stem

collar

seed leaf

primary root

secondary root

root system

root hairs

root cap

blade

radicle

margin

tip

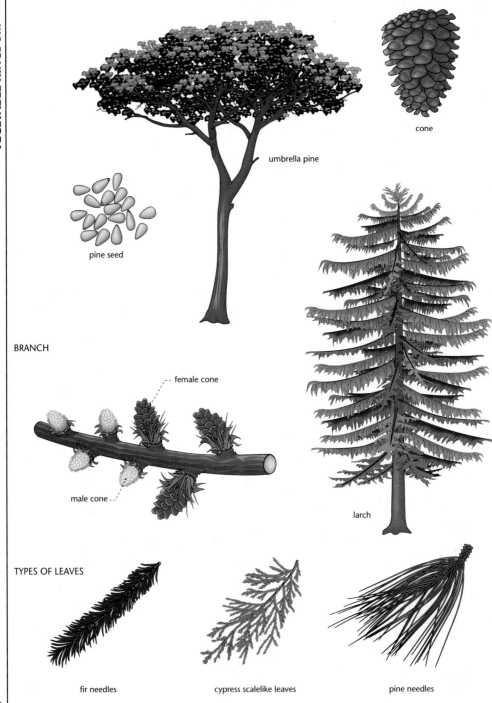

cone

umbrella pine

pine seed

BRANCH

female cone

male cone

larch

TYPES OF LEAVES

fir needles

cypress scalelike leaves

pine needles

STRUCTURE OF A TREE

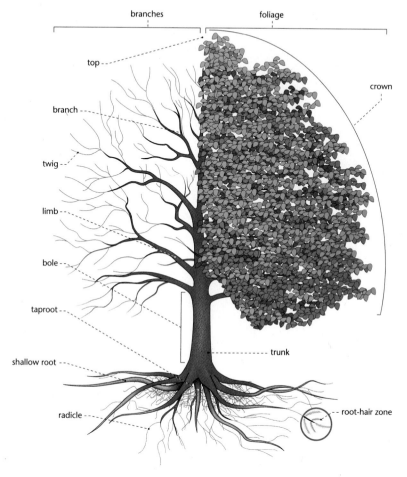

branches

foliage

top

crown

branch

twig

limb

bole

taproot

trunk

shallow root

radicle

root-hair zone

CROSS SECTION OF A TRUNK

wood ray

pith

annual ring

bark

heartwood

phloem

sapwood

cambium

STUMP

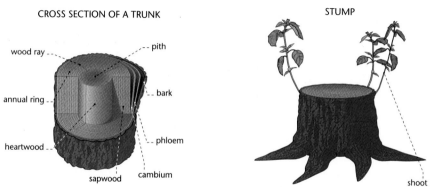

shoot

STRUCTURE OF A FLOWER

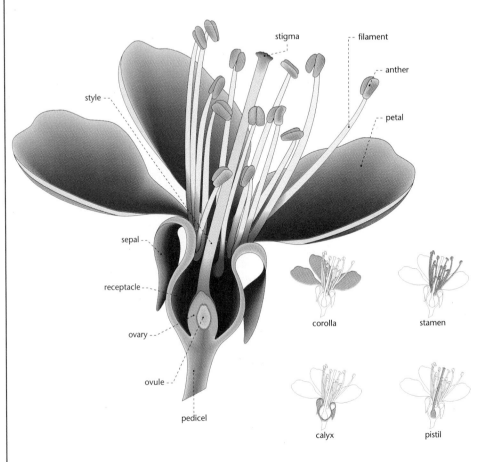

stigma

filament

anther

style

petal

sepal

receptacle

ovary

ovule

pedicel

corolla

stamen

calyx

pistil

TYPES OF INFLORESCENCES

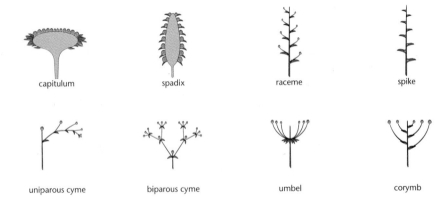

capitulum

spadix

raceme

spike

uniparous cyme

biparous cyme

umbel

corymb

GRAPE

VINE STOCK

MATURING STEPS

flowering

fruition

ripening

ripeness

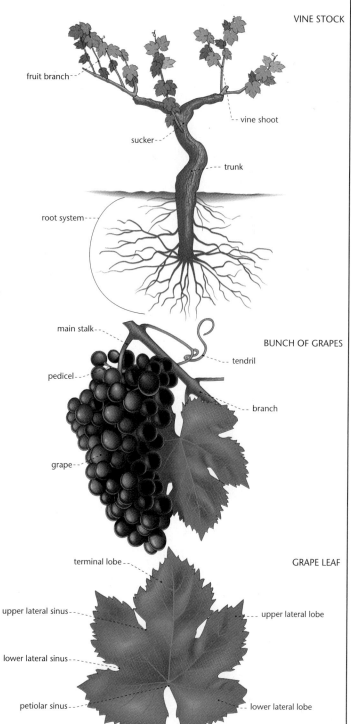

fruit branch

vine shoot

sucker

trunk

root system

BUNCH OF GRAPES

main stalk

tendril

pedicel

branch

grape

GRAPE LEAF

terminal lobe

upper lateral sinus

upper lateral lobe

lower lateral sinus

petiolar sinus

lower lateral lobe

61

VEGETABLE KINGDOM

SECTION OF A BERRY

MAJOR TYPES OF BERRIES

GRAPE

usual terms   technical terms

style

skin --- --- exocarp

pip -- --- seed

flesh --- --- mesocarp

--- funiculus

stalk --- ---

--- pedicel

SECTION OF A RASPBERRY

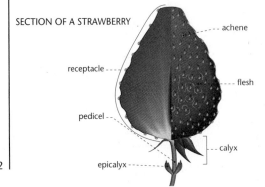

--- drupelet

seed ---

receptacle ---

--- sepal

--- pedicel

SECTION OF A STRAWBERRY

--- achene

receptacle ---

--- flesh

pedicel ---

--- calyx

epicalyx ---

black currant

currant

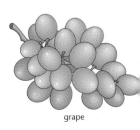

grape

gooseberry

blueberry

huckleberry

cranberry

STONE FLESHY FRUITS

SECTION OF A STONE FRUIT

PEACH

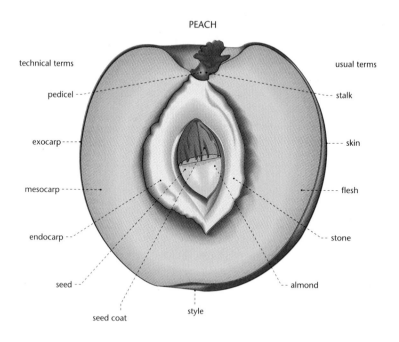

technical terms

usual terms

pedicel ---- stalk

exocarp ---- skin

mesocarp ---- flesh

endocarp ---- stone

seed ---- almond

seed coat   style

MAJOR TYPES OF STONE FRUITS

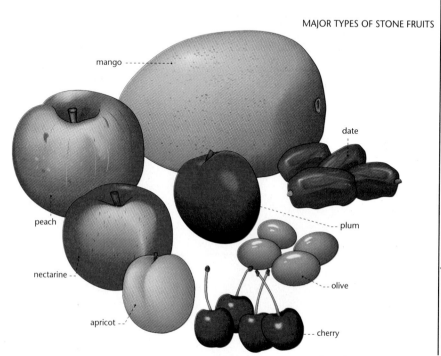

mango

date

peach

plum

nectarine

olive

apricot

cherry

63

VEGETABLE KINGDOM

SECTION OF A POME FRUIT

APPLE

technical terms   usual terms

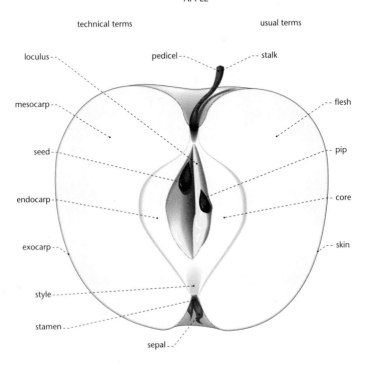

loculus
pedicel
stalk

mesocarp
flesh

seed
pip

endocarp
core

exocarp
skin

style

stamen

sepal

MAJOR TYPES OF POME FRUITS

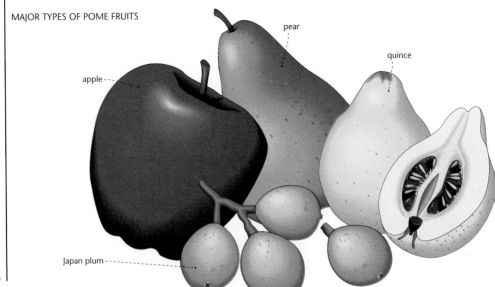

pear

quince

apple

Japan plum

FLESHY FRUITS: CITRUS FRUITS

SECTION OF A CITRUS FRUIT

ORANGE

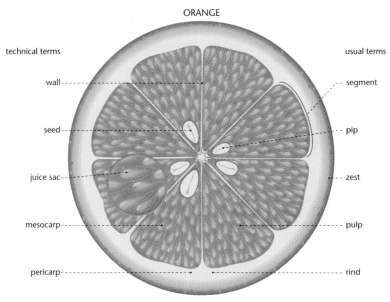

technical terms

wall

seed

juice sac

mesocarp

pericarp

usual terms

segment

pip

zest

pulp

rind

MAJOR TYPES OF CITRUS FRUITS

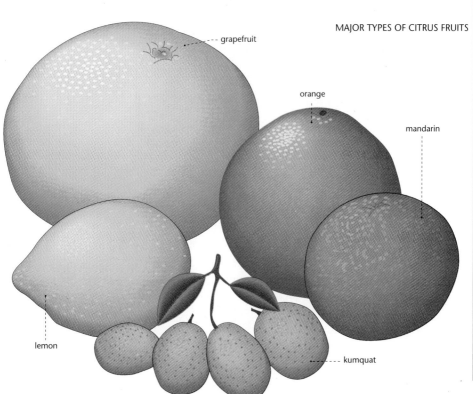

grapefruit

orange

mandarin

lemon

kumquat

SECTION OF A HAZELNUT

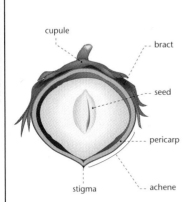

cupule

bract

seed

pericarp

stigma

achene

SECTION OF A WALNUT

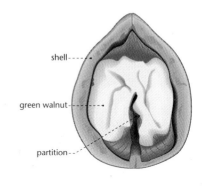

shell

green walnut

partition

HUSK

MAJOR TYPES OF NUTS

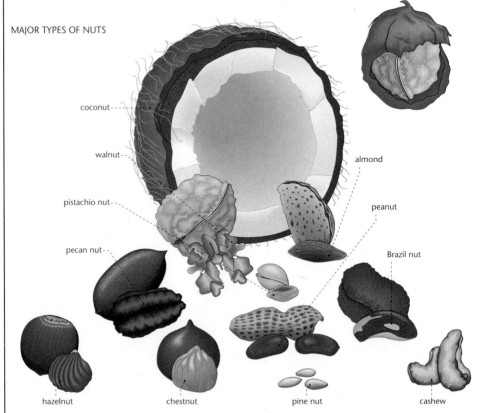

coconut

walnut

almond

pistachio nut

peanut

pecan nut

Brazil nut

hazelnut

chestnut

pine nut

cashew

VARIOUS DRY FRUITS

SECTION OF A FOLLICLE

SECTION OF A SILIQUE

star anise

follicle

seed

suture

mustard

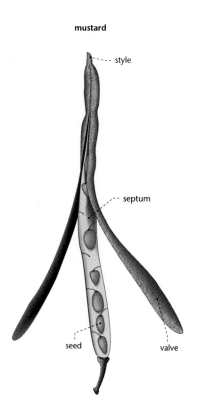

style

septum

seed

valve

SECTION OF A LEGUME

pea

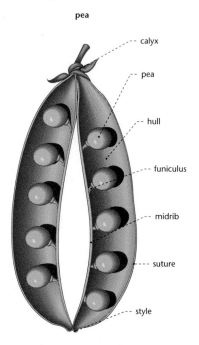

calyx

pea

hull

funiculus

midrib

suture

style

SECTION OF A CAPSULE

poppy

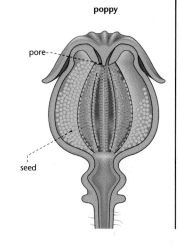

pore

seed

67

VEGETABLE KINGDOM

MAJOR TYPES OF TROPICAL FRUITS

litchi

Japanese persimmon

papaya

banana

kiwi

pomegranate

Indian fig

cherimoya

guava

avocado

pineapple

VEGETABLES

FRUIT VEGETABLES

autumn squash

watermelon

pumpkin

cantaloupe

muskmelon

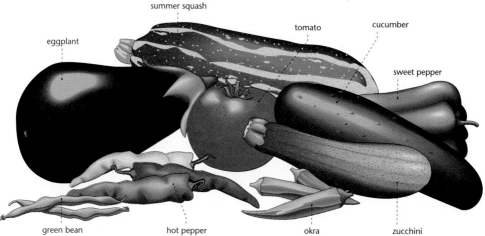

summer squash

tomato

cucumber

eggplant

sweet pepper

green bean

hot pepper

okra

zucchini

INFLORESCENT VEGETABLES

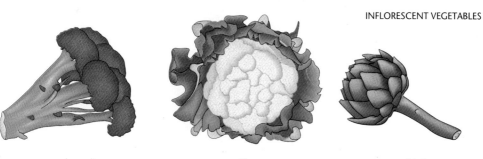

broccoli

cauliflower

artichoke

69

VEGETABLE KINGDOM

SECTION OF A BULB

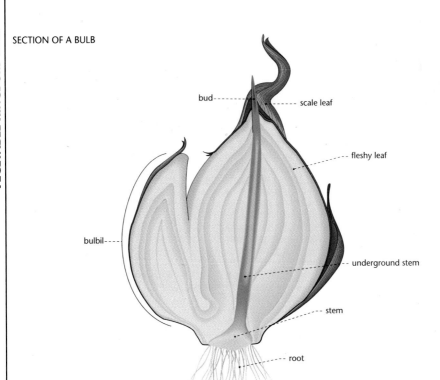

bud - - - - - - - scale leaf

- - - - - - fleshy leaf

bulbil - - - - -

- - - - - - underground stem

- - - - - - stem

- - - - - root

BULB VEGETABLES

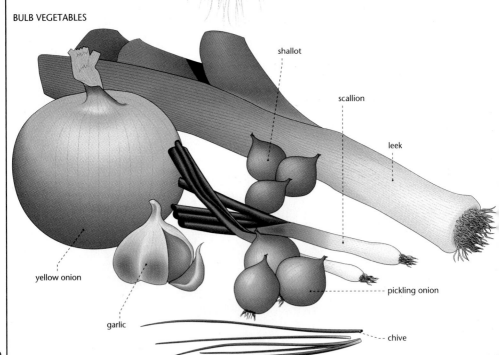

shallot

scallion

leek

yellow onion

garlic

pickling onion

chive

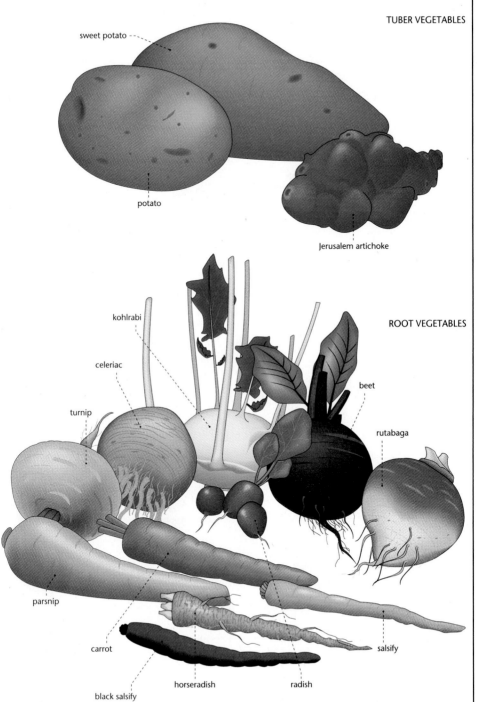

TUBER VEGETABLES

sweet potato

potato

Jerusalem artichoke

ROOT VEGETABLES

kohlrabi

celeriac

turnip

beet

rutabaga

parsnip

carrot

black salsify

horseradish

radish

salsify

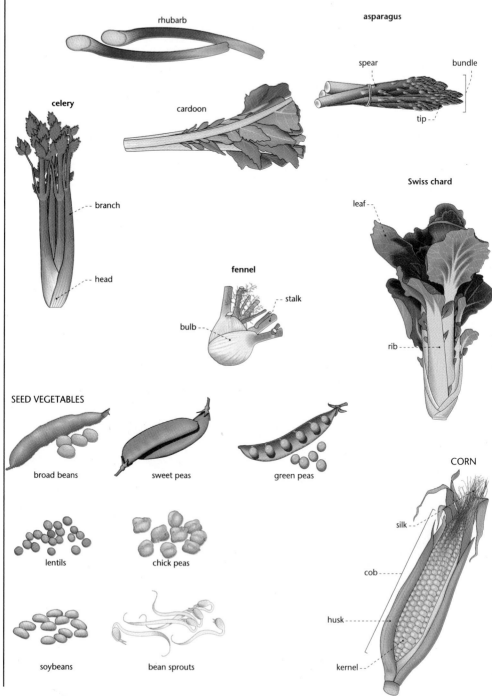

STALK VEGETABLES

rhubarb

asparagus

spear

bundle

tip

celery

cardoon

Swiss chard

leaf

branch

head

fennel

stalk

bulb

rib

SEED VEGETABLES

broad beans

sweet peas

green peas

CORN

lentils

chick peas

silk

cob

husk

soybeans

bean sprouts

kernel

VEGETABLES

LEAF VEGETABLES

corn salad

watercress

chicory

Brussels sprouts

curled kale

grape leaf

garden sorrel

spinach

curled endive

broad-leaved endive

romaine lettuce

dandelion

white cabbage

cabbage lettuce

green cabbage

Chinese cabbage

73

VEGETABLE KINGDOM

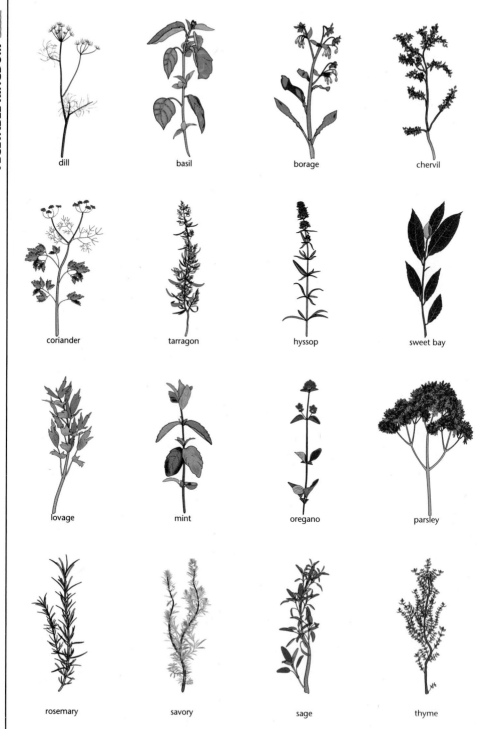

dill

basil

borage

chervil

coriander

tarragon

hyssop

sweet bay

lovage

mint

oregano

parsley

rosemary

savory

sage

thyme

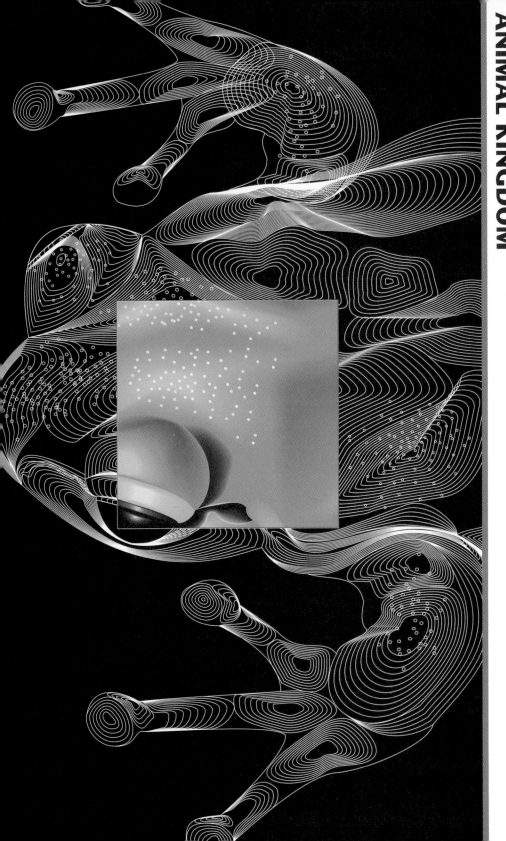

CONTENTS

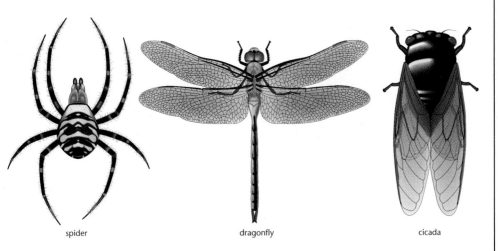

spider

dragonfly

cicada

fly

ladybug

ant

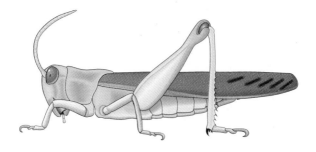

grasshopper

CATERPILLAR

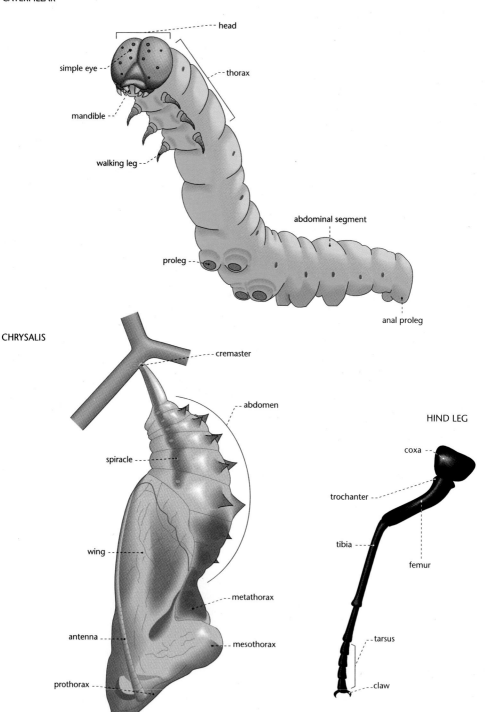

CHRYSALIS

HIND LEG

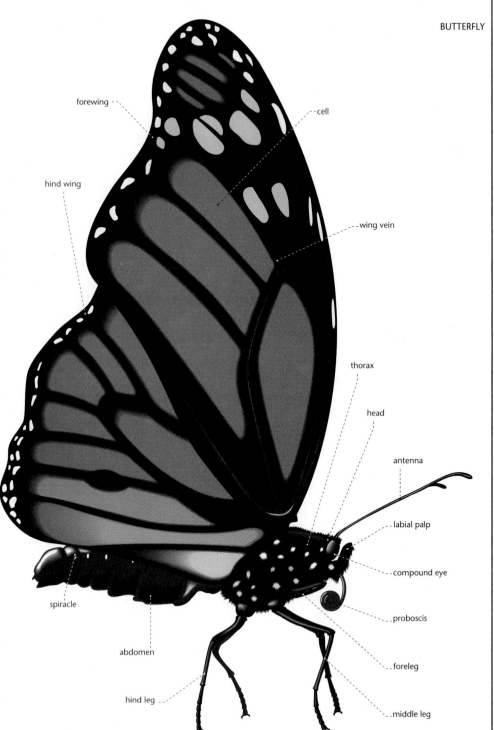

forewing

cell

hind wing

wing vein

thorax

head

antenna

labial palp

compound eye

proboscis

spiracle

foreleg

abdomen

hind leg

middle leg

WORKER

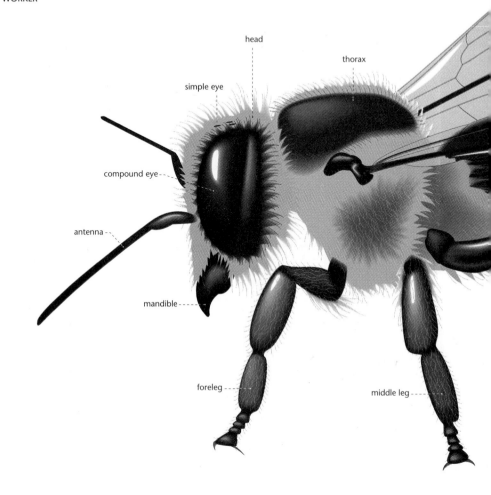

- head
- thorax
- simple eye
- compound eye
- antenna
- mandible
- foreleg
- middle leg

FORELEG (OUTER SURFACE)

MIDDLE LEG (OUTER SURFACE)

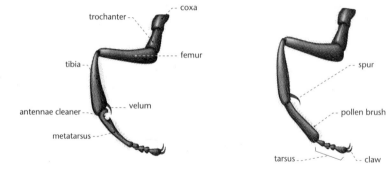

- coxa
- trochanter
- femur
- tibia
- antennae cleaner
- velum
- metatarsus
- spur
- pollen brush
- tarsus
- claw

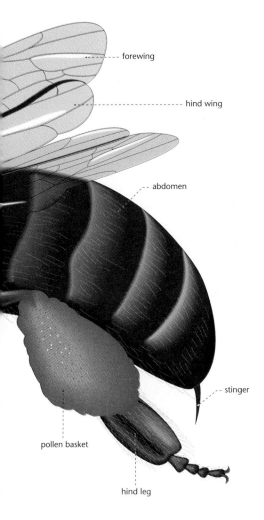

forewing

hind wing

abdomen

stinger

pollen basket

hind leg

queen

drone

worker

MOUTHPARTS

HIND LEG (INNER SURFACE)

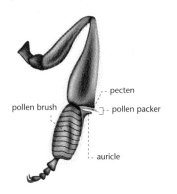

pecten

pollen brush

pollen packer

auricle

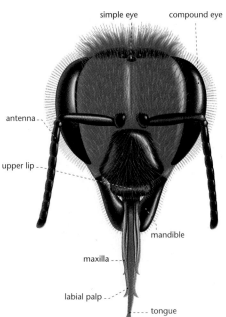

simple eye

compound eye

antenna

upper lip

mandible

maxilla

labial palp

tongue

81

HONEYCOMB SECTION

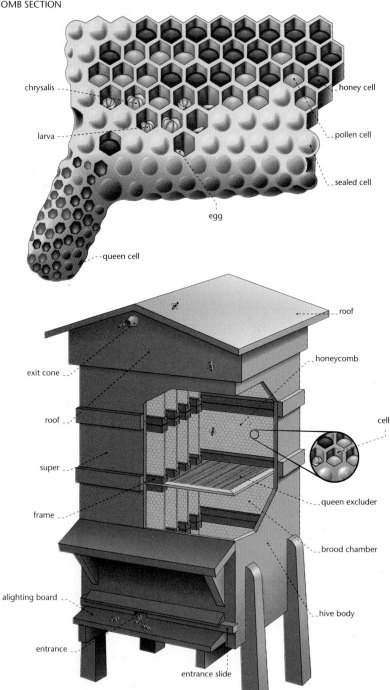

chrysalis
larva
honey cell
pollen cell
sealed cell
egg
queen cell

HIVE

roof
honeycomb
exit cone
roof
cell
super
queen excluder
frame
brood chamber
alighting board
hive body
entrance
entrance slide

GASTROPOD

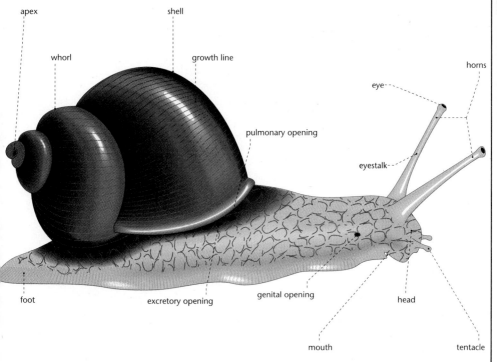

apex

whorl

shell

growth line

pulmonary opening

eye

horns

eyestalk

foot

excretory opening

genital opening

head

mouth

tentacle

limpet

common periwinkle

whelk

FROG

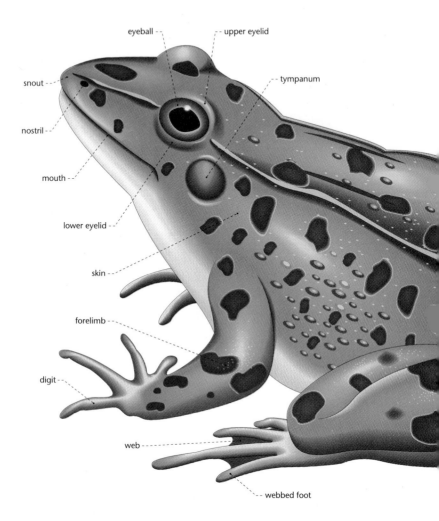

eyeball

upper eyelid

tympanum

snout

nostril

mouth

lower eyelid

skin

forelimb

digit

web

webbed foot

LIFE CYCLE OF THE FROG

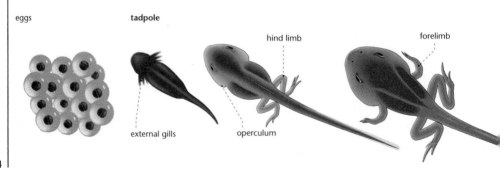

eggs

tadpole

hind limb

forelimb

external gills

operculum

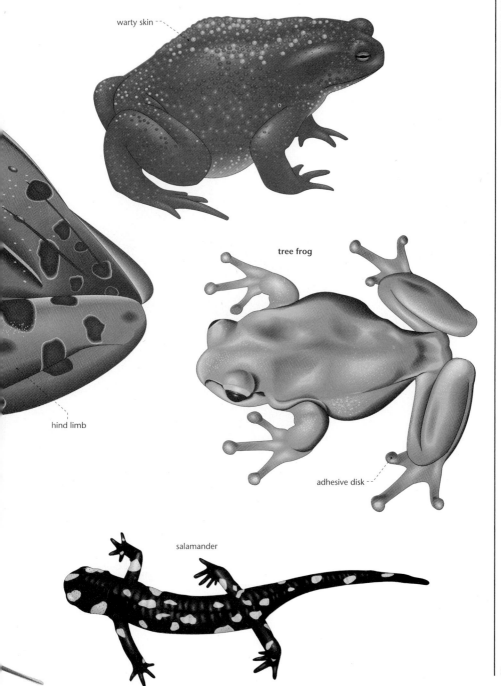

toad

warty skin

hind limb

tree frog

adhesive disk

salamander

MORPHOLOGY

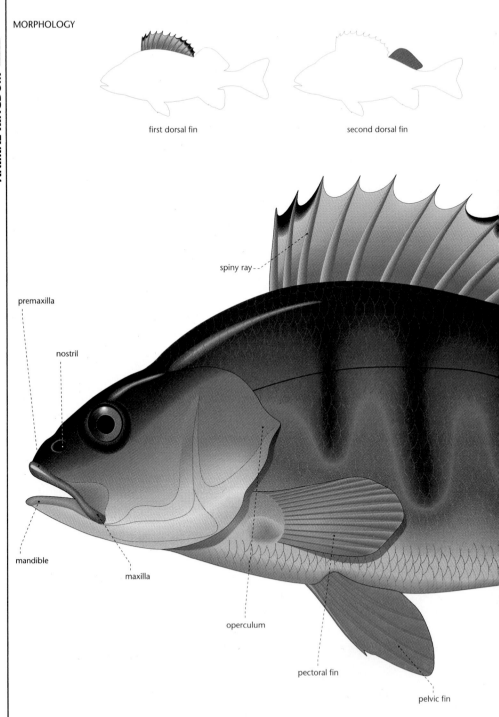

first dorsal fin

second dorsal fin

spiny ray

premaxilla

nostril

mandible

maxilla

operculum

pectoral fin

pelvic fin

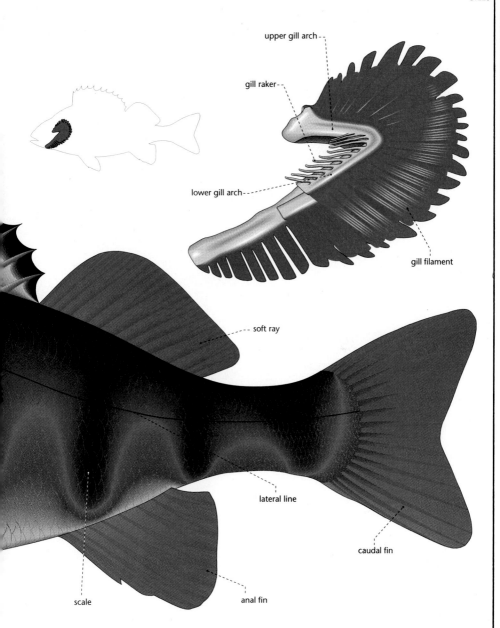

upper gill arch

gill raker

lower gill arch

gill filament

soft ray

lateral line

scale

anal fin

caudal fin

ANATOMY

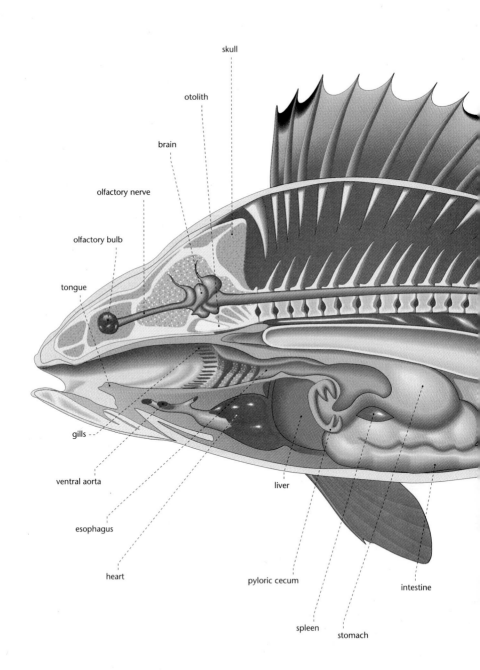

skull

otolith

brain

olfactory nerve

olfactory bulb

tongue

gills

ventral aorta

esophagus

heart

liver

pyloric cecum

intestine

spleen

stomach

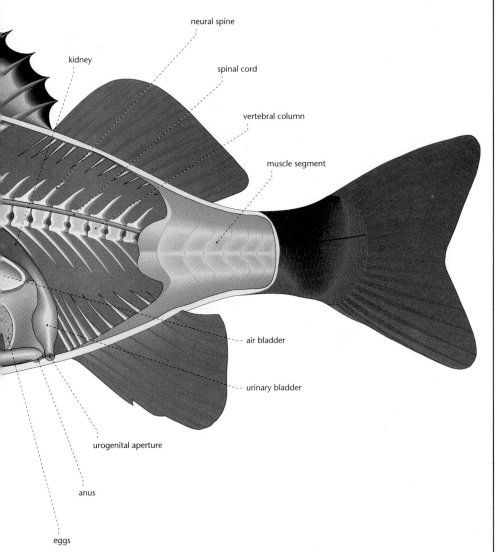

neural spine

kidney

spinal cord

vertebral column

muscle segment

air bladder

urinary bladder

urogenital aperture

anus

eggs

ANIMAL KINGDOM

LOBSTER

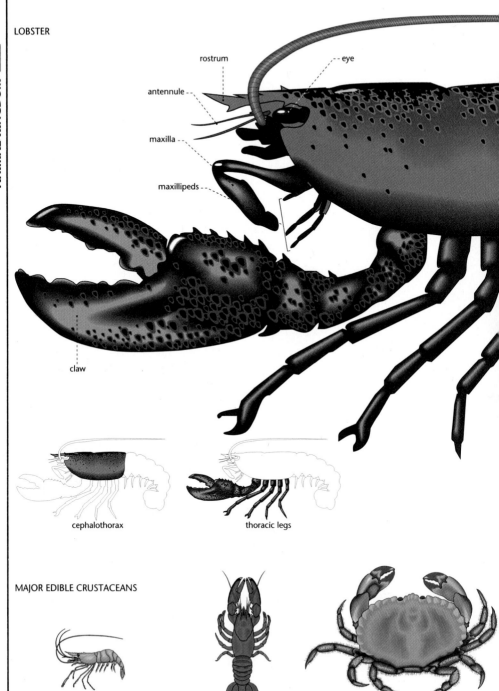

rostrum

eye

antennule

maxilla

maxillipeds

claw

cephalothorax

thoracic legs

MAJOR EDIBLE CRUSTACEANS

shrimp

crayfish

crab

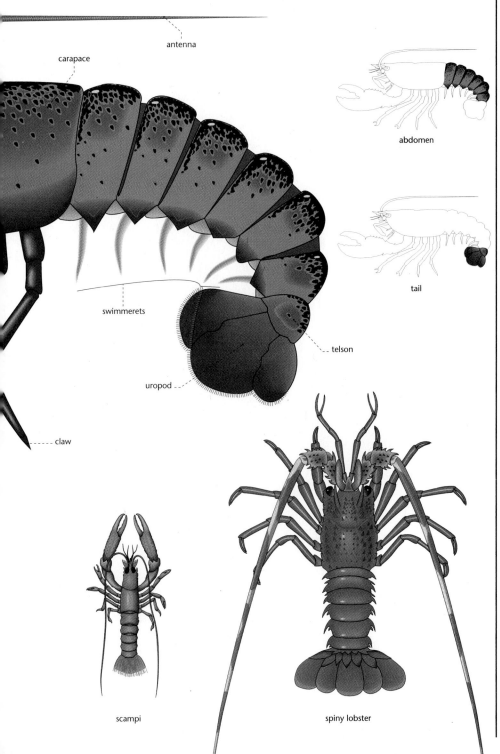

antenna

carapace

swimmerets

telson

uropod

claw

abdomen

tail

scampi

spiny lobster

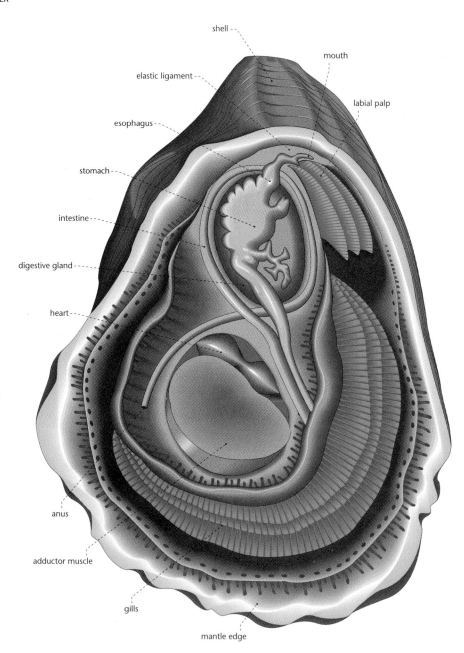

shell

mouth

elastic ligament

labial palp

esophagus

stomach

intestine

digestive gland

heart

anus

adductor muscle

gills

mantle edge

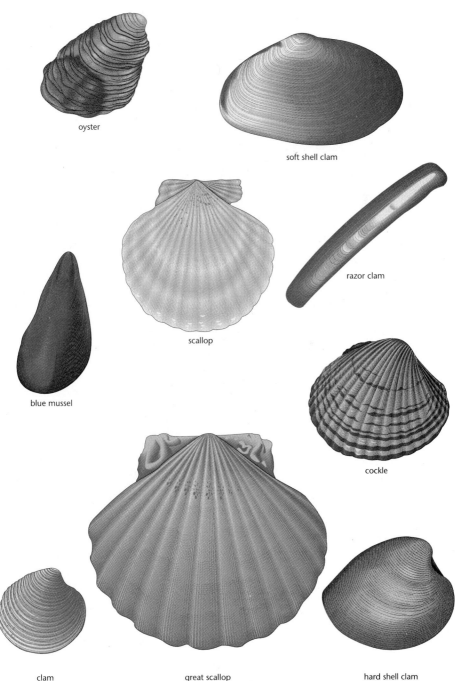

oyster

soft shell clam

scallop

razor clam

blue mussel

cockle

clam

great scallop

hard shell clam

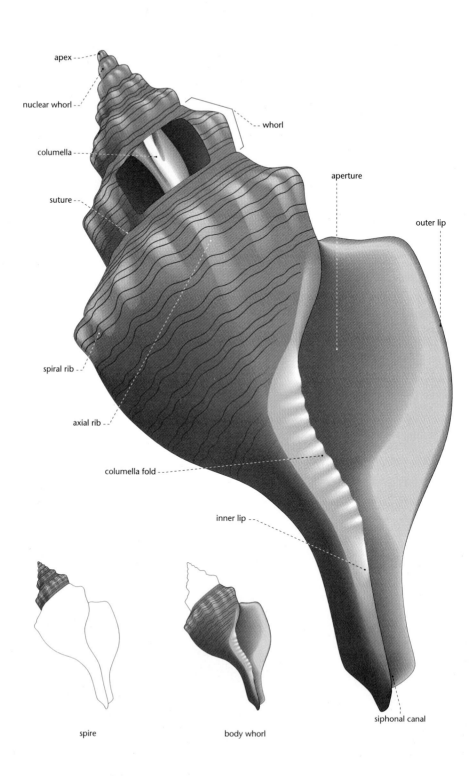

apex

nuclear whorl

columella

suture

whorl

aperture

outer lip

spiral rib

axial rib

columella fold

inner lip

siphonal canal

spire

body whorl

BIVALVE SHELL

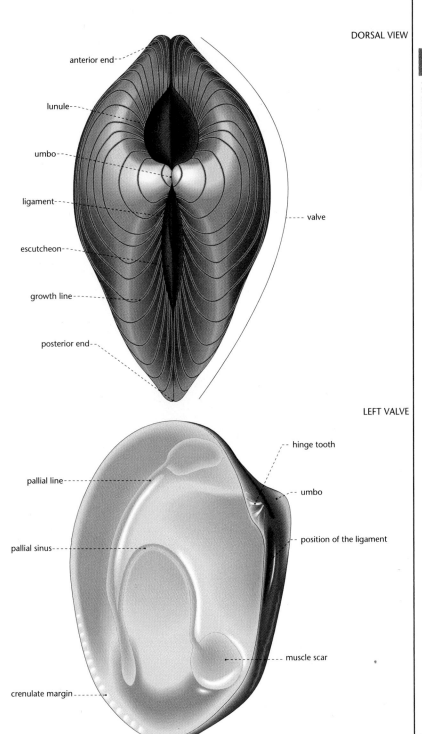

DORSAL VIEW

anterior end

lunule

umbo

ligament

escutcheon

growth line

posterior end

valve

LEFT VALVE

hinge tooth

umbo

position of the ligament

pallial line

pallial sinus

muscle scar

crenulate margin

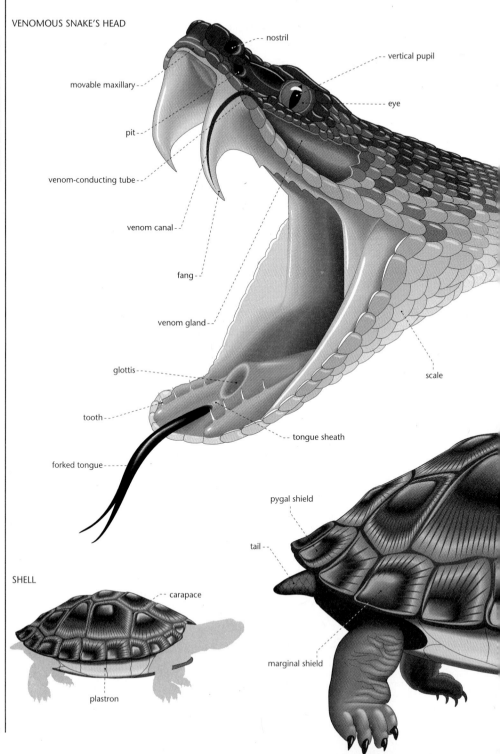

VENOMOUS SNAKE'S HEAD

nostril

vertical pupil

movable maxillary

eye

pit

venom-conducting tube

venom canal

fang

venom gland

glottis

tooth

scale

tongue sheath

forked tongue

pygal shield

tail

SHELL

carapace

marginal shield

plastron

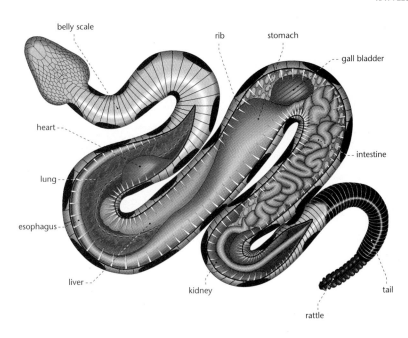

belly scale

rib

stomach

gall bladder

heart

intestine

lung

esophagus

liver

kidney

tail

rattle

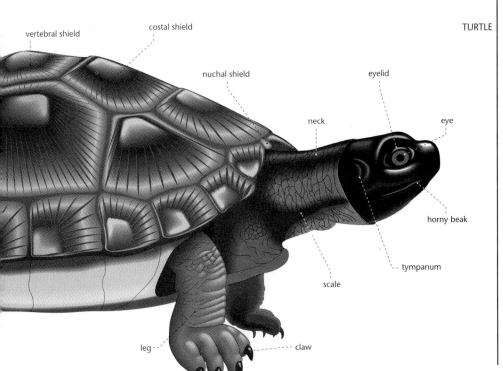

vertebral shield

costal shield

nuchal shield

eyelid

neck

eye

horny beak

tympanum

scale

leg

claw

TYPES OF JAWS

BEAVER

RODENT'S JAW

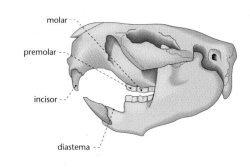

LION

CARNIVORE'S JAW

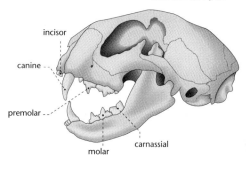

HORSE

HERBIVORE'S JAW

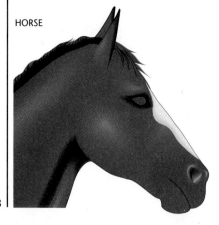

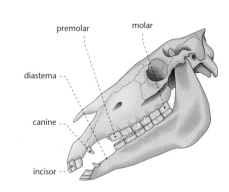

MAJOR TYPES OF HORNS

horns of mouflon

horns of giraffe

horns of rhinoceros

MAJOR TYPES OF TUSKS

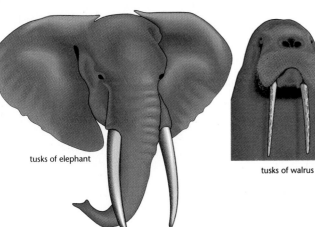

tusks of elephant

tusks of walrus

tusks of wart hog

TYPES OF HOOFS

one-toe hoof

two-toed hoof

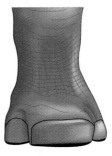

three-toed hoof

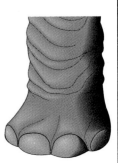

four-toed hoof

99

MORPHOLOGY

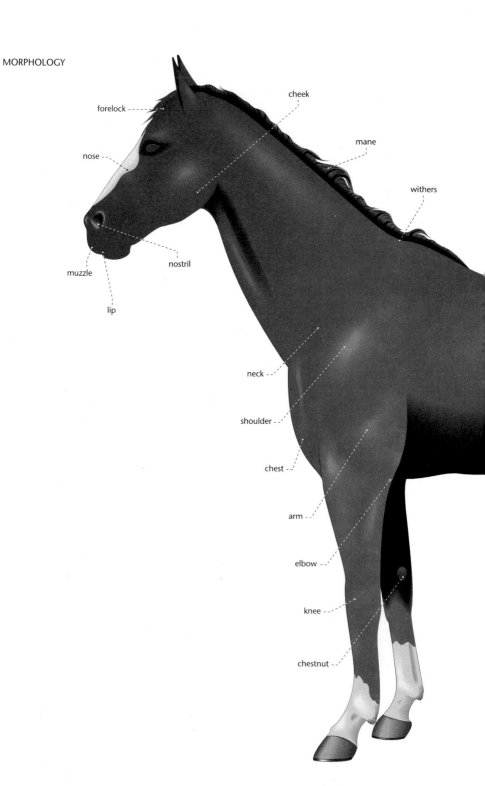

forelock

cheek

mane

nose

withers

muzzle

nostril

lip

neck

shoulder

chest

arm

elbow

knee

chestnut

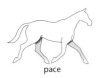

pace

walk

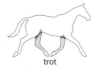

trot

gallop

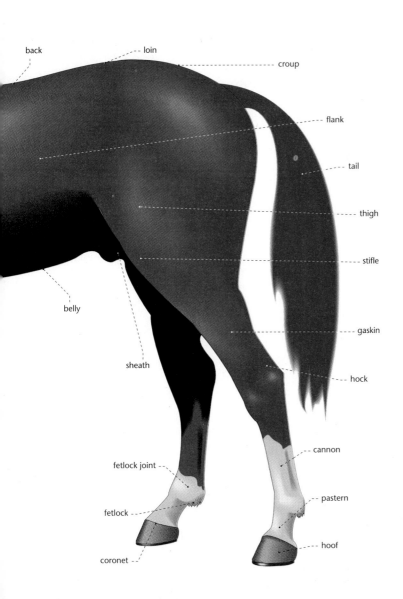

back

loin

croup

flank

tail

thigh

stifle

belly

gaskin

sheath

hock

cannon

fetlock joint

pastern

fetlock

hoof

coronet

ANIMAL KINGDOM

SKELETON

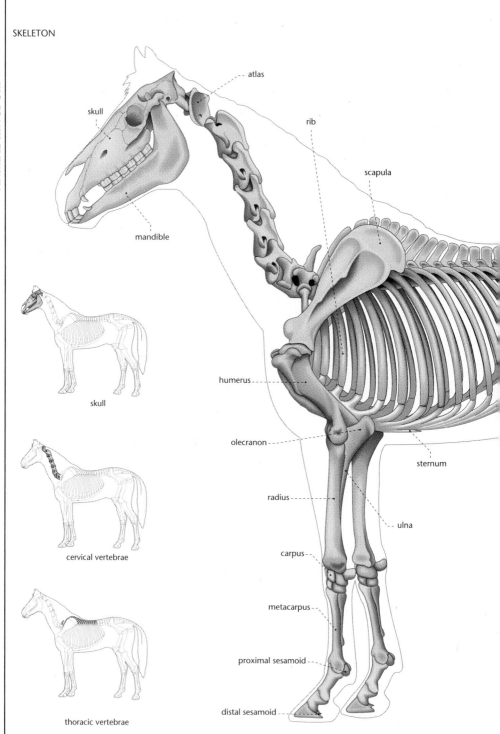

atlas

skull

rib

scapula

mandible

skull

cervical vertebrae

thoracic vertebrae

humerus

olecranon

sternum

radius

ulna

carpus

metacarpus

proximal sesamoid

distal sesamoid

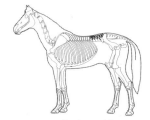

lumbar vertebrae

sacral vertebrae

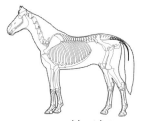

caudal vertebrae

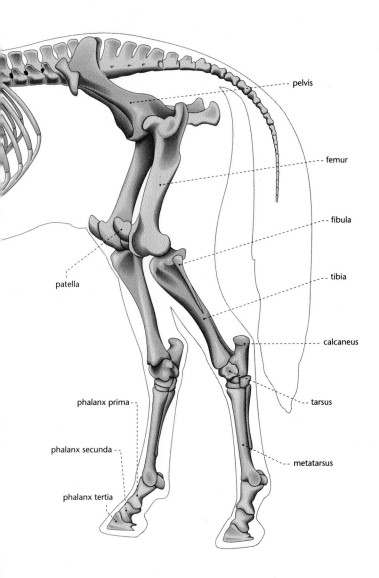

pelvis

femur

fibula

tibia

patella

calcaneus

tarsus

phalanx prima

metatarsus

phalanx secunda

phalanx tertia

PLANTAR SURFACE OF THE HOOF

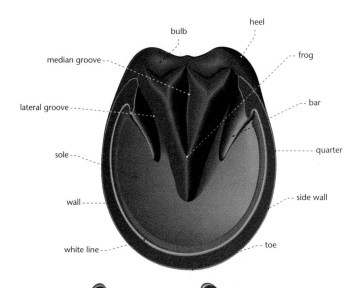

bulb

heel

median groove

frog

lateral groove

bar

sole

quarter

wall

side wall

white line

toe

HORSESHOE

HOOF

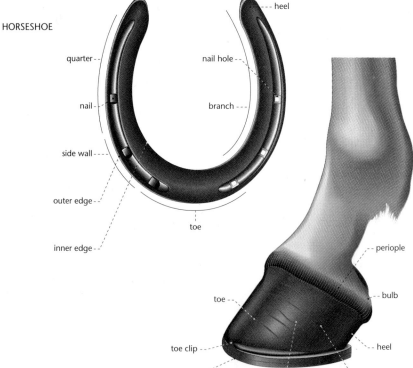

heel

quarter

nail hole

nail

branch

side wall

outer edge

inner edge

toe

periople

bulb

toe

heel

toe clip

horseshoe

side wall

quarter

DEER FAMILY

DEER ANTLERS

fork

palm

crown tine

pearl

royal antler

gutter

surroyal antler

bay antler

beam

brow tine

burr

pearls

pedicle

KINDS OF DEER

caribou

white-tailed deer

moose

wapiti

105

MORPHOLOGY

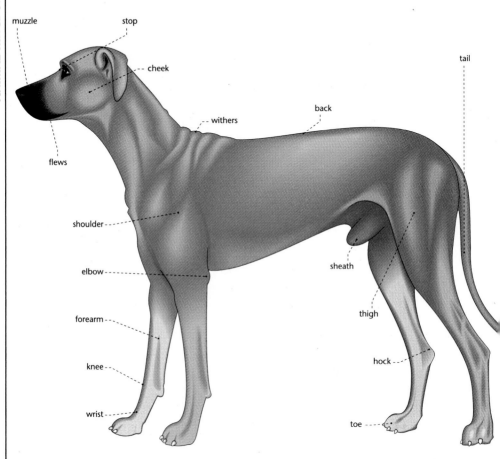

muzzle

stop

cheek

tail

back

withers

flews

shoulder

elbow

forearm

knee

wrist

sheath

thigh

hock

toe

DOG'S FOREPAW

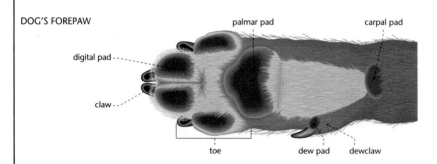

palmar pad

carpal pad

digital pad

claw

toe

dew pad

dewclaw

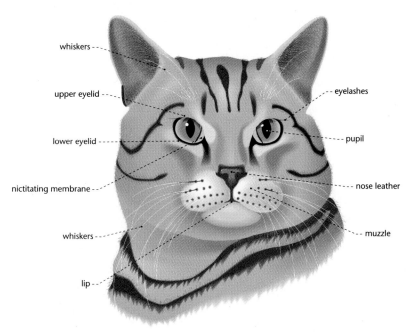

CAT'S HEAD

whiskers

upper eyelid

lower eyelid

nictitating membrane

whiskers

lip

eyelashes

pupil

nose leather

muzzle

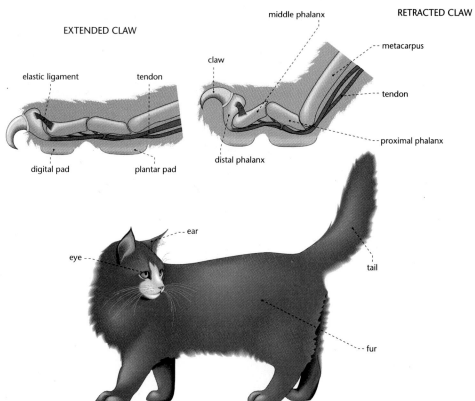

RETRACTED CLAW

middle phalanx

EXTENDED CLAW

elastic ligament

tendon

claw

metacarpus

tendon

proximal phalanx

distal phalanx

digital pad

plantar pad

ear

eye

tail

fur

MORPHOLOGY

bill

nape

back

chin

throat

wing covert

breast

wing

abdomen

tarsus

inner toe

middle toe

outer toe

claw

hind toe

thigh

flank

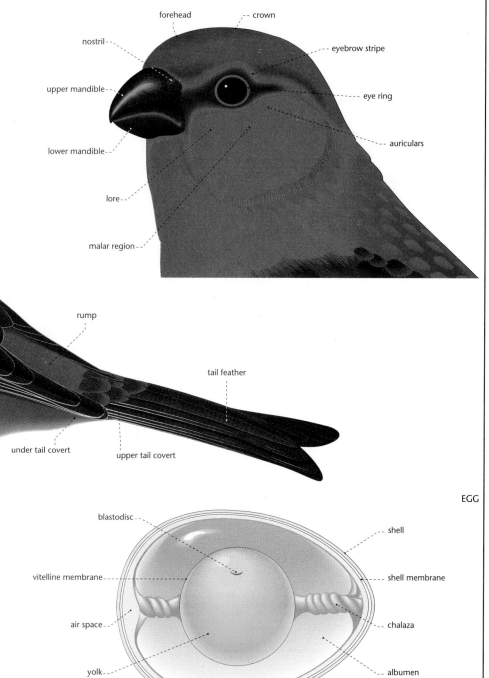

forehead

crown

nostril

eyebrow stripe

upper mandible

eye ring

lower mandible

auriculars

lore

malar region

rump

tail feather

under tail covert

upper tail covert

EGG

blastodisc

shell

vitelline membrane

shell membrane

air space

chalaza

yolk

albumen

WING

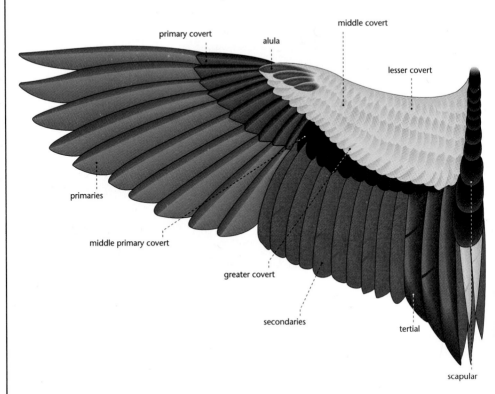

middle covert

lesser covert

primary covert

alula

primaries

middle primary covert

greater covert

secondaries

tertial

scapular

CONTOUR FEATHER

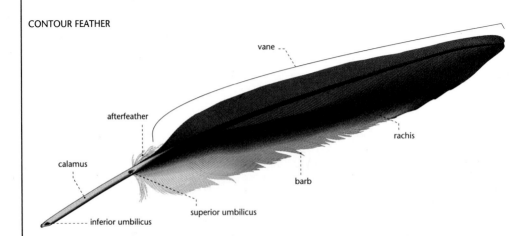

vane

afterfeather

rachis

calamus

barb

superior umbilicus

inferior umbilicus

PRINCIPAL TYPES OF BILLS

bird of prey

aquatic bird

wading bird

granivorous bird

insectivorous bird

PRINCIPAL TYPES OF FEET

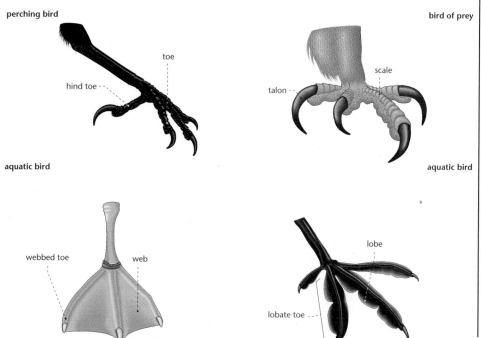

perching bird

toe

hind toe

bird of prey

talon

scale

aquatic bird

webbed toe

web

aquatic bird

lobe

lobate toe

BAT

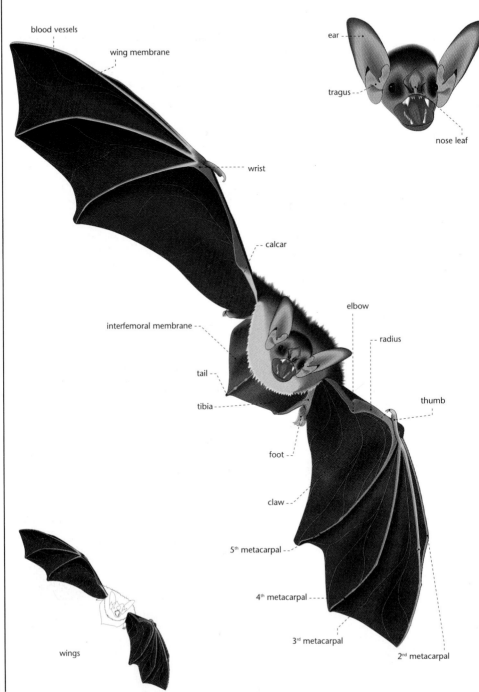

BAT'S HEAD

ear

tragus

nose leaf

blood vessels

wing membrane

wrist

calcar

elbow

radius

interfemoral membrane

tail

thumb

tibia

foot

claw

5th metacarpal

4th metacarpal

3rd metacarpal

2nd metacarpal

wings

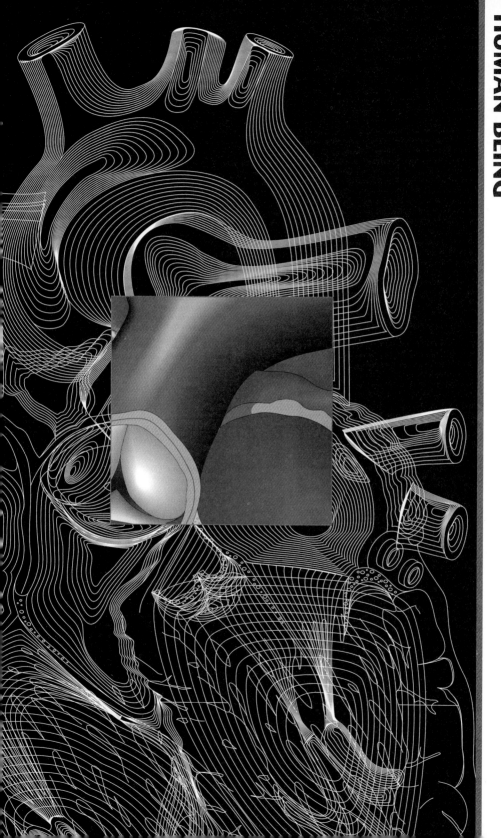

CONTENTS

PLANT CELL

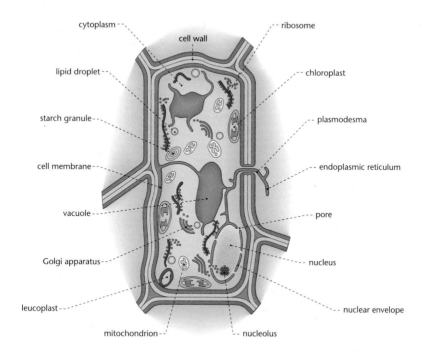

cytoplasm

cell wall

lipid droplet

starch granule

cell membrane

vacuole

Golgi apparatus

leucoplast

mitochondrion

ribosome

chloroplast

plasmodesma

endoplasmic reticulum

pore

nucleus

nuclear envelope

nucleolus

ANIMAL CELL

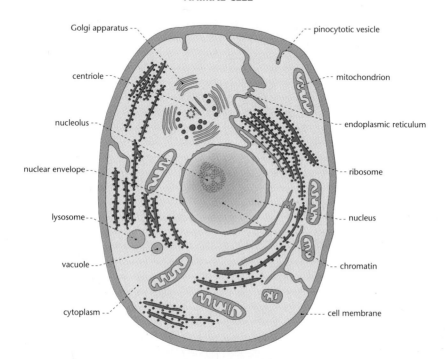

Golgi apparatus

centriole

nucleolus

nuclear envelope

lysosome

vacuole

cytoplasm

pinocytotic vesicle

mitochondrion

endoplasmic reticulum

ribosome

nucleus

chromatin

cell membrane

HUMAN BODY

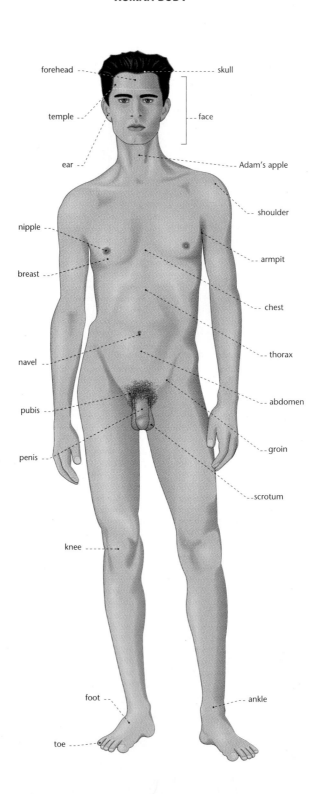

forehead

skull

temple

face

ear

Adam's apple

shoulder

nipple

armpit

breast

chest

thorax

navel

abdomen

pubis

penis

groin

scrotum

knee

foot

ankle

toe

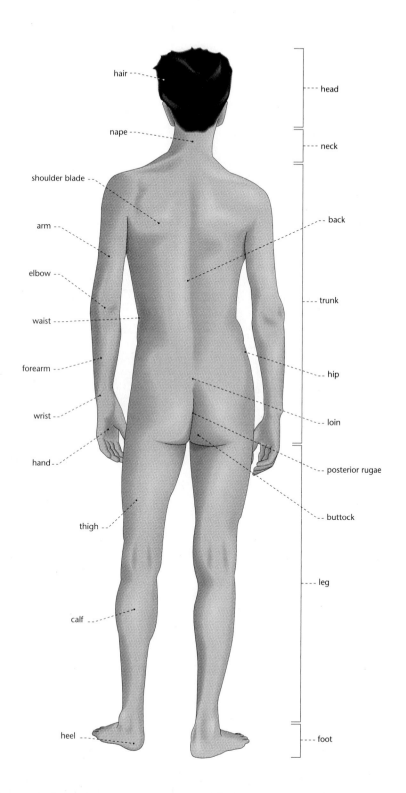

hair ----- head

nape ----- neck

shoulder blade --- back

arm ---- trunk

elbow ---

waist ----- hip

forearm ----- loin

wrist ---- posterior rugae

hand --- buttock

thigh ---

calf ---- leg

heel ----- foot

117

HUMAN BODY

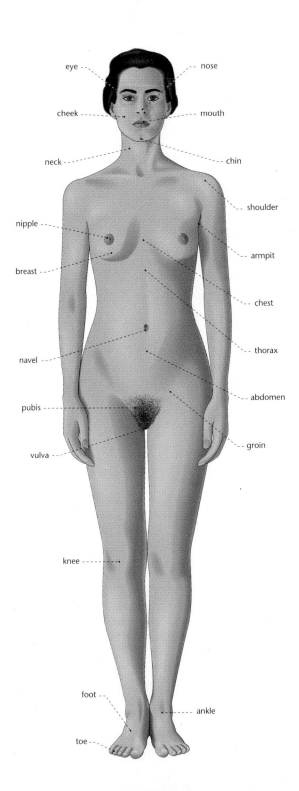

eye

nose

cheek

mouth

neck

chin

shoulder

nipple

armpit

breast

chest

thorax

navel

abdomen

pubis

groin

vulva

knee

foot

ankle

toe

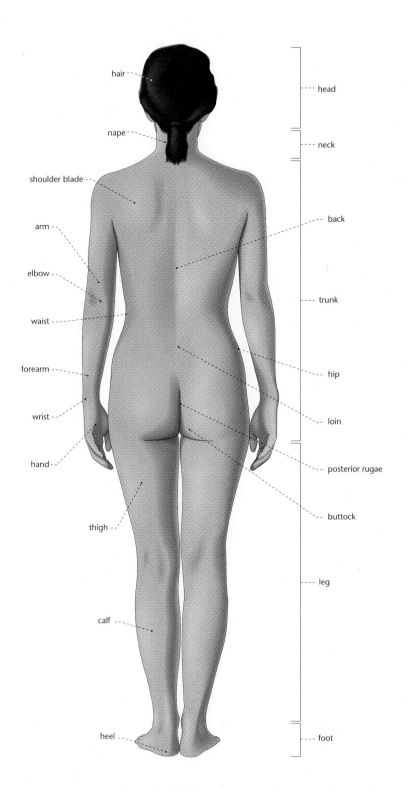

hair

nape

shoulder blade

arm

elbow

waist

forearm

wrist

hand

thigh

calf

heel

head

neck

back

trunk

hip

loin

posterior rugae

buttock

leg

foot

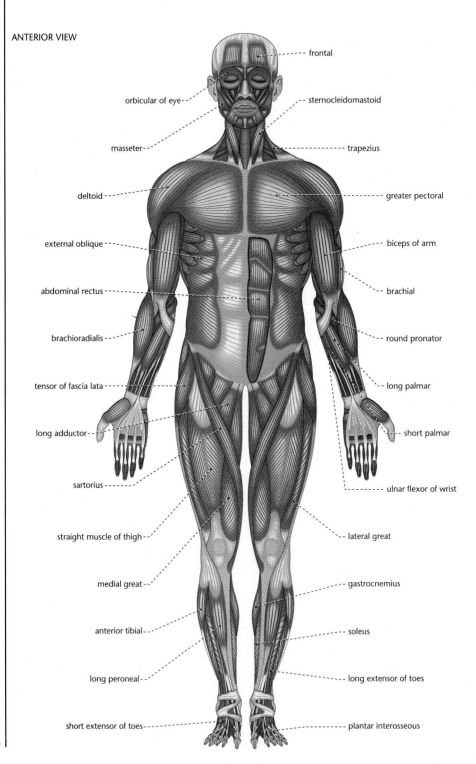

ANTERIOR VIEW

frontal

orbicular of eye

sternocleidomastoid

masseter

trapezius

deltoid

greater pectoral

external oblique

biceps of arm

abdominal rectus

brachial

brachioradialis

round pronator

tensor of fascia lata

long palmar

long adductor

short palmar

sartorius

ulnar flexor of wrist

straight muscle of thigh

lateral great

medial great

gastrocnemius

anterior tibial

soleus

long peroneal

long extensor of toes

short extensor of toes

plantar interosseous

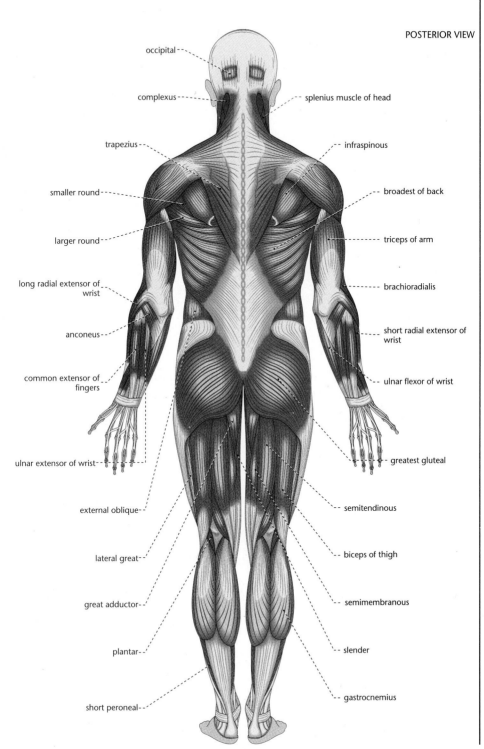

occipital

complexus

splenius muscle of head

trapezius

infraspinous

smaller round

broadest of back

larger round

triceps of arm

long radial extensor of wrist

brachioradialis

anconeus

short radial extensor of wrist

common extensor of fingers

ulnar flexor of wrist

ulnar extensor of wrist

greatest gluteal

external oblique

semitendinous

lateral great

biceps of thigh

great adductor

semimembranous

plantar

slender

short peroneal

gastrocnemius

SKELETON

ANTERIOR VIEW

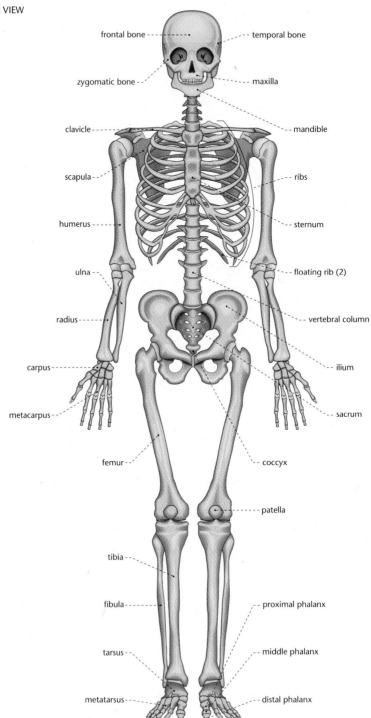

frontal bone - - - - - - - - - - - - - temporal bone

zygomatic bone - - - - - - - - - - - maxilla

clavicle - - - - - - - - - - - mandible

scapula - - - - - ribs

humerus - - - - - sternum

ulna - - - - - floating rib (2)

radius - - - - - vertebral column

carpus - - - - - - - - - - - ilium

metacarpus - - - - - - - - sacrum

femur - - - - - - coccyx

patella - - - - - -

tibia - - - - -

fibula - - - - - - - - - proximal phalanx

tarsus - - - - middle phalanx

metatarsus - - - - - - - distal phalanx

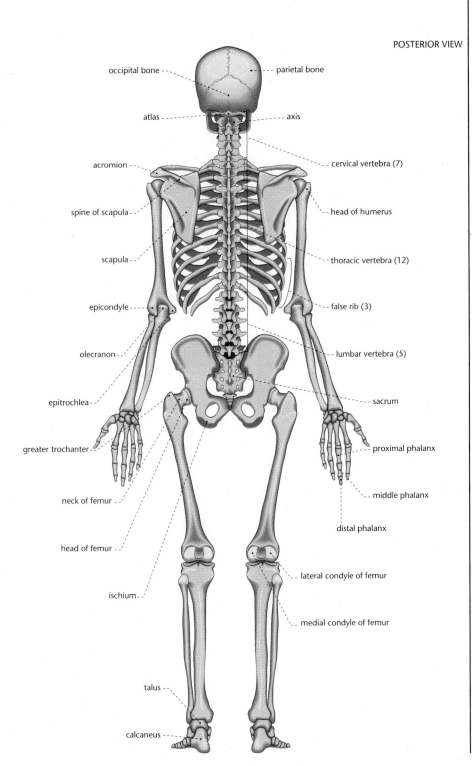

occipital bone

parietal bone

atlas

axis

cervical vertebra (7)

acromion

spine of scapula

head of humerus

scapula

thoracic vertebra (12)

epicondyle

false rib (3)

olecranon

lumbar vertebra (5)

epitrochlea

sacrum

greater trochanter

proximal phalanx

neck of femur

middle phalanx

head of femur

distal phalanx

ischium

lateral condyle of femur

medial condyle of femur

talus

calcaneus

HUMAN BEING

BLOOD CIRCULATION

SCHEMA OF CIRCULATION

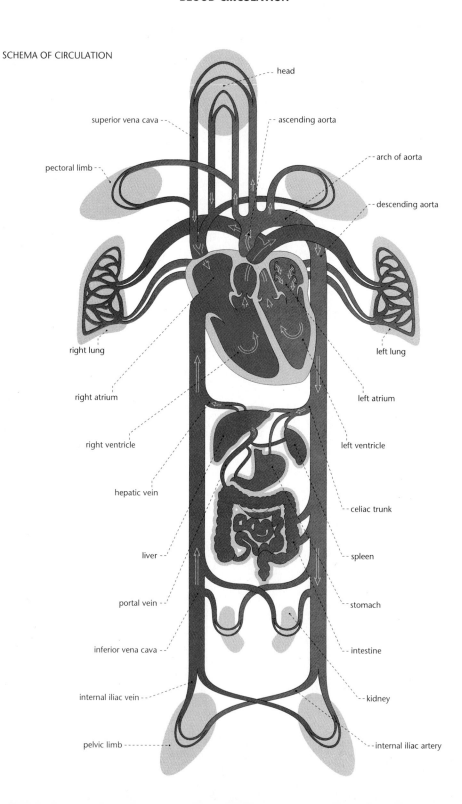

head

superior vena cava

ascending aorta

arch of aorta

pectoral limb

descending aorta

right lung

left lung

right atrium

left atrium

right ventricle

left ventricle

hepatic vein

celiac trunk

liver

spleen

portal vein

stomach

inferior vena cava

intestine

internal iliac vein

kidney

pelvic limb

internal iliac artery

124

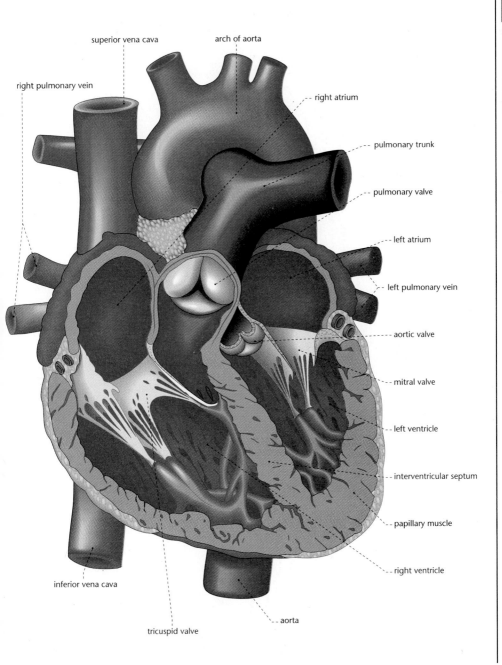

superior vena cava

arch of aorta

right pulmonary vein

right atrium

pulmonary trunk

pulmonary valve

left atrium

left pulmonary vein

aortic valve

mitral valve

left ventricle

interventricular septum

papillary muscle

right ventricle

inferior vena cava

tricuspid valve

aorta

BLOOD CIRCULATION

PRINCIPAL VEINS AND ARTERIES

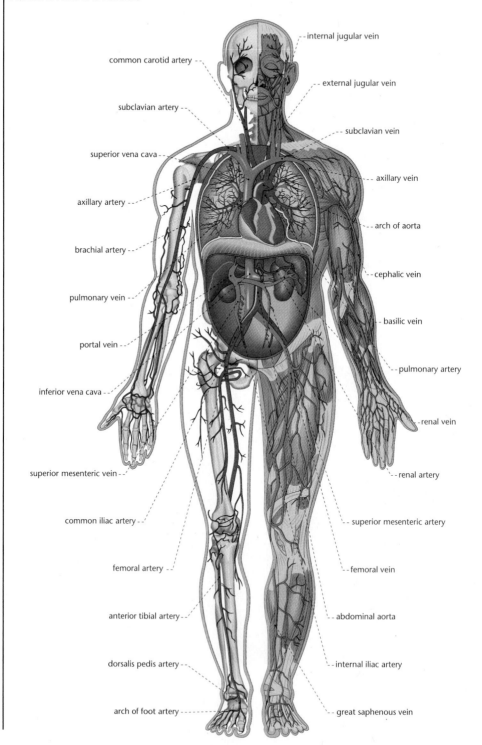

internal jugular vein

common carotid artery

external jugular vein

subclavian artery

subclavian vein

superior vena cava

axillary vein

axillary artery

arch of aorta

brachial artery

cephalic vein

pulmonary vein

basilic vein

portal vein

pulmonary artery

inferior vena cava

renal vein

superior mesenteric vein

renal artery

common iliac artery

superior mesenteric artery

femoral artery

femoral vein

anterior tibial artery

abdominal aorta

dorsalis pedis artery

internal iliac artery

arch of foot artery

great saphenous vein

MALE GENITAL ORGANS

SAGITTAL SECTION

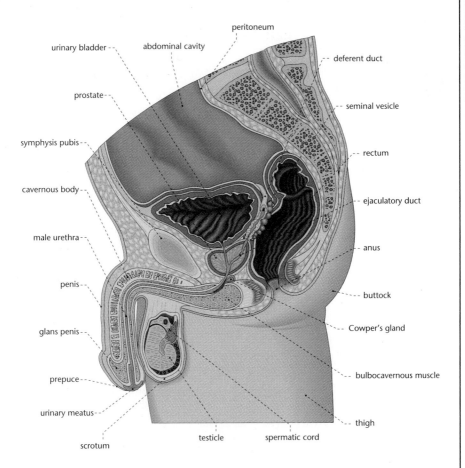

peritoneum

urinary bladder

abdominal cavity

deferent duct

prostate

seminal vesicle

symphysis pubis

rectum

cavernous body

ejaculatory duct

male urethra

anus

penis

buttock

glans penis

Cowper's gland

prepuce

bulbocavernous muscle

urinary meatus

thigh

scrotum

testicle

spermatic cord

SPERMATOZOON

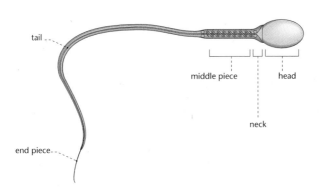

tail

middle piece

head

neck

end piece

127

FEMALE GENITAL ORGANS

EGG

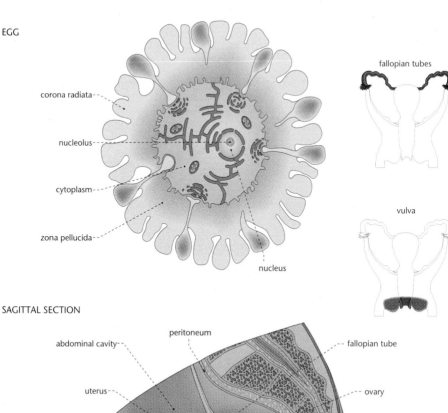

corona radiata

nucleolus

cytoplasm

zona pellucida

nucleus

fallopian tubes

vulva

SAGITTAL SECTION

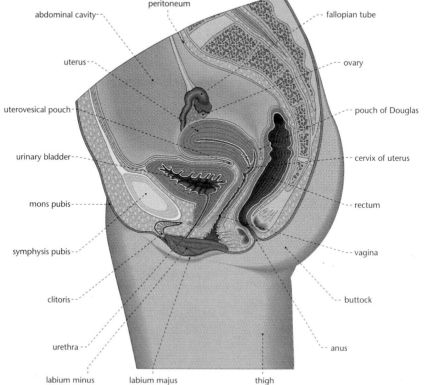

abdominal cavity

peritoneum

fallopian tube

uterus

ovary

uterovesical pouch

pouch of Douglas

urinary bladder

cervix of uterus

mons pubis

rectum

symphysis pubis

vagina

clitoris

buttock

urethra

anus

labium minus

labium majus

thigh

FEMALE GENITAL ORGANS

POSTERIOR VIEW

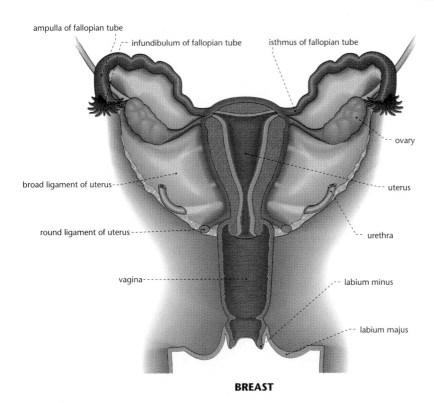

ampulla of fallopian tube

infundibulum of fallopian tube

isthmus of fallopian tube

ovary

broad ligament of uterus

uterus

round ligament of uterus

urethra

vagina

labium minus

labium majus

BREAST

SAGITTAL SECTION

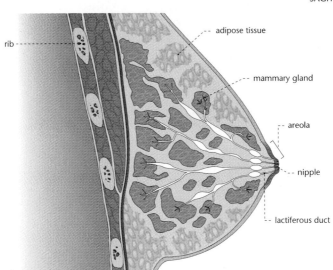

rib

adipose tissue

mammary gland

areola

nipple

lactiferous duct

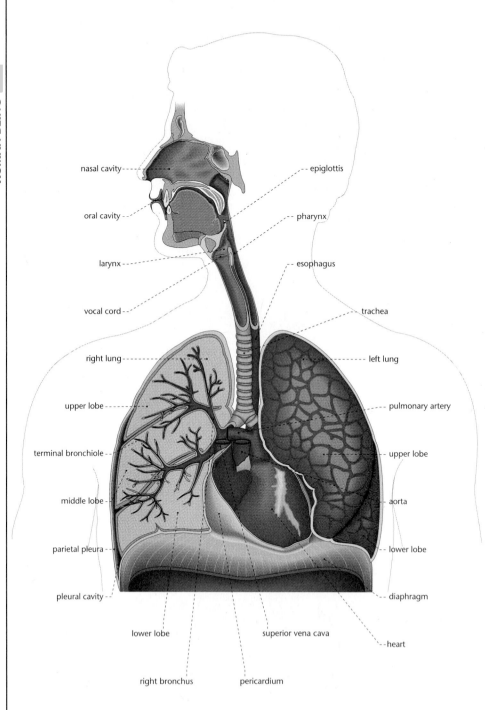

nasal cavity
oral cavity
larynx
vocal cord
right lung
upper lobe
terminal bronchiole
middle lobe
parietal pleura
pleural cavity
lower lobe
right bronchus
pericardium
epiglottis
pharynx
esophagus
trachea
left lung
pulmonary artery
upper lobe
aorta
lower lobe
diaphragm
superior vena cava
heart

DIGESTIVE SYSTEM

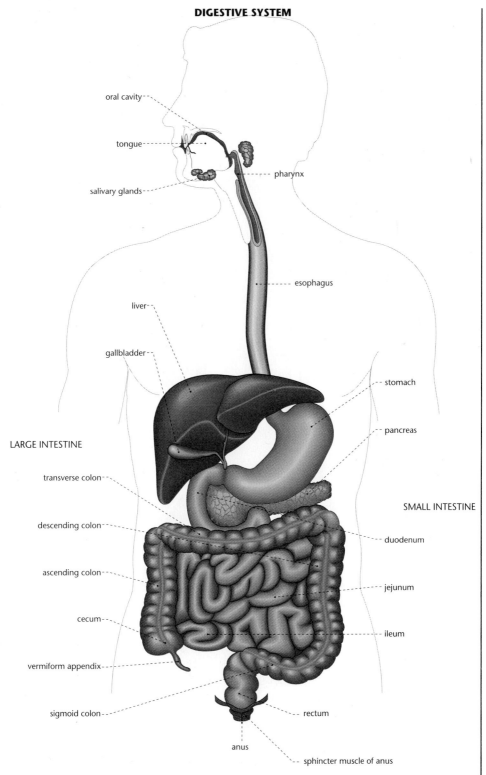

oral cavity

tongue

salivary glands

pharynx

esophagus

liver

gallbladder

stomach

pancreas

LARGE INTESTINE

transverse colon

descending colon

ascending colon

cecum

vermiform appendix

sigmoid colon

anus

duodenum

SMALL INTESTINE

jejunum

ileum

rectum

sphincter muscle of anus

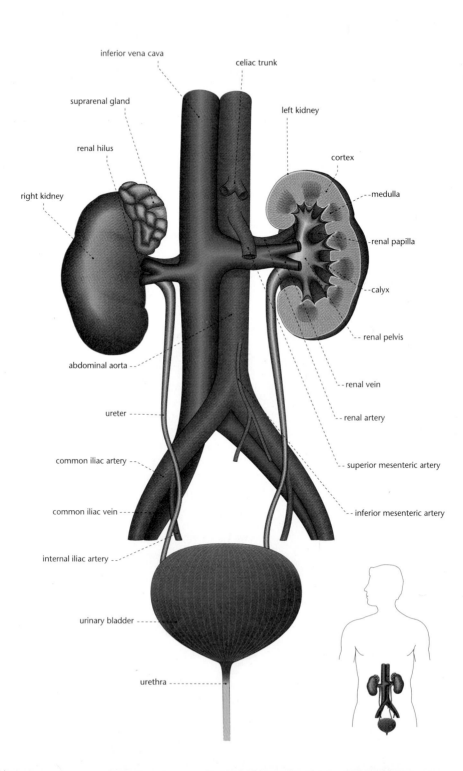

inferior vena cava

celiac trunk

suprarenal gland

left kidney

renal hilus

cortex

right kidney

medulla

renal papilla

calyx

renal pelvis

abdominal aorta

ureter

renal vein

common iliac artery

renal artery

common iliac vein

superior mesenteric artery

internal iliac artery

inferior mesenteric artery

urinary bladder

urethra

PERIPHERAL NERVOUS SYSTEM

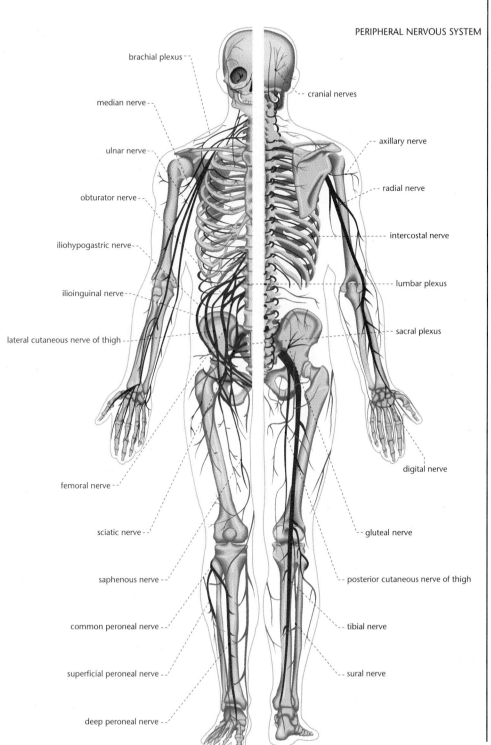

brachial plexus

median nerve

ulnar nerve

obturator nerve

iliohypogastric nerve

ilioinguinal nerve

lateral cutaneous nerve of thigh

femoral nerve

sciatic nerve

saphenous nerve

common peroneal nerve

superficial peroneal nerve

deep peroneal nerve

cranial nerves

axillary nerve

radial nerve

intercostal nerve

lumbar plexus

sacral plexus

digital nerve

gluteal nerve

posterior cutaneous nerve of thigh

tibial nerve

sural nerve

CENTRAL NERVOUS SYSTEM

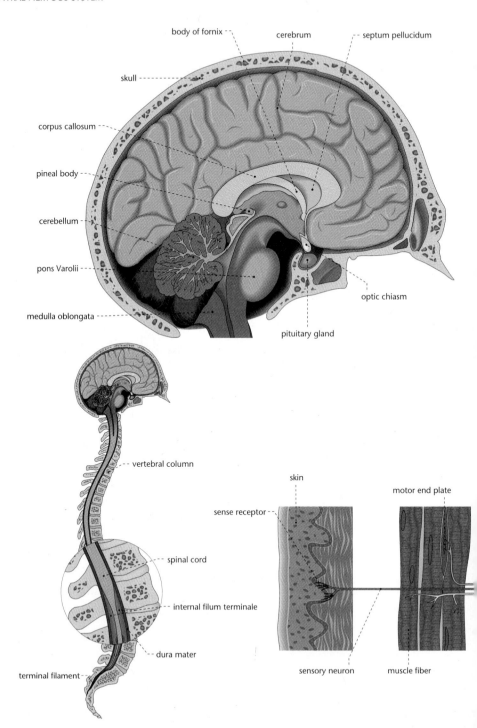

body of fornix

cerebrum

septum pellucidum

skull

corpus callosum

pineal body

cerebellum

pons Varolii

medulla oblongata

optic chiasm

pituitary gland

vertebral column

skin

sense receptor

motor end plate

spinal cord

internal filum terminale

dura mater

terminal filament

sensory neuron

muscle fiber

LUMBAR VERTEBRA

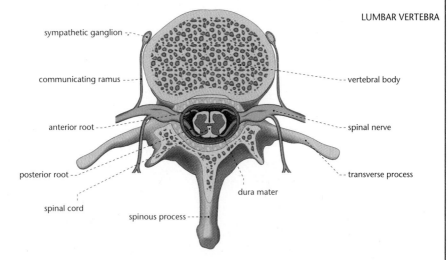

sympathetic ganglion

communicating ramus

anterior root

posterior root

spinal cord

spinous process

vertebral body

spinal nerve

transverse process

dura mater

CHAIN OF NEURONS

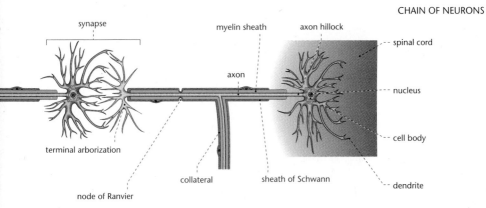

synapse

myelin sheath

axon hillock

spinal cord

axon

nucleus

cell body

terminal arborization

node of Ranvier

collateral

sheath of Schwann

dendrite

SENSORY IMPULSE

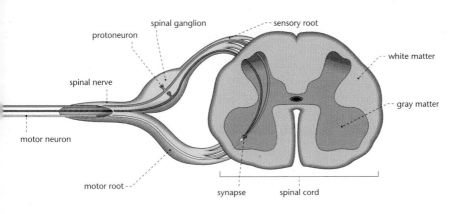

spinal ganglion

protoneuron

sensory root

spinal nerve

white matter

gray matter

motor neuron

motor root

synapse

spinal cord

SKIN

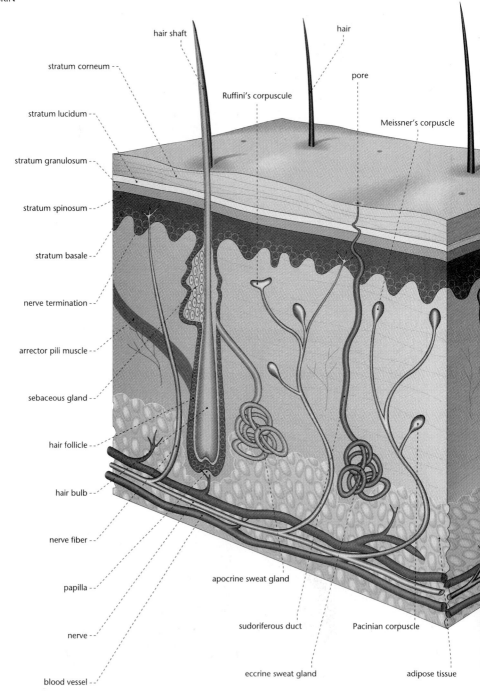

hair shaft

hair

stratum corneum

Ruffini's corpuscle

pore

Meissner's corpuscle

stratum lucidum

stratum granulosum

stratum spinosum

stratum basale

nerve termination

arrector pili muscle

sebaceous gland

hair follicle

hair bulb

nerve fiber

papilla

apocrine sweat gland

nerve

sudoriferous duct

Pacinian corpuscle

blood vessel

eccrine sweat gland

adipose tissue

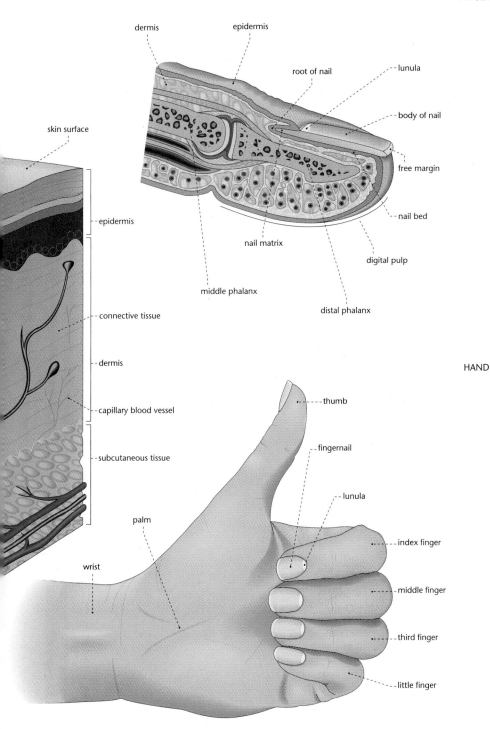

dermis

epidermis

root of nail

lunula

body of nail

free margin

nail bed

digital pulp

distal phalanx

nail matrix

middle phalanx

skin surface

epidermis

connective tissue

dermis

capillary blood vessel

subcutaneous tissue

HAND

thumb

fingernail

lunula

index finger

middle finger

third finger

little finger

palm

wrist

137

PARTS OF THE EAR

AUDITORY OSSICLES

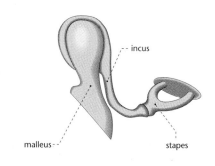

incus

malleus

stapes

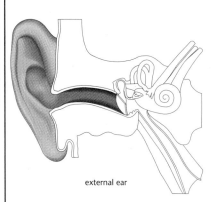

external ear

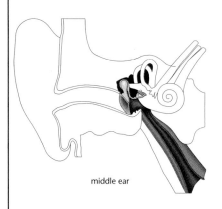

middle ear

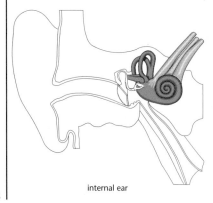

internal ear

auricle

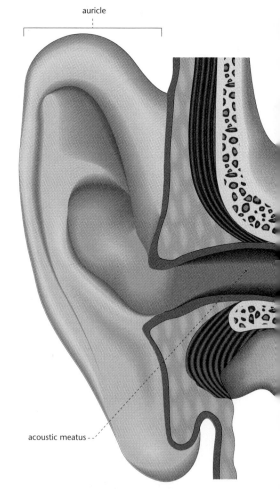

acoustic meatus

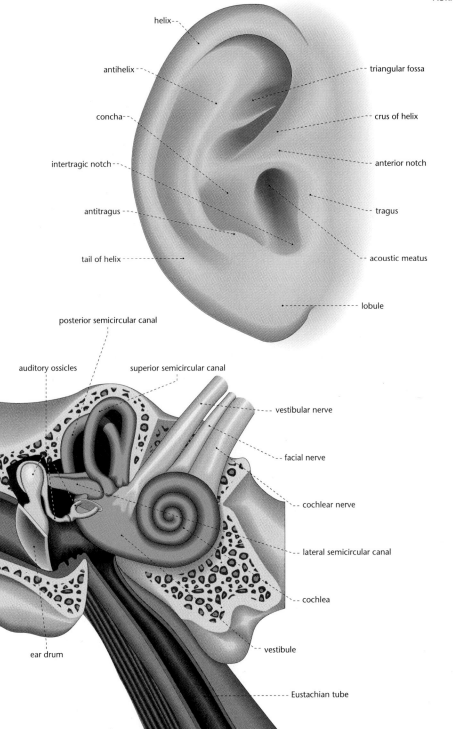

helix

antihelix

concha

intertragic notch

antitragus

tail of helix

triangular fossa

crus of helix

anterior notch

tragus

acoustic meatus

lobule

posterior semicircular canal

auditory ossicles

superior semicircular canal

vestibular nerve

facial nerve

cochlear nerve

lateral semicircular canal

cochlea

vestibule

ear drum

Eustachian tube

EYE

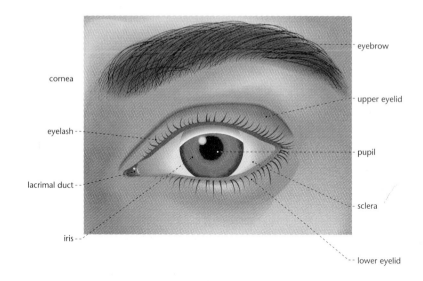

eyebrow

cornea

upper eyelid

eyelash

pupil

lacrimal duct

sclera

iris

lower eyelid

EYEBALL

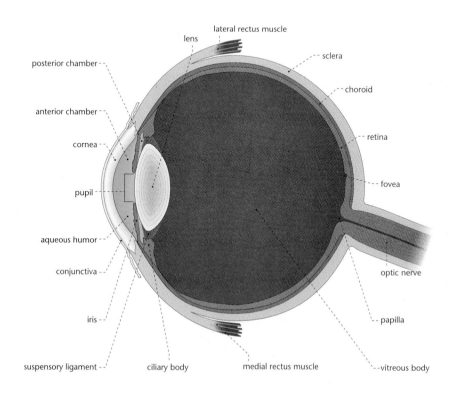

lateral rectus muscle

lens

sclera

posterior chamber

choroid

anterior chamber

retina

cornea

fovea

pupil

aqueous humor

conjunctiva

optic nerve

iris

papilla

suspensory ligament

ciliary body

medial rectus muscle

vitreous body

EXTERNAL NOSE

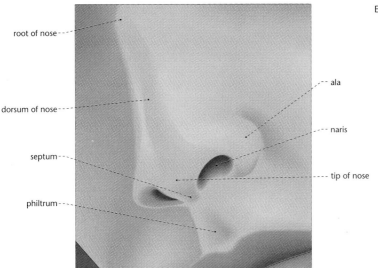

root of nose

dorsum of nose

septum

philtrum

ala

naris

tip of nose

NASAL FOSSAE

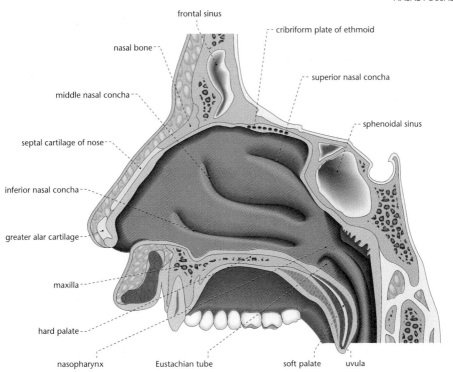

frontal sinus

cribriform plate of ethmoid

nasal bone

superior nasal concha

middle nasal concha

septal cartilage of nose

sphenoidal sinus

inferior nasal concha

greater alar cartilage

maxilla

hard palate

nasopharynx

Eustachian tube

soft palate

uvula

MOUTH

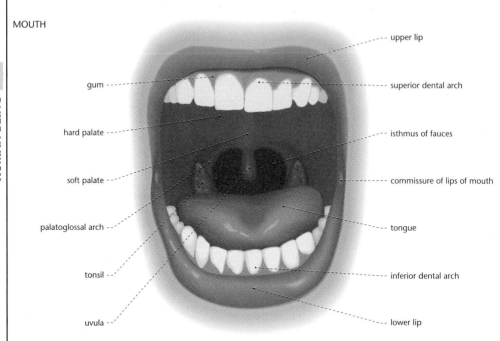

upper lip

gum

superior dental arch

hard palate

isthmus of fauces

soft palate

commissure of lips of mouth

palatoglossal arch

tongue

tonsil

inferior dental arch

uvula

lower lip

SAGITTAL SECTION

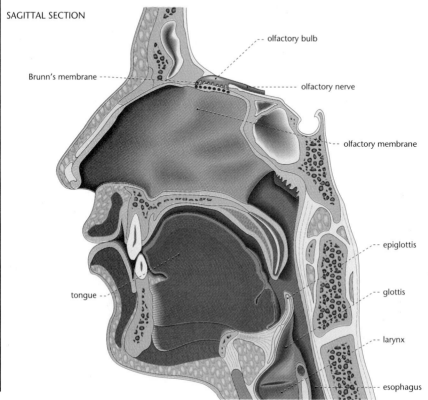

olfactory bulb

Brunn's membrane

olfactory nerve

olfactory membrane

epiglottis

glottis

tongue

larynx

esophagus

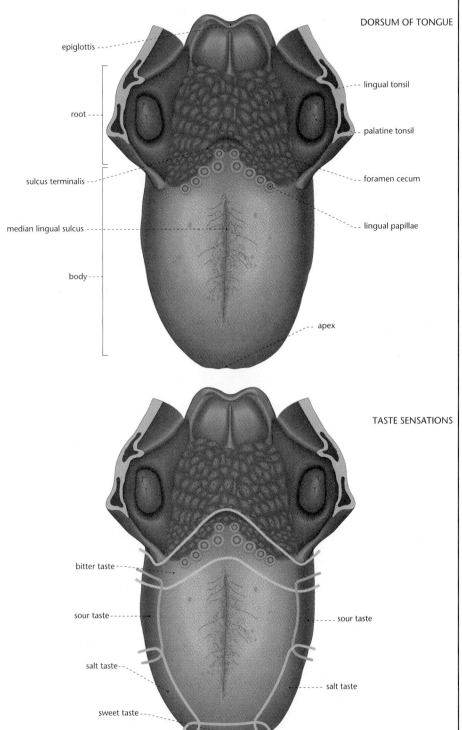

DORSUM OF TONGUE

epiglottis

lingual tonsil

root

palatine tonsil

sulcus terminalis

foramen cecum

median lingual sulcus

lingual papillae

body

apex

TASTE SENSATIONS

bitter taste

sour taste

sour taste

salt taste

salt taste

sweet taste

HUMAN DENTURE

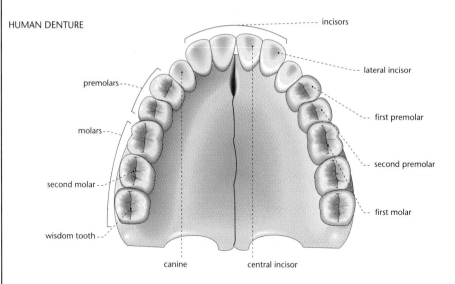

incisors

lateral incisor

first premolar

second premolar

first molar

premolars

molars

second molar

wisdom tooth

canine

central incisor

CROSS SECTION OF A MOLAR

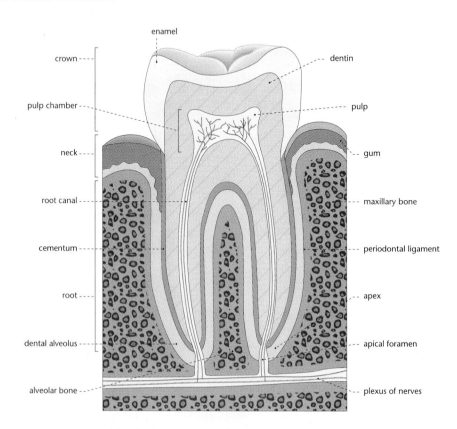

enamel

crown

dentin

pulp chamber

pulp

neck

gum

root canal

maxillary bone

cementum

periodontal ligament

root

apex

dental alveolus

apical foramen

alveolar bone

plexus of nerves

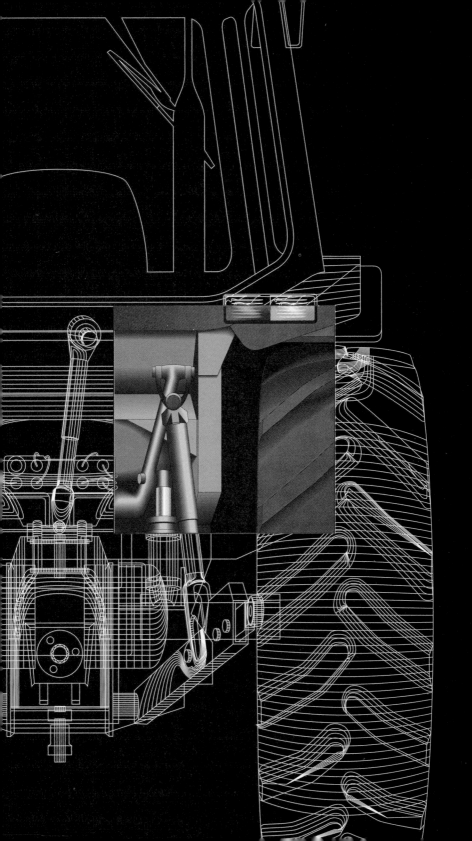

CONTENTS

FARMING

TRACTOR

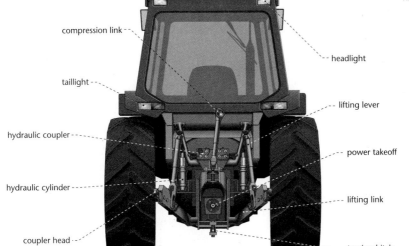

compression link

headlight

taillight

lifting lever

hydraulic coupler

power takeoff

hydraulic cylinder

lifting link

coupler head

towing hitch

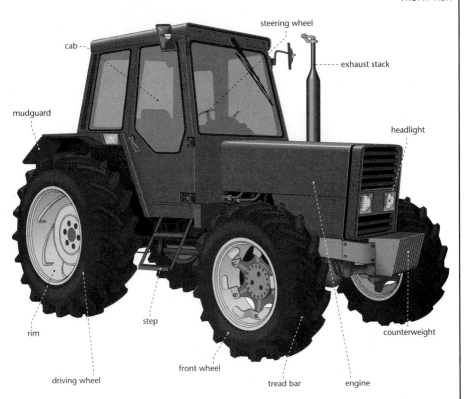

steering wheel

cab

exhaust stack

mudguard

headlight

rim

counterweight

step

driving wheel

front wheel

tread bar

engine

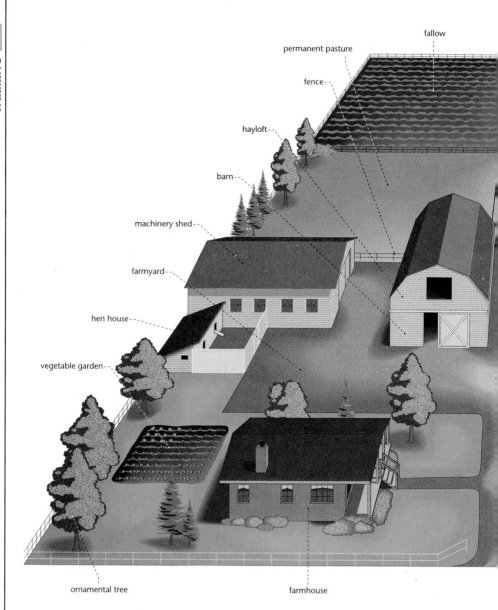

fallow

permanent pasture

fence

hayloft

barn

machinery shed

farmyard

hen house

vegetable garden

ornamental tree

farmhouse

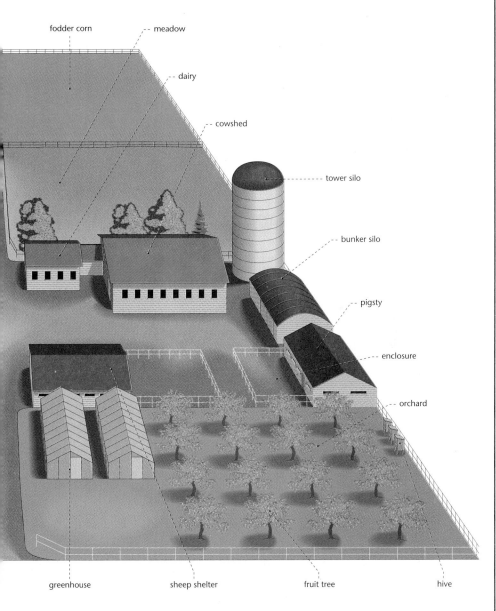

fodder corn

meadow

dairy

cowshed

tower silo

bunker silo

pigsty

enclosure

orchard

greenhouse

sheep shelter

fruit tree

hive

hen

chick

rooster

duck

goose

turkey

goat

lamb

sheep

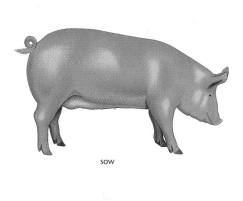

sow

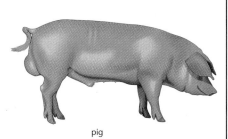

pig

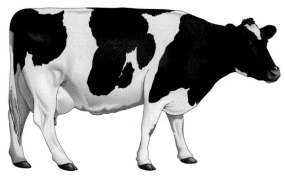

cow

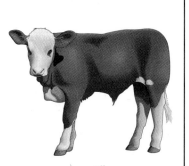

calf

ox

PRINCIPAL TYPES OF CEREALS

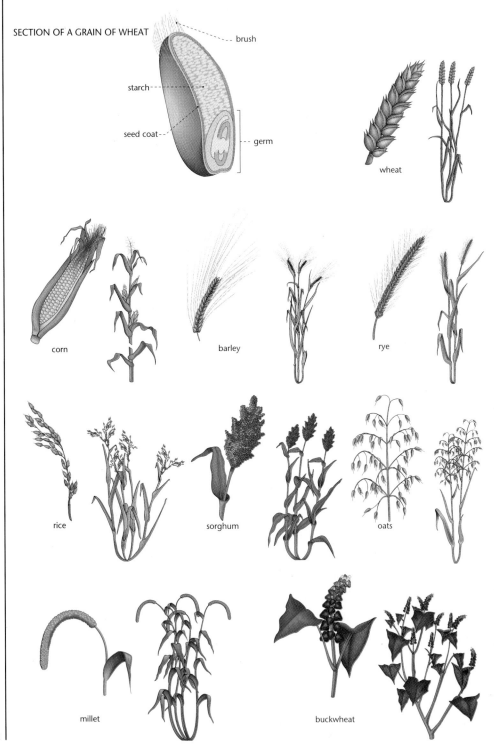

SECTION OF A GRAIN OF WHEAT

brush

starch

seed coat

germ

wheat

corn

barley

rye

rice

sorghum

oats

millet

buckwheat

BREAD

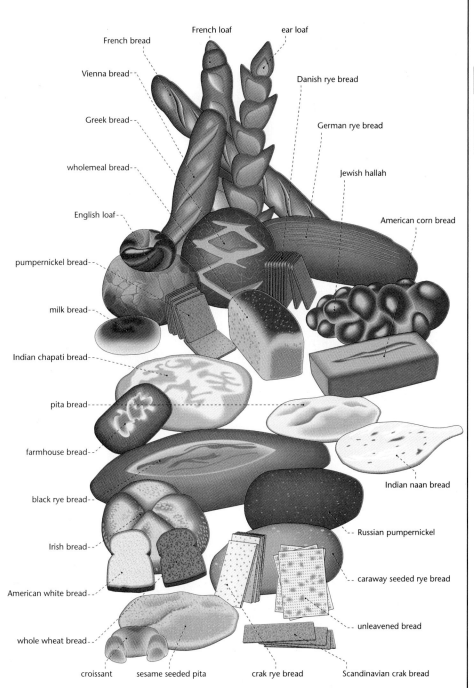

French loaf

ear loaf

French bread

Vienna bread

Danish rye bread

Greek bread

German rye bread

wholemeal bread

Jewish hallah

English loaf

American corn bread

pumpernickel bread

milk bread

Indian chapati bread

pita bread

farmhouse bread

Indian naan bread

black rye bread

Russian pumpernickel

Irish bread

caraway seeded rye bread

American white bread

unleavened bread

whole wheat bread

croissant   sesame seeded pita   crak rye bread   Scandinavian crak bread

153

STEPS FOR CULTIVATING SOIL

PLOWING SOIL

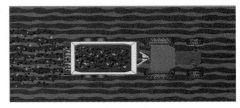

ribbing plow

FERTILIZING SOIL

manure spreader

PULVERIZING SOIL

tandem disk harrow

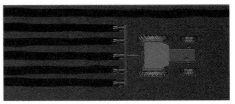

cultivator

PLANTING

seed drill

MOWING

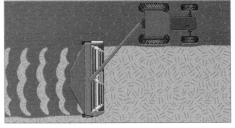

flail mower

TEDDING

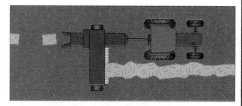

rake

HARVESTING

hay baler

HARVESTING

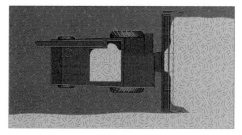

combine harvester

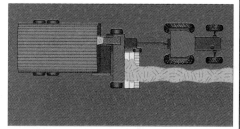

forage harvester

ENSILING

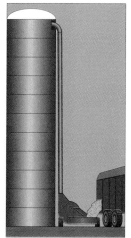

forage blower

PLOWING SOIL

RIBBING PLOW

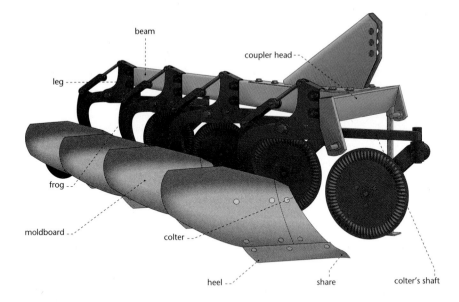

beam

coupler head

leg

frog

moldboard

colter

heel

share

colter's shaft

FERTILIZING SOIL

MANURE SPREADER

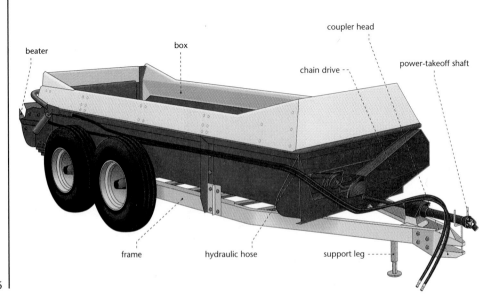

beater

box

coupler head

chain drive

power-takeoff shaft

frame

hydraulic hose

support leg

TANDEM DISK HARROW

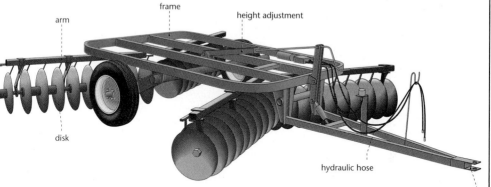

arm

frame

height adjustment

disk

hydraulic hose

coupler head

CULTIVATOR

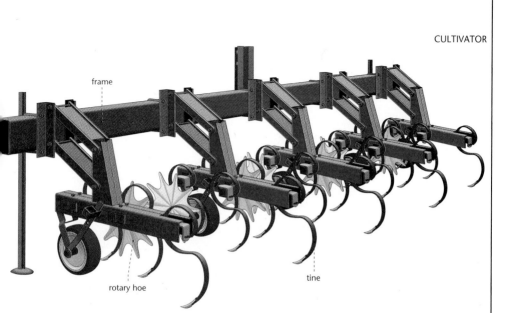

frame

rotary hoe

tine

157

SEED DRILL

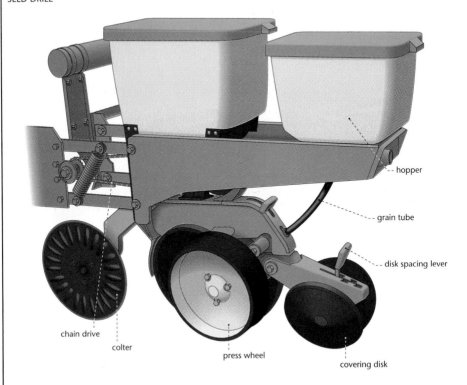

hopper

grain tube

disk spacing lever

chain drive

colter

press wheel

covering disk

MOWING

FLAIL MOWER

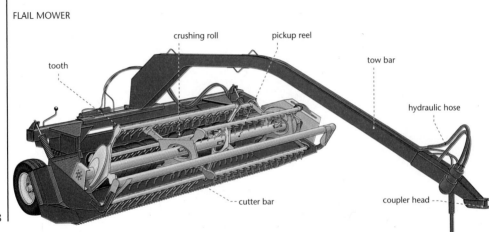

crushing roll

pickup reel

tooth

tow bar

hydraulic hose

cutter bar

coupler head

TEDDING

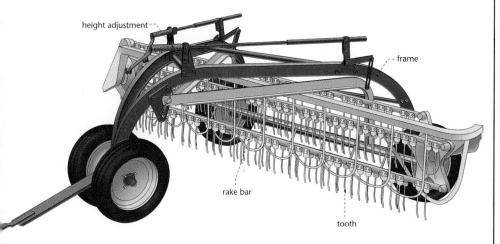

height adjustment

frame

rake bar

tooth

HARVESTING

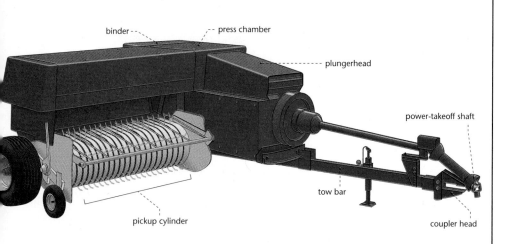

binder

press chamber

plungerhead

power-takeoff shaft

tow bar

pickup cylinder

coupler head

COMBINE HARVESTER

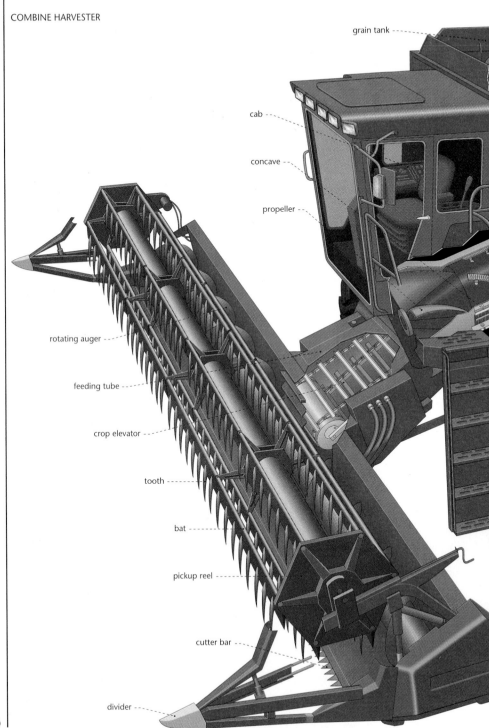

grain tank

cab

concave

propeller

rotating auger

feeding tube

crop elevator

tooth

bat

pickup reel

cutter bar

divider

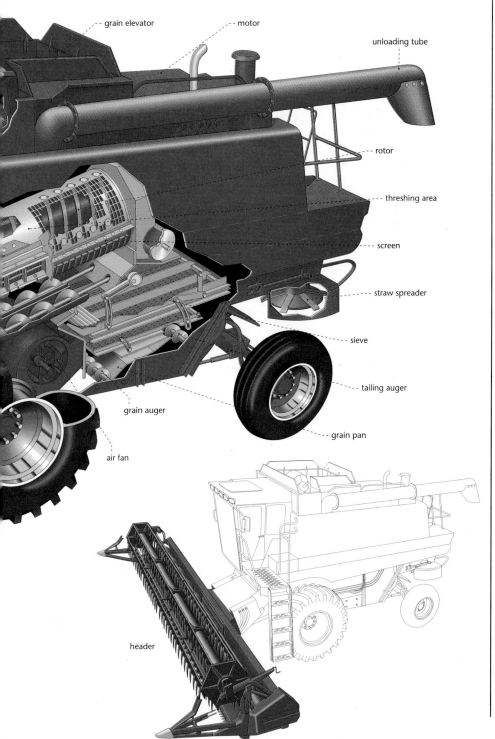

grain elevator

motor

unloading tube

rotor

threshing area

screen

straw spreader

sieve

tailing auger

grain auger

grain pan

air fan

header

FARMING

FORAGE HARVESTER

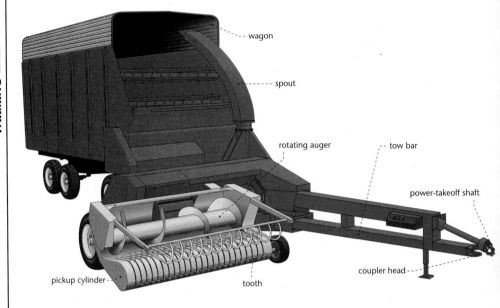

wagon

spout

rotating auger

tow bar

power-takeoff shaft

pickup cylinder

tooth

coupler head

ENSILING

FORAGE BLOWER

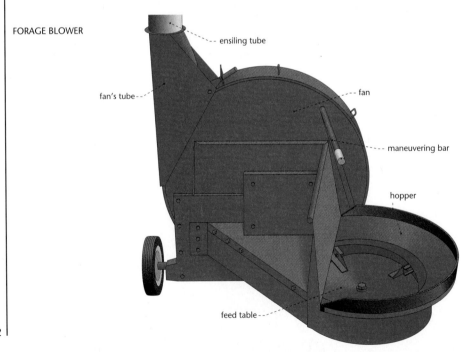

ensiling tube

fan's tube

fan

maneuvering bar

hopper

feed table

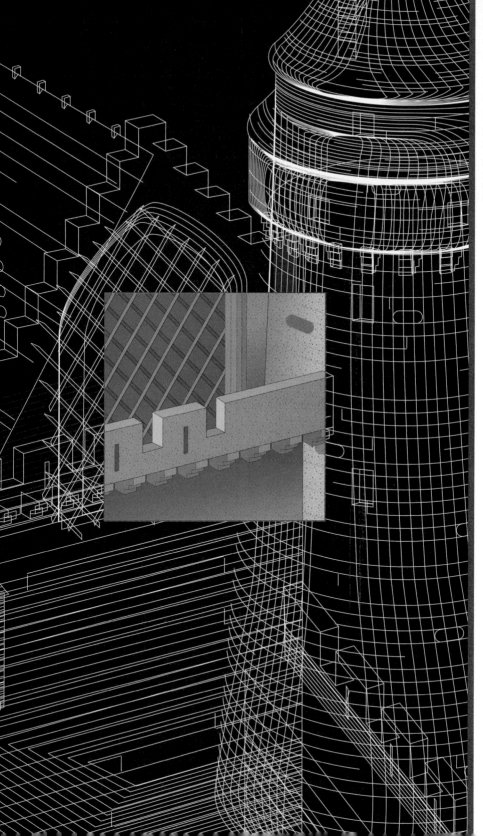

CONTENTS

ARCHITECTURE

igloo

wigwam

yurt

isba

hut

hut

tepee

pile dwelling

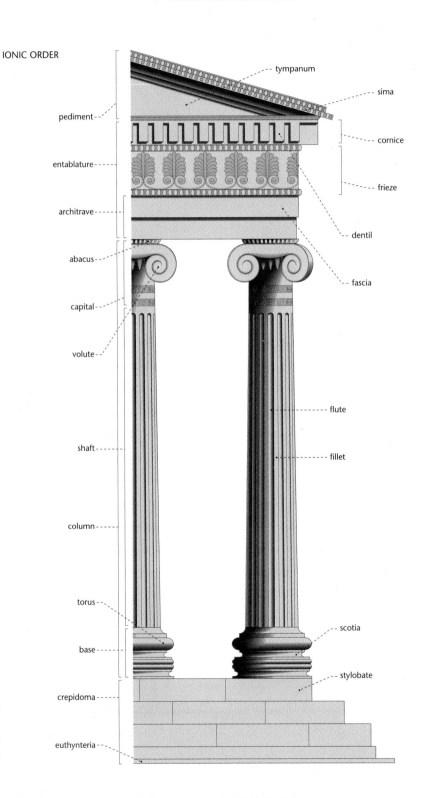

IONIC ORDER

tympanum

sima

pediment

cornice

entablature

frieze

architrave

abacus

dentil

capital

fascia

volute

flute

shaft

fillet

column

torus

scotia

base

stylobate

crepidoma

euthynteria

DORIC ORDER

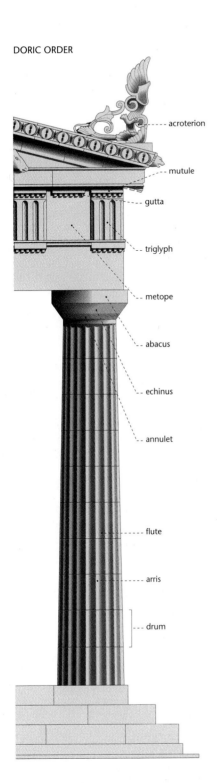

acroterion

mutule

gutta

triglyph

metope

abacus

echinus

annulet

flute

arris

drum

CORINTHIAN ORDER

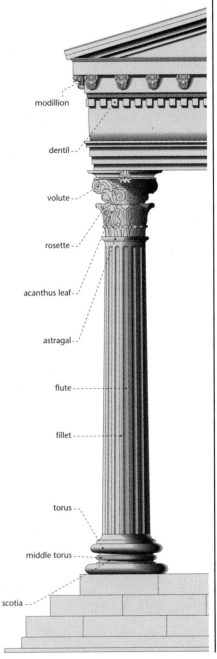

modillion

dentil

volute

rosette

acanthus leaf

astragal

flute

fillet

torus

middle torus

scotia

GREEK TEMPLE

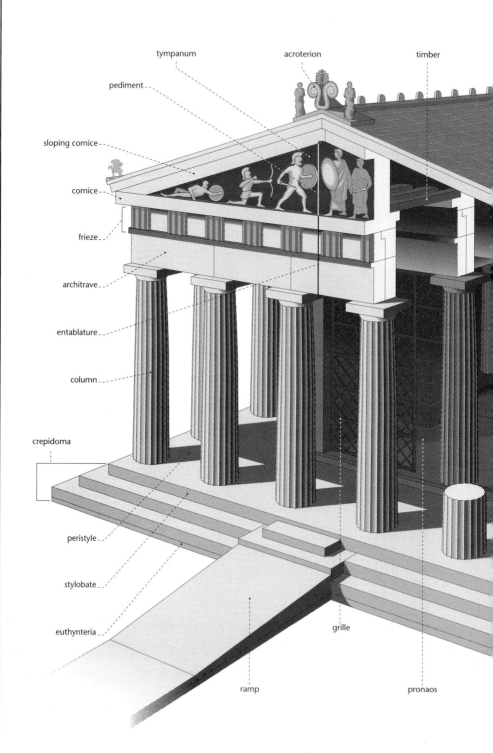

tympanum

acroterion

timber

pediment

sloping cornice

cornice

frieze

architrave

entablature

column

crepidoma

peristyle

stylobate

euthynteria

ramp

grille

pronaos

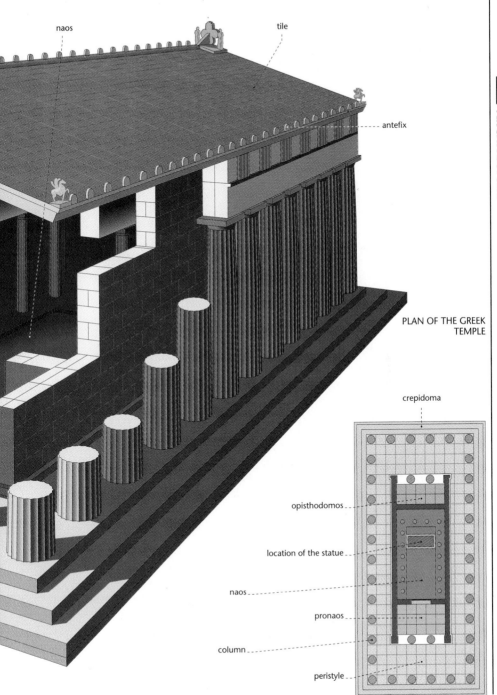

naos

tile

antefix

PLAN OF THE GREEK
TEMPLE

crepidoma

opisthodomos

location of the statue

naos

pronaos

column

peristyle

169

ROMAN HOUSE

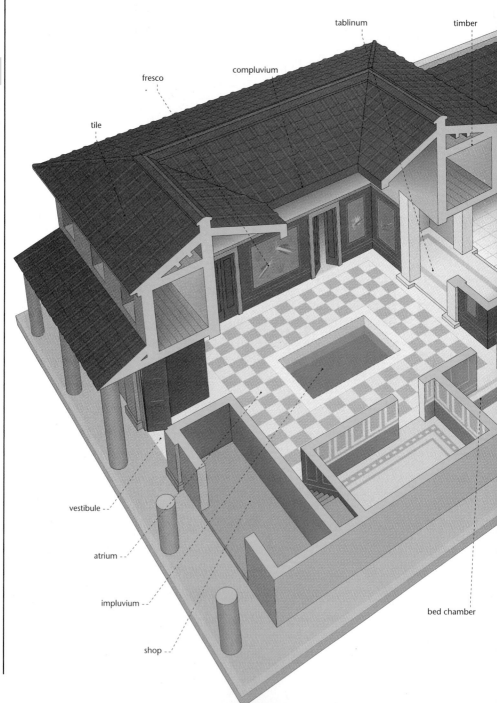

tablinum

timber

fresco

compluvium

tile

vestibule

atrium

impluvium

shop

bed chamber

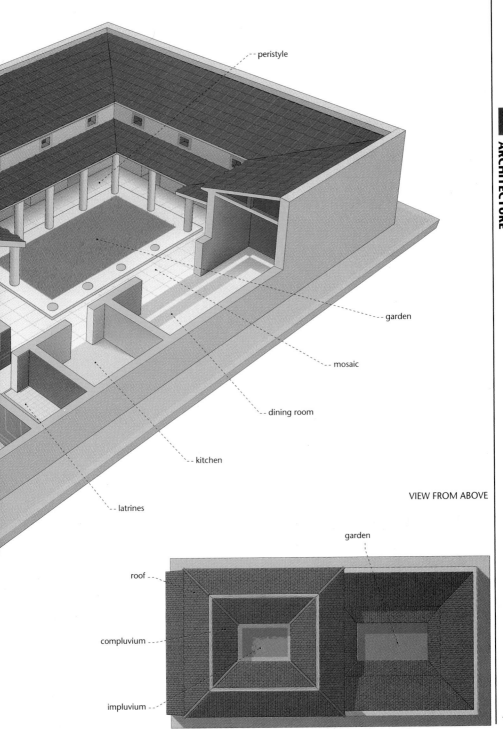

peristyle

garden

mosaic

dining room

kitchen

VIEW FROM ABOVE

latrines

garden

roof

compluvium

impluvium

171

MOSQUE

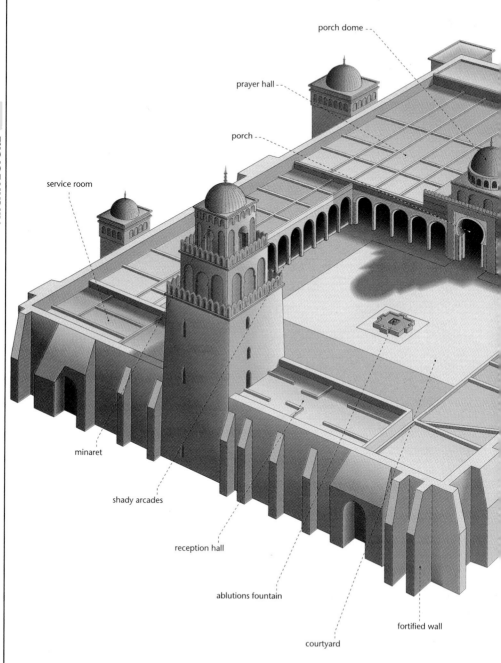

porch dome

prayer hall

porch

service room

minaret

shady arcades

reception hall

ablutions fountain

courtyard

fortified wall

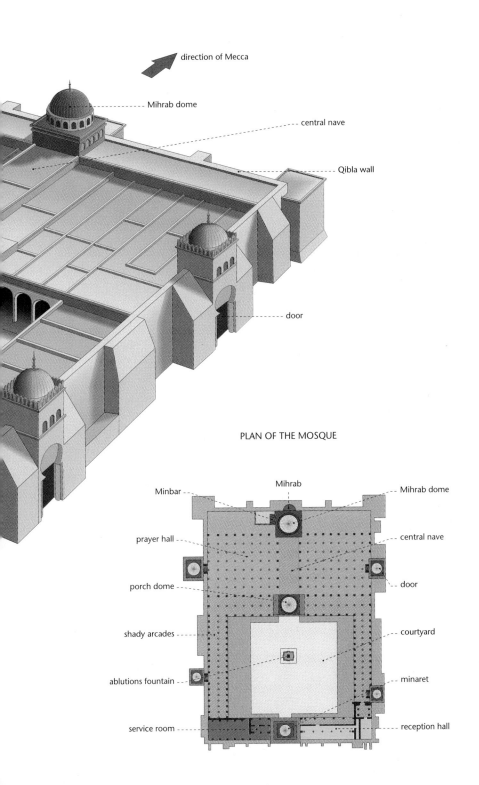

direction of Mecca

Mihrab dome

central nave

Qibla wall

door

PLAN OF THE MOSQUE

Minbar

Mihrab

Mihrab dome

prayer hall

central nave

porch dome

door

shady arcades

courtyard

ablutions fountain

minaret

service room

reception hall

ARCHITECTURE

SEMICIRCULAR ARCH

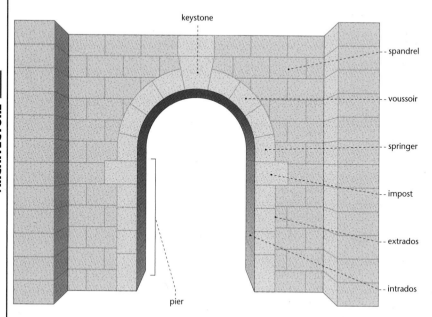

keystone

- spandrel

- voussoir

- springer

- impost

- extrados

- intrados

pier

TYPES OF ARCHES

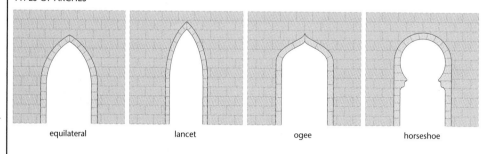

| equilateral | lancet | ogee | horseshoe |

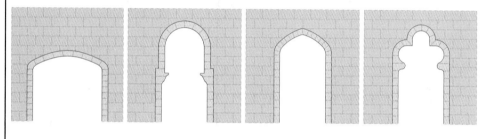

| basket handle | stilted | Tudor | trefoil |

GOTHIC CATHEDRAL

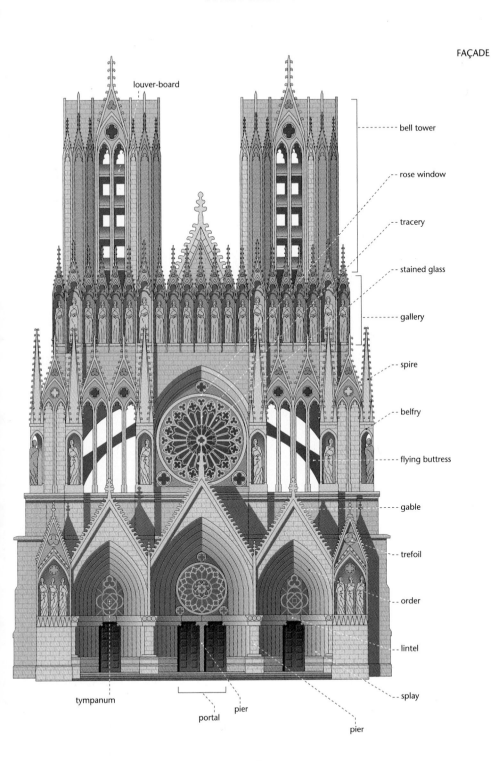

louver-board

bell tower

rose window

tracery

stained glass

gallery

spire

belfry

flying buttress

gable

trefoil

order

lintel

splay

tympanum

portal

pier

pier

CATHEDRAL

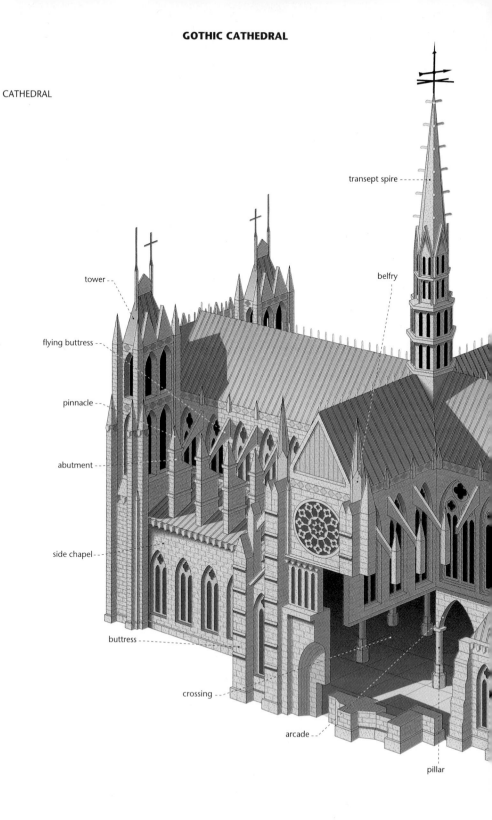

transept spire

belfry

tower

flying buttress

pinnacle

abutment

side chapel

buttress

crossing

arcade

pillar

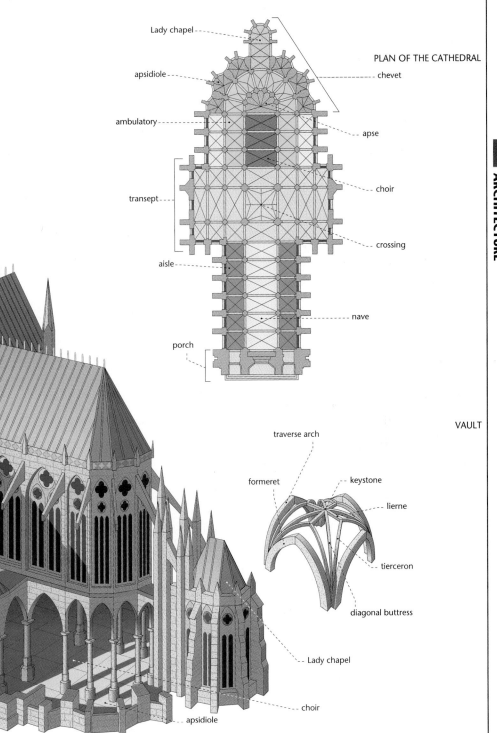

PLAN OF THE CATHEDRAL

Lady chapel

apsidiole

ambulatory

transept

aisle

porch

chevet

apse

choir

crossing

nave

VAULT

traverse arch

formeret

keystone

lierne

tierceron

diagonal buttress

Lady chapel

choir

apsidiole

VAUBAN FORTIFICATION

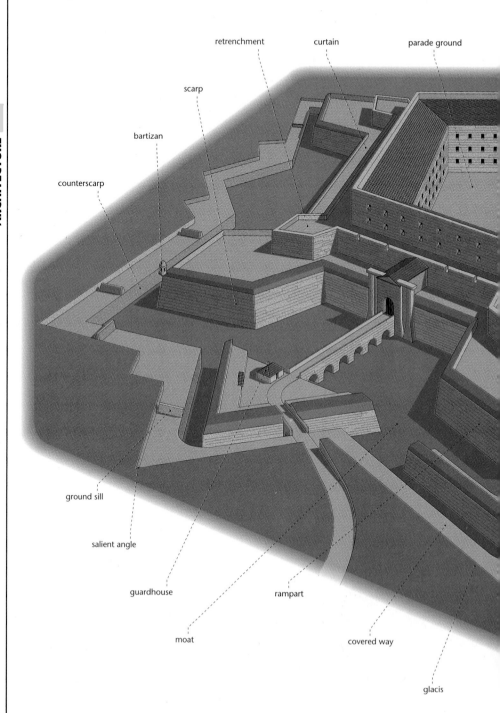

retrenchment

curtain

parade ground

scarp

bartizan

counterscarp

ground sill

salient angle

guardhouse

moat

rampart

covered way

glacis

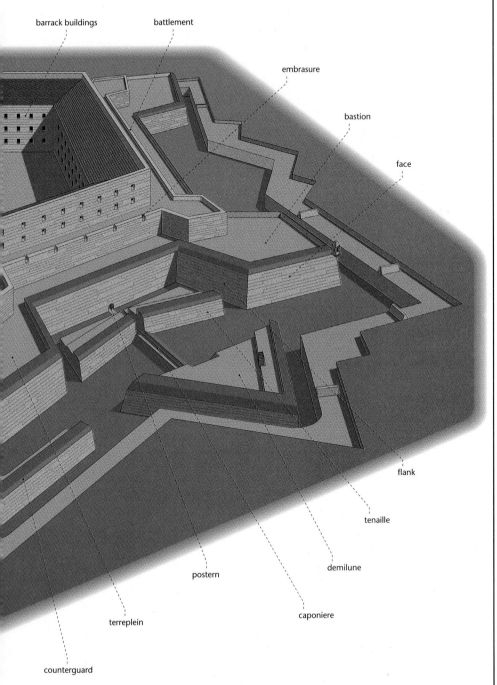

barrack buildings

battlement

embrasure

bastion

face

flank

tenaille

demilune

caponiere

postern

terreplein

counterguard

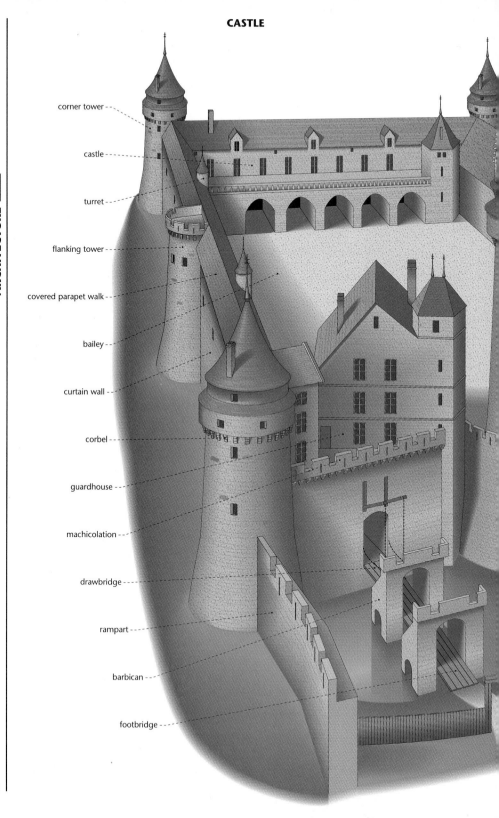

corner tower

castle

turret

flanking tower

covered parapet walk

bailey

curtain wall

corbel

guardhouse

machicolation

drawbridge

rampart

barbican

footbridge

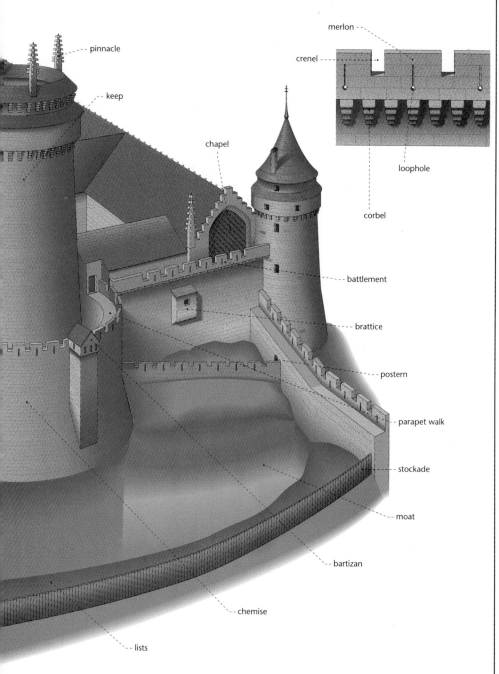

merlon

crenel

loophole

corbel

pinnacle

keep

chapel

battlement

brattice

postern

parapet walk

stockade

moat

bartizan

chemise

lists

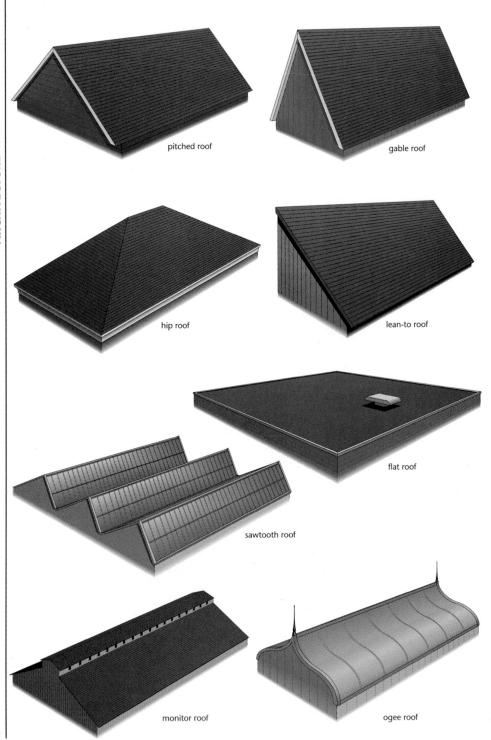

pitched roof

gable roof

hip roof

lean-to roof

flat roof

sawtooth roof

monitor roof

ogee roof

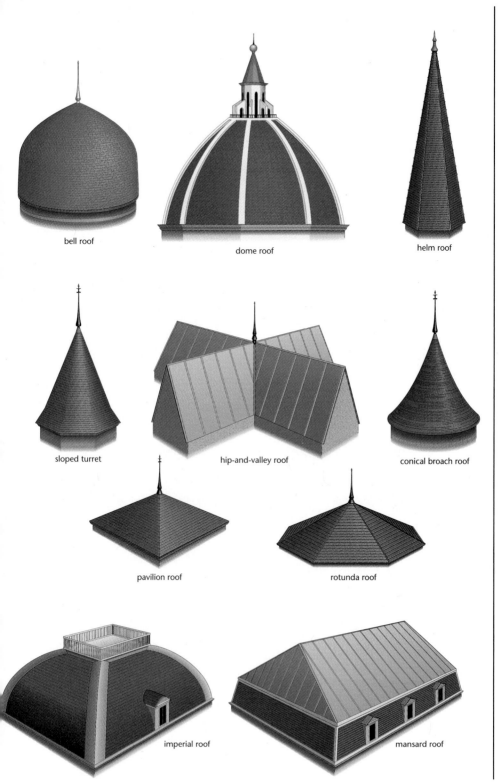

bell roof

dome roof

helm roof

sloped turret

hip-and-valley roof

conical broach roof

pavilion roof

rotunda roof

imperial roof

mansard roof

ARCHITECTURE

square
park
cathedral
convention center
passenger station
office tower
median strip

planetarium
railroad
traffic island
boulevard

street
delivery ramp
freeway

hotel

skyscraper

restaurant

church

high-rise apartment

street light

parking lot

trade building

office building

museum

stadium

CROSS SECTION OF A STREET

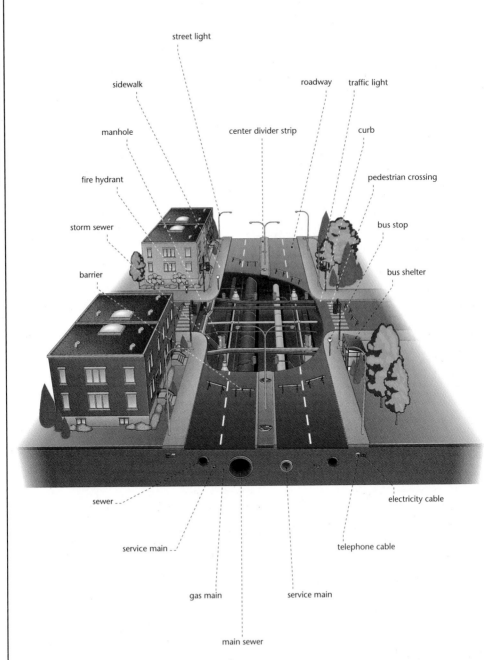

street light

sidewalk

roadway   traffic light

manhole

center divider strip   curb

fire hydrant

pedestrian crossing

storm sewer

bus stop

barrier

bus shelter

sewer

electricity cable

service main

telephone cable

gas main

service main

main sewer

CITY HOUSES

cottage

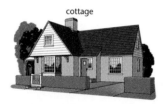

single-family home

apartment building

semi-detached cottage

town houses

high-rise apartment

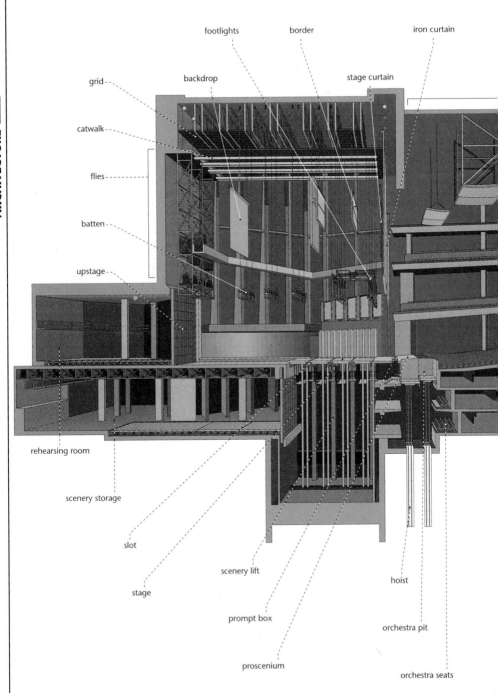

footlights

border

iron curtain

grid

backdrop

stage curtain

catwalk

flies

batten

upstage

rehearsing room

scenery storage

slot

scenery lift

stage

hoist

prompt box

orchestra pit

proscenium

orchestra seats

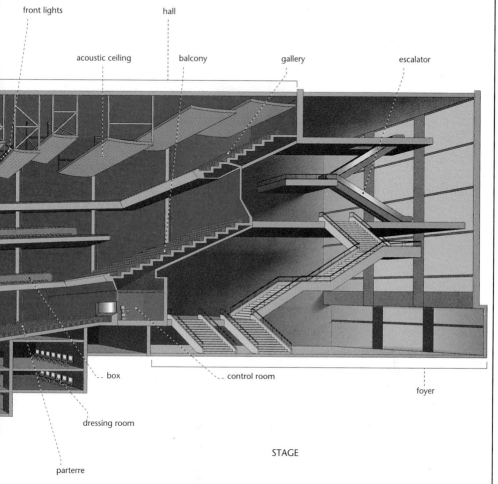

front lights

hall

acoustic ceiling

balcony

gallery

escalator

box

control room

foyer

dressing room

parterre

STAGE

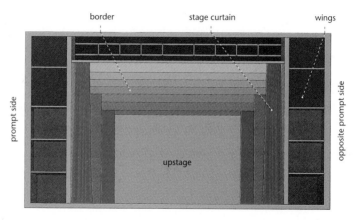

border

stage curtain

wings

prompt side

opposite prompt side

upstage

189

OFFICE BUILDING

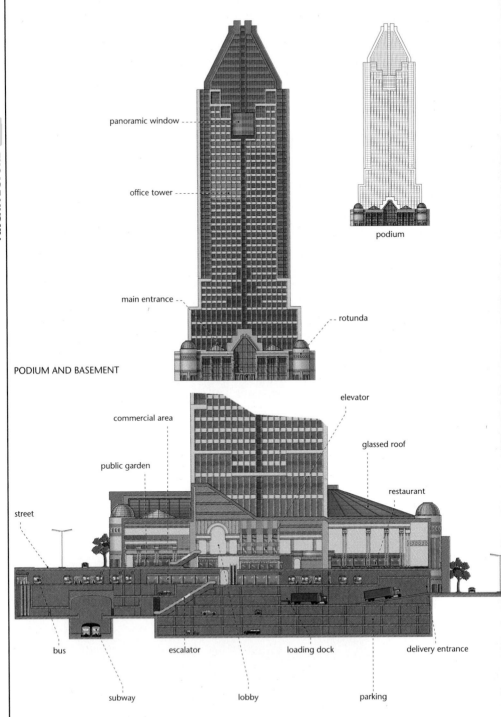

panoramic window

office tower

main entrance

rotunda

podium

PODIUM AND BASEMENT

elevator

commercial area

glassed roof

public garden

restaurant

street

bus

escalator

loading dock

delivery entrance

subway

lobby

parking

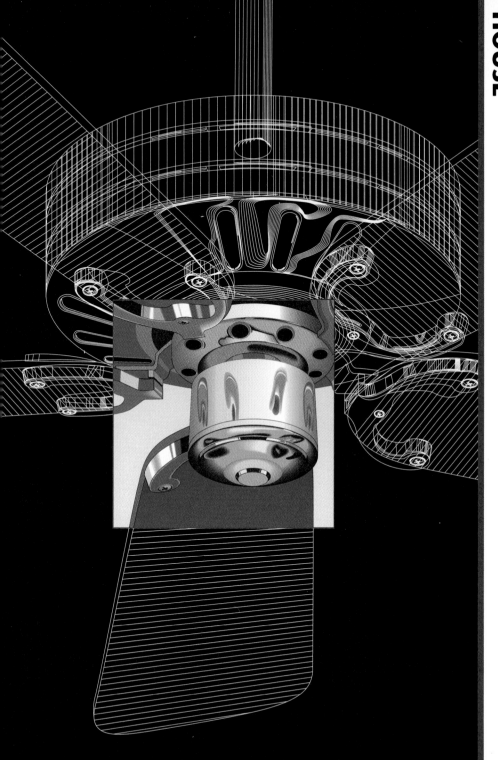

CONTENTS

HOUSE

BLUEPRINT READING

ELEVATION

SITE PLAN

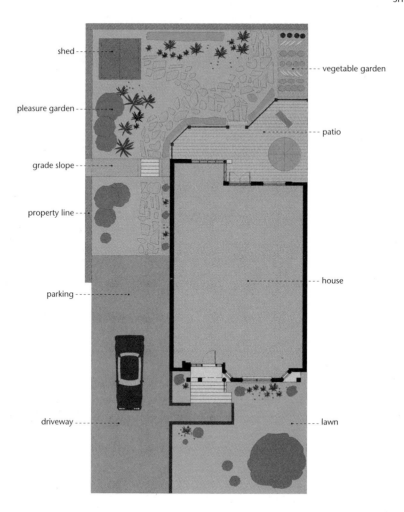

shed

vegetable garden

pleasure garden

patio

grade slope

property line

house

parking

driveway

lawn

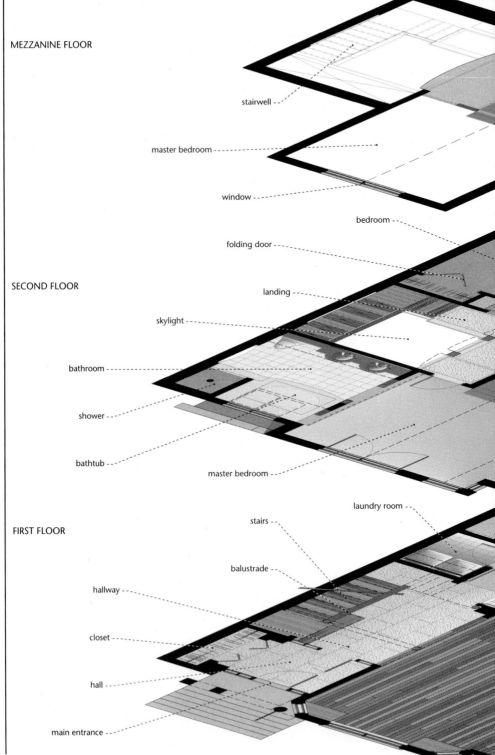

MEZZANINE FLOOR

stairwell

master bedroom

window

bedroom

folding door

SECOND FLOOR

landing

skylight

bathroom

shower

bathtub

master bedroom

laundry room

stairs

FIRST FLOOR

balustrade

hallway

closet

hall

main entrance

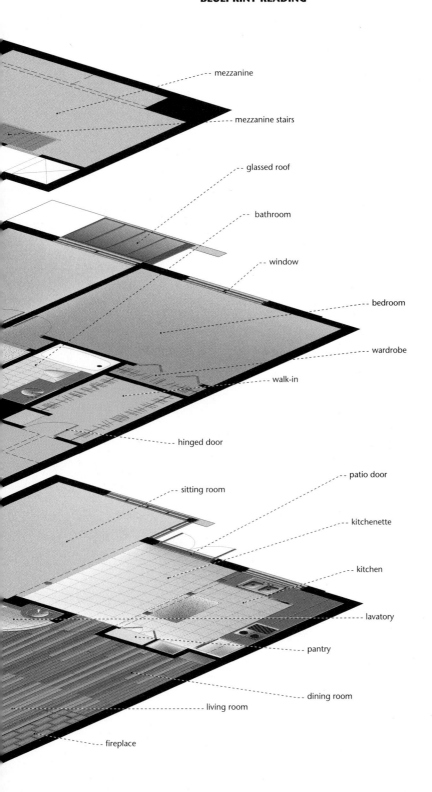

mezzanine

mezzanine stairs

glassed roof

bathroom

window

bedroom

wardrobe

walk-in

hinged door

patio door

sitting room

kitchenette

kitchen

lavatory

pantry

dining room

living room

fireplace

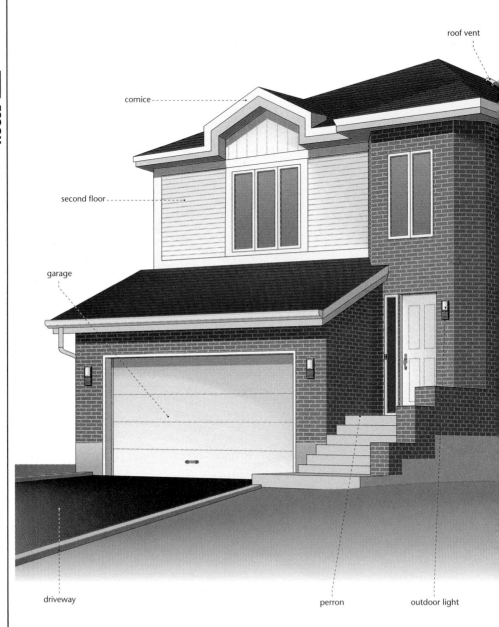

roof vent

cornice

second floor

garage

driveway

perron

outdoor light

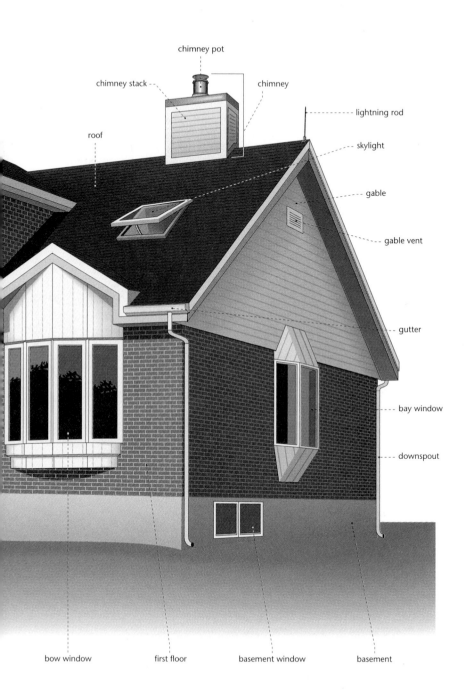

chimney pot

chimney stack

chimney

roof

lightning rod

skylight

gable

gable vent

gutter

bay window

downspout

bow window

first floor

basement window

basement

FRAME

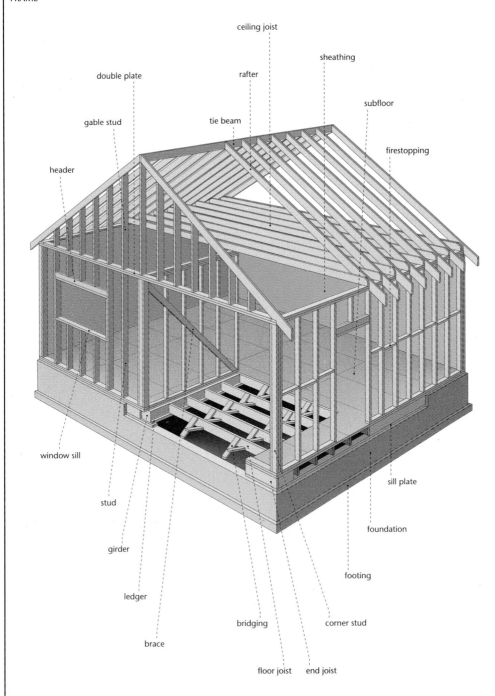

ceiling joist

sheathing

double plate

rafter

subfloor

gable stud

tie beam

firestopping

header

window sill

stud

girder

ledger

brace

bridging

floor joist

end joist

corner stud

footing

foundation

sill plate

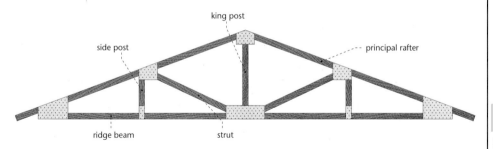

king post

side post

principal rafter

ridge beam

strut

FOUNDATIONS

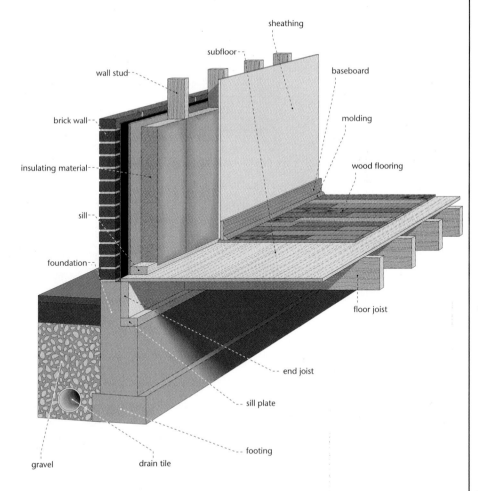

sheathing

subfloor

wall stud

baseboard

brick wall

molding

insulating material

wood flooring

sill

foundation

floor joist

end joist

sill plate

footing

gravel

drain tile

WOOD FLOORING

WOOD FLOORING ON CEMENT SCREED

WOOD FLOORING ON WOODEN STRUCTURE

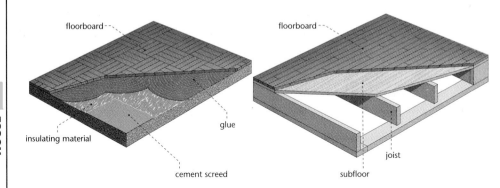

floorboard

insulating material

glue

cement screed

floorboard

joist

subfloor

WOOD FLOORING ARRANGEMENTS

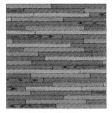

overlay flooring

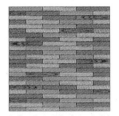

strip flooring with alternate joints

herringbone parquet

herringbone pattern

inlaid parquet

basket weave pattern

Arenberg parquet

Chantilly parquet

Versailles parquet

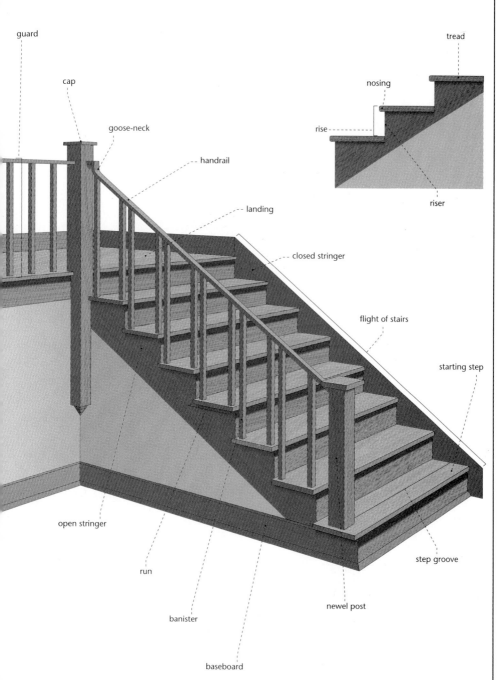

guard

cap

goose-neck

tread

nosing

rise

riser

handrail

landing

closed stringer

flight of stairs

starting step

HOUSE

open stringer

run

banister

newel post

step groove

baseboard

DOOR

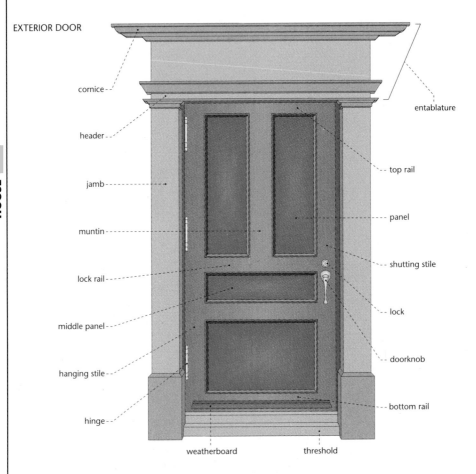

EXTERIOR DOOR

- cornice
- header
- jamb
- muntin
- lock rail
- middle panel
- hanging stile
- hinge

- entablature
- top rail
- panel
- shutting stile
- lock
- doorknob
- bottom rail

weatherboard threshold

TYPES OF DOORS

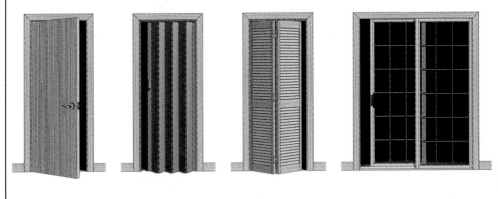

conventional door   sliding folding door   folding door   sliding door

202

WINDOW

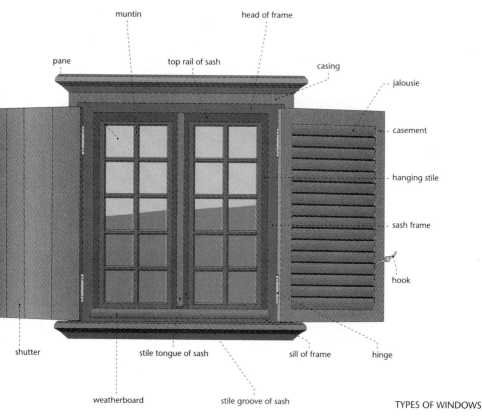

muntin

head of frame

pane

top rail of sash

casing

jalousie

casement

hanging stile

sash frame

hook

shutter

stile tongue of sash

sill of frame

hinge

weatherboard

stile groove of sash

TYPES OF WINDOWS

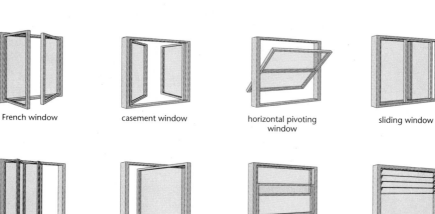

French window

casement window

horizontal pivoting
window

sliding window

sliding folding window

vertical pivoting window

sash window

louvered window

FIREPLACE

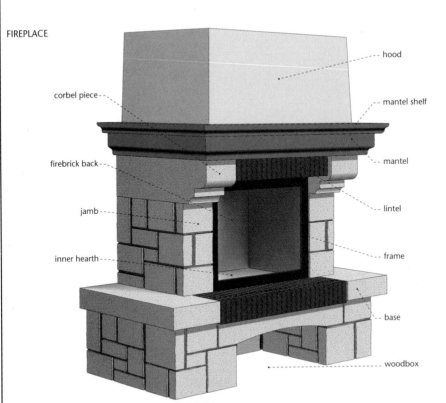

hood

corbel piece

mantel shelf

mantel

firebrick back

lintel

jamb

inner hearth

frame

base

woodbox

SLOW-BURNING STOVE

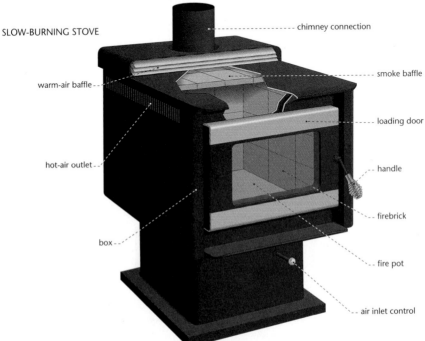

chimney connection

smoke baffle

warm-air baffle

loading door

hot-air outlet

handle

firebrick

box

fire pot

air inlet control

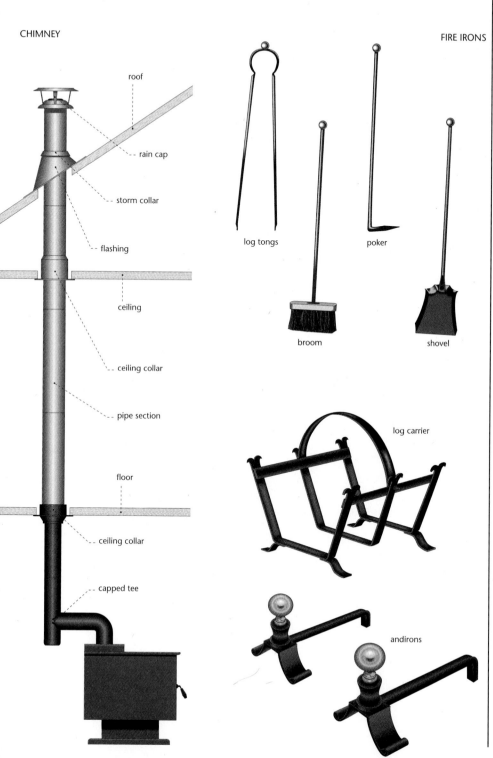

roof

rain cap

storm collar

flashing

ceiling

ceiling collar

pipe section

floor

ceiling collar

capped tee

log tongs

poker

broom

shovel

log carrier

andirons

FORCED WARM-AIR SYSTEM

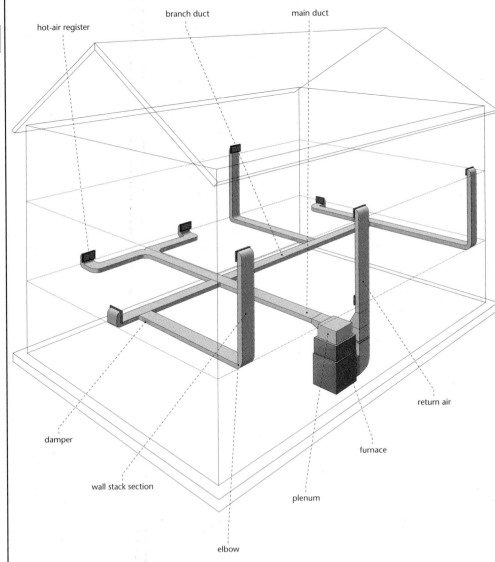

branch duct

main duct

hot-air register

damper

wall stack section

elbow

plenum

furnace

return air

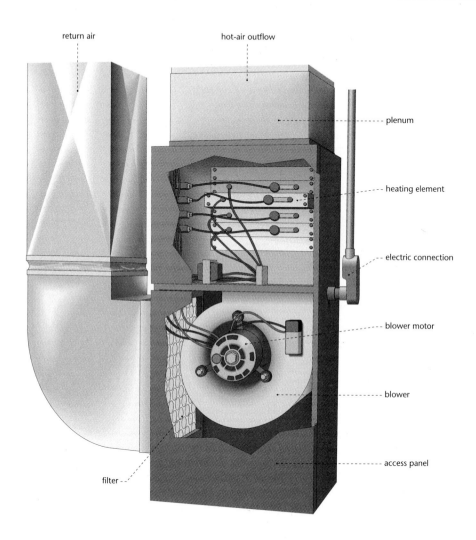

return air

hot-air outflow

plenum

heating element

electric connection

blower motor

blower

access panel

filter

TYPES OF REGISTERS

baseboard register

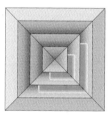

ceiling register

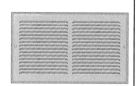

wall register

FORCED HOT-WATER SYSTEM

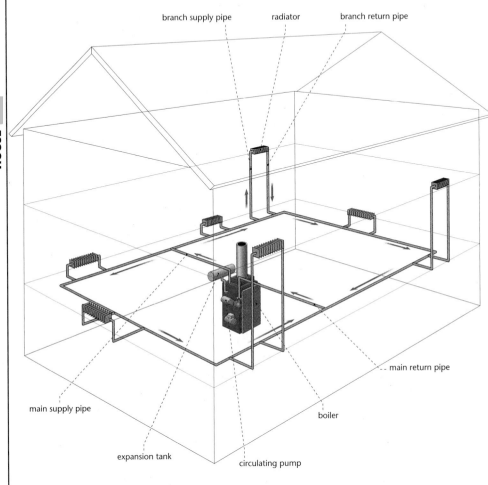

branch supply pipe   radiator   branch return pipe

main return pipe

main supply pipe

boiler

expansion tank

circulating pump

COLUMN RADIATOR

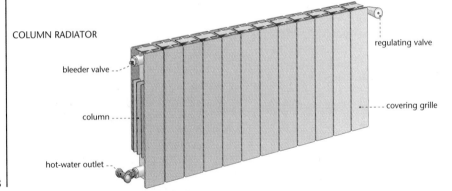

regulating valve

bleeder valve

covering grille

column

hot-water outlet

BOILER

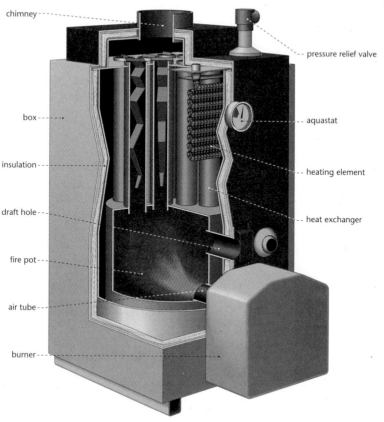

chimney

box

insulation

draft hole

fire pot

air tube

burner

pressure relief valve

aquastat

heating element

heat exchanger

OIL BURNER

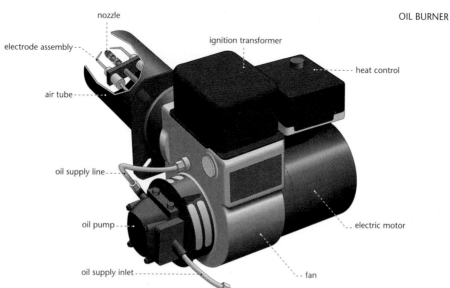

nozzle

electrode assembly

air tube

oil supply line

oil pump

oil supply inlet

ignition transformer

heat control

electric motor

fan

HUMIDIFIER

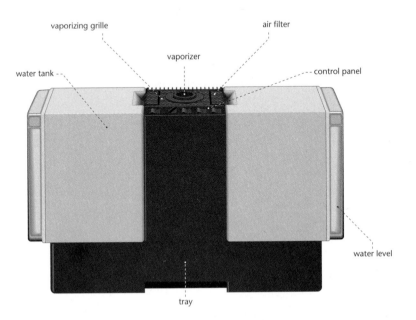

vaporizing grille

vaporizer

air filter

water tank

control panel

water level

tray

HYGROMETER

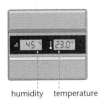

humidity   temperature

air purifier

ELECTRIC BASEBOARD RADIATOR

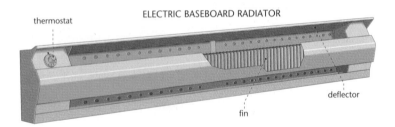

thermostat

deflector

fin

HOUSE

CONVECTOR

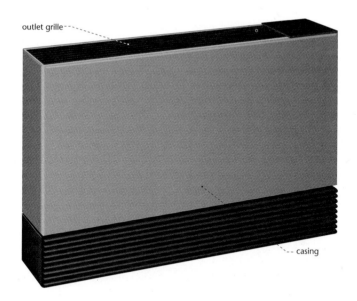

outlet grille

casing

AUXILIARY HEATING

radiant heater

oil-filled heater

fan heater

HEAT PUMP

OUTDOOR UNIT

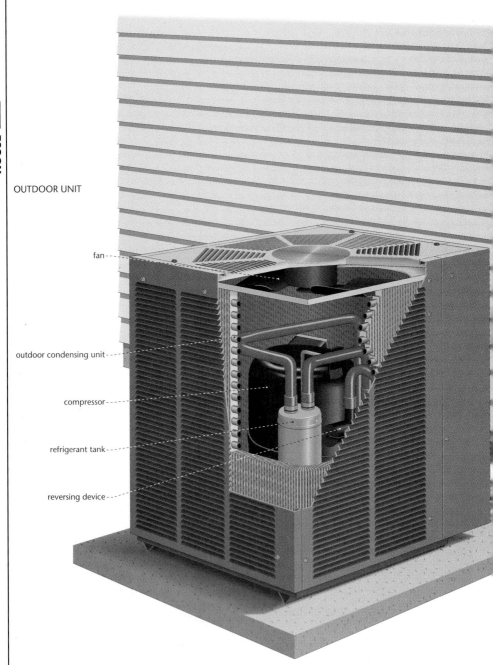

fan

outdoor condensing unit

compressor

refrigerant tank

reversing device

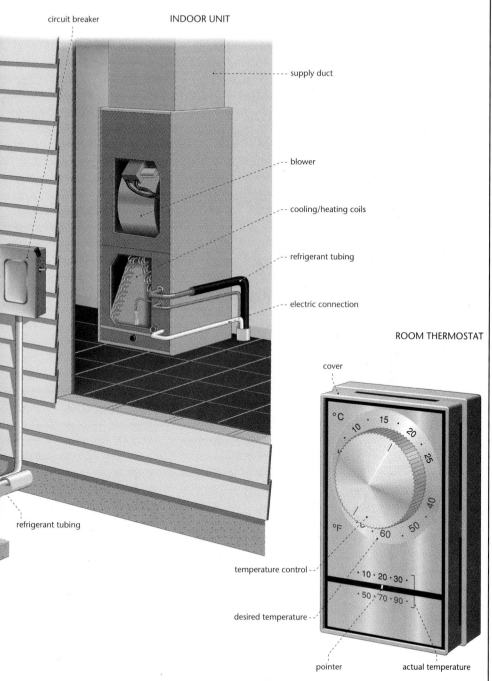

circuit breaker   INDOOR UNIT

supply duct

blower

cooling/heating coils

refrigerant tubing

electric connection

refrigerant tubing

ROOM THERMOSTAT

cover

°C

°F

temperature control

desired temperature

pointer

actual temperature

AIR CONDITIONING

CEILING FAN

rod

motor

blade

ROOM AIR CONDITIONER

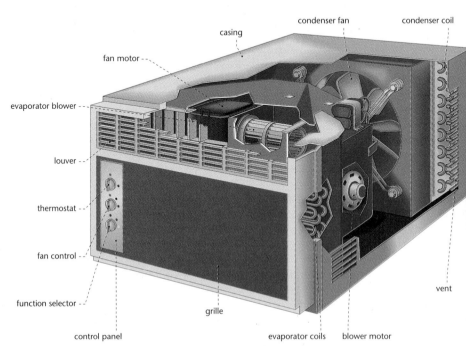

condenser fan

condenser coil

casing

fan motor

evaporator blower

louver

thermostat

fan control

function selector

control panel

grille

evaporator coils

blower motor

vent

PLUMBING SYSTEM

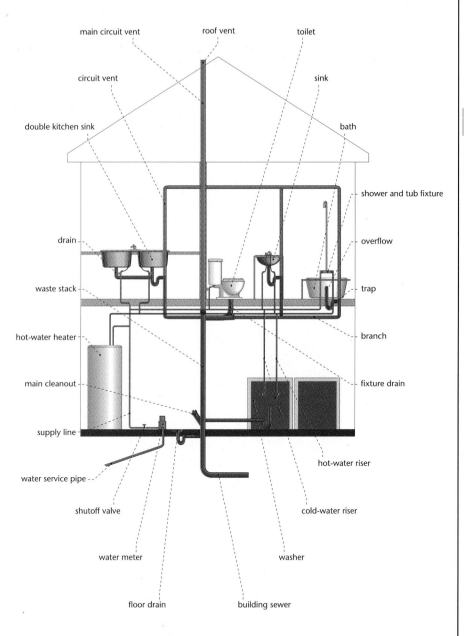

main circuit vent

roof vent

toilet

circuit vent

sink

double kitchen sink

bath

shower and tub fixture

drain

overflow

waste stack

trap

hot-water heater

branch

main cleanout

fixture drain

supply line

hot-water riser

water service pipe

shutoff valve

cold-water riser

water meter

washer

floor drain

building sewer

ventilating circuit   draining circuit   cold-water circuit   hot-water circuit

PEDESTAL-TYPE SUMP PUMP

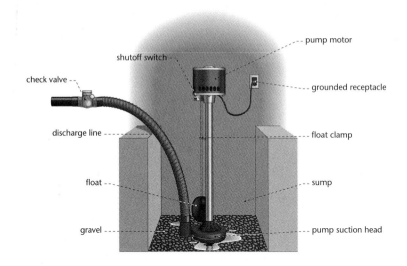

pump motor

shutoff switch

check valve

grounded receptacle

discharge line

float clamp

float

sump

gravel

pump suction head

SEPTIC TANK

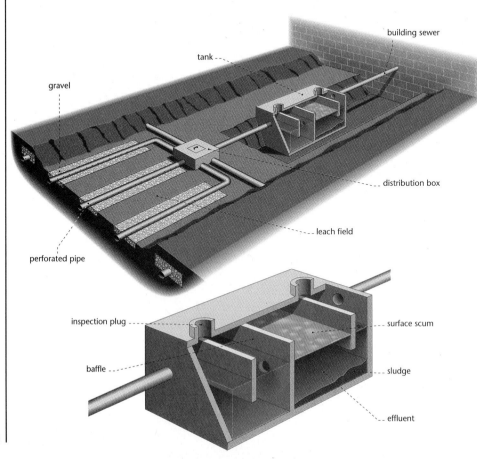

building sewer

tank

gravel

distribution box

leach field

perforated pipe

inspection plug

surface scum

baffle

sludge

effluent

HOUSE FURNITURE

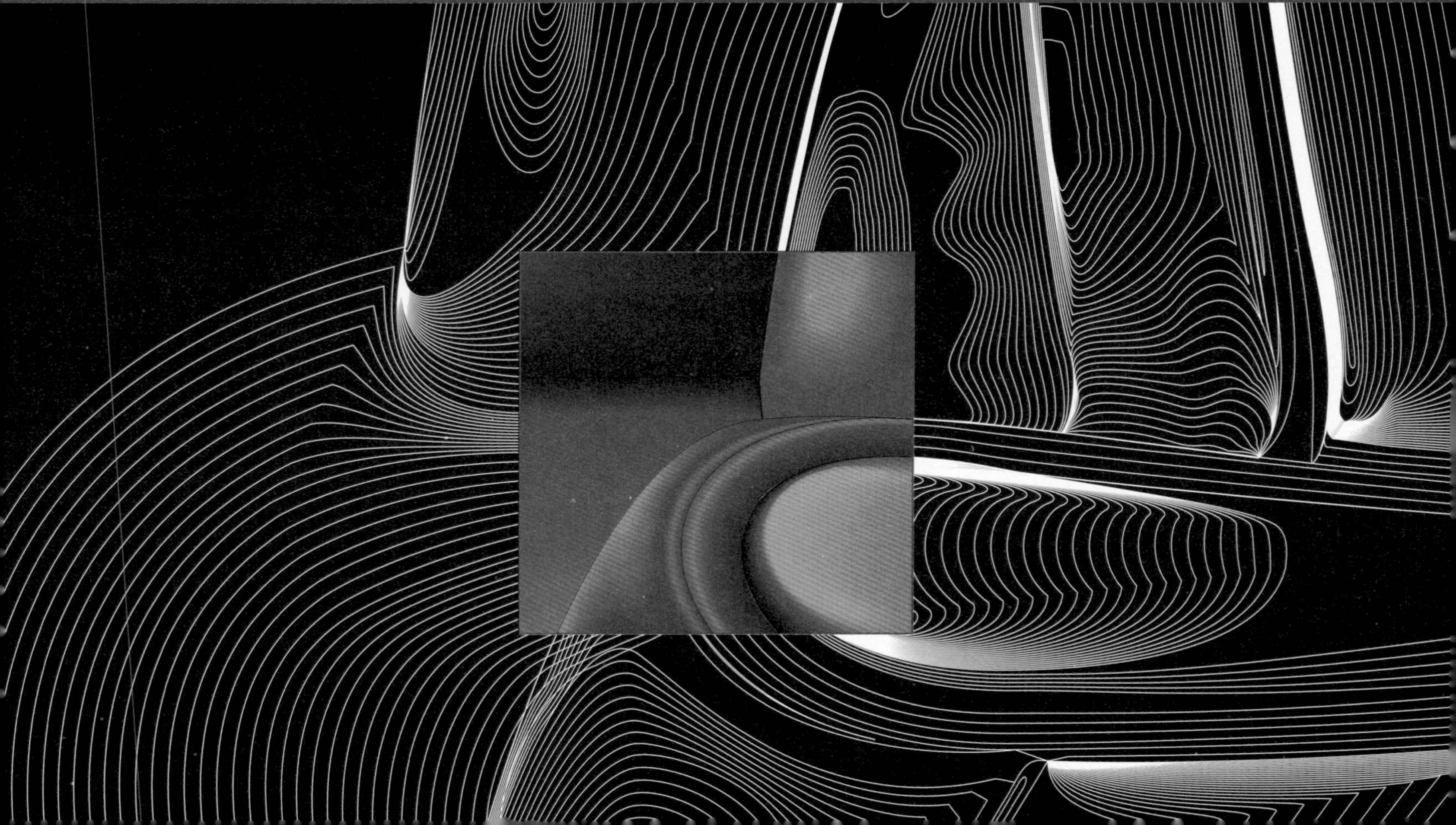

CONTENTS

TABLE

GATE-LEG TABLE

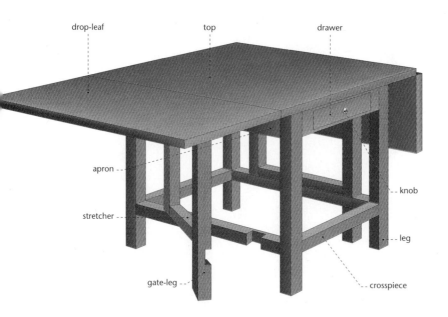

drop-leaf

top

drawer

apron

stretcher

knob

leg

gate-leg

crosspiece

TYPES OF TABLES

extension table

top

extension

serving cart

nest of tables

HOUSE FURNITURE

PARTS

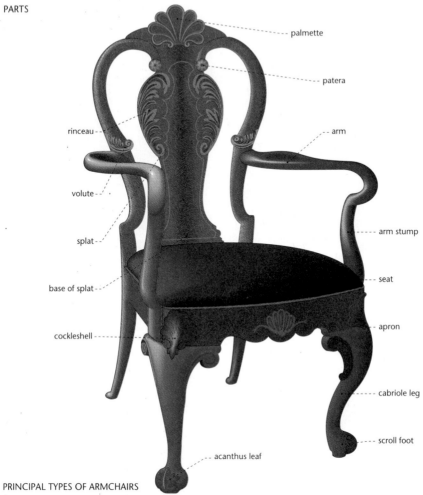

palmette

patera

rinceau

arm

volute

arm stump

splat

seat

base of splat

apron

cockleshell

cabriole leg

scroll foot

acanthus leaf

PRINCIPAL TYPES OF ARMCHAIRS

bergère

cabriolet

director's chair

sofa

love seat

récamier

chesterfield

méridienne

Wassily chair

rocking chair

club chair

221

HOUSE FURNITURE

banquette

ottoman

bean bag chair

bench

bar stool

footstool

step chair

SIDE CHAIR

ear

top rail

cross rail

stile

apron

spindle

rear leg

front leg

back

seat

support

TYPES OF CHAIRS

chaise longue

stacking chairs

rocking chair

folding chair

PARTS

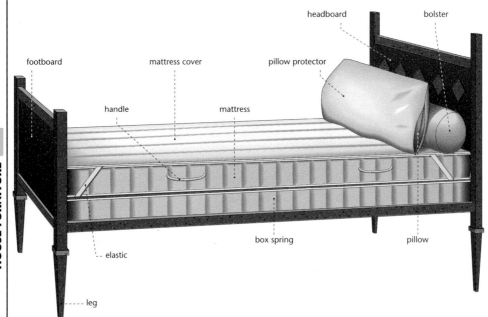

headboard

bolster

footboard

mattress cover

pillow protector

handle

mattress

box spring

pillow

elastic

leg

LINEN

sham

pillowcase

scatter cushion

comforter

neckroll

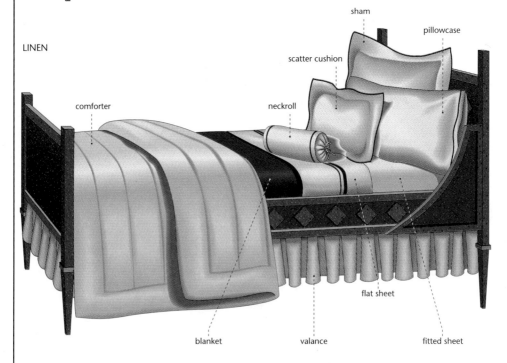

flat sheet

blanket

valance

fitted sheet

224

ARMOIRE

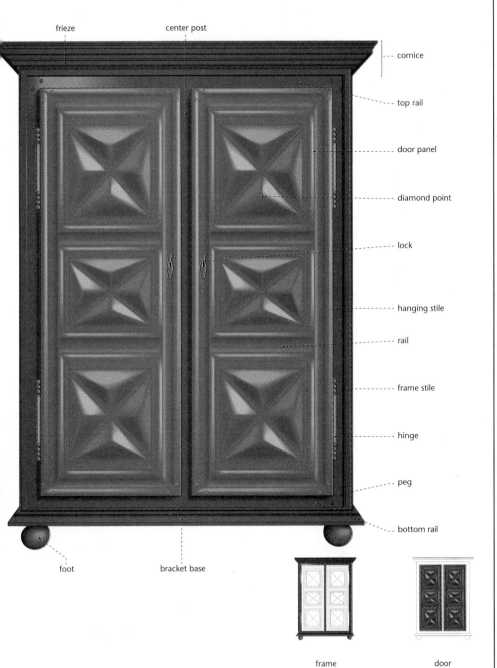

frieze

center post

cornice

top rail

door panel

diamond point

lock

hanging stile

rail

frame stile

hinge

peg

bottom rail

foot

bracket base

frame

door

linen chest

dresser

drawer

chiffonier

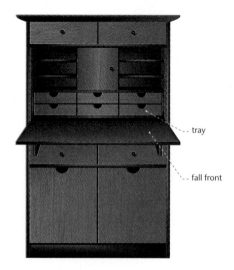

tray

fall front

secretary

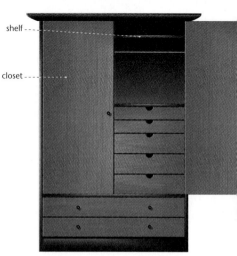

shelf

closet

wardrobe

display cabinet

cocktail cabinet

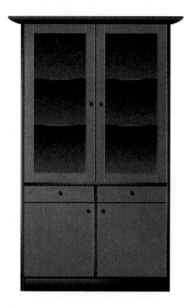

glass-fronted display cabinet

corner cupboard

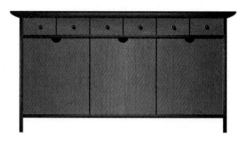

buffet

HOUSE FURNITURE

TYPES OF CURTAINS

GLASS CURTAIN

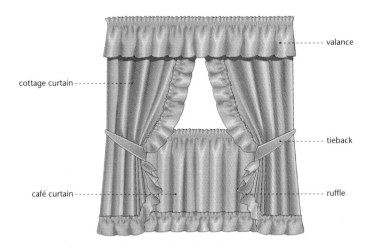

valance

cottage curtain

tieback

café curtain

ruffle

ATTACHED CURTAIN

LOOSE CURTAIN

TYPES OF PLEATS

box pleat

pinch pleat

inverted pleat

CURTAIN

overdrapery

holdback

sheer curtain

cornice

draw drapery

cord tieback

tassel

BALLOON CURTAIN

CRISSCROSS CURTAINS

fringe trimming

panel

TYPES OF HEADINGS

draped swag

pencil pleat heading

pleated heading

shirred heading

HOUSE FURNITURE

CURTAIN POLE

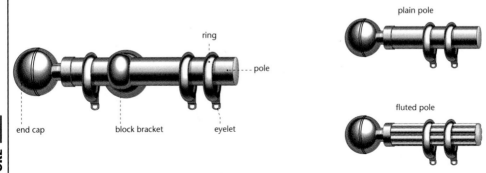

plain pole

ring

pole

end cap

block bracket

eyelet

fluted pole

single curtain rod

double curtain rod

CURTAIN TRACK

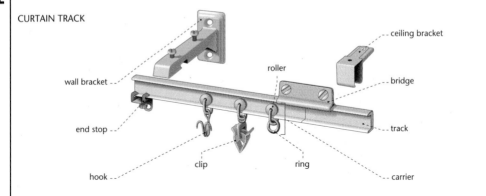

ceiling bracket

roller

wall bracket

bridge

end stop

track

hook

clip

ring

carrier

TRAVERSE ROD

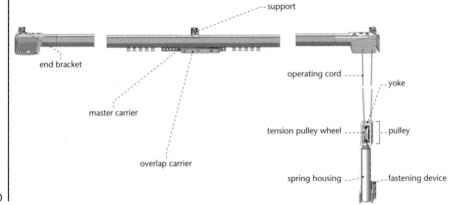

support

end bracket

operating cord

yoke

master carrier

tension pulley wheel

pulley

overlap carrier

spring housing

fastening device

ROLLER SHADE

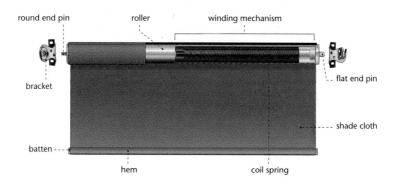

round end pin
roller
winding mechanism
bracket
flat end pin
shade cloth
batten
hem
coil spring

VENETIAN BLIND

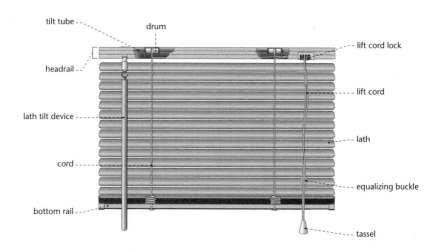

tilt tube
drum
lift cord lock
headrail
lift cord
lath tilt device
lath
cord
equalizing buckle
bottom rail
tassel

roll-up blind

roman shade

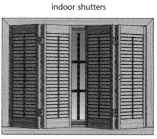

indoor shutters

INCANDESCENT LAMP

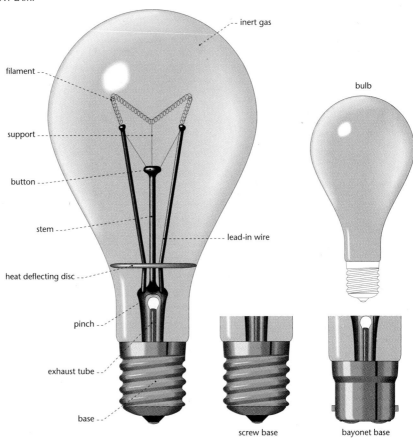

inert gas

filament

support

button

stem

lead-in wire

heat deflecting disc

pinch

exhaust tube

base

bulb

screw base

bayonet base

FLUORESCENT TUBE

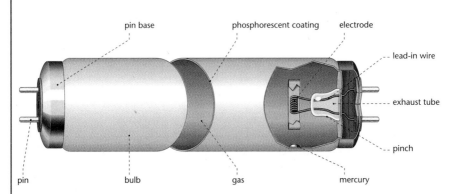

pin base

phosphorescent coating

electrode

lead-in wire

exhaust tube

pinch

pin

bulb

gas

mercury

TUNGSTEN-HALOGEN LAMP

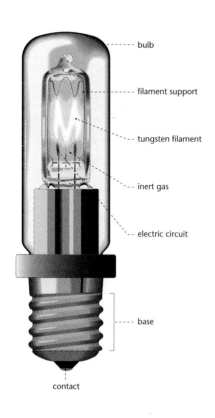

bulb

filament support

tungsten filament

inert gas

electric circuit

base

contact

ENERGY SAVING BULB

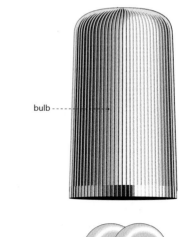

bulb

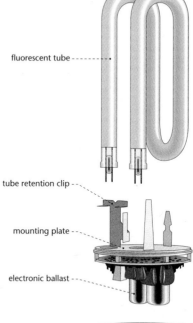

fluorescent tube

tube retention clip

mounting plate

electronic ballast

TUNGSTEN-HALOGEN LAMP

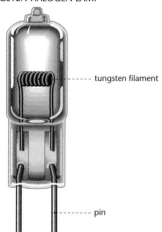

tungsten filament

pin

housing

base

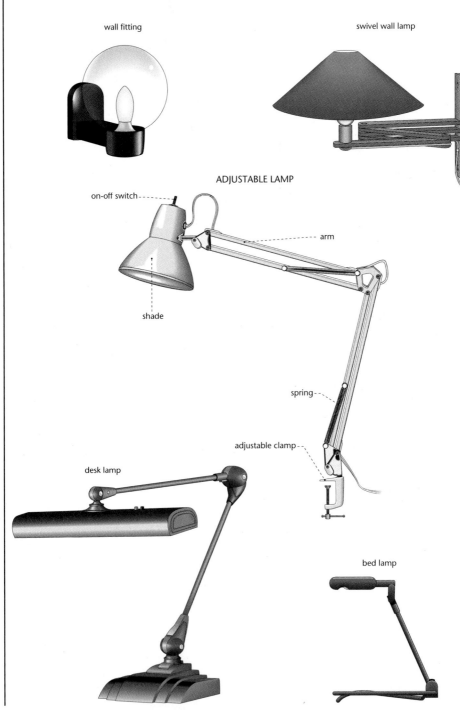

wall fitting

swivel wall lamp

ADJUSTABLE LAMP

on-off switch

arm

shade

spring

adjustable clamp

desk lamp

bed lamp

TRACK LIGHTING

bar frame

transformer

contact lever

spot

post lantern

clamp spotlight

wall lantern

strip light

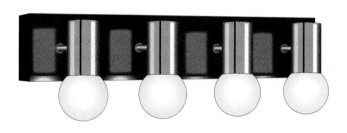

HOUSE FURNITURE

CHANDELIER

bobeche

crystal drop

crystal button

column

floor lamp

hanging pendant

ceiling fitting

table lamp

shade

stand

base

port glass

sparkling wine glass

brandy snifter

liqueur glass

white wine glass

bordeaux glass

burgundy glass

Alsace glass

old-fashioned glass

highball glass

cocktail glass

water goblet

decanter

small decanter

champagne flute

beer mug

237

demitasse

cup

coffee mug

creamer

sugar bowl

pepper shaker

salt shaker

gravy boat

butter dish

ramekin

soup bowl

rim soup bowl

dinner plate

salad plate

bread and butter plate

teapot

platter

vegetable bowl

fish platter

hors d'oeuvre dish

water pitcher

salad bowl

salad dish

soup tureen

SILVERWARE

KNIFE

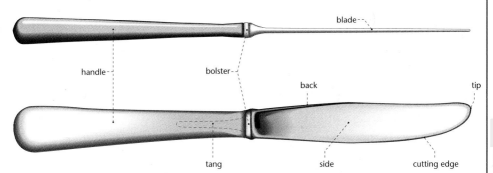

blade

handle

bolster

back

tip

tang

side

cutting edge

PRINCIPAL TYPES OF KNIVES

butter knife

dessert knife

fish knife

cheese knife

dinner knife

steak knife

FORK

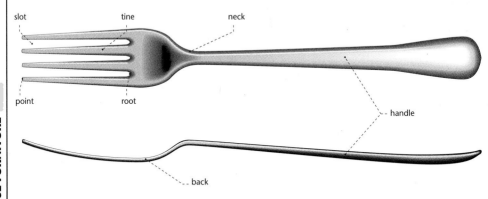

slot   tine   neck

point   root

handle

back

PRINCIPAL TYPES OF FORKS

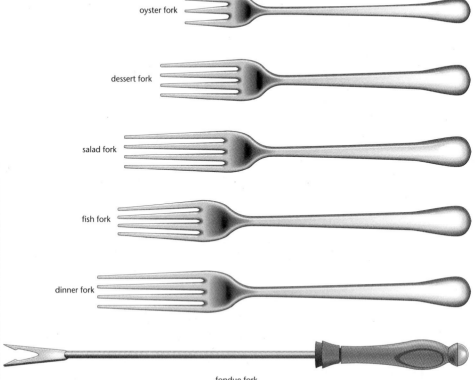

oyster fork

dessert fork

salad fork

fish fork

dinner fork

fondue fork

SPOON

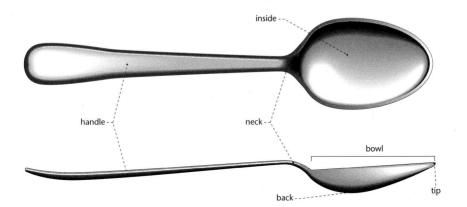

inside

handle

neck

bowl

back

tip

PRINCIPAL TYPES OF SPOONS

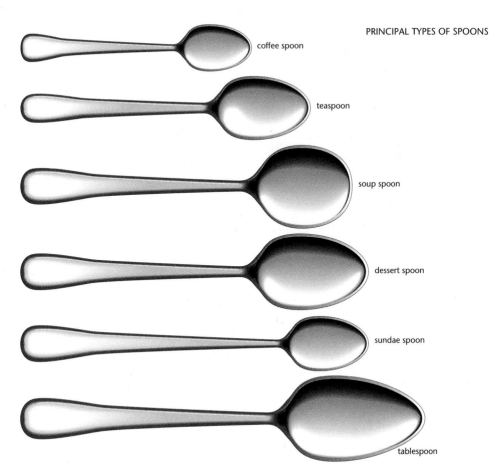

coffee spoon

teaspoon

soup spoon

dessert spoon

sundae spoon

tablespoon

HOUSE FURNITURE

KITCHEN KNIFE

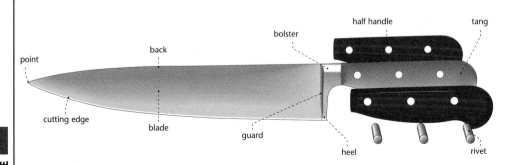

point · cutting edge · back · blade · bolster · guard · heel · half handle · tang · rivet

TYPES OF KITCHEN KNIVES

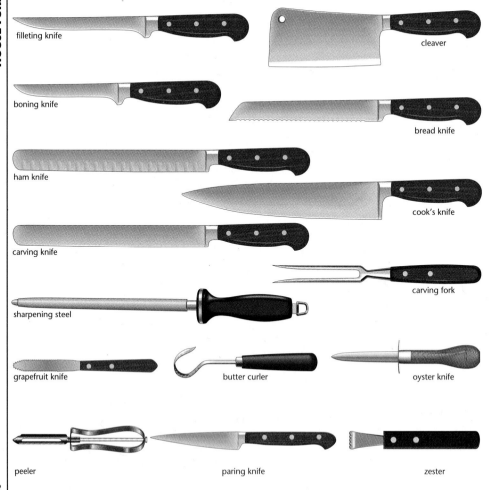

filleting knife · cleaver · boning knife · bread knife · ham knife · cook's knife · carving knife · carving fork · sharpening steel · grapefruit knife · butter curler · oyster knife · peeler · paring knife · zester

FOR STRAINING AND DRAINING

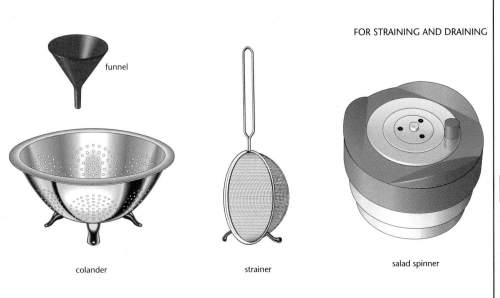

funnel

colander

strainer

salad spinner

FOR GRINDING AND GRATING

pestle

mortar

nutcracker

garlic press

citrus juicer

meat grinder

grater

pasta maker

KITCHEN UTENSILS

SET OF UTENSILS

ladle

potato masher

turner

spatula

draining spoon

skimmer

FOR OPENING

FOR MEASURING

bottle opener

kitchen timer

egg timer

wine waiter corkscrew

meat thermometer

lever corkscrew

measuring spoons

can opener

kitchen scale

measuring cups

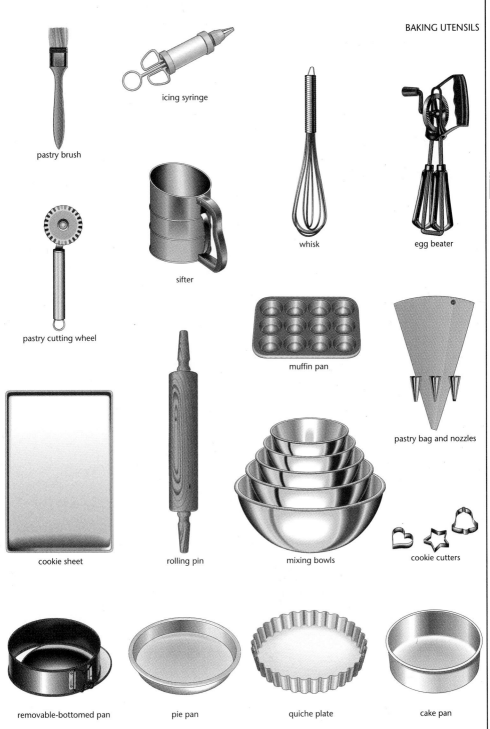

pastry brush

icing syringe

whisk

egg beater

pastry cutting wheel

sifter

muffin pan

pastry bag and nozzles

cookie sheet

rolling pin

mixing bowls

cookie cutters

removable-bottomed pan

pie pan

quiche plate

cake pan

245

MISCELLANEOUS UTENSILS

stoner

ice cream scoop

poultry shears

spaghetti tongs

baster

tongs

vegetable brush

tea ball

snail tongs

dredger

egg slicer

snail dish

COFFEE MAKERS

AUTOMATIC DRIP COFFEE MAKER

lid

reservoir

basket

water level

carafe

signal lamp

warming plate

on-off switch

PERCOLATOR

spout

signal lamp

VACUUM COFFEE MAKER

upper bowl

stem

lower bowl

plunger

Neapolitan coffee maker

espresso coffee maker

WOK SET

lid

rack

wok

burner ring

FISH POACHER

rack

lid

FONDUE SET

fondue pot

stand

burner

roasting pans

PRESSURE COOKER

pressure regulator

safety valve

Dutch oven

stock pot

frying pan

pancake pan

couscous kettle

egg poacher

sauté pan

vegetable steamer

double boiler

saucepan

BLENDER

cap

container

cutting blade

motor unit

push button

HAND MIXER

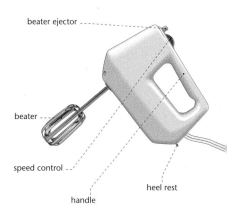

beater ejector

beater

speed control

handle

heel rest

HAND BLENDER

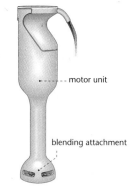

motor unit

blending attachment

TABLE MIXER

beater ejector

beater

tilt-back head

mixing bowl

turntable

speed control

stand

BEATERS

four blade beater

spiral beater

wire beater

dough hook

FOOD PROCESSOR

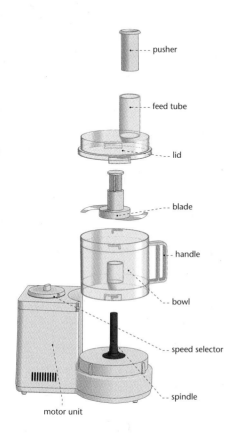

pusher

feed tube

lid

blade

handle

bowl

speed selector

spindle

motor unit

CITRUS JUICER

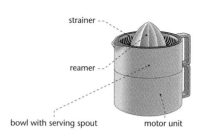

strainer

reamer

bowl with serving spout

motor unit

JUICER

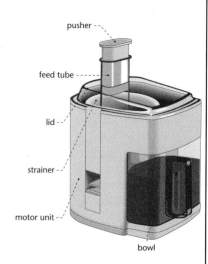

pusher

feed tube

lid

strainer

motor unit

bowl

ICE CREAM FREEZER

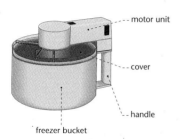

motor unit

cover

handle

freezer bucket

DOMESTIC APPLIANCES

KETTLE

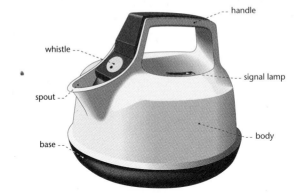

handle

whistle

signal lamp

spout

base

body

TOASTER

slot

bread guide

lever

handle

temperature control

DEEP FRYER

basket

rack

lid

timer

filter

thermostat

signal lamp

WAFFLE IRON

handle

lid

plate

hinge

plate

temperature selector

MICROWAVE OVEN

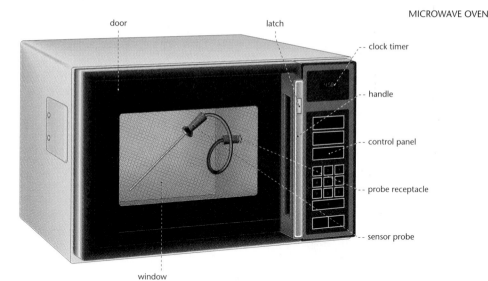

door

latch

clock timer

handle

control panel

probe receptacle

sensor probe

window

GRIDDLE

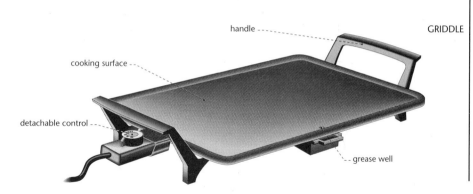

handle

cooking surface

detachable control

grease well

REFRIGERATOR

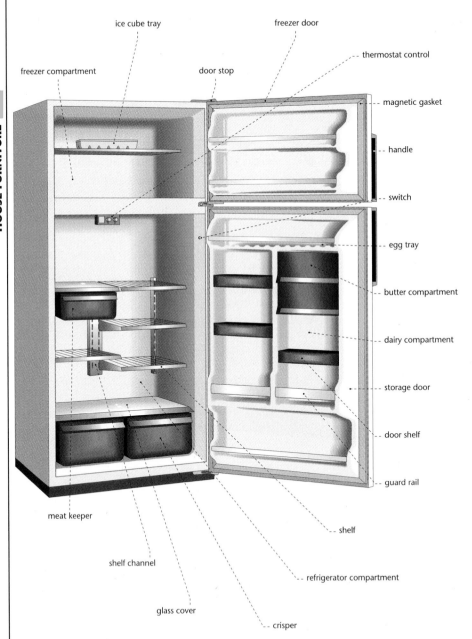

ice cube tray

freezer door

thermostat control

freezer compartment

door stop

magnetic gasket

handle

switch

egg tray

butter compartment

dairy compartment

storage door

door shelf

guard rail

meat keeper

shelf

shelf channel

refrigerator compartment

glass cover

crisper

RANGE HOOD

filter

ELECTRIC RANGE

clock timer

oven control knob

signal lamp

control knob

control panel

surface element

cooktop edge

cooktop

handle

backguard

timed outlet

oven

rack

window

drawer

trim ring

drip bowl

terminal

tubular element

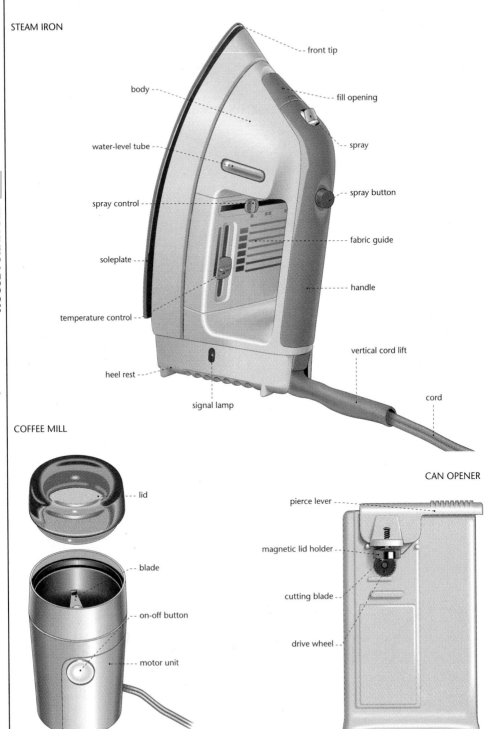

STEAM IRON

front tip

body

fill opening

water-level tube

spray

spray button

spray control

fabric guide

soleplate

handle

temperature control

vertical cord lift

heel rest

cord

signal lamp

COFFEE MILL

lid

CAN OPENER

blade

pierce lever

magnetic lid holder

on-off button

cutting blade

motor unit

drive wheel

DOMESTIC APPLIANCES

CONTROL PANEL

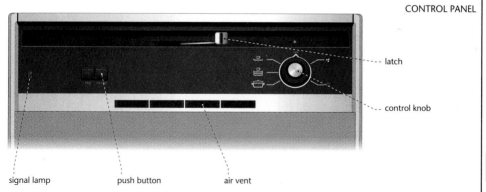

latch

control knob

signal lamp

push button

air vent

DISHWASHER

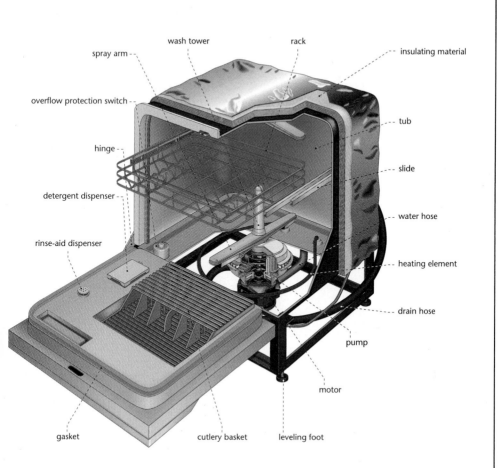

spray arm

wash tower

rack

insulating material

overflow protection switch

hinge

detergent dispenser

rinse-aid dispenser

tub

slide

water hose

heating element

drain hose

pump

motor

gasket

cutlery basket

leveling foot

257

WASHER

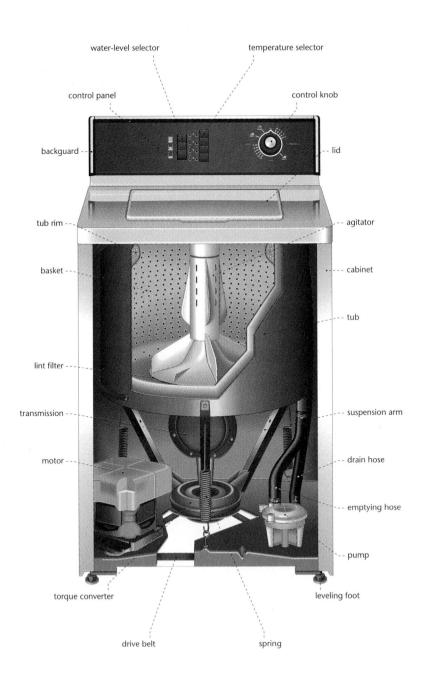

water-level selector

temperature selector

control panel

control knob

backguard

lid

tub rim

agitator

basket

cabinet

tub

lint filter

transmission

suspension arm

motor

drain hose

emptying hose

pump

torque converter

leveling foot

drive belt

spring

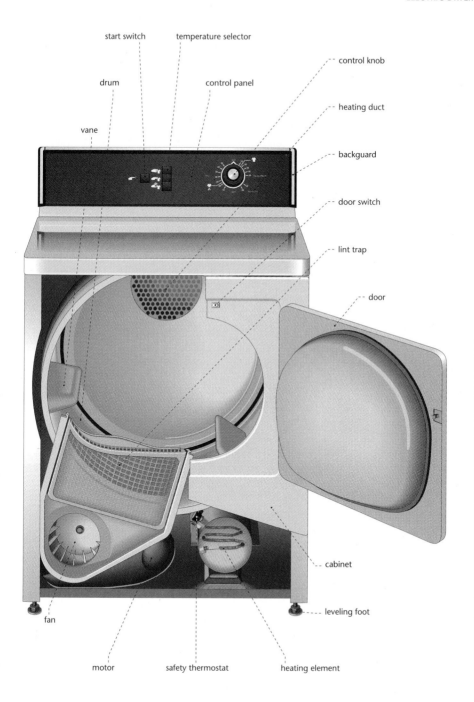

start switch

temperature selector

drum

control panel

vane

control knob

heating duct

backguard

door switch

lint trap

door

cabinet

leveling foot

fan

motor

safety thermostat

heating element

HOUSE FURNITURE

HAND VACUUM CLEANER

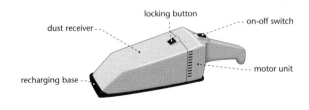

locking button — on-off switch

dust receiver

recharging base — motor unit

CANISTER VACUUM CLEANER

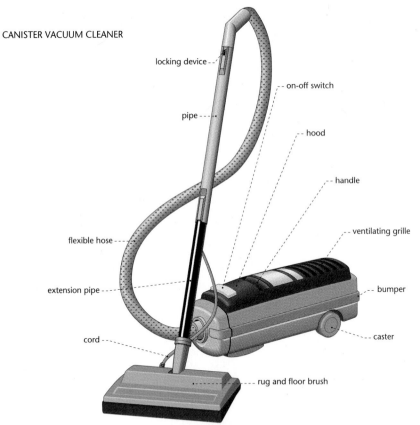

locking device

on-off switch

pipe — hood

handle

flexible hose — ventilating grille

extension pipe — bumper

cord — caster

rug and floor brush

CLEANING TOOLS

upholstery nozzle — crevice tool — floor brush — dusting brush

GARDENING

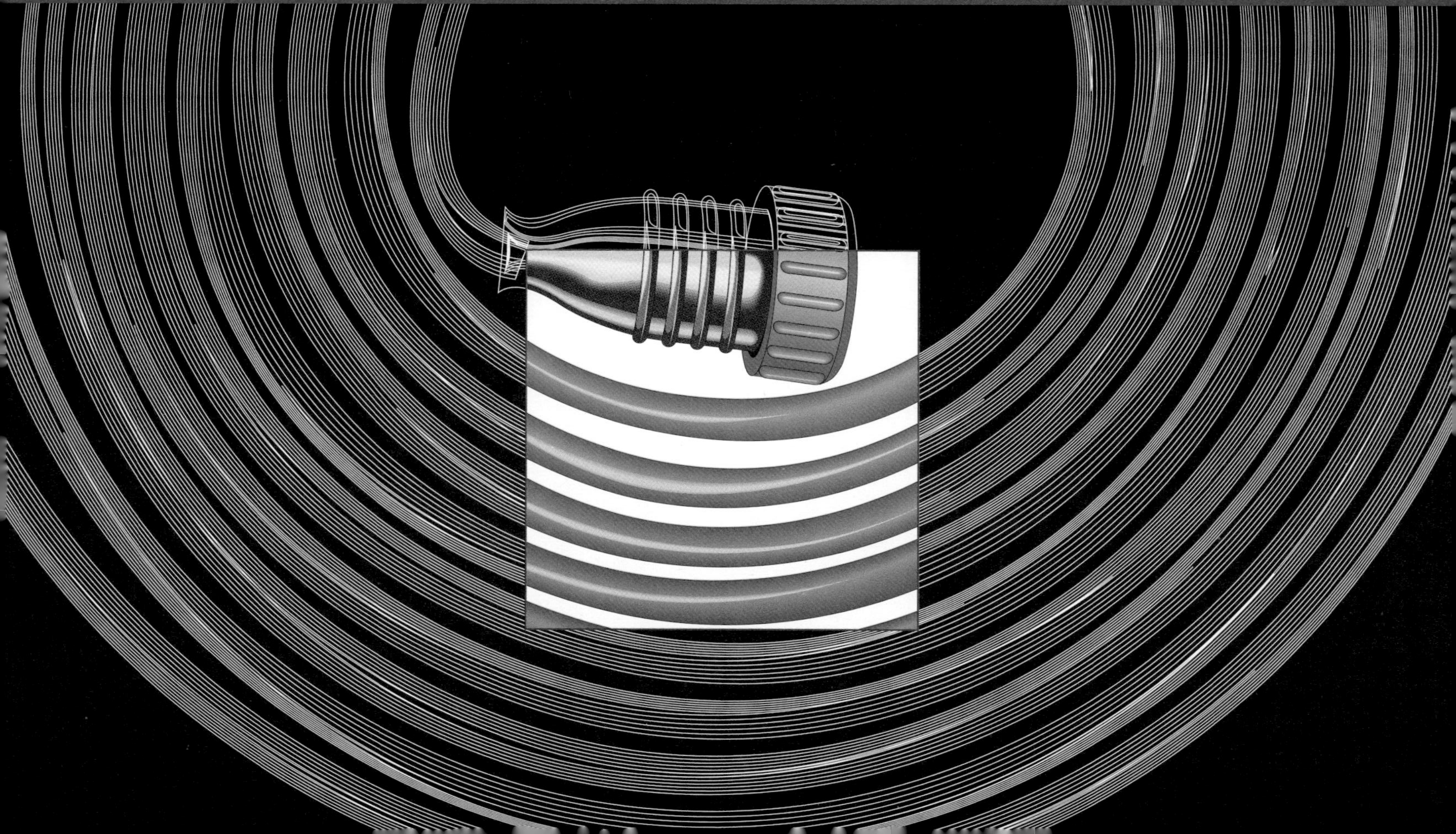

CONTENTS

GARDENING

PLEASURE GARDEN

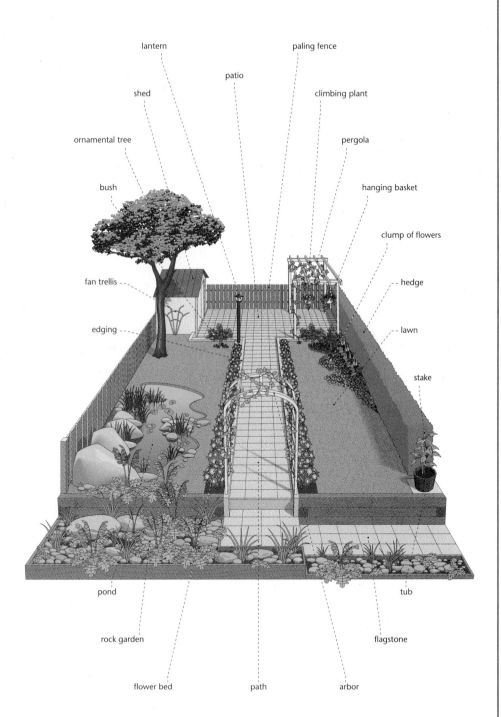

lantern

paling fence

patio

shed

climbing plant

ornamental tree

pergola

bush

hanging basket

clump of flowers

fan trellis

hedge

edging

lawn

stake

pond

tub

rock garden

flagstone

flower bed

path

arbor

pistol nozzle

sprayer

spray nozzle

arm

oscillating sprinkler

REVOLVING SPRINKLER

IMPULSE SPRINKLER

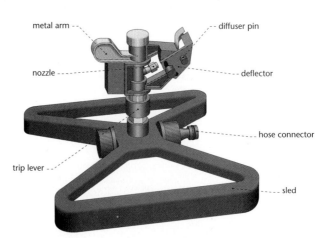

metal arm

diffuser pin

nozzle

deflector

hose connector

trip lever

sled

HOSE TROLLEY

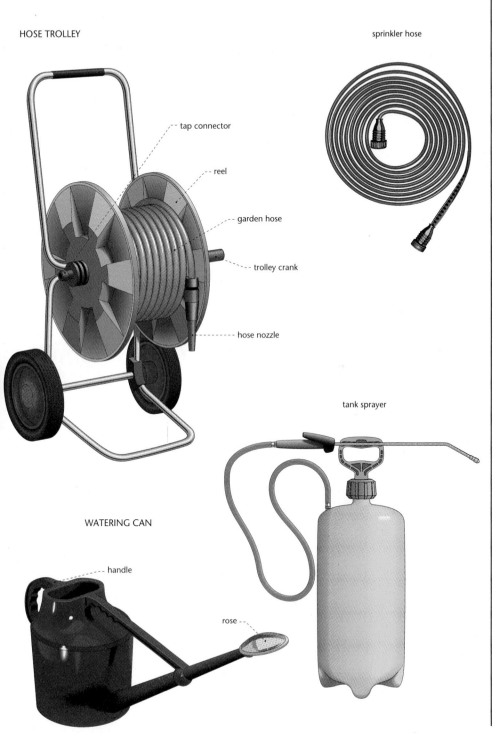

sprinkler hose

tap connector

reel

garden hose

trolley crank

hose nozzle

tank sprayer

WATERING CAN

handle

rose

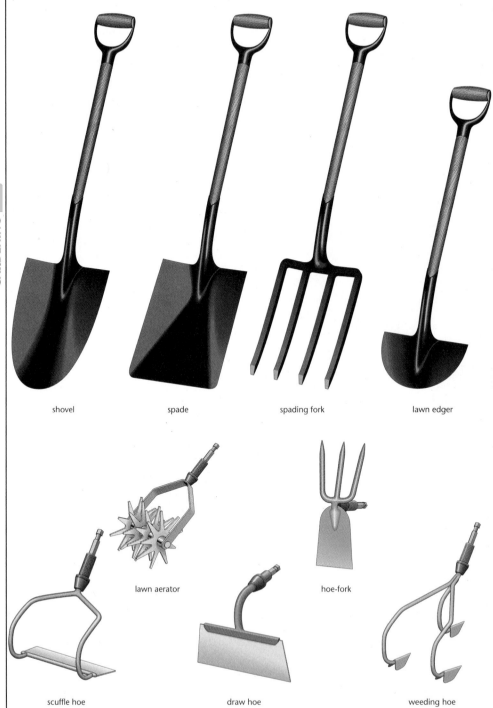

shovel

spade

spading fork

lawn edger

lawn aerator

hoe-fork

scuffle hoe

draw hoe

weeding hoe

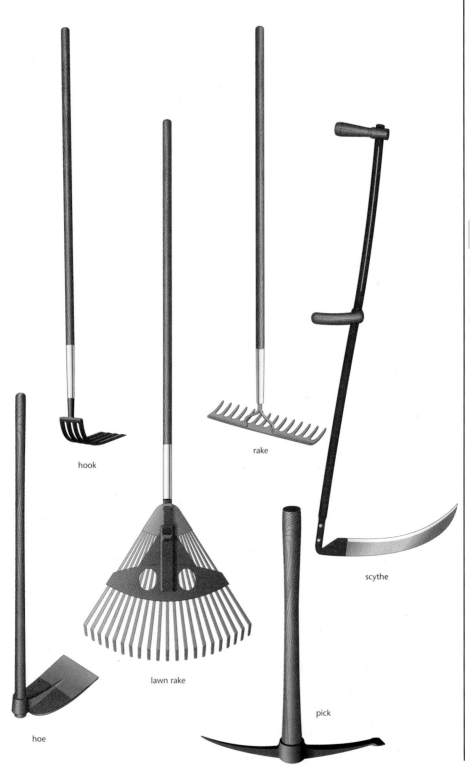

hook

rake

hoe

lawn rake

pick

scythe

TOOLS AND EQUIPMENT

hand fork

weeder

trowel

small hand cultivator

seeder

garden line

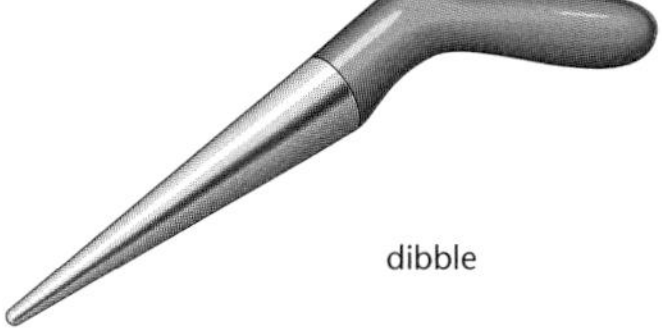

dibble

bulb dibble

HEDGE TRIMMER

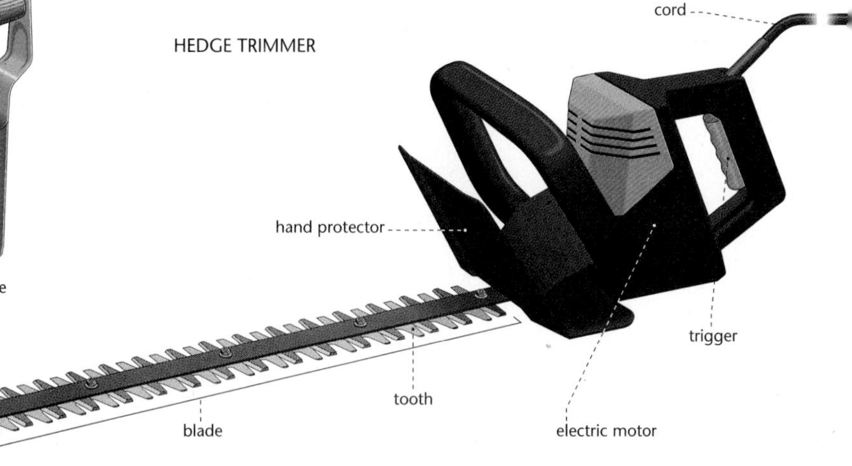

cord

hand protector

tooth

blade

electric motor

trigger

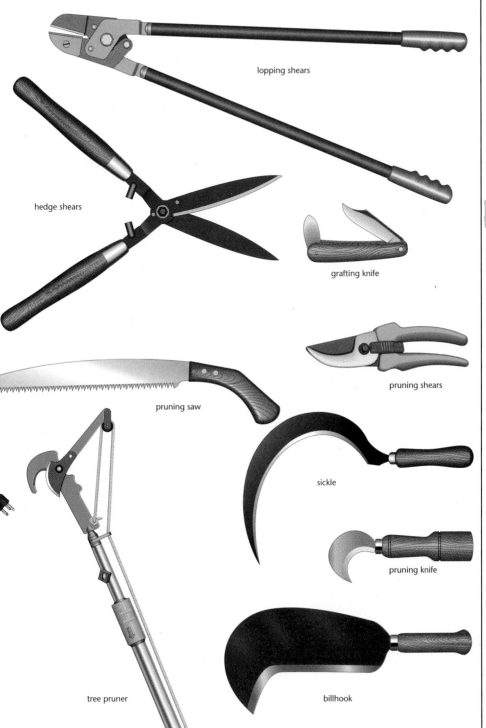

lopping shears

hedge shears

grafting knife

pruning shears

pruning saw

sickle

pruning knife

tree pruner

billhook

spreader

MOTORIZED EARTH AUGER

handle

control cable

starting cable

auger bit

motor

WHEELBARROW

tray

roller

handle

leg

wheel

HAND MOWER

blade

cutting cylinder

EDGER

cord

electric motor

security casing

nylon yarn

POWER MOWER

handle

safety handle

speed control

ignition key

grassbox

starter

filler cap

deflector

motor

accelerator cable

spark plug

casing

CHAINSAW

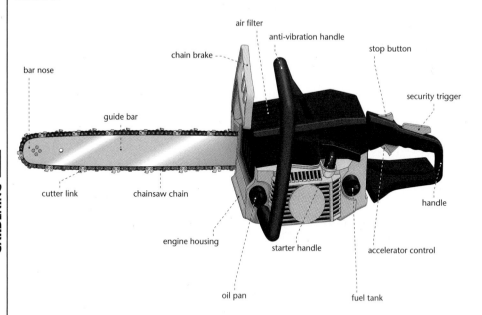

air filter

anti-vibration handle

stop button

chain brake

bar nose

security trigger

guide bar

handle

cutter link

chainsaw chain

engine housing

starter handle

accelerator control

oil pan

fuel tank

TILLER

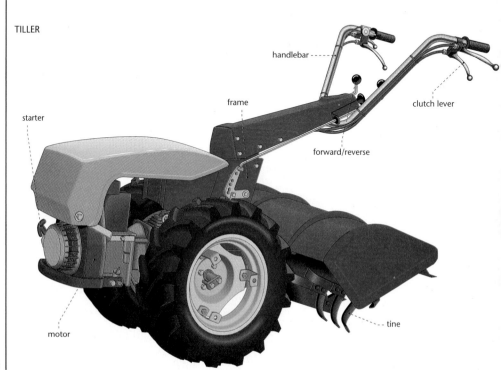

handlebar

frame

clutch lever

starter

forward/reverse

motor

tine

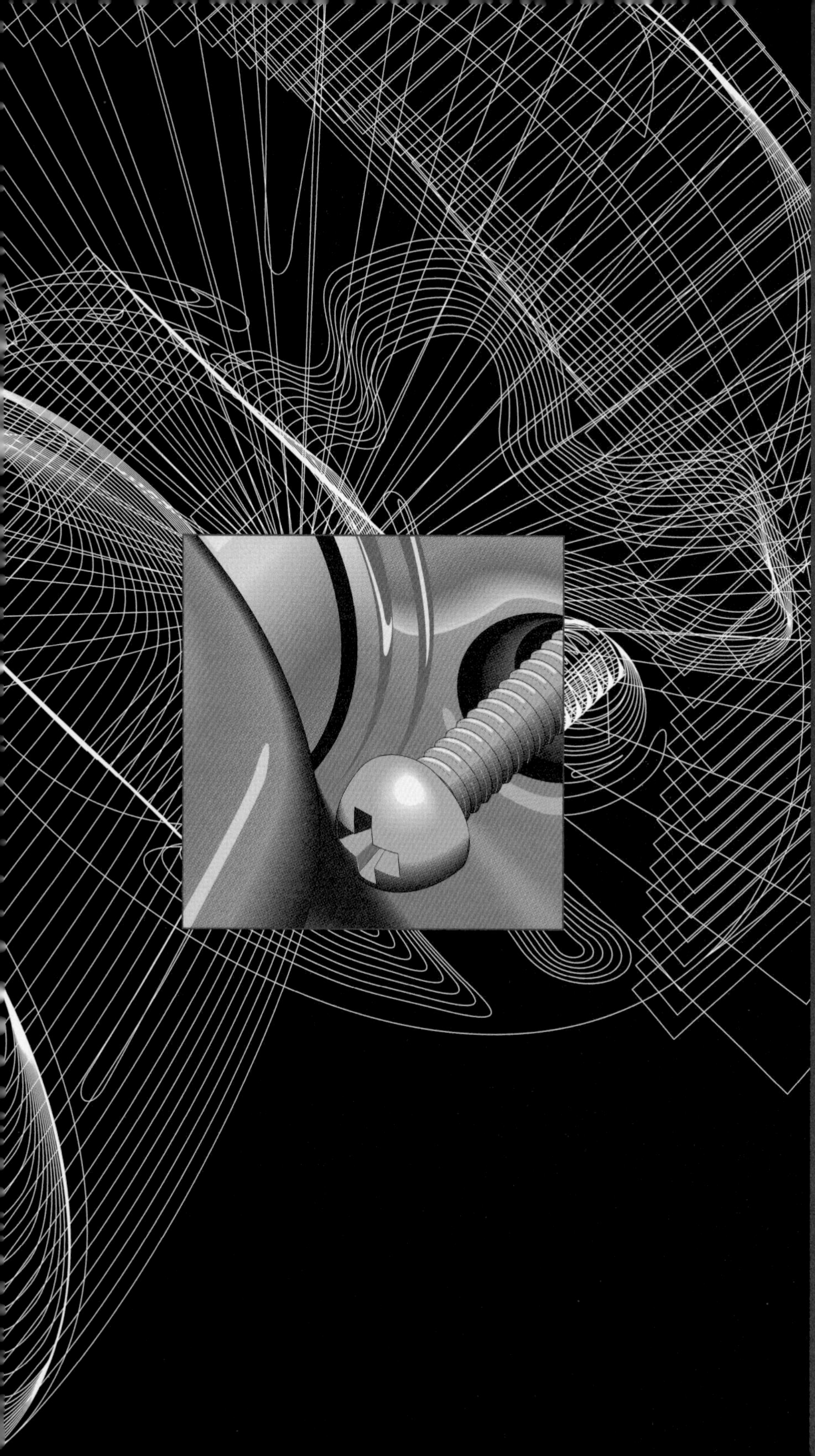

DO-IT-YOURSELF

CONTENTS

CLAW HAMMER

claw

cheek

handle

eye

face

wood chisel

carpenter's hammer

MALLET

head

BALL-PEEN HAMMER

ball peen

NAIL

head

shank

framing square

tip

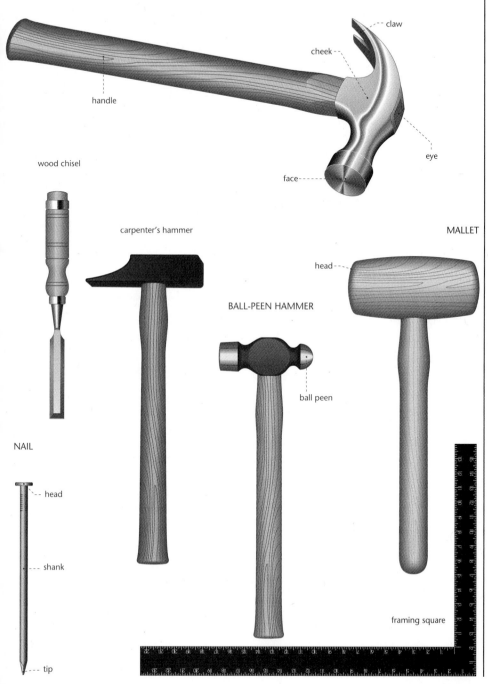

CARPENTRY: TOOLS

DO-IT-YOURSELF

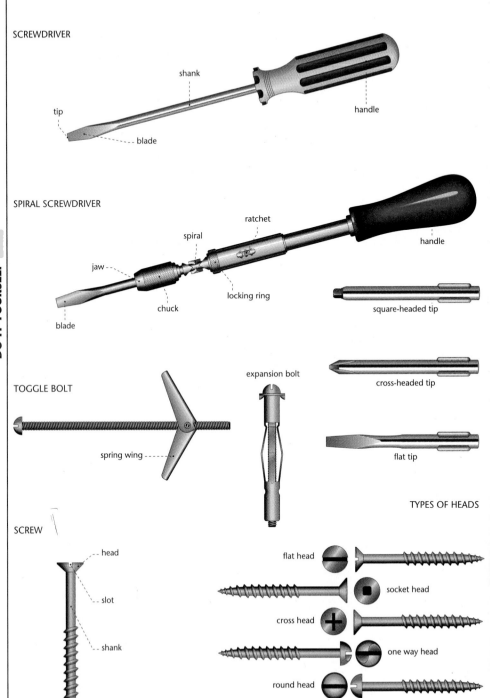

SCREWDRIVER

shank

tip

handle

blade

SPIRAL SCREWDRIVER

ratchet

spiral

handle

jaw

chuck

locking ring

blade

square-headed tip

cross-headed tip

TOGGLE BOLT

expansion bolt

spring wing

flat tip

TYPES OF HEADS

SCREW

head

slot

shank

thread

flat head

socket head

cross head

one way head

round head

oval head

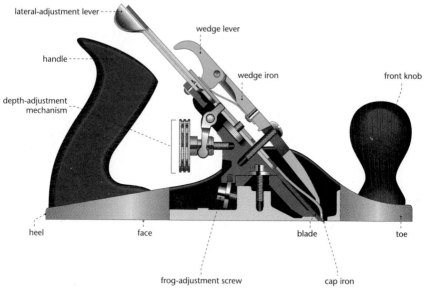

lateral-adjustment lever

wedge lever

handle

wedge iron

front knob

depth-adjustment mechanism

heel

face

blade

toe

frog-adjustment screw

cap iron

HACKSAW

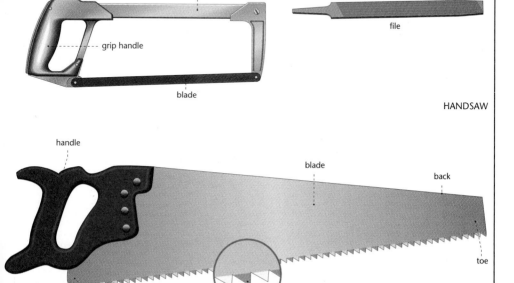

adjustable frame

file

grip handle

blade

HANDSAW

handle

blade

back

toe

heel

tooth

SLIP JOINT PLIERS

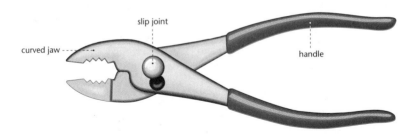

slip joint

curved jaw

handle

RIB JOINT PLIERS

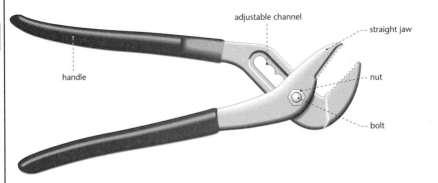

adjustable channel

straight jaw

handle

nut

bolt

LOCKING PLIERS

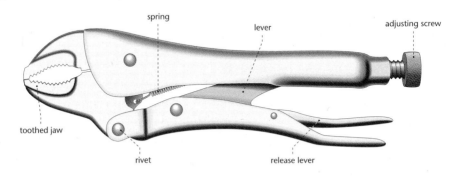

spring

lever

adjusting screw

toothed jaw

rivet

release lever

WASHERS

flat washer

lock washer

internal tooth lock washer

external tooth lock washer

DO-IT-YOURSELF

278

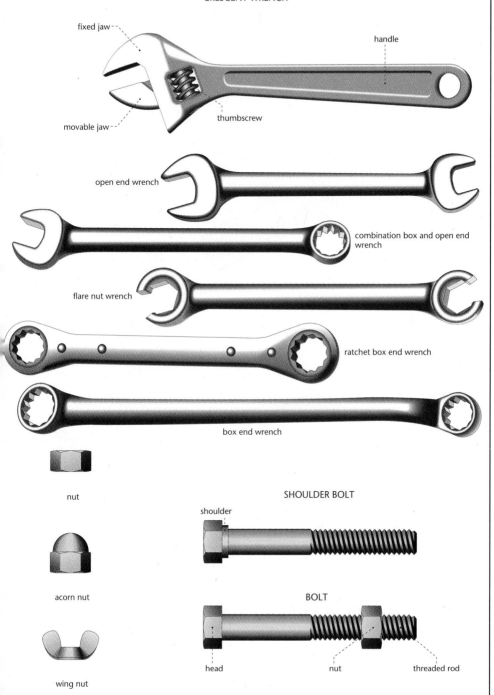

CRESCENT WRENCH

fixed jaw

handle

movable jaw

thumbscrew

open end wrench

combination box and open end wrench

flare nut wrench

ratchet box end wrench

box end wrench

nut

SHOULDER BOLT

shoulder

acorn nut

BOLT

head

nut

threaded rod

wing nut

ELECTRIC DRILL

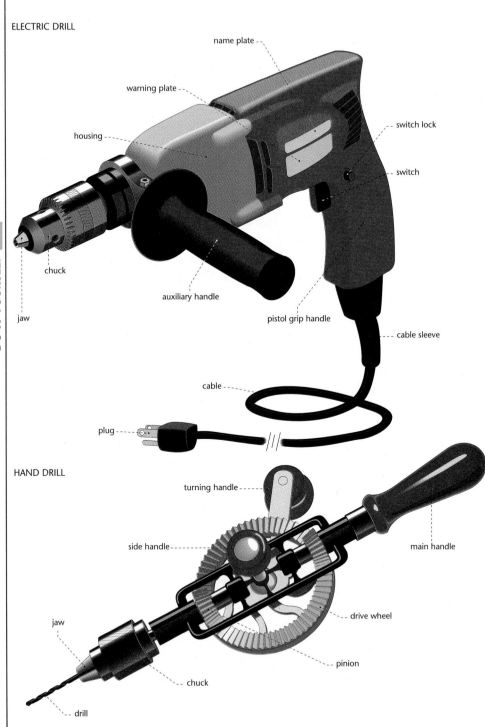

name plate

warning plate

housing

switch lock

switch

chuck

jaw

auxiliary handle

pistol grip handle

cable sleeve

cable

plug

HAND DRILL

turning handle

side handle

main handle

jaw

drive wheel

chuck

pinion

drill

DO-IT-YOURSELF

280

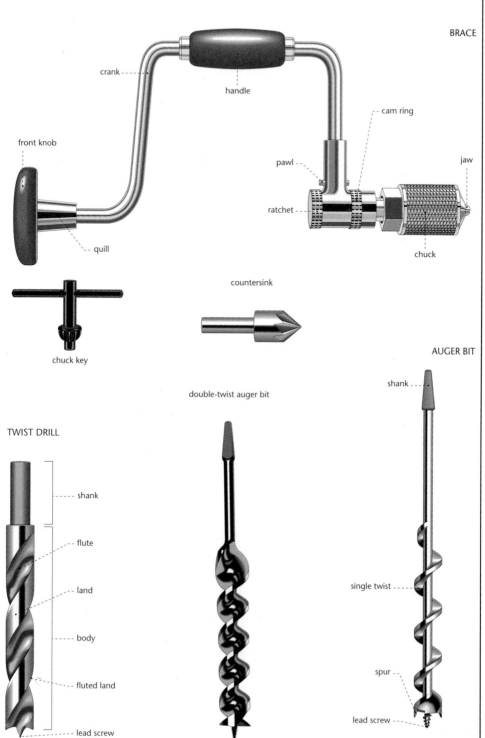

BRACE

crank

handle

cam ring

front knob

pawl

jaw

ratchet

quill

chuck

chuck key

countersink

AUGER BIT

shank

double-twist auger bit

TWIST DRILL

shank

flute

land

body

fluted land

lead screw

single twist

spur

lead screw

DO-IT-YOURSELF

C-CLAMP

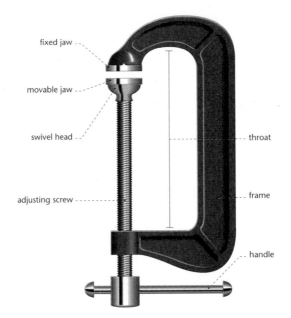

fixed jaw

movable jaw

swivel head

throat

adjusting screw

frame

handle

VISE

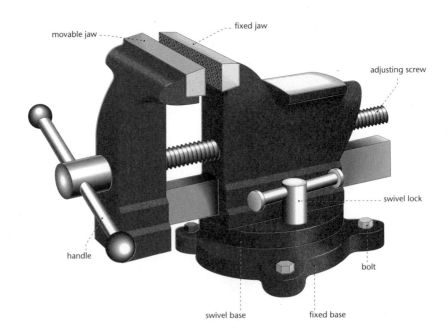

movable jaw

fixed jaw

adjusting screw

handle

swivel lock

bolt

swivel base

fixed base

head
motor
cord sleeve
switch
guide handle
depth adjustment
collet
base
tool holder

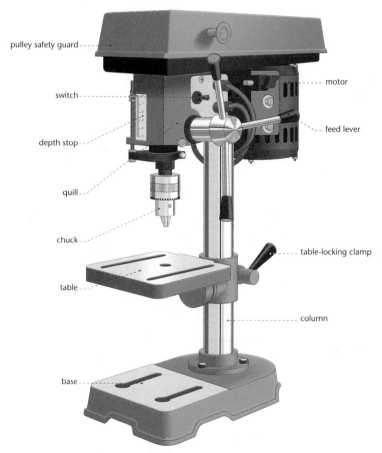

pulley safety guard
motor
switch
depth stop
feed lever
quill
chuck
table-locking clamp
table
column
base

CIRCULAR SAW BLADE

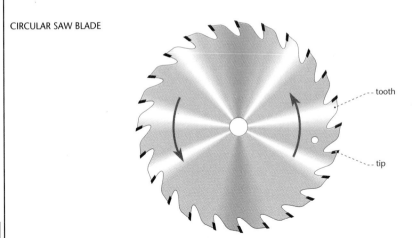

tooth

tip

CIRCULAR SAW

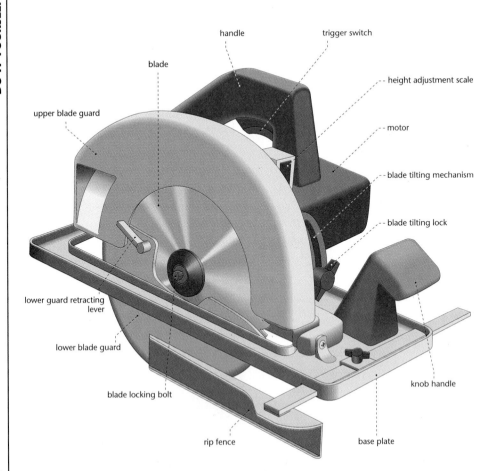

handle

trigger switch

blade

height adjustment scale

upper blade guard

motor

blade tilting mechanism

blade tilting lock

lower guard retracting lever

lower blade guard

blade locking bolt

knob handle

rip fence

base plate

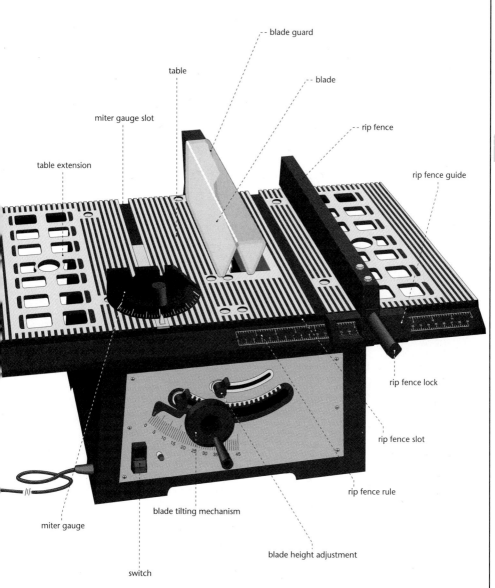

blade guard

table

blade

miter gauge slot

rip fence

table extension

rip fence guide

rip fence lock

rip fence slot

rip fence rule

blade tilting mechanism

miter gauge

blade height adjustment

switch

BASIC BUILDING MATERIALS

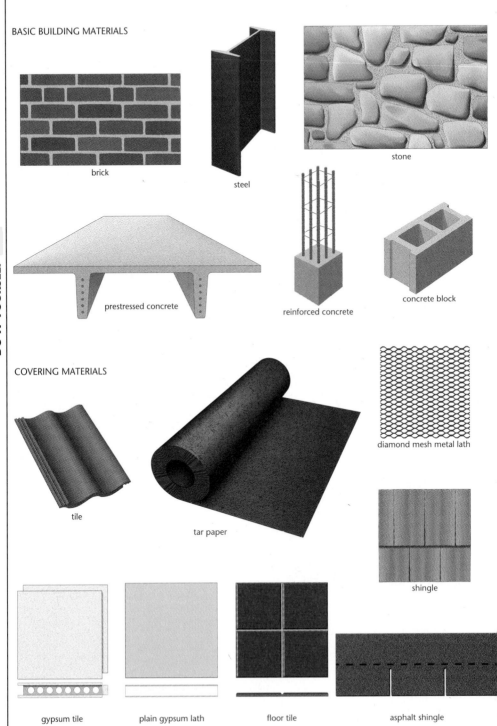

brick

steel

stone

prestressed concrete

reinforced concrete

concrete block

COVERING MATERIALS

tile

tar paper

diamond mesh metal lath

shingle

gypsum tile

plain gypsum lath

floor tile

asphalt shingle

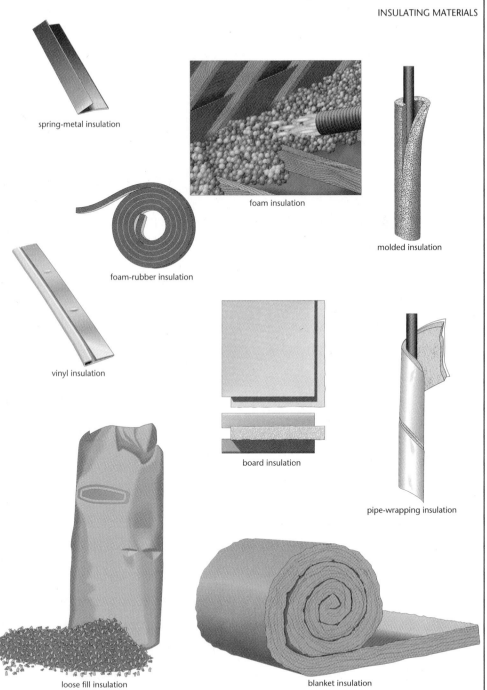

spring-metal insulation

foam insulation

molded insulation

foam-rubber insulation

vinyl insulation

board insulation

pipe-wrapping insulation

loose fill insulation

blanket insulation

WOOD

SECTION OF A LOG

BOARD

WOOD-BASED MATERIALS

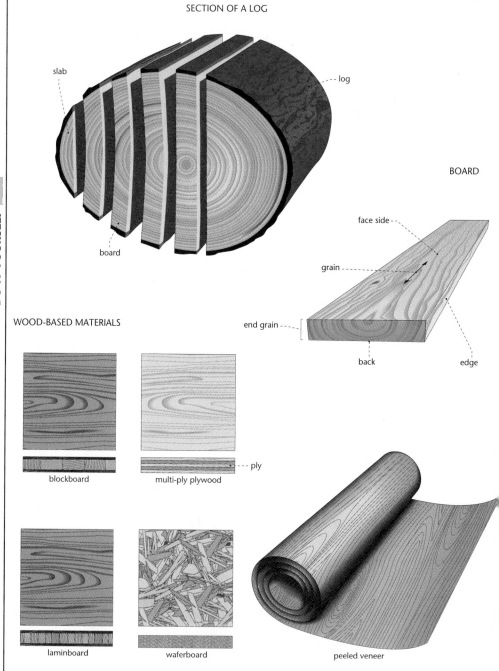

slab

log

board

face side

grain

end grain

back

edge

blockboard

multi-ply plywood

ply

laminboard

waferboard

peeled veneer

hardboard

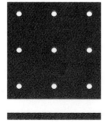

perforated hardboard

plastic-laminated particle board

particle board

LOCK

GENERAL VIEW

lock

dead bolt

escutcheon

faceplate

latch bolt

rose

door handle

MORTISE LOCK

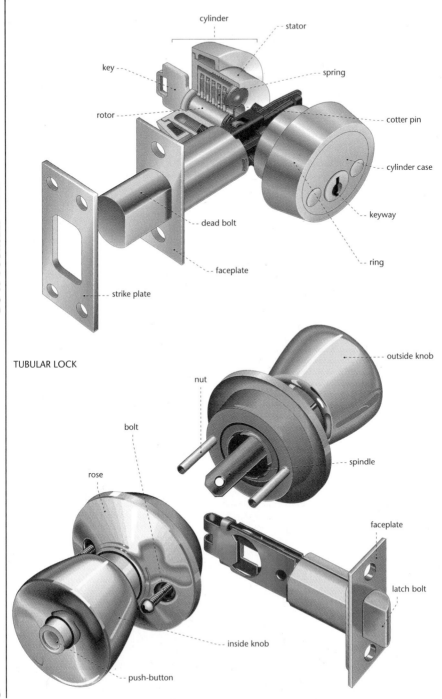

cylinder

stator

key

spring

rotor

cotter pin

cylinder case

keyway

dead bolt

ring

faceplate

strike plate

TUBULAR LOCK

outside knob

nut

bolt

spindle

rose

faceplate

latch bolt

inside knob

push-button

MASONRY

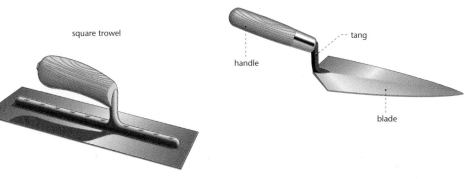

MASON'S TROWEL

square trowel

handle

tang

blade

bricklayer's hammer

hawk

joint filler

spirit level

CAULKING GUN

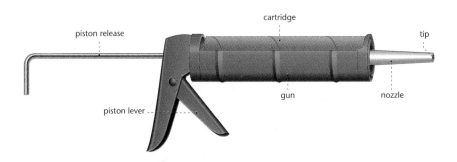

cartridge

piston release

tip

piston lever

gun

nozzle

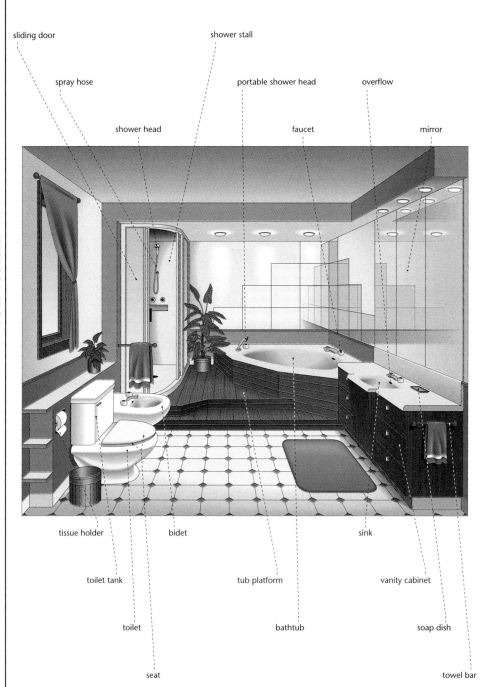

sliding door

shower stall

spray hose

portable shower head

overflow

shower head

faucet

mirror

tissue holder

bidet

sink

toilet tank

tub platform

vanity cabinet

toilet

bathtub

soap dish

seat

towel bar

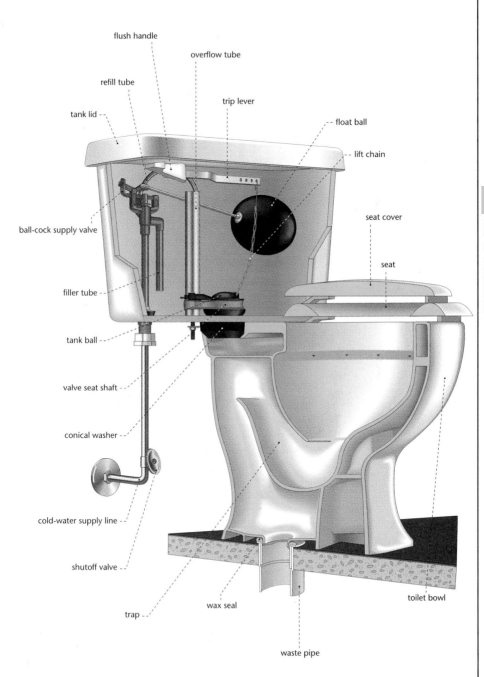

flush handle

overflow tube

refill tube

trip lever

tank lid

float ball

lift chain

ball-cock supply valve

seat cover

seat

filler tube

tank ball

valve seat shaft

conical washer

cold-water supply line

shutoff valve

trap

wax seal

toilet bowl

waste pipe

STEM FAUCET

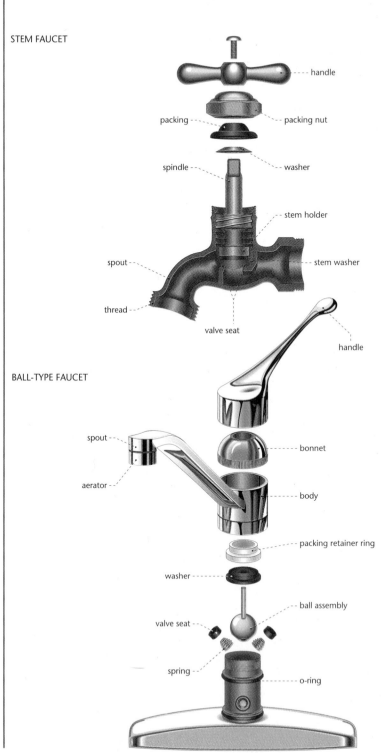

handle

packing · · · · · · · · · · · · · packing nut

washer

spindle · · · ·

stem holder

spout · · · · · · · · · · · · · · · stem washer

thread · · · · ·

valve seat

handle

BALL-TYPE FAUCET

spout · · · ·

bonnet

aerator · · · ·

body

packing retainer ring

washer · · · · · · · ·

ball assembly

valve seat · · · ·

spring

o-ring

handle

bonnet

cylinder

spout

seal

aerator

water inlet

escutcheon

CARTRIDGE FAUCET

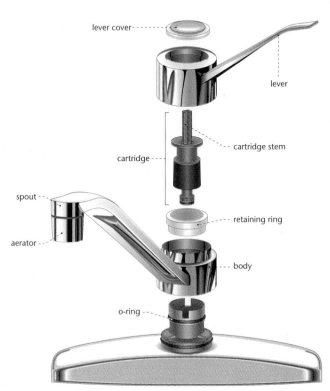

lever cover

lever

cartridge stem

cartridge

spout

retaining ring

aerator

body

o-ring

GARBAGE DISPOSAL SINK

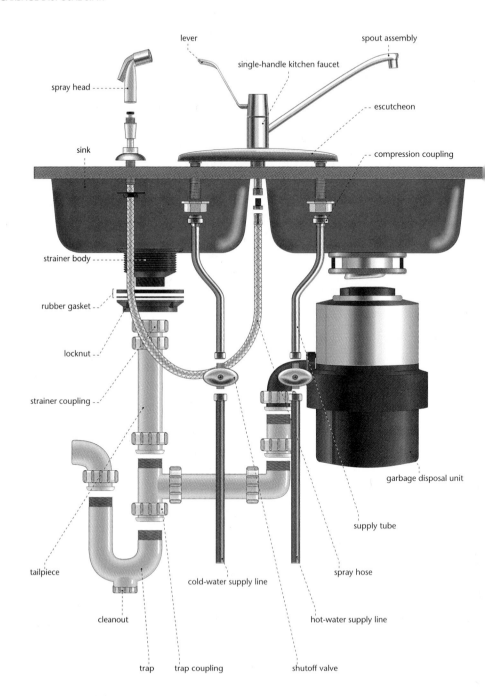

lever

spout assembly

single-handle kitchen faucet

spray head

escutcheon

sink

compression coupling

strainer body

rubber gasket

locknut

strainer coupling

garbage disposal unit

supply tube

tailpiece

spray hose

cold-water supply line

cleanout

hot-water supply line

trap   trap coupling   shutoff valve

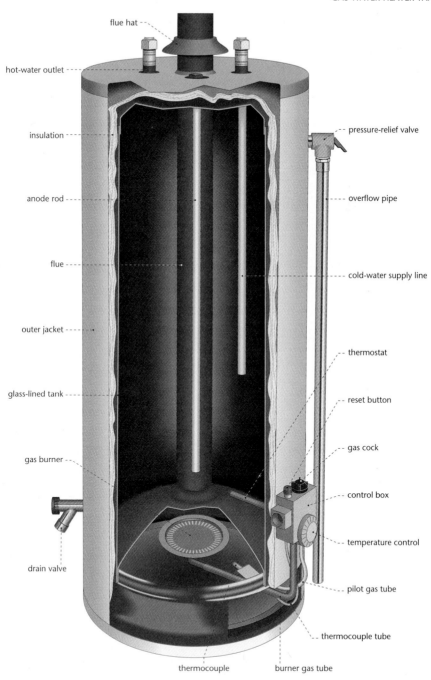

flue hat

hot-water outlet

insulation

anode rod

flue

outer jacket

glass-lined tank

gas burner

drain valve

thermocouple

burner gas tube

pressure-relief valve

overflow pipe

cold-water supply line

thermostat

reset button

gas cock

control box

temperature control

pilot gas tube

thermocouple tube

WASHER

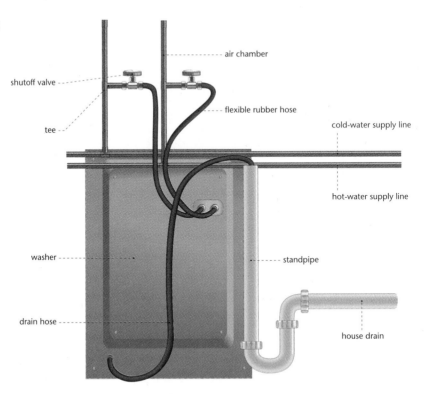

air chamber

shutoff valve

flexible rubber hose

tee

cold-water supply line

hot-water supply line

washer

standpipe

drain hose

house drain

DISHWASHER

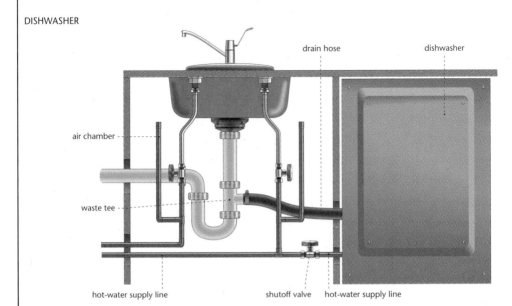

drain hose

dishwasher

air chamber

waste tee

hot-water supply line

shutoff valve

hot-water supply line

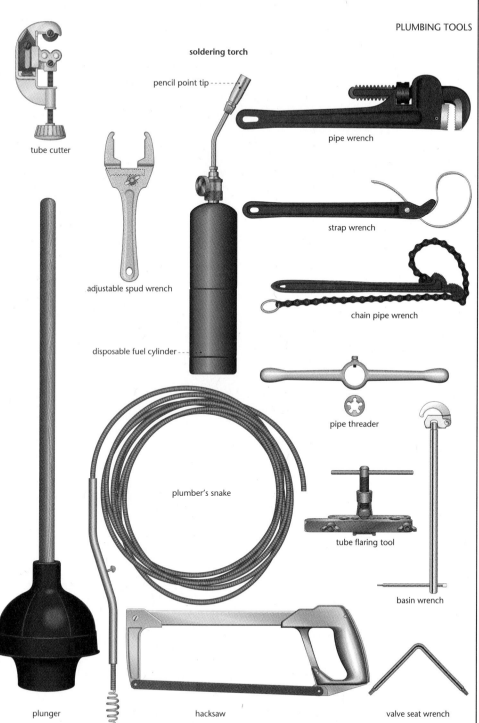

tube cutter

soldering torch

pencil point tip

pipe wrench

adjustable spud wrench

strap wrench

chain pipe wrench

disposable fuel cylinder

pipe threader

plumber's snake

tube flaring tool

basin wrench

plunger

hacksaw

valve seat wrench

MECHANICAL CONNECTORS

compression fitting

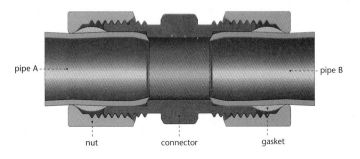

pipe A — — — — — pipe B

nut   connector   gasket

flare joint

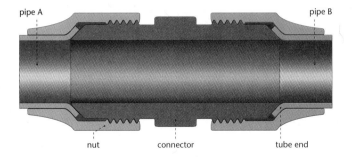

pipe A   pipe B

nut   connector   tube end

union

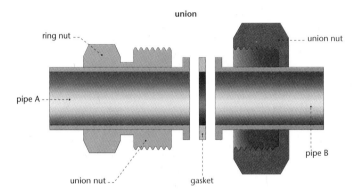

ring nut — — —   — — — union nut

pipe A — — — —

union nut — — —   gasket   pipe B

DO-IT-YOURSELF

steel to plastic

copper to plastic

copper to steel

FITTINGS

45° elbow

elbow

U-bend

tee

Y-branch

offset

trap

square head plug

cap

flush bushing

nipple

reducing coupling

threaded cap

pipe coupling

hexagon bushing

DO-IT-YOURSELF

301

STEPLADDER

EXTENSION LADDER

top

tool shelf

step

rung

side rail

step stool

brace

pulley

locking device

PLATFORM LADDER

safety rail

shelf

platform

frame

hoisting rope

step

rubber tip

anti-slip shoe

DO-IT-YOURSELF

straight ladder

foldaway ladder

hook ladder

rope ladder

multi-purpose ladder

ladder scaffold

fruit-picking ladder

rolling ladder

SPRAY PAINT GUN

spreader adjustment screw

fluid adjustment screw

nozzle

air valve

air cap

gun body

trigger

air hose connection

vent hole

SCRAPER

blade

knurled bolt

container

handle

BRUSH

PAINT ROLLER

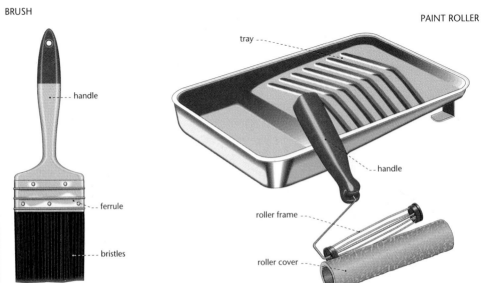

tray

handle

handle

ferrule

roller frame

roller cover

bristles

304

SOLDERING AND WELDING

soldering iron

SOLDERING GUN

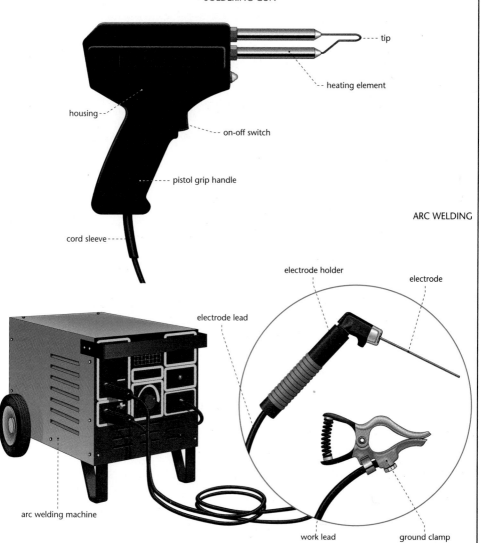

tip

heating element

housing

on-off switch

pistol grip handle

cord sleeve

ARC WELDING

electrode holder

electrode

electrode lead

arc welding machine

work lead

ground clamp

SOLDERING AND WELDING

CUTTING TORCH

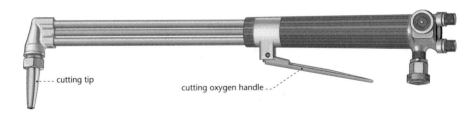

cutting tip

cutting oxygen handle

WELDING TORCH

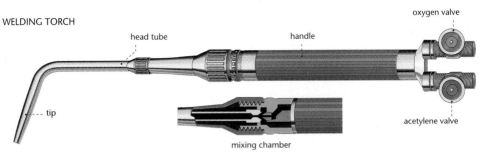

oxygen valve

head tube

handle

tip

acetylene valve

mixing chamber

OXYACETYLENE WELDING

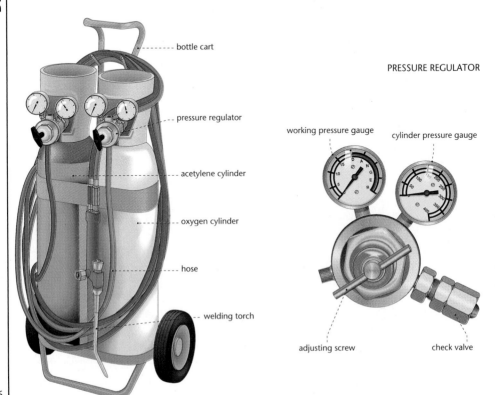

bottle cart

pressure regulator

acetylene cylinder

oxygen cylinder

hose

welding torch

PRESSURE REGULATOR

working pressure gauge

cylinder pressure gauge

adjusting screw

check valve

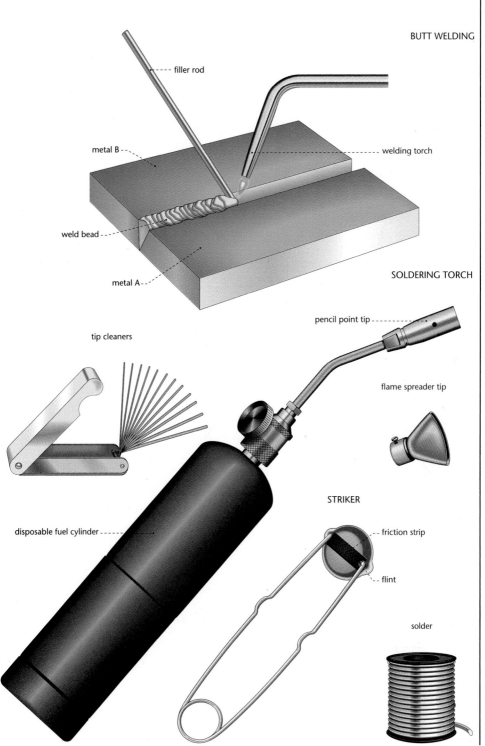

BUTT WELDING

filler rod

metal B

welding torch

weld bead

metal A

SOLDERING TORCH

pencil point tip

tip cleaners

flame spreader tip

STRIKER

disposable fuel cylinder

friction strip

flint

solder

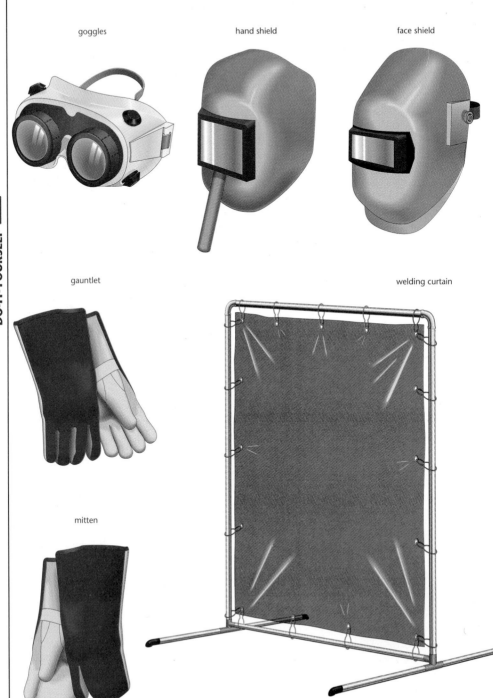

goggles

hand shield

face shield

gauntlet

welding curtain

mitten

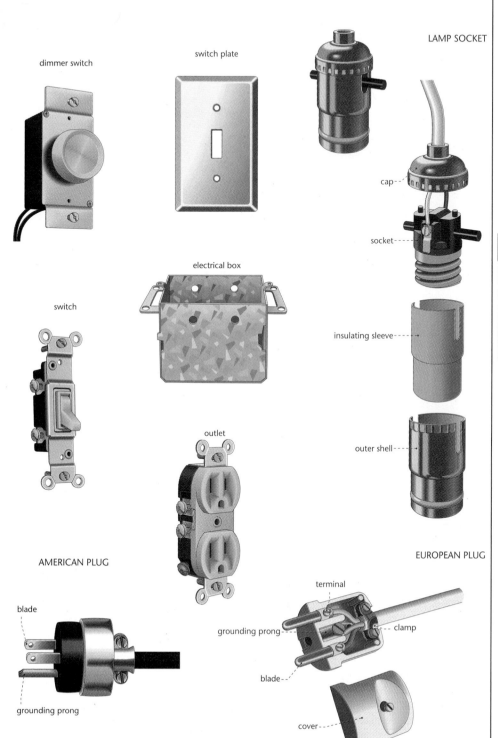

dimmer switch

switch plate

LAMP SOCKET

cap

socket

insulating sleeve

outer shell

electrical box

switch

outlet

AMERICAN PLUG

blade

grounding prong

EUROPEAN PLUG

terminal

grounding prong

clamp

blade

cover

DO-IT-YOURSELF

ELECTRICIAN'S TOOLS

voltage tester

multimeter

housing

probe

digital display

data hold

auto/manual range

selector switch

cord

input terminal

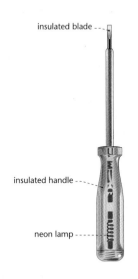

insulated blade

insulated handle

neon lamp

continuity tester

drop light

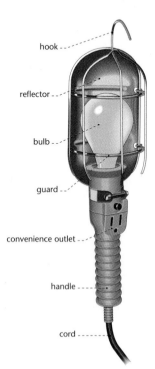

hook

reflector

bulb

guard

convenience outlet

handle

cord

neon tester

receptacle analyzer

high-voltage tester

DO-IT-YOURSELF

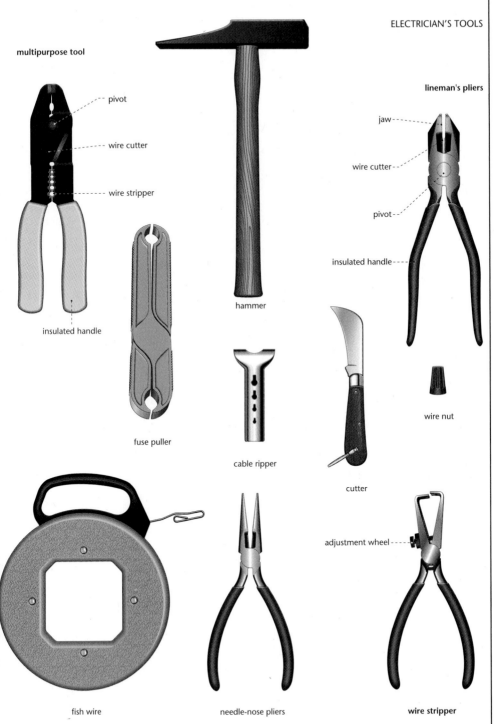

multipurpose tool

pivot

wire cutter

wire stripper

insulated handle

fuse puller

hammer

cable ripper

cutter

lineman's pliers

jaw

wire cutter

pivot

insulated handle

wire nut

fish wire

needle-nose pliers

adjustment wheel

wire stripper

FUSE BOX

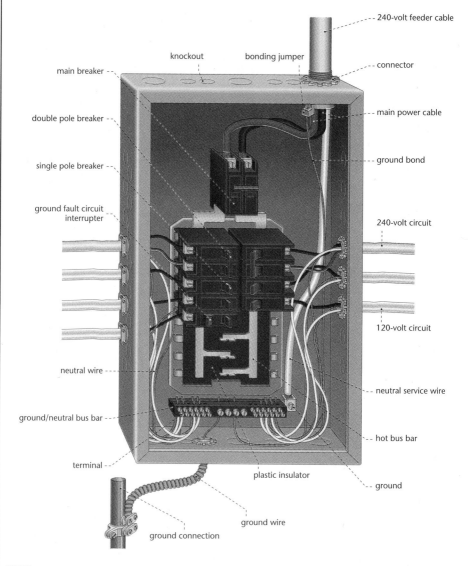

240-volt feeder cable

knockout

bonding jumper

connector

main breaker

main power cable

double pole breaker

ground bond

single pole breaker

ground fault circuit interrupter

240-volt circuit

120-volt circuit

neutral wire

neutral service wire

ground/neutral bus bar

hot bus bar

terminal

ground

plastic insulator

ground wire

ground connection

FUSES

cartridge fuse

plug fuse

knife-blade cartridge fuse

CLOTHING

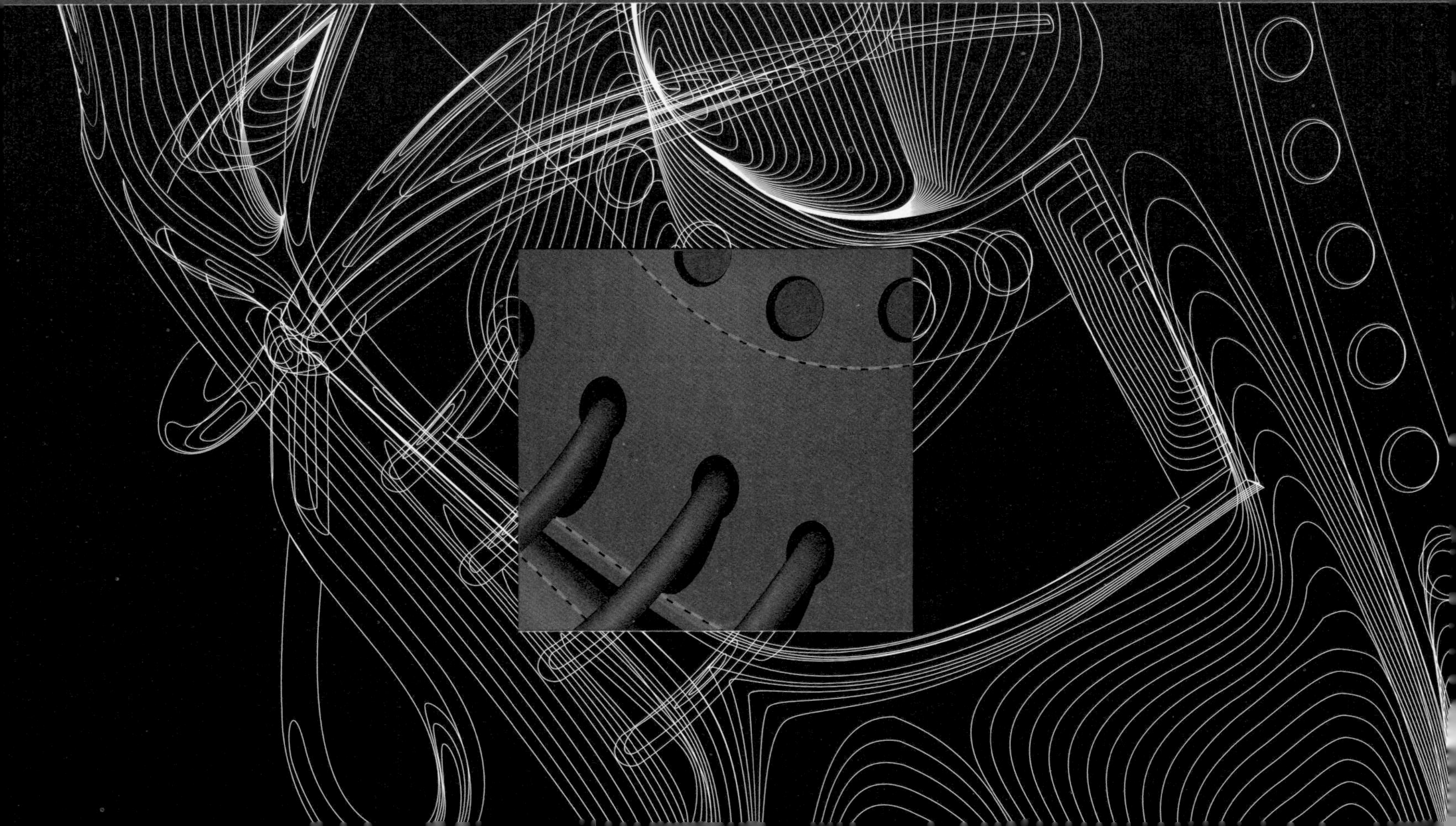

CONTENTS

CLOTHING

ELEMENTS OF ANCIENT COSTUME

PEPLOS

TOGA

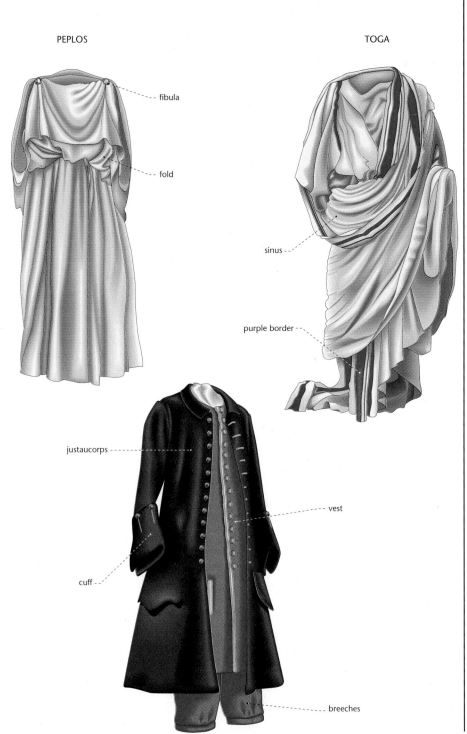

fibula

fold

sinus

purple border

justaucorps

vest

cuff

breeches

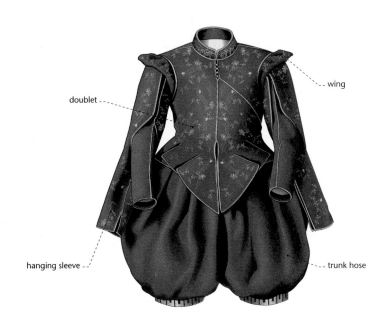

wing

doublet

hanging sleeve

trunk hose

COTEHARDIE

DRESS WITH BUSTLE

caraco jacket

floating sleeve

vertical pocket

bustle

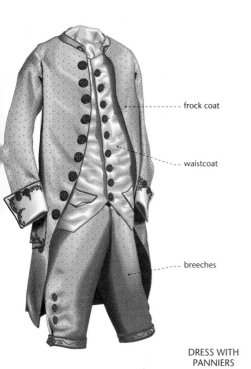

houppelande

frock coat

waistcoat

breeches

DRESS WITH
PANNIERS

ruffle

stomacker

DRESS WITH CRINOLINE

short sleeve

sleeve

fringe

hennin

bicorne

tricorne

fraise

collaret

heeled shoe

crakow

MEN'S CLOTHING

RAINCOAT

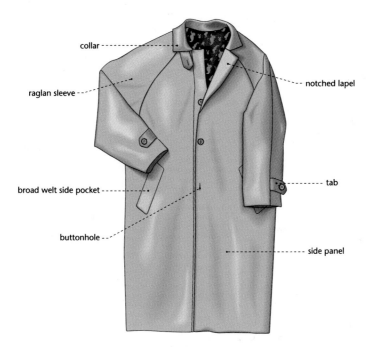

collar

notched lapel

raglan sleeve

broad welt side pocket

tab

buttonhole

side panel

TRENCH COAT

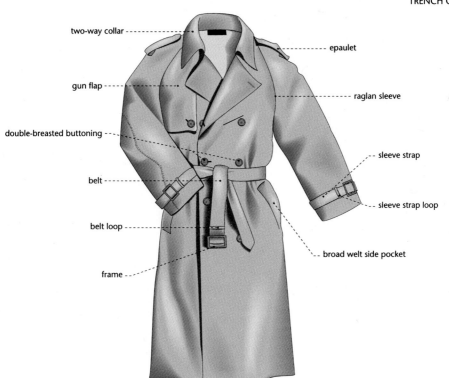

two-way collar

epaulet

gun flap

raglan sleeve

double-breasted buttoning

sleeve strap

belt

sleeve strap loop

belt loop

broad welt side pocket

frame

DUFFLE COAT

hood

yoke

frog

patch pocket

toggle fastening

OVERCOAT

notched lapel

breast pocket

breast dart

WINDBREAKER

flap pocket

waistband

drawstring

CLOTHING

three-quarter coat

PARKA

zipper   snap-fastening tab

JACKET

sheepskin jacket

snap fastener

hand-warmer pocket   elastic waistband

CLOTHING

DOUBLE-BREASTED JACKET

lining
peaked lapel
collar
breast welt pocket
sleeve
flap
outside ticket pocket
patch pocket

side back vent

VEST

V-neck
lining
welt
front
seaming
welt pocket
adjustable waist tab

SINGLE-BREASTED JACKET

notch
lining
pocket handkerchief
lapel
sleeve
front
flap pocket

back
center back vent

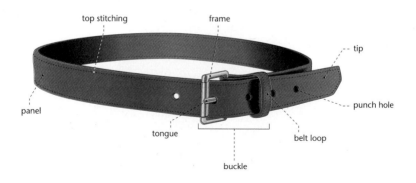

BELT

top stitching

frame

tip

panel

tongue

punch hole

belt loop

buckle

SUSPENDERS

PANTS

elastic webbing

adjustment slide

leather end

button loop

suspender clip

back pocket

waistband

belt loop

front top pocket

waistband extension

fly

knife pleat

crease

cuff

MEN'S CLOTHING

SHIRT

yoke

set-in sleeve

collar

breast pocket

collar point

buttoned placket

front

pointed tab end

button

cuff

shirttail

buttondown collar

ascot tie

spread collar

collar stay

bow tie

NECKTIE

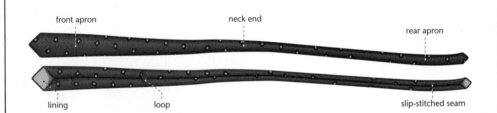

front apron

neck end

rear apron

lining

loop

slip-stitched seam

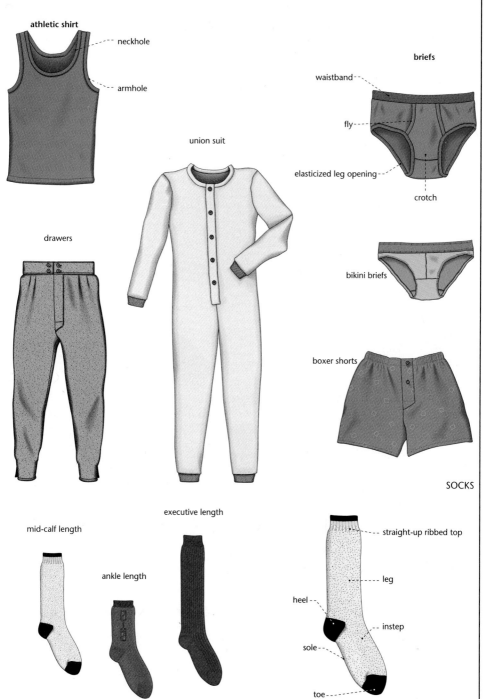

athletic shirt

neckhole

armhole

briefs

waistband

fly

elasticized leg opening

crotch

union suit

drawers

bikini briefs

boxer shorts

executive length

mid-calf length

ankle length

straight-up ribbed top

leg

heel

instep

sole

toe

CLOTHING

CLOTHING

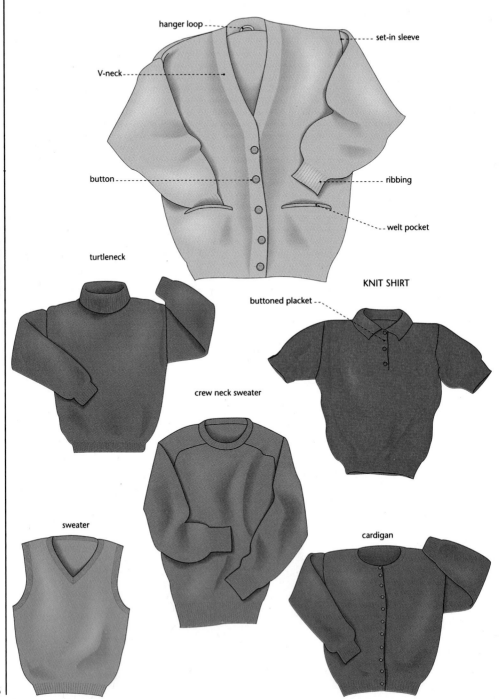

V-NECK CARDIGAN

hanger loop

set-in sleeve

V-neck

button

ribbing

welt pocket

turtleneck

KNIT SHIRT

buttoned placket

crew neck sweater

sweater

cardigan

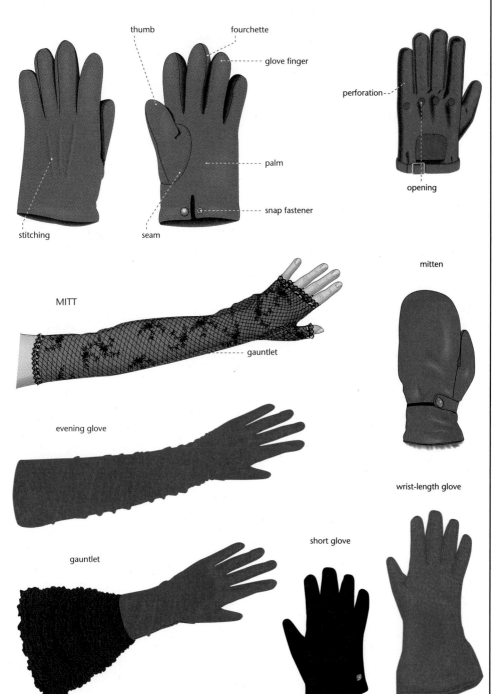

DRIVING GLOVE

thumb

fourchette

glove finger

perforation

palm

snap fastener

opening

stitching

seam

CLOTHING

MITT

mitten

gauntlet

evening glove

wrist-length glove

gauntlet

short glove

FELT HAT

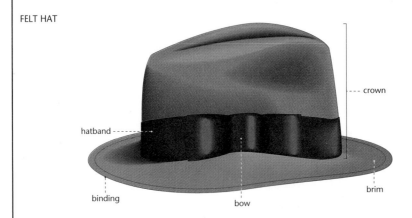

crown

hatband

binding

bow

brim

boater

top hat

derby

HUNTING CAP

ear flap

shapka

CAP

crown

peak

garrison cap

skullcap

panama

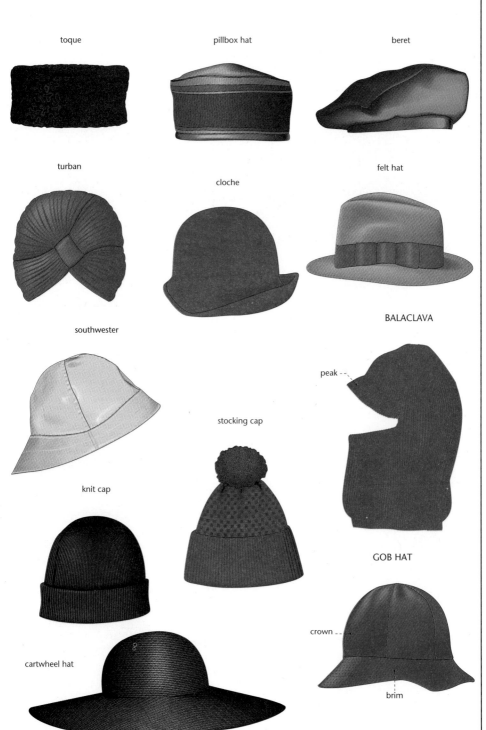

toque

pillbox hat

beret

turban

cloche

felt hat

southwester

BALACLAVA

peak

stocking cap

knit cap

GOB HAT

cartwheel hat

crown

brim

TYPES OF COATS

pea jacket

tailored collar

hand warmer pocket

mock pocket

car coat

raglan

raglan sleeve

fly front closing

broad welt side pocket

back belt

pelerine

pelerine

seam pocket

cape

arm slit

overcoat

top coat

poncho

suit

jacket

skirt

jacket

TYPES OF DRESSES

sheath dress

princess dress

coat dress

drop waist dress

trapeze dress

sundress

polo dress

house dress

shirtwaist dress

jumper

wraparound dress

tunic dress

TYPES OF SKIRTS

CLOTHING

yoke skirt

sheath skirt

gored skirt

ruffled skirt

sarong

wraparound skirt

straight skirt

culottes

kilt

gather skirt

TYPES OF PLEATS

inverted pleat

kick pleat

accordion pleat

knife pleat

top stitched pleat

TYPES OF PANTS

Bermuda shorts

shorts

ski pants

jeans

pedal pushers

knickers

footstrap

jumpsuit

overalls

bell bottoms

classic blouse

middy

polo shirt

smock

yoke

gather

tunic

wrap-over top

mini shirtdress

body shirt

over-blouse

shirttail

crotch piece

JACKETS, VEST AND SWEATERS

safari jacket

blazer

gusset pocket

bolero

spencer

vest

twin-set

turtleneck

V-neck cardigan

inset pocket

seam pocket

broad welt side pocket

hand warmer pouch

gusset pocket

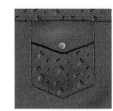

flap pocket

patch pocket

welt pocket

CLOTHING

TYPES OF SLEEVES

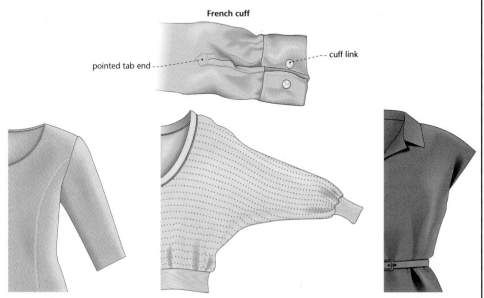

French cuff

pointed tab end ---- ---- cuff link

three-quarter sleeve

batwing sleeve

cap sleeve

TYPES OF SLEEVES

bishop sleeve

leg-of-mutton sleeve

puff sleeve

tailored sleeve

epaulet sleeve

kimono sleeve

shirt sleeve

raglan sleeve

pagoda sleeve

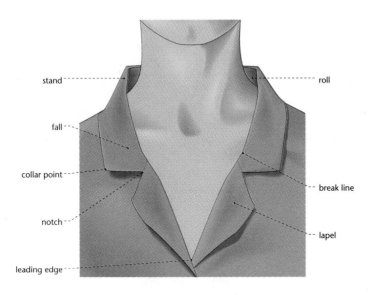

stand

roll

fall

collar point

break line

notch

lapel

leading edge

TYPES OF COLLARS

shirt collar

tailored collar

dog ear collar

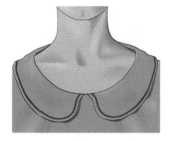

Peter Pan collar

shawl collar

collaret

TYPES OF COLLARS

bertha collar

bow collar

sailor collar

mandarin collar

jabot

stand-up collar

polo collar

cowl neck

turtleneck

CLOTHING

plunging neckline

bateau neck

square neck

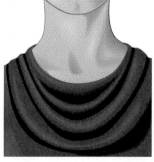

draped neck

round neck

sweetheart neckline

draped neckline

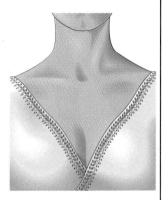

V-shaped neck

HOSE

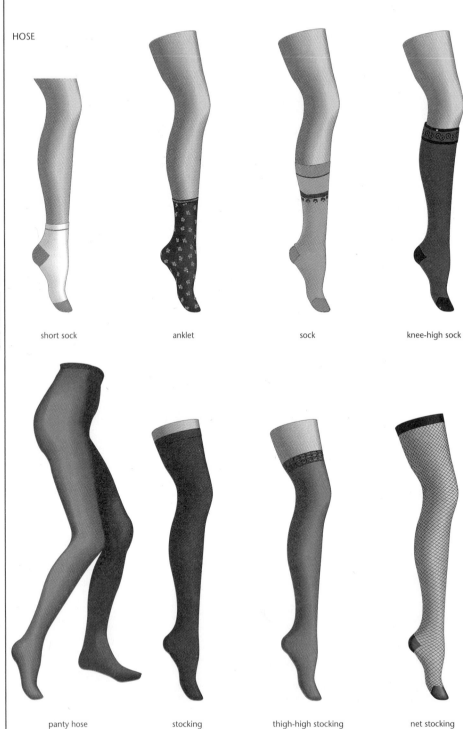

short sock

anklet

sock

knee-high sock

panty hose

stocking

thigh-high stocking

net stocking

CLOTHING

body suit

teddy

camisole

foundation slip

slip

princess seaming

half-slip

CLOTHING

UNDERWEAR

décolleté bra

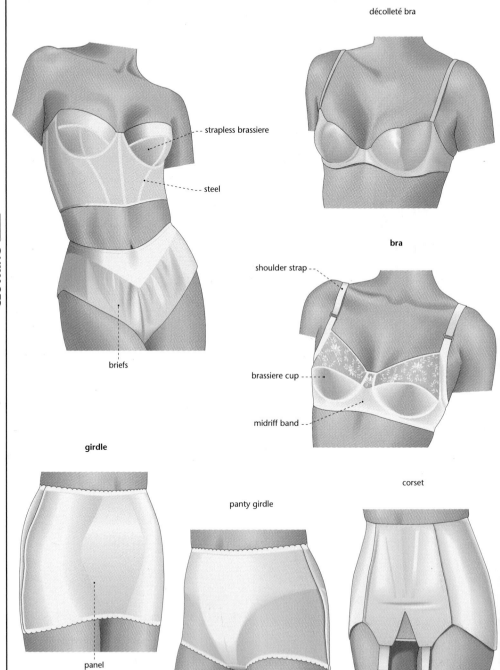

strapless brassiere

steel

briefs

bra

shoulder strap

brassiere cup

midriff band

girdle

panty girdle

corset

panel

346

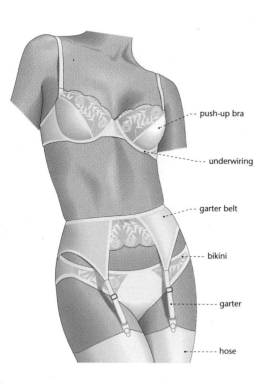

--- push-up bra

--- underwiring

--- garter belt

--- bikini

---- garter

------ hose

corselette

panty corselette

wasp-waisted corset

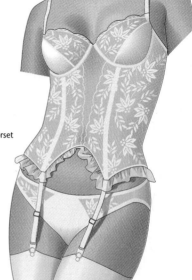

347

NIGHTWEAR

nightgown

baby doll

kimono

pajamas

negligee

bathrobe

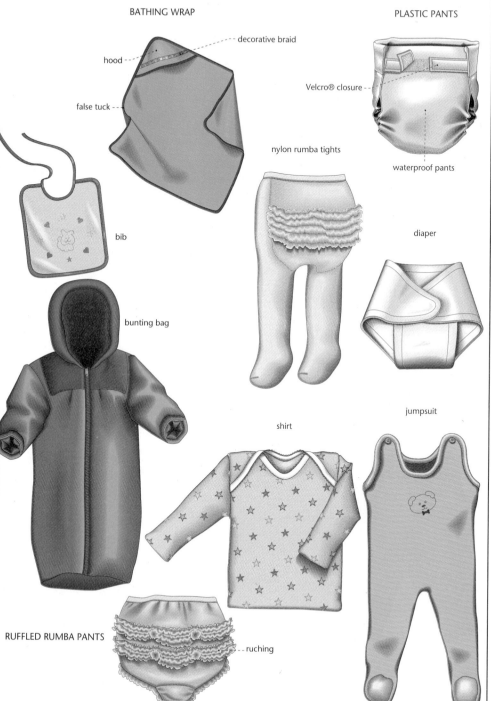

BATHING WRAP

decorative braid

hood

false tuck

PLASTIC PANTS

Velcro® closure

waterproof pants

nylon rumba tights

bib

diaper

bunting bag

shirt

jumpsuit

RUFFLED RUMBA PANTS

ruching

BLANKET SLEEPERS

SLEEPERS

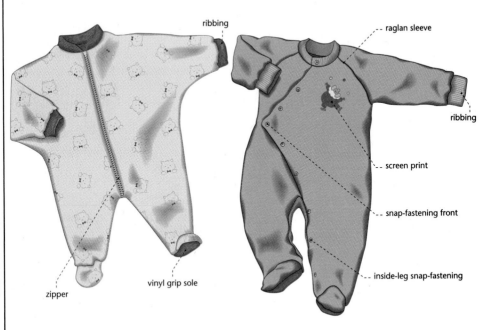

ribbing

raglan sleeve

ribbing

screen print

snap-fastening front

inside-leg snap-fastening

zipper

vinyl grip sole

HIGH-BACK OVERALLS

GROW SLEEPERS

adjustable strap

patch pocket

bib

top stitching

fly

inside-leg snap-fastening

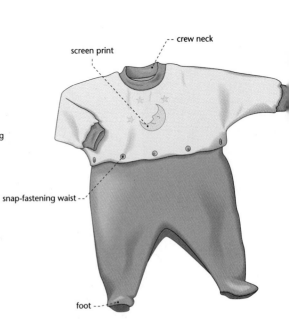

screen print

crew neck

snap-fastening waist

foot

TRAINING SET

CROSSOVER BACK STRAPS OVERALLS

polojama

button strap

bib

tank top

shorts

SNOWSUIT

drawstring hood

fly front closing

rompers

jumpsuit

T-shirt dress

CLOTHING

RUNNING SHOE

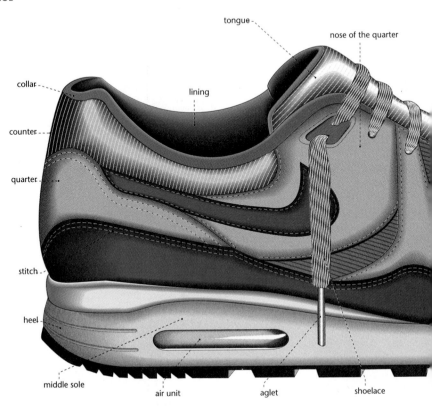

tongue

nose of the quarter

collar

lining

counter

quarter

stitch

heel

middle sole

air unit

aglet

shoelace

TRAINING SUIT

hooded sweat shirt

sweat pants

sweat shirt

swimming trunks

swimsuit

eyelet

vamp

punch hole

outsole

stud

leotard

footless tights

leg-warmer

boxer shorts

pants

anorak

tank top

353

PARTS OF A SHOE

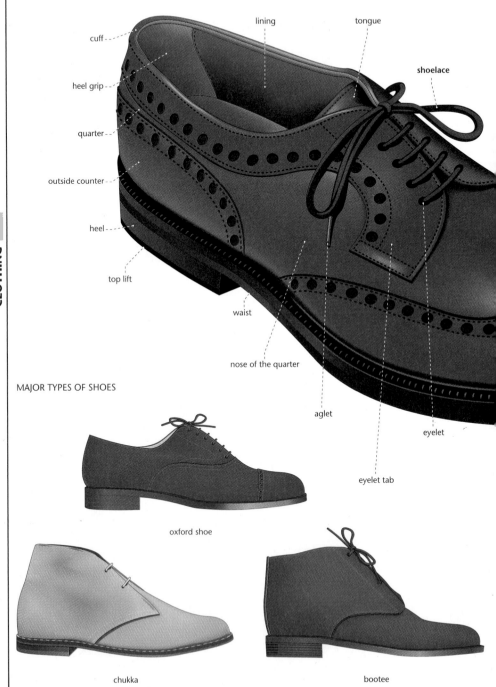

cuff

lining

tongue

shoelace

heel grip

quarter

outside counter

heel

top lift

waist

nose of the quarter

aglet

eyelet

eyelet tab

MAJOR TYPES OF SHOES

oxford shoe

chukka

bootee

tennis shoe

blucher oxford

moccasin

vamp

stitch

punch hole

perforated toe cap

welt

outsole

loafer

mule

heavy duty boot

rubber

CLOTHING

MAJOR TYPES OF SHOES

sling back shoe

pump

sandal

T-strap shoe

one-bar shoe

ballerina

casual shoe

boot

sandal

thong

ankle boot

clog

espadrille

thigh-boot

sandal

ACCESSORIES

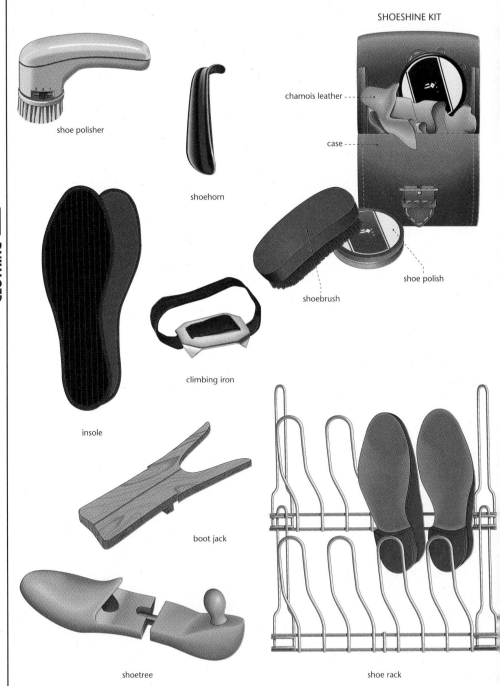

shoe polisher

shoehorn

chamois leather ---

case ---

shoe polish

shoebrush

climbing iron

insole

boot jack

shoetree

shoe rack

PERSONAL ADORNMENT

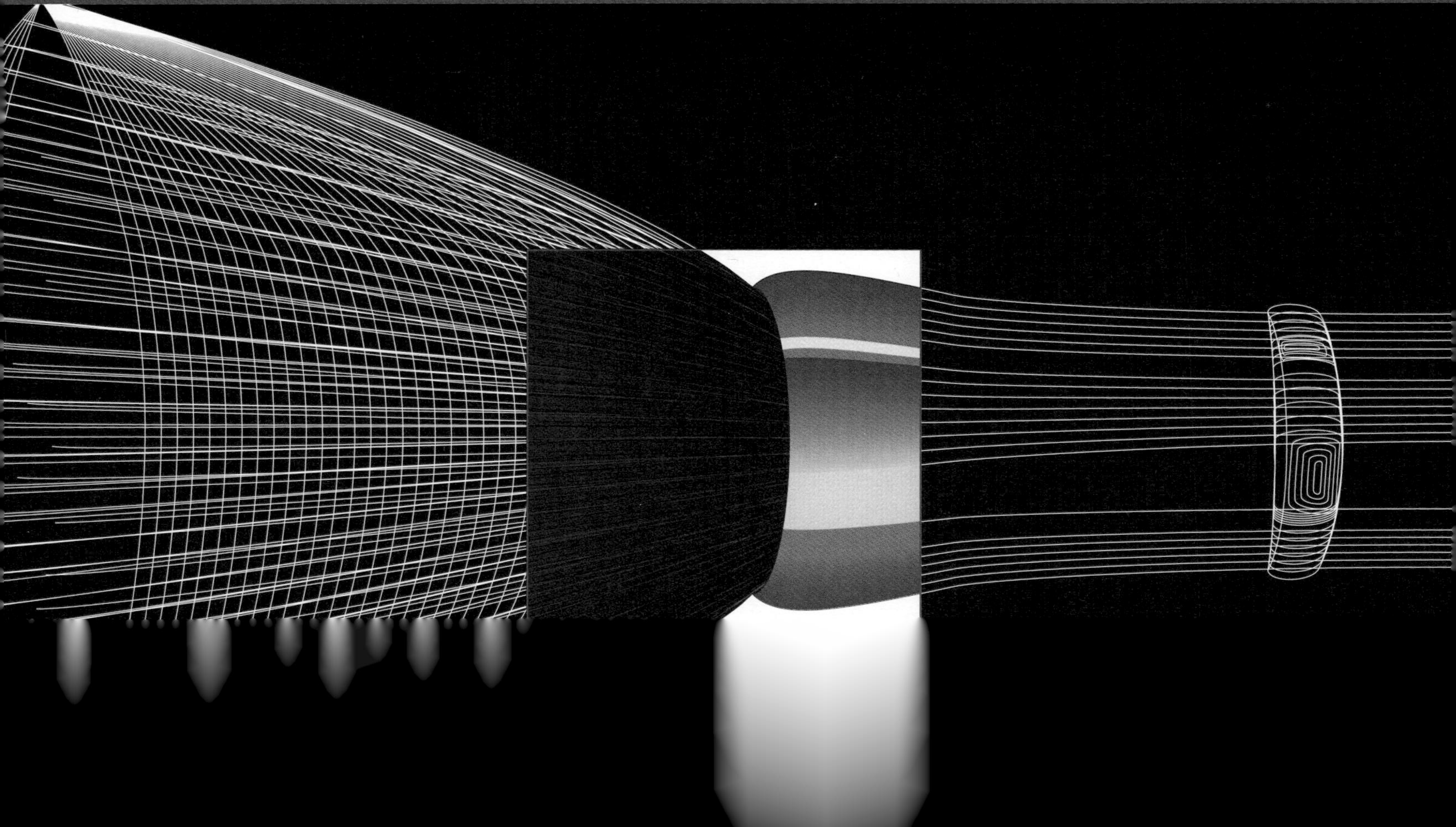

CONTENTS

PERSONAL ADORNMENT

JEWELRY

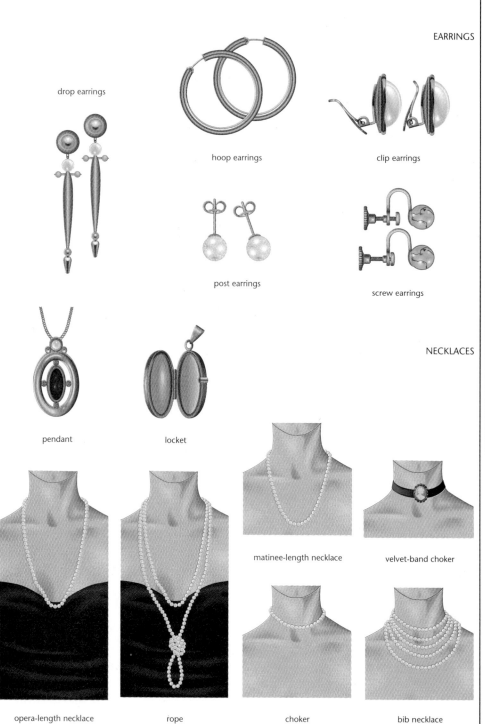

drop earrings

hoop earrings

clip earrings

post earrings

screw earrings

pendant

locket

matinee-length necklace

velvet-band choker

opera-length necklace

rope

choker

bib necklace

CUT FOR GEMSTONES

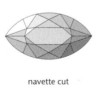

navette cut

baguette cut

oval cut

French cut

pear-shaped cut

briolette cut

table cut

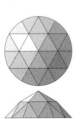

rose cut

cabochon cut

step cut

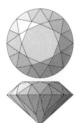

brilliant full cut

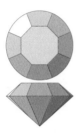

eight cut

scissors cut

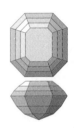

emerald cut

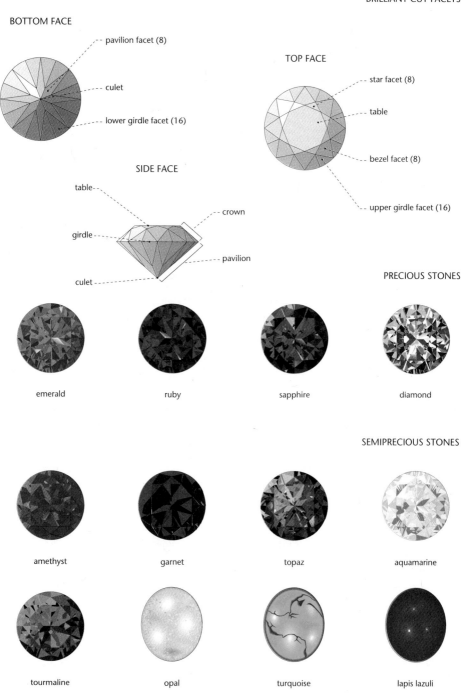

BRILLIANT CUT FACETS

BOTTOM FACE

- pavilion facet (8)
- culet
- lower girdle facet (16)

TOP FACE

- star facet (8)
- table
- bezel facet (8)
- upper girdle facet (16)

SIDE FACE

table
crown
girdle
pavilion
culet

PRECIOUS STONES

emerald

ruby

sapphire

diamond

SEMIPRECIOUS STONES

amethyst

garnet

topaz

aquamarine

tourmaline

opal

turquoise

lapis lazuli

PERSONAL ADORNMENT

363

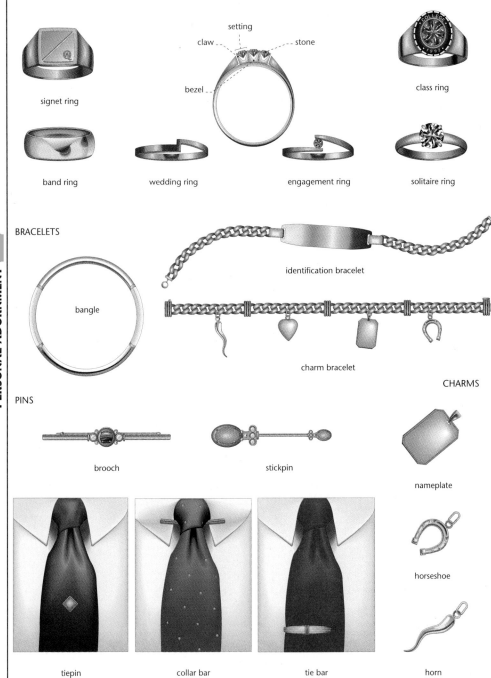

RINGS

signet ring

setting

claw

stone

bezel

class ring

band ring

wedding ring

engagement ring

solitaire ring

BRACELETS

bangle

identification bracelet

charm bracelet

CHARMS

PINS

brooch

stickpin

nameplate

tiepin

collar bar

tie bar

horseshoe

horn

MANICURE

MANICURE SET

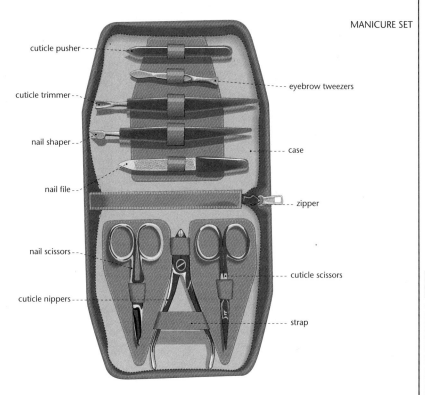

cuticle pusher

cuticle trimmer

nail shaper

nail file

nail scissors

cuticle nippers

eyebrow tweezers

case

zipper

cuticle scissors

strap

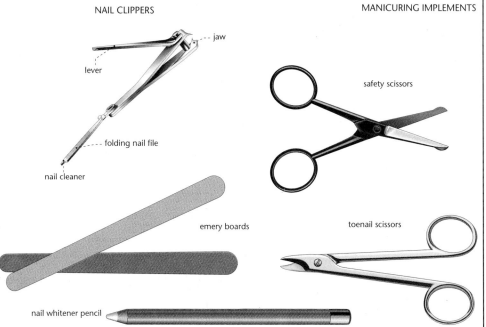

NAIL CLIPPERS

jaw

lever

folding nail file

nail cleaner

MANICURING IMPLEMENTS

safety scissors

emery boards

toenail scissors

nail whitener pencil

365

PERSONAL ADORNMENT

FACIAL MAKEUP

fan brush

loose powder brush

loose powder

liquid foundation

powder puff

blusher brush ----

compact

pressed powder

powder blusher

LIP MAKEUP

lipbrush

lipstick

lipliner

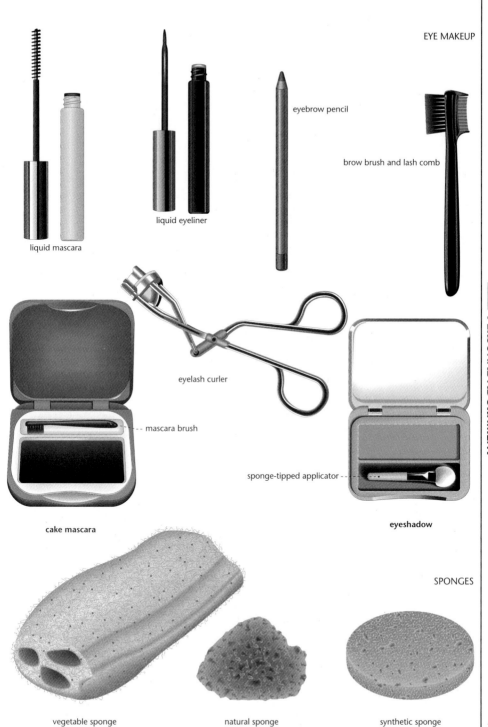

eyebrow pencil

brow brush and lash comb

liquid eyeliner

liquid mascara

eyelash curler

mascara brush

sponge-tipped applicator

cake mascara

eyeshadow

SPONGES

vegetable sponge

natural sponge

synthetic sponge

LIGHTED MIRROR

side mirror

dual swivel mirror

lighting

base

on-off switch

HAIRBRUSHES

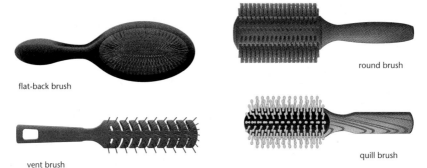

flat-back brush

round brush

vent brush

quill brush

COMBS

teaser comb

rake comb

tail comb

pitchfork comb

Afro pick

barber comb

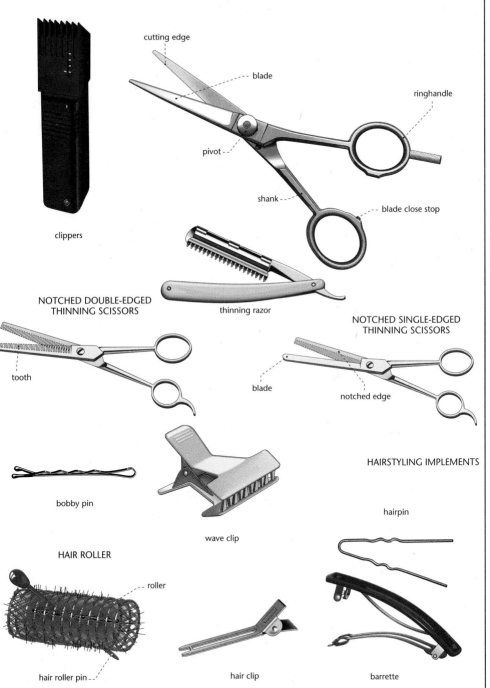

HAIRCUTTING SCISSORS

cutting edge

blade

ringhandle

pivot

shank

blade close stop

clippers

thinning razor

NOTCHED DOUBLE-EDGED
THINNING SCISSORS

tooth

blade

NOTCHED SINGLE-EDGED
THINNING SCISSORS

notched edge

HAIRSTYLING IMPLEMENTS

bobby pin

hairpin

wave clip

HAIR ROLLER

roller

hair roller pin

hair clip

barrette

CURLING IRON

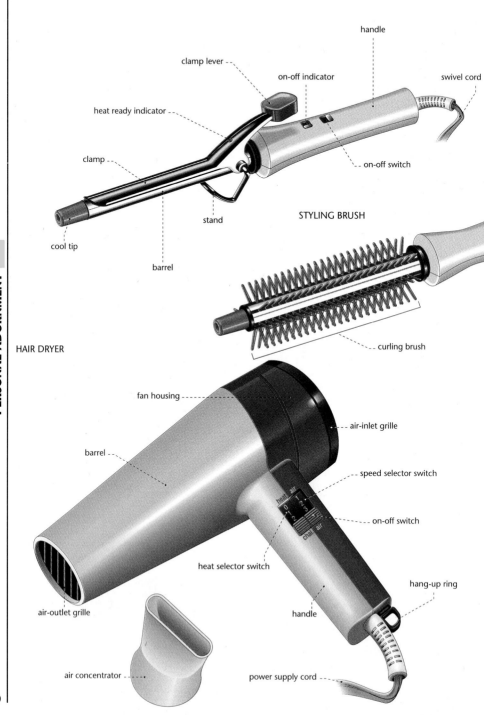

handle

clamp lever

on-off indicator

heat ready indicator

swivel cord

clamp

on-off switch

cool tip

stand

STYLING BRUSH

barrel

curling brush

HAIR DRYER

fan housing

air-inlet grille

barrel

speed selector switch

on-off switch

heat selector switch

hang-up ring

air-outlet grille

handle

air concentrator

power supply cord

PERSONAL ARTICLES

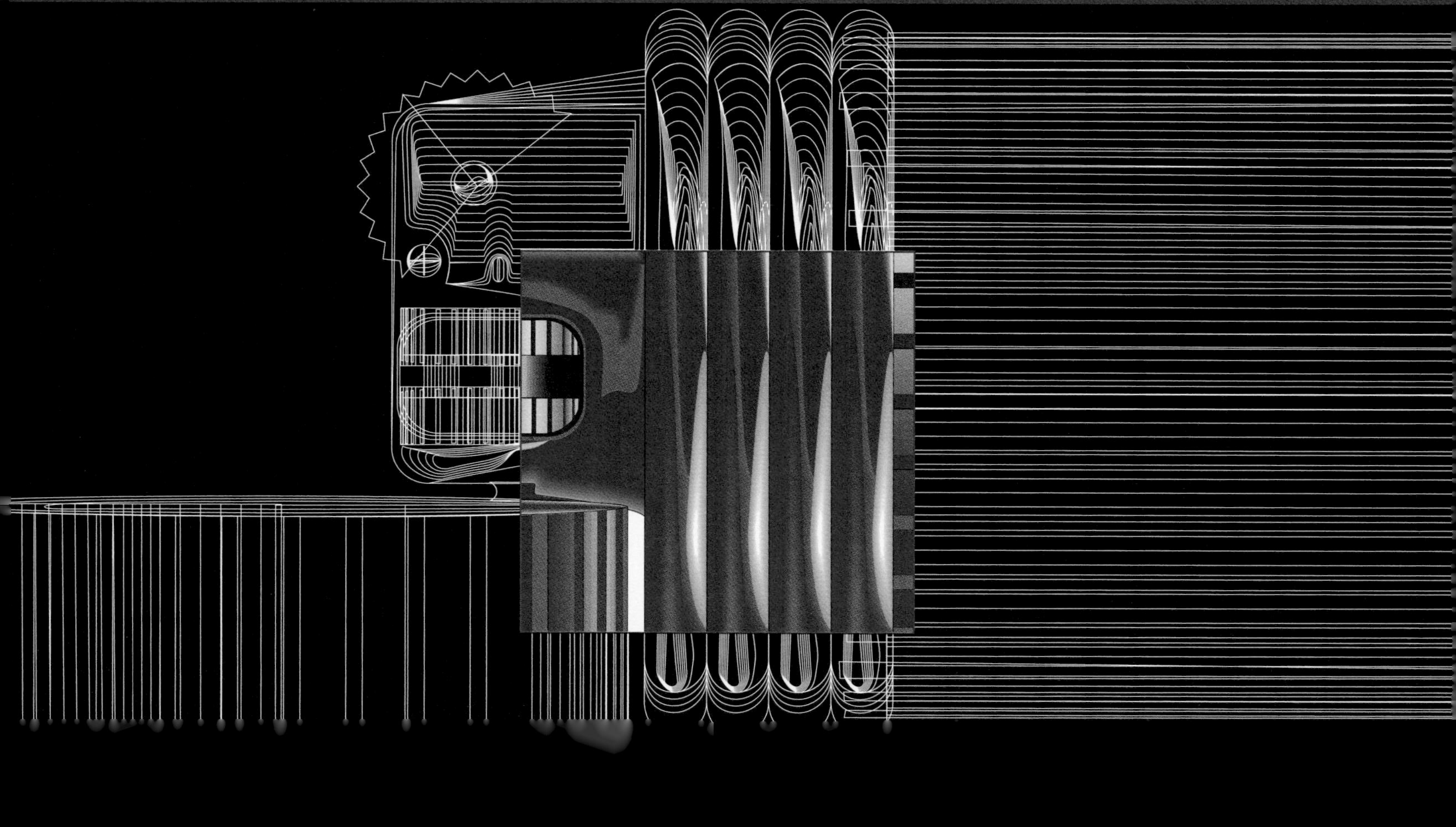

CONTENTS

PERSONAL ARTICLES

DENTAL CARE

TOOTHBRUSH

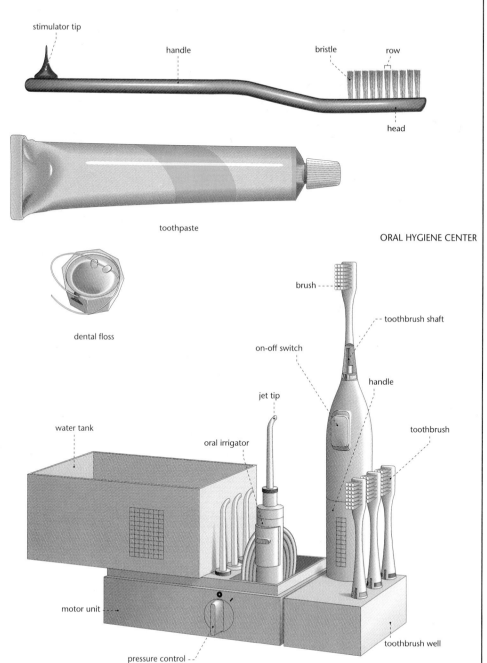

stimulator tip

handle

bristle

row

head

toothpaste

dental floss

ORAL HYGIENE CENTER

brush

toothbrush shaft

on-off switch

handle

jet tip

toothbrush

water tank

oral irrigator

motor unit

toothbrush well

pressure control

RAZORS

ELECTRIC RAZOR

floating head - - - - trimmer

screen - -

closeness setting

housing

charging light

on-off switch

charge indicator - - -

charging plug - - - - - - - -

power cord

cleaning brush

STRAIGHT RAZOR

blade

pivot

handle

plug adapter

DOUBLE-EDGE RAZOR

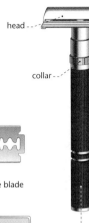

head - -

collar - - -

handle

bristle

disposable razor

double-edge blade

blade injector

SHAVING BRUSH   shaving mug

374

UMBRELLA AND STICK

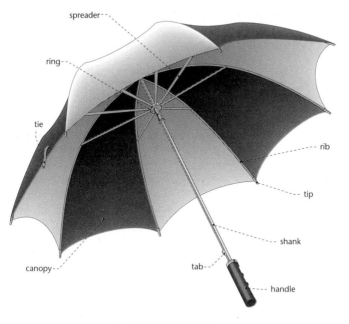

spreader

ring

tie

rib

tip

shank

canopy

tab

handle

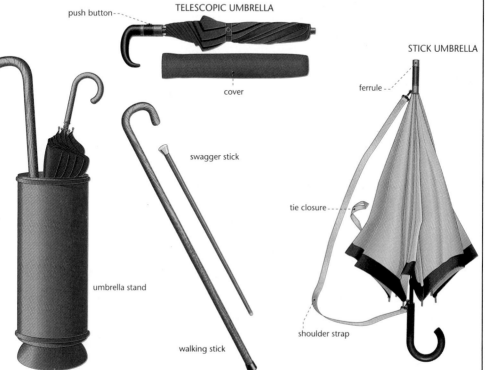

TELESCOPIC UMBRELLA

push button

cover

STICK UMBRELLA

ferrule

swagger stick

tie closure

umbrella stand

shoulder strap

walking stick

EYEGLASSES PARTS

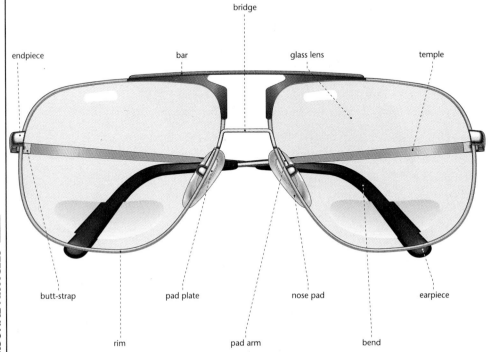

bridge

endpiece

bar

glass lens

temple

butt-strap

pad plate

nose pad

earpiece

rim

pad arm

bend

BIFOCAL LENS

distance

rim

reading

FRAMES

half-glasses

scissors-glasses

sunglasses

pince-nez

lorgnette

monocle

opera glasses

LEATHER GOODS

ATTACHÉ CASE

divider ---

clasp

pocket ---

expandable file pouch

hinge ---

lining ---

pen holder

frame

handle ---

combination lock

BRIEFCASE

BOTTOM-FOLD PORTFOLIO

retractable handle

tab ---

exterior pocket

gusset ---

key lock

underarm portfolio

writing case

eyeglasses case

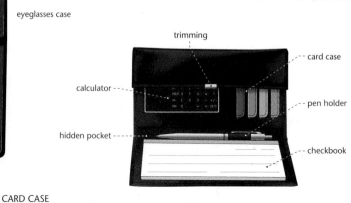

trimming

calculator

hidden pocket

card case

pen holder

checkbook

CARD CASE

bill compartment

windows

tab

slot

window

key case

billfold

purse

wallet

checkbook

passport case

coin purse

PERSONAL ARTICLES

379

men's bag

SATCHEL BAG

handle

flap

clasp

lock

pouch

SHOULDER BAG

buckle

shoulder strap

ACCORDION BAG

gusset

tote bag

duffel bag

hobo bag

sea bag

box bag

clutch bag

DRAWSTRING BAG

eyelet

drawstring

front pocket

duffel bag

muff

shopping bag

carrier bag

LUGGAGE

CARRY-ON BAG

tote bag

handle

exterior pocket

shoulder strap

VANITY CASE

mirror

hinge

cosmetic tray

GARMENT BAG

zipper

utility case

LUGGAGE CARRIER

frame

luggage elastic

stand

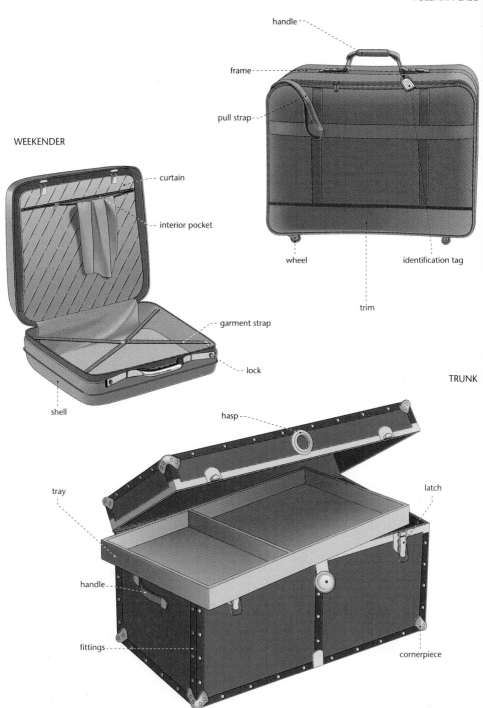

PULLMAN CASE

handle

frame

pull strap

wheel   identification tag

trim

WEEKENDER

curtain

interior pocket

garment strap

lock

shell

TRUNK

hasp

tray

latch

handle

fittings

cornerpiece

SMOKING ACCESSORIES

CIGAR

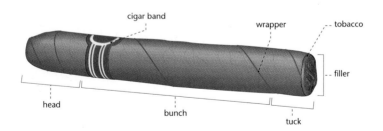

cigar band

wrapper

tobacco

head

bunch

filler

tuck

cigarette holder

CIGARETTE

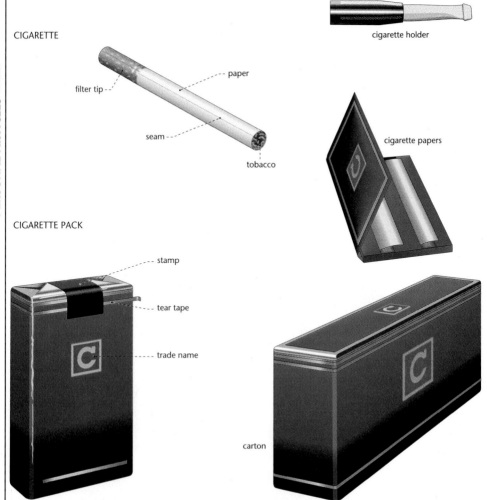

paper

filter tip

seam

tobacco

cigarette papers

CIGARETTE PACK

stamp

tear tape

trade name

carton

384

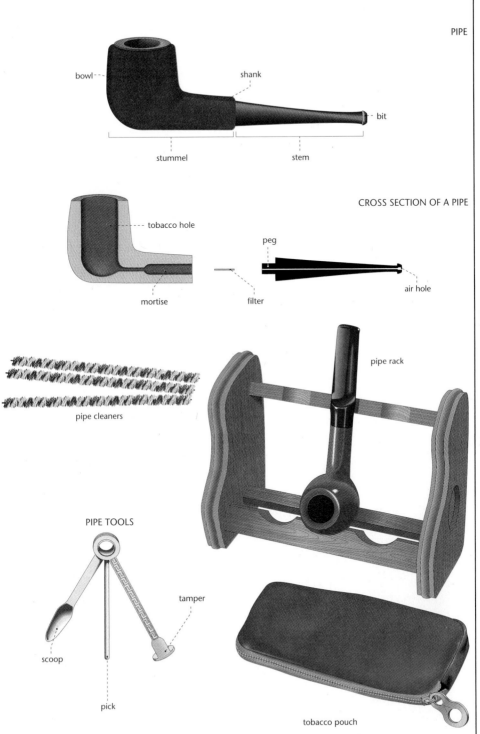

bowl

shank

bit

stummel

stem

CROSS SECTION OF A PIPE

tobacco hole

peg

mortise

filter

air hole

pipe cleaners

pipe rack

PIPE TOOLS

tamper

scoop

pick

tobacco pouch

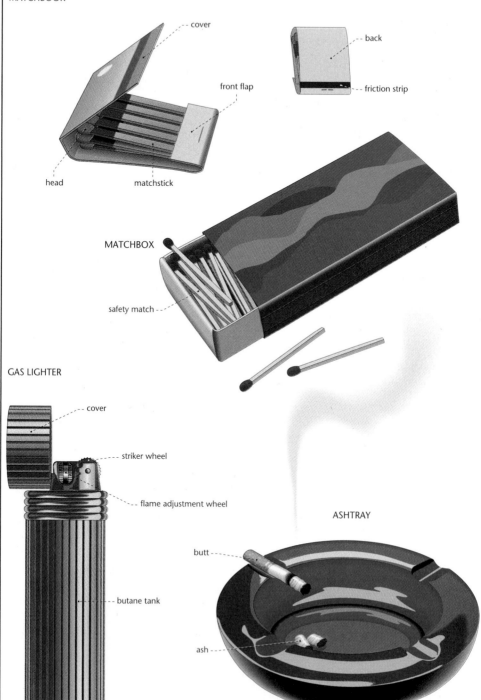

MATCHBOOK

cover

back

front flap

friction strip

head

matchstick

MATCHBOX

safety match

GAS LIGHTER

cover

striker wheel

flame adjustment wheel

ASHTRAY

butt

butane tank

ash

COMMUNICATIONS

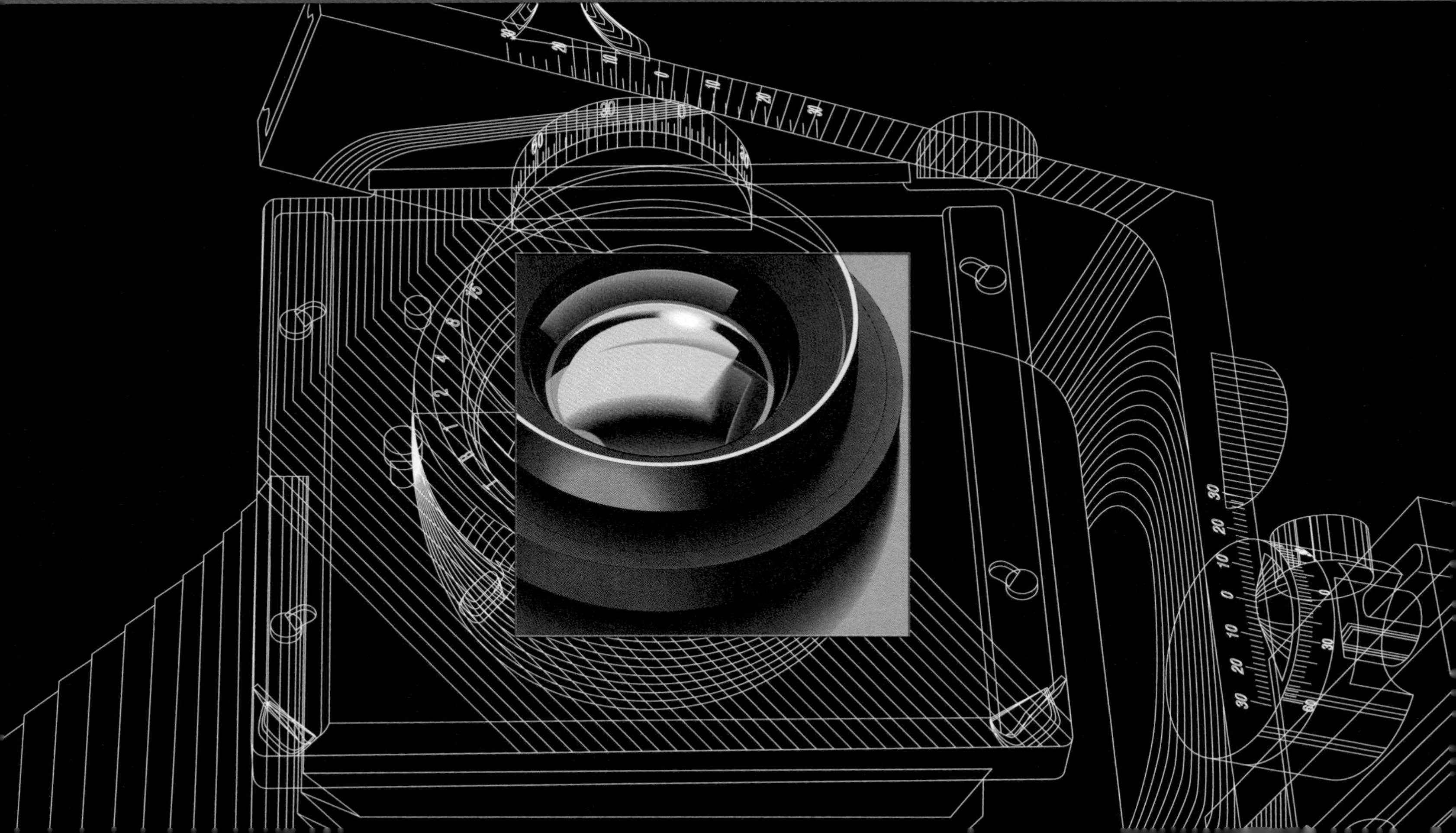

CONTENTS

COMMUNICATIONS

WRITING INSTRUMENTS

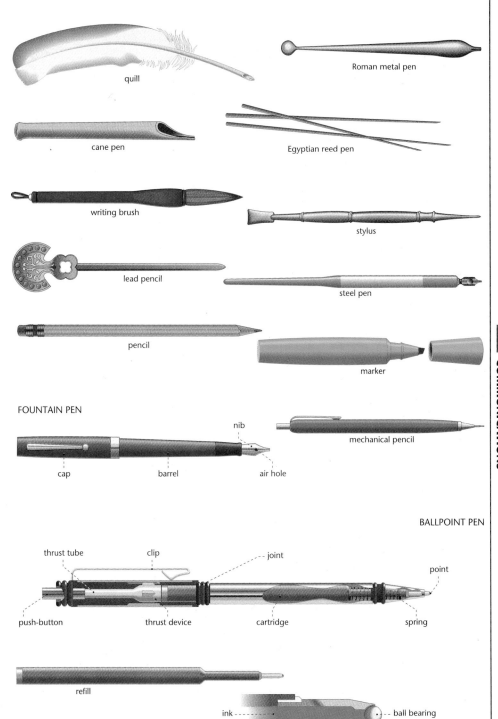

quill

Roman metal pen

cane pen

Egyptian reed pen

writing brush

stylus

lead pencil

steel pen

pencil

marker

FOUNTAIN PEN

nib

mechanical pencil

cap

barrel

air hole

BALLPOINT PEN

thrust tube

clip

joint

point

push-button

thrust device

cartridge

spring

refill

ink

ball bearing

CROSS SECTION OF A REFLEX CAMERA

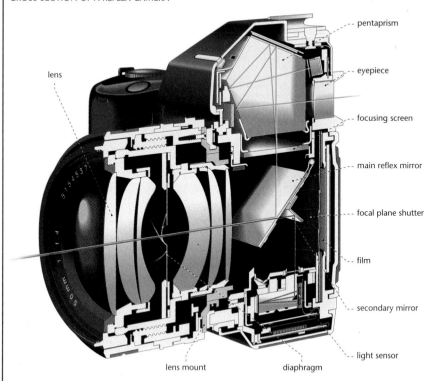

lens

pentaprism

eyepiece

focusing screen

main reflex mirror

focal plane shutter

film

secondary mirror

light sensor

lens mount

diaphragm

CAMERA BACK

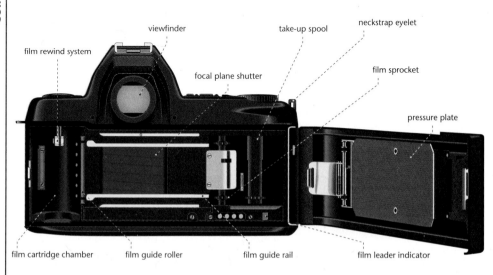

viewfinder

take-up spool

neckstrap eyelet

film rewind system

focal plane shutter

film sprocket

pressure plate

film cartridge chamber

film guide roller

film guide rail

film leader indicator

film rewind knob

control panel

exposure adjustment knob

on/off switch

command control dial

hot-shoe contact

accessory shoe

film advance mode

film speed

multiple exposure mode

exposure mode

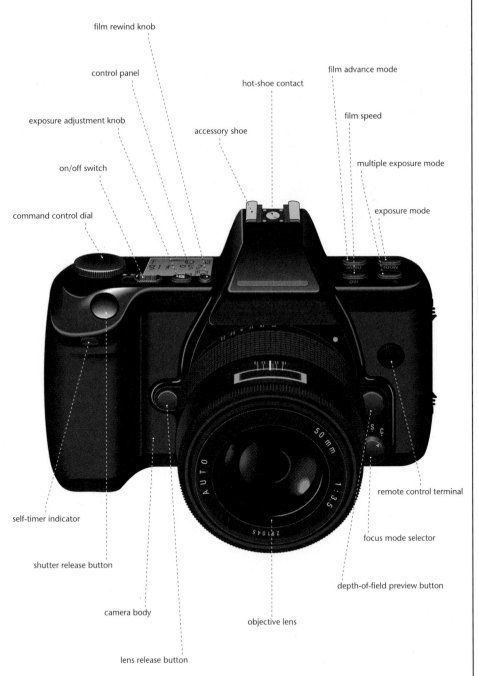

self-timer indicator

shutter release button

camera body

lens release button

objective lens

remote control terminal

focus mode selector

depth-of-field preview button

LENSES

standard lens

lens

distance scale

focus setting ring

depth-of-field scale

lens aperture scale

wide-angle lens

bayonet mount

LENS ACCESSORIES

lens cap

lens hood

zoom lens

semi-fisheye lens

color filter

close-up lens

polarizing filter

objective lens

telephoto lens

fisheye lens

tele-converter

COMMUNICATIONS

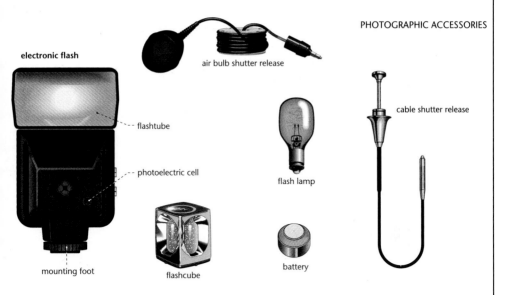

electronic flash

air bulb shutter release

cable shutter release

flashtube

photoelectric cell

flash lamp

mounting foot

flashcube

battery

TRIPOD

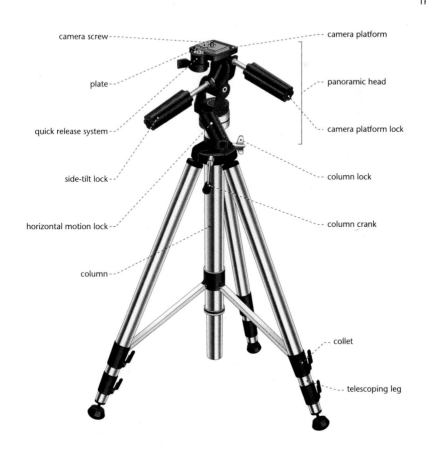

camera screw

plate

quick release system

side-tilt lock

horizontal motion lock

column

camera platform

panoramic head

camera platform lock

column lock

column crank

collet

telescoping leg

COMMUNICATIONS

STILL CAMERAS

rangefinder

underwater camera

Polaroid® Land camera

single-lens reflex camera

disposable camera

twin-lens reflex camera

view camera

pocket camera

medium format SLR (6 × 6)

disk camera

stereo camera

still video camera

film leader   perforation

still video film disk

cassette film

film disk

cartridge film

sheet film

roll film

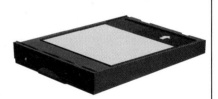

film pack

EXPOSURE METER

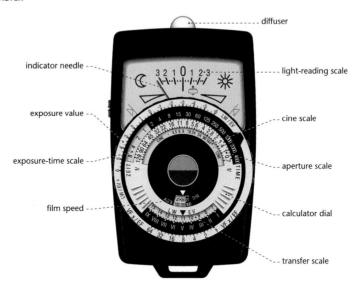

diffuser

indicator needle

light-reading scale

exposure value

cine scale

exposure-time scale

aperture scale

film speed

calculator dial

transfer scale

SPOTMETER

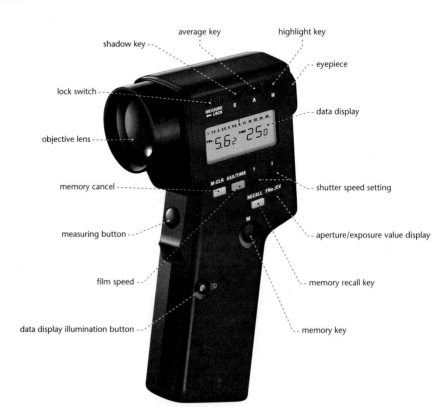

average key

highlight key

shadow key

eyepiece

lock switch

data display

objective lens

memory cancel

shutter speed setting

measuring button

aperture/exposure value display

film speed

memory recall key

data display illumination button

memory key

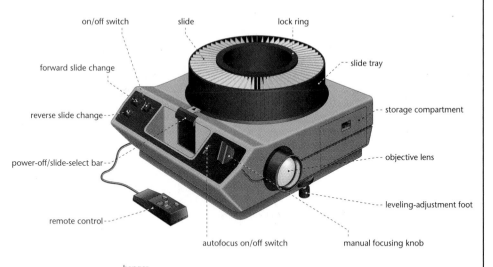

on/off switch

slide

lock ring

forward slide change

slide tray

reverse slide change

storage compartment

power-off/slide-select bar

objective lens

leveling-adjustment foot

remote control

autofocus on/off switch

manual focusing knob

hanger

PROJECTION SCREEN

saddle

push-button

pull bail

tube

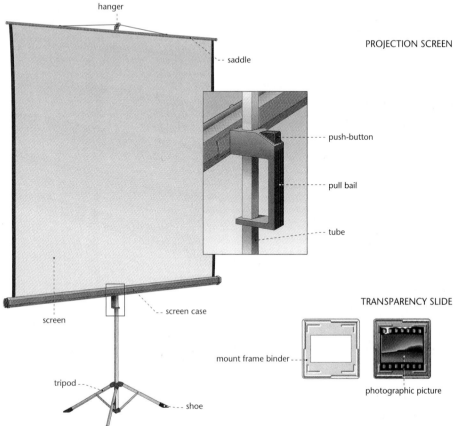

screen

screen case

tripod

shoe

TRANSPARENCY SLIDE

mount frame binder

photographic picture

COMMUNICATIONS

DEVELOPING TANK

cap

lid

reel

tank

lightbox

timer

guillotine trimmer

safelight

film drying cabinet

easel

contact printer

NEGATIVE CARRIER

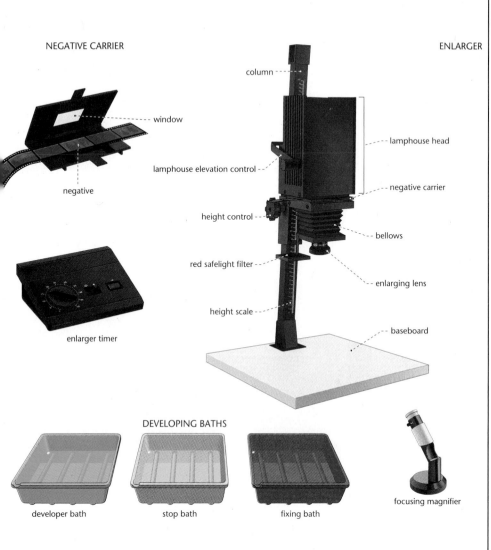

window

negative

enlarger timer

ENLARGER

column

lamphouse head

lamphouse elevation control

negative carrier

height control

bellows

red safelight filter

enlarging lens

height scale

baseboard

DEVELOPING BATHS

developer bath

stop bath

fixing bath

focusing magnifier

PRINT WASHER

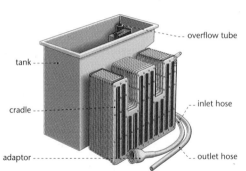

overflow tube

tank

cradle

inlet hose

adaptor

outlet hose

print drying rack

SOUND REPRODUCING SYSTEM

SYSTEM COMPONENTS

COMMUNICATIONS

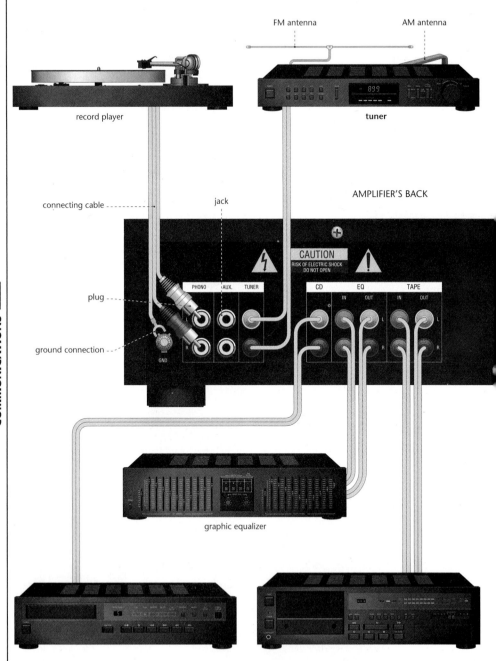

FM antenna

AM antenna

record player

tuner

connecting cable

jack

AMPLIFIER'S BACK

CAUTION
RISK OF ELECTRIC SHOCK
DO NOT OPEN

PHONO   AUX.   TUNER   CD   EQ   TAPE
                                    IN   OUT   IN   OUT

plug

ground connection

GND

graphic equalizer

compact disk player

cassette tape deck

400

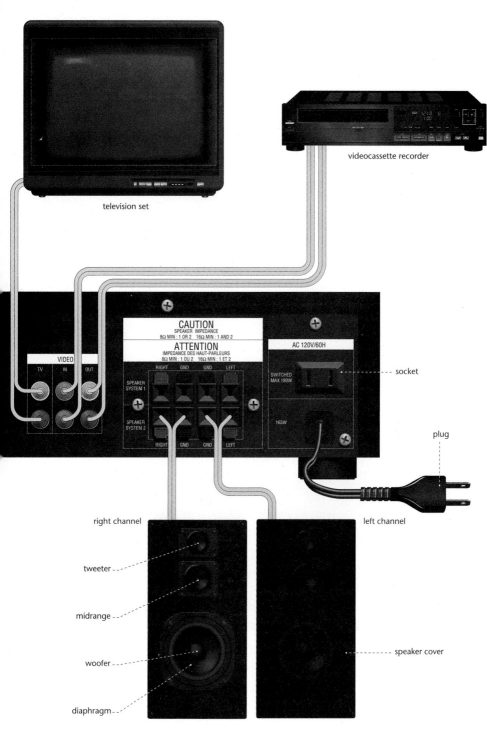

television set

videocassette recorder

CAUTION
SPEAKER IMPEDANCE
8Ω MIN : 1 OR 2   16Ω MIN : 1 AND 2
ATTENTION
IMPEDANCE DES HAUT-PARLEURS
8Ω MIN : 1 OU 2   16Ω MIN : 1 ET 2

AC 120V/60H

VIDEO

TV   IN   OUT

RIGHT   GND   GND   LEFT

SPEAKER
SYSTEM 1

SPEAKER
SYSTEM 2

RIGHT   GND   GND   LEFT

SWITCHED
MAX 180W

165W

socket

plug

right channel

left channel

tweeter

midrange

woofer

diaphragm

speaker cover

loudspeakers

SOUND REPRODUCING SYSTEM

COMMUNICATIONS

TUNER

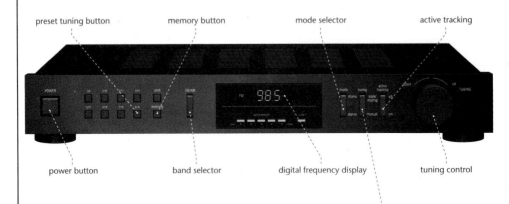

preset tuning button memory button mode selector active tracking

power button band selector digital frequency display tuning control

tuning mode

AMPLIFIER

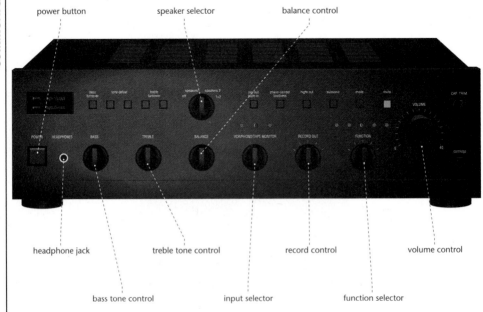

power button speaker selector balance control

headphone jack treble tone control record control volume control

bass tone control input selector function selector

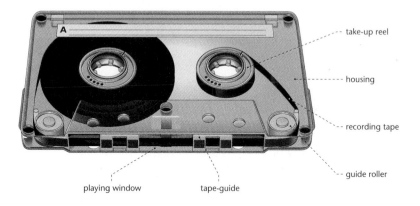

take-up reel

housing

recording tape

guide roller

playing window   tape-guide

counter reset button   tape selector   fast-forward button

eject button   tape counter   play button   peak level meter

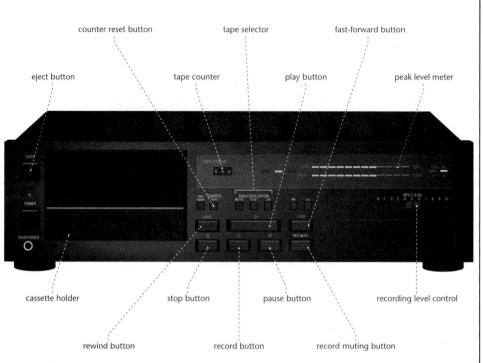

cassette holder   stop button   pause button   recording level control

rewind button   record button   record muting button

RECORD

RECORD PLAYER

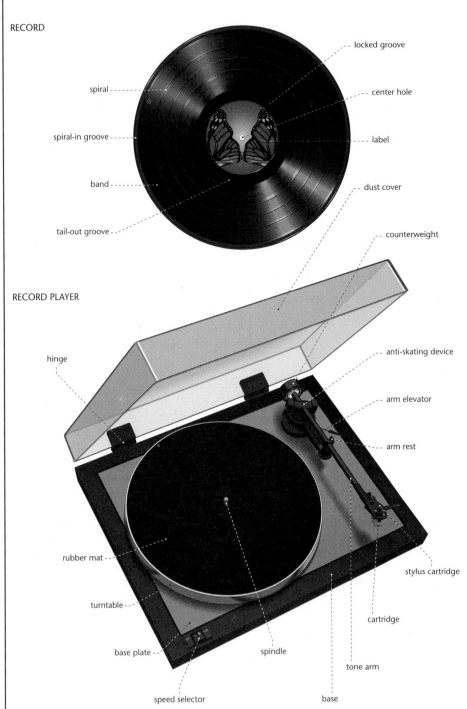

locked groove

spiral

center hole

spiral-in groove

label

band

dust cover

tail-out groove

counterweight

hinge

anti-skating device

arm elevator

arm rest

rubber mat

stylus cartridge

turntable

cartridge

base plate

spindle

tone arm

speed selector

base

COMPACT DISK

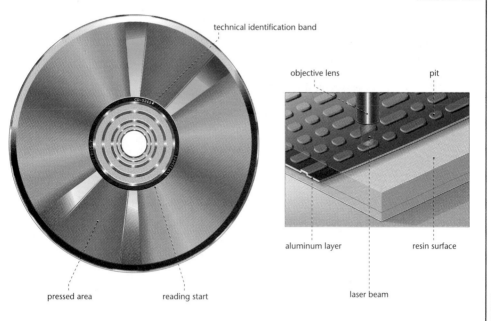

technical identification band

objective lens

pit

aluminum layer

resin surface

pressed area

reading start

laser beam

COMPACT DISK PLAYER

track number

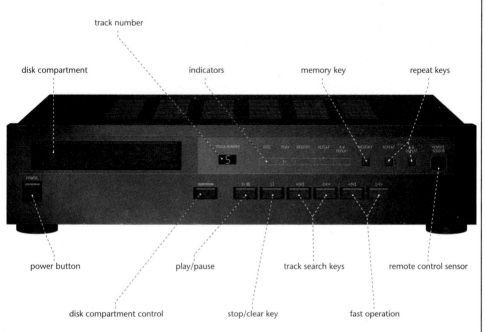

disk compartment

indicators

memory key

repeat keys

power button

play/pause

remote control sensor

disk compartment control

stop/clear key

fast operation

track search keys

DYNAMIC MICROPHONE

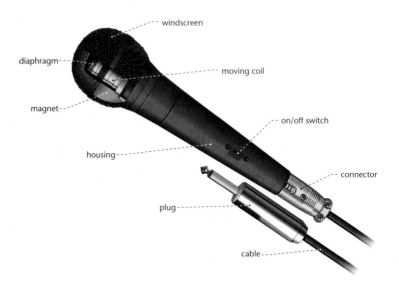

windscreen

diaphragm

moving coil

magnet

on/off switch

housing

connector

plug

cable

HEADPHONES

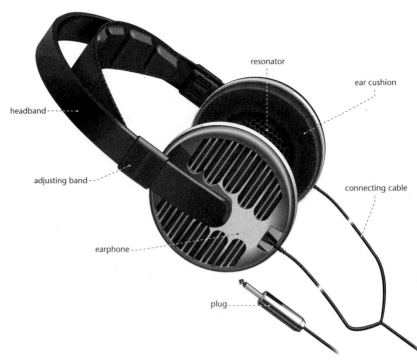

resonator

ear cushion

headband

adjusting band

connecting cable

earphone

plug

studio

microphone

announcer turret

on-air warning light

tone leader generator

clock

volume unit meters

audio monitor

cartridge tape recorder

digital audio tape recorder

compact disk player

cassette deck

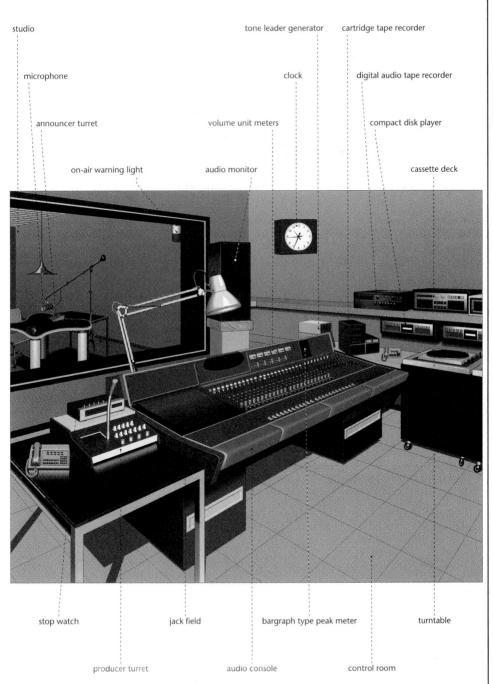

stop watch

jack field

bargraph type peak meter

turntable

producer turret

audio console

control room

PERSONAL RADIO CASSETTE
PLAYER

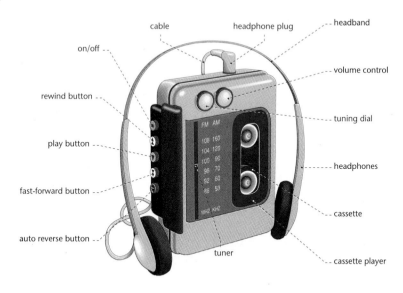

cable

headphone plug

headband

on/off

volume control

rewind button

tuning dial

play button

headphones

fast-forward button

cassette

auto reverse button

cassette player

tuner

FM AM

108 160
104 120
100 90
96 70
92 60
88 53

MHZ KHZ

PORTABLE CD RADIO CASSETTE
RECORDER

stereo control

handle

mode selectors

antenna

compact disk player

on/off/volume

headphone jack

compact disk

compact disk player
controls

speaker

tuner

tuning control

power plug

cassette

cassette player

cassette player controls

VIDEO CAMERA

eyepiece

power zoom button

electronic viewfinder

white balance sensor

accessory shoe

cassette eject switch

videotape operation controls

viewfinder adjustment keys

built-in microphone

DATA SET

ZERO MEM

ADJUST

RESET

SELECT

00425

EDIT SEARCH

SPEED

EXPOSURE

FOCUS

WHITE BAL

FADER

AUTO LOCK

BATT

macro set button

cassette compartment

zoom lens

data display

battery eject switch

lens hood

shooting adjustment keys

battery

edit/search buttons

TELEVISION SET

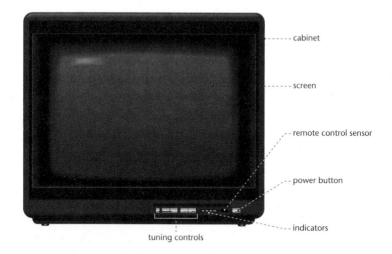

cabinet

screen

remote control sensor

power button

indicators

tuning controls

PICTURE TUBE

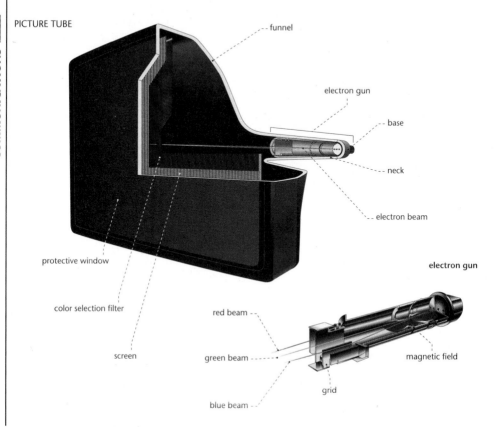

funnel

electron gun

base

neck

electron beam

protective window

color selection filter

screen

electron gun

red beam

green beam

blue beam

grid

magnetic field

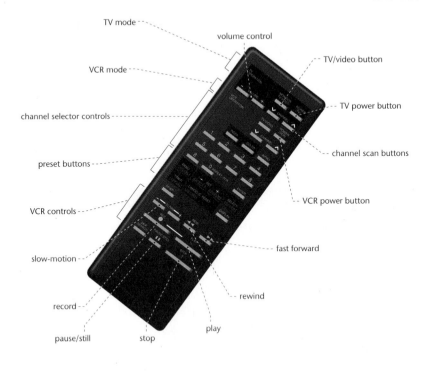

TV mode

volume control

VCR mode

TV/video button

TV power button

channel selector controls

preset buttons

channel scan buttons

VCR controls

VCR power button

slow-motion

fast forward

record

rewind

pause/still

stop

play

VIDEOCASSETTE RECORDER

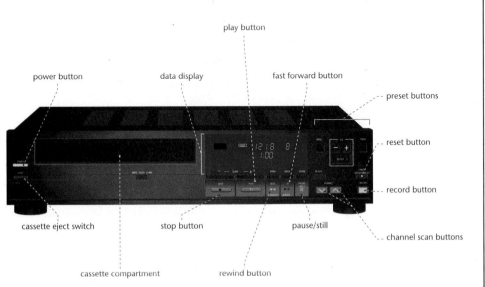

play button

power button

data display

fast forward button

preset buttons

reset button

record button

cassette eject switch

stop button

pause/still

channel scan buttons

cassette compartment

rewind button

STUDIO AND CONTROL ROOMS

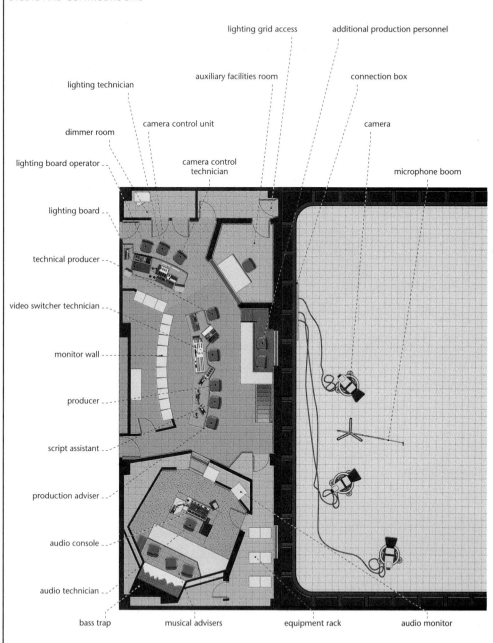

lighting grid access

additional production personnel

auxiliary facilities room

connection box

lighting technician

camera control unit

camera

dimmer room

camera control
technician

lighting board operator

microphone boom

lighting board

technical producer

video switcher technician

monitor wall

producer

script assistant

production adviser

audio console

audio technician

bass trap

musical advisers

equipment rack

audio monitor

 studio floor

lighting/camera control
area

 audio control room

production control room

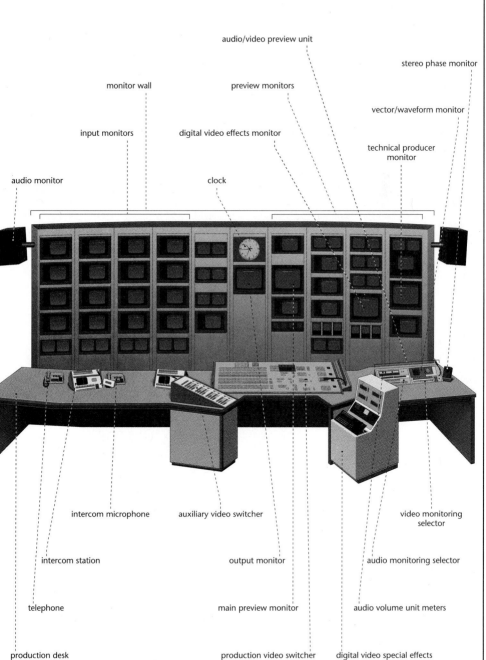

audio/video preview unit

stereo phase monitor

monitor wall

preview monitors

vector/waveform monitor

input monitors

digital video effects monitor

technical producer
monitor

audio monitor

clock

intercom microphone

auxiliary video switcher

video monitoring
selector

intercom station

output monitor

audio monitoring selector

telephone

main preview monitor

audio volume unit meters

production desk

production video switcher

digital video special effects

STUDIO FLOOR

floodlight on pantograph

spotlight

test pattern

lighting grid

curtain

floodlight

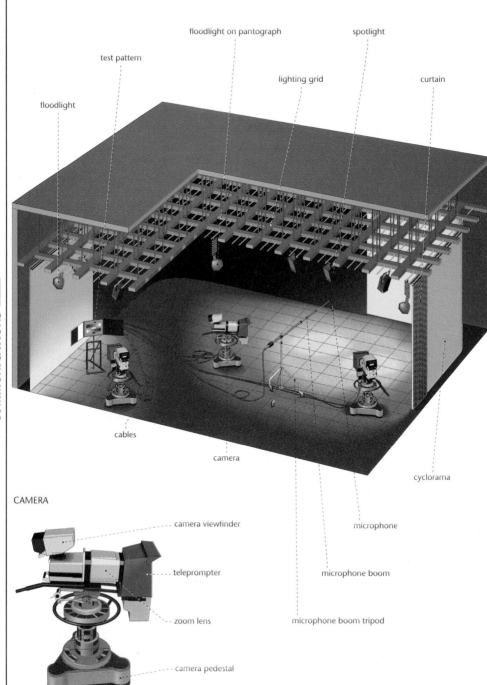

cables

camera

cyclorama

CAMERA

camera viewfinder

microphone

teleprompter

microphone boom

zoom lens

microphone boom tripod

camera pedestal

MOBILE UNIT

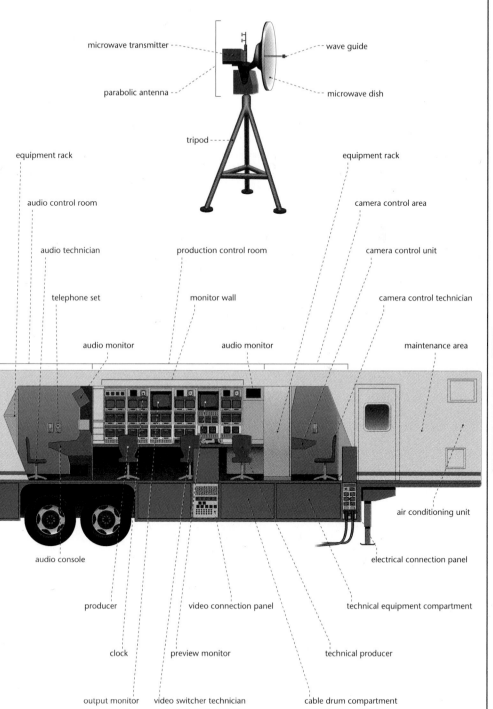

microwave transmitter

wave guide

parabolic antenna

microwave dish

tripod

equipment rack

equipment rack

audio control room

camera control area

audio technician

camera control unit

telephone set

production control room

camera control technician

monitor wall

audio monitor

audio monitor

maintenance area

audio console

air conditioning unit

producer

electrical connection panel

video connection panel

clock

technical equipment compartment

preview monitor

technical producer

output monitor

video switcher technician

cable drum compartment

BROADCAST SATELLITE COMMUNICATION

satellite

local station

cable distributor

private broadcasting network

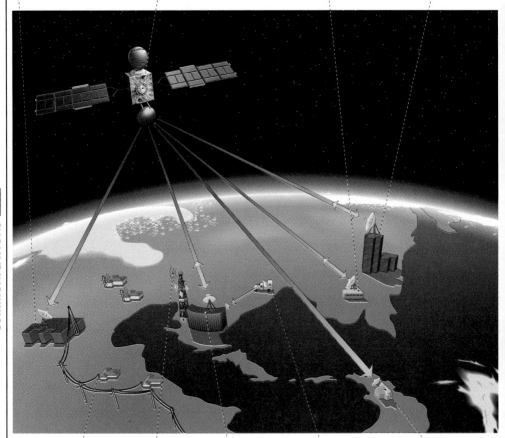

distribution by cable network

direct home reception

Hertzian wave transmission

mobile unit

national broadcasting network

TELECOMMUNICATIONS BY SATELLITE

industrial communications   teleport

air communications   military communications   maritime communications

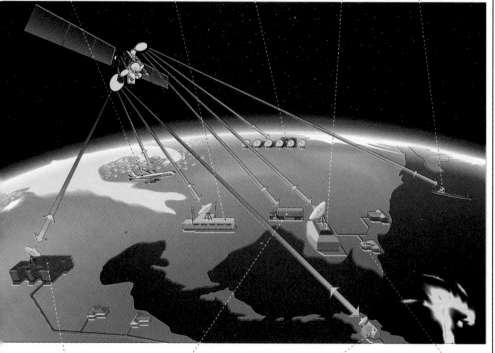

telephone network   road communications   personal communications   consumer

TELECOMMUNICATIONS BY TELEPHONE NETWORK

computer communication

facsimile machine

telex

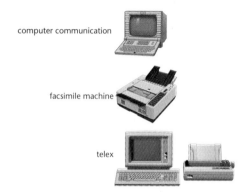

cellular telephone

telephone set

417

TELECOMMUNICATION SATELLITES

EXAMPLES OF SATELLITES

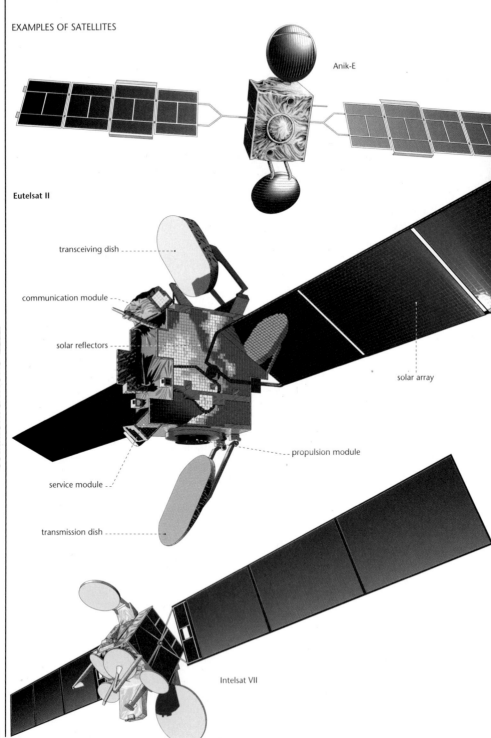

Anik-E

Eutelsat II

transceiving dish

communication module

solar reflectors

solar array

propulsion module

service module

transmission dish

Intelsat VII

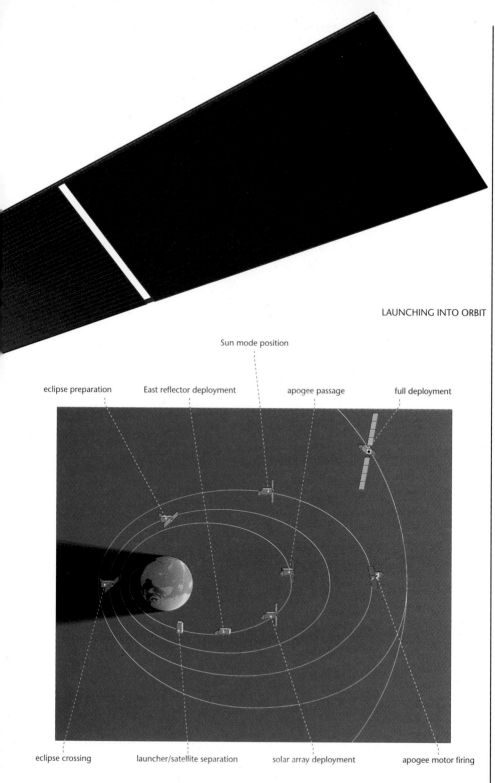

Sun mode position

eclipse preparation

East reflector deployment

apogee passage

full deployment

eclipse crossing

launcher/satellite separation

solar array deployment

apogee motor firing

TELEPHONE ANSWERING
MACHINE

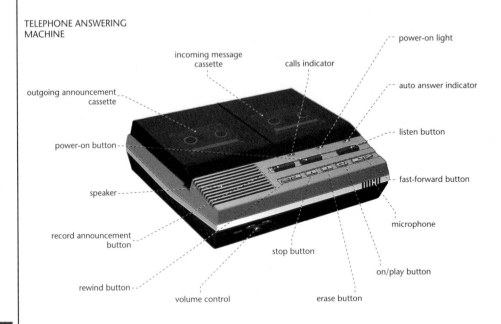

outgoing announcement cassette

incoming message cassette

calls indicator

power-on light

auto answer indicator

power-on button

listen button

speaker

fast-forward button

record announcement button

microphone

rewind button

stop button

on/play button

volume control

erase button

TELEPHONE SET

receiver

display

handset

on/off light

receiver volume control

transmitter

display setting

handset cord

ringing volume control

push buttons

telephone index

automatic dialer index

memory button

function selectors

terminal

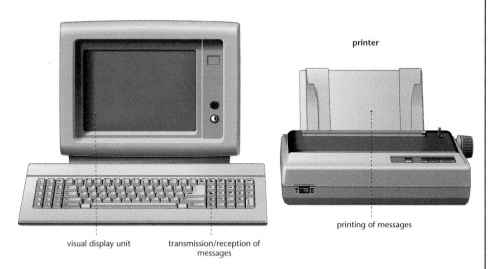

printer

visual display unit   transmission/reception of messages

printing of messages

FACSIMILE MACHINE

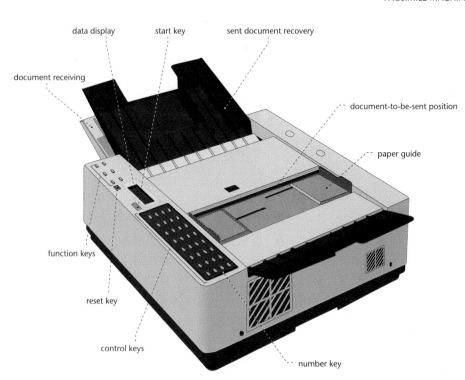

document receiving

data display   start key   sent document recovery

document-to-be-sent position

paper guide

function keys

reset key

control keys

number key

421

TYPES OF TELEPHONES

cordless telephone

telecommunication terminal

housing

visual display unit

function keys

numeric keyboard

operation keys

alphanumeric keyboard

keyboard

call director telephone

portable cellular telephone

pay phone

coin slot

volume control

display

handset

next call

armored cord

language display button

push buttons

card reader

push-button telephone

coin return bucket

CONTENTS

ROAD TRANSPORT

AUTOMOBILE 425

TRUCKING 440

MOTORCYCLE 442

SNOWMOBILE 445

BICYCLE 446

CARAVAN..449

ROAD SYSTEM 450

SERVICE STATION 453

FIXED BRIDGES 454

MOVABLE BRIDGES..457

RAIL TRANSPORT

HIGH-SPEED TRAIN 458

TYPES OF PASSENGER CARS 460

PASSENGER STATION 462

RAILROAD STATION..464

YARD..465

RAILROAD TRACK...466

DIESEL-ELECTRIC LOCOMOTIVE 468

CAR..470

TYPES OF FREIGHT CARS 472

SUBWAY TRANSPORT

SUBWAY...474

MARITIME TRANSPORT

FOUR-MASTED BARK...478

TYPES OF SAILS 482

TYPES OF RIGS 482

ANCHOR...483

NAVIGATION DEVICES 484

MARITIME SIGNALS 486

MARITIME BUOYAGE SYSTEM 488

HARBOR..490

CANAL LOCK 492

HOVERCRAFT 492

FERRY 494

CONTAINER SHIP 494

HYDROFOIL BOAT..495

PASSENGER LINER..496

AIR TRANSPORT

LONG-RANGE JET 498

TYPES OF TAIL SHAPES 498

TYPES OF WING SHAPES 499

FLIGHT DECK 500

TURBOFAN ENGINE 501

AIRPORT..502

HELICOPTER...508

SPACE TRANSPORT

ROCKET 509

SPACE SHUTTLE 510

SPACESUIT...512

TRANSPORT

AUTOMOBILE

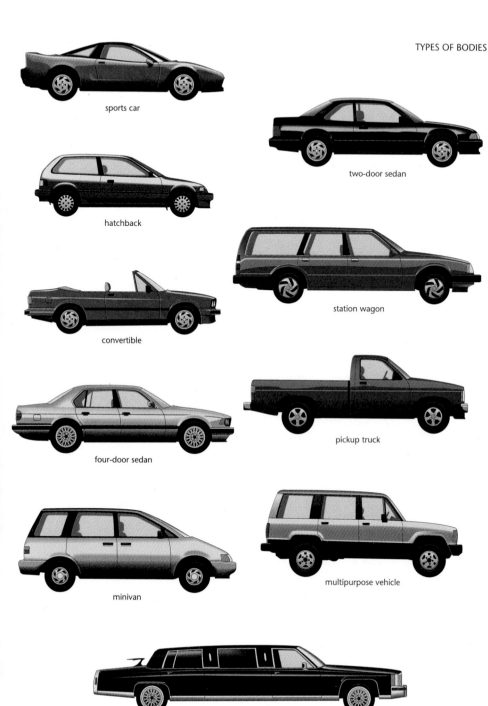

sports car

two-door sedan

hatchback

station wagon

convertible

four-door sedan

pickup truck

minivan

multipurpose vehicle

limousine

BODY

windshield

windshield wiper

cowl

outside mirror

washer nozzle

hood

headlight

grille

bumper

shield

fender

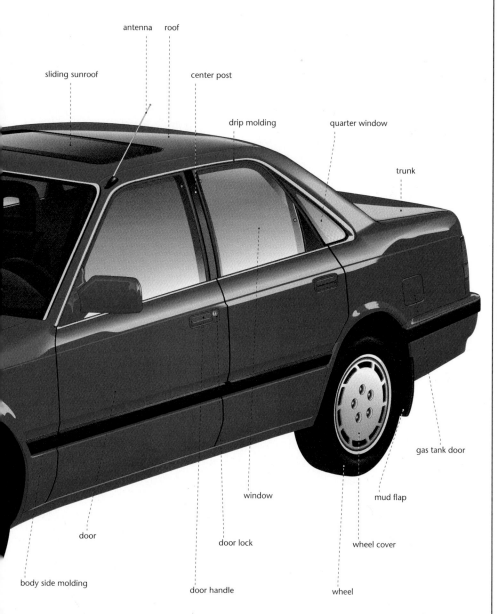

antenna   roof

sliding sunroof

center post

drip molding

quarter window

trunk

gas tank door

window

mud flap

door

door lock

wheel cover

body side molding

door handle

wheel

ROAD TRANSPORT

BUCKET SEAT

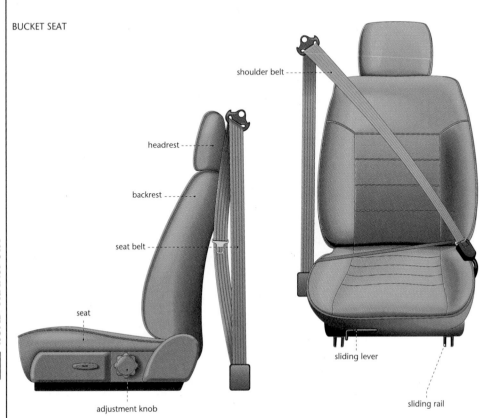

shoulder belt

headrest

backrest

seat belt

seat

adjustment knob

sliding lever

sliding rail

REAR SEAT

armrest

webbing

buckle

bench seat

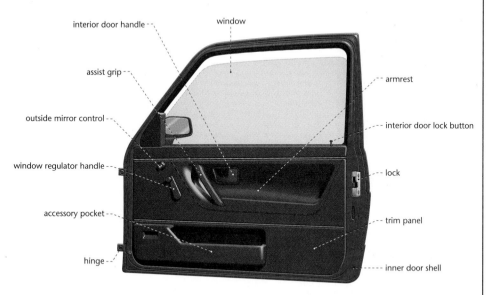

interior door handle

window

assist grip

armrest

outside mirror control

interior door lock button

window regulator handle

lock

accessory pocket

trim panel

hinge

inner door shell

headlights

high beam

turn signal

low beam

side-marker light

fog light

taillights

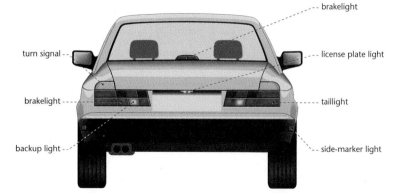

turn signal

brakelight

license plate light

brakelight

taillight

backup light

side-marker light

429

DASHBOARD

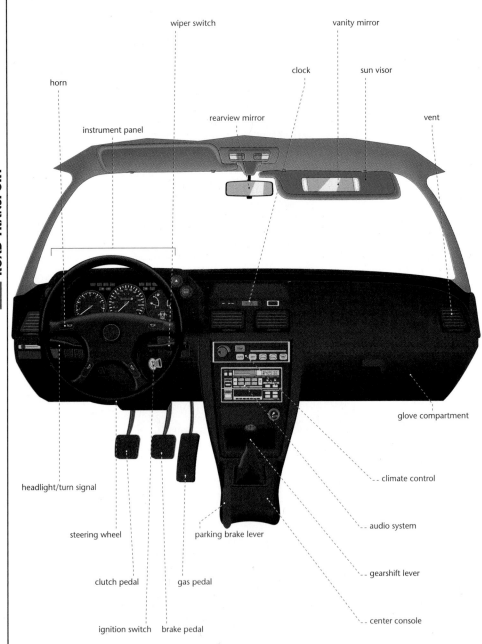

wiper switch

vanity mirror

clock

sun visor

horn

rearview mirror

vent

instrument panel

headlight/turn signal

glove compartment

climate control

audio system

steering wheel

parking brake lever

gearshift lever

clutch pedal

gas pedal

center console

ignition switch

brake pedal

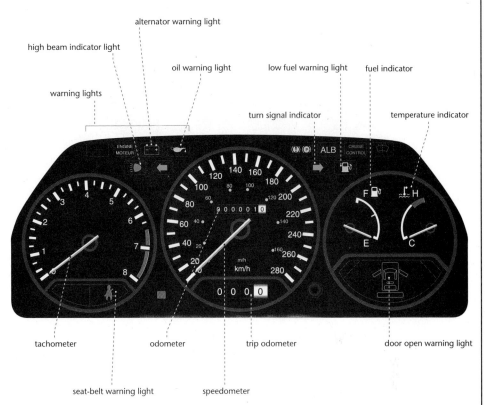

alternator warning light

high beam indicator light

oil warning light

low fuel warning light

fuel indicator

warning lights

turn signal indicator

temperature indicator

tachometer

odometer

trip odometer

door open warning light

seat-belt warning light

speedometer

WINDSHIELD WIPER

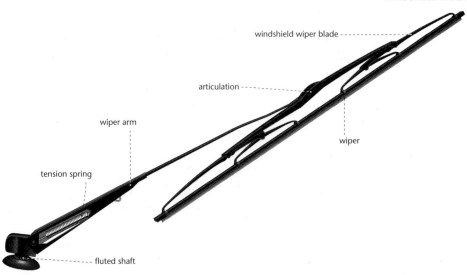

windshield wiper blade

articulation

wiper arm

wiper

tension spring

fluted shaft

431

ROAD TRANSPORT

DISK BRAKE

brake line

caliper

piston

brake pad

disk

DRUM BRAKE

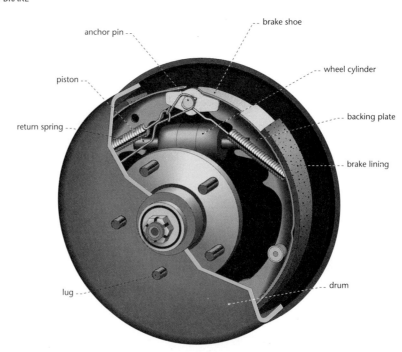

brake shoe

anchor pin

wheel cylinder

piston

backing plate

return spring

brake lining

lug

drum

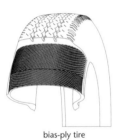

bias-ply tire

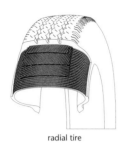

radial tire

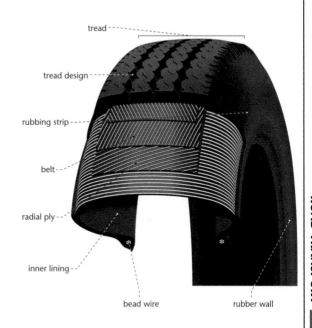

STEEL BELTED RADIAL TIRE

tread

tread design

rubbing strip

belt

radial ply

inner lining

bead wire

rubber wall

TIRE

tread design

rubbing strip

technical specifications

bead

rubber wall

WHEEL

disk

rim

rim flange

GASOLINE ENGINE

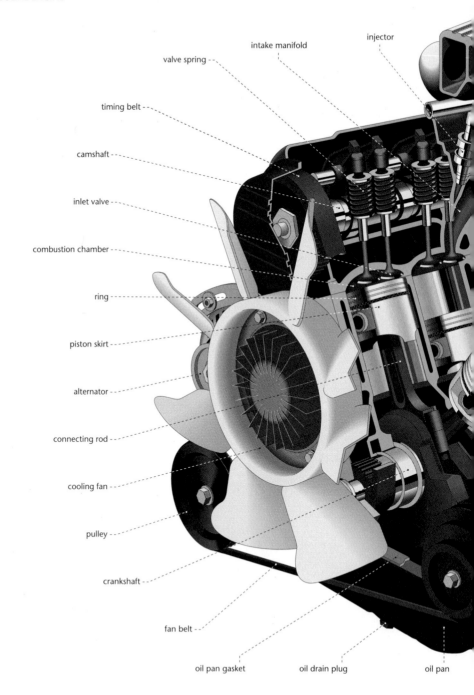

valve spring

intake manifold

injector

timing belt

camshaft

inlet valve

combustion chamber

ring

piston skirt

alternator

connecting rod

cooling fan

pulley

crankshaft

fan belt

oil pan gasket

oil drain plug

oil pan

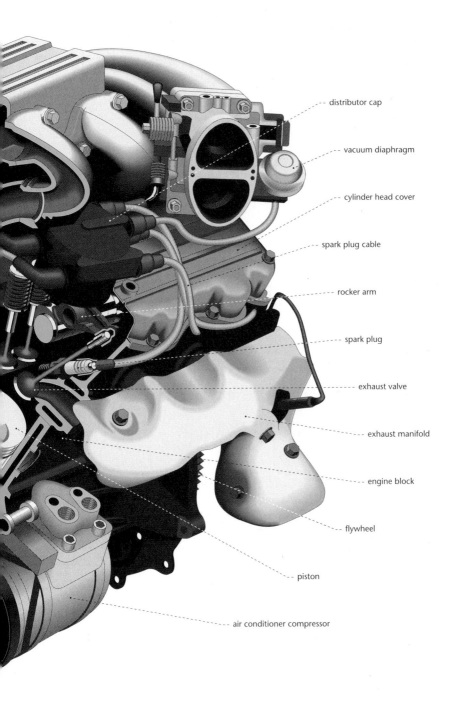

distributor cap

vacuum diaphragm

cylinder head cover

spark plug cable

rocker arm

spark plug

exhaust valve

exhaust manifold

engine block

flywheel

piston

air conditioner compressor

TYPES OF ENGINES

FOUR-STROKE-CYCLE ENGINE

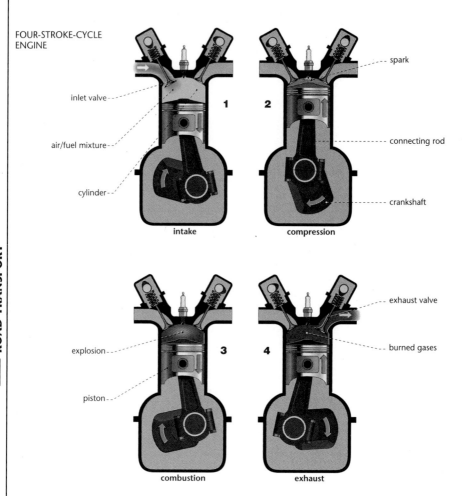

inlet valve

air/fuel mixture

cylinder

spark

connecting rod

crankshaft

1 intake

2 compression

explosion

piston

exhaust valve

burned gases

3 combustion

4 exhaust

TWO-STROKE-CYCLE ENGINE

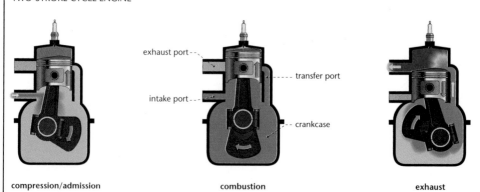

exhaust port

transfer port

intake port

crankcase

compression/admission

combustion

exhaust

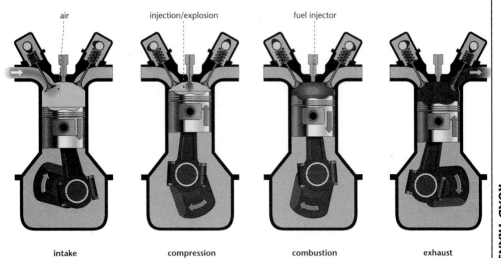

air injection/explosion fuel injector

intake   compression   combustion   exhaust

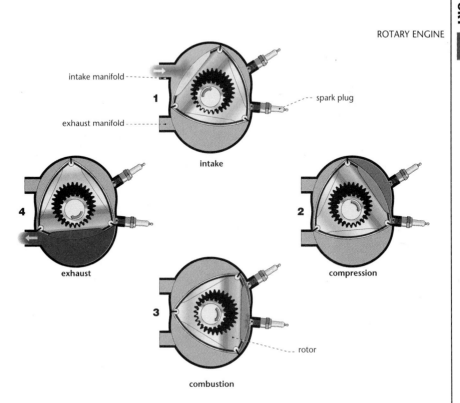

intake manifold

exhaust manifold

1

spark plug

intake

4

2

exhaust

compression

3

rotor

combustion

ROAD TRANSPORT

RADIATOR

filler cap

grille

cooling fan

fan thermostat

electric motor

radiator hose

TURBO-COMPRESSOR ENGINE

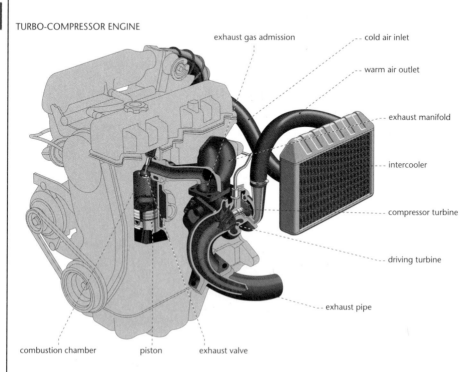

exhaust gas admission

cold air inlet

warm air outlet

exhaust manifold

intercooler

compressor turbine

driving turbine

exhaust pipe

combustion chamber

piston

exhaust valve

438

SPARK PLUG

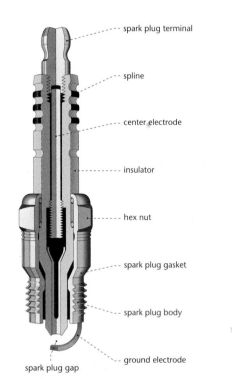

spark plug terminal

spline

center electrode

insulator

hex nut

spark plug gasket

spark plug body

ground electrode

spark plug gap

EXHAUST SYSTEM

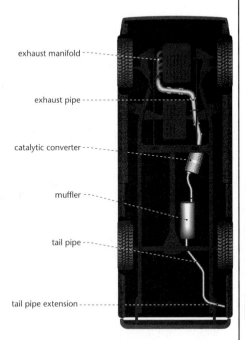

exhaust manifold

exhaust pipe

catalytic converter

muffler

tail pipe

tail pipe extension

BATTERY

positive terminal

battery cover

negative terminal

liquid/gas separator

hydrometer

positive plate strap

battery case

negative plate strap

positive plate

negative plate

plate grid

separator

TRUCK TRACTOR

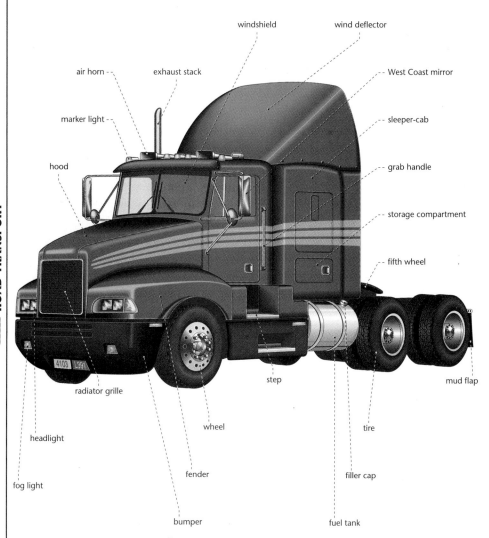

windshield

wind deflector

air horn

exhaust stack

West Coast mirror

marker light

sleeper-cab

hood

grab handle

storage compartment

fifth wheel

mud flap

step

radiator grille

tire

wheel

headlight

filler cap

fender

fog light

bumper

fuel tank

TANDEM TRACTOR TRAILER

truck tractor

semitrailer

truck trailer

SEMITRAILER

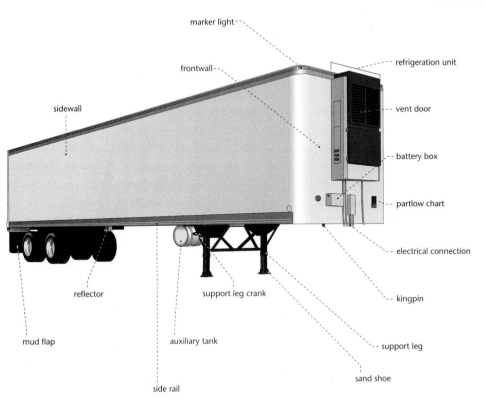

marker light

refrigeration unit

frontwall

vent door

sidewall

battery box

partlow chart

electrical connection

reflector

support leg crank

kingpin

mud flap

auxiliary tank

support leg

sand shoe

side rail

FLATBED

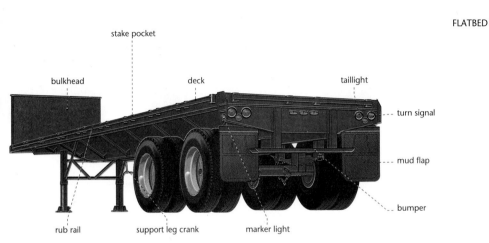

stake pocket

bulkhead

deck

taillight

turn signal

mud flap

bumper

rub rail

support leg crank

marker light

441

SIDE VIEW

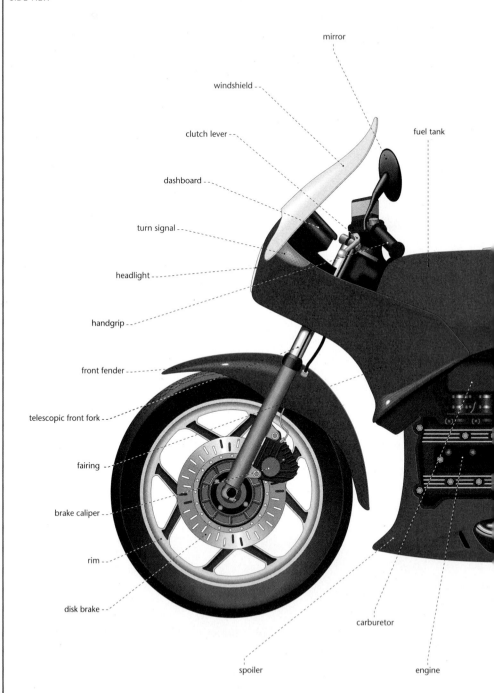

mirror

windshield

clutch lever

fuel tank

dashboard

turn signal

headlight

handgrip

front fender

telescopic front fork

fairing

brake caliper

rim

disk brake

carburetor

spoiler

engine

bubble

visor

air inlet

chin protector

visor hinge

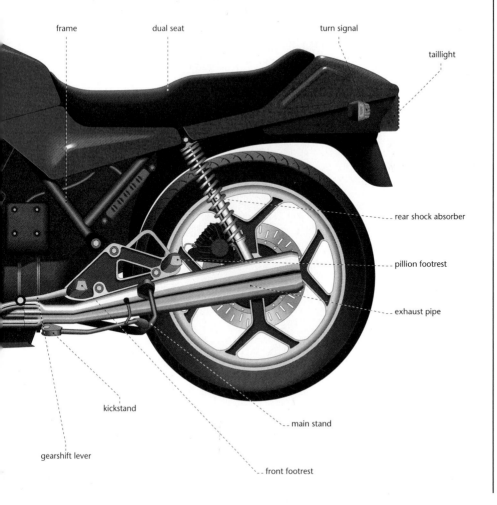

frame

dual seat

turn signal

taillight

rear shock absorber

pillion footrest

exhaust pipe

kickstand

main stand

gearshift lever

front footrest

VIEW FROM ABOVE

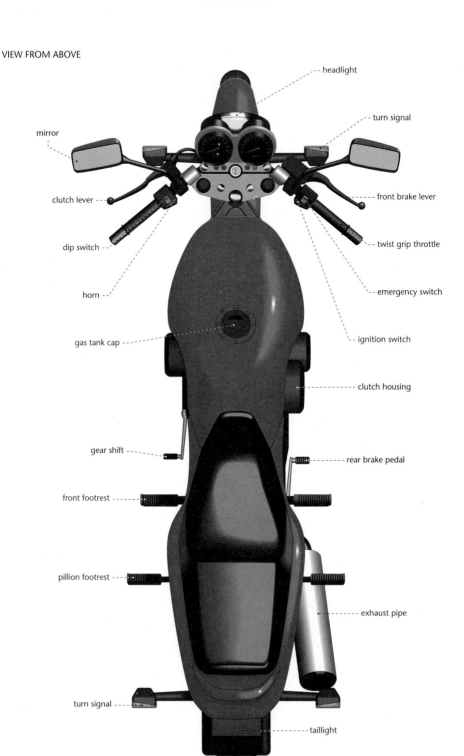

headlight

turn signal

mirror

clutch lever

front brake lever

dip switch

twist grip throttle

horn

emergency switch

gas tank cap

ignition switch

clutch housing

gear shift

rear brake pedal

front footrest

pillion footrest

exhaust pipe

turn signal

taillight

MOTORCYCLE DASHBOARD

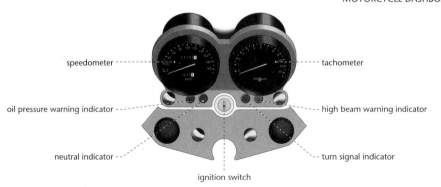

speedometer

tachometer

oil pressure warning indicator

high beam warning indicator

neutral indicator

turn signal indicator

ignition switch

SNOWMOBILE

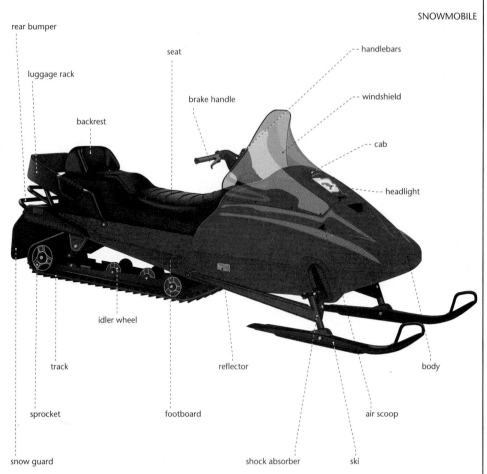

rear bumper

seat

handlebars

luggage rack

brake handle

windshield

backrest

cab

headlight

idler wheel

track

reflector

body

sprocket

footboard

air scoop

snow guard

shock absorber

ski

445

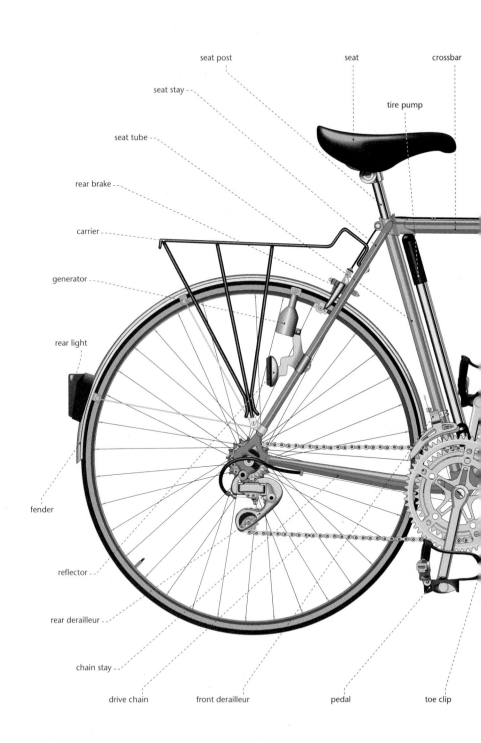

seat post

seat

crossbar

seat stay

tire pump

seat tube

rear brake

carrier

generator

rear light

fender

reflector

rear derailleur

chain stay

drive chain

front derailleur

pedal

toe clip

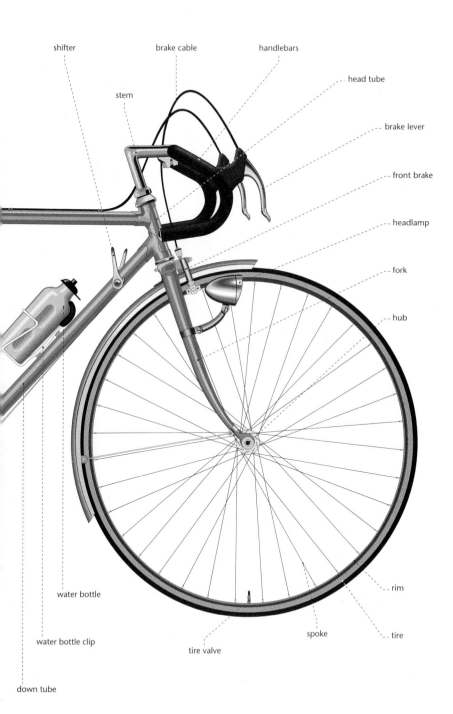

shifter

brake cable

handlebars

stem

head tube

brake lever

front brake

headlamp

fork

hub

water bottle

water bottle clip

down tube

tire valve

spoke

rim

tire

BICYCLE

POWER TRAIN

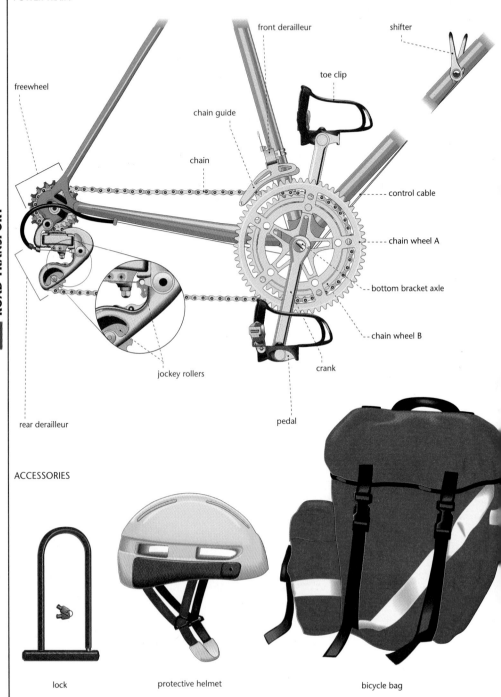

front derailleur

shifter

toe clip

freewheel

chain guide

chain

control cable

chain wheel A

bottom bracket axle

chain wheel B

jockey rollers

crank

rear derailleur

pedal

ACCESSORIES

lock

protective helmet

bicycle bag

CARAVAN

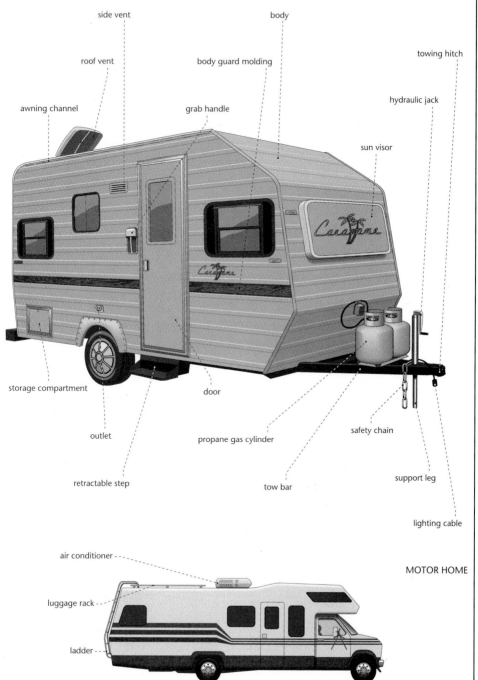

side vent

body

roof vent

body guard molding

towing hitch

awning channel

grab handle

hydraulic jack

sun visor

storage compartment

door

outlet

propane gas cylinder

safety chain

retractable step

tow bar

support leg

lighting cable

air conditioner

MOTOR HOME

luggage rack

ladder

CROSS SECTION OF A ROAD

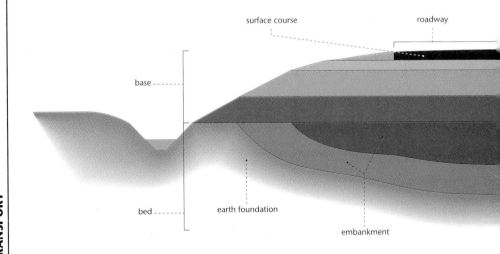

surface course

roadway

base

bed

earth foundation

embankment

MAJOR TYPES OF INTERCHANGES

cloverleaf

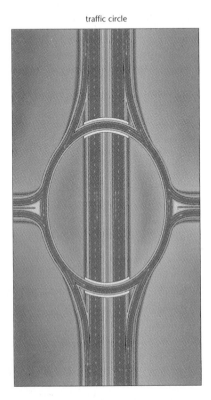

traffic circle

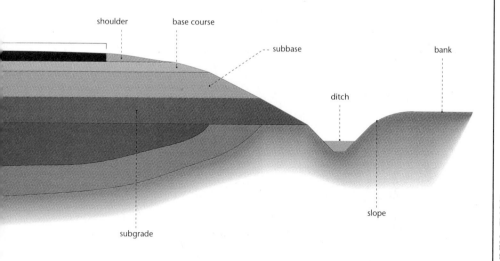

shoulder

base course

subbase

bank

ditch

subgrade

slope

diamond interchange

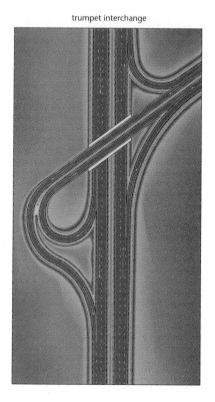

trumpet interchange

CLOVERLEAF

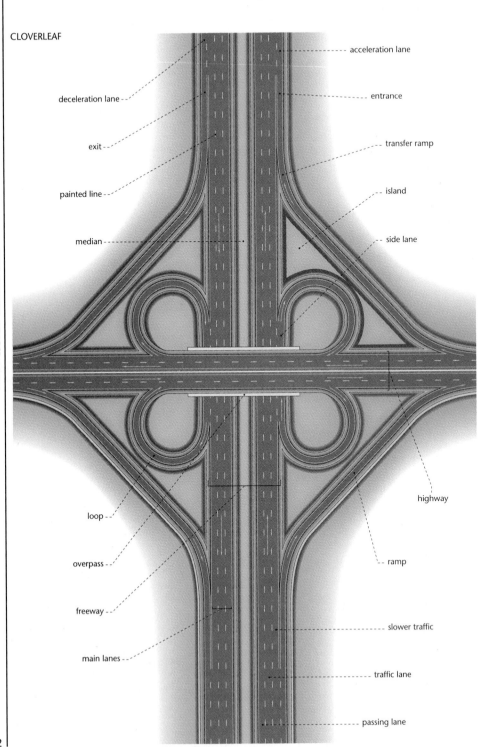

acceleration lane

deceleration lane

entrance

exit

transfer ramp

painted line

island

median

side lane

loop

highway

overpass

freeway

ramp

main lanes

slower traffic

traffic lane

passing lane

GASOLINE PUMP

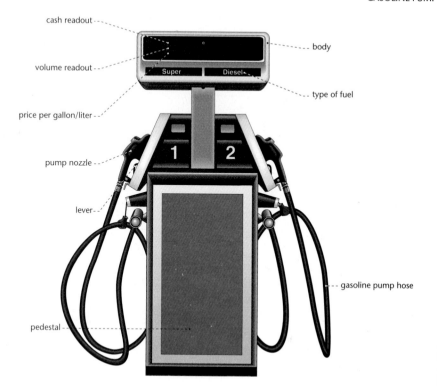

cash readout

volume readout

price per gallon/liter

pump nozzle

lever

pedestal

body

type of fuel

gasoline pump hose

Super   Diesel

1   2

SERVICE STATION

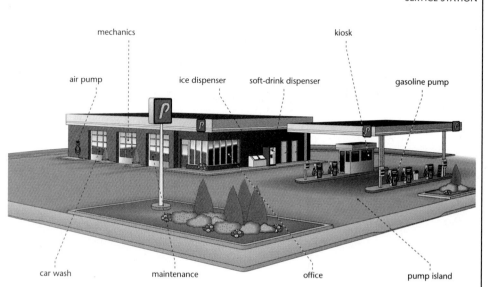

mechanics

kiosk

air pump

ice dispenser

soft-drink dispenser

gasoline pump

car wash

maintenance

office

pump island

FIXED BRIDGES

BEAM BRIDGE

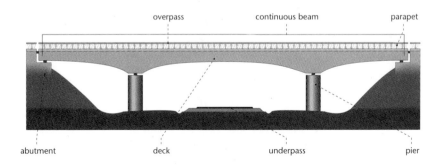

overpass   continuous beam   parapet

abutment   deck   underpass   pier

ROAD TRANSPORT

TYPES OF BEAM BRIDGES

multiple-span beam bridge

simple-span beam bridge

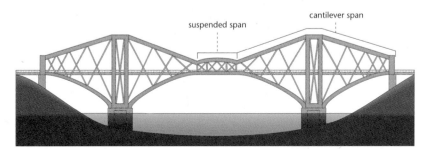

suspended span   cantilever span

cantilever bridge

viaduct

454

ARCH BRIDGE

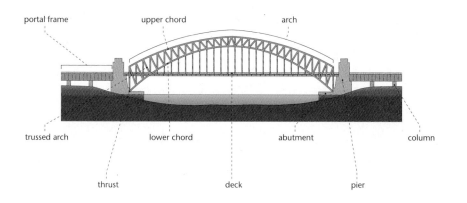

portal frame

upper chord

arch

trussed arch

lower chord

abutment

column

thrust

deck

pier

TYPES OF ARCH BRIDGES

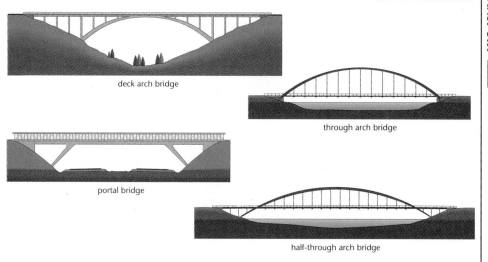

deck arch bridge

through arch bridge

portal bridge

half-through arch bridge

TYPES OF ARCHES

fixed arch

two-hinged arch

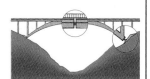

three-hinged arch

SUSPENSION BRIDGE

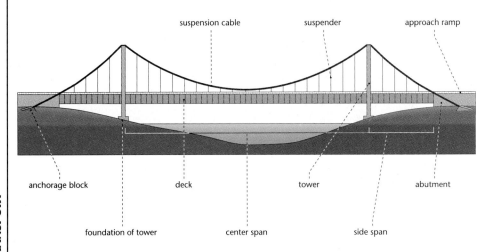

suspension cable

suspender

approach ramp

anchorage block

deck

tower

abutment

foundation of tower

center span

side span

CABLE-STAYED BRIDGES

fan cable stays

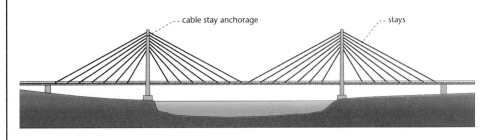

cable stay anchorage

stays

harp cable stays

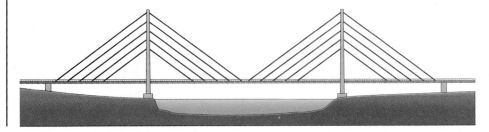

MOVABLE BRIDGES

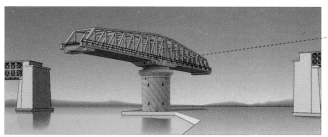

SWING BRIDGE — turntable

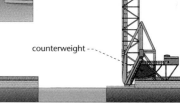

SINGLE-LEAF BASCULE BRIDGE — counterweight

FLOATING BRIDGE

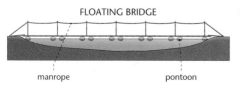

manrope — pontoon

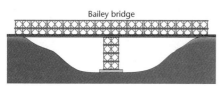

Bailey bridge

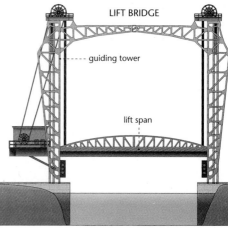

LIFT BRIDGE — guiding tower — lift span

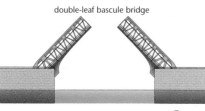

double-leaf bascule bridge

TRANSPORTER BRIDGE

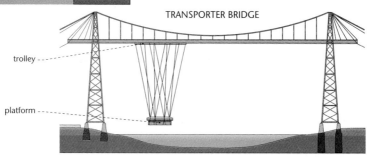

trolley — platform

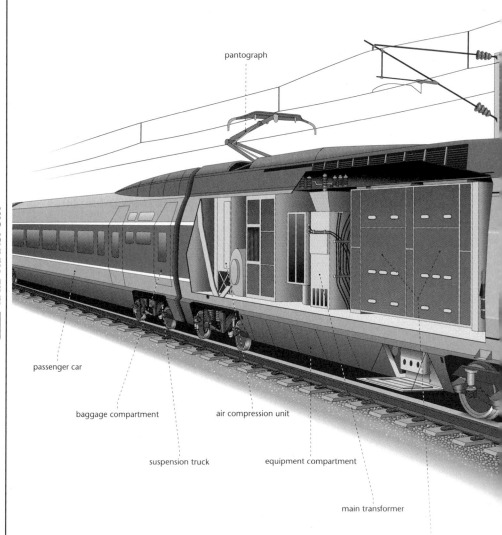

pantograph

passenger car

baggage compartment

air compression unit

suspension truck

equipment compartment

main transformer

motor unit

catenary

headlight

driver's cab

power car

headlight

position light

motor truck

pilot

coupling guide device

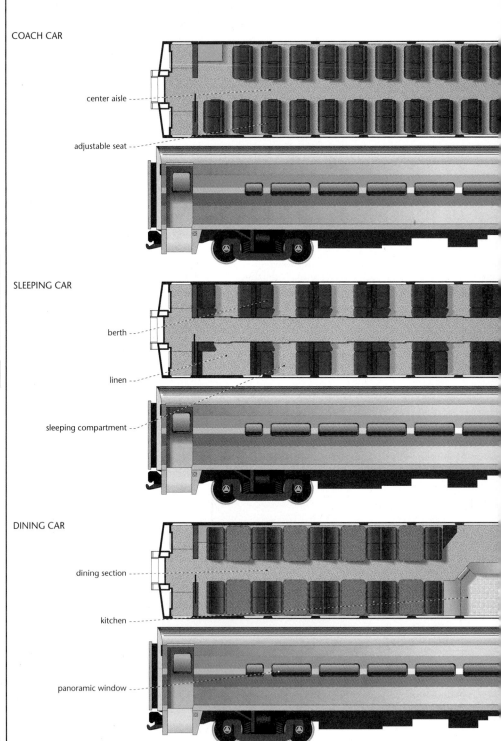

COACH CAR

center aisle

adjustable seat

SLEEPING CAR

berth

linen

sleeping compartment

DINING CAR

dining section

kitchen

panoramic window

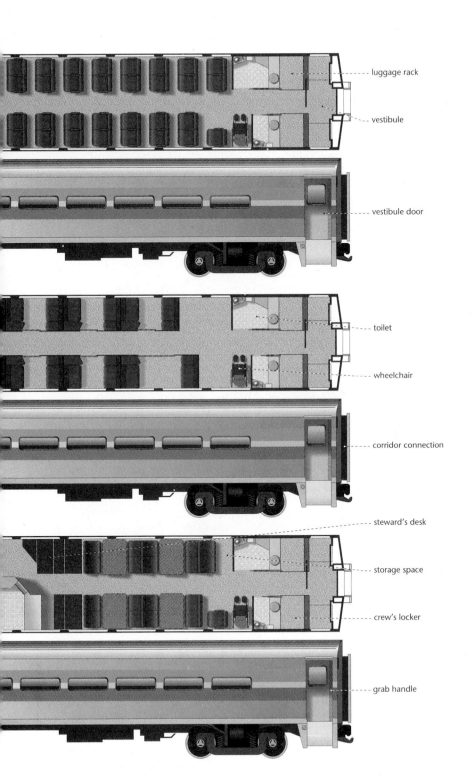

luggage rack

vestibule

vestibule door

toilet

wheelchair

corridor connection

steward's desk

storage space

crew's locker

grab handle

office

glassed roof

indicator board

parcels office

baggage room

passenger train

platform edge

passenger platform

gate

booking hall

platform number

metal structure   baggage cart

departure time indicator   ticket collector   baggage lockers

destination   platform entrance   track

schedules   ticket control

station platform

passenger station

suburban commuter railroad

parking

footbridge

commuter train

subsidiary track

platform shelter

main line

level crossing

semaphore

bumper

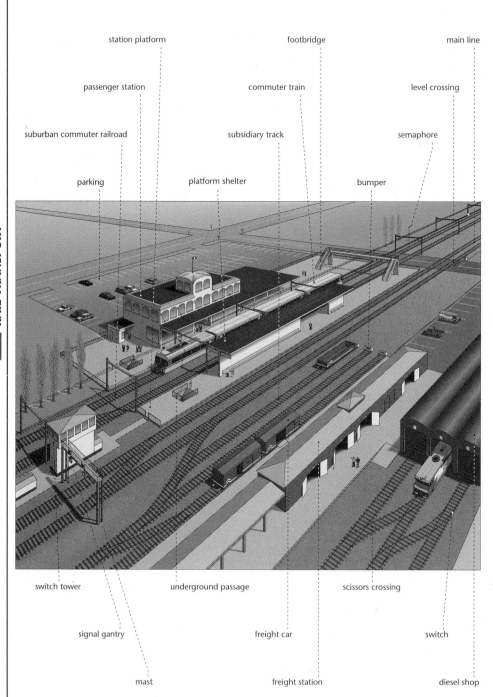

switch tower

signal gantry

mast

underground passage

freight car

freight station

scissors crossing

switch

diesel shop

YARD

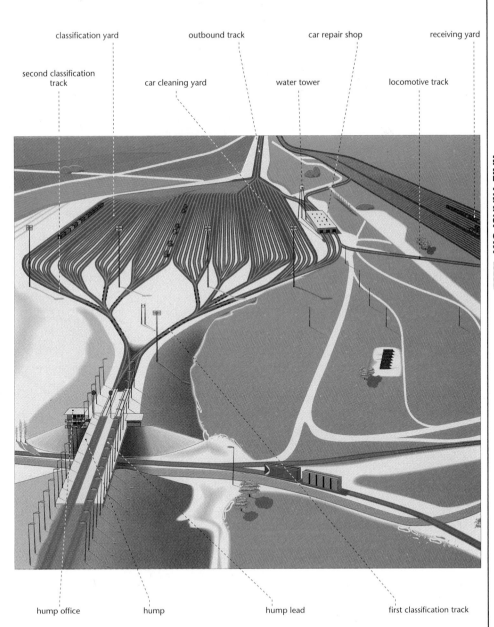

classification yard

outbound track

car repair shop

receiving yard

second classification track

car cleaning yard

water tower

locomotive track

hump office

hump

hump lead

first classification track

RAILROAD TRACK

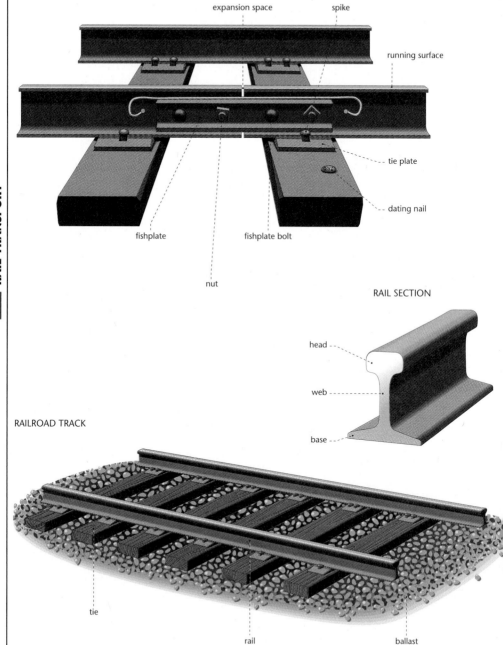

RAIL JOINT

expansion space

spike

running surface

tie plate

dating nail

fishplate

fishplate bolt

nut

RAIL SECTION

head

web

base

RAILROAD TRACK

tie

rail

ballast

REMOTE-CONTROLLED SWITCH

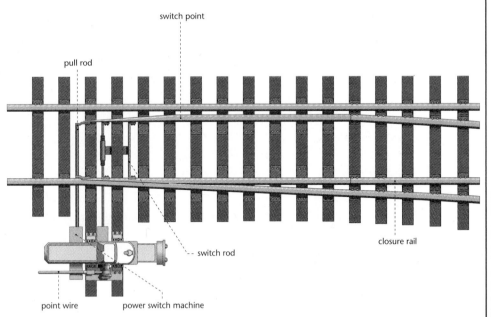

switch point

pull rod

closure rail

switch rod

point wire

power switch machine

MANUALLY-OPERATED SWITCH

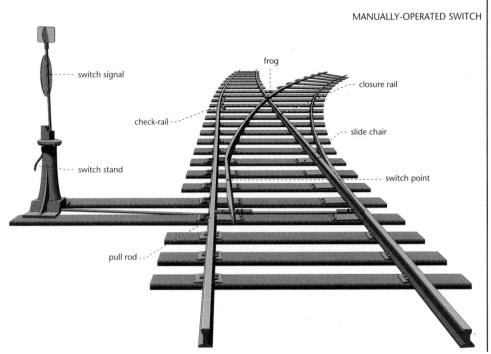

frog

switch signal

closure rail

check-rail

slide chair

switch stand

switch point

pull rod

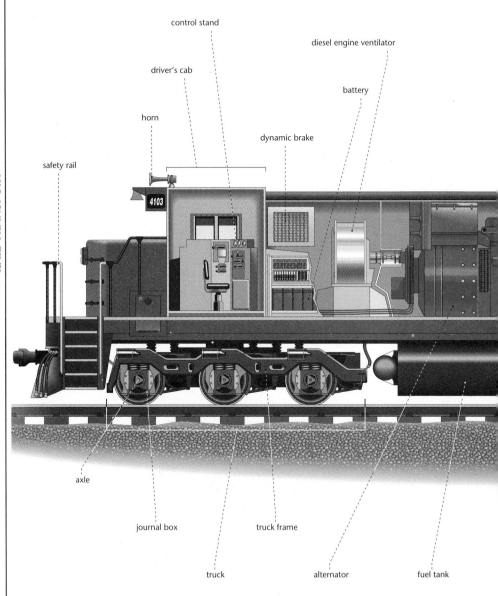

control stand

diesel engine ventilator

driver's cab

battery

horn

dynamic brake

safety rail

4103

axle

journal box

truck frame

truck

alternator

fuel tank

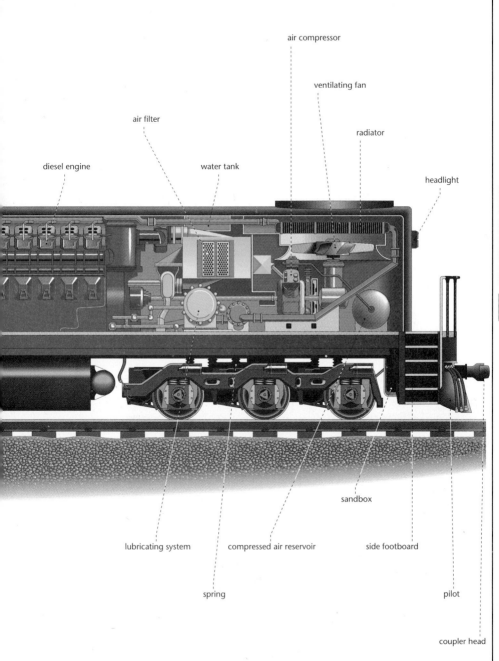

air compressor

ventilating fan

air filter

radiator

diesel engine

water tank

headlight

sandbox

lubricating system

compressed air reservoir

side footboard

spring

pilot

coupler head

BOX CAR

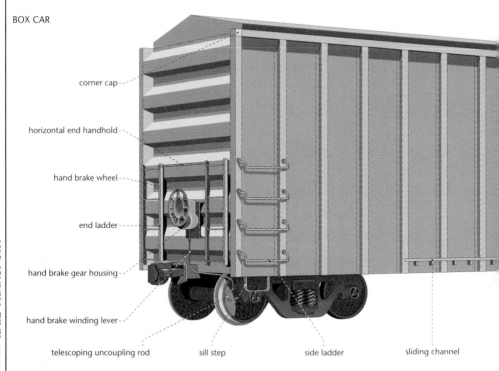

corner cap

horizontal end handhold

hand brake wheel

end ladder

hand brake gear housing

hand brake winding lever

telescoping uncoupling rod

sill step

side ladder

sliding channel

CONTAINER

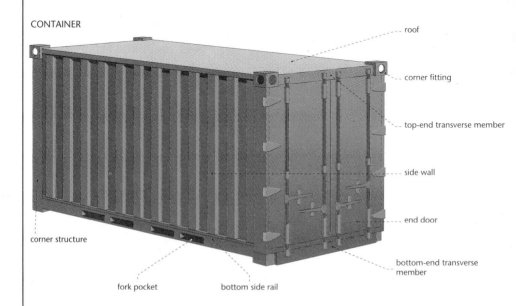

roof

corner fitting

top-end transverse member

side wall

end door

bottom-end transverse member

corner structure

fork pocket

bottom side rail

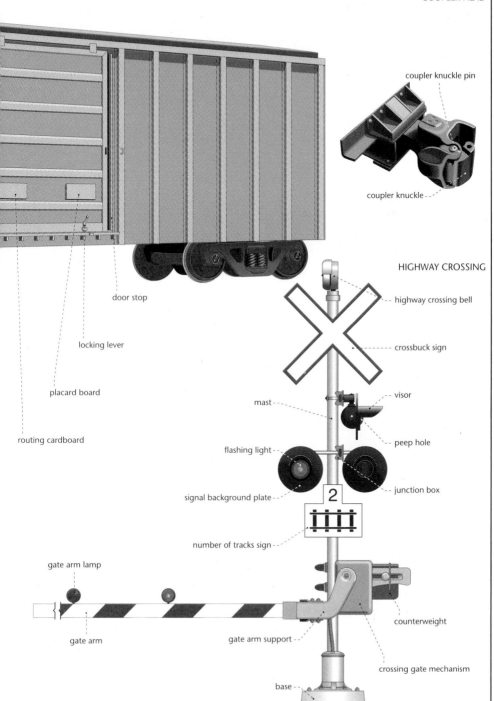

coupler knuckle pin

coupler knuckle

HIGHWAY CROSSING

highway crossing bell

crossbuck sign

door stop

visor

mast

locking lever

peep hole

flashing light

placard board

junction box

signal background plate

routing cardboard

number of tracks sign

gate arm lamp

gate arm

gate arm support

counterweight

crossing gate mechanism

base

TYPES OF FREIGHT CARS

box car

tank car

wood chip car

livestock car

hopper car

hard top gondola

hopper ore car

refrigerator car

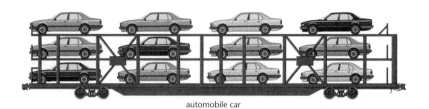

automobile car

container car

piggyback car

flat car

bulkhead flat car

gondola car

depressed-center flat car

caboose

SUBWAY STATION

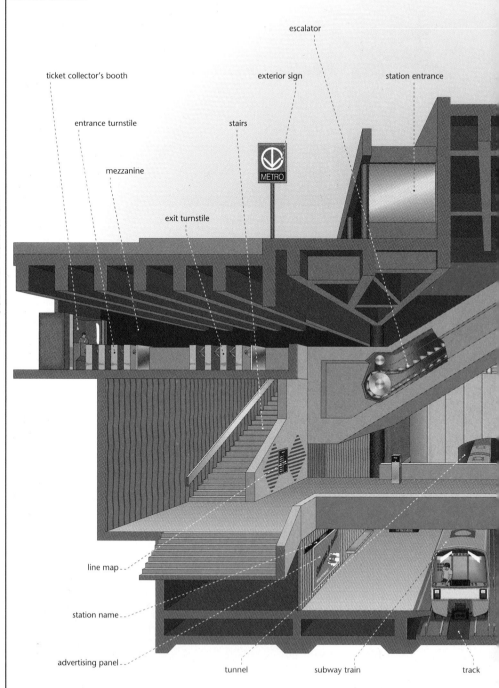

escalator

ticket collector's booth

exterior sign

station entrance

entrance turnstile

stairs

mezzanine

exit turnstile

METRO

line map

station name

advertising panel

tunnel

subway train

track

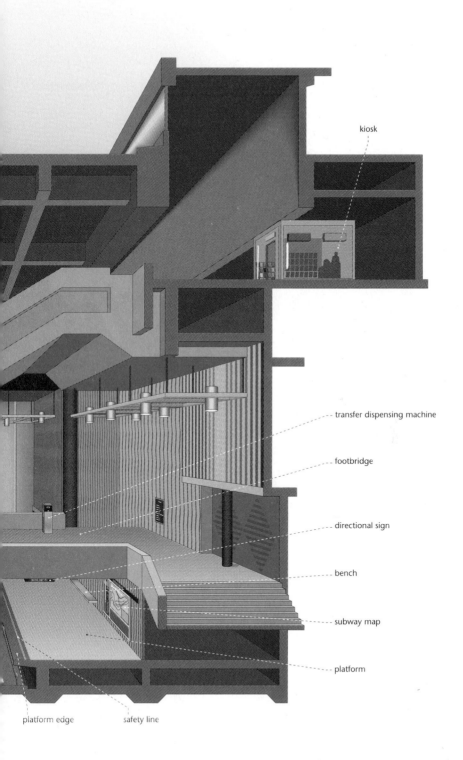

kiosk

transfer dispensing machine

footbridge

directional sign

bench

subway map

platform

platform edge   safety line

TRUCK AND TRACK

SUBWAY TRANSPORT

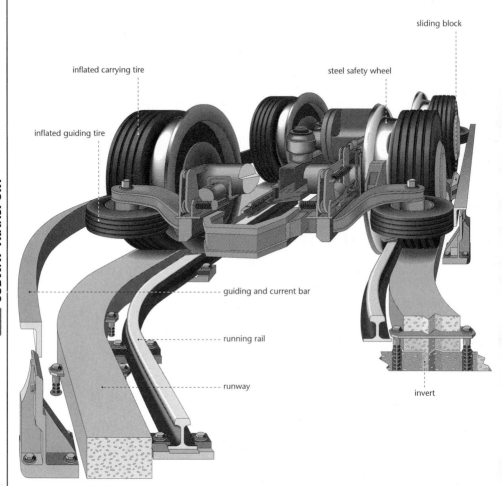

sliding block

inflated carrying tire

steel safety wheel

inflated guiding tire

guiding and current bar

running rail

runway

invert

SUBWAY TRAIN

motor car

passenger car

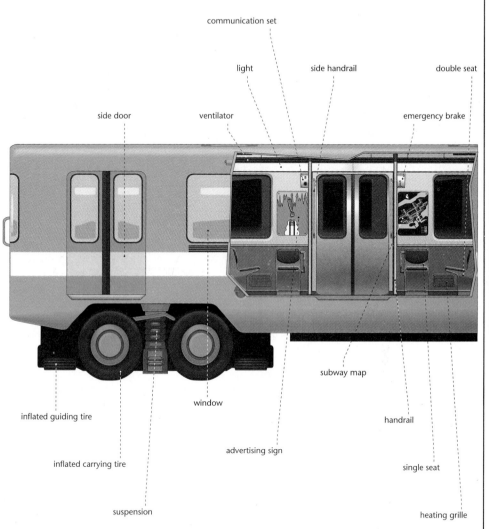

communication set

light

side handrail

double seat

side door

ventilator

emergency brake

inflated guiding tire

subway map

window

handrail

inflated carrying tire

advertising sign

single seat

suspension

heating grille

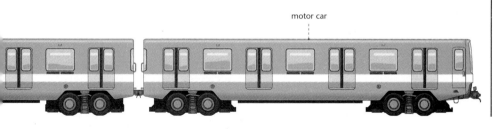

motor car

MASTING AND RIGGING

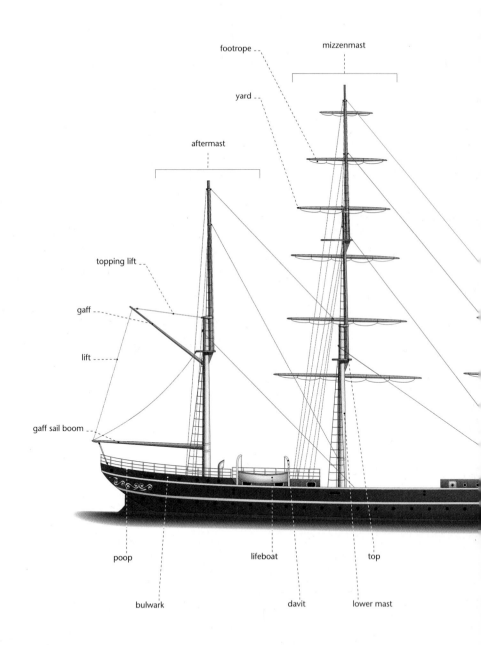

footrope

mizzenmast

yard

aftermast

topping lift

gaff

lift

gaff sail boom

poop

lifeboat

top

bulwark

davit

lower mast

mainmast

foremast

pole

fore-royal mast

fore-topgallant mast

masthead

fore-topmast

stay

staysail-stay

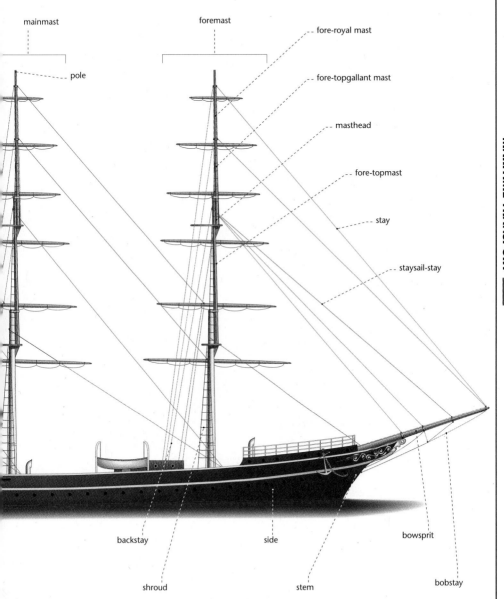

backstay

side

bowsprit

shroud

stem

bobstay

SAILS

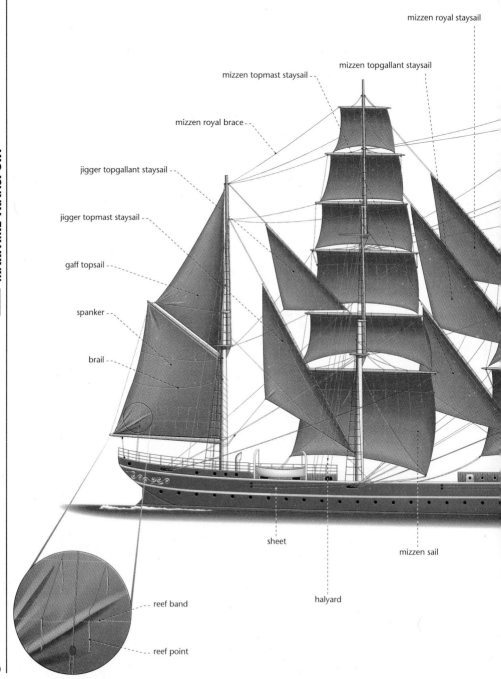

mizzen royal staysail

mizzen topgallant staysail

mizzen topmast staysail

mizzen royal brace

jigger topgallant staysail

jigger topmast staysail

gaff topsail

spanker

brail

sheet

mizzen sail

halyard

reef band

reef point

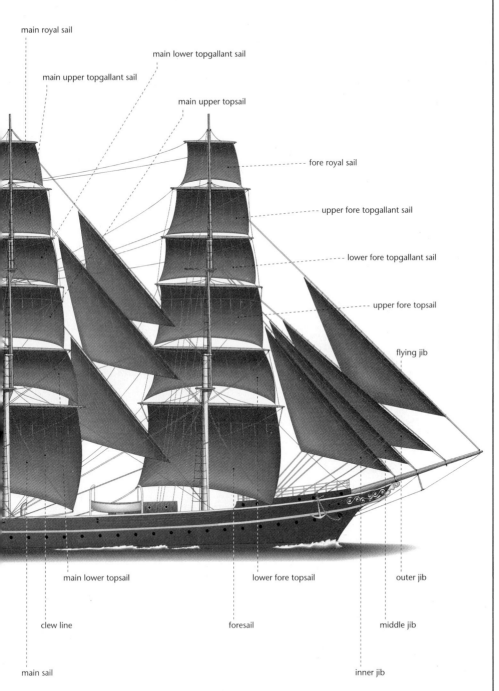

main royal sail

main lower topgallant sail

main upper topgallant sail

main upper topsail

fore royal sail

upper fore topgallant sail

lower fore topgallant sail

upper fore topsail

flying jib

main lower topsail

clew line

foresail

lower fore topsail

outer jib

middle jib

main sail

inner jib

TYPES OF SAILS

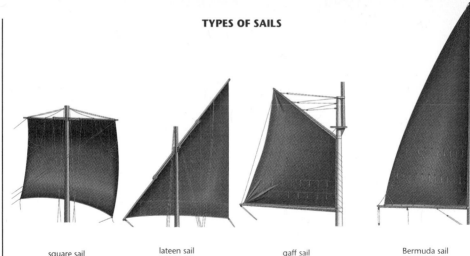

square sail   lateen sail   gaff sail   Bermuda sail

TYPES OF RIGS

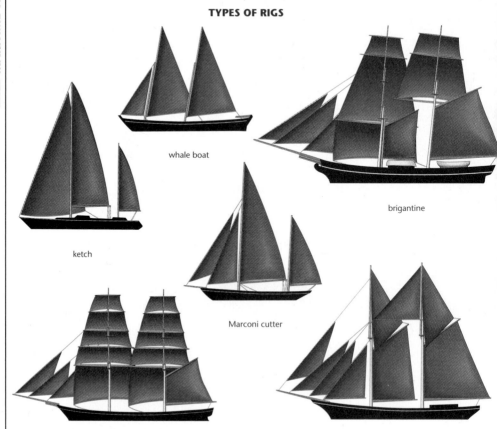

whale boat

ketch

brigantine

Marconi cutter

brig

schooner

ANCHOR

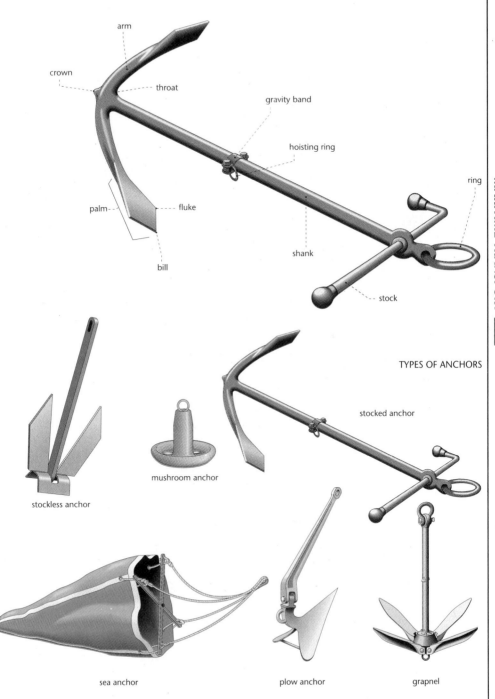

SHIP'S ANCHOR

arm

crown

throat

gravity band

hoisting ring

ring

palm

fluke

bill

shank

stock

TYPES OF ANCHORS

stocked anchor

stockless anchor

mushroom anchor

sea anchor

plow anchor

grapnel

483

SEXTANT

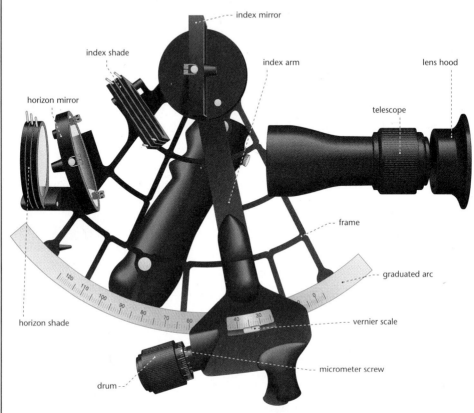

index mirror

index shade

index arm

lens hood

horizon mirror

telescope

frame

graduated arc

horizon shade

vernier scale

micrometer screw

drum

LIQUID COMPASS

sliding cover

glass dome

compass card

pivot

bowl

ECHO SOUNDER

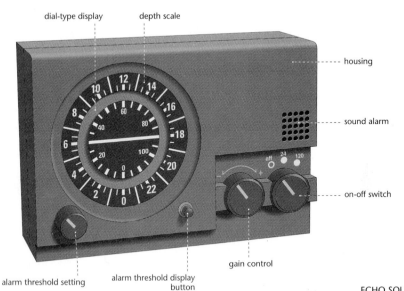

dial-type display

depth scale

housing

sound alarm

off 24 120

on-off switch

gain control

alarm threshold setting

alarm threshold display button

ECHO SOUNDER PROBE

transducer

transmission cable

plug

CROSS SECTION OF A LIQUID COMPASS

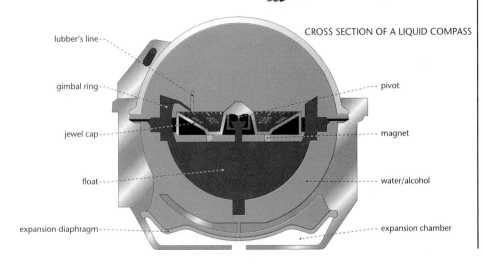

lubber's line

gimbal ring

pivot

jewel cap

magnet

float

water/alcohol

expansion diaphragm

expansion chamber

485

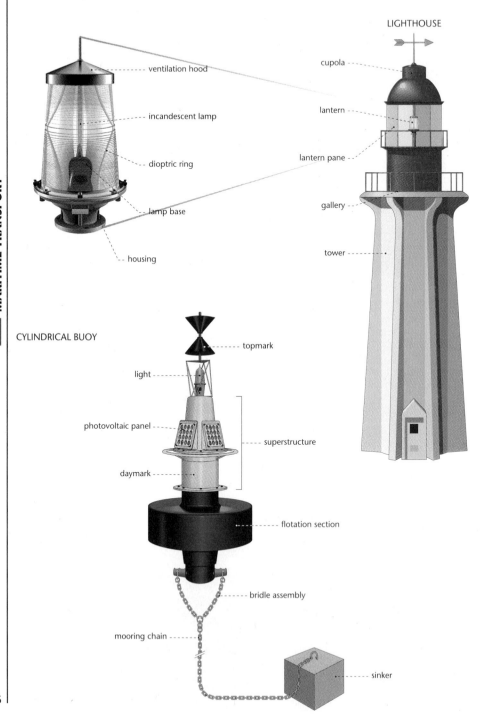

LIGHTHOUSE LANTERN

LIGHTHOUSE

ventilation hood

incandescent lamp

dioptric ring

lamp base

housing

cupola

lantern

lantern pane

gallery

tower

MARITIME TRANSPORT

CYLINDRICAL BUOY

topmark

light

photovoltaic panel

superstructure

daymark

flotation section

bridle assembly

mooring chain

sinker

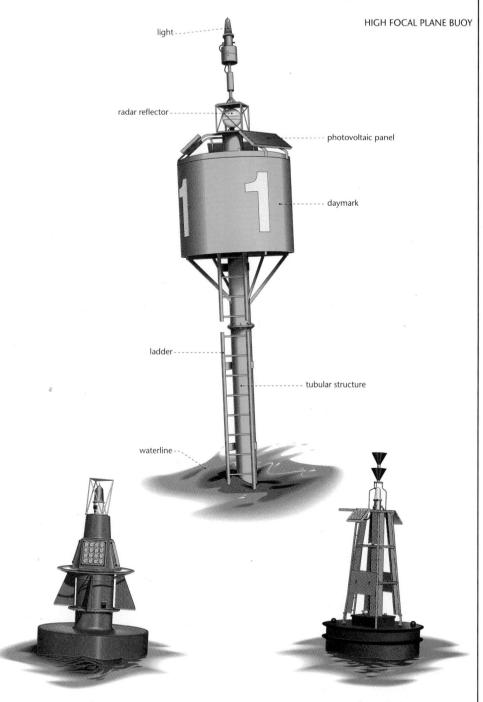

light

radar reflector

photovoltaic panel

daymark

ladder

tubular structure

waterline

conical buoy

pillar buoy

MARITIME BUOYAGE SYSTEM

CARDINAL MARKS

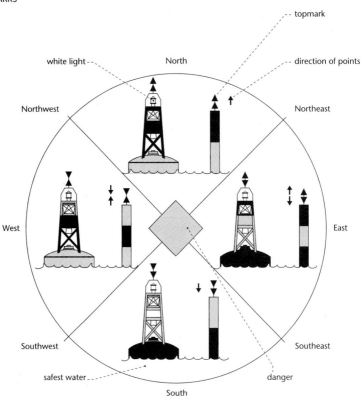

white light · · ·
topmark
direction of points
North
Northwest
Northeast
West
East
Southwest
Southeast
safest water
danger
South

BUOYAGE REGIONS

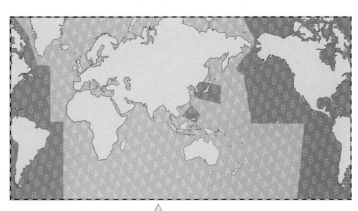

port hand   starboard hand

RHYTHM OF MARKS BY NIGHT

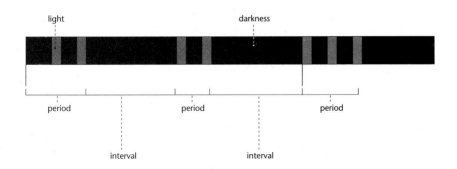

DAYMARKS (REGION B)

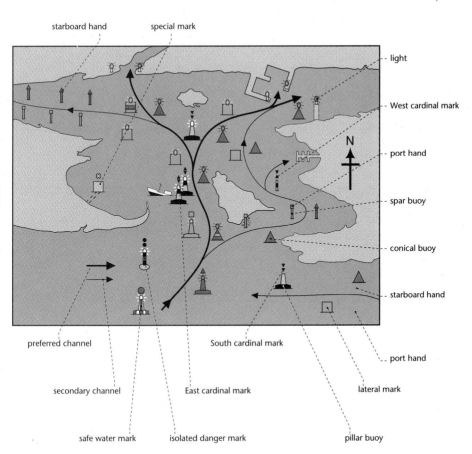

gate

transit shed

dry dock

quayside crane

quay

bulk terminal

canal lock

floating crane

container-loading bridge

silos

dock

quay ramp

grain terminal

container ship

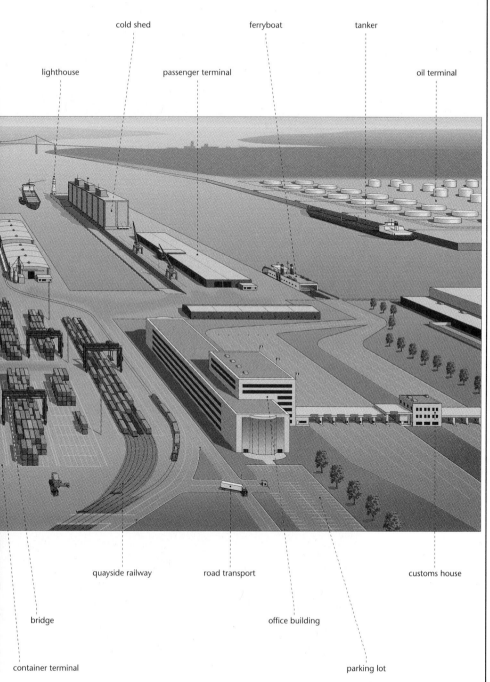

cold shed

ferryboat

tanker

lighthouse

passenger terminal

oil terminal

quayside railway

road transport

customs house

bridge

office building

container terminal

parking lot

CANAL LOCK

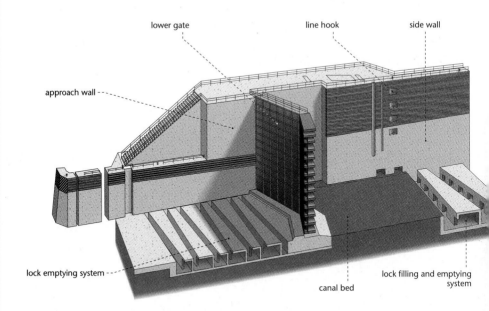

lower gate

line hook

side wall

approach wall

lock emptying system

lock filling and emptying system

canal bed

HOVERCRAFT

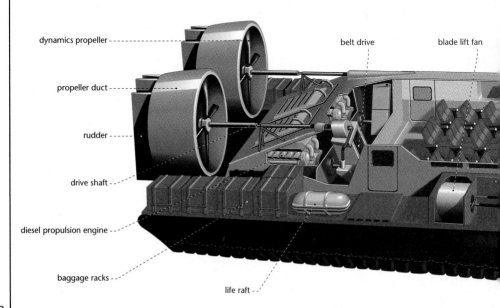

dynamics propeller

belt drive

blade lift fan

propeller duct

rudder

drive shaft

diesel propulsion engine

baggage racks

life raft

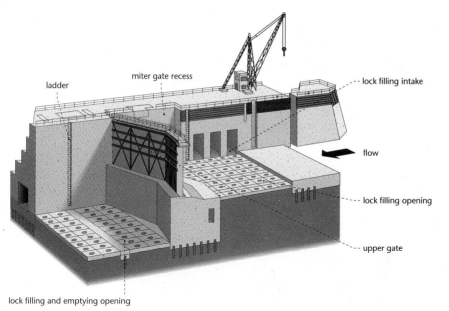

ladder

miter gate recess

lock filling intake

flow

lock filling opening

upper gate

lock filling and emptying opening

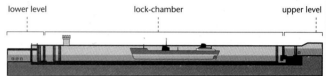

lower level

lock-chamber

upper level

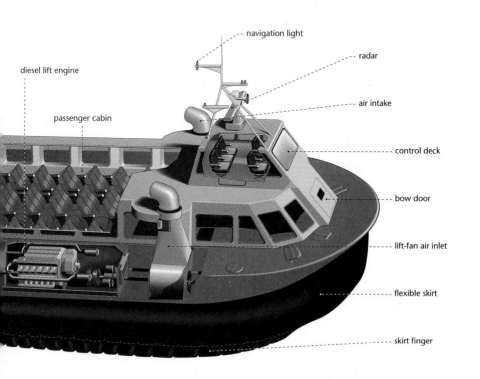

diesel lift engine

navigation light

radar

air intake

passenger cabin

control deck

bow door

lift-fan air inlet

flexible skirt

skirt finger

FERRY

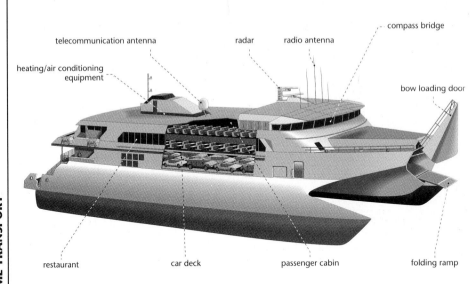

telecommunication antenna

heating/air conditioning equipment

radar

radio antenna

compass bridge

bow loading door

restaurant

car deck

passenger cabin

folding ramp

CONTAINER SHIP

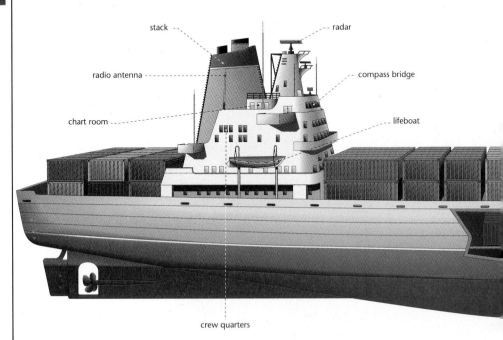

stack

radar

radio antenna

compass bridge

chart room

lifeboat

crew quarters

HYDROFOIL BOAT

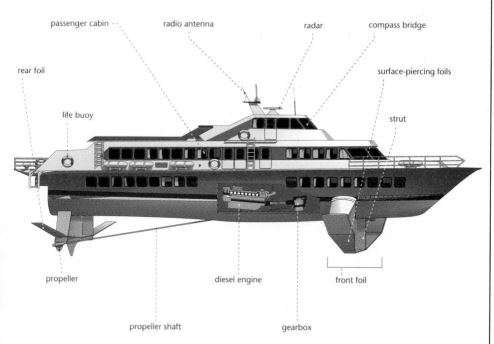

passenger cabin

radio antenna

radar

compass bridge

rear foil

surface-piercing foils

life buoy

strut

propeller

diesel engine

front foil

propeller shaft

gearbox

container

container hold

masthead light

forecastle

anchor-windlass room

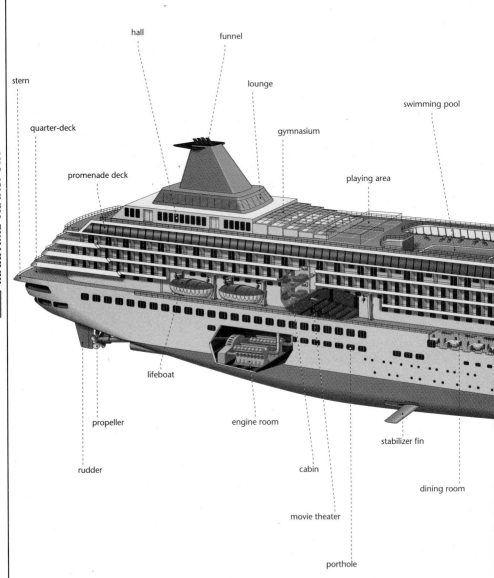

stern

quarter-deck

hall

funnel

lounge

swimming pool

gymnasium

promenade deck

playing area

lifeboat

propeller

engine room

rudder

cabin

stabilizer fin

dining room

movie theater

porthole

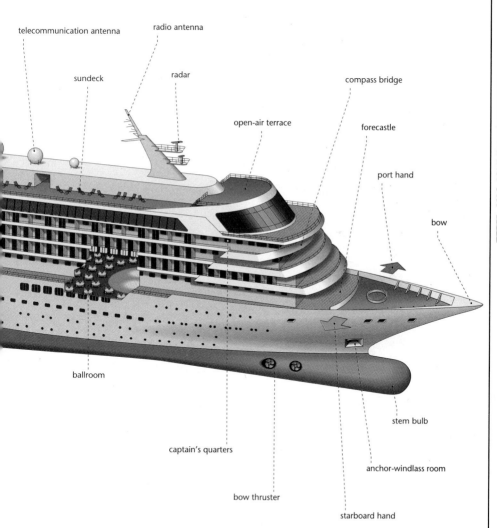

telecommunication antenna

radio antenna

sundeck

radar

compass bridge

open-air terrace

forecastle

port hand

bow

ballroom

captain's quarters

bow thruster

starboard hand

anchor-windlass room

stem bulb

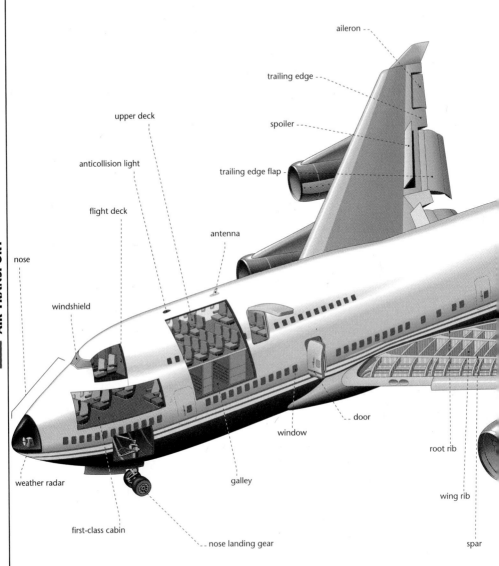

aileron

trailing edge

spoiler

trailing edge flap

upper deck

anticollision light

flight deck

antenna

nose

windshield

weather radar

first-class cabin

nose landing gear

galley

window

door

root rib

wing rib

spar

TYPES OF TAIL SHAPES

fuselage mounted tail unit

fin-mounted tail unit

triple tail unit

T-tail unit

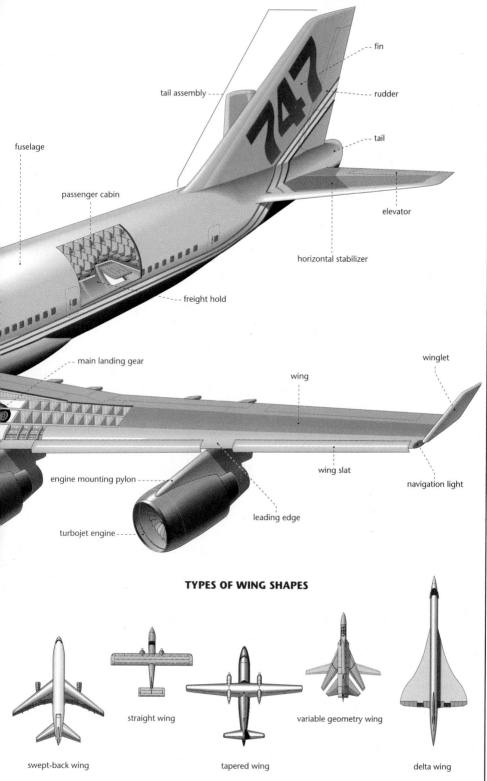

fin

tail assembly

rudder

fuselage

tail

passenger cabin

elevator

horizontal stabilizer

freight hold

main landing gear

winglet

wing

engine mounting pylon

wing slat

navigation light

leading edge

turbojet engine

TYPES OF WING SHAPES

straight wing

variable geometry wing

swept-back wing

tapered wing

delta wing

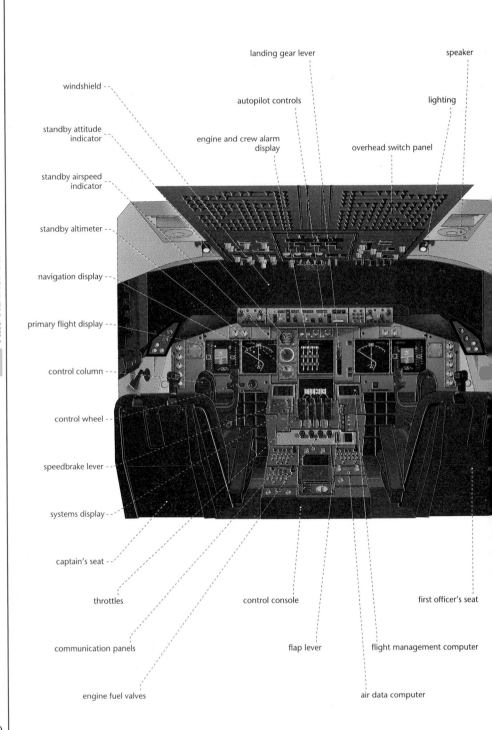

landing gear lever

speaker

windshield

autopilot controls

lighting

standby attitude
indicator

engine and crew alarm
display

overhead switch panel

standby airspeed
indicator

standby altimeter

navigation display

primary flight display

control column

control wheel

speedbrake lever

systems display

captain's seat

throttles

control console

first officer's seat

communication panels

flap lever

flight management computer

engine fuel valves

air data computer

TURBOFAN ENGINE

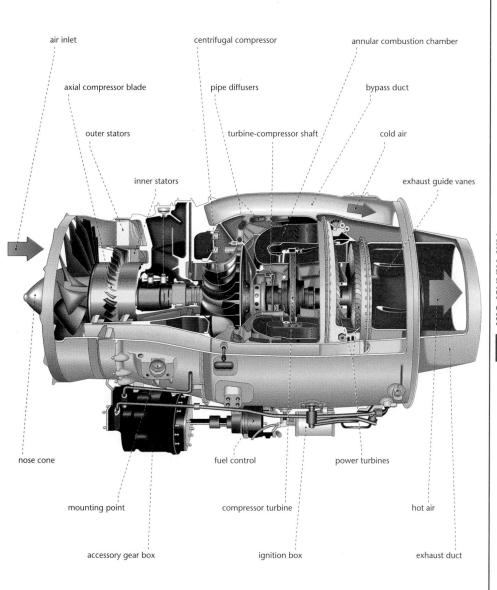

air inlet

centrifugal compressor

annular combustion chamber

axial compressor blade

pipe diffusers

bypass duct

outer stators

turbine-compressor shaft

cold air

inner stators

exhaust guide vanes

nose cone

fuel control

power turbines

mounting point

compressor turbine

hot air

accessory gear box

ignition box

exhaust duct

fan

compression

combustion

exhaust

control tower cab

access road

high-speed exit taxiway

control tower

taxiway

by-pass taxiway

apron

apron

taxiway

service road

maintenance hangar

passenger terminal

parking area

telescopic corridor

boarding walkway

radial passenger loading area

service area

taxiway line

AIR TRANSPORT

PASSENGER TERMINAL

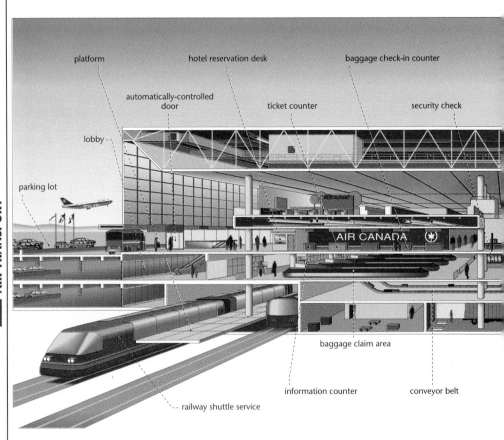

platform

automatically-controlled door

hotel reservation desk

ticket counter

baggage check-in counter

security check

lobby

parking lot

AIR CANADA

baggage claim area

information counter

conveyor belt

railway shuttle service

RUNWAY

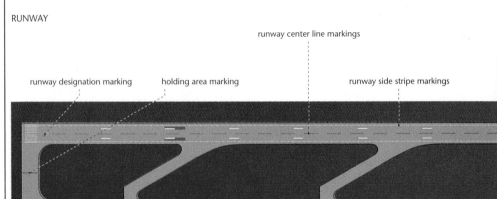

runway center line markings

runway designation marking

holding area marking

runway side stripe markings

504

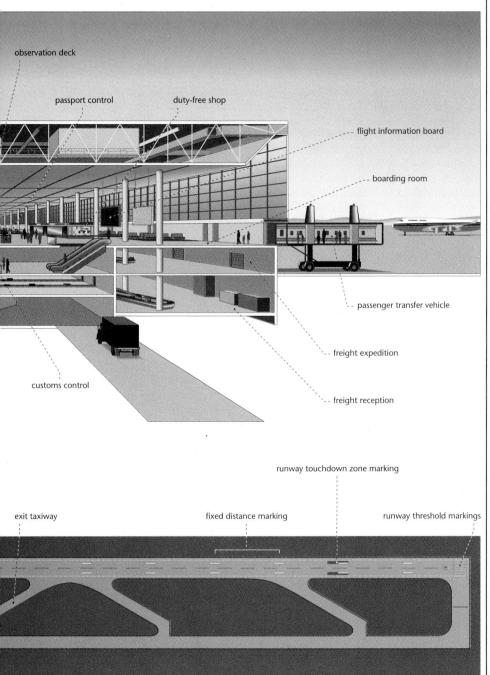

observation deck

passport control

duty-free shop

flight information board

boarding room

customs control

passenger transfer vehicle

freight expedition

freight reception

runway touchdown zone marking

exit taxiway

fixed distance marking

runway threshold markings

AIR TRANSPORT

GROUND AIRPORT EQUIPMENT

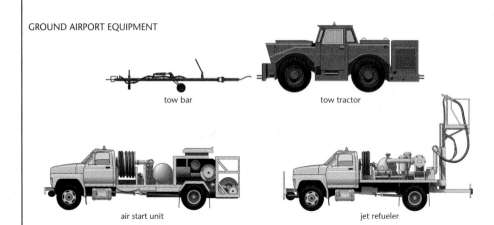

tow bar

tow tractor

air start unit

jet refueler

electrical power unit

ground air conditioner

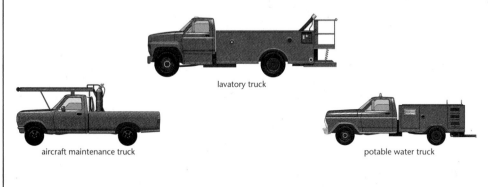

lavatory truck

aircraft maintenance truck

potable water truck

127

wheel chock

boom truck

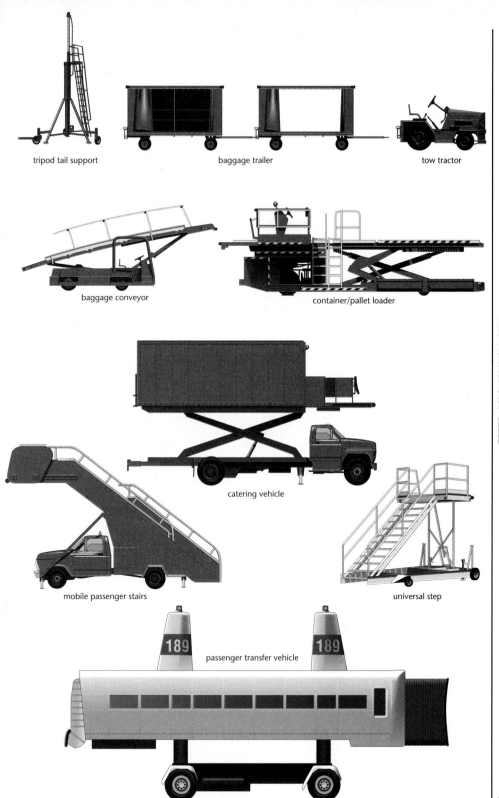

tripod tail support

baggage trailer

tow tractor

baggage conveyor

container/pallet loader

catering vehicle

mobile passenger stairs

universal step

passenger transfer vehicle

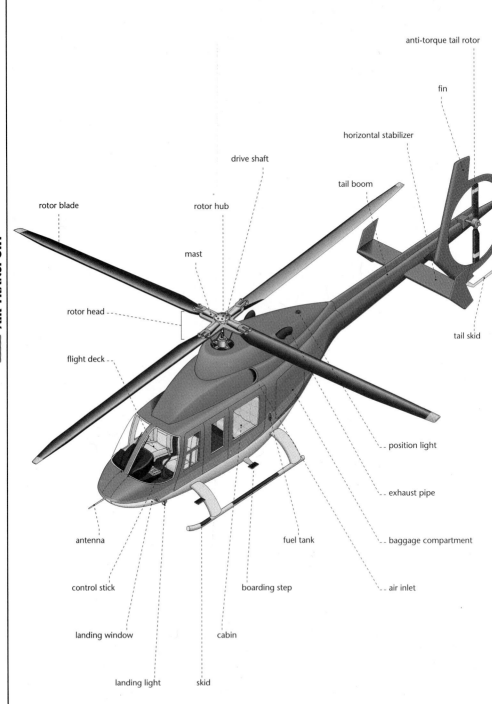

anti-torque tail rotor

fin

horizontal stabilizer

drive shaft

tail boom

rotor blade

rotor hub

mast

tail skid

rotor head

flight deck

position light

exhaust pipe

antenna

fuel tank

baggage compartment

control stick

boarding step

air inlet

landing window

cabin

landing light

skid

ROCKET

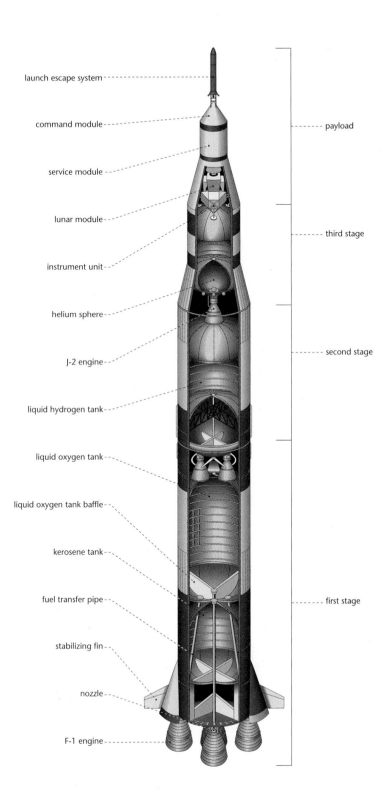

launch escape system

command module

service module

lunar module

instrument unit

helium sphere

J-2 engine

liquid hydrogen tank

liquid oxygen tank

liquid oxygen tank baffle

kerosene tank

fuel transfer pipe

stabilizing fin

nozzle

F-1 engine

payload

third stage

second stage

first stage

SPACE SHUTTLE

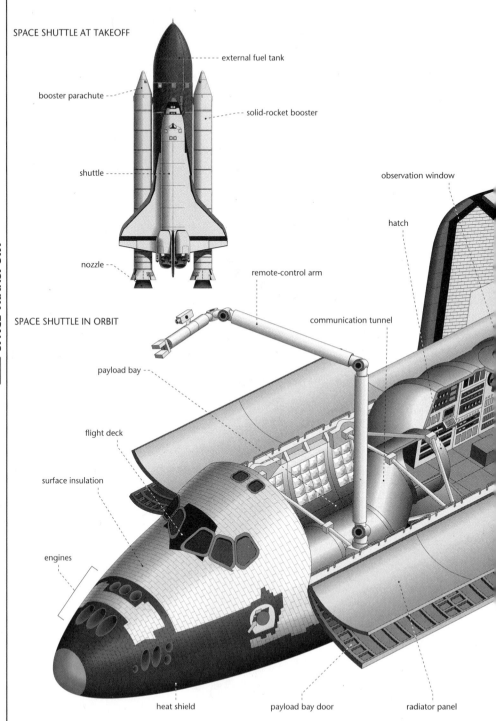

SPACE SHUTTLE AT TAKEOFF

external fuel tank

booster parachute

solid-rocket booster

shuttle

observation window

hatch

nozzle

remote-control arm

communication tunnel

SPACE SHUTTLE IN ORBIT

payload bay

flight deck

surface insulation

engines

heat shield

payload bay door

radiator panel

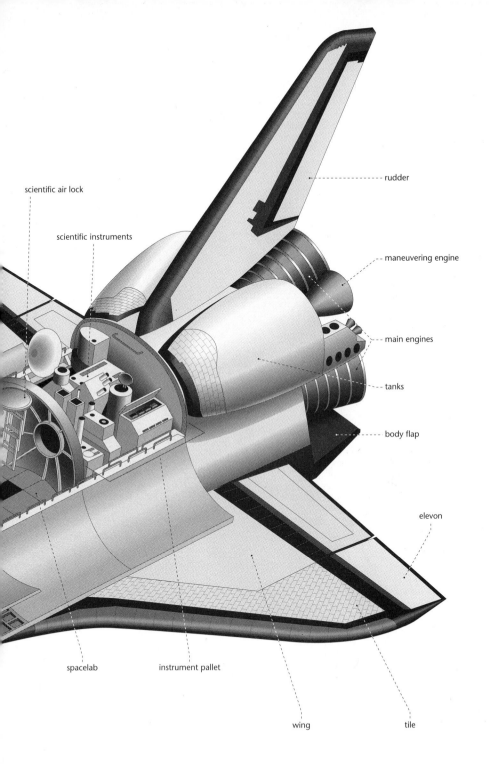

scientific air lock

scientific instruments

rudder

maneuvering engine

main engines

tanks

body flap

elevon

spacelab

instrument pallet

wing

tile

SPACESUIT

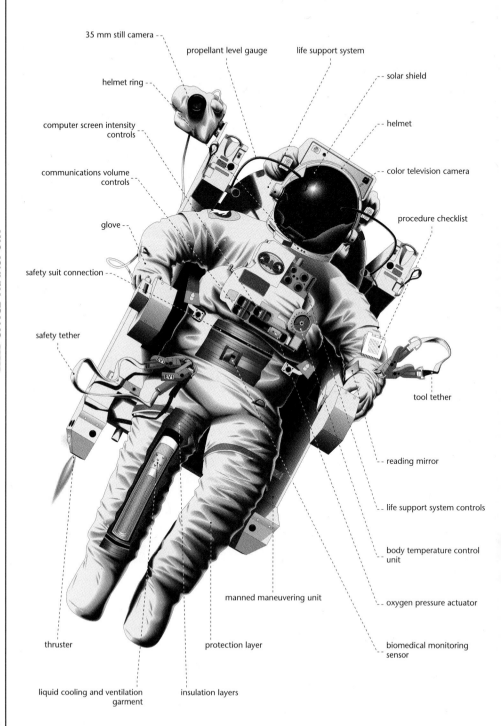

35 mm still camera

helmet ring

computer screen intensity
controls

communications volume
controls

glove

safety suit connection

safety tether

propellant level gauge

life support system

solar shield

helmet

color television camera

procedure checklist

tool tether

reading mirror

life support system controls

body temperature control
unit

oxygen pressure actuator

biomedical monitoring
sensor

thruster

liquid cooling and ventilation
garment

insulation layers

protection layer

manned maneuvering unit

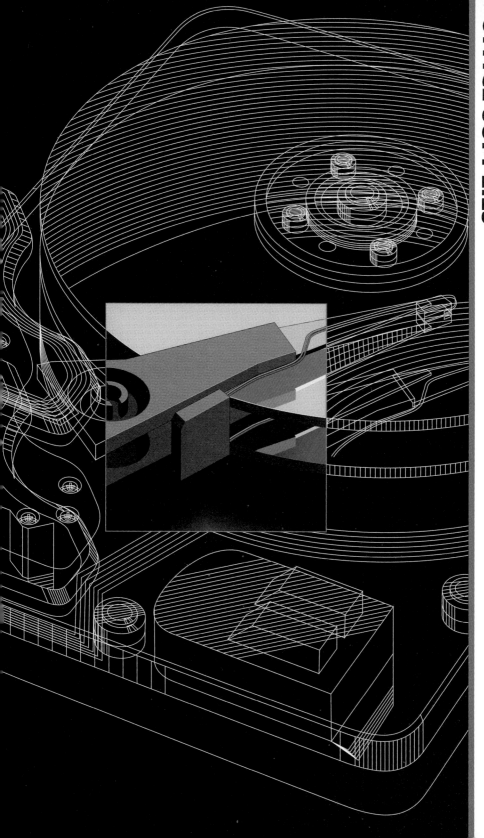

CONTENTS

OFFICE SUPPLIES

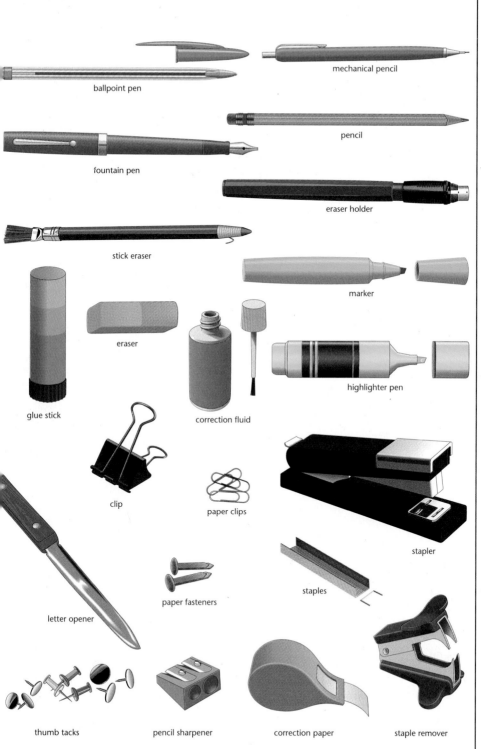

ballpoint pen

mechanical pencil

pencil

fountain pen

eraser holder

stick eraser

marker

glue stick

eraser

correction fluid

highlighter pen

clip

paper clips

stapler

letter opener

paper fasteners

staples

staple remover

thumb tacks

pencil sharpener

correction paper

rubber stamp

stamp pad

tape dispenser

bill-file

dater

numbering machine

stamp rack

paper punch

label maker

moistener

rotary file

letter scale

pencil sharpener

telephone index

INDEX CARD DRAWER

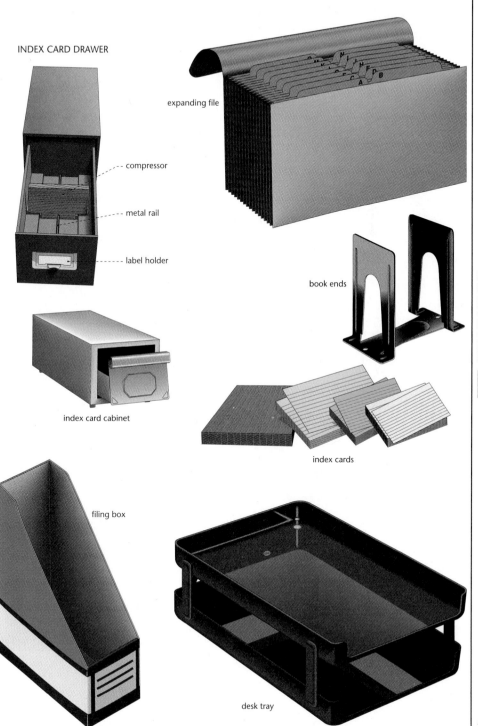

expanding file

- - - - compressor

- - - - metal rail

- - - - label holder

book ends

index card cabinet

index cards

filing box

desk tray

tear-off calendar

appointment book

calendar pad

account book

memo pad

self-adhesive labels

tab

archboard

window tab

hanging file

file guides

folder

clipboard

post binder

spring binder

document folder

ring binder

dividers

spiral binder

clamp binder

fastener binder

executive desk

swivel-tilter armchair

desk mat

credenza

partition

lateral filing cabinet

COMPUTER TABLE

PRINTER TABLE

paper catcher

adjustable platen

modesty panel

paper tray

paper feed channel

mobile filing unit

mobile drawer unit

typist's chair

return

SECRETARIAL DESK

display cabinet

coat hook

stationery cabinet

coat tree

locker

coat rack

CALCULATOR

POCKET CALCULATOR

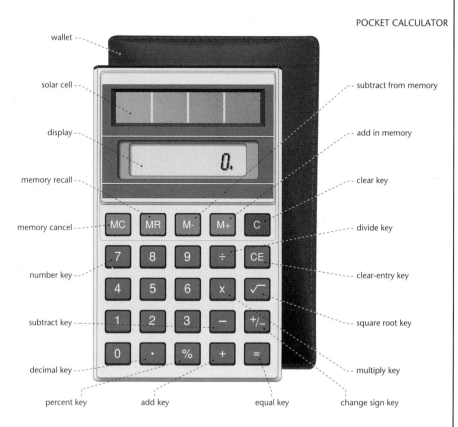

wallet

solar cell

display

memory recall

memory cancel

number key

subtract key

decimal key

percent key

add key

equal key

subtract from memory

add in memory

clear key

divide key

clear-entry key

square root key

multiply key

change sign key

PRINTING CALCULATOR

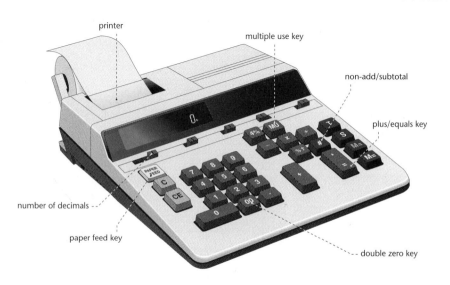

printer

multiple use key

non-add/subtotal

plus/equals key

number of decimals

paper feed key

double zero key

523

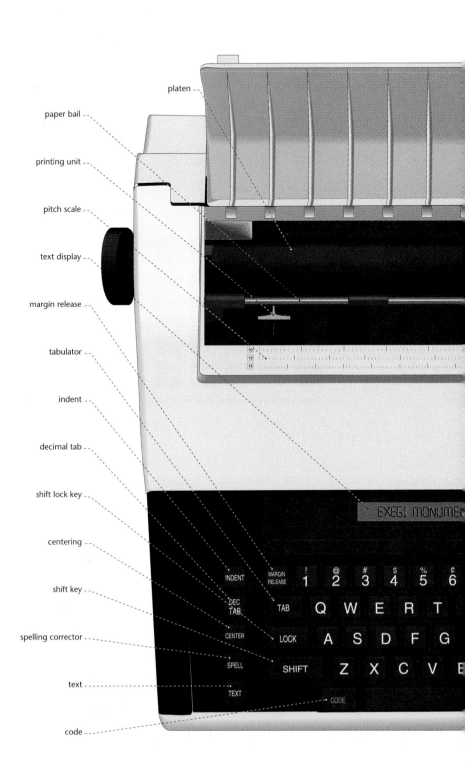

platen

paper bail

printing unit

pitch scale

text display

margin release

tabulator

indent

decimal tab

shift lock key

centering

shift key

spelling corrector

text

code

EXEGI MONUMEN

MARGIN RELEASE 1 2 3 4 5 6

INDENT TAB Q W E R T

DEC TAB LOCK A S D F G

CENTER SHIFT Z X C V E

SPELL

TEXT CODE

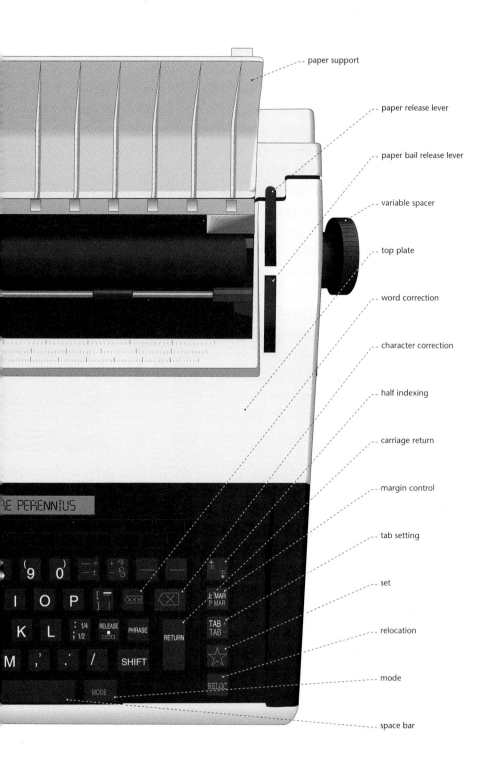

paper support

paper release lever

paper bail release lever

variable spacer

top plate

word correction

character correction

half indexing

carriage return

margin control

tab setting

set

relocation

mode

space bar

INPUT DEVICES

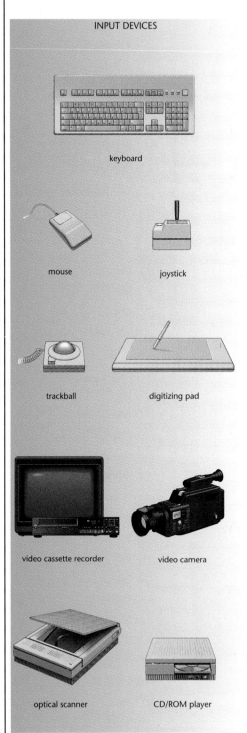

keyboard

mouse

joystick

trackball

digitizing pad

video cassette recorder

video camera

optical scanner

CD/ROM player

COMMUNICATION DEVICES

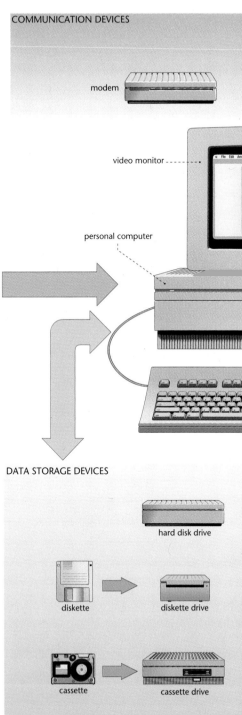

modem

video monitor

personal computer

DATA STORAGE DEVICES

hard disk drive

diskette

diskette drive

cassette

cassette drive

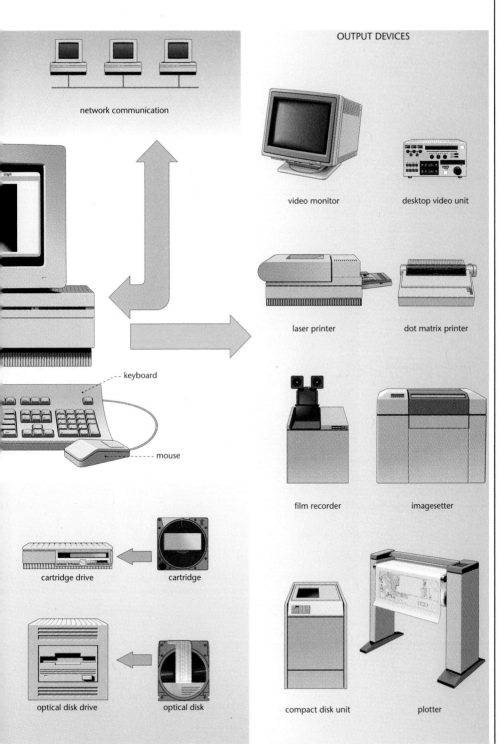

network communication

OUTPUT DEVICES

video monitor

desktop video unit

laser printer

dot matrix printer

keyboard

mouse

film recorder

imagesetter

cartridge drive

cartridge

optical disk drive

optical disk

compact disk unit

plotter

PERSONAL COMPUTER (VIEW FROM ABOVE)

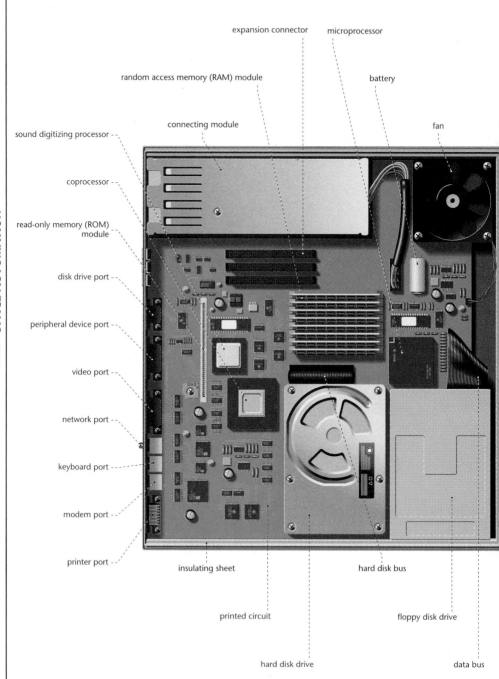

expansion connector

microprocessor

random access memory (RAM) module

battery

connecting module

fan

sound digitizing processor

coprocessor

read-only memory (ROM) module

disk drive port

peripheral device port

video port

network port

keyboard port

modem port

printer port

insulating sheet

hard disk bus

printed circuit

floppy disk drive

hard disk drive

data bus

VIDEO MONITOR

vertical control

horizontal control

centering control

contrast control

power indicator

power switch

brightness control

FLOPPY DISK

MINI-FLOPPY DISK

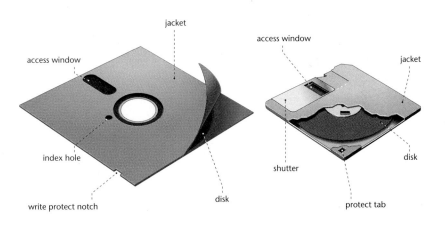

jacket

access window

access window

jacket

index hole

disk

write protect notch

disk

shutter

protect tab

HARD DISK DRIVE

actuator arm

actuator arm motor

disk

disk motor

read/write head

529

BASIC COMPONENTS

KEYBOARD

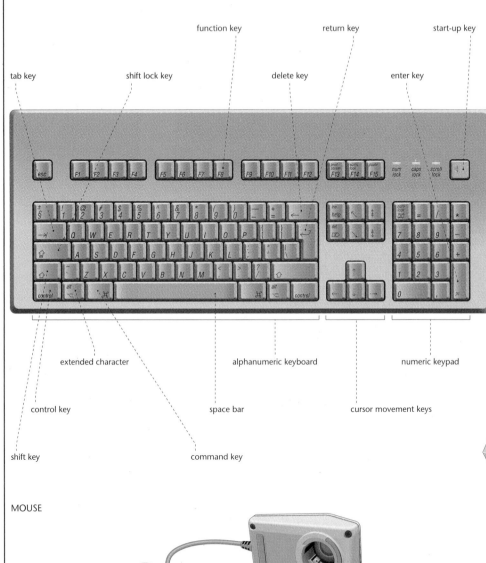

function key

return key

start-up key

tab key

shift lock key

delete key

enter key

extended character

alphanumeric keyboard

numeric keypad

control key

space bar

cursor movement keys

shift key

command key

MOUSE

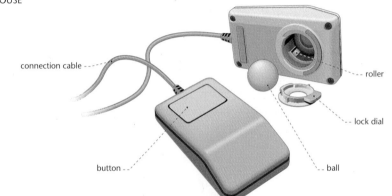

connection cable

roller

lock dial

button

ball

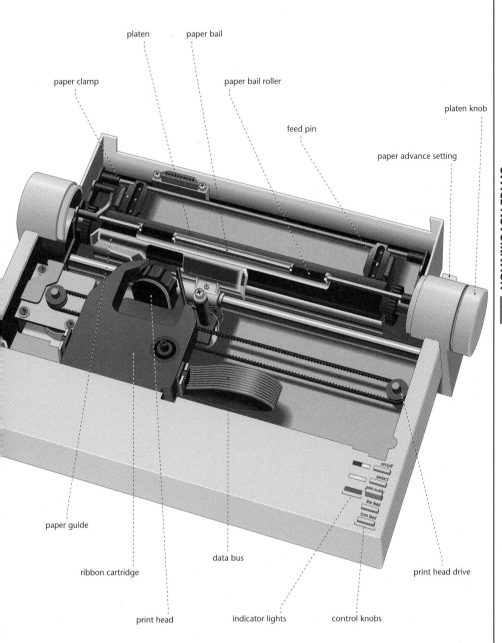

platen

paper bail

paper clamp

paper bail roller

platen knob

feed pin

paper advance setting

on/off

select

print quality

line feed

form feed

paper guide

data bus

ribbon cartridge

print head drive

print head

indicator lights

control knobs

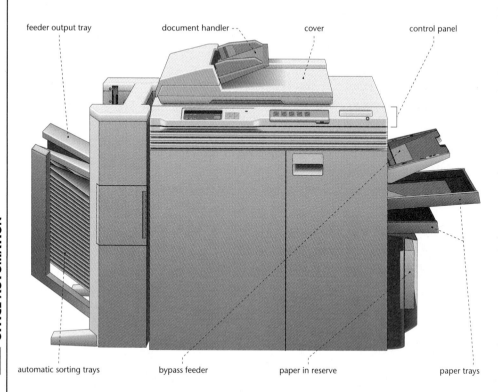

feeder output tray

document handler - -

cover

control panel

automatic sorting trays

bypass feeder

paper in reserve

paper trays

CONTROL PANEL

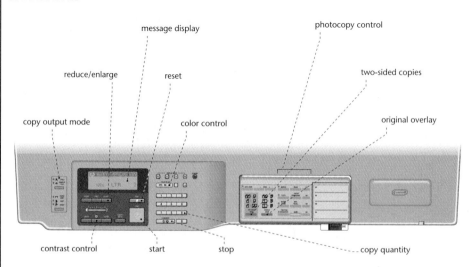

message display

photocopy control

reduce/enlarge

reset

two-sided copies

copy output mode

color control

original overlay

contrast control

start

stop

copy quantity

MUSIC

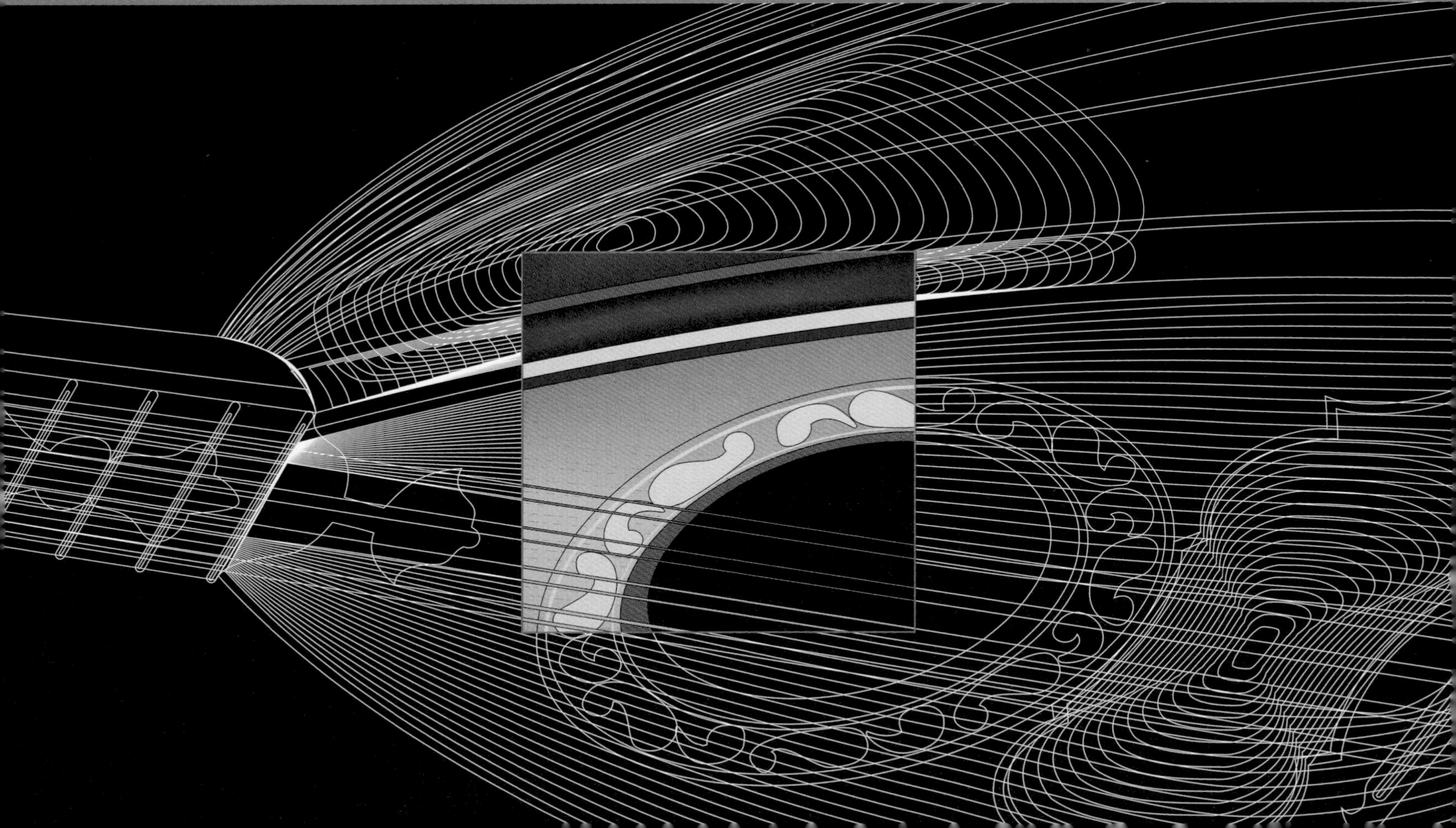

CONTENTS

MUSIC

TRADITIONAL MUSICAL INSTRUMENTS

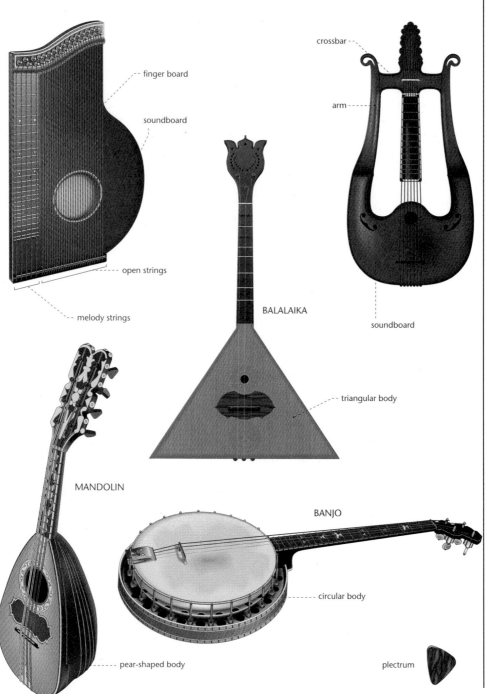

ZITHER

finger board

soundboard

open strings

melody strings

LYRE

crossbar

arm

soundboard

BALALAIKA

triangular body

MANDOLIN

BANJO

circular body

pear-shaped body

plectrum

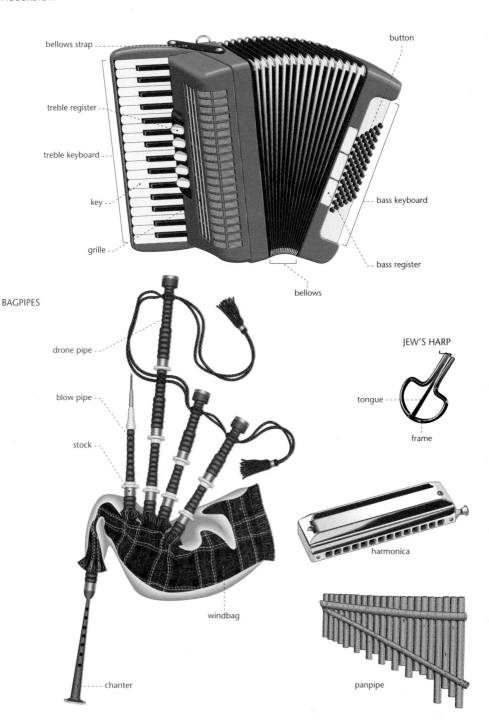

ACCORDION

bellows strap

treble register

treble keyboard

key

grille

button

bass keyboard

bass register

bellows

BAGPIPES

drone pipe

blow pipe

stock

windbag

chanter

JEW'S HARP

tongue

frame

harmonica

panpipe

MUSIC

536

MUSICAL NOTATION

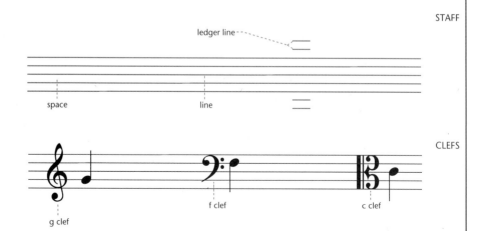

ledger line

space   line

CLEFS

f clef   c clef

g clef

TIME SIGNATURES

bar line

two-two time   four-four time   repeat mark

three-four time

SCALE

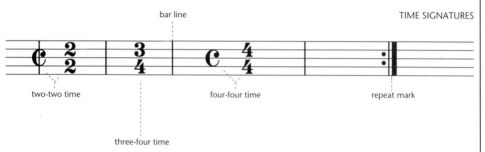

c   d   e   f   g   a   b   c

MUSIC

INTERVALS

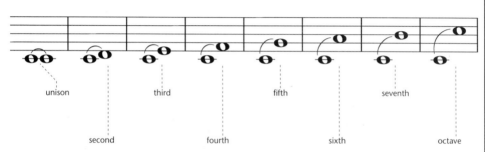

unison   third   fifth   seventh

second   fourth   sixth   octave

MUSICAL NOTATION

NOTE SYMBOLS

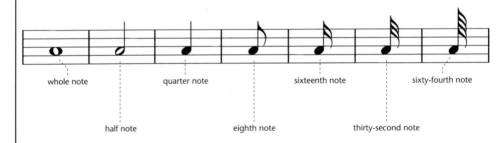

whole note   quarter note   sixteenth note   sixty-fourth note

half note   eighth note   thirty-second note

REST SYMBOLS

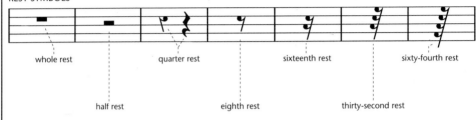

whole rest   quarter rest   sixteenth rest   sixty-fourth rest

half rest   eighth rest   thirty-second rest

ACCIDENTALS

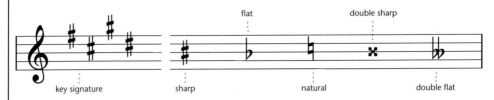

flat   double sharp

key signature   sharp   natural   double flat

ORNAMENTS

appoggiatura   trill   turn   mordent

MUSIC

538

CHORD

OTHER SIGNS

accent mark

arpeggio

tie

pause

MUSICAL ACCESSORIES

MUSIC STAND

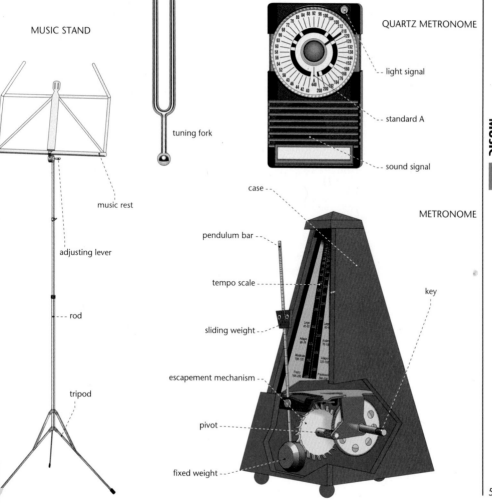

tuning fork

QUARTZ METRONOME

light signal

standard A

sound signal

music rest

adjusting lever

rod

tripod

case

METRONOME

pendulum bar

tempo scale

sliding weight

key

escapement mechanism

pivot

fixed weight

UPRIGHT PIANO

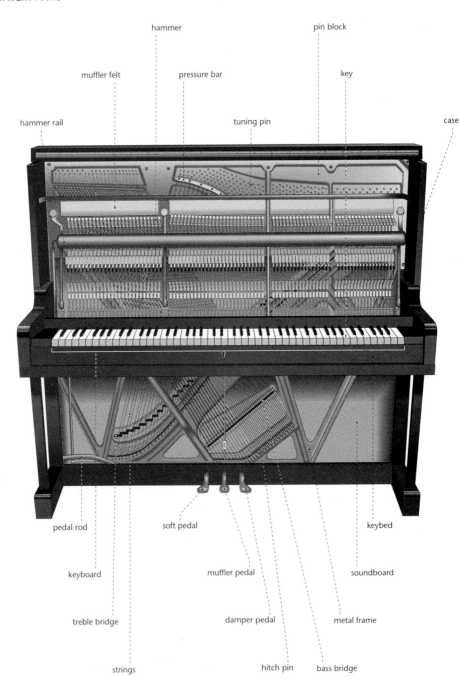

hammer

pin block

muffler felt

pressure bar

key

hammer rail

tuning pin

case

pedal rod

soft pedal

keybed

keyboard

muffler pedal

soundboard

treble bridge

damper pedal

metal frame

strings

hitch pin

bass bridge

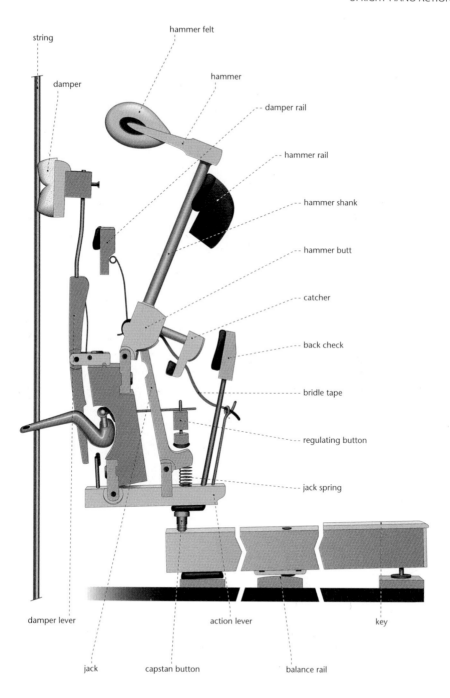

string

damper

hammer felt

hammer

damper rail

hammer rail

hammer shank

hammer butt

catcher

back check

bridle tape

regulating button

jack spring

damper lever

action lever

key

jack

capstan button

balance rail

ORGAN

ORGAN CONSOLE

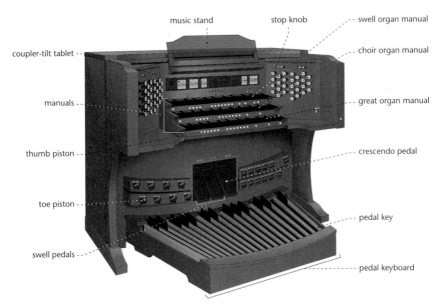

music stand · stop knob · swell organ manual

coupler-tilt tablet · choir organ manual

manuals · great organ manual

thumb piston · crescendo pedal

toe piston · pedal key

swell pedals · pedal keyboard

FLUE PIPE

REED PIPE

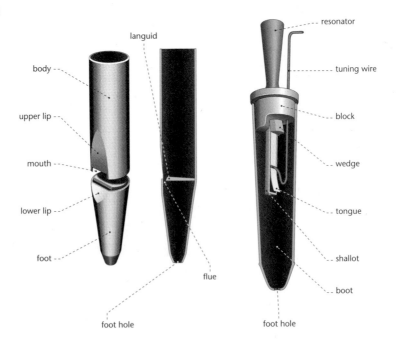

languid

body · resonator

upper lip · tuning wire

mouth · block

lower lip · wedge

foot · tongue

· shallot

flue · boot

foot hole · foot hole

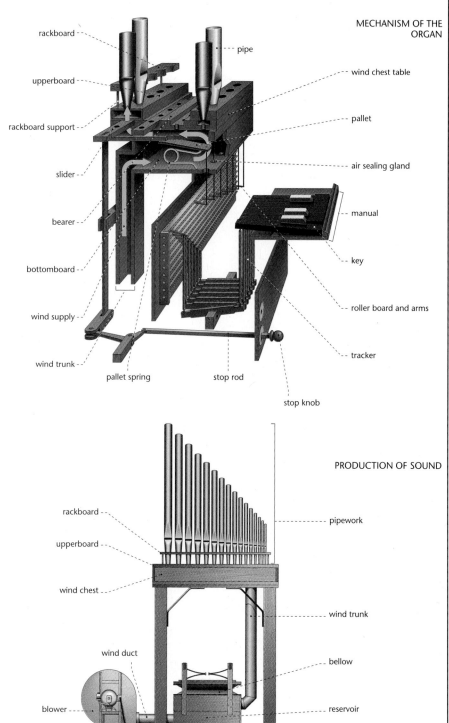

MECHANISM OF THE ORGAN

rackboard

pipe

upperboard

wind chest table

rackboard support

pallet

slider

air sealing gland

bearer

manual

bottomboard

key

wind supply

roller board and arms

wind trunk

tracker

pallet spring

stop rod

stop knob

PRODUCTION OF SOUND

rackboard

pipework

upperboard

wind chest

wind trunk

wind duct

bellow

blower

reservoir

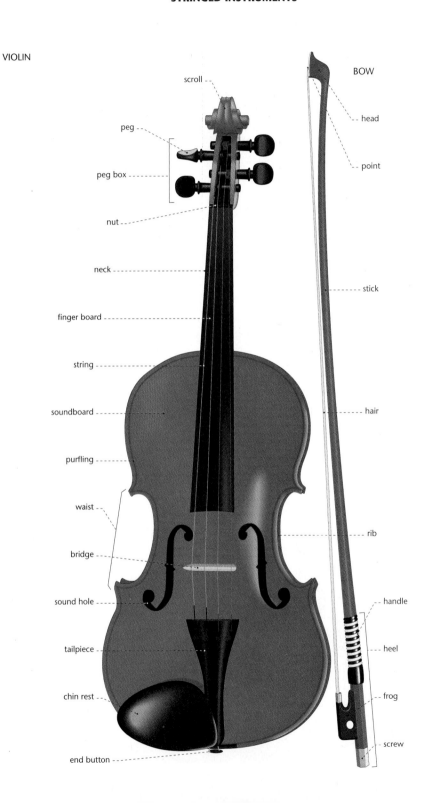

VIOLIN

scroll

peg

peg box

nut

neck

finger board

string

soundboard

purfling

waist

bridge

sound hole

tailpiece

chin rest

end button

BOW

head

point

stick

hair

rib

handle

heel

frog

screw

MUSIC

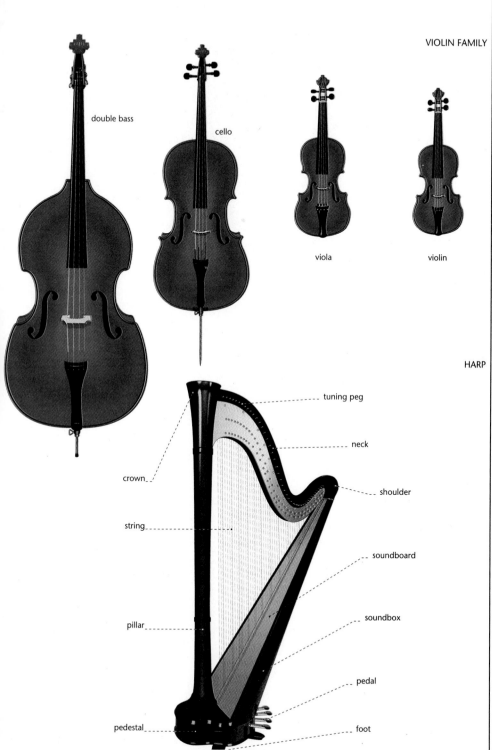

double bass

cello

viola

violin

tuning peg

neck

crown

shoulder

string

soundboard

pillar

soundbox

pedal

pedestal

foot

ACOUSTIC GUITAR

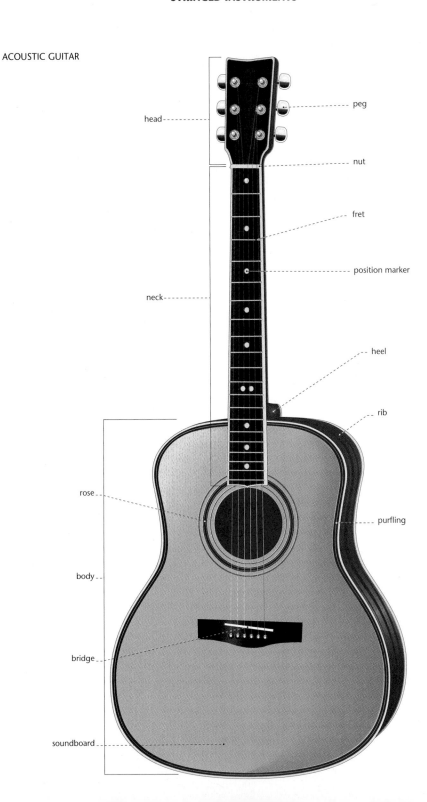

peg

head

nut

fret

position marker

neck

heel

rib

rose

purfling

body

bridge

soundboard

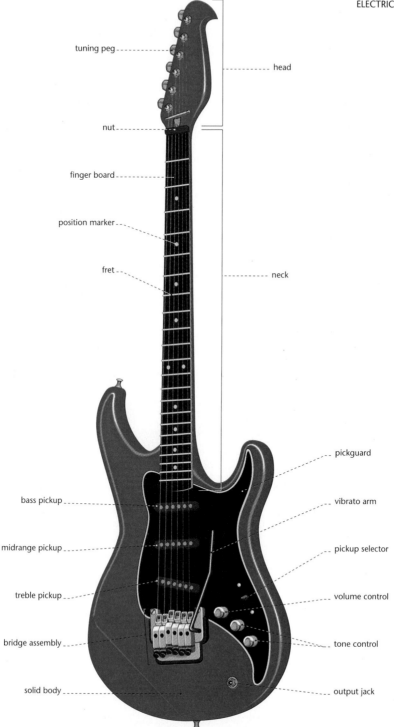

tuning peg

head

nut

finger board

position marker

fret

neck

pickguard

bass pickup

vibrato arm

midrange pickup

pickup selector

treble pickup

volume control

bridge assembly

tone control

solid body

output jack

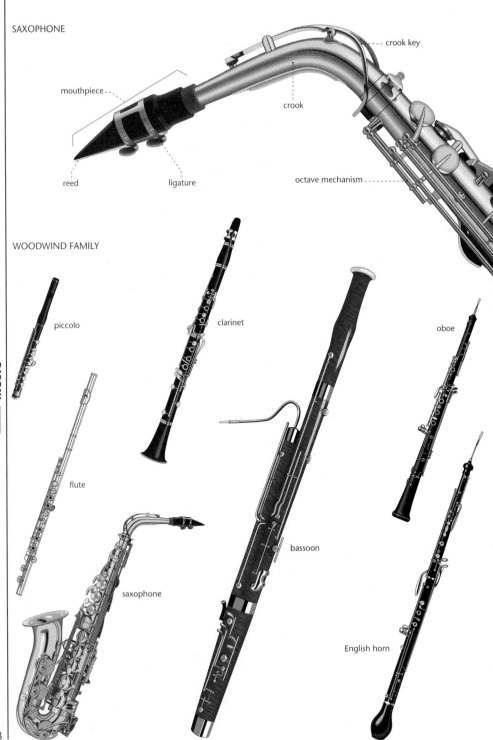

WIND INSTRUMENTS

SAXOPHONE

crook key

mouthpiece

crook

reed

ligature

octave mechanism

WOODWIND FAMILY

piccolo

clarinet

oboe

flute

saxophone

bassoon

English horn

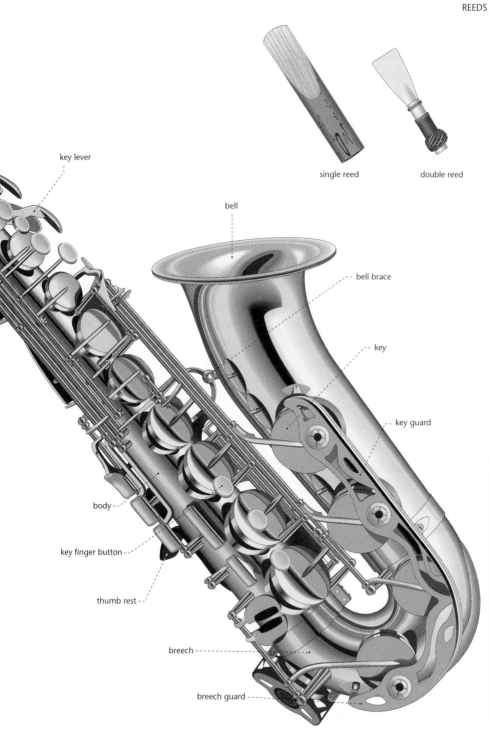

REEDS

single reed

double reed

key lever

bell

bell brace

key

key guard

body

key finger button

thumb rest

breech

breech guard

MUSIC

549

TRUMPET

BRASS FAMILY

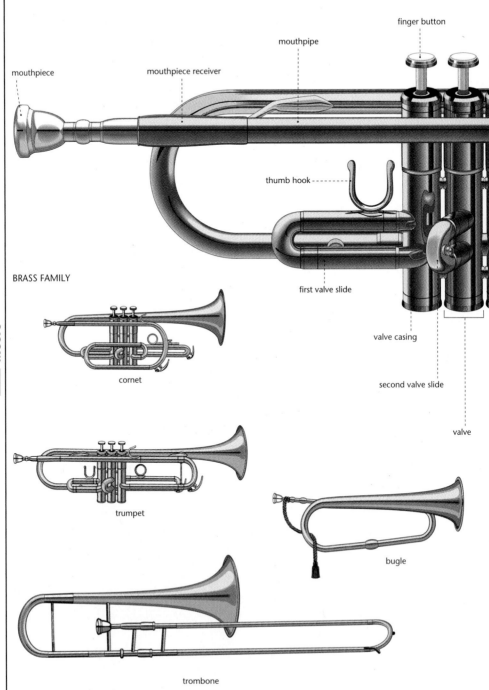

finger button

mouthpipe

mouthpiece

mouthpiece receiver

thumb hook

first valve slide

valve casing

second valve slide

valve

cornet

trumpet

bugle

trombone

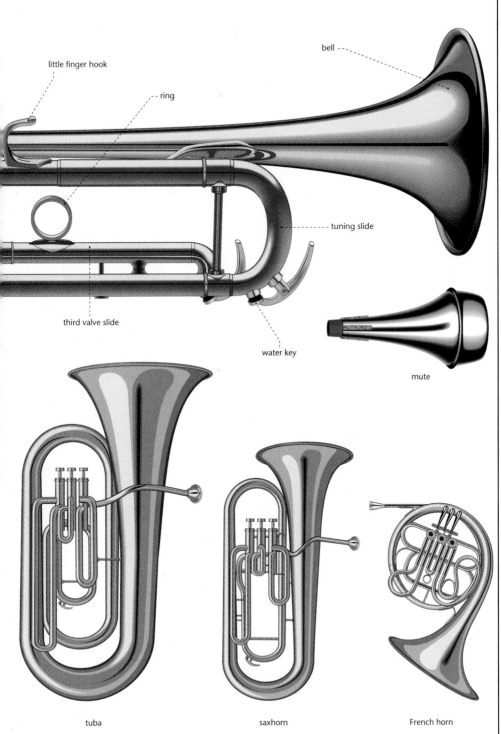

little finger hook

ring

bell

tuning slide

third valve slide

water key

mute

tuba

saxhorn

French horn

DRUMS

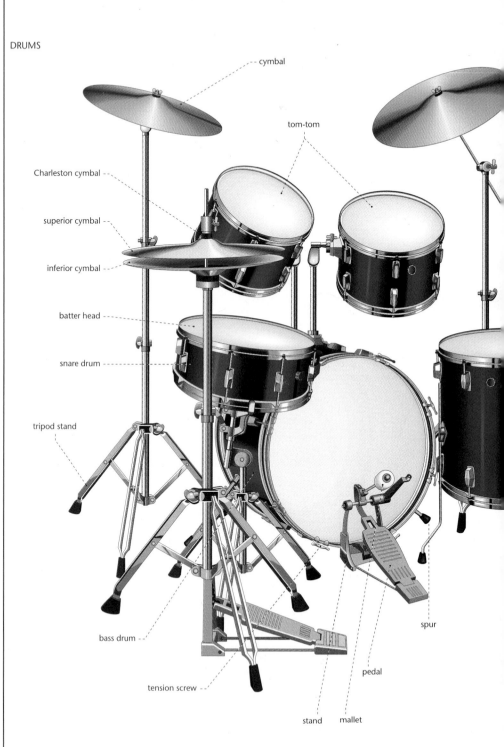

cymbal

tom-tom

Charleston cymbal

superior cymbal

inferior cymbal

batter head

snare drum

tripod stand

bass drum

tension screw

stand

mallet

pedal

spur

SNARE DRUM

lug

tension rod

snare

snare strainer

snare head

sticks

wire brush

mallets

tenor drum

KETTLEDRUM

batter head

metal counterhoop

tie rod

tuning gauge

shell

strut

tension rod

leg

crown

caster

foot

pedal

PERCUSSION INSTRUMENTS

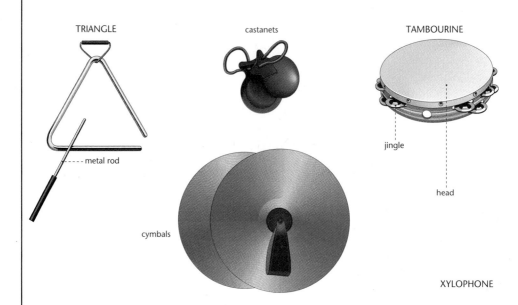

TRIANGLE

metal rod

castanets

TAMBOURINE

jingle

head

cymbals

XYLOPHONE

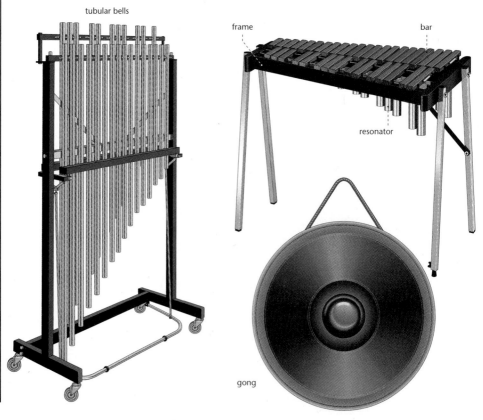

tubular bells

frame

bar

resonator

gong

ELECTRONIC INSTRUMENTS

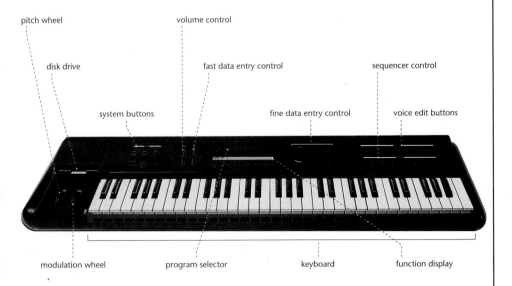

pitch wheel

volume control

disk drive

fast data entry control

sequencer control

system buttons

fine data entry control

voice edit buttons

modulation wheel

program selector

keyboard

function display

ELECTRONIC PIANO

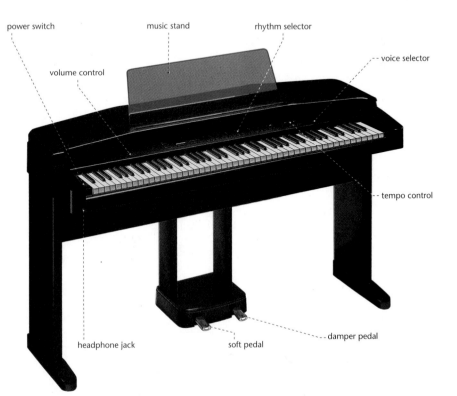

power switch

music stand

rhythm selector

voice selector

volume control

tempo control

headphone jack

soft pedal

damper pedal

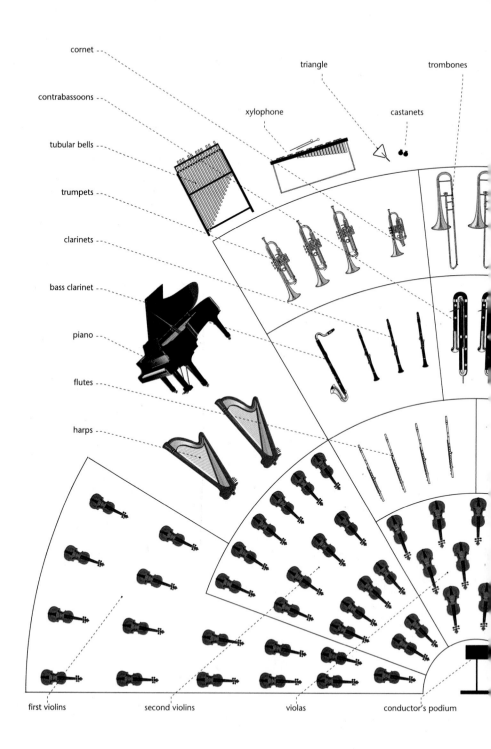

cornet

contrabassoons

tubular bells

trumpets

clarinets

bass clarinet

piano

flutes

harps

triangle

trombones

xylophone

castanets

first violins

second violins

violas

conductor's podium

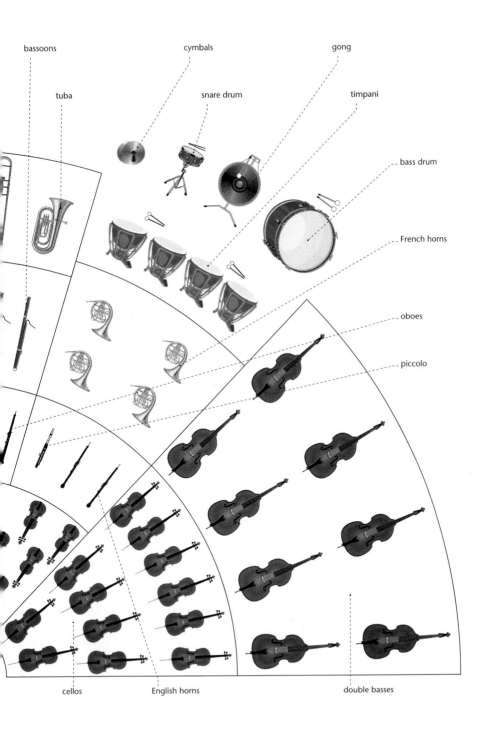

bassoons

tuba

cymbals

snare drum

gong

timpani

bass drum

French horns

oboes

piccolo

cellos

English horns

double basses

EXAMPLES OF INSTRUMENTAL GROUPS

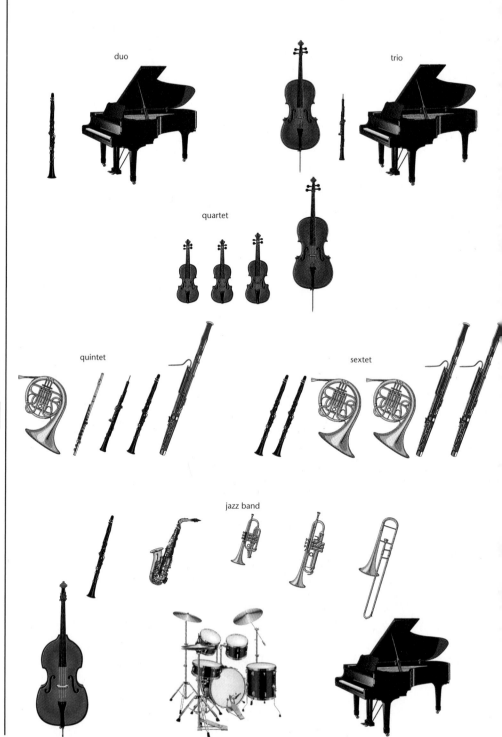

duo

trio

quartet

quintet

sextet

jazz band

CREATIVE LEISURE ACTIVITIES

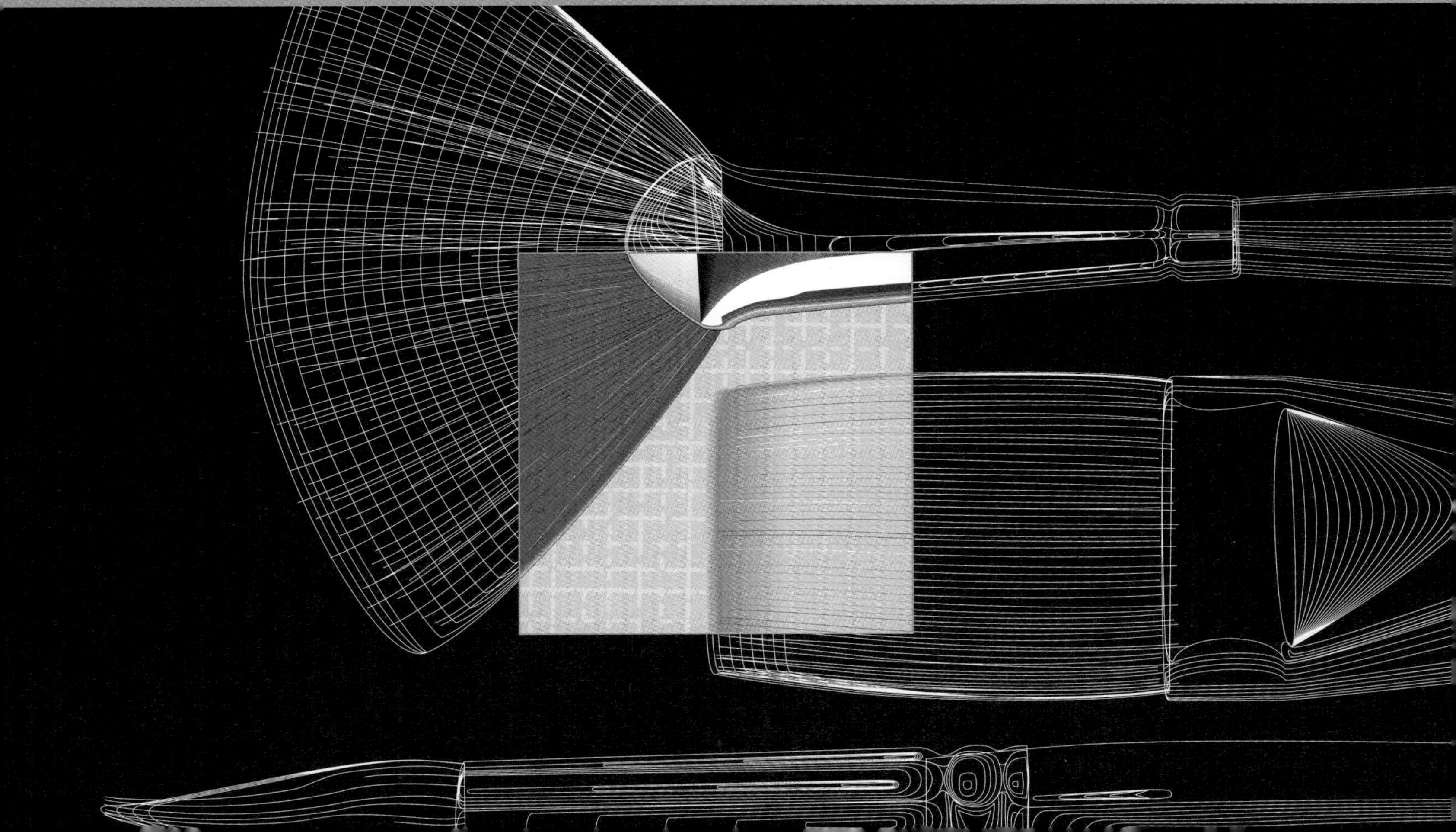

CONTENTS

SEWING

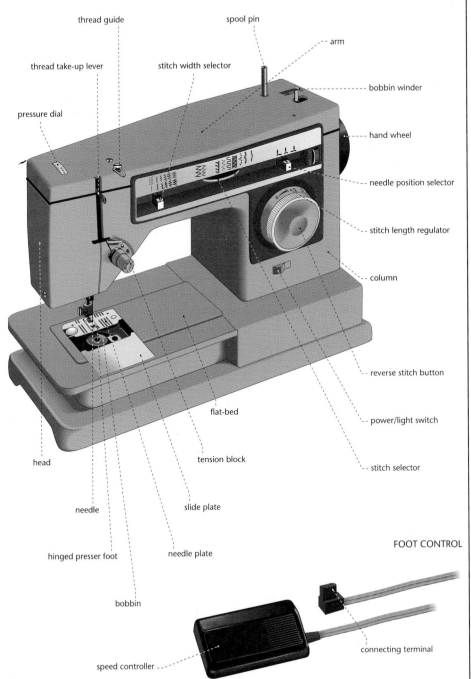

thread guide

spool pin

arm

thread take-up lever

stitch width selector

bobbin winder

pressure dial

hand wheel

needle position selector

stitch length regulator

column

reverse stitch button

flat-bed

power/light switch

tension block

stitch selector

head

slide plate

needle

hinged presser foot

needle plate

bobbin

FOOT CONTROL

speed controller

connecting terminal

CREATIVE LEISURE ACTIVITIES

PRESSER FOOT

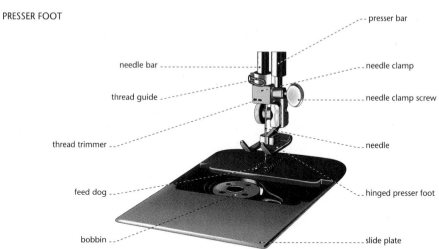

presser bar

needle bar

needle clamp

thread guide

needle clamp screw

thread trimmer

needle

feed dog

hinged presser foot

bobbin

slide plate

NEEDLE

TENSION BLOCK

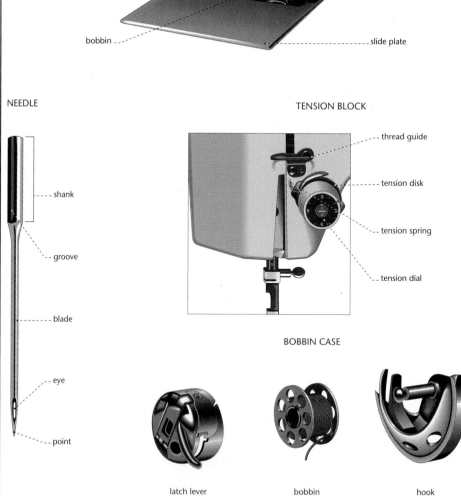

shank

groove

blade

eye

point

thread guide

tension disk

tension spring

tension dial

BOBBIN CASE

latch lever

bobbin

hook

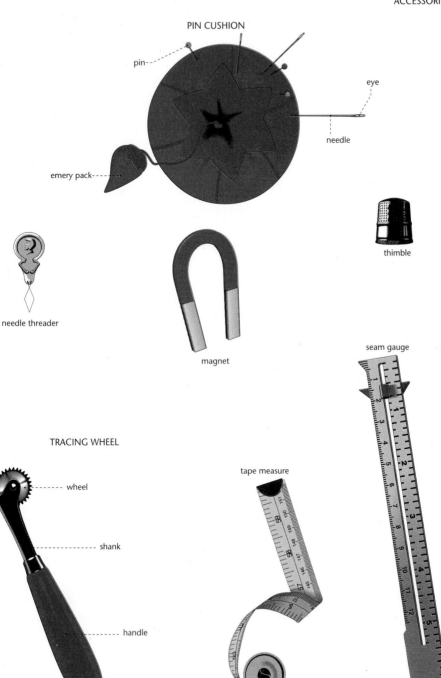

PIN CUSHION

pin

eye

needle

emery pack

thimble

needle threader

magnet

seam gauge

TRACING WHEEL

wheel

shank

handle

tape measure

ACCESSORIES

scissors

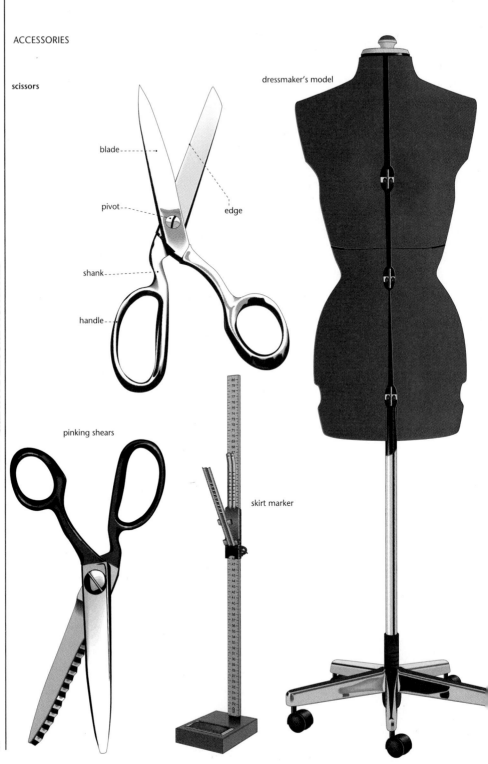

blade

pivot

edge

shank

handle

dressmaker's model

pinking shears

skirt marker

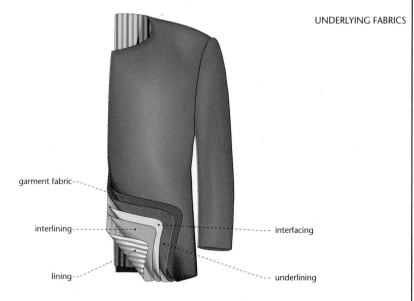

garment fabric

interlining

lining

interfacing

underlining

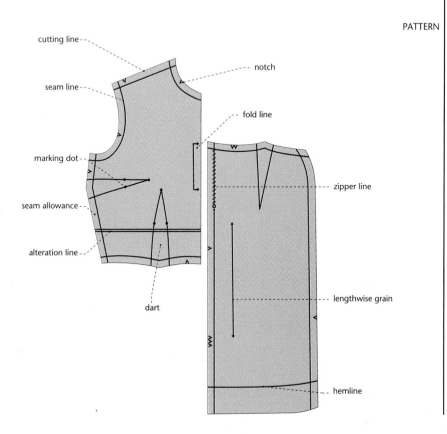

cutting line

seam line

marking dot

seam allowance

alteration line

notch

fold line

zipper line

lengthwise grain

hemline

dart

FASTENERS

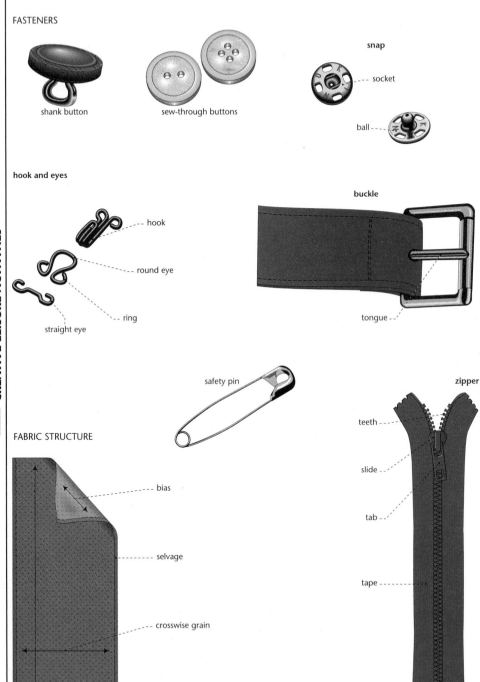

shank button

sew-through buttons

snap

socket

ball

hook and eyes

hook

round eye

ring

straight eye

buckle

tongue

safety pin

zipper

teeth

slide

tab

tape

stop

FABRIC STRUCTURE

bias

selvage

crosswise grain

lengthwise grain

KNITTING

KNITTING NEEDLES

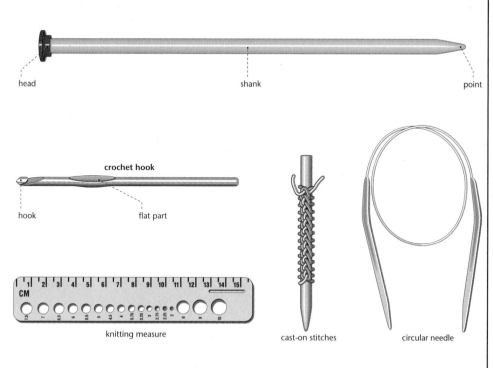

head   shank   point

crochet hook

hook   flat part

knitting measure

cast-on stitches

circular needle

STITCH PATTERNS

sample   stocking stitch   garter stitch

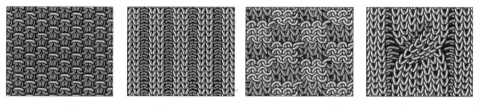

moss stitch   rib stitch   basket stitch   cable stitch

NEEDLE BED AND CARRIAGES

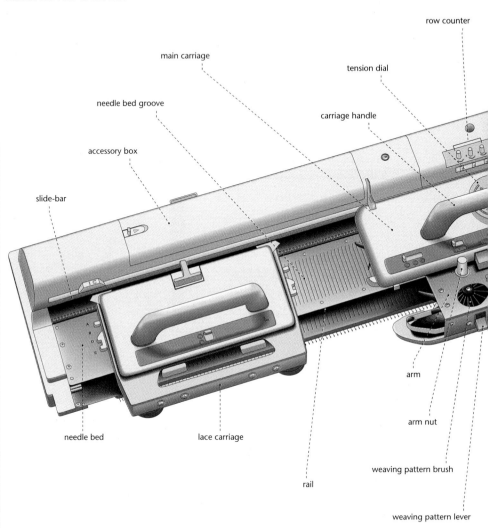

row counter

main carriage

tension dial

needle bed groove

carriage handle

accessory box

slide-bar

arm

arm nut

needle bed

lace carriage

weaving pattern brush

rail

weaving pattern lever

LATCH NEEDLE

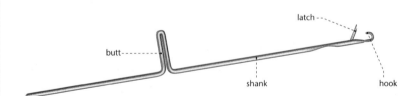

latch

butt

shank

hook

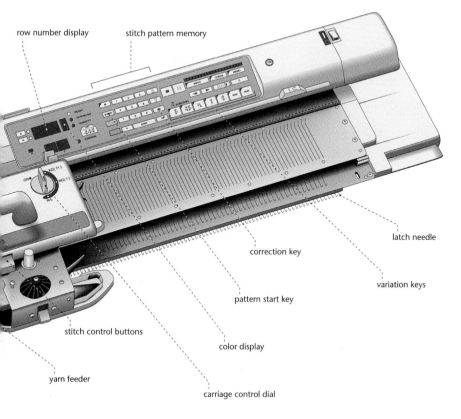

row number display

stitch pattern memory

latch needle

correction key

variation keys

pattern start key

stitch control buttons

color display

yarn feeder

carriage control dial

TENSION BLOCK

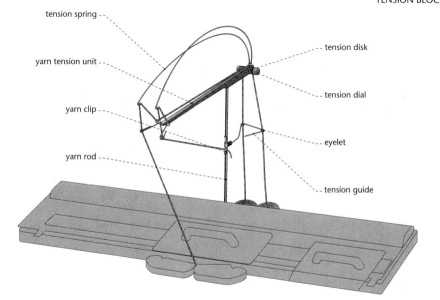

tension spring

tension disk

yarn tension unit

tension dial

yarn clip

eyelet

yarn rod

tension guide

PILLOW

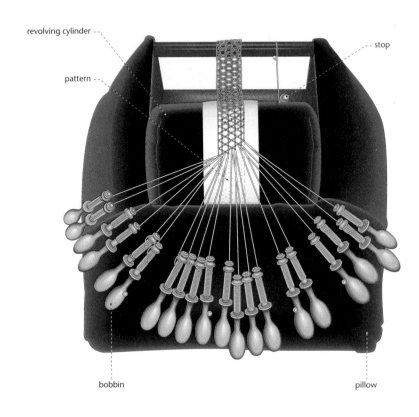

revolving cylinder

pattern

stop

bobbin

pillow

pricker

BOBBIN

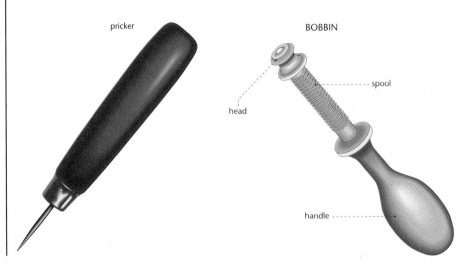

spool

head

handle

EMBROIDERY

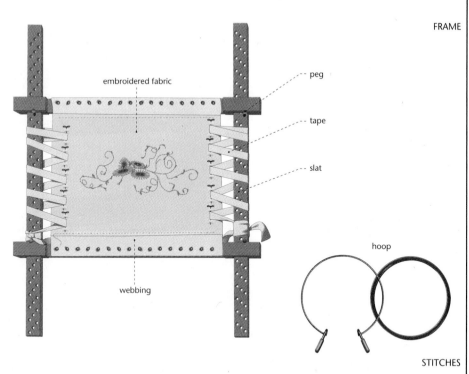

FRAME

embroidered fabric

peg

tape

slat

webbing

hoop

STITCHES

cross stitches

herringbone stitch

chevron stitch

flat stitches

long and short stitch

fishbone stitch

couched stitches

Romanian couching stitch

Oriental couching stitch

knot stitches

bullion stitch

French knot stitch

loop stitches

chain stitch

feather stitch

571

LOW WARP LOOM

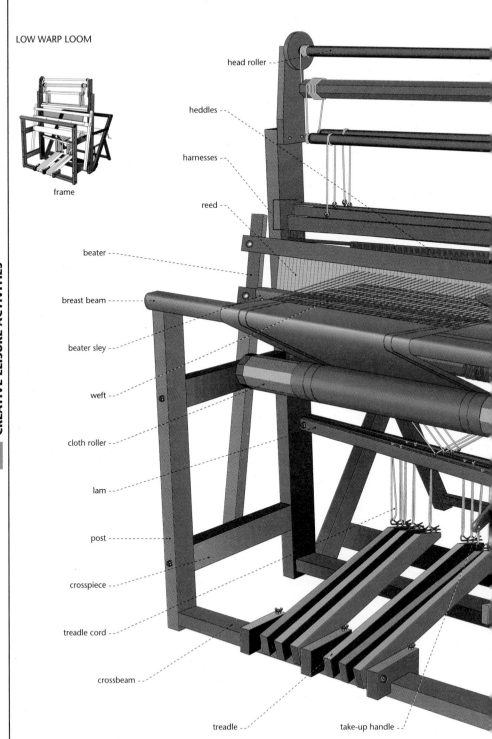

frame

head roller

heddles

harnesses

reed

beater

breast beam

beater sley

weft

cloth roller

lam

post

crosspiece

treadle cord

crossbeam

treadle

take-up handle

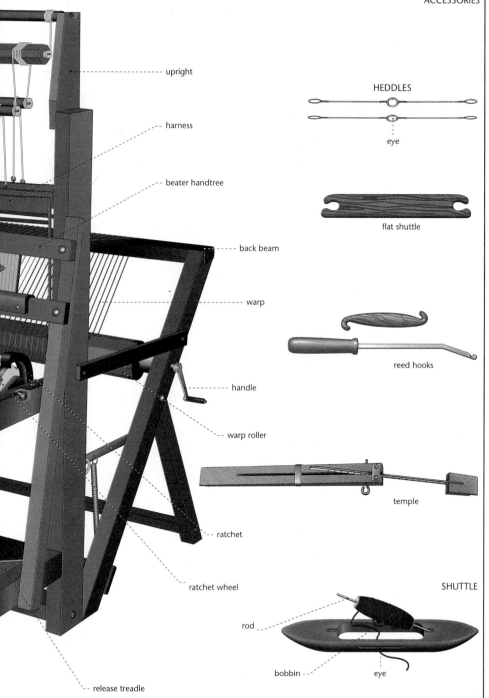

upright

harness

beater handtree

back beam

warp

handle

warp roller

ratchet

ratchet wheel

release treadle

HEDDLES

eye

flat shuttle

reed hooks

temple

SHUTTLE

rod

bobbin

eye

HIGH WARP LOOM

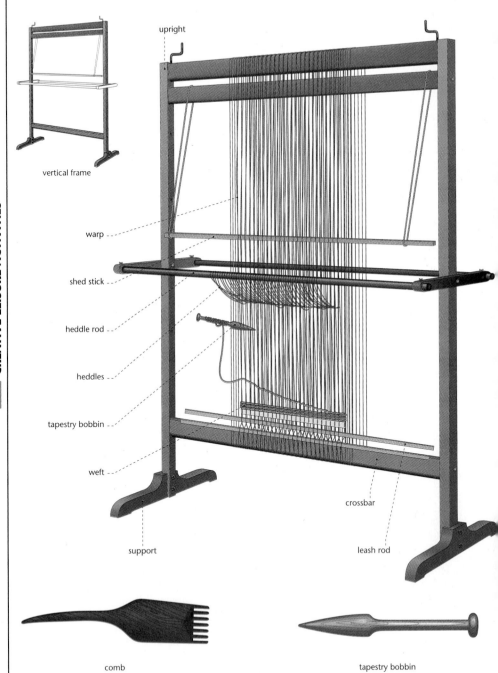

vertical frame

upright

warp

shed stick

heddle rod

heddles

tapestry bobbin

weft

support

crossbar

leash rod

comb

tapestry bobbin

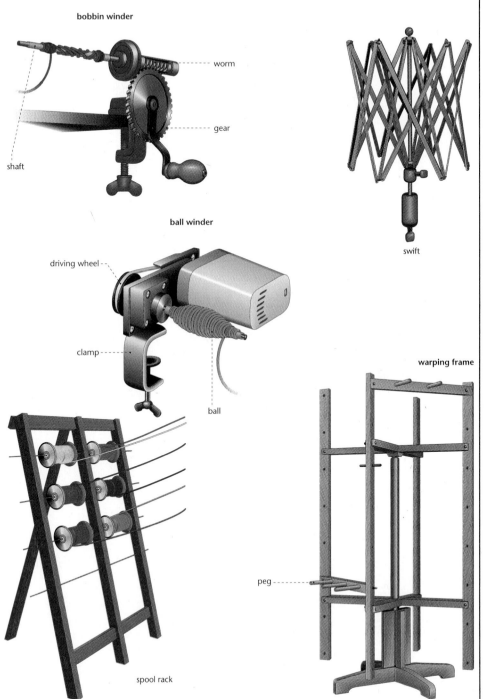

bobbin winder

worm

gear

shaft

swift

ball winder

driving wheel

clamp

ball

warping frame

peg

spool rack

DIAGRAM OF WEAVING PRINCIPLE

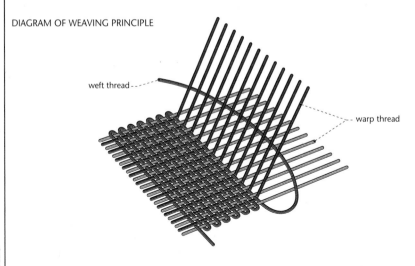

weft thread

warp thread

BASIC WEAVES

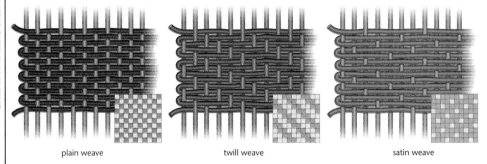

plain weave

twill weave

satin weave

OTHER TECHNIQUES

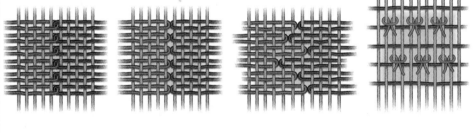

interlock

slit

hatching

knot

576

FINE BOOKBINDING

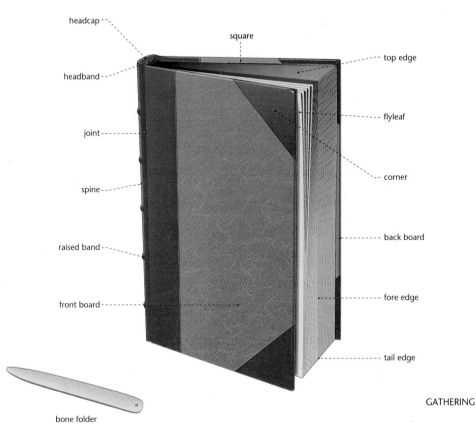

headcap

square

top edge

headband

flyleaf

joint

corner

spine

back board

raised band

fore edge

front board

tail edge

bone folder

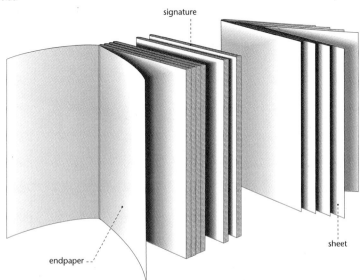

signature

sheet

endpaper

TRIMMING

board cutter

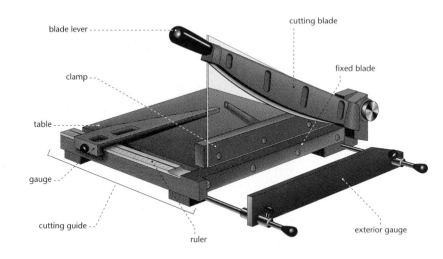

blade lever

cutting blade

clamp

fixed blade

table

gauge

cutting guide

ruler

exterior gauge

SAWING-IN

tenon saw

groove

SEWING

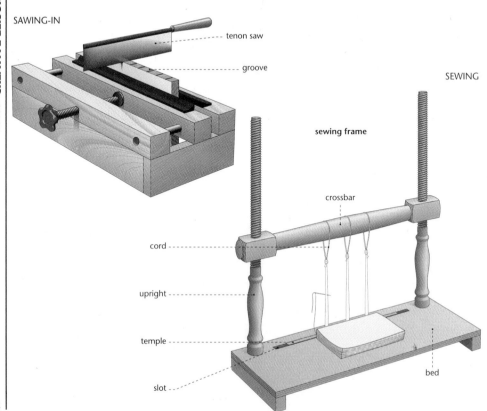

sewing frame

crossbar

cord

upright

temple

slot

bed

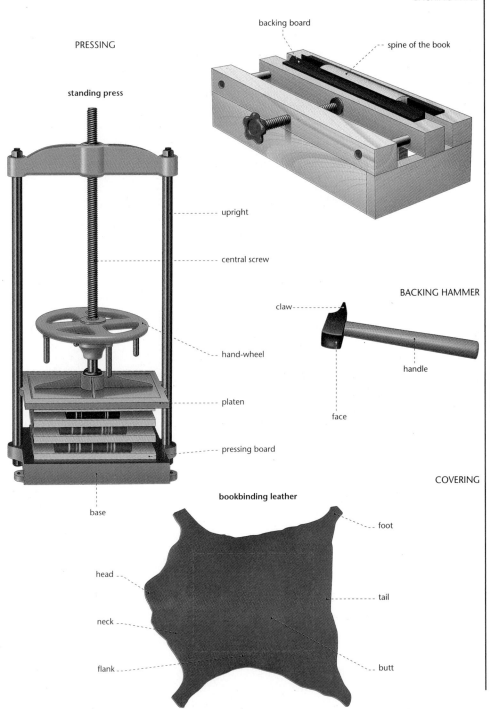

BACKING PRESS

backing board

spine of the book

PRESSING

standing press

upright

central screw

BACKING HAMMER

claw

hand-wheel

handle

platen

face

pressing board

COVERING

bookbinding leather

base

foot

head

neck

flank

tail

butt

579

RELIEF PRINTING

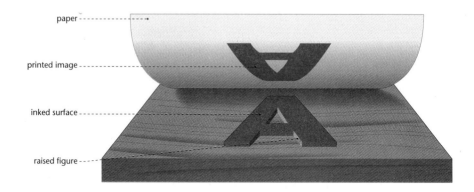

INTAGLIO PRINTING

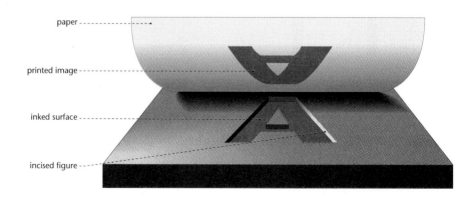

LITHOGRAPHIC PRINTING

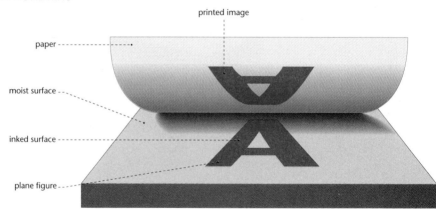

RELIEF PRINTING PROCESS

EQUIPMENT

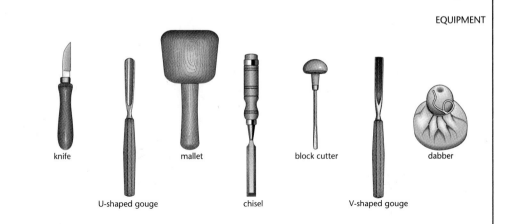

knife

U-shaped gouge

mallet

chisel

block cutter

V-shaped gouge

dabber

ink

brayer

INKING SLAB

ink

spatula

ETCHING PRESS

woodcut

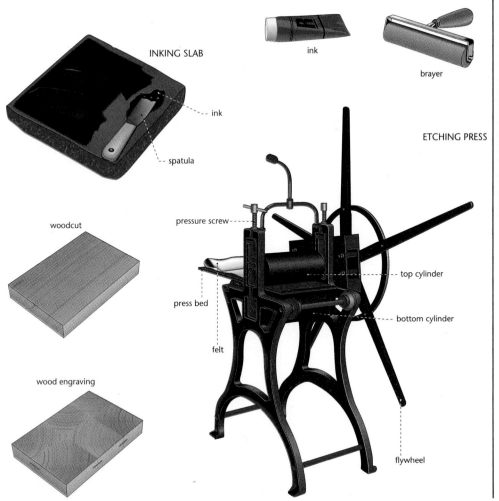

pressure screw

top cylinder

press bed

bottom cylinder

felt

wood engraving

flywheel

581

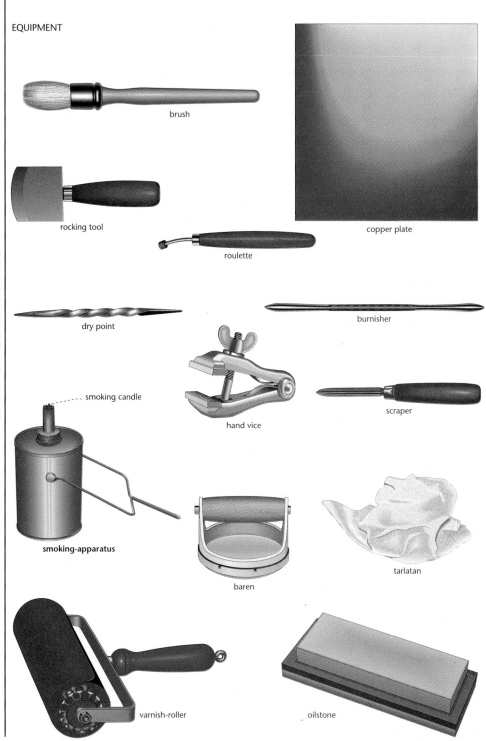

EQUIPMENT

brush

rocking tool

roulette

copper plate

dry point

burnisher

smoking candle

hand vice

scraper

smoking-apparatus

baren

tarlatan

varnish-roller

oilstone

CREATIVE LEISURE ACTIVITIES

LITHOGRAPHY

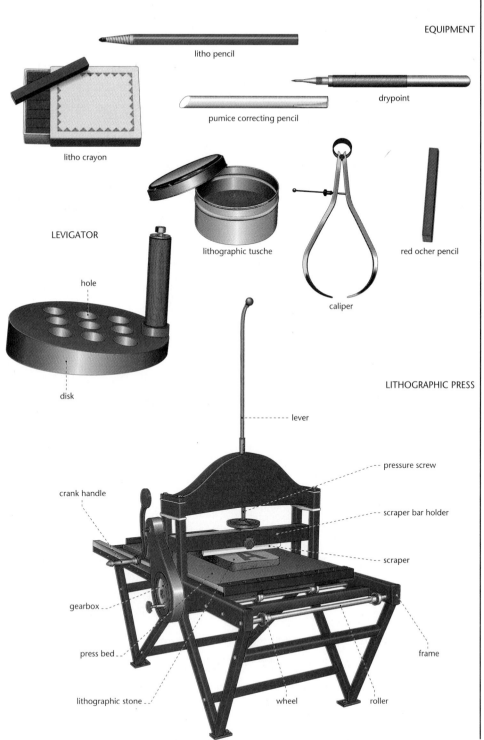

litho pencil

litho crayon

pumice correcting pencil

drypoint

LEVIGATOR

lithographic tusche

red ocher pencil

hole

caliper

disk

LITHOGRAPHIC PRESS

lever

pressure screw

crank handle

scraper bar holder

scraper

gearbox

press bed

frame

lithographic stone

wheel

roller

POTTERY

TURNING

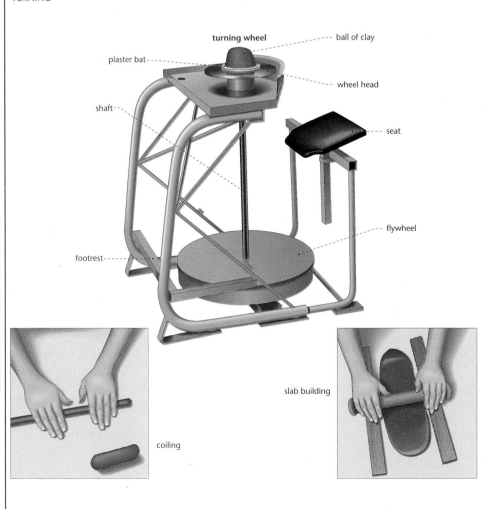

turning wheel — ball of clay

plaster bat —

— wheel head

shaft —

— seat

— flywheel

footrest —

coiling

slab building

TOOLS

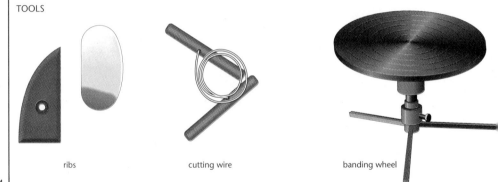

ribs

cutting wire

banding wheel

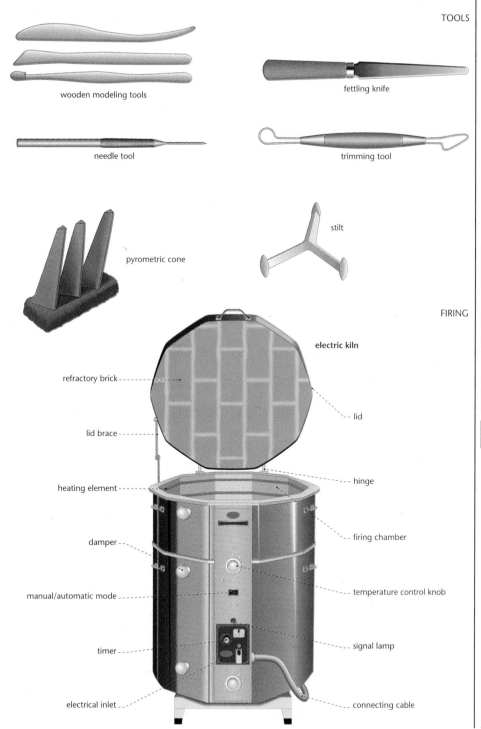

wooden modeling tools

fettling knife

needle tool

trimming tool

stilt

pyrometric cone

electric kiln

refractory brick

lid

lid brace

heating element

hinge

firing chamber

damper

manual/automatic mode

temperature control knob

timer

signal lamp

electrical inlet

connecting cable

WOOD CARVING

STEPS

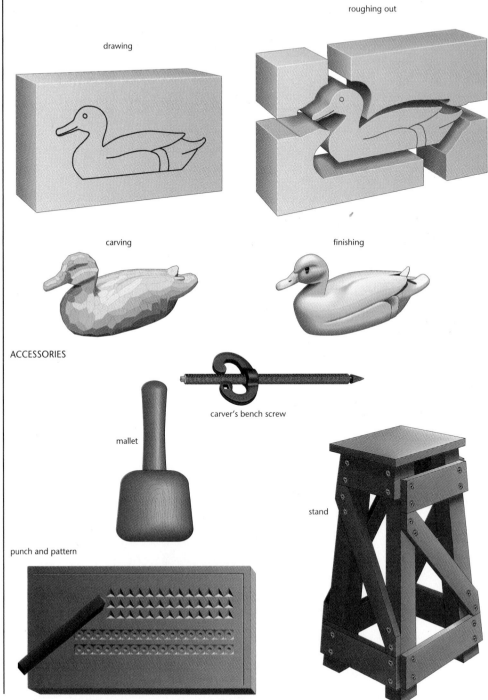

roughing out

drawing

carving

finishing

ACCESSORIES

carver's bench screw

mallet

stand

punch and pattern

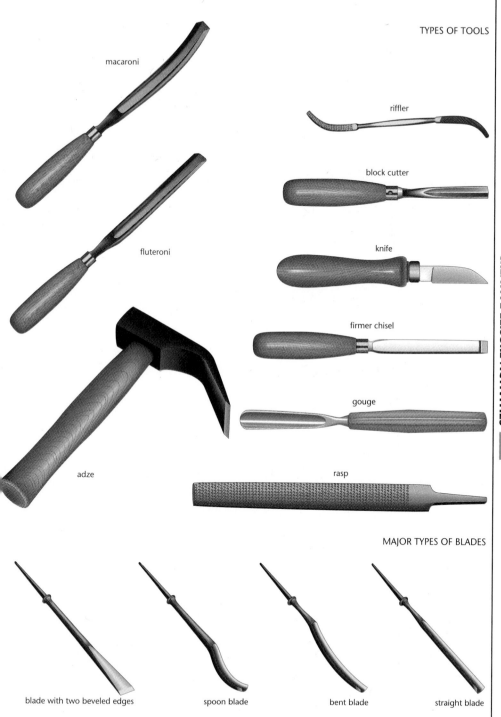

macaroni

riffler

block cutter

fluteroni

knife

firmer chisel

adze

gouge

rasp

MAJOR TYPES OF BLADES

blade with two beveled edges

spoon blade

bent blade

straight blade

MAJOR TECHNIQUES

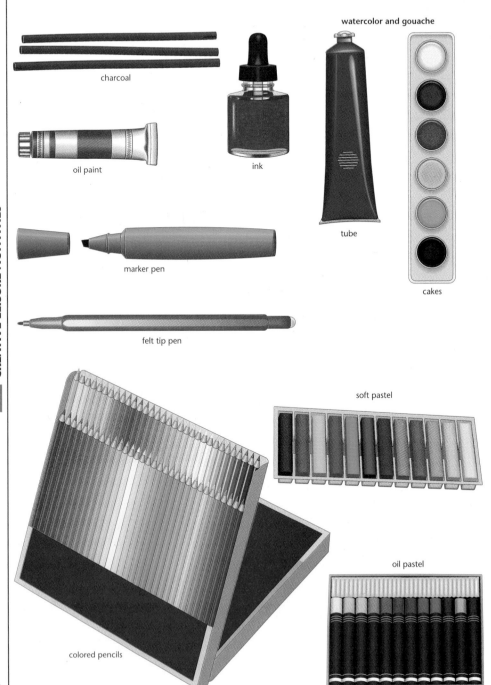

charcoal

oil paint

ink

watercolor and gouache

tube

cakes

marker pen

felt tip pen

soft pastel

oil pastel

colored pencils

reservoir-nib pen

sumie

brush

painting knife

flat brush

fan brush

spatula

SUPPORTS

paper

cardboard

canvas

panel

AIRBRUSH

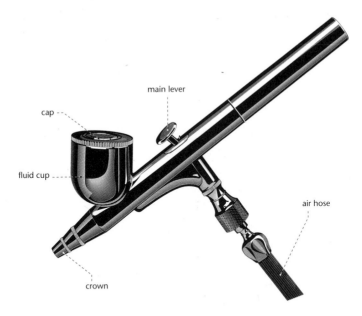

main lever

cap

fluid cup

air hose

crown

CROSS SECTION OF AN AIRBRUSH

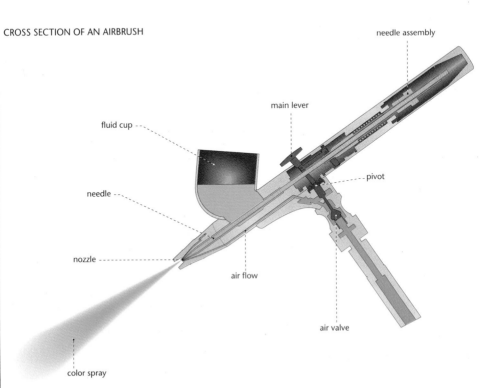

needle assembly

main lever

fluid cup

pivot

needle

nozzle

air flow

air valve

color spray

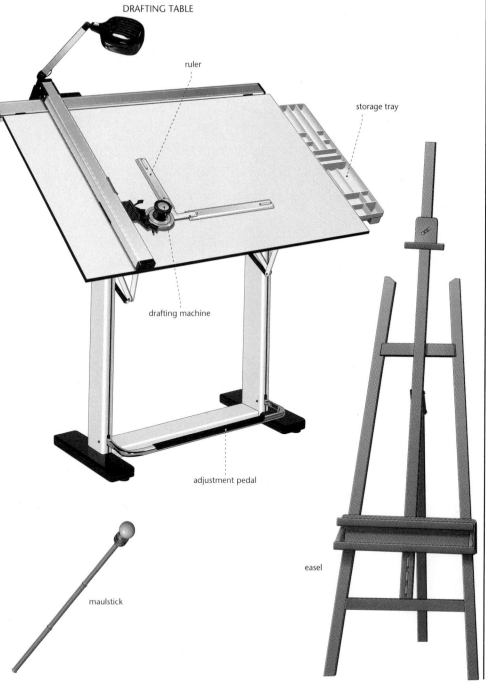

DRAFTING TABLE

ruler

storage tray

drafting machine

adjustment pedal

maulstick

easel

ACCESSORIES

color chart

palette with hollows

dipper

palette with dipper

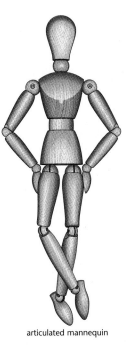

articulated mannequin

UTILITY LIQUIDS

varnish

linseed oil

turpentine

fixative

SPORTS

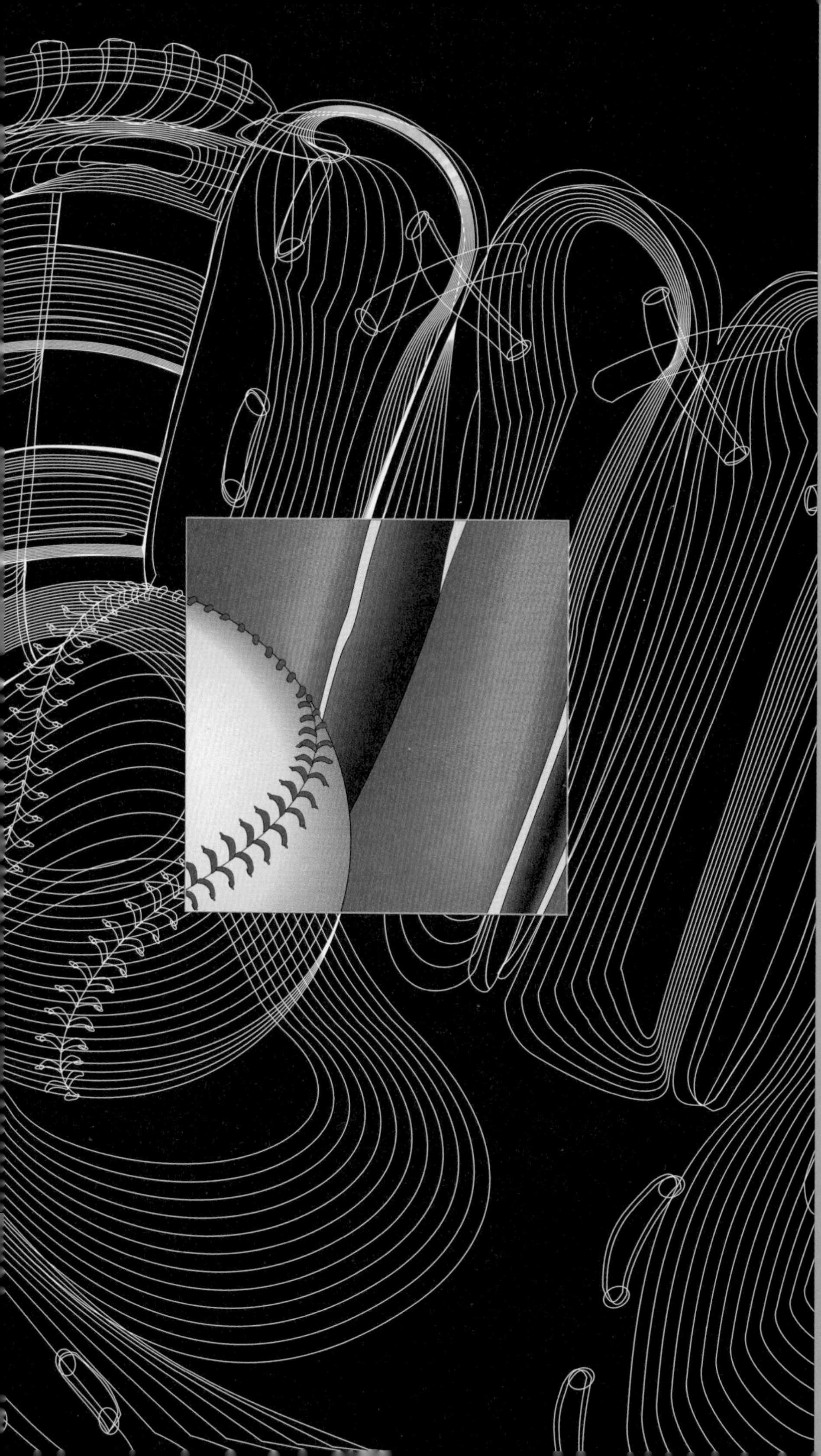

CONTENTS

TEAM GAMES

BASEBALL 595
CRICKET 598
SOCCER 600
FOOTBALL 602
RUGBY 606
FIELD HOCKEY 607
ICE HOCKEY 608
BASKETBALL 610
NETBALL 611
HANDBALL 612
VOLLEYBALL 613
TENNIS 614
SQUASH 616
RACQUETBALL 617
BADMINTON 618
TABLE TENNIS 619
CURLING 620

WATER SPORTS

SWIMMING 621
DIVING 624
WATER POLO 626
SCUBA DIVING 627
SAILING 628
SAILBOARD 631
ROWING AND SCULLING 632
WATER SKIING 633

AERIAL SPORTS

BALLOONING 634
SKY DIVING 635
PARAGLIDING 636
HANG GLIDING 637
GLIDING 638

WINTER SPORTS

ALPINE SKIING 640
CROSS-COUNTRY SKIING 642
BOBSLED 643
LUGE..643
SKATING 644
ROLLER SKATE 645
SNOWSHOE...645

EQUESTRIAN SPORTS

RIDING 646
TYPES OF BITS...650
HORSE RACING 651
HARNESS RACING...652

ATHLETICS

TRACK AND FIELD ATHLETICS..654
GYMNASTICS...659
WEIGHTLIFTING 662
FITNESS EQUIPMENT 663

COMBAT SPORTS

FENCING 666
JUDO 668
BOXING 669

LEISURE SPORTS

FISHING 670
BILLIARDS 673
GOLF 676
MOUNTAINEERING 680
BOWLS AND PETANQUE 682
BOWLING 683
ARCHERY...684

CAMPING

CAMPING 685
KNOTS 691
CABLE 692

BASEBALL

BATTER

CATCHER

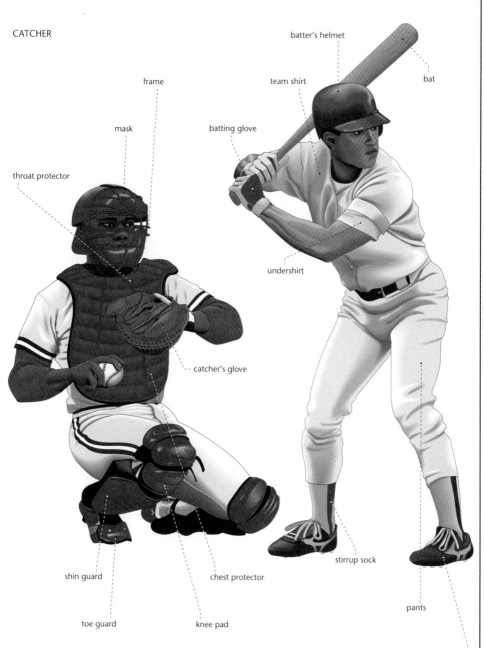

frame

batter's helmet

team shirt

bat

mask

batting glove

throat protector

undershirt

catcher's glove

shin guard

chest protector

toe guard

knee pad

stirrup sock

pants

spiked shoe

TEAM GAMES

595

BASEBALL

BAT

knob

handle

crest

hitting area

BASEBALL

$2\ {}^{13}/_{16} - 2\ {}^{29}/_{32}$ in

BASEBALL, CROSS SECTION

yarn ball

cork ball

cover

stitches

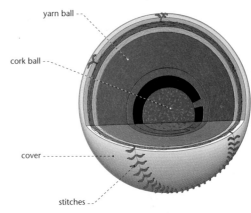

FIELDER'S GLOVE

web

strap

thumb

finger

palm

heel

lace

TEAM GAMES

596

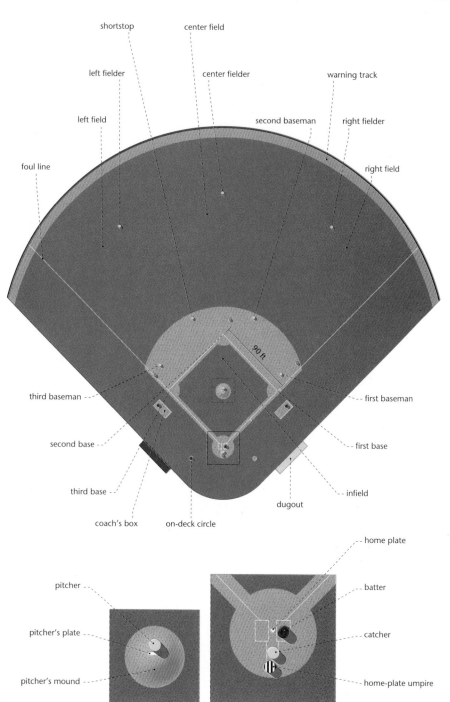

shortstop

center field

left fielder

center fielder

warning track

left field

second baseman

right fielder

foul line

right field

third baseman ---

first baseman

second base ---

first base

third base ---

infield

dugout

coach's box

on-deck circle

home plate

pitcher ---

batter

pitcher's plate ---

catcher

pitcher's mound ---

home-plate umpire

90 ft

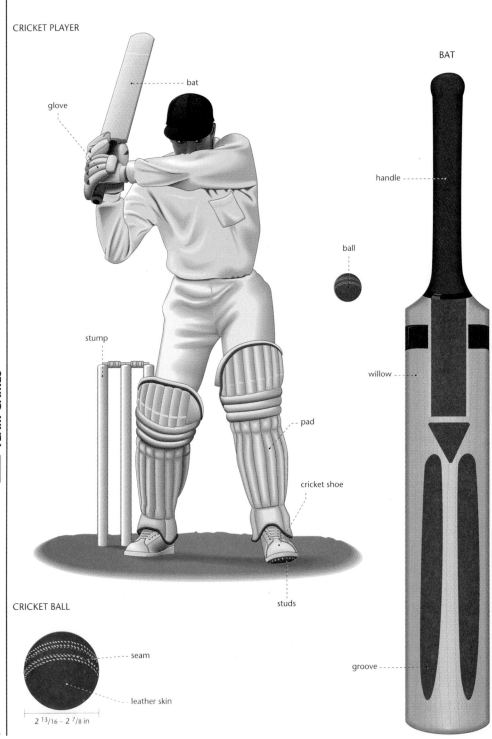

CRICKET PLAYER

bat

glove

BAT

handle

ball

stump

willow

pad

cricket shoe

studs

CRICKET BALL

groove

seam

leather skin

2 13/16 – 2 7/8 in

WICKET

FIELD

bail

stump

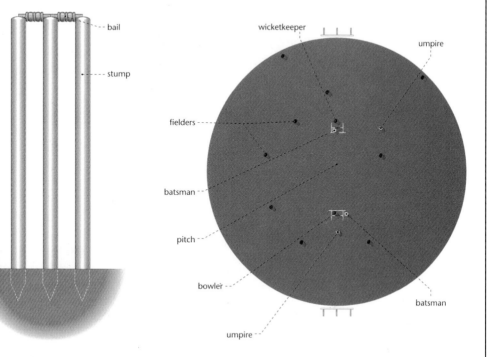

wicketkeeper

umpire

fielders

batsman

pitch

bowler

batsman

umpire

PITCH

wicketkeeper

wicket

run

batsman

return crease

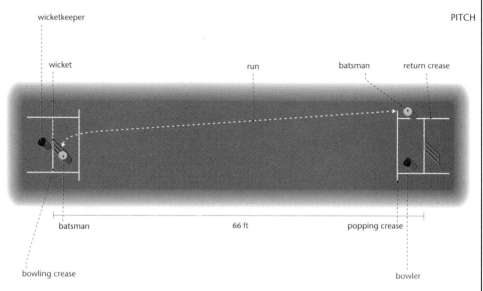

batsman

66 ft

popping crease

bowling crease

bowler

SOCCER

TEAM GAMES

SOCCER PLAYER

SOCCER BALL

team shirt

8 1/2 in

shorts

shin guard

soccer shoe

interchangeable studs

600

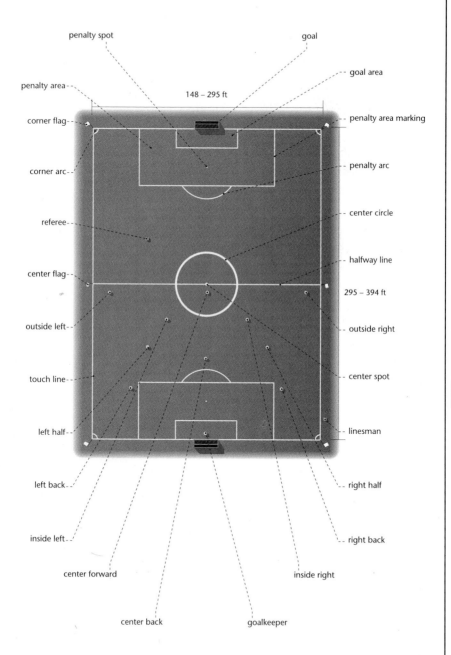

penalty spot

goal

goal area

penalty area

148 – 295 ft

penalty area marking

corner flag

penalty arc

corner arc

center circle

referee

halfway line

center flag

295 – 394 ft

outside left

outside right

touch line

center spot

left half

linesman

left back

right half

inside left

right back

center forward

inside right

center back

goalkeeper

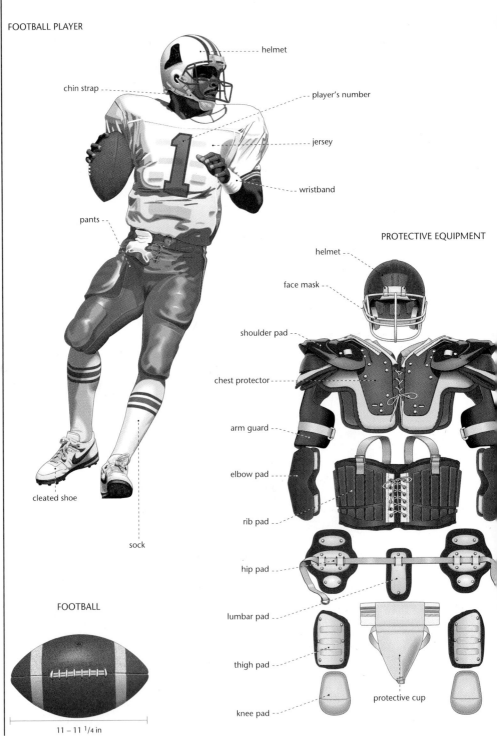

FOOTBALL PLAYER

helmet

chin strap

player's number

jersey

wristband

pants

PROTECTIVE EQUIPMENT

helmet

face mask

shoulder pad

chest protector

arm guard

elbow pad

rib pad

hip pad

lumbar pad

thigh pad

protective cup

knee pad

cleated shoe

sock

TEAM GAMES

FOOTBALL

11 – 11 ¹/₄ in

602

OFFENSE

DEFENSE

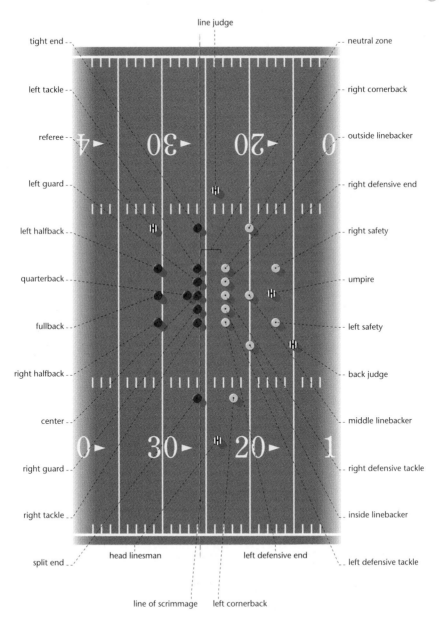

tight end

left tackle

referee

left guard

left halfback

quarterback

fullback

right halfback

center

right guard

right tackle

split end   head linesman

line judge

neutral zone

right cornerback

outside linebacker

right defensive end

right safety

umpire

left safety

back judge

middle linebacker

right defensive tackle

inside linebacker

left defensive end   left defensive tackle

line of scrimmage   left cornerback

TEAM GAMES

PLAYING FIELD FOR AMERICAN FOOTBALL

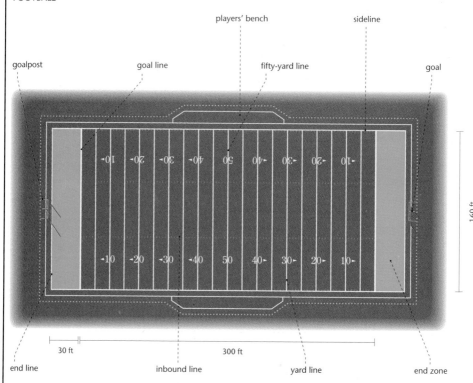

players' bench

sideline

goalpost

goal line

fifty-yard line

goal

160 ft

30 ft

300 ft

end line

inbound line

yard line

end zone

PLAYING FIELD FOR CANADIAN FOOTBALL

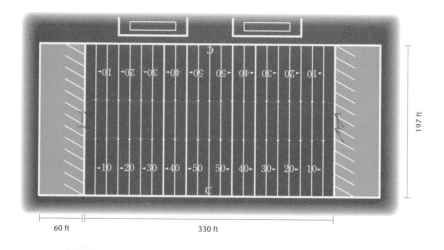

197 ft

60 ft

330 ft

TEAM GAMES

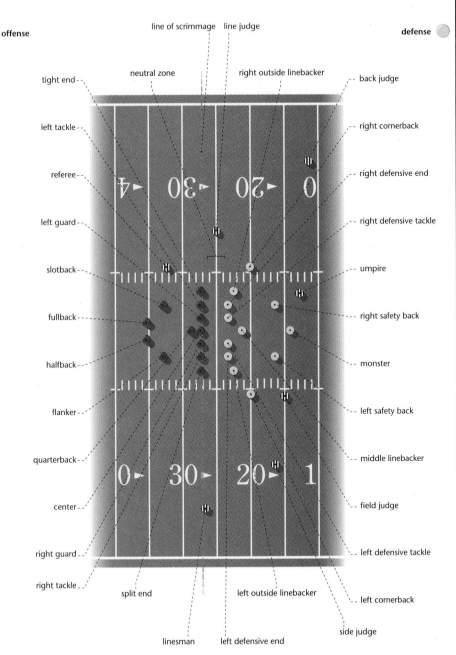

offense

defense

line of scrimmage   line judge

neutral zone   right outside linebacker

tight end

left tackle

referee

left guard

slotback

fullback

halfback

flanker

quarterback

center

right guard

right tackle

back judge

right cornerback

right defensive end

right defensive tackle

umpire

right safety back

monster

left safety back

middle linebacker

field judge

left defensive tackle

left cornerback

split end   left outside linebacker   side judge

linesman   left defensive end

TEAM GAMES

RUGBY

FIELD

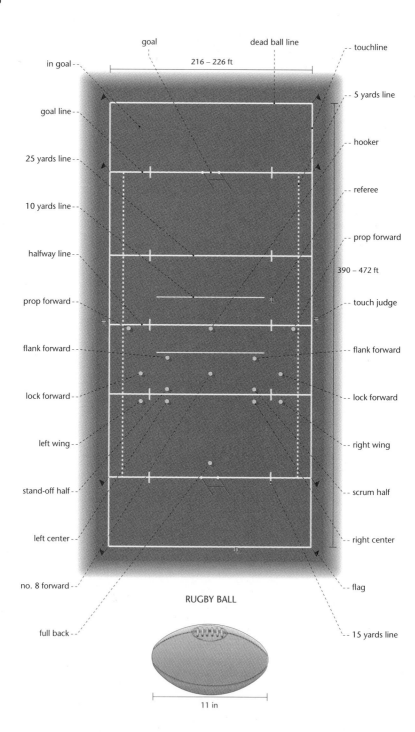

goal

dead ball line

-- touchline

in goal --

216 – 226 ft

-- 5 yards line

goal line --

-- hooker

25 yards line --

-- referee

10 yards line --

-- prop forward

halfway line --

390 – 472 ft

prop forward --

-- touch judge

flank forward --

-- flank forward

lock forward --

-- lock forward

left wing --

-- right wing

stand-off half --

-- scrum half

left center --

-- right center

no. 8 forward --

-- flag

RUGBY BALL

full back --

-- 15 yards line

11 in

FIELD HOCKEY

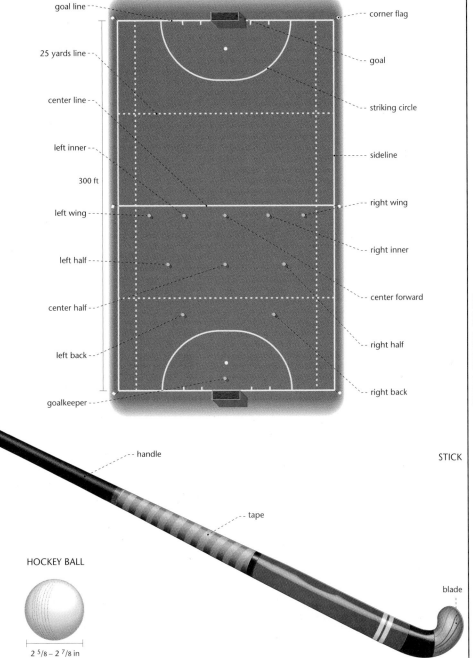

180 ft

goal line

corner flag

goal

striking circle

25 yards line

center line

left inner

300 ft

sideline

left wing

right wing

left half

right inner

center half

center forward

left back

right half

goalkeeper

right back

handle

STICK

tape

HOCKEY BALL

blade

2 5/8 – 2 7/8 in

ICE HOCKEY

RINK

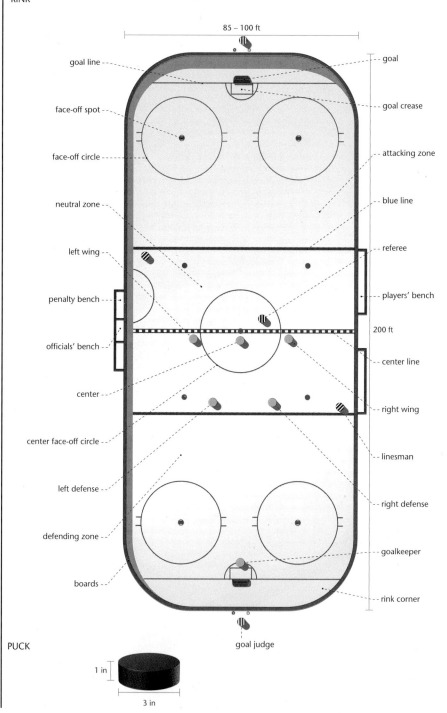

85 – 100 ft

goal line

goal

face-off spot

goal crease

face-off circle

attacking zone

neutral zone

blue line

left wing

referee

penalty bench

players' bench

200 ft

officials' bench

center line

center

center face-off circle

linesman

left defense

right defense

defending zone

boards

goalkeeper

rink corner

PUCK

goal judge

right wing

1 in

3 in

608

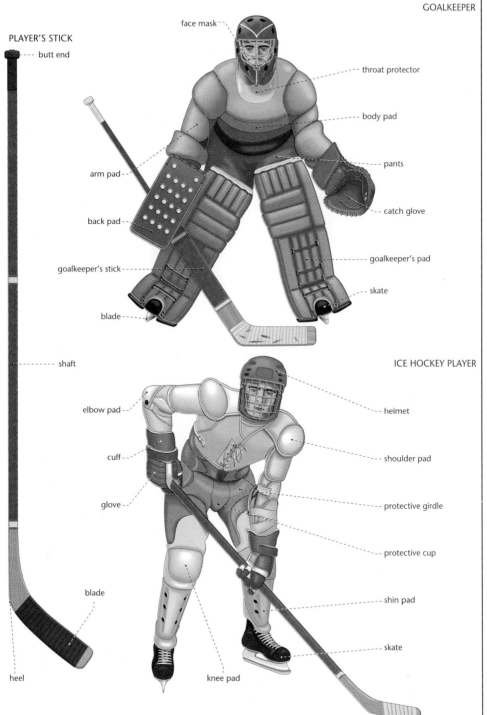

PLAYER'S STICK

butt end

face mask

throat protector

body pad

arm pad

pants

back pad

catch glove

goalkeeper's stick

goalkeeper's pad

blade

skate

shaft

ICE HOCKEY PLAYER

elbow pad

helmet

cuff

shoulder pad

glove

protective girdle

protective cup

blade

shin pad

skate

heel

knee pad

BASKETBALL

COURT

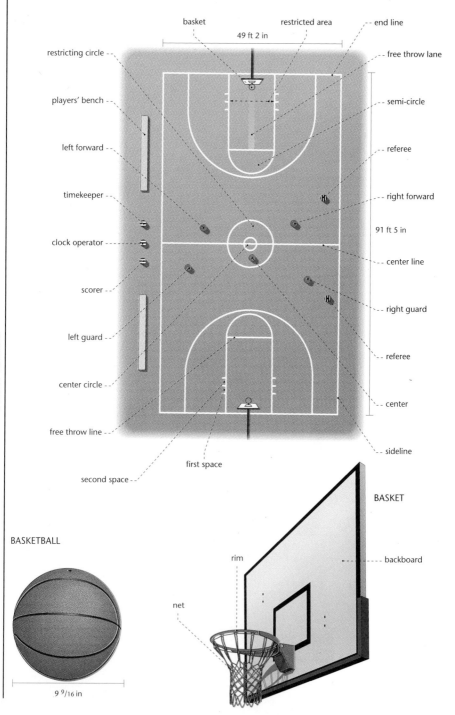

basket

restricted area

end line

49 ft 2 in

restricting circle

free throw lane

players' bench

semi-circle

left forward

referee

timekeeper

right forward

clock operator

91 ft 5 in

center line

scorer

right guard

left guard

referee

center circle

center

free throw line

sideline

first space

second space

BASKET

BASKETBALL

rim

backboard

net

9 9/16 in

NETBALL

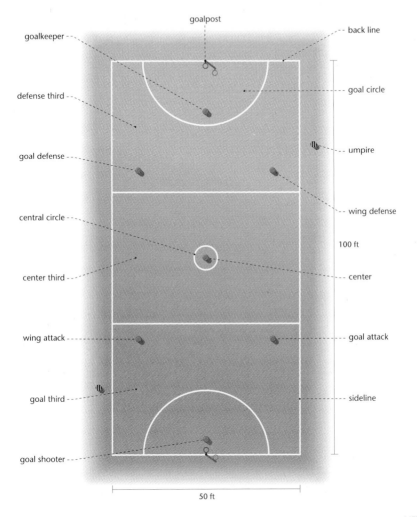

goalpost

goalkeeper

back line

goal circle

defense third

umpire

goal defense

wing defense

central circle

100 ft

center third

center

wing attack

goal attack

goal third

sideline

goal shooter

50 ft

NETBALL

8 5/8 – 8 3/4 in

COURT

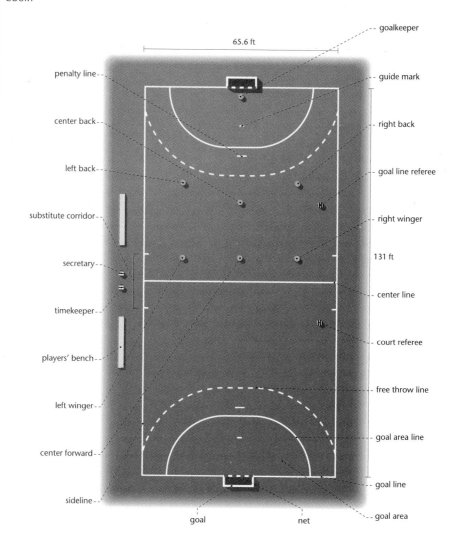

65.6 ft

goalkeeper

penalty line

guide mark

center back

right back

left back

goal line referee

substitute corridor

right winger

secretary

131 ft

timekeeper

center line

court referee

players' bench

free throw line

left winger

goal area line

center forward

goal line

sideline

goal area

goal

net

HANDBALL

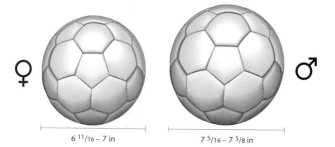

♀ 6 ¹¹/₁₆ – 7 in

♂ 7 ⁵/₁₆ – 7 ⁵/₈ in

VOLLEYBALL

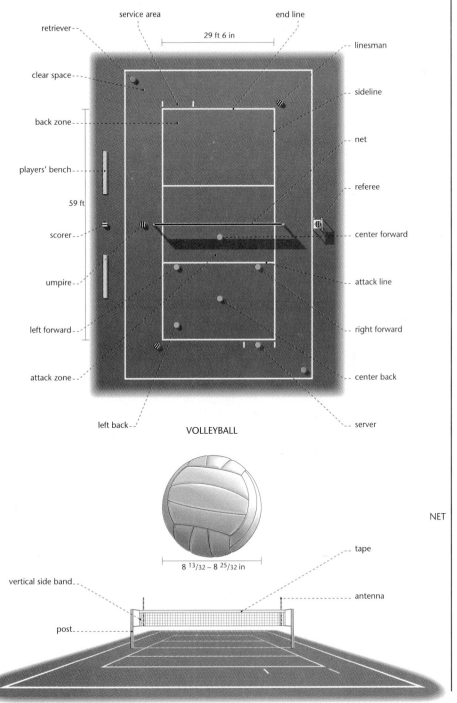

retriever

service area

end line

29 ft 6 in

linesman

clear space

sideline

back zone

net

players' bench

referee

59 ft

scorer

center forward

umpire

attack line

left forward

right forward

attack zone

center back

left back

server

VOLLEYBALL

8 13/32 – 8 25/32 in

tape

vertical side band

antenna

post

COURT

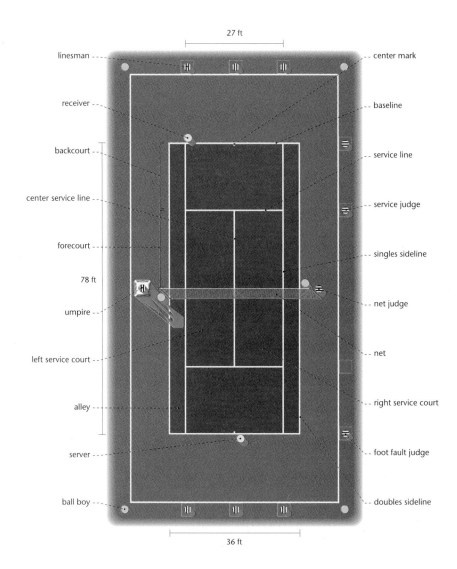

27 ft

linesman ---- center mark

receiver --- baseline

backcourt --- service line

center service line --- service judge

forecourt --- singles sideline

78 ft

umpire --- net judge

left service court --- net

alley --- right service court

server --- foot fault judge

ball boy --- doubles sideline

36 ft

NET

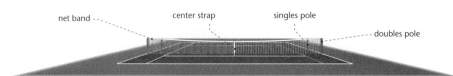

net band --- center strap --- singles pole --- doubles pole

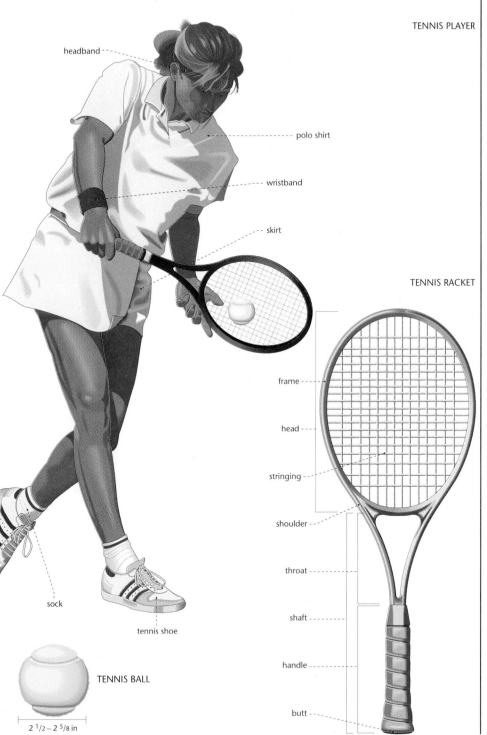

TENNIS PLAYER

headband

polo shirt

wristband

skirt

TENNIS RACKET

frame

head

stringing

shoulder

throat

shaft

handle

butt

sock

tennis shoe

TENNIS BALL

2 $\frac{1}{2}$ – 2 $\frac{5}{8}$ in

SQUASH

SQUASH BALL

SQUASH RACKET

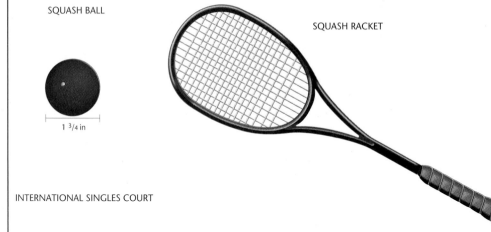

1 3/4 in

INTERNATIONAL SINGLES COURT

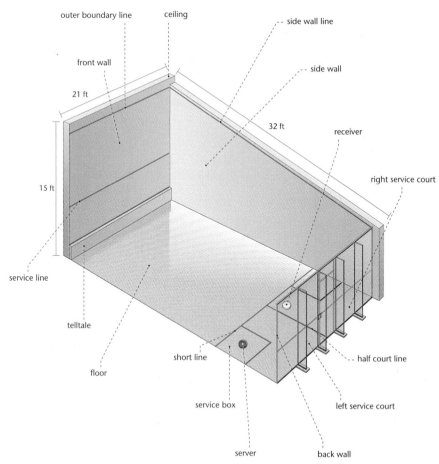

outer boundary line

ceiling

side wall line

front wall

side wall

21 ft

32 ft

receiver

15 ft

right service court

service line

telltale

short line

half court line

floor

service box

left service court

server

back wall

616

RACQUETBALL

RACQUETBALL RACKET

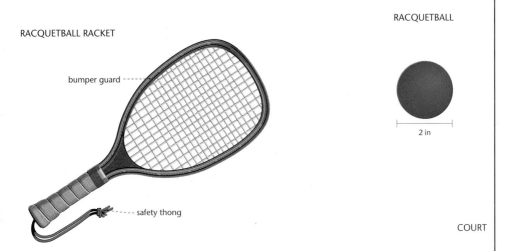

bumper guard

safety thong

RACQUETBALL

2 in

COURT

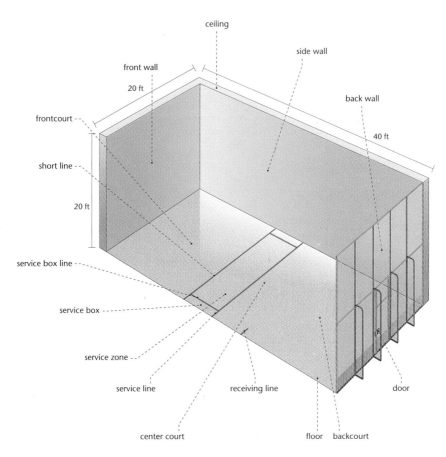

ceiling

side wall

front wall

back wall

20 ft

40 ft

frontcourt

short line

20 ft

service box line

service box

service zone

service line

receiving line

door

center court

floor   backcourt

BADMINTON

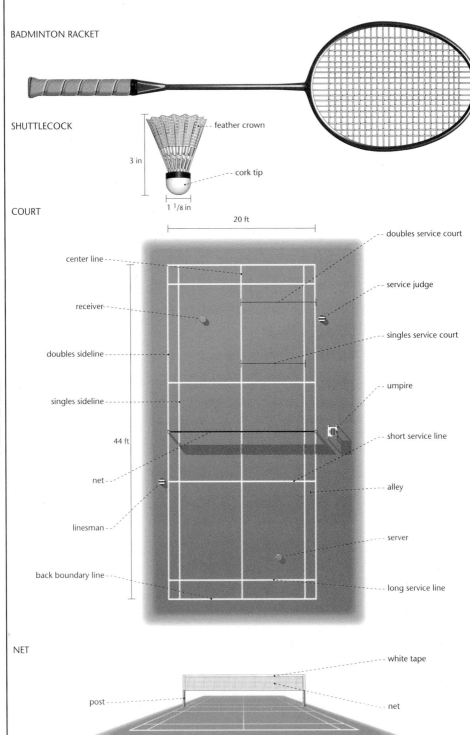

BADMINTON RACKET

SHUTTLECOCK

feather crown

3 in

cork tip

1 1/8 in

COURT

20 ft

doubles service court

center line

service judge

receiver

singles service court

doubles sideline

umpire

singles sideline

44 ft

short service line

net

alley

linesman

server

back boundary line

long service line

NET

white tape

post

net

TABLE TENNIS

TABLE

mesh

side line

net

upper edge

playing surface

white tape

center line

end line

net support

6 in

9 ft

5 ft

leg

1 1/2 in

table tennis ball

TYPES OF GRIPS

TABLE TENNIS PADDLE

face

penholder grip

covering

handle

blade

shake-hands grip

CURLING

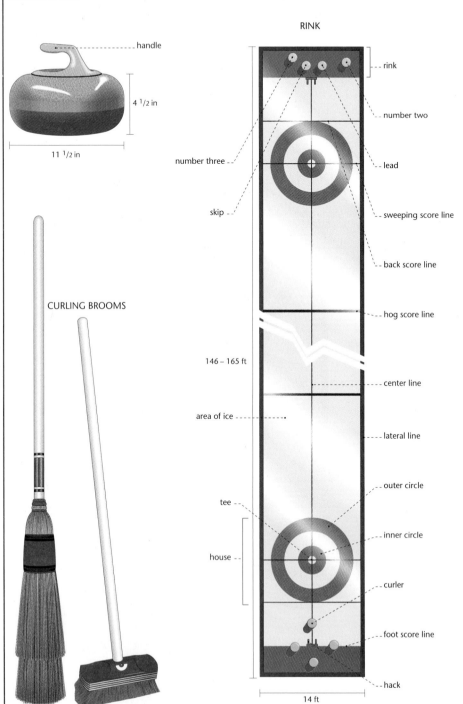

CURLING STONE

handle

4 1/2 in

11 1/2 in

CURLING BROOMS

RINK

rink

number two

number three

lead

skip

sweeping score line

back score line

hog score line

146 – 165 ft

center line

area of ice

lateral line

outer circle

tee

inner circle

house

curler

foot score line

hack

14 ft

SWIMMING

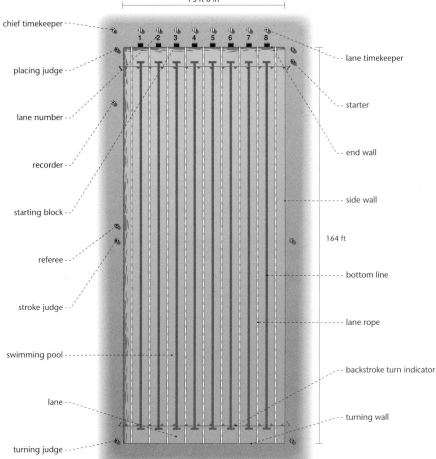

COMPETITIVE COURSE

75 ft 6 in

chief timekeeper

placing judge

lane number

recorder

starting block

referee

stroke judge

swimming pool

lane

turning judge

lane timekeeper

starter

end wall

side wall

164 ft

bottom line

lane rope

backstroke turn indicator

turning wall

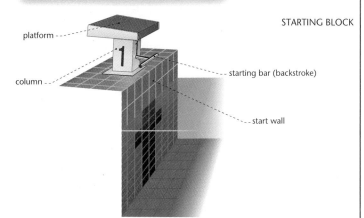

STARTING BLOCK

platform

column

starting bar (backstroke)

start wall

WATER SPORTS

TYPES OF STROKES

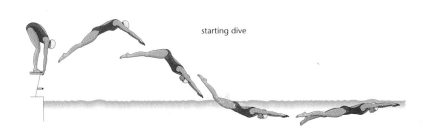

starting dive

FRONT CRAWL STROKE

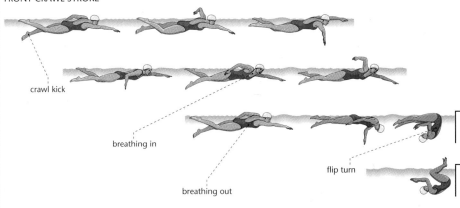

crawl kick

breathing in

breathing out

flip turn

turning wall

BREASTSTROKE

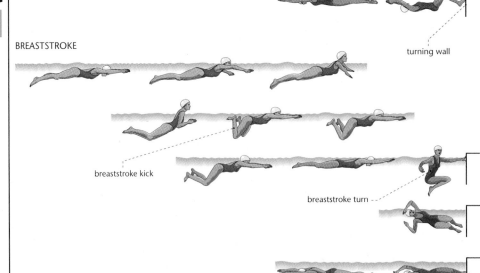

breaststroke kick

breaststroke turn

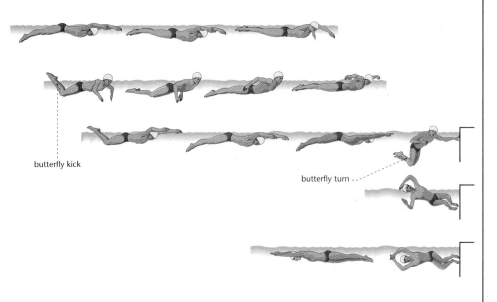

butterfly kick

butterfly turn

BACKSTROKE START

BACKSTROKE

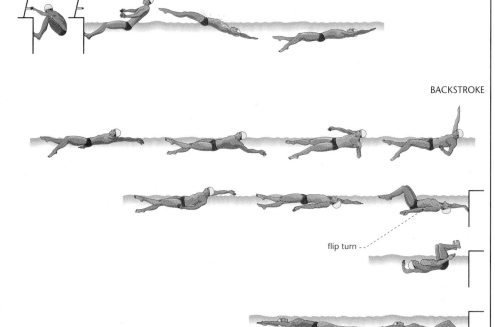

flip turn

DIVING

DIVING INSTALLATIONS

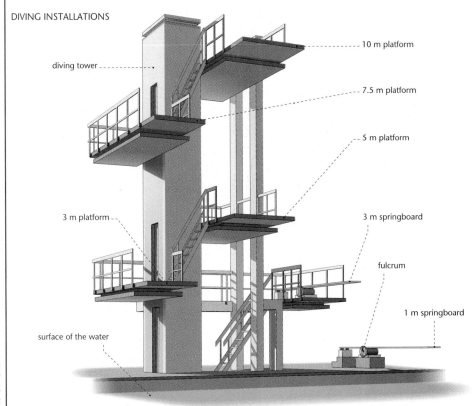

diving tower

10 m platform

7.5 m platform

5 m platform

3 m platform

3 m springboard

fulcrum

1 m springboard

surface of the water

STARTING POSITIONS

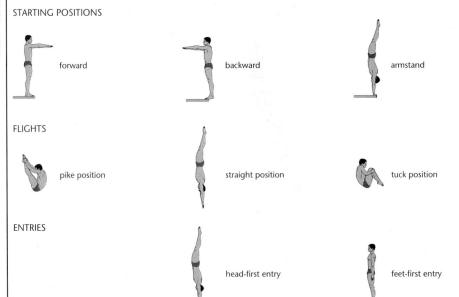

forward

backward

armstand

FLIGHTS

pike position

straight position

tuck position

ENTRIES

head-first entry

feet-first entry

FORWARD DIVE

BACKWARD DIVE

ARMSTAND DIVE

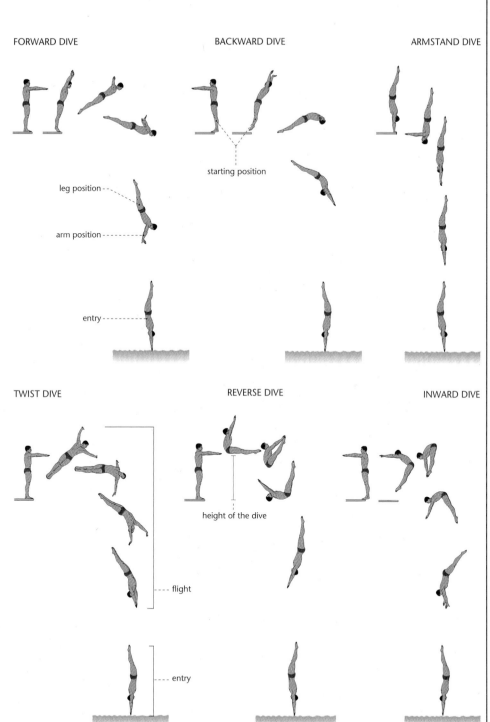

starting position

leg position

arm position

entry

TWIST DIVE

REVERSE DIVE

INWARD DIVE

height of the dive

flight

entry

PLAYING AREA

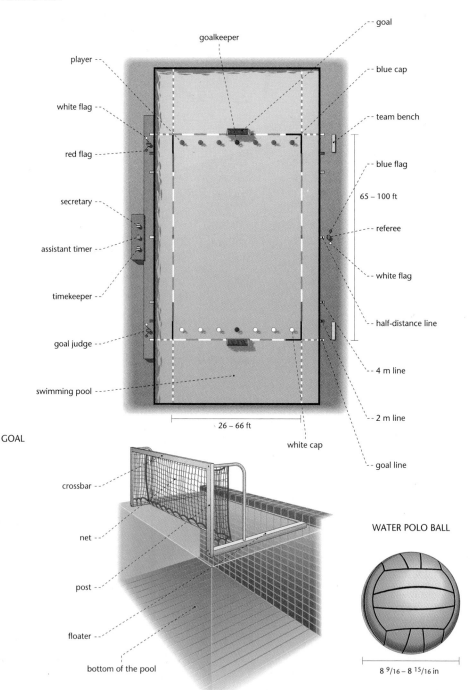

goal

goalkeeper

player

blue cap

white flag

team bench

red flag

blue flag

65 – 100 ft

secretary

referee

assistant timer

timekeeper

white flag

goal judge

half-distance line

swimming pool

4 m line

26 – 66 ft

2 m line

white cap

goal line

GOAL

crossbar

net

post

floater

bottom of the pool

WATER POLO BALL

8 9/16 – 8 15/16 in

SCUBA DIVING

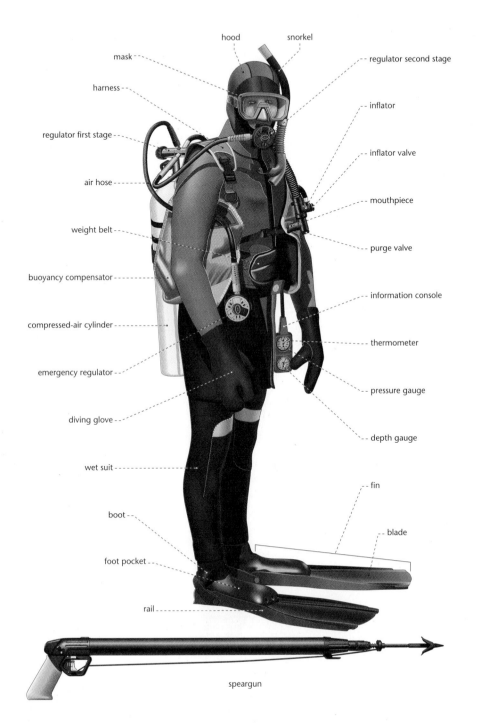

hood

snorkel

mask

harness

regulator first stage

air hose

weight belt

buoyancy compensator

compressed-air cylinder

emergency regulator

diving glove

wet suit

boot

foot pocket

rail

regulator second stage

inflator

inflator valve

mouthpiece

purge valve

information console

thermometer

pressure gauge

depth gauge

fin

blade

speargun

SAILBOAT

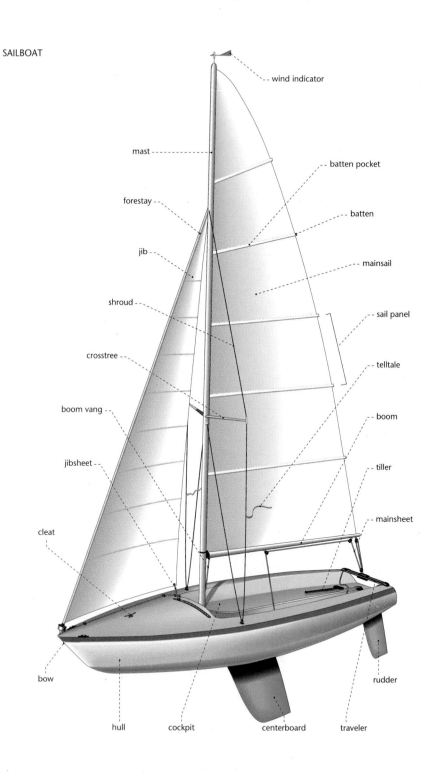

wind indicator

mast

batten pocket

forestay

batten

jib

mainsail

shroud

sail panel

crosstree

telltale

boom vang

boom

jibsheet

tiller

cleat

mainsheet

bow

rudder

hull

cockpit

centerboard

traveler

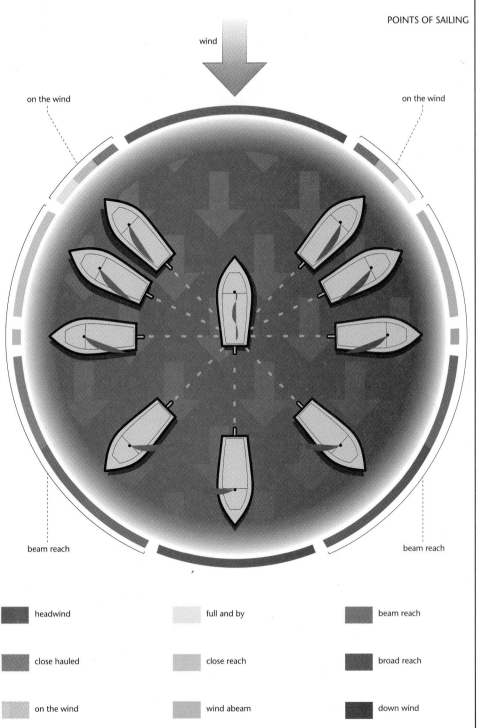

wind

on the wind

on the wind

beam reach

beam reach

headwind	full and by	beam reach
close hauled	close reach	broad reach
on the wind	wind abeam	down wind

UPPERWORKS

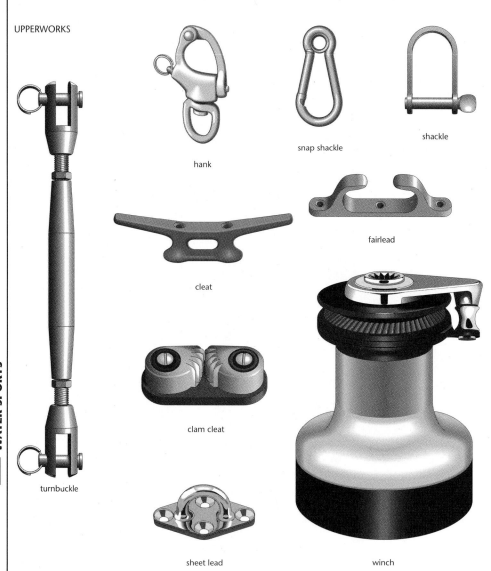

hank

snap shackle

shackle

cleat

fairlead

turnbuckle

clam cleat

sheet lead

winch

TRAVELER

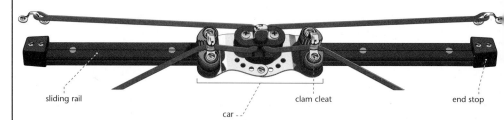

sliding rail

car

clam cleat

end stop

SAILBOARD

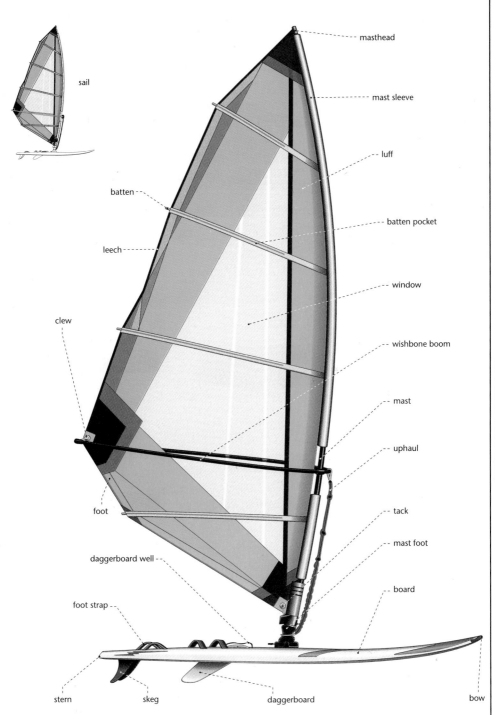

sail

masthead

mast sleeve

luff

batten

batten pocket

leech

window

clew

wishbone boom

mast

uphaul

foot

tack

daggerboard well

mast foot

foot strap

board

stern

skeg

daggerboard

bow

ROWING AND SCULLING

SCULLING (TWO OARS)

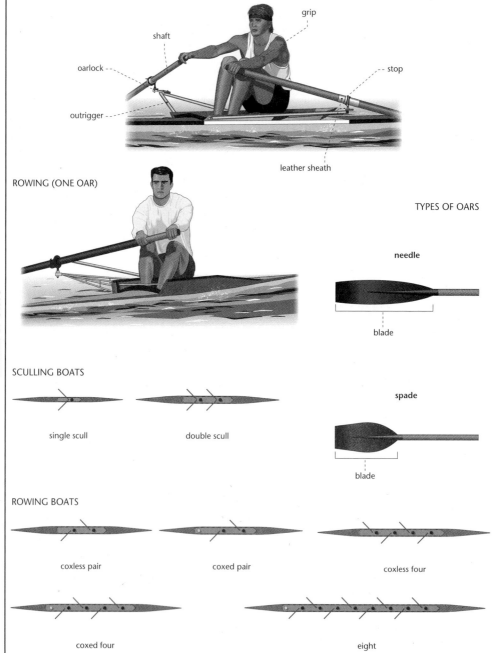

grip

shaft

oarlock

stop

outrigger

leather sheath

ROWING (ONE OAR)

TYPES OF OARS

needle

blade

SCULLING BOATS

spade

single scull

double scull

blade

ROWING BOATS

coxless pair

coxed pair

coxless four

coxed four

eight

WATER SKIING

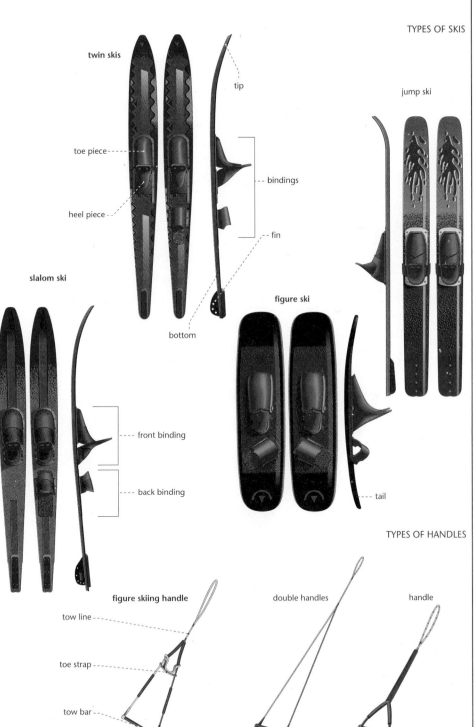

twin skis

tip

toe piece

heel piece

bindings

fin

slalom ski

jump ski

front binding

back binding

bottom

figure ski

tail

TYPES OF HANDLES

figure skiing handle

tow line

toe strap

tow bar

double handles

handle

WATER SPORTS

633

BALLOON

parachute valve

panel

webbing

envelope

balloon

wind guard

basket suspension cables

burner

basket

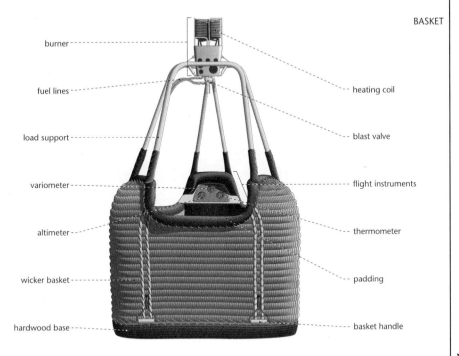

burner

fuel lines

load support

variometer

altimeter

wicker basket

hardwood base

heating coil

blast valve

flight instruments

thermometer

padding

basket handle

SKY DIVING

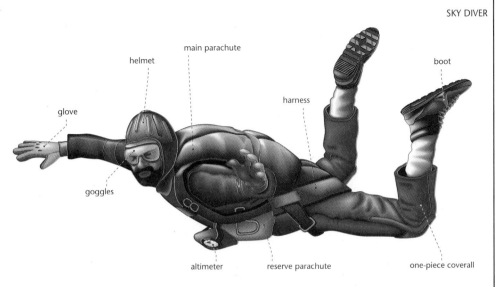

SKY DIVER

main parachute

helmet

boot

glove

harness

goggles

altimeter

reserve parachute

one-piece coverall

CANOPY

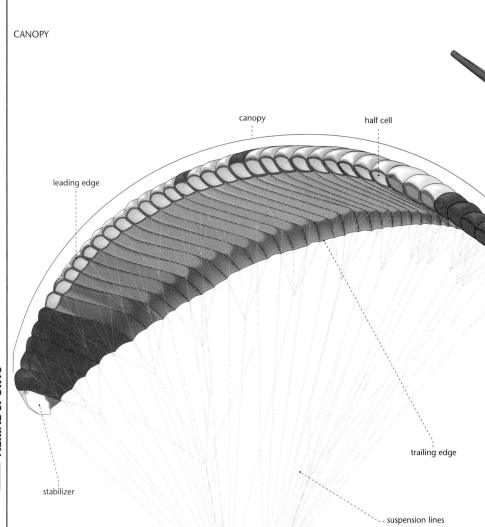

canopy

half cell

leading edge

trailing edge

stabilizer

suspension lines

helmet

brake loop

riser

harness

saddle

paragliding pilot

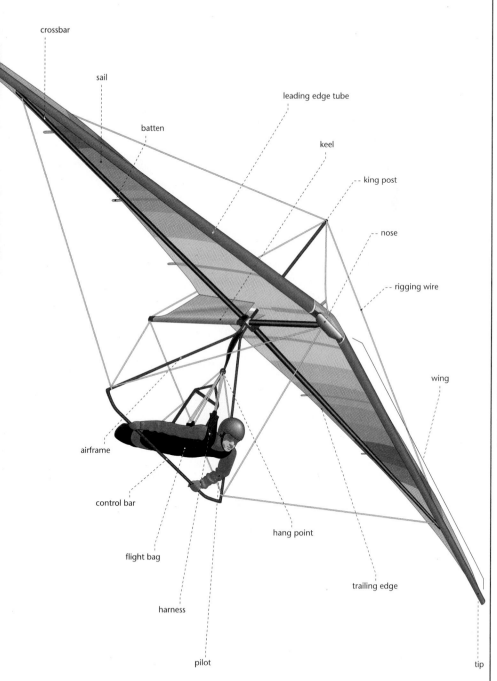

crossbar

sail

batten

leading edge tube

keel

king post

nose

rigging wire

wing

airframe

control bar

hang point

flight bag

trailing edge

harness

pilot

tip

GLIDER

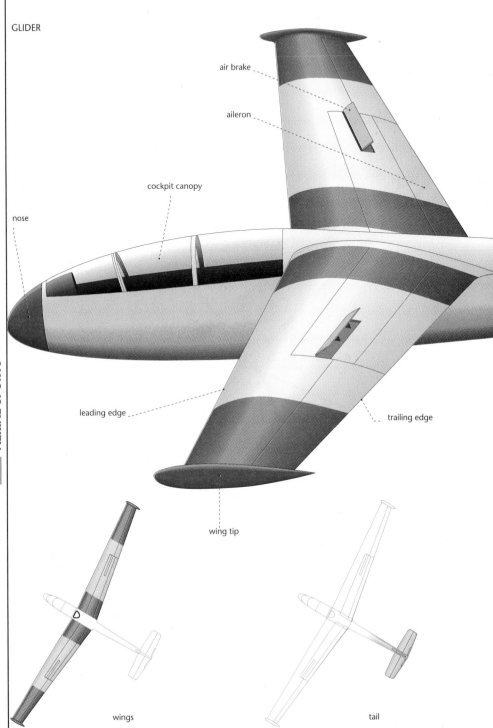

air brake

aileron

cockpit canopy

nose

leading edge

trailing edge

wing tip

wings

tail

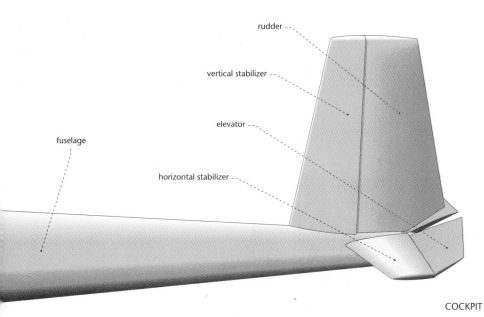

rudder

vertical stabilizer

elevator

fuselage

horizontal stabilizer

COCKPIT

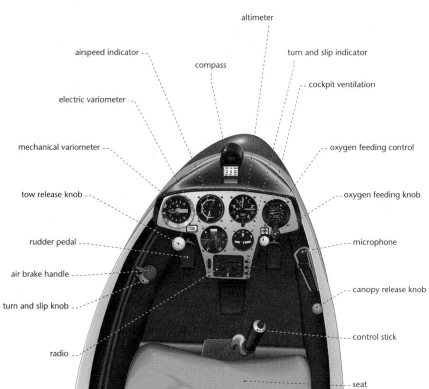

altimeter

airspeed indicator

compass

turn and slip indicator

cockpit ventilation

electric variometer

mechanical variometer

oxygen feeding control

tow release knob

oxygen feeding knob

rudder pedal

microphone

air brake handle

turn and slip knob

canopy release knob

radio

control stick

seat

ALPINE SKIER

ski hat

ski goggles

ski suit

ski glove

handle

wrist strap

ski pole

bottom

shovel

edge

ski stop

heel piece

ski boot

tip

toe piece

SAFETY BINDING

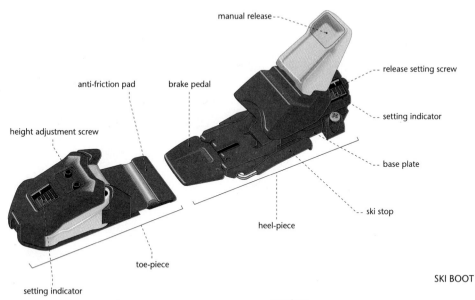

manual release

release setting screw

setting indicator

base plate

ski stop

heel-piece

anti-friction pad

brake pedal

height adjustment screw

toe-piece

setting indicator

SKI BOOT

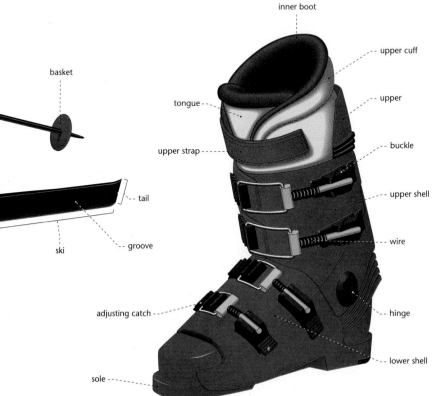

inner boot

upper cuff

tongue

upper

upper strap

buckle

basket

upper shell

tail

wire

ski

groove

adjusting catch

hinge

sole

lower shell

CROSS-COUNTRY SKIER

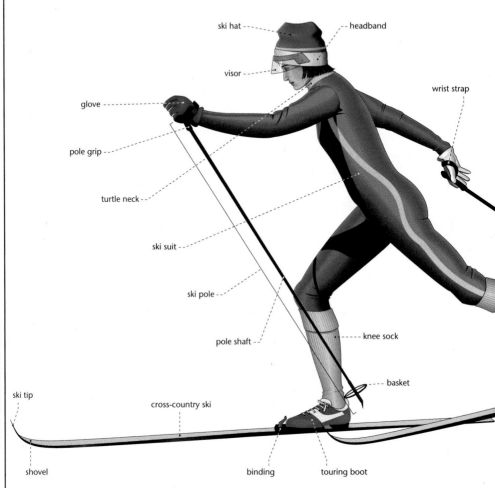

ski hat

headband

visor

wrist strap

glove

pole grip

turtle neck

ski suit

ski pole

pole shaft

knee sock

ski tip

cross-country ski

basket

shovel

binding

touring boot

CROSS-COUNTRY SKI

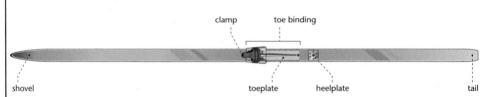

clamp

toe binding

shovel

toeplate

heelplate

tail

LUGE

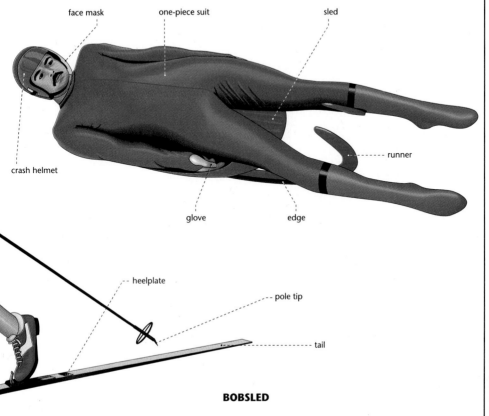

face mask

one-piece suit

sled

crash helmet

glove

edge

runner

heelplate

pole tip

tail

BOBSLED

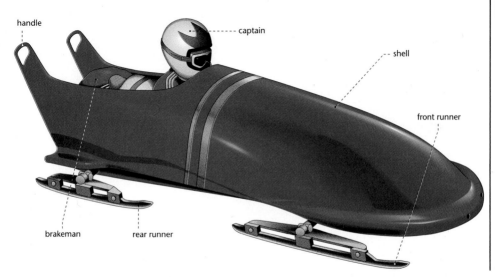

handle

captain

shell

front runner

brakeman

rear runner

FIGURE SKATE

tongue

lining

hook

backstay

lace

boot

eyelet

heel

sole

stanchion

toe pick

edge

blade

HOCKEY SKATE

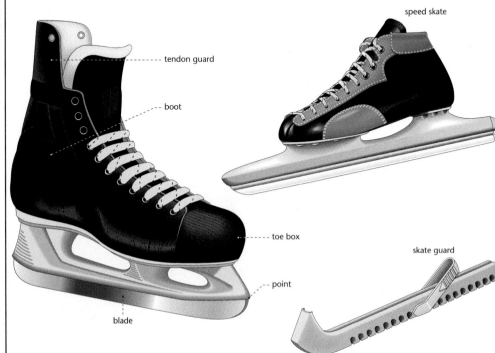

speed skate

tendon guard

boot

toe box

skate guard

point

blade

SNOWSHOE

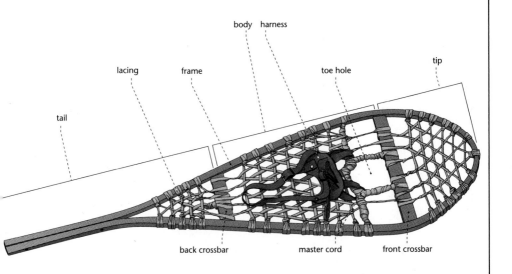

body   harness

lacing   frame   toe hole   tip

tail

back crossbar   master cord   front crossbar

ROLLER SKATE

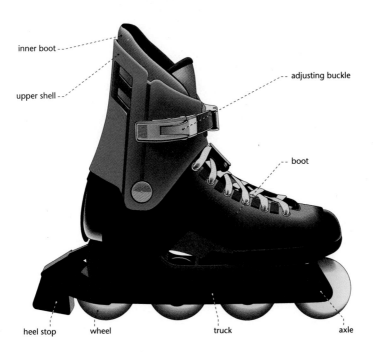

inner boot

adjusting buckle

upper shell

boot

heel stop   wheel   truck   axle

COMPETITION RING

EQUESTRIAN SPORTS

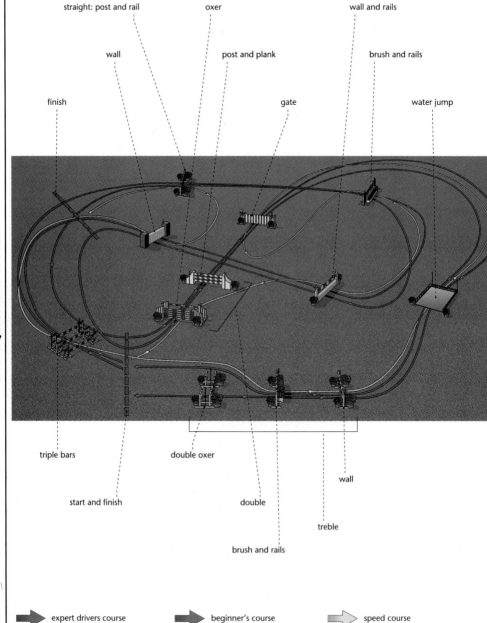

straight: post and rail

oxer

wall and rails

wall

post and plank

brush and rails

finish

gate

water jump

triple bars

double oxer

start and finish

double

wall

treble

brush and rails

expert drivers course

beginner's course

speed course

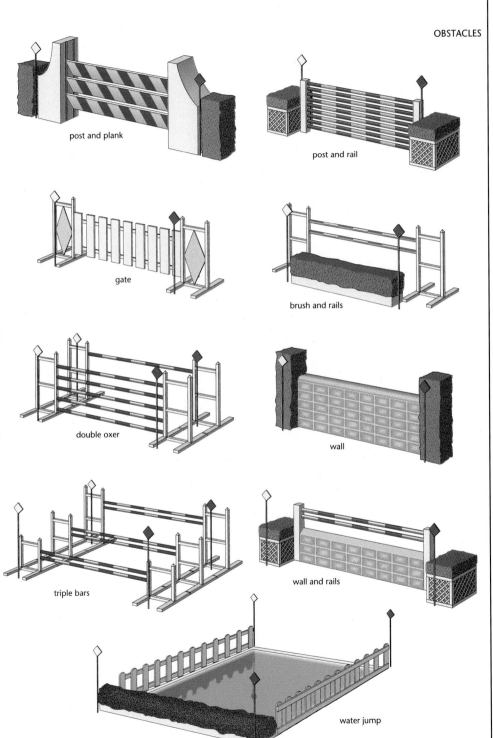

post and plank

post and rail

gate

brush and rails

double oxer

wall

triple bars

wall and rails

water jump

RIDER

EQUESTRIAN SPORTS

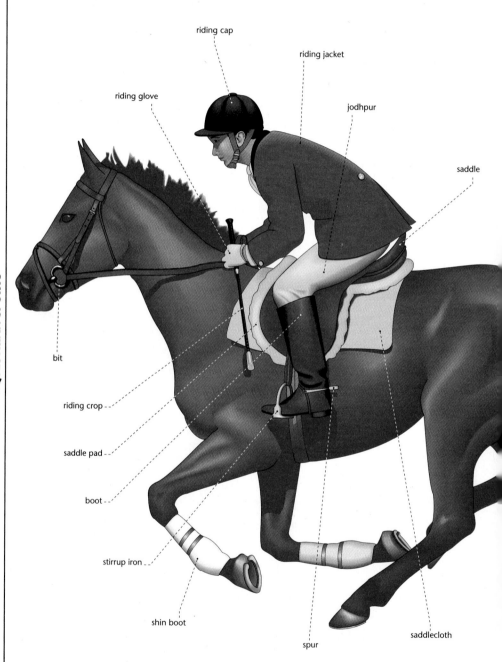

riding cap

riding jacket

riding glove

jodhpur

saddle

bit

riding crop

saddle pad

boot

stirrup iron

shin boot

spur

saddlecloth

648

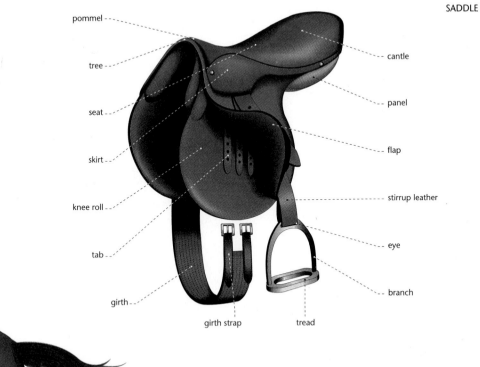

pommel

tree

seat

skirt

knee roll

tab

girth

girth strap

cantle

panel

flap

stirrup leather

eye

branch

tread

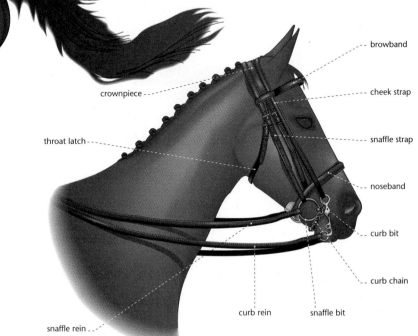

crownpiece

throat latch

snaffle rein

curb rein

snaffle bit

browband

cheek strap

snaffle strap

noseband

curb bit

curb chain

TYPES OF BITS

SNAFFLE BIT

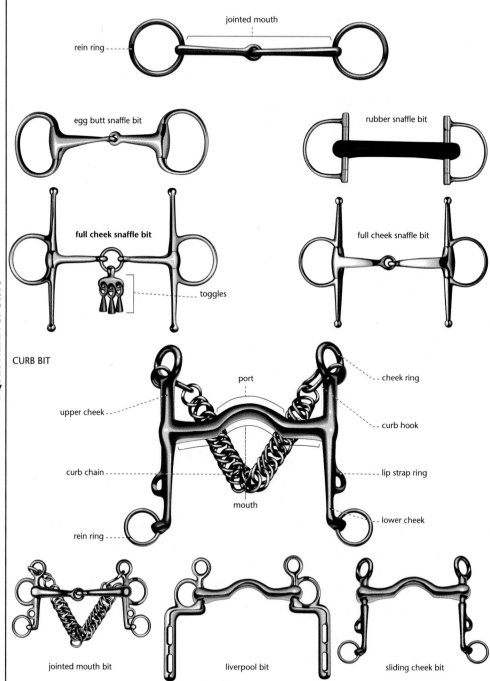

rein ring

jointed mouth

egg butt snaffle bit

rubber snaffle bit

full cheek snaffle bit

full cheek snaffle bit

toggles

CURB BIT

port

cheek ring

upper cheek

curb hook

curb chain

lip strap ring

mouth

rein ring

lower cheek

jointed mouth bit

liverpool bit

sliding cheek bit

HORSE RACING

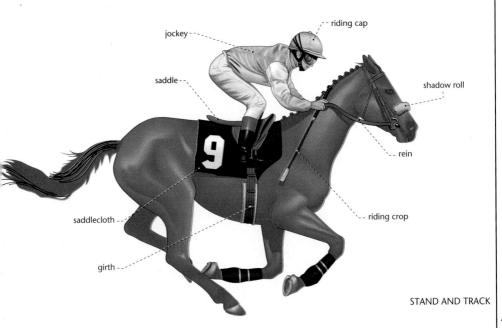

jockey

riding cap

saddle

shadow roll

rein

saddlecloth

riding crop

girth

STAND AND TRACK

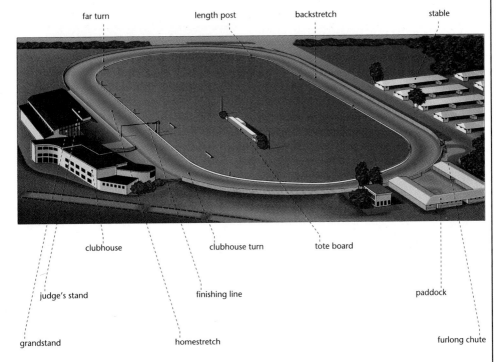

far turn

length post

backstretch

stable

clubhouse

clubhouse turn

tote board

judge's stand

finishing line

paddock

grandstand

homestretch

furlong chute

STANDARDBRED PACER

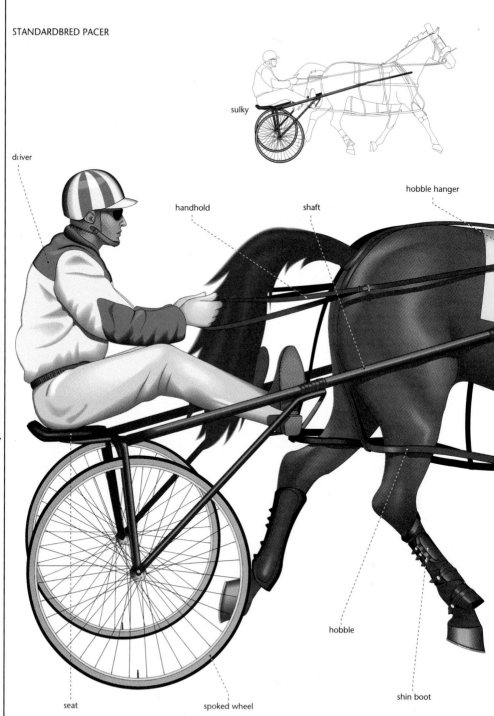

sulky

driver

handhold

shaft

hobble hanger

hobble

shin boot

seat

spoked wheel

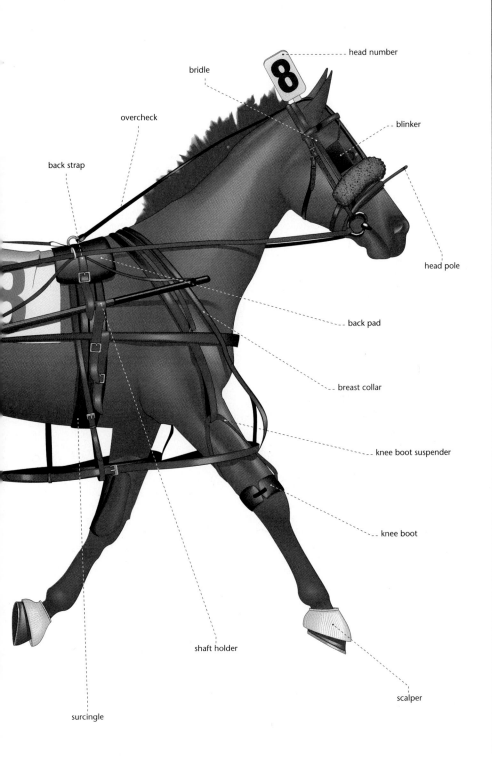

head number

bridle

overcheck

blinker

back strap

head pole

back pad

breast collar

knee boot suspender

knee boot

shaft holder

scalper

surcingle

ARENA

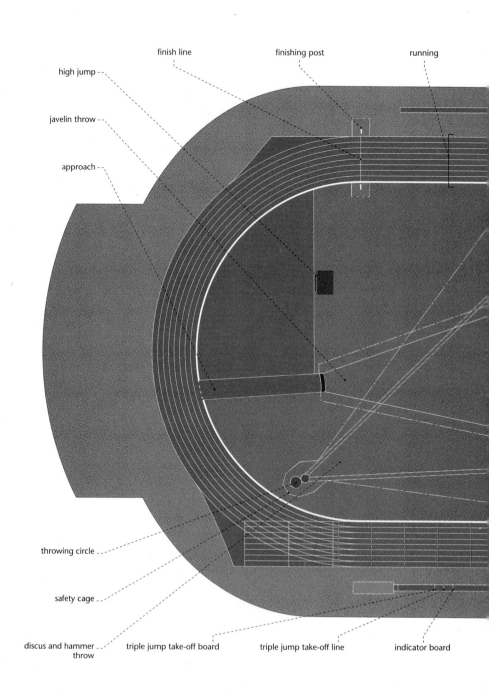

finish line

finishing post

running

high jump

javelin throw

approach

throwing circle

safety cage

discus and hammer throw

triple jump take-off board

triple jump take-off line

indicator board

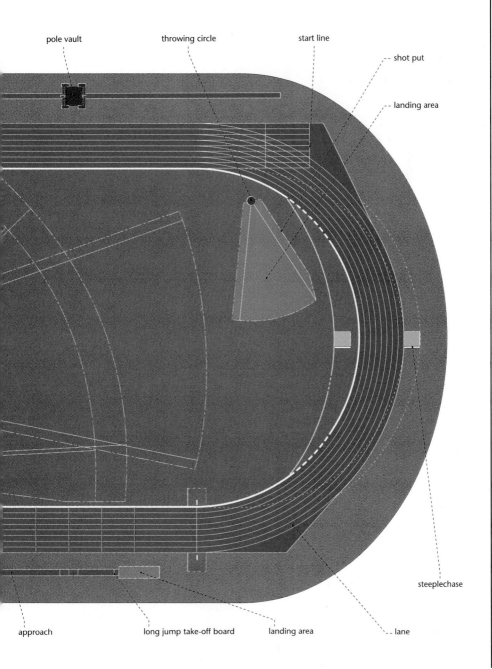

pole vault

throwing circle

start line

shot put

landing area

steeplechase

approach

long jump take-off board

landing area

lane

STARTING BLOCK

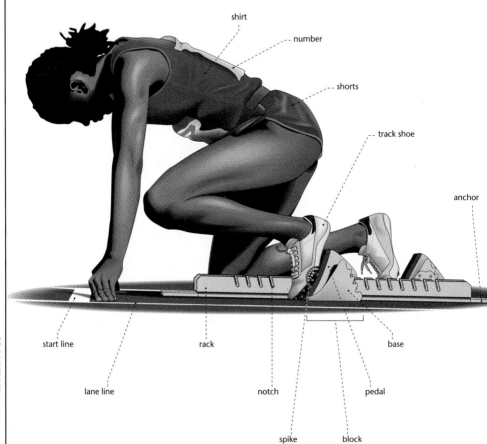

shirt

number

shorts

track shoe

anchor

start line

rack

base

lane line

notch

pedal

spike

block

hurdle

steeplechase hurdle

pole

crossbar

upright

landing area

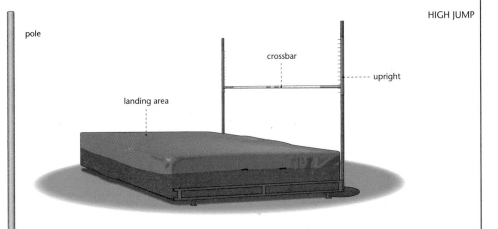

POLE VAULT

upright

crossbar

landing area

ATHLETICS

planting box

approach

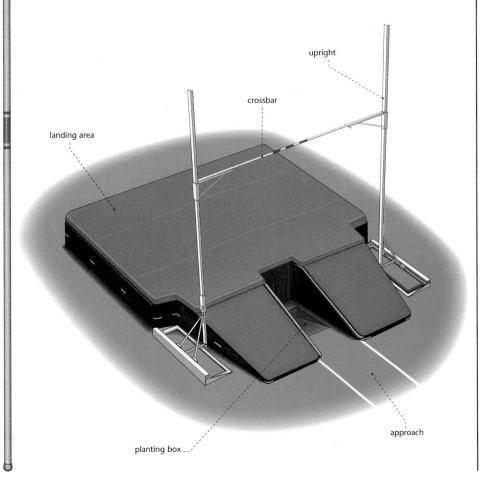

THROWINGS

javelins

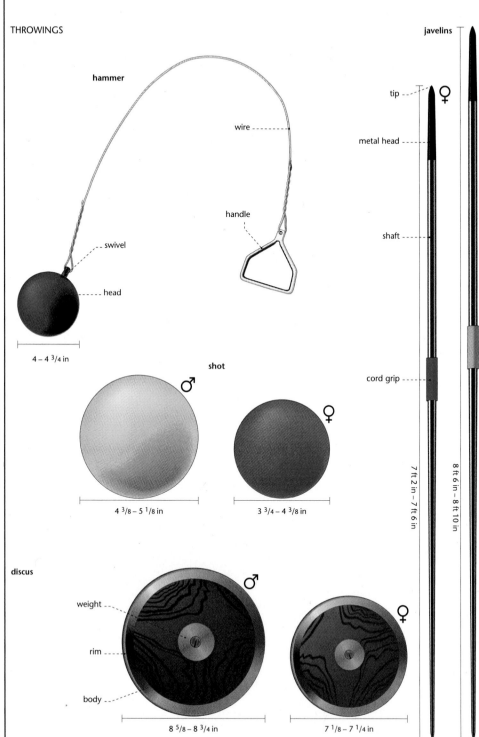

hammer

wire

handle

swivel

head

4 – 4 3/4 in

tip

metal head

shaft

cord grip

shot

4 3/8 – 5 1/8 in

3 3/4 – 4 3/8 in

7 ft 2 in – 7 ft 6 in

8 ft 6 in – 8 ft 10 in

discus

weight

rim

body

8 5/8 – 8 3/4 in

7 1/8 – 7 1/4 in

ATHLETICS

658

GYMNASTICS

vaulting horse

top bar

low bar

adjusting tube

springboard

BALANCE BEAM

beam

upright

height adjustment

TRAMPOLINE

safety pad

bed

leg

spring

frame

ATHLETICS

659

RINGS

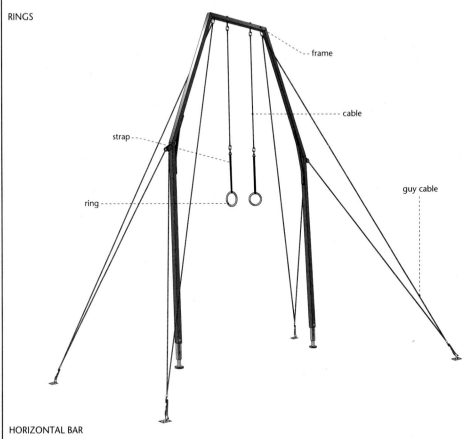

frame

cable

strap

guy cable

ring

HORIZONTAL BAR

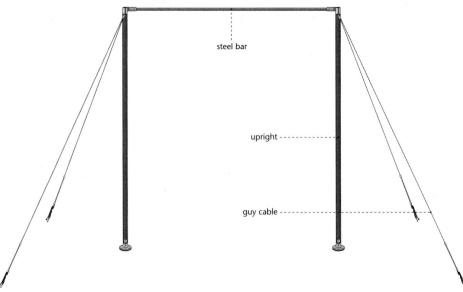

steel bar

upright

guy cable

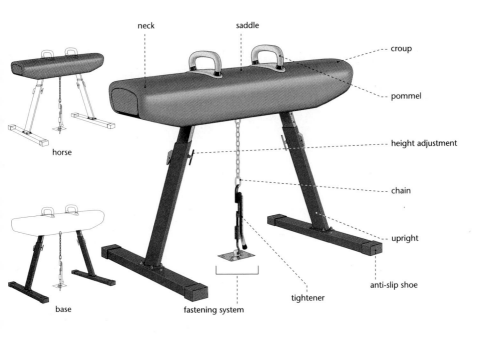

neck

saddle

croup

pommel

height adjustment

chain

upright

anti-slip shoe

horse

tightener

base

fastening system

ATHLETICS

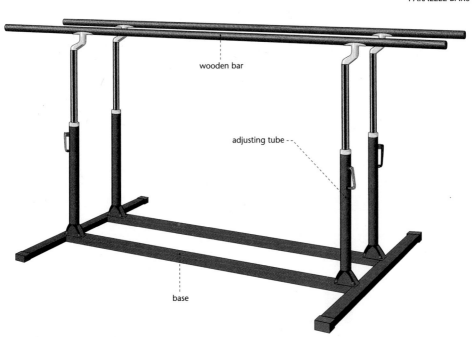

wooden bar

adjusting tube

base

WEIGHTLIFTER

bar

gauze bandage

sleeveless jersey

weightlifting belt

trunks

weightlifting shoe

strap

ATHLETICS

TWO-HAND SNATCH

TWO-HAND CLEAN AND JERK

FITNESS EQUIPMENT

WEIGHT STACK EXERCISE UNIT

cable

pectoral deck

lateral bar

press bar

bench

leg curl bar

leg extension bar

triceps bar

weights

BARBELL

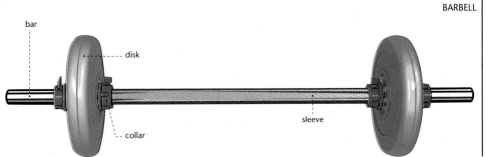

bar

disk

collar

sleeve

FITNESS EQUIPMENT

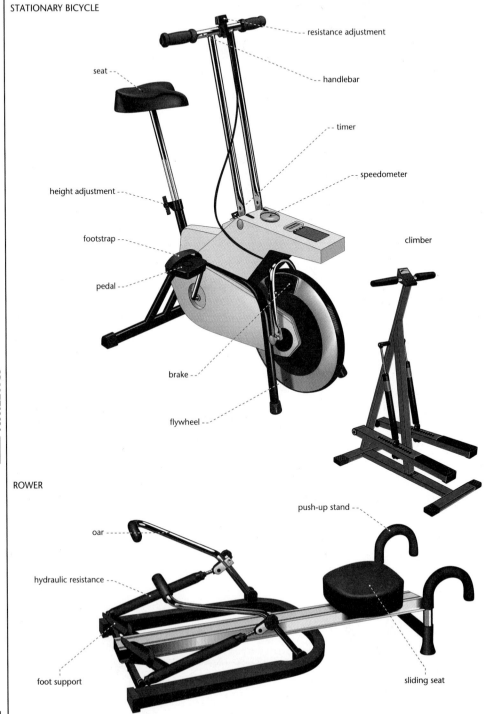

STATIONARY BICYCLE

resistance adjustment

handlebar

seat

timer

speedometer

height adjustment

climber

footstrap

pedal

brake

flywheel

ROWER

push-up stand

oar

hydraulic resistance

foot support

sliding seat

DUMBBELL

handgrips

weight   bar

ankle/wrist weight

jump rope

TWIST BAR

grip

tension spring

chest expander

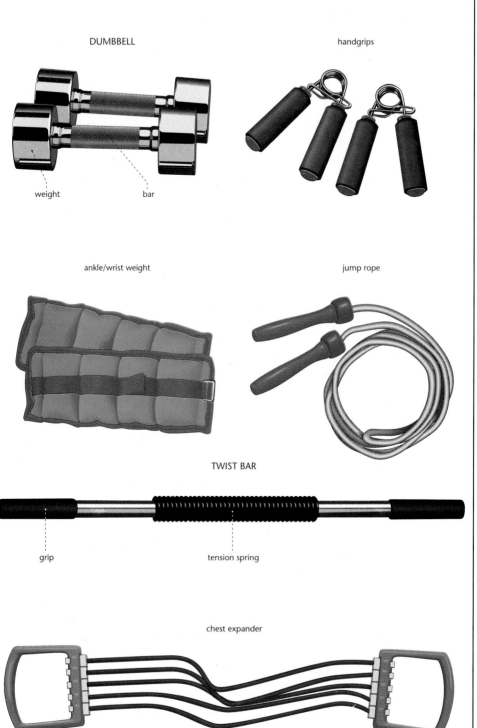

FENCING

PARTS OF THE WEAPON

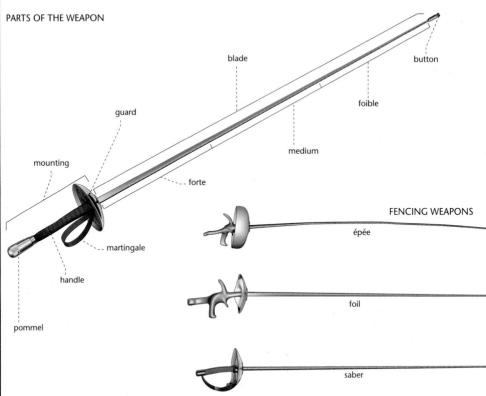

blade

button

guard

foible

medium

mounting

forte

martingale

handle

pommel

FENCING WEAPONS

épée

foil

saber

PISTE

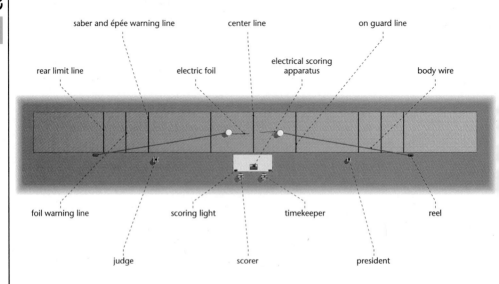

saber and épée warning line

center line

on guard line

rear limit line

electric foil

electrical scoring apparatus

body wire

foil warning line

scoring light

timekeeper

reel

judge

scorer

president

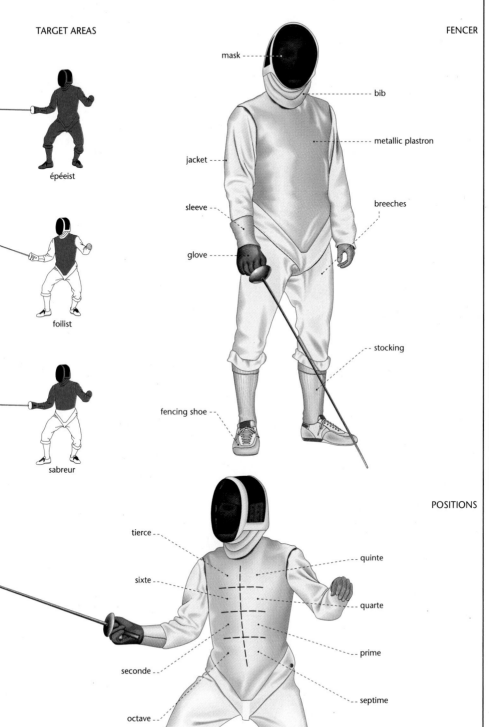

TARGET AREAS

épéeist

foilist

sabreur

FENCER

mask

bib

metallic plastron

jacket

sleeve

breeches

glove

stocking

fencing shoe

POSITIONS

tierce

quinte

sixte

quarte

seconde

prime

octave

septime

JUDO

JUDO SUIT

jacket

belt

trousers

EXAMPLES OF HOLDS

arm lock

holding

major outer reaping throw

one-arm shoulder throw

major inner reaping throw

naked strangle

stomach throw

sweeping hip throw

MAT

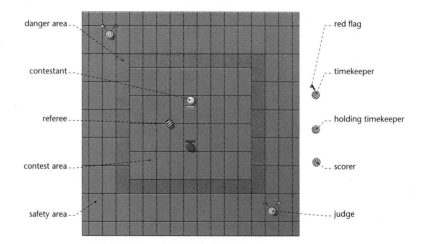

danger area

contestant

referee

contest area

safety area

red flag

timekeeper

holding timekeeper

scorer

judge

BOXING

RING

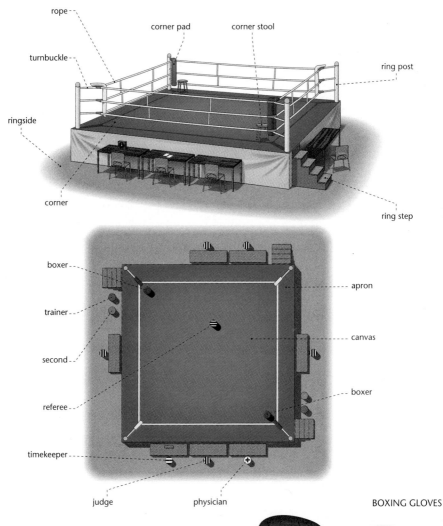

rope

corner pad

corner stool

turnbuckle

ring post

ringside

corner

ring step

boxer

apron

trainer

second

canvas

referee

boxer

timekeeper

judge

physician

BOXING GLOVES

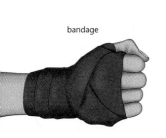

bandage

mouthpiece

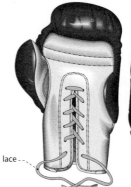

lace

14 OZ

669

FISHING

FLY ROD

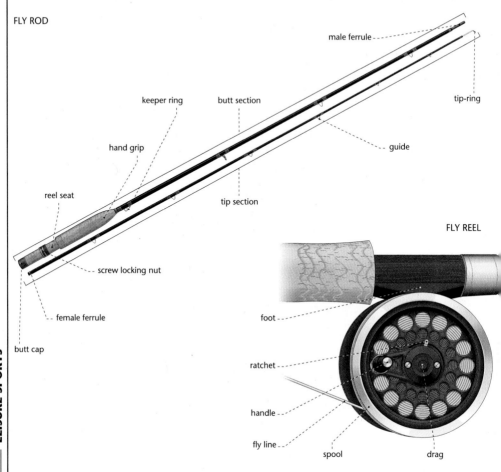

male ferrule

tip-ring

keeper ring

butt section

guide

hand grip

reel seat

tip section

screw locking nut

female ferrule

butt cap

FLY REEL

foot

ratchet

handle

fly line

spool

drag

ARTIFICIAL FLY

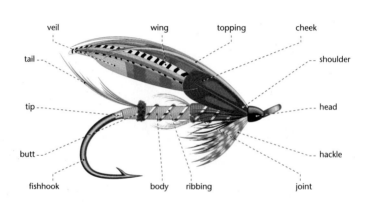

veil

wing

topping

cheek

tail

shoulder

tip

head

butt

hackle

fishhook

body

ribbing

joint

LEISURE SPORTS

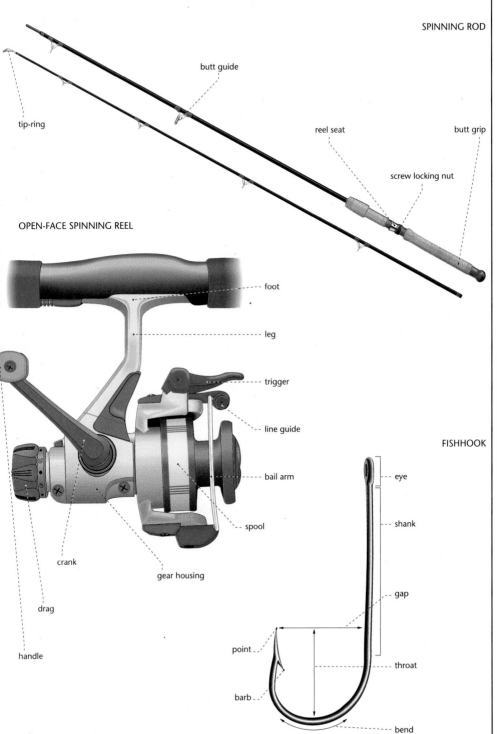

SPINNING ROD

butt guide

tip-ring

reel seat

butt grip

screw locking nut

OPEN-FACE SPINNING REEL

foot

leg

trigger

line guide

bail arm

spool

crank

gear housing

drag

handle

FISHHOOK

eye

shank

gap

throat

point

barb

bend

FISHING

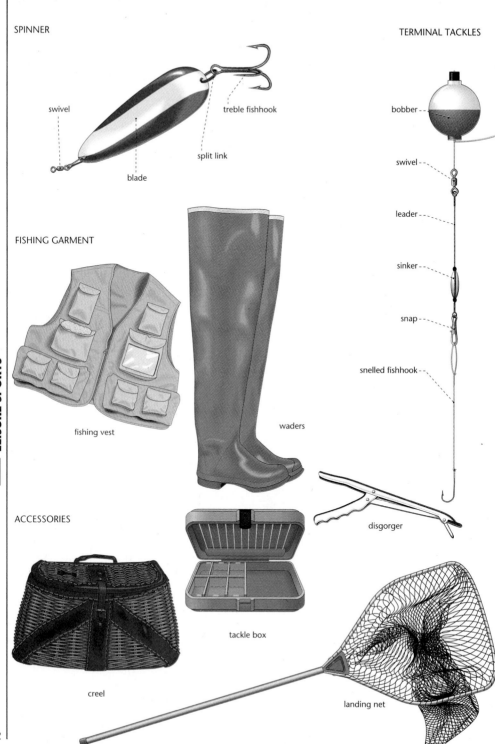

SPINNER

TERMINAL TACKLES

swivel

treble fishhook

split link

blade

bobber

swivel

leader

sinker

snap

snelled fishhook

FISHING GARMENT

fishing vest

waders

ACCESSORIES

disgorger

tackle box

creel

landing net

672

BILLIARDS

CAROM BILLIARDS

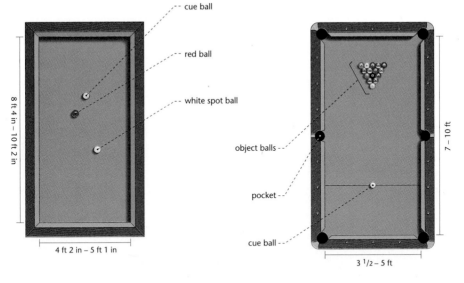

cue ball

red ball

white spot ball

8 ft 4 in – 10 ft 2 in

4 ft 2 in – 5 ft 1 in

POOL

object balls

pocket

cue ball

7 – 10 ft

3 1/2 – 5 ft

ENGLISH BILLIARDS

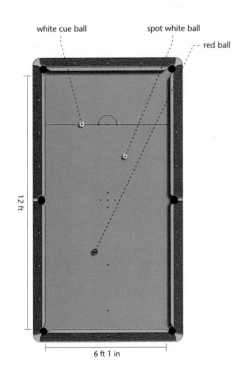

white cue ball

spot white ball

red ball

12 ft

6 ft 1 in

SNOOKER

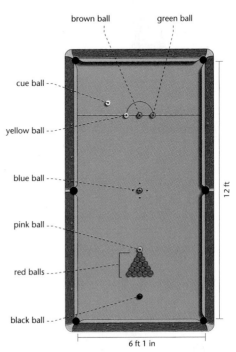

brown ball

green ball

cue ball

yellow ball

blue ball

pink ball

red balls

black ball

12 ft

6 ft 1 in

LEISURE SPORTS

673

ENGLISH BILLIARDS AND SNOOKER

TABLE

balk line spot

center spot

balk area

«D»

bottom pocket

head cushion

balk line

hook

center pocket

BRIDGE

shaft

notch

end-piece

rack

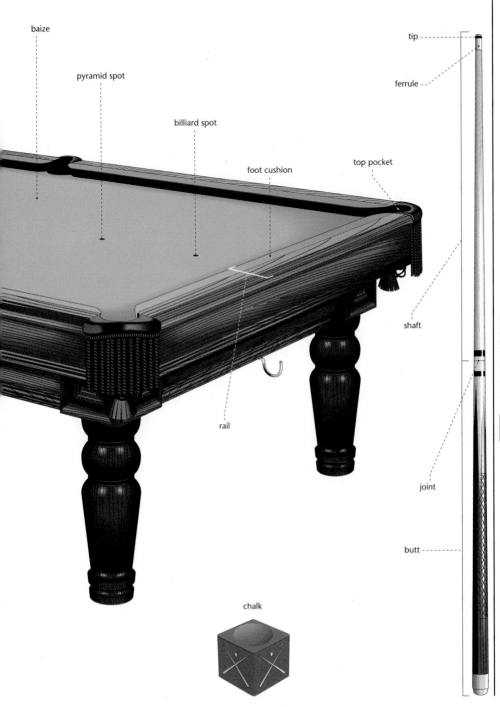

baize

pyramid spot

billiard spot

foot cushion

top pocket

tip

ferrule

shaft

rail

joint

butt

chalk

LEISURE SPORTS

675

COURSE

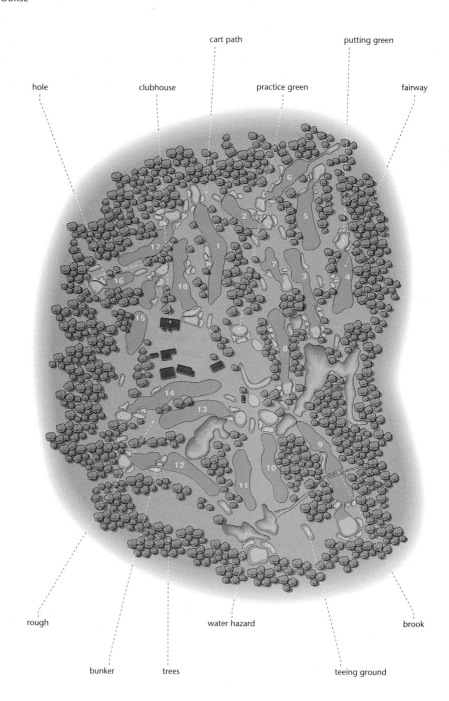

cart path

hole

clubhouse

practice green

putting green

fairway

rough

water hazard

brook

bunker

trees

teeing ground

CROSS SECTION OF A GOLF BALL

GOLF BALL

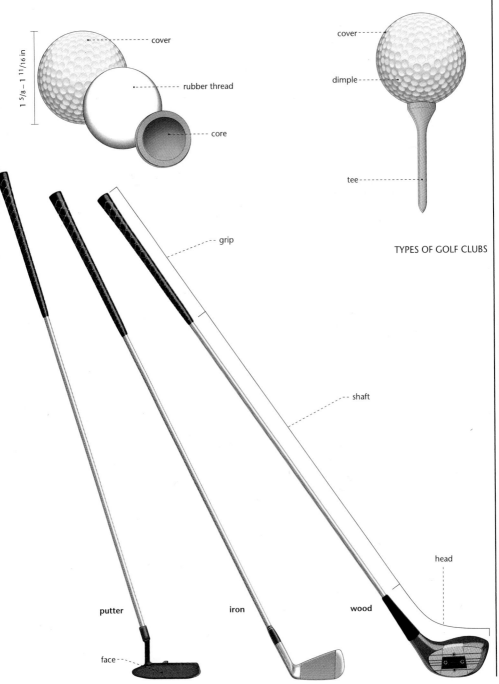

1 5/8 – 1 11/16 in

cover

rubber thread

core

cover

dimple

tee

grip

TYPES OF GOLF CLUBS

shaft

head

putter

iron

wood

face

GOLF

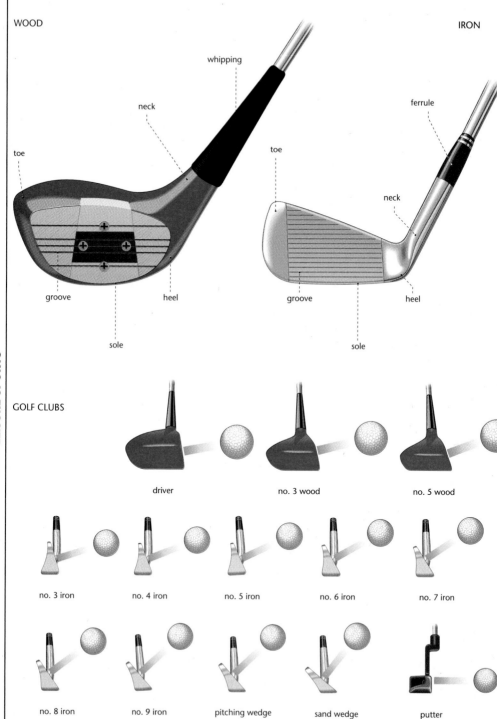

WOOD

IRON

whipping

neck

ferrule

toe

toe

neck

groove

heel

groove

heel

sole

sole

GOLF CLUBS

driver

no. 3 wood

no. 5 wood

no. 3 iron

no. 4 iron

no. 5 iron

no. 6 iron

no. 7 iron

no. 8 iron

no. 9 iron

pitching wedge

sand wedge

putter

golf glove

head cover

golf shoe

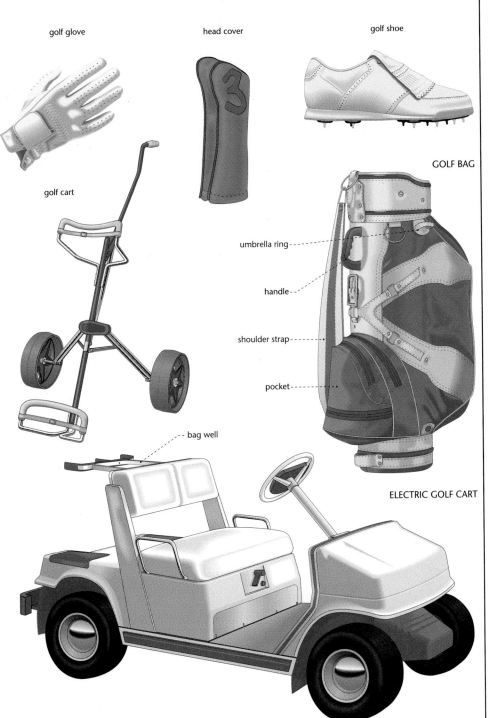

GOLF BAG

golf cart

umbrella ring

handle

shoulder strap

pocket

bag well

ELECTRIC GOLF CART

MOUNTAINEER

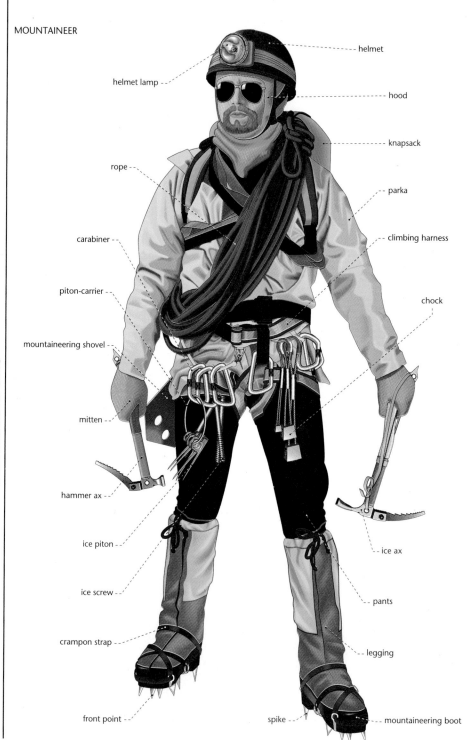

helmet lamp

helmet

hood

knapsack

rope

parka

climbing harness

carabiner

chock

piton-carrier

mountaineering shovel

mitten

hammer ax

ice piton

ice ax

ice screw

pants

crampon strap

legging

front point

spike

mountaineering boot

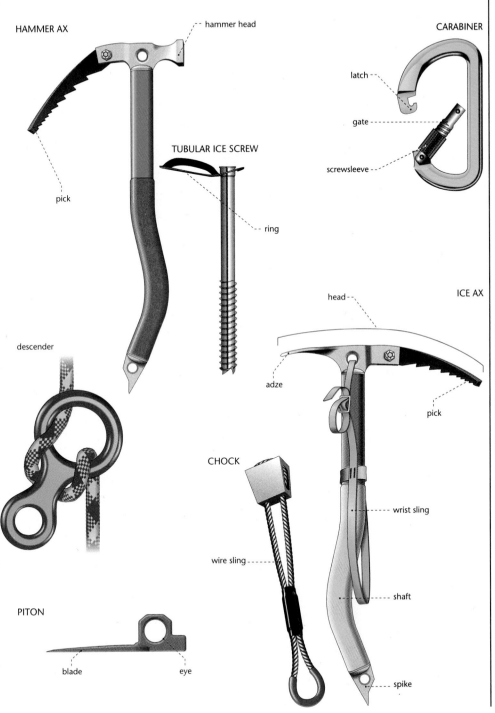

HAMMER AX

hammer head

CARABINER

latch

gate

screwsleeve

pick

TUBULAR ICE SCREW

ring

ICE AX

head

adze

pick

descender

CHOCK

wrist sling

wire sling

shaft

PITON

blade

eye

spike

GREEN

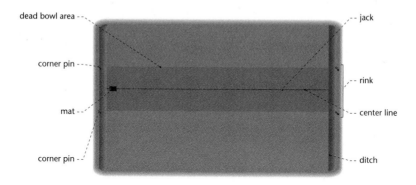

dead bowl area

corner pin

mat

corner pin

jack

rink

center line

ditch

DELIVERY

forward swing

delivery

follow-through

bowl

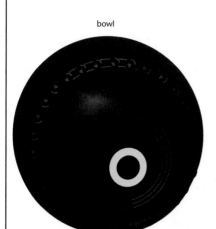

petanque bowl

jack

BOWLING

BOWLING BALL

tenpin

duckpin

candlepin

duckpin

fivepin

pin

pocket

headpin

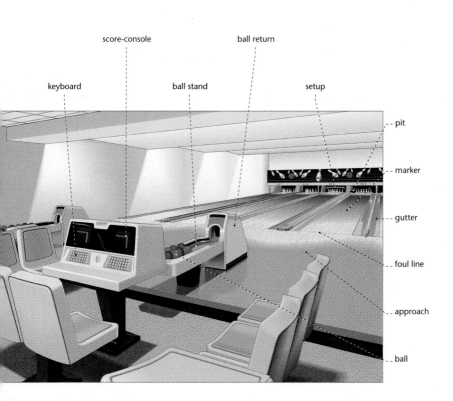

score-console

ball return

keyboard

ball stand

setup

pit

marker

gutter

foul line

approach

ball

ARCHERY

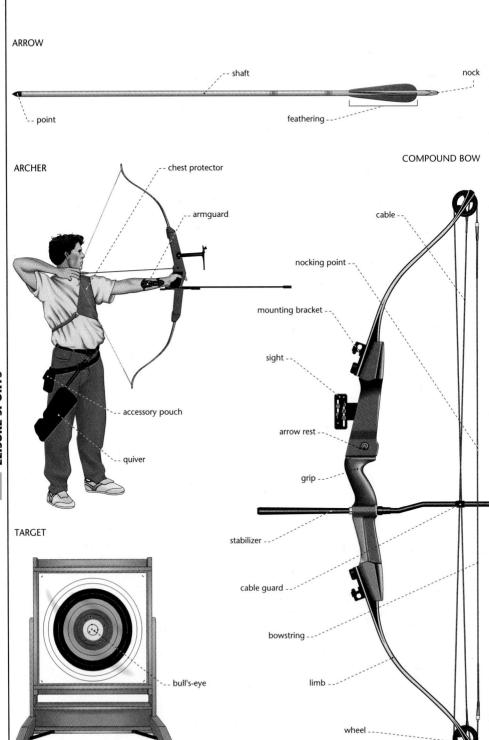

ARROW

shaft

nock

point

feathering

ARCHER

COMPOUND BOW

chest protector

cable

armguard

nocking point

mounting bracket

sight

accessory pouch

arrow rest

quiver

grip

TARGET

stabilizer

cable guard

bowstring

bull's-eye

limb

wheel

TWO-PERSON TENT

rainfly

door

canopy

strainer

zipper

inner tent

elastic strainer

guy line

stake

FAMILY TENT

living room

bedroom

window canopy

screen window

elastic strainer

sewn-in floor

wall

guy line

canvas divider

frame

stake loop

PUP TENT

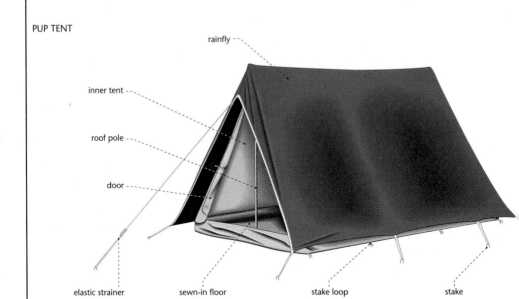

rainfly

inner tent

roof pole

door

elastic strainer

sewn-in floor

stake loop

stake

MAJOR TYPES OF TENTS

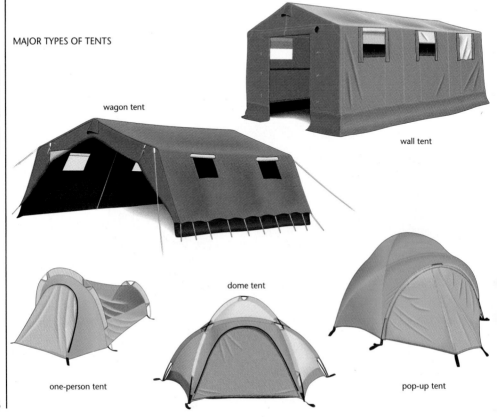

wagon tent

wall tent

one-person tent

dome tent

pop-up tent

foam pad

self-inflating mattress

air mattress

inflator

inflator-deflator

folding cot

SLEEPING BAGS

mummy

semi-mummy

rectangular

CAMPING EQUIPMENT

SWISS ARMY KNIFE

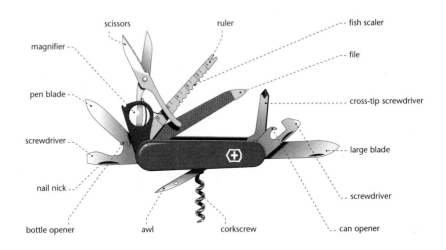

magnifier
scissors
ruler
fish scaler
file
pen blade
cross-tip screwdriver
screwdriver
large blade
nail nick
screwdriver
bottle opener
awl
corkscrew
can opener

COOKING SET

cup
coffee pot
saucepan
frying pan
plate
handle

CUTLERY SET

belt loop
spoon
fork
sheath
knife

lantern

globe

burner frame

pressure regulator

leakproof cap

tank

pump

heater

single-burner camp stove

two-burner camp stove

burner

control valve

wire support

tank

CAMPING

CAMPING EQUIPMENT

thermos

water carrier

canteen

hurricane lamp

cooler

folding grill

TOOLS

hatchet

leather sheath

sheath

knife

folding shovel

bow saw

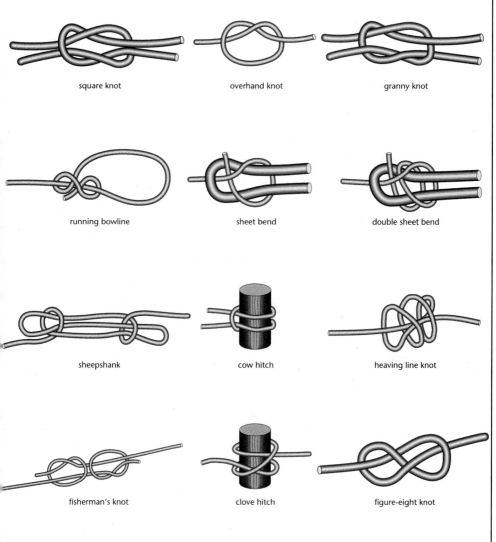

square knot

overhand knot

granny knot

running bowline

sheet bend

double sheet bend

sheepshank

cow hitch

heaving line knot

fisherman's knot

clove hitch

figure-eight knot

common whipping

bowline

bowline on a bight

KNOTS

SHORT SPLICE

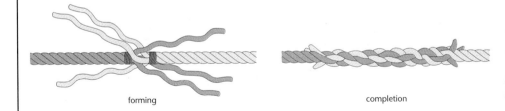

forming

completion

CABLE

TWISTED ROPE

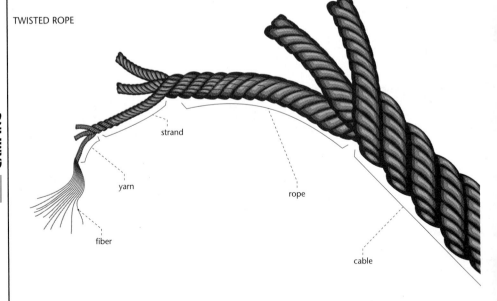

strand

yarn

fiber

rope

cable

BRAIDED ROPE

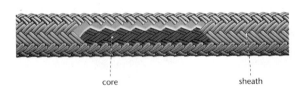

core

sheath

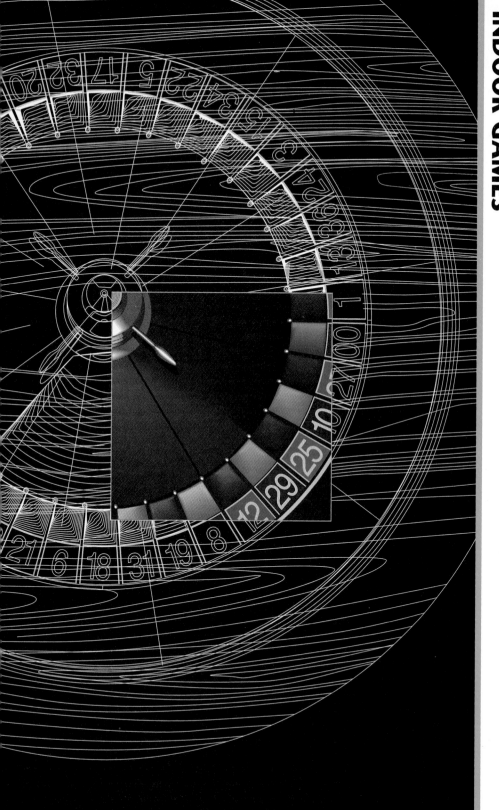

CONTENTS

INDOOR GAMES

CARD GAMES

SYMBOLS

heart

diamond

club

spade

Joker

Ace

King

Queen

Jack

STANDARD POKER HANDS

royal flush

straight flush

four-of-a-kind

full house

flush

straight

three-of-a-kind

two pairs

one pair

high card

DOMINOES

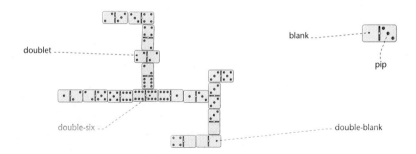

doublet

blank

pip

double-six

double-blank

CHESS

CHESSBOARD

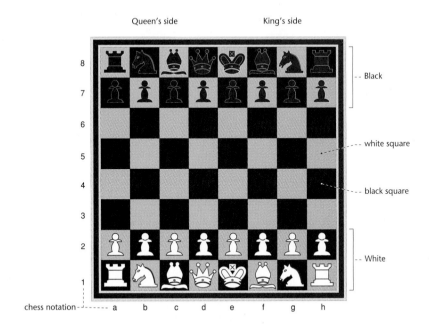

Queen's side   King's side

- - Black

- - - white square

- - - black square

- - White

chess notation - - - - - - - a   b   c   d   e   f   g   h

INDOOR GAMES

TYPES OF MOVEMENTS

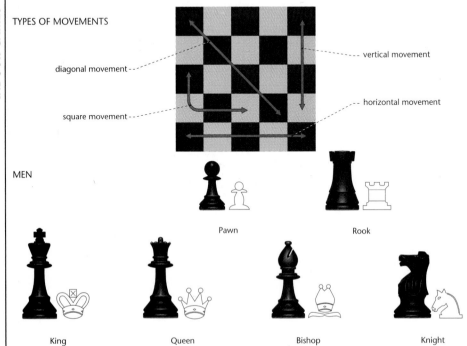

diagonal movement - - -

- - - vertical movement

square movement - - -

- - - horizontal movement

MEN

Pawn

Rook

King

Queen

Bishop

Knight

BACKGAMMON

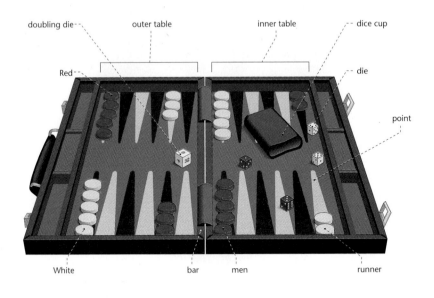

doubling die · · outer table · · inner table · · dice cup

Red · · · die

point

White · · bar · · men · · runner

GO

BOARD

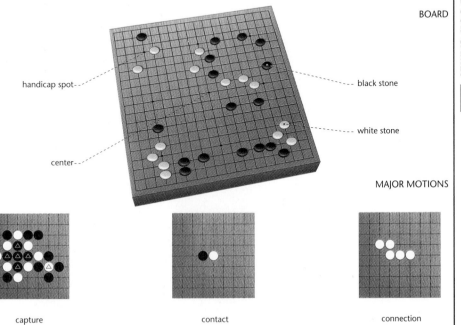

handicap spot · · · black stone

white stone

center · ·

MAJOR MOTIONS

capture · · · contact · · · connection

GAME OF DARTS

DARTBOARD

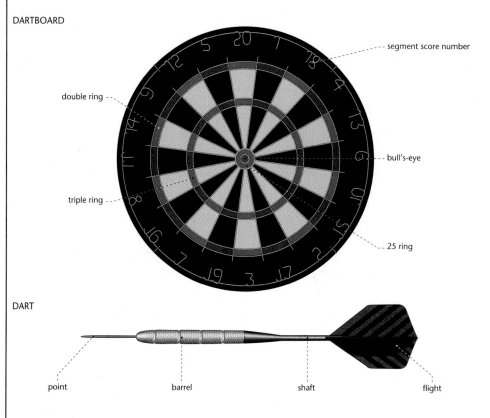

segment score number

double ring

bull's-eye

triple ring

25 ring

DART

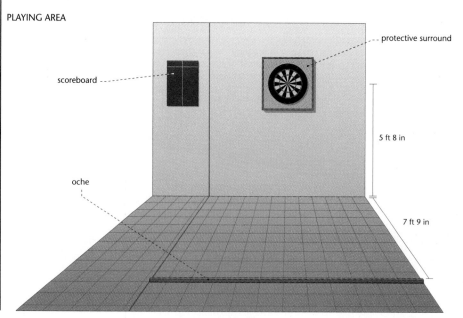

point

barrel

shaft

flight

PLAYING AREA

protective surround

scoreboard

5 ft 8 in

oche

7 ft 9 in

VIDEO ENTERTAINMENT SYSTEM

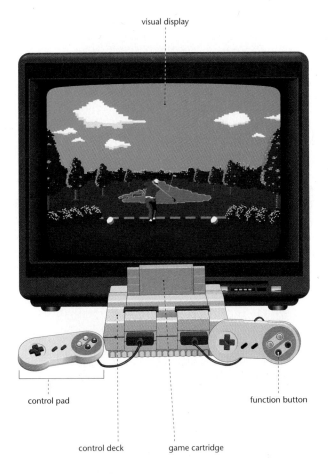

visual display

control pad

control deck

game cartridge

function button

DICE

poker die

ordinary die

ROULETTE TABLE

AMERICAN ROULETTE WHEEL

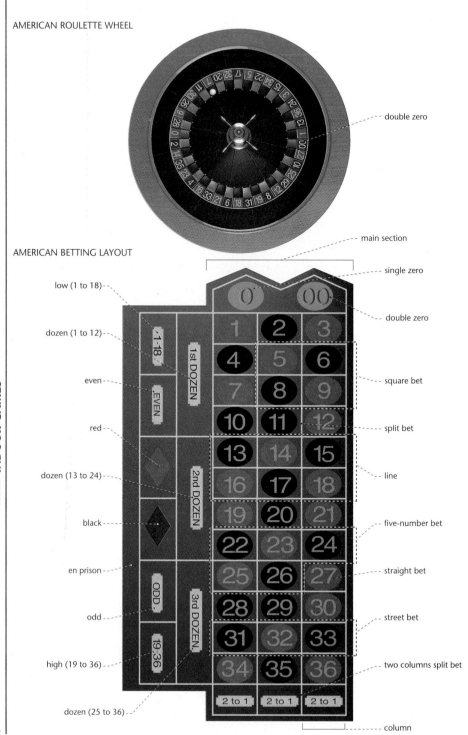

double zero

AMERICAN BETTING LAYOUT

main section

single zero

double zero

low (1 to 18)

dozen (1 to 12)

even

red

dozen (13 to 24)

black

en prison

odd

high (19 to 36)

dozen (25 to 36)

square bet

split bet

line

five-number bet

straight bet

street bet

two columns split bet

column

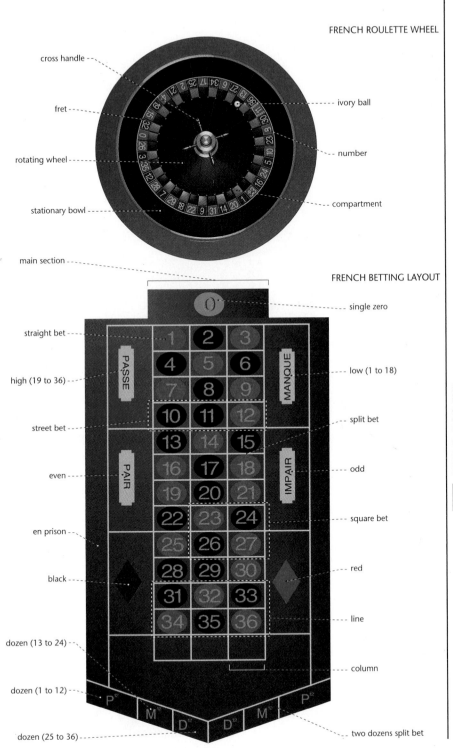

FRENCH ROULETTE WHEEL

cross handle

fret

rotating wheel

stationary bowl

ivory ball

number

compartment

main section

FRENCH BETTING LAYOUT

single zero

straight bet

high (19 to 36)

street bet

even

en prison

black

dozen (13 to 24)

dozen (1 to 12)

dozen (25 to 36)

PASSE

MANQUE

PAIR

IMPAIR

low (1 to 18)

split bet

odd

square bet

red

line

column

two dozens split bet

casing

coin slot

symbol

lever

coin reject slot

winning line

payout tray

CROSS SECTION

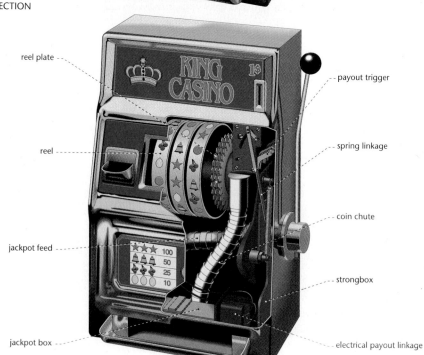

reel plate

payout trigger

reel

spring linkage

coin chute

jackpot feed

strongbox

jackpot box

electrical payout linkage

MEASURING DEVICES

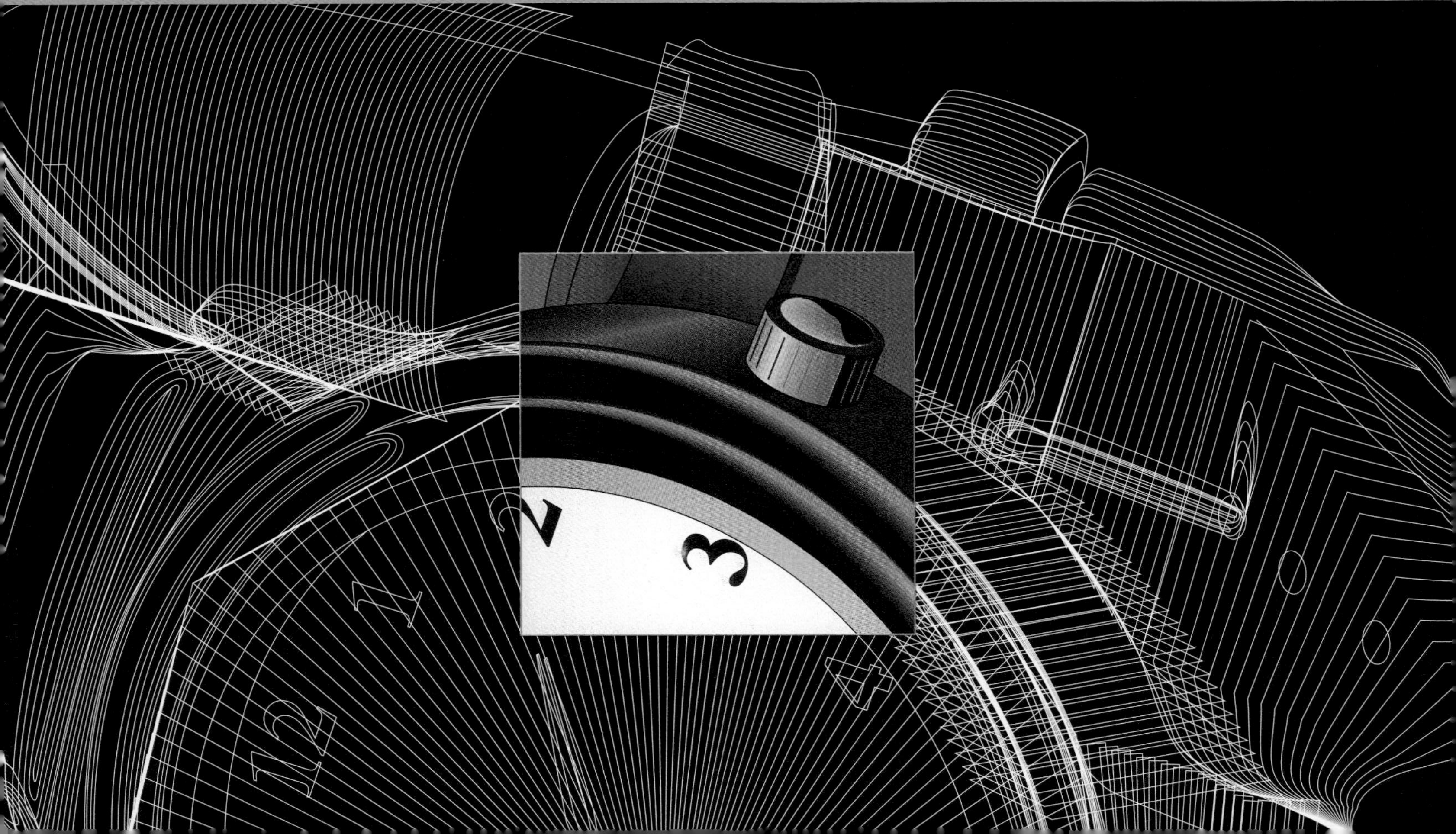

CONTENTS

MEASURING DEVICES

MEASURE OF TEMPERATURE

THERMOMETER

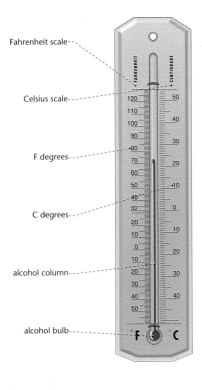

Fahrenheit scale

Celsius scale

F degrees

C degrees

alcohol column

alcohol bulb

CLINICAL THERMOMETER

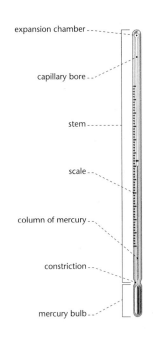

expansion chamber

capillary bore

stem

scale

column of mercury

constriction

mercury bulb

BIMETALLIC THERMOMETER

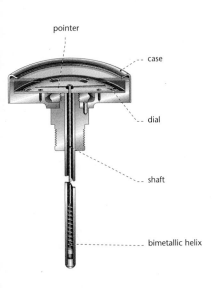

pointer

case

dial

shaft

bimetallic helix

ROOM THERMOSTAT

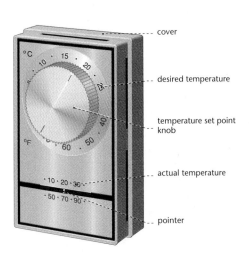

cover

desired temperature

temperature set point knob

actual temperature

pointer

MEASURE OF TIME

STOPWATCH

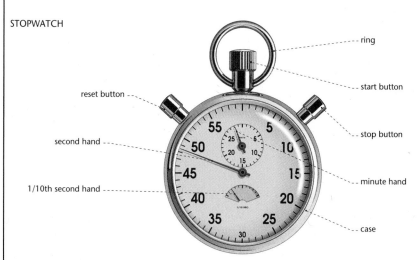

ring

start button

reset button

stop button

second hand

1/10th second hand

minute hand

case

MECHANICAL WATCH

strap

jewel

fourth wheel

escape wheel

third wheel

hairspring

crown

center wheel

winder

ratchet wheel

click

ANALOG WATCH

dial

DIGITAL WATCH

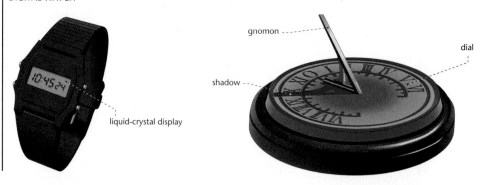

gnomon

dial

shadow

liquid-crystal display

SUNDIAL

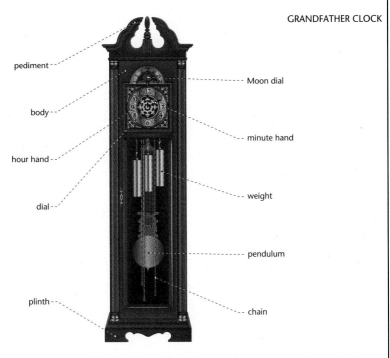

pediment

Moon dial

body

minute hand

hour hand

weight

dial

pendulum

plinth

chain

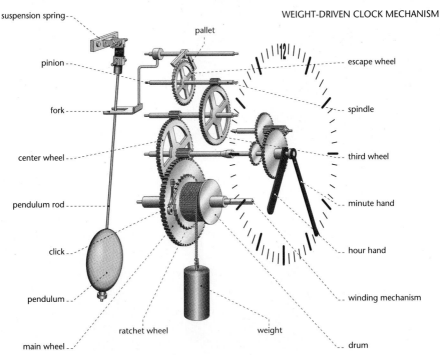

suspension spring

pallet

escape wheel

pinion

spindle

fork

third wheel

center wheel

minute hand

pendulum rod

hour hand

click

pendulum

winding mechanism

main wheel

ratchet wheel

weight

drum

BEAM BALANCE

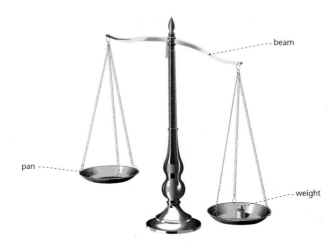

beam

pan

weight

STEELYARD

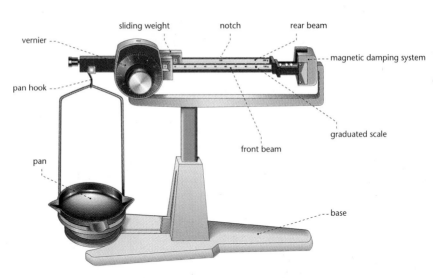

sliding weight

notch

rear beam

vernier

magnetic damping system

pan hook

graduated scale

pan

front beam

base

MEASURING DEVICES

ROBERVAL'S BALANCE

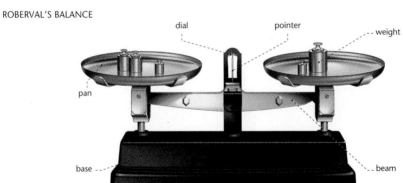

dial

pointer

weight

pan

base

beam

SPRING BALANCE

ELECTRONIC SCALES

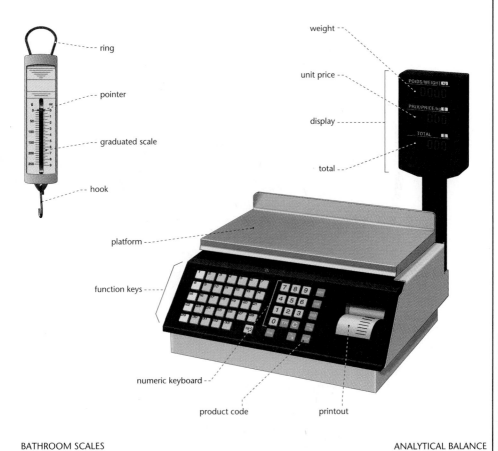

ring

pointer

graduated scale

hook

weight

unit price

display

total

platform

function keys

numeric keyboard

product code

printout

BATHROOM SCALES

digital display

weighing platform

ANALYTICAL BALANCE

glass case

door access

pan

leveling screw

BAROMETER/THERMOMETER

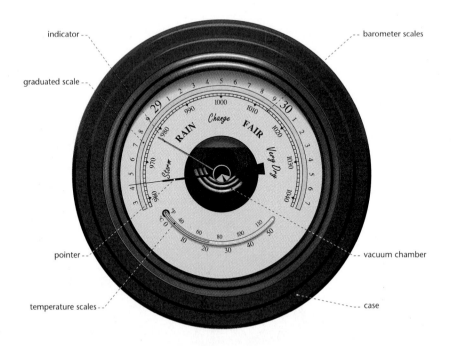

indicator

graduated scale

barometer scales

pointer

vacuum chamber

temperature scales

case

TENSIOMETER

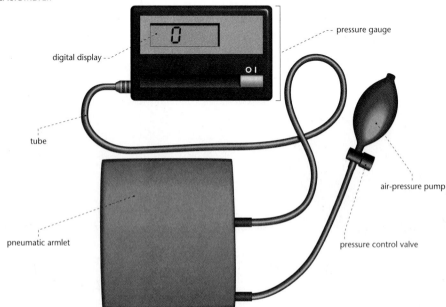

pressure gauge

digital display

tube

air-pressure pump

pneumatic armlet

pressure control valve

MEASURING DEVICES

MEASURE OF LENGTH

TAPE MEASURE

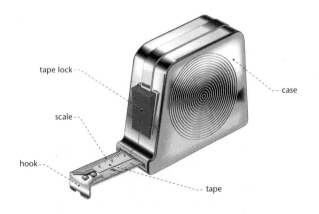

tape lock

scale

hook

case

tape

MEASURE OF DISTANCE

PEDOMETER

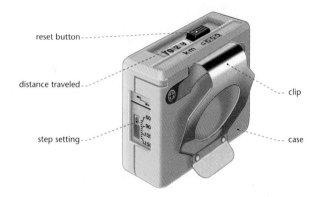

reset button

distance traveled

step setting

clip

case

MEASURE OF THICKNESS

MICROMETER CALIPER

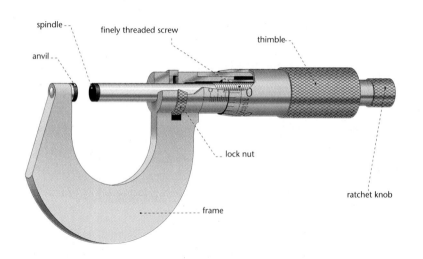

spindle

finely threaded screw

thimble

anvil

lock nut

frame

ratchet knob

MEASURING DEVICES

711

WATT-HOUR METER

EXTERIOR VIEW

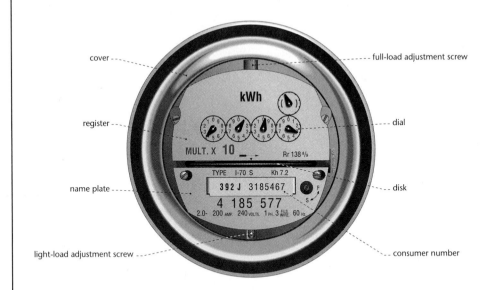

cover

full-load adjustment screw

register

dial

name plate

disk

light-load adjustment screw

consumer number

MECHANISM

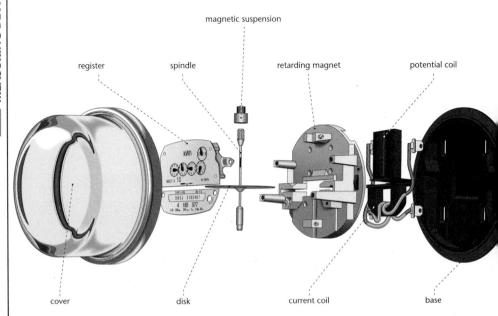

magnetic suspension

register   spindle   retarding magnet   potential coil

cover   disk   current coil   base

MEASURING DEVICES

THEODOLITE

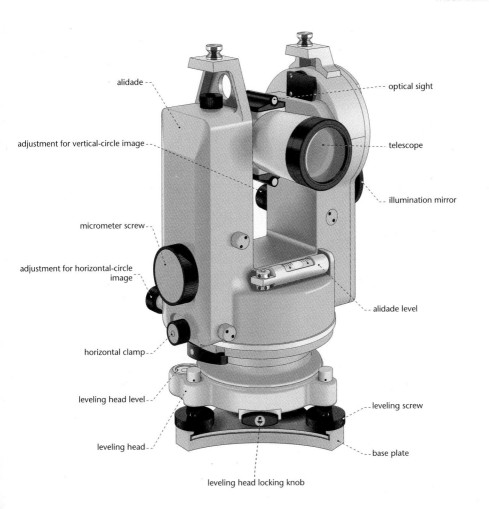

alidade

optical sight

adjustment for vertical-circle image

telescope

illumination mirror

micrometer screw

adjustment for horizontal-circle image

alidade level

horizontal clamp

leveling head level

leveling screw

leveling head

base plate

leveling head locking knob

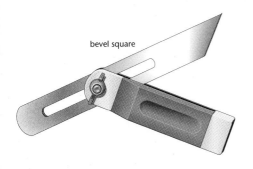

bevel square

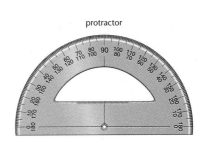

protractor

713

MEASURE OF SEISMIC WAVES

MEASURING DEVICES

DETECTION OF SEISMIC WAVES

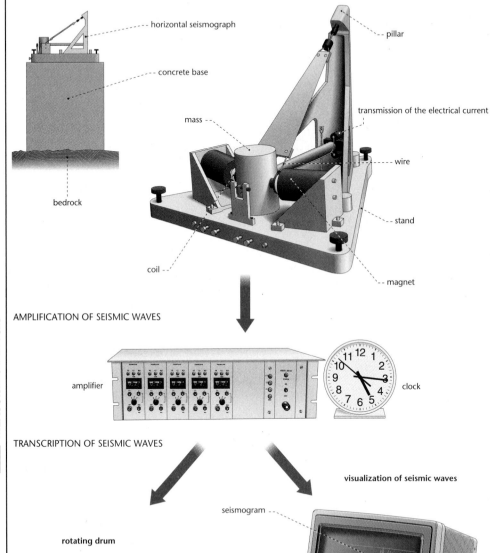

horizontal seismograph

concrete base

bedrock

pillar

transmission of the electrical current

mass

wire

stand

coil

magnet

AMPLIFICATION OF SEISMIC WAVES

amplifier

clock

TRANSCRIPTION OF SEISMIC WAVES

visualization of seismic waves

seismogram

rotating drum

pen

drum

sheet of paper

714

OPTICAL INSTRUMENTS

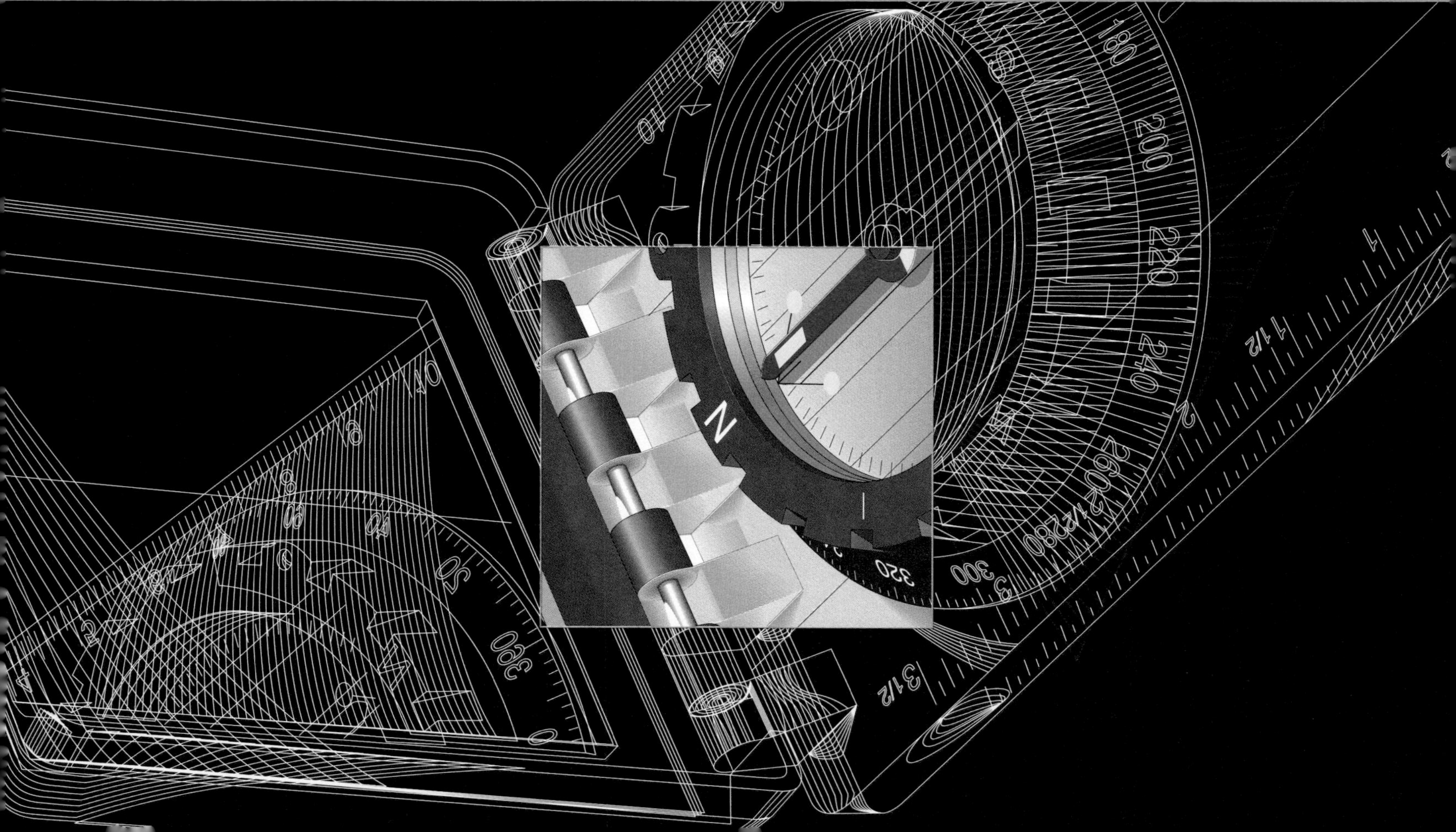

CONTENTS

OPTICAL INSTRUMENTS

ELECTRON MICROSCOPE

CROSS SECTION OF AN ELECTRON MICROSCOPE

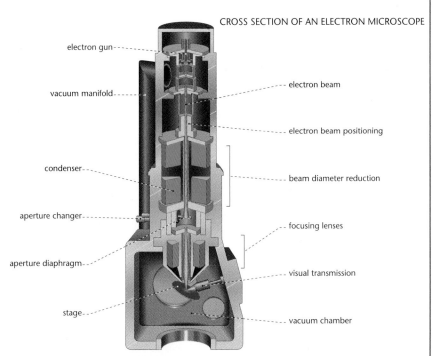

electron gun

vacuum manifold

condenser

aperture changer

aperture diaphragm

stage

electron beam

electron beam positioning

beam diameter reduction

focusing lenses

visual transmission

vacuum chamber

ELECTRON MICROSCOPE ELEMENTS

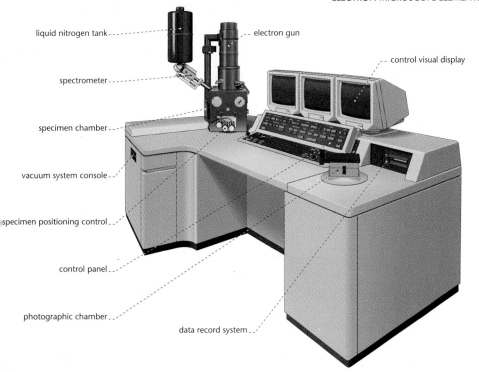

liquid nitrogen tank

spectrometer

specimen chamber

vacuum system console

specimen positioning control

control panel

photographic chamber

electron gun

control visual display

data record system

BINOCULAR MICROSCOPE

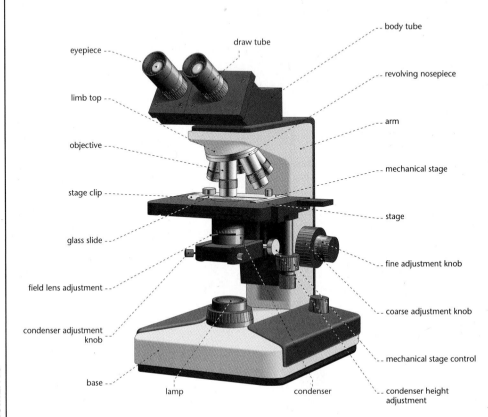

eyepiece

draw tube

body tube

limb top

revolving nosepiece

objective

arm

stage clip

mechanical stage

glass slide

stage

field lens adjustment

fine adjustment knob

condenser adjustment knob

coarse adjustment knob

base

mechanical stage control

lamp

condenser

condenser height adjustment

TELESCOPIC SIGHT

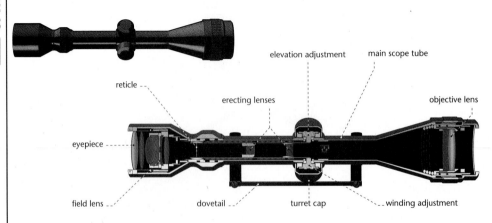

elevation adjustment

main scope tube

reticle

erecting lenses

objective lens

eyepiece

field lens

dovetail

turret cap

winding adjustment

PRISM BINOCULARS

eyepiece

lens system

Porro prism

hinge

objective lens

focusing ring

central focusing wheel

bridge

body

MAGNETIC COMPASS

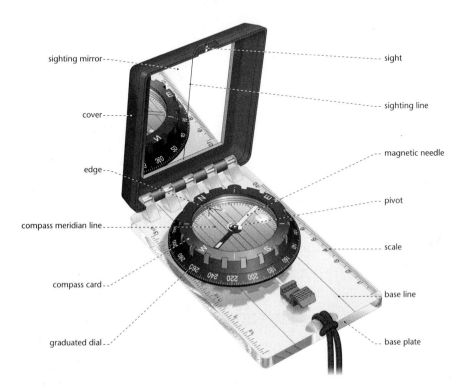

sighting mirror

cover

edge

compass meridian line

compass card

graduated dial

sight

sighting line

magnetic needle

pivot

scale

base line

base plate

REFLECTING TELESCOPE

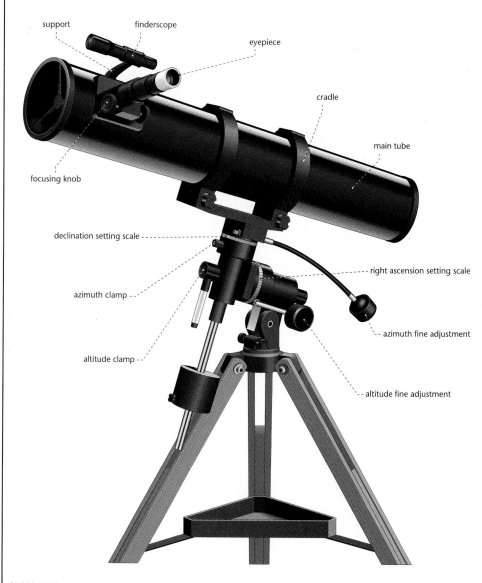

support

finderscope

eyepiece

cradle

main tube

focusing knob

declination setting scale

right ascension setting scale

azimuth clamp

altitude clamp

azimuth fine adjustment

altitude fine adjustment

CROSS SECTION OF A REFLECTING TELESCOPE

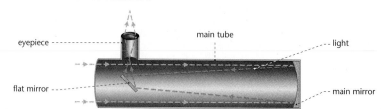

eyepiece

main tube

light

flat mirror

main mirror

REFRACTING TELESCOPE

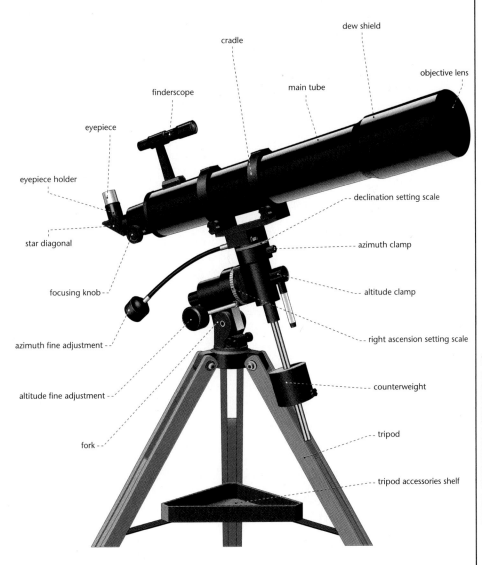

dew shield

cradle

objective lens

finderscope

main tube

eyepiece

eyepiece holder

declination setting scale

star diagonal

azimuth clamp

altitude clamp

focusing knob

right ascension setting scale

azimuth fine adjustment

altitude fine adjustment

counterweight

fork

tripod

tripod accessories shelf

CROSS SECTION OF A REFRACTING TELESCOPE

eyepiece

light

main tube

objective lens

LENSES

CONVERGING LENSES

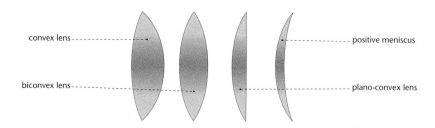

convex lens ---- · ---- positive meniscus

biconvex lens ---- · ---- plano-convex lens

DIVERGING LENSES

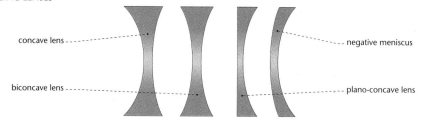

concave lens ---- · ---- negative meniscus

biconcave lens ---- · ---- plano-concave lens

RADAR

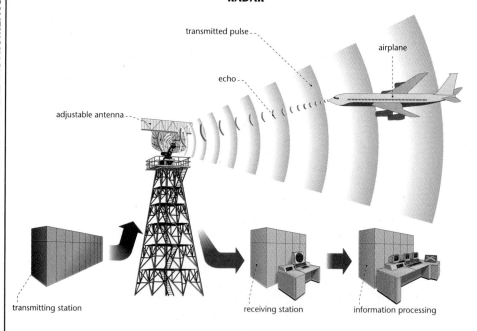

transmitted pulse

airplane

echo

adjustable antenna

transmitting station

receiving station

information processing

CONTENTS

HEALTH AND SAFETY

FIRST AID KIT

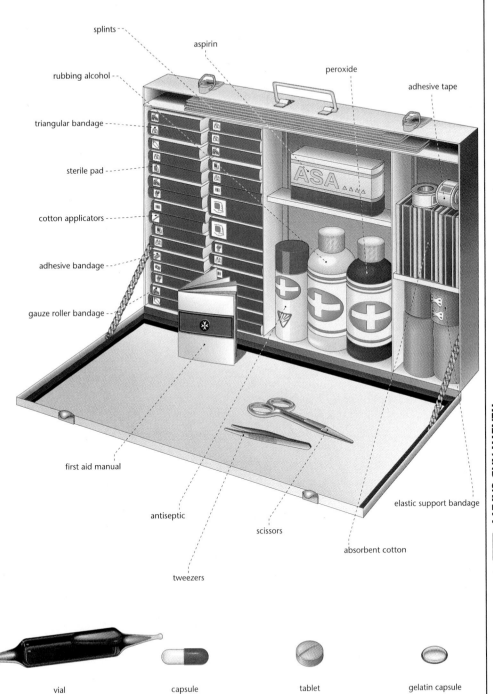

splints

aspirin

peroxide

rubbing alcohol

adhesive tape

triangular bandage

sterile pad

cotton applicators

adhesive bandage

gauze roller bandage

first aid manual

antiseptic

scissors

elastic support bandage

absorbent cotton

tweezers

vial

capsule

tablet

gelatin capsule

FIRST AID EQUIPMENT

STETHOSCOPE

SYRINGE

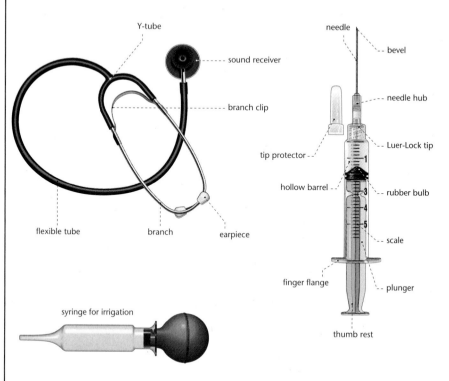

Y-tube

sound receiver

branch clip

flexible tube

branch

earpiece

needle

bevel

needle hub

Luer-Lock tip

tip protector

hollow barrel

rubber bulb

1

3
4
5

scale

finger flange

plunger

thumb rest

syringe for irrigation

COT

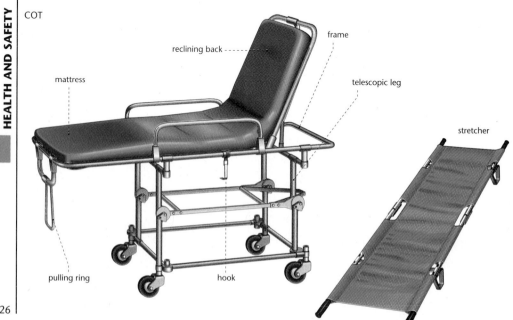

reclining back

frame

mattress

telescopic leg

stretcher

pulling ring

hook

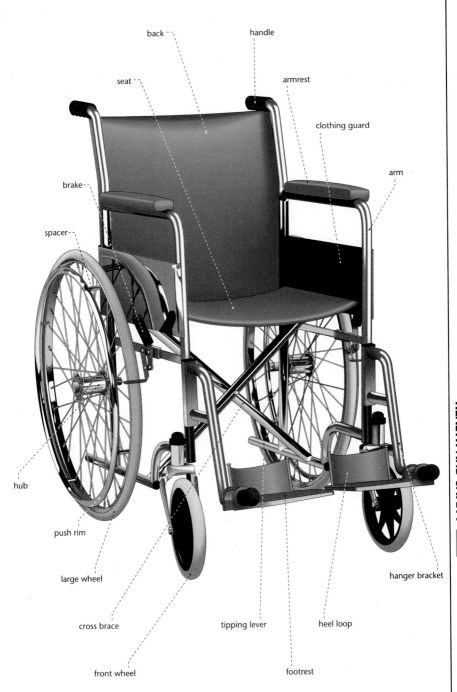

back

handle

seat

armrest

clothing guard

arm

brake

spacer

hub

push rim

large wheel

cross brace

front wheel

tipping lever

footrest

heel loop

hanger bracket

WALKING AIDS

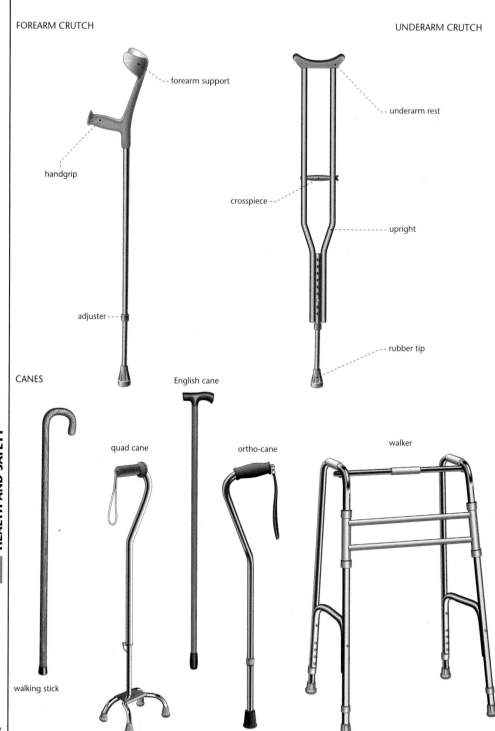

FOREARM CRUTCH

forearm support

handgrip

adjuster

UNDERARM CRUTCH

underarm rest

crosspiece

upright

rubber tip

CANES

English cane

quad cane

ortho-cane

walker

walking stick

EAR PROTECTION

SAFETY EARMUFF

ear plugs

headband

foam cushion

EYE PROTECTION

safety glasses

safety goggles

HEAD PROTECTION

SAFETY CAP

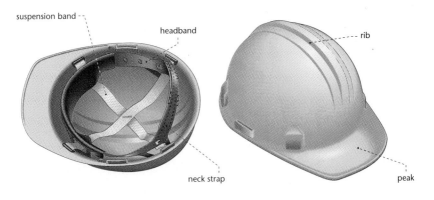

suspension band

headband

rib

neck strap

peak

RESPIRATORY SYSTEM PROTECTION

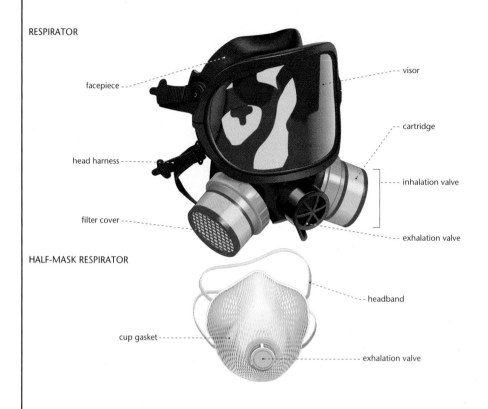

RESPIRATOR

facepiece

visor

cartridge

head harness

inhalation valve

filter cover

exhalation valve

HALF-MASK RESPIRATOR

headband

cup gasket

exhalation valve

SAFETY VEST

reflective stripe

FEET PROTECTION

toe guard

SAFETY BOOT

reinforced toe

ENERGY

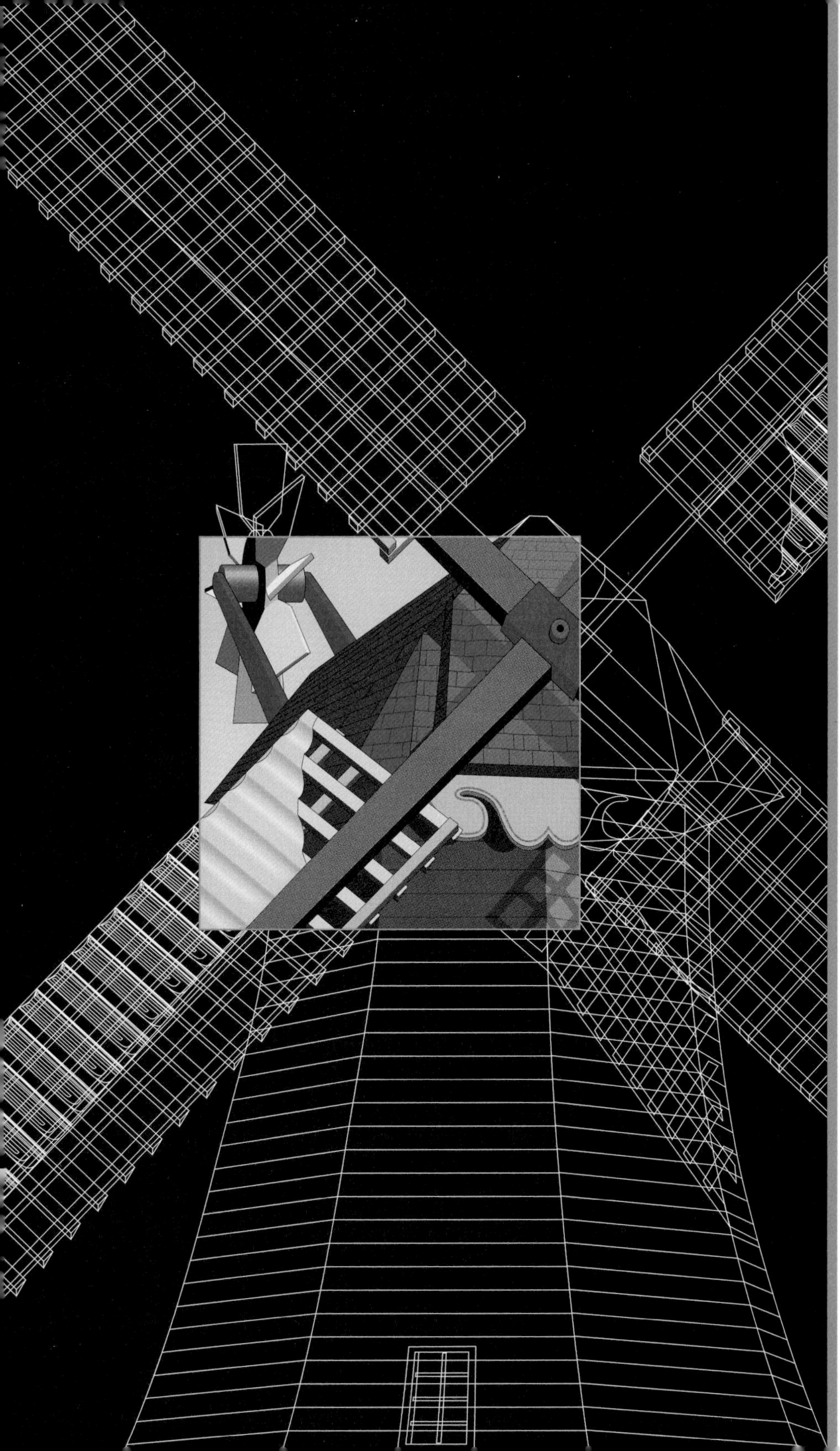

CONTENTS

ENERGY

COAL MINE

face   bench

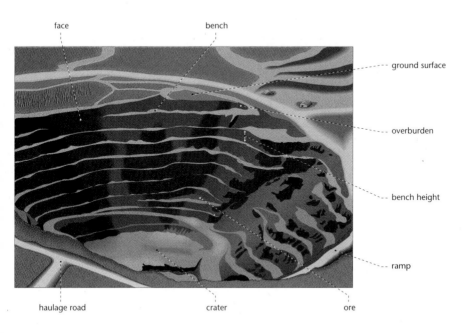

ground surface

overburden

bench height

ramp

haulage road   crater   ore

STRIP MINE

dump   conveyor

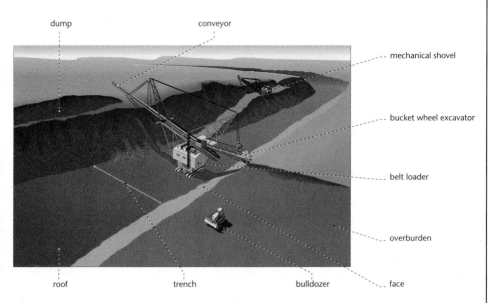

mechanical shovel

bucket wheel excavator

belt loader

overburden

roof   trench   bulldozer   face

ENERGY

733

COAL MINE

JACKLEG DRILL

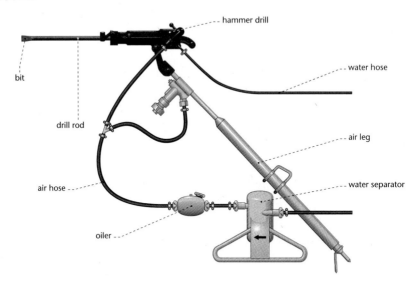

hammer drill

water hose

bit

drill rod

air leg

water separator

air hose

oiler

PITHEAD

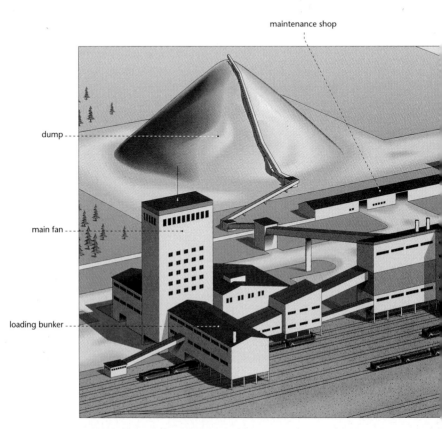

maintenance shop

dump

main fan

loading bunker

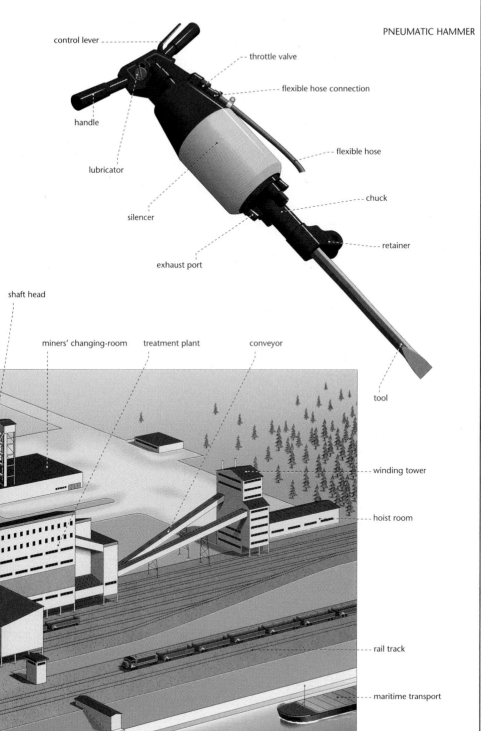

PNEUMATIC HAMMER

control lever

throttle valve

flexible hose connection

handle

flexible hose

lubricator

chuck

silencer

retainer

exhaust port

tool

shaft head

miners' changing-room   treatment plant   conveyor

winding tower

hoist room

rail track

maritime transport

UNDERGROUND MINE

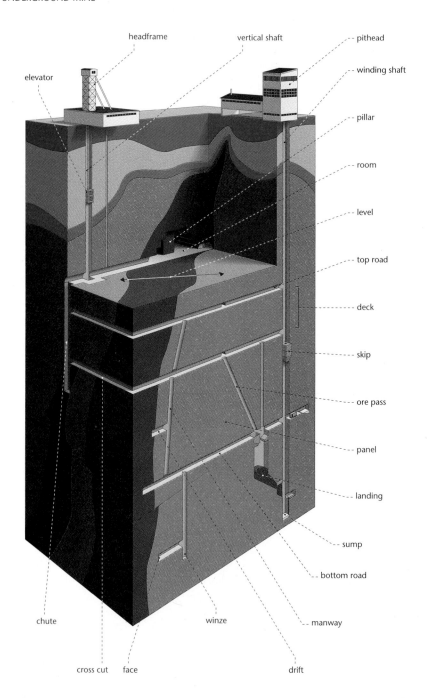

headframe

vertical shaft

pithead

elevator

winding shaft

pillar

room

level

top road

deck

skip

ore pass

panel

landing

sump

bottom road

manway

chute

winze

cross cut

face

drift

OIL

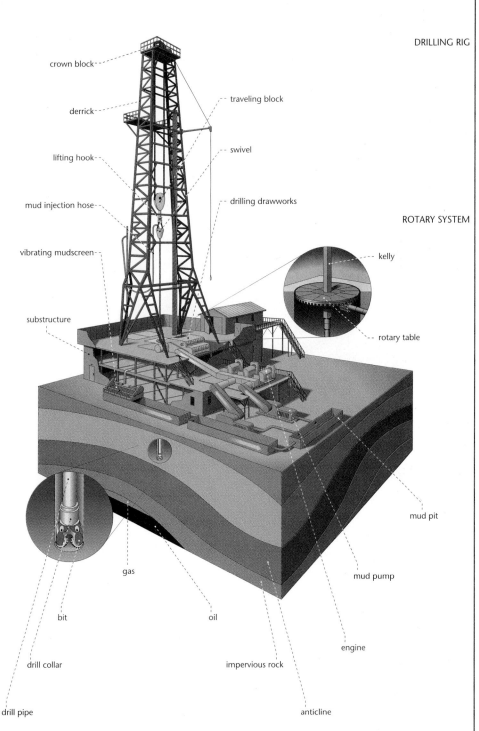

crown block

derrick

traveling block

lifting hook

swivel

mud injection hose

drilling drawworks

ROTARY SYSTEM

vibrating mudscreen

kelly

substructure

rotary table

mud pit

gas

mud pump

bit

oil

engine

drill collar

impervious rock

drill pipe

anticline

PRODUCTION PLATFORM

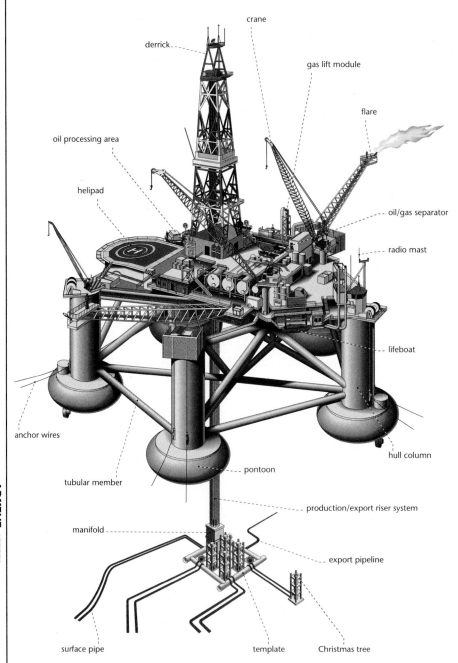

crane

derrick

gas lift module

flare

oil processing area

helipad

oil/gas separator

radio mast

lifeboat

anchor wires

hull column

tubular member

pontoon

manifold

production/export riser system

export pipeline

surface pipe

template

Christmas tree

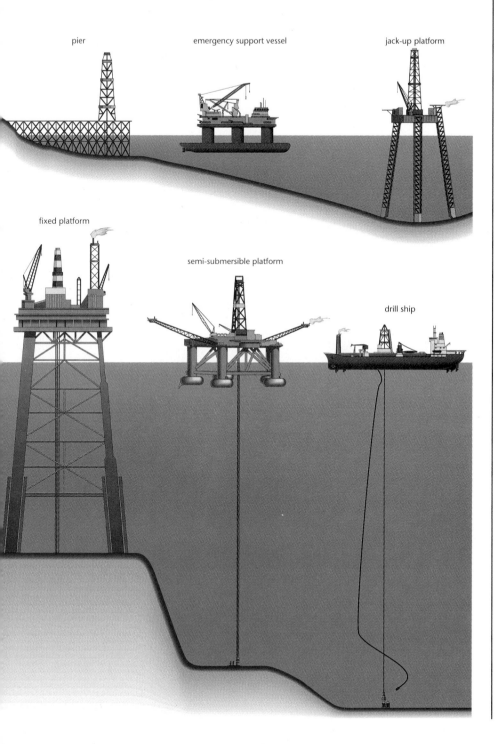

pier

emergency support vessel

jack-up platform

fixed platform

semi-submersible platform

drill ship

OIL

CHRISTMAS TREE

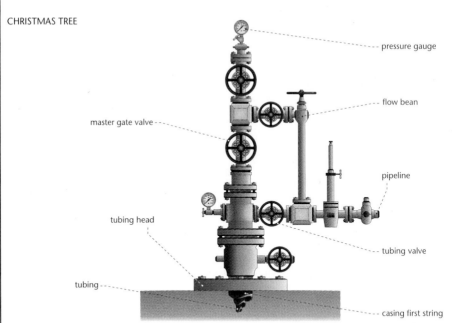

pressure gauge

flow bean

master gate valve

pipeline

tubing head

tubing valve

tubing

casing first string

CRUDE-OIL PIPELINE

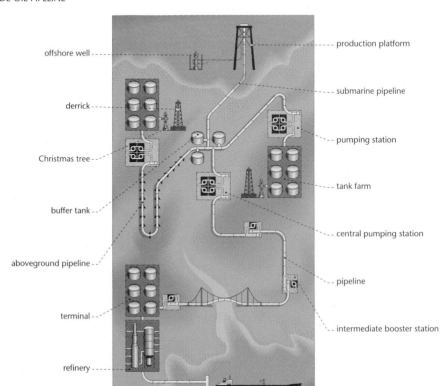

offshore well

production platform

derrick

submarine pipeline

Christmas tree

pumping station

buffer tank

tank farm

aboveground pipeline

central pumping station

terminal

pipeline

refinery

intermediate booster station

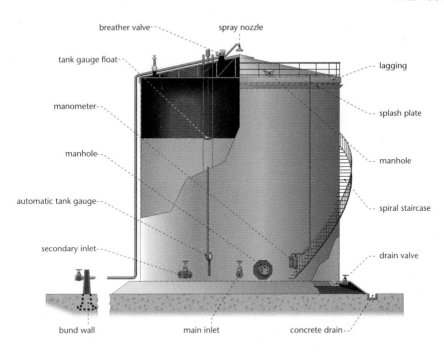

breather valve

spray nozzle

tank gauge float

lagging

manometer

splash plate

manhole

manhole

automatic tank gauge

spiral staircase

secondary inlet

drain valve

bund wall

main inlet

concrete drain

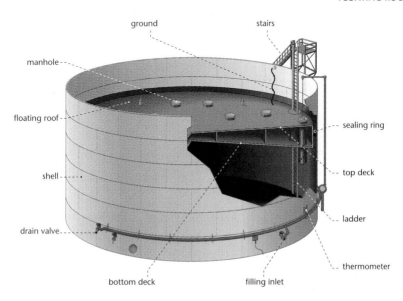

ground

stairs

manhole

floating roof

sealing ring

shell

top deck

ladder

drain valve

bottom deck

filling inlet

thermometer

TANK TRAILER

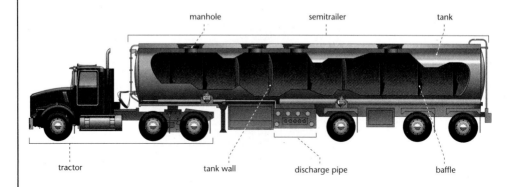

manhole   semitrailer   tank

tractor   tank wall   discharge pipe   baffle

TANKER

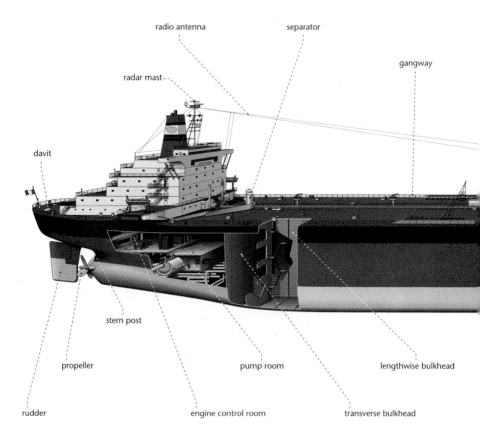

radio antenna   separator

radar mast

gangway

davit

stern post

propeller

rudder   engine control room   transverse bulkhead

pump room   lengthwise bulkhead

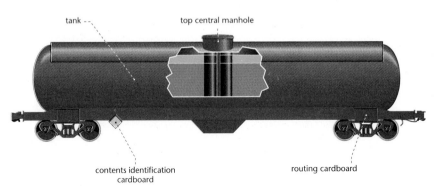

tank

top central manhole

contents identification
cardboard

routing cardboard

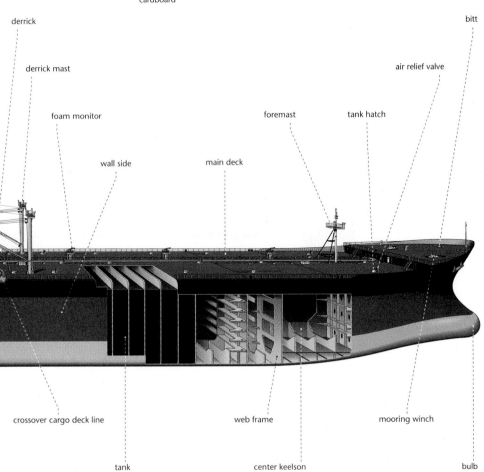

derrick

bitt

derrick mast

air relief valve

foam monitor

foremast

tank hatch

wall side

main deck

crossover cargo deck line

web frame

mooring winch

tank

center keelson

bulb

REFINERY PRODUCTS

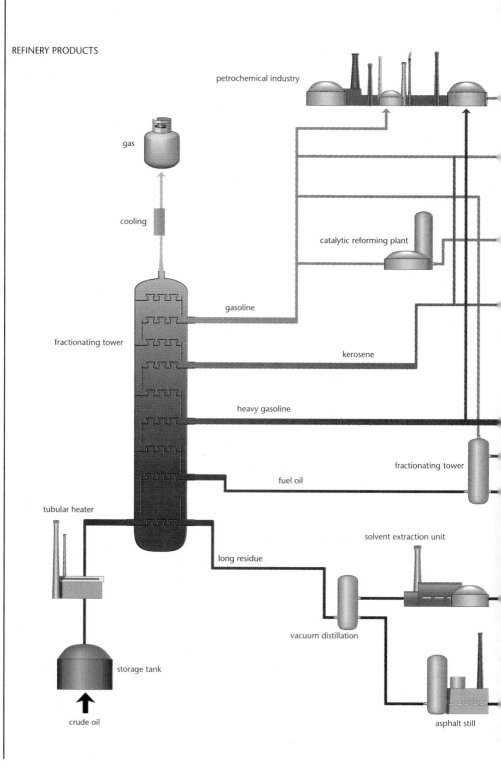

petrochemical industry

gas

cooling

catalytic reforming plant

gasoline

fractionating tower

kerosene

heavy gasoline

fractionating tower

fuel oil

tubular heater

solvent extraction unit

long residue

vacuum distillation

storage tank

crude oil

asphalt still

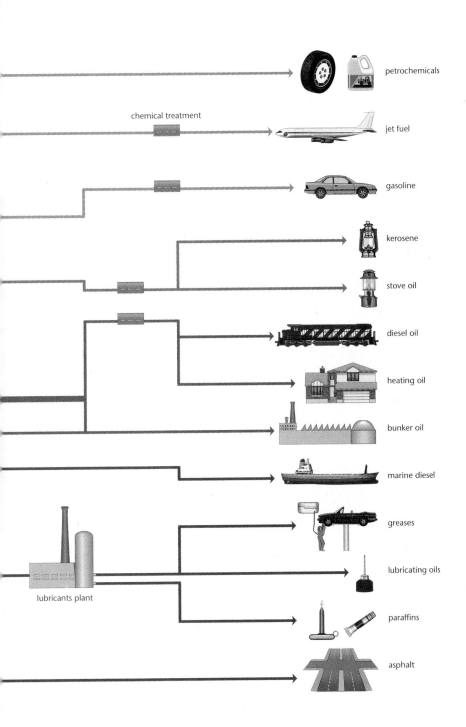

petrochemicals

chemical treatment

jet fuel

gasoline

kerosene

stove oil

diesel oil

heating oil

bunker oil

marine diesel

greases

lubricating oils

lubricants plant

paraffins

asphalt

HYDROELECTRIC COMPLEX

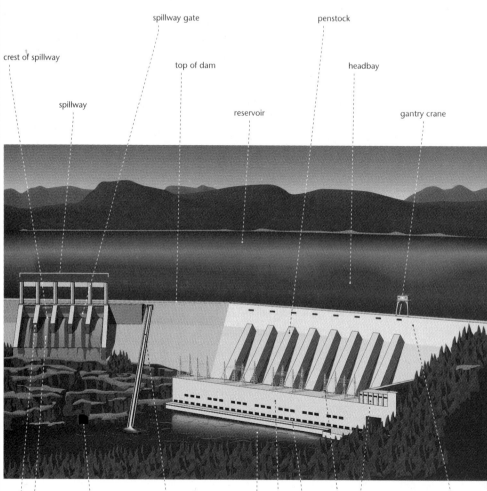

spillway gate

penstock

crest of spillway

top of dam

headbay

spillway

reservoir

gantry crane

log chute

control room

diversion canal

dam

spillway chute

afterbay

bushing

training wall

powerhouse

machine hall

gate

gantry crane

transformer

circuit breaker

bushing

lightning arrester

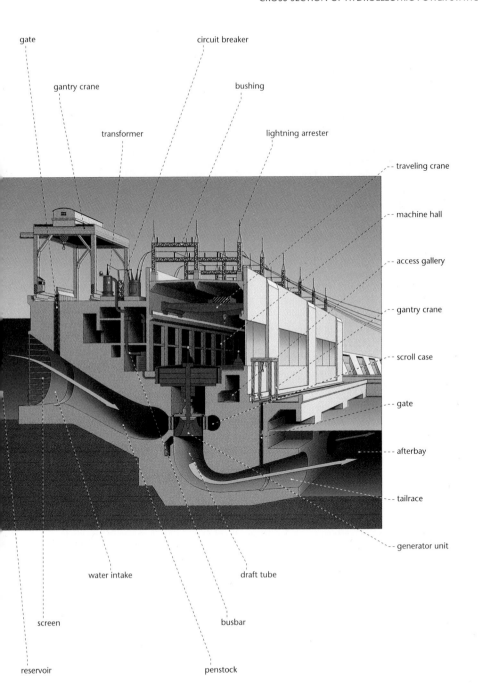

-- traveling crane

--- machine hall

--- access gallery

--- gantry crane

--- scroll case

--- gate

--- afterbay

--- tailrace

--- generator unit

water intake

draft tube

screen

busbar

reservoir

penstock

embankment dam

CROSS SECTION OF AN EMBANKMENT DAM

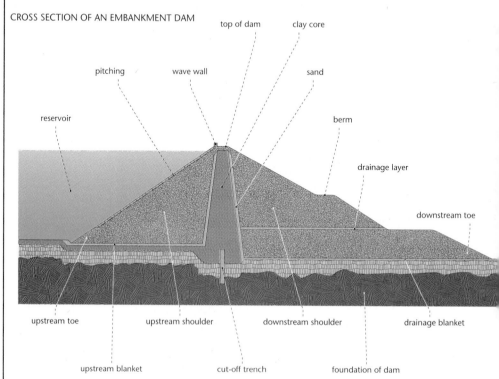

top of dam

clay core

pitching

wave wall

sand

reservoir

berm

drainage layer

downstream toe

upstream toe

upstream shoulder

downstream shoulder

drainage blanket

upstream blanket

cut-off trench

foundation of dam

ENERGY

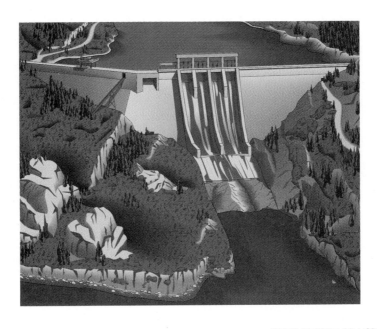

CROSS SECTION OF A GRAVITY DAM

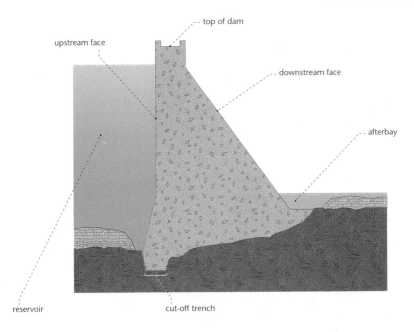

upstream face

top of dam

downstream face

afterbay

reservoir

cut-off trench

arch dam

CROSS SECTION OF AN ARCH DAM

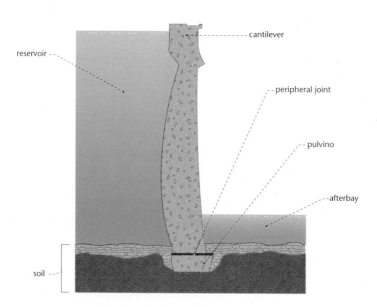

reservoir

cantilever

peripheral joint

pulvino

afterbay

soil

CROSS SECTION OF A BUTTRESS DAM

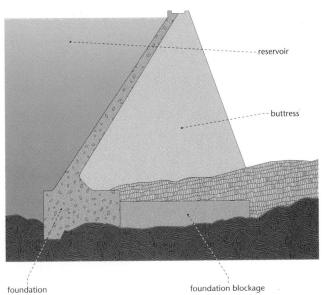

reservoir

buttress

foundation

foundation blockage

TIDAL POWER PLANT

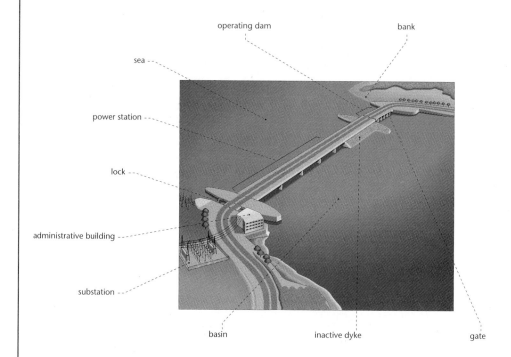

operating dam

bank

sea

power station

lock

administrative building

substation

basin

inactive dyke

gate

CROSS SECTION OF POWER PLANT

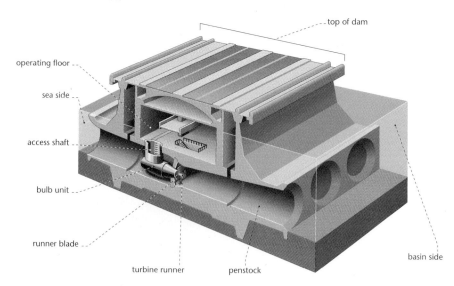

top of dam

operating floor

sea side

access shaft

bulb unit

runner blade

turbine runner

penstock

basin side

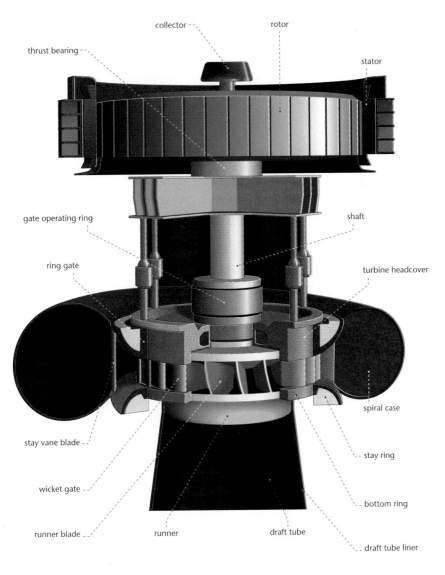

collector

rotor

thrust bearing

stator

gate operating ring

shaft

ring gate

turbine headcover

stay vane blade

spiral case

wicket gate

stay ring

bottom ring

runner blade

runner

draft tube

draft tube liner

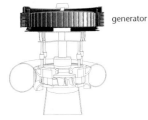

generator

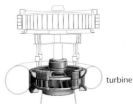

turbine

FRANCIS RUNNER

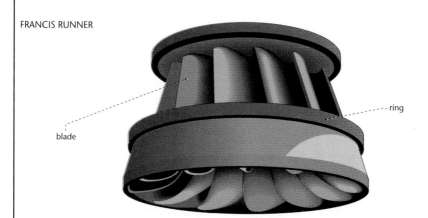

blade

ring

KAPLAN RUNNER

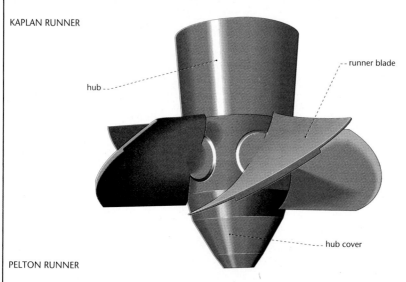

hub

runner blade

hub cover

PELTON RUNNER

bucket ring

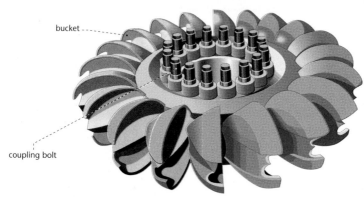

bucket

coupling bolt

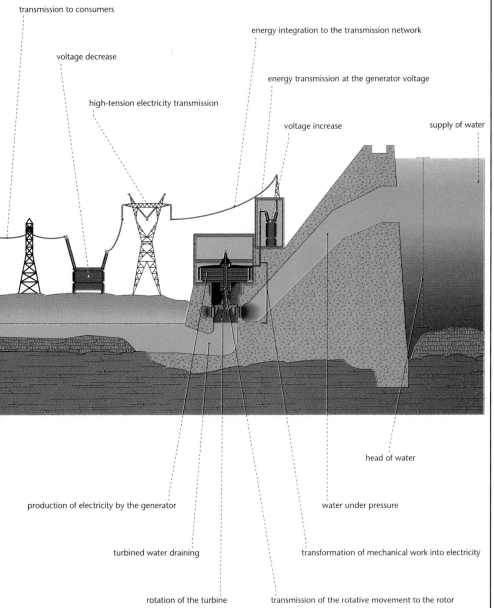

transmission to consumers

voltage decrease

high-tension electricity transmission

energy integration to the transmission network

energy transmission at the generator voltage

voltage increase

supply of water

head of water

production of electricity by the generator

water under pressure

turbined water draining

transformation of mechanical work into electricity

rotation of the turbine

transmission of the rotative movement to the rotor

ENERGY

PYLON

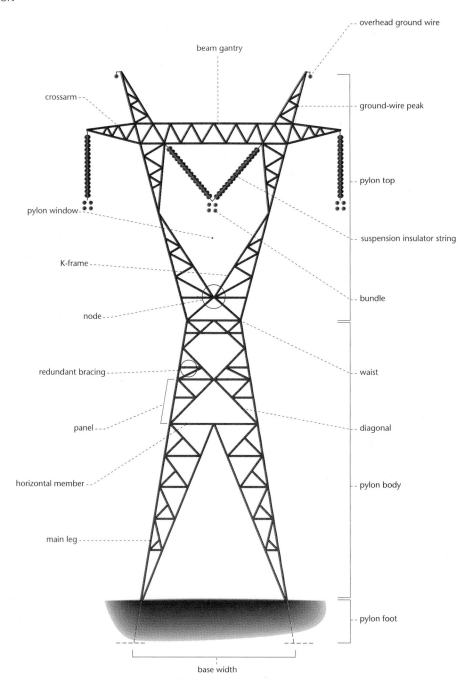

overhead ground wire

beam gantry

crossarm

ground-wire peak

pylon top

pylon window

suspension insulator string

K-frame

node

bundle

redundant bracing

waist

panel

diagonal

horizontal member

pylon body

main leg

pylon foot

base width

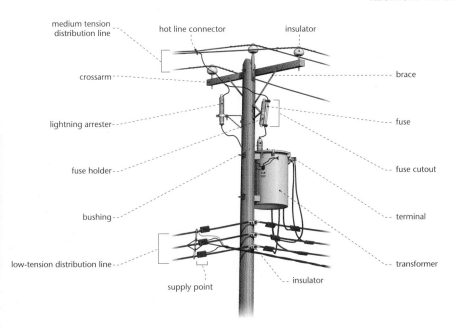

medium tension distribution line

hot line connector

insulator

crossarm

brace

lightning arrester

fuse

fuse holder

fuse cutout

bushing

terminal

low-tension distribution line

transformer

supply point

insulator

OVERHEAD CONNECTION

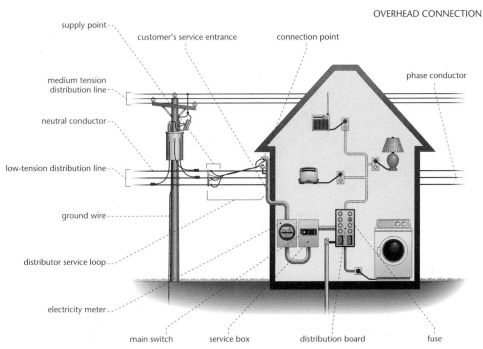

supply point

customer's service entrance

connection point

phase conductor

medium tension distribution line

neutral conductor

low-tension distribution line

ground wire

distributor service loop

electricity meter

main switch

service box

distribution board

fuse

ENERGY

NUCLEAR GENERATING STATION

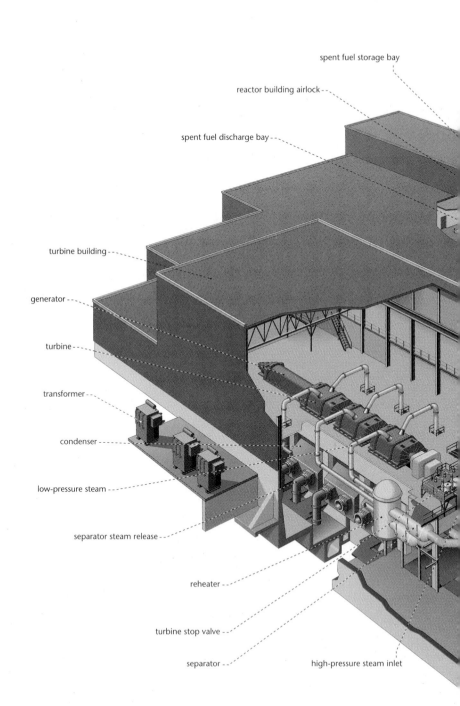

spent fuel storage bay

reactor building airlock

spent fuel discharge bay

turbine building

generator

turbine

transformer

condenser

low-pressure steam

separator steam release

reheater

turbine stop valve

separator

high-pressure steam inlet

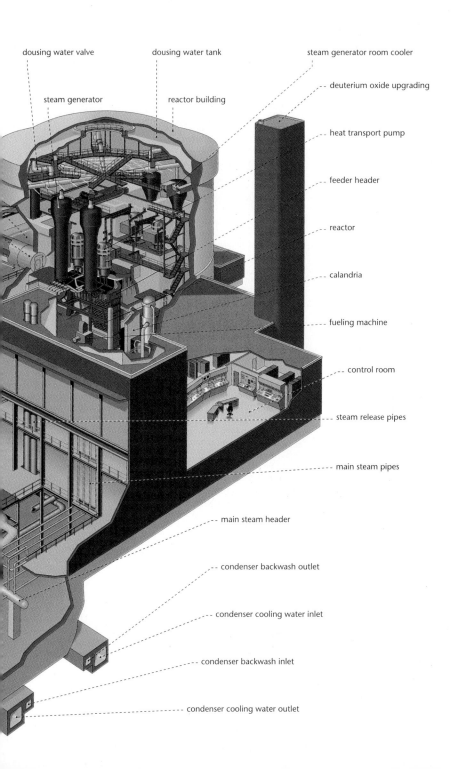

dousing water valve

dousing water tank

steam generator room cooler

deuterium oxide upgrading

steam generator

reactor building

heat transport pump

feeder header

reactor

calandria

fueling machine

control room

steam release pipes

main steam pipes

main steam header

condenser backwash outlet

condenser cooling water inlet

condenser backwash inlet

condenser cooling water outlet

CARBON DIOXIDE REACTOR

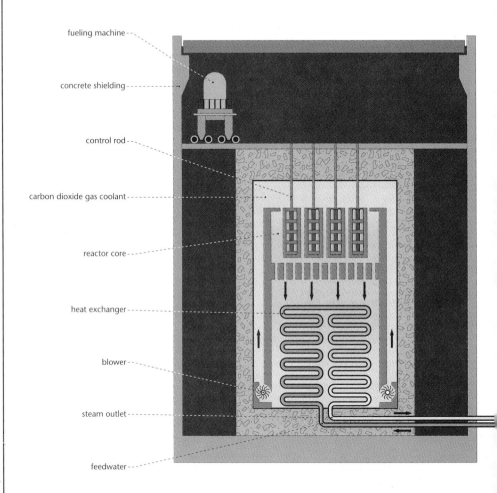

fueling machine

concrete shielding

control rod

carbon dioxide gas coolant

reactor core

heat exchanger

blower

steam outlet

feedwater

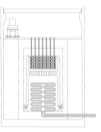

fuel: natural uranium

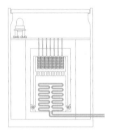

moderator: graphite

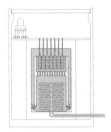

coolant: carbon dioxide

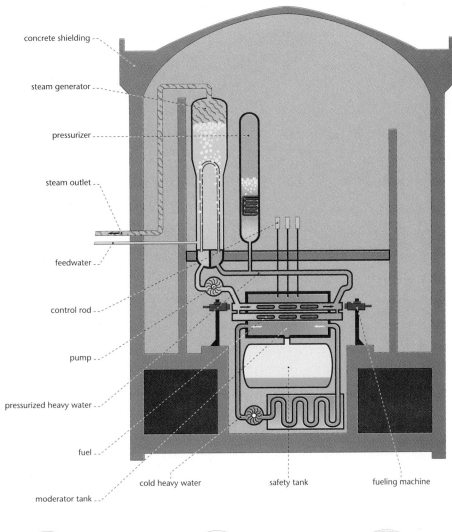

concrete shielding

steam generator

pressurizer

steam outlet

feedwater

control rod

pump

pressurized heavy water

fuel

moderator tank

cold heavy water

safety tank

fueling machine

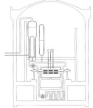

fuel: natural uranium

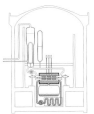

moderator: heavy water

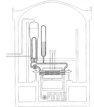

coolant: pressurized heavy water

PRESSURIZED-WATER REACTOR

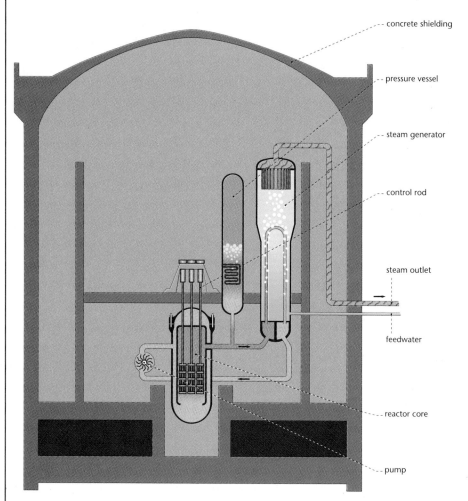

concrete shielding

pressure vessel

steam generator

control rod

steam outlet

feedwater

reactor core

pump

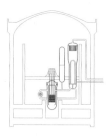

fuel: enriched uranium

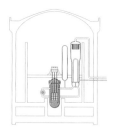

moderator: natural water

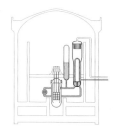

coolant: pressurized water

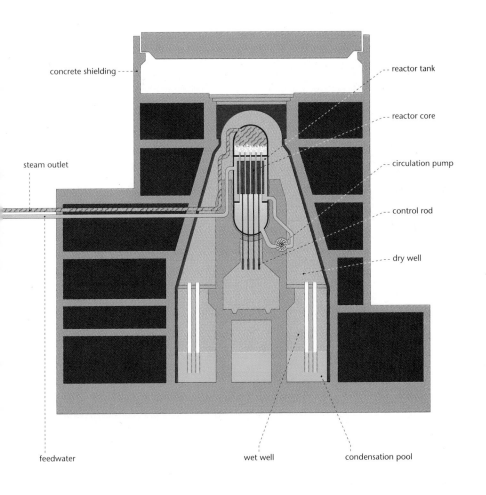

concrete shielding

reactor tank

reactor core

circulation pump

steam outlet

control rod

dry well

feedwater

wet well

condensation pool

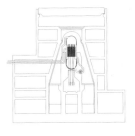

fuel: enriched uranium

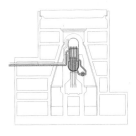

moderator: natural water

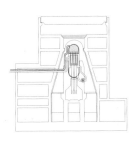

coolant: boiling water

FUEL HANDLING SEQUENCE

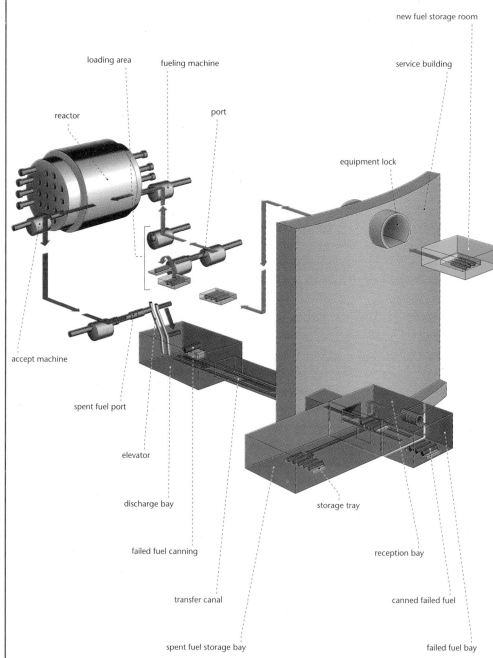

new fuel storage room

loading area

fueling machine

service building

reactor

port

equipment lock

accept machine

spent fuel port

elevator

discharge bay

storage tray

failed fuel canning

reception bay

transfer canal

canned failed fuel

spent fuel storage bay

failed fuel bay

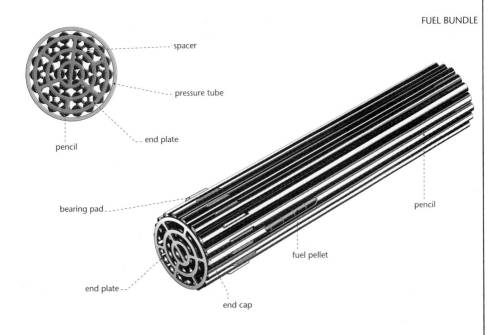

spacer

pressure tube

end plate

pencil

bearing pad

end plate

end cap

fuel pellet

pencil

NUCLEAR REACTOR

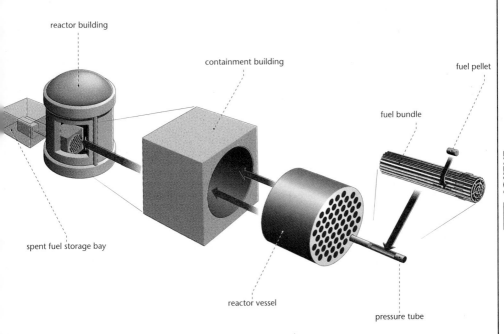

reactor building

containment building

fuel pellet

fuel bundle

spent fuel storage bay

reactor vessel

pressure tube

ENERGY

NUCLEAR ENERGY

PRODUCTION OF ELECTRICITY FROM NUCLEAR ENERGY

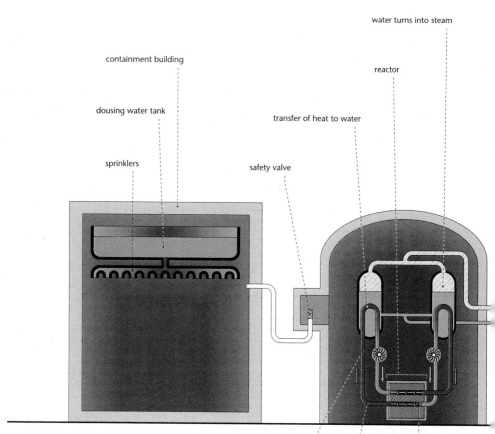

water turns into steam

containment building

reactor

dousing water tank

transfer of heat to water

sprinklers

safety valve

coolant transfers the heat to the steam generator

heat production

fission of uranium fuel

fuel

moderator

coolant

steam pressure drives turbine

electricity transmission

voltage increase

turbine shaft turns generator

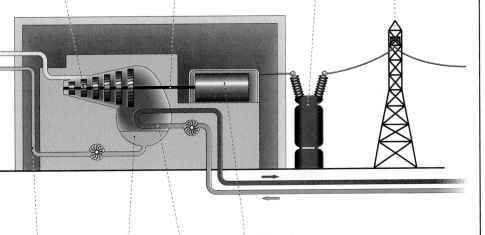

electricity production

water cools the used steam

condensation of steam into water

water is pumped back into the steam generator

SOLAR ENERGY

SOLAR CELL

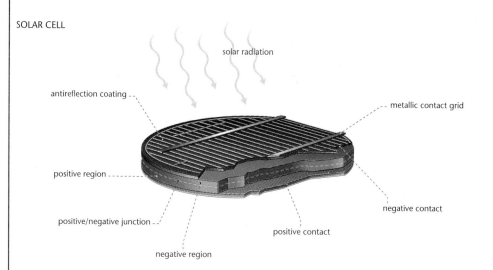

solar radiation

antireflection coating

metallic contact grid

positive region

positive/negative junction

negative contact

positive contact

negative region

FLAT-PLATE SOLAR COLLECTOR

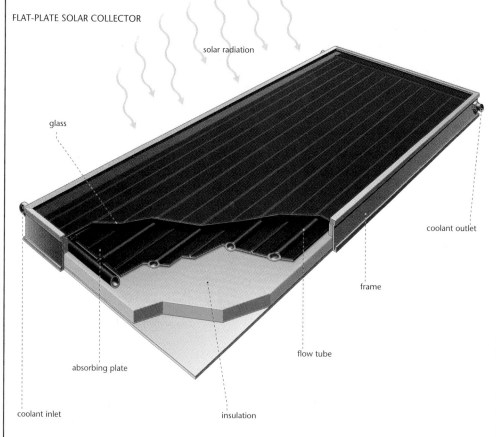

solar radiation

glass

coolant outlet

frame

flow tube

absorbing plate

coolant inlet

insulation

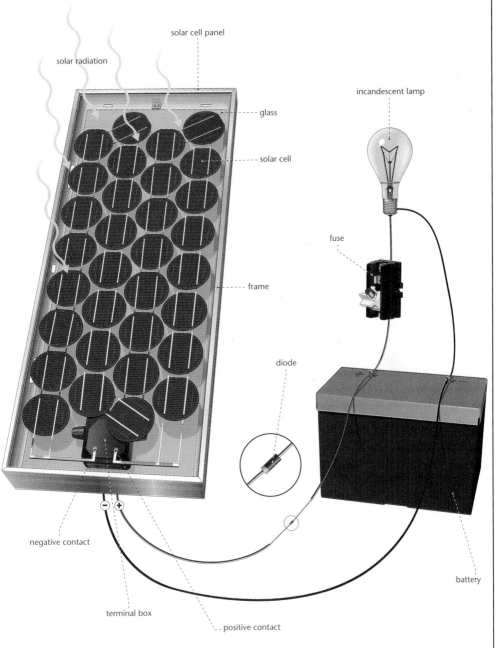

solar cell panel

solar radiation

glass

solar cell

incandescent lamp

frame

fuse

diode

negative contact

terminal box

positive contact

battery

SOLAR FURNACE

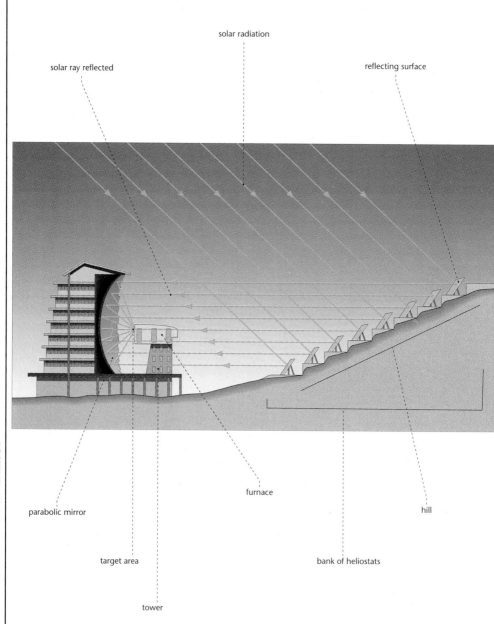

solar radiation

solar ray reflected

reflecting surface

parabolic mirror

furnace

hill

target area

bank of heliostats

tower

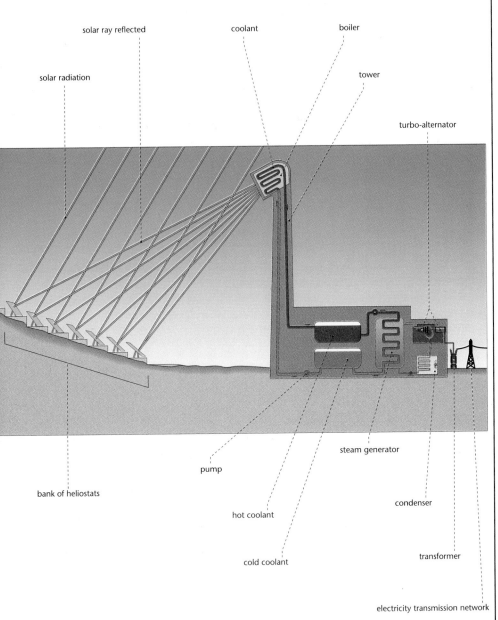

solar ray reflected

coolant

boiler

solar radiation

tower

turbo-alternator

bank of heliostats

pump

steam generator

condenser

hot coolant

transformer

cold coolant

electricity transmission network

SOLAR ENERGY

SOLAR HOUSE

solar radiation

solar collector

ventilation

Trombe wall

heat exchanger

circulating pump

water-heater tank

pool

expansion tank

water main

circulating pump

heat exchanger

storage tank

filter

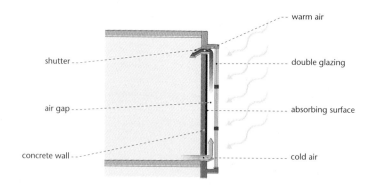

TROMBE WALL

warm air

shutter

double glazing

air gap

absorbing surface

concrete wall

cold air

WIND ENERGY

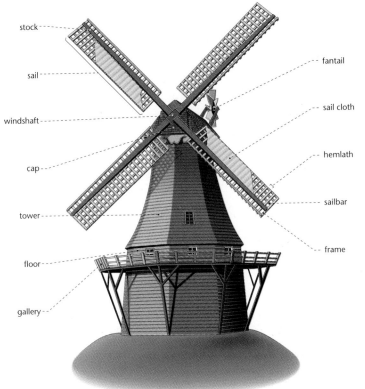

stock

sail

windshaft

cap

tower

floor

gallery

fantail

sail cloth

hemlath

sailbar

frame

POST MILL

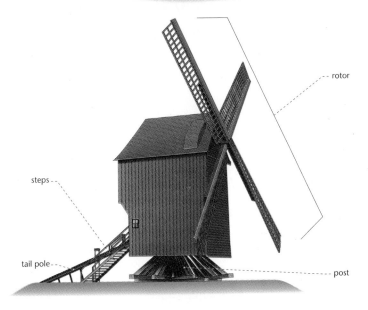

rotor

steps

tail pole

post

ENERGY

HORIZONTAL-AXIS WIND TURBINE

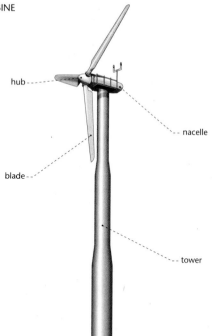

hub ---

nacelle

blade ---

tower

VERTICAL-AXIS WIND TURBINE

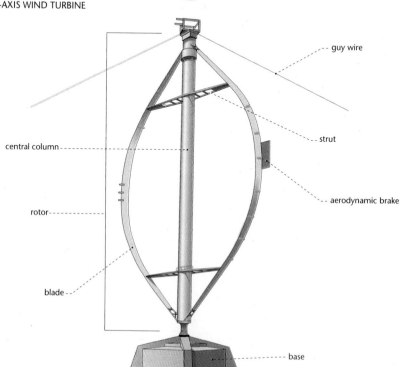

guy wire

strut

central column ---

aerodynamic brake

rotor ---

blade ---

base

HEAVY MACHINERY

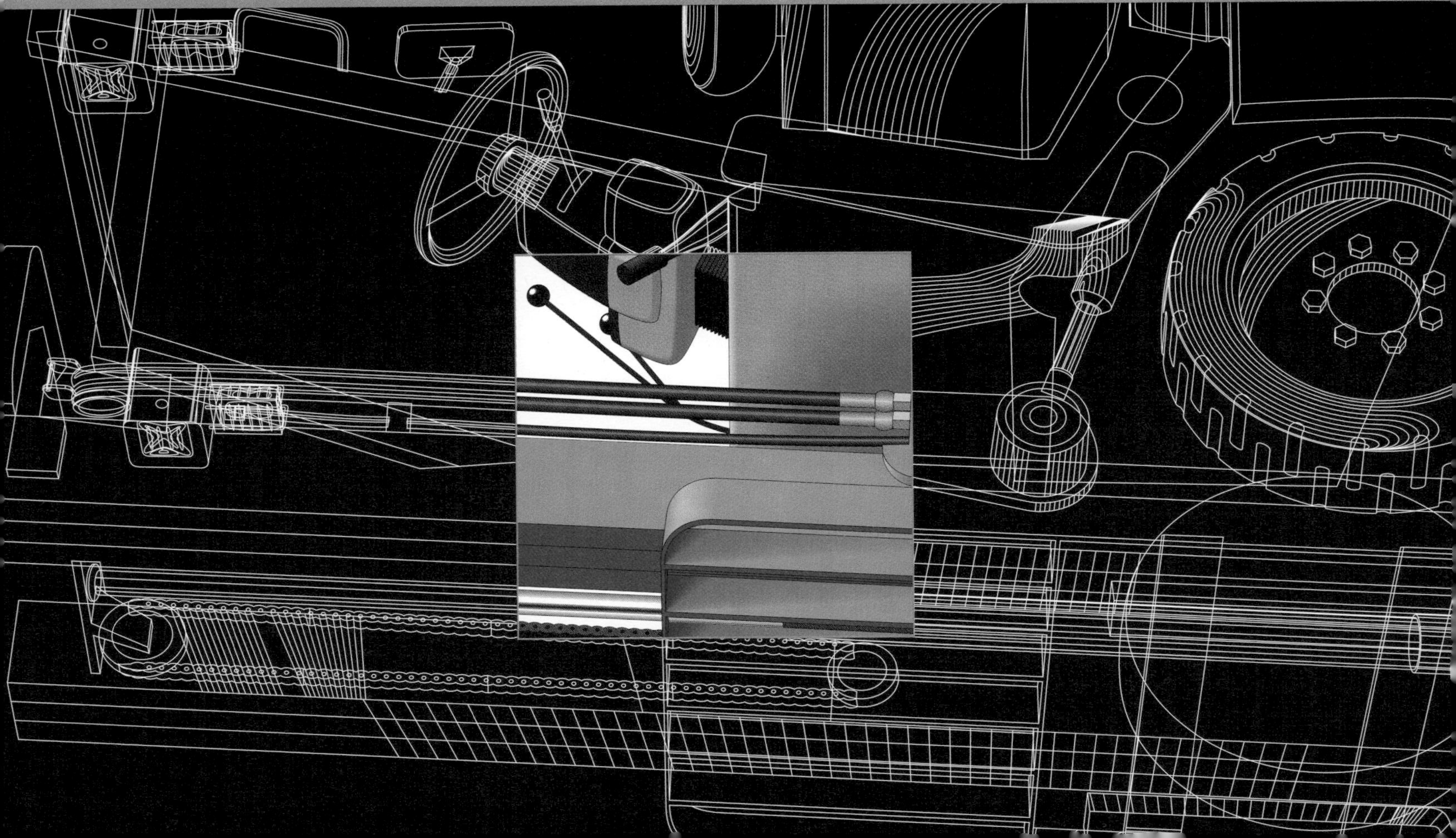

CONTENTS

HEAVY MACHINERY

FIRE PREVENTION

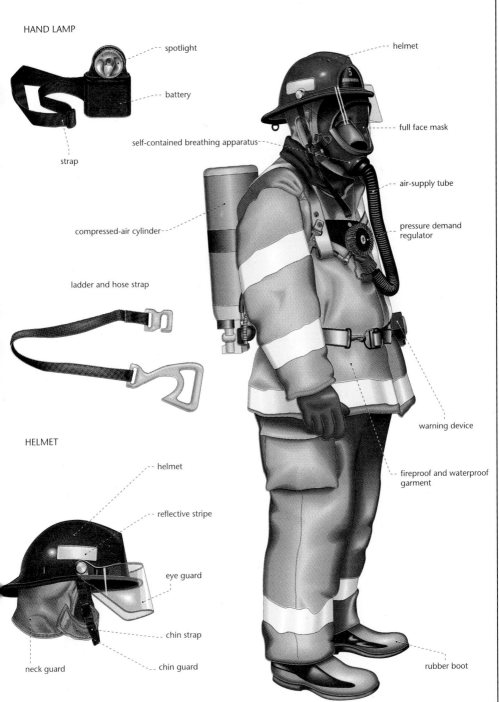

FIREMAN

HAND LAMP

- spotlight
- battery
- strap

helmet

full face mask

air-supply tube

pressure demand regulator

self-contained breathing apparatus

compressed-air cylinder

ladder and hose strap

warning device

fireproof and waterproof garment

HELMET

- helmet
- reflective stripe
- eye guard
- chin strap
- chin guard
- neck guard

rubber boot

FIRE ENGINE

PUMPER

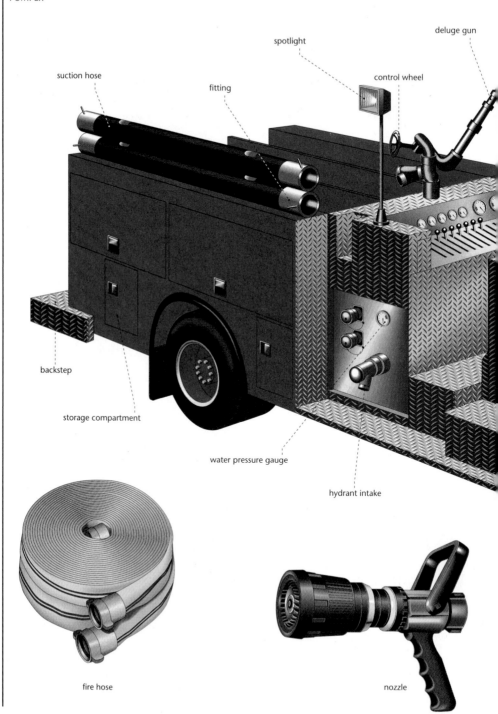

spotlight

deluge gun

suction hose

fitting

control wheel

backstep

storage compartment

water pressure gauge

hydrant intake

fire hose

nozzle

dividing breeching

control panel

horn

light bar

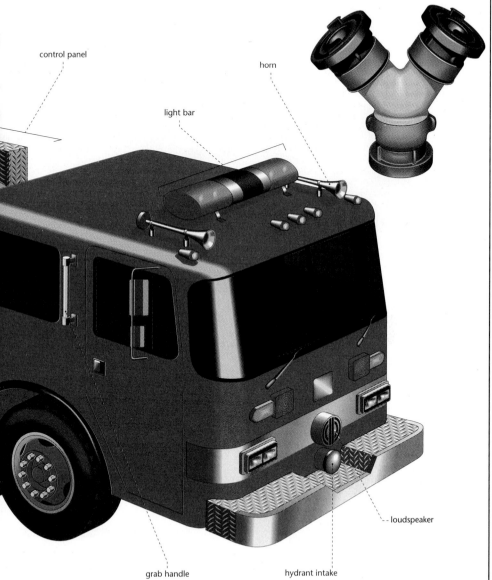

loudspeaker

grab handle

hydrant intake

fire hydrant wrench

FIRE ENGINE

AERIAL LADDER TRUCK

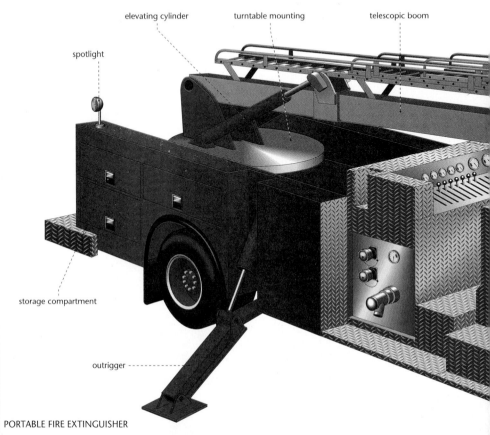

elevating cylinder

turntable mounting

telescopic boom

spotlight

storage compartment

outrigger

PORTABLE FIRE EXTINGUISHER

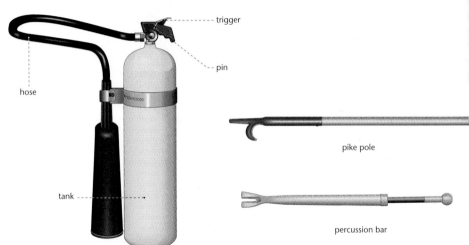

trigger

pin

hose

tank

pike pole

percussion bar

tower ladder

mars light

top ladder

ladder pipe nozzle

hook ladder

fireman's hatchet

WHEEL LOADER

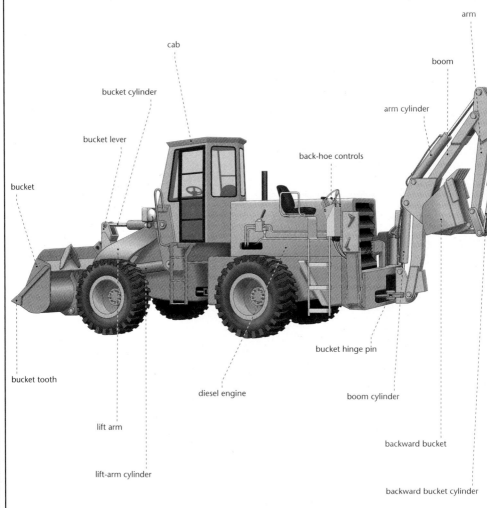

arm

boom

cab

bucket cylinder

arm cylinder

bucket lever

back-hoe controls

bucket

bucket tooth

lift arm

lift-arm cylinder

diesel engine

bucket hinge pin

boom cylinder

backward bucket

backward bucket cylinder

front-end loader

wheel tractor

back-hoe

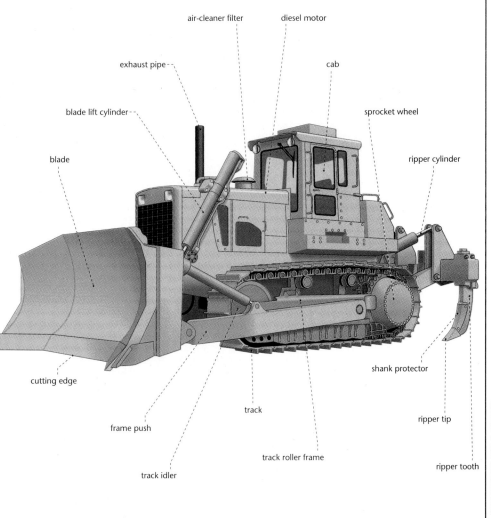

air-cleaner filter

diesel motor

exhaust pipe

cab

blade lift cylinder

sprocket wheel

blade

ripper cylinder

cutting edge

shank protector

frame push

track

ripper tip

track roller frame

track idler

ripper tooth

blade

crawler tractor

ripper

SCRAPER

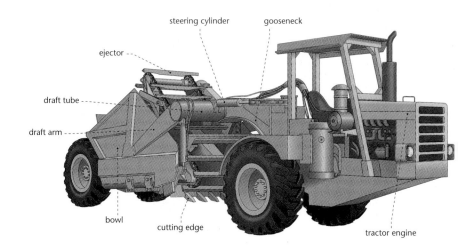

steering cylinder

gooseneck

ejector

draft tube

draft arm

bowl

cutting edge

tractor engine

GRADER

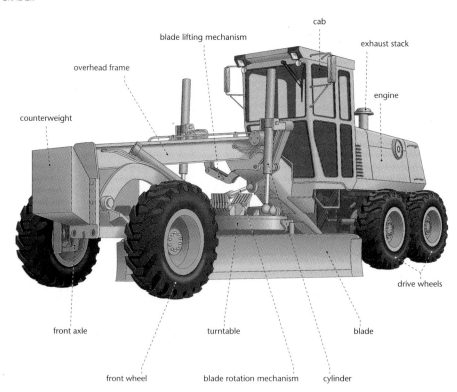

cab

blade lifting mechanism

exhaust stack

overhead frame

engine

counterweight

drive wheels

front axle

turntable

blade

front wheel

blade rotation mechanism

cylinder

HEAVY MACHINERY

HEAVY MACHINERY

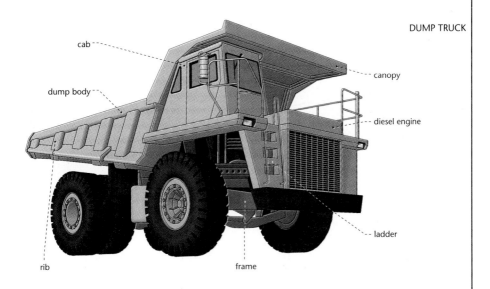

cab

dump body

canopy

diesel engine

ladder

rib

frame

HYDRAULIC SHOVEL

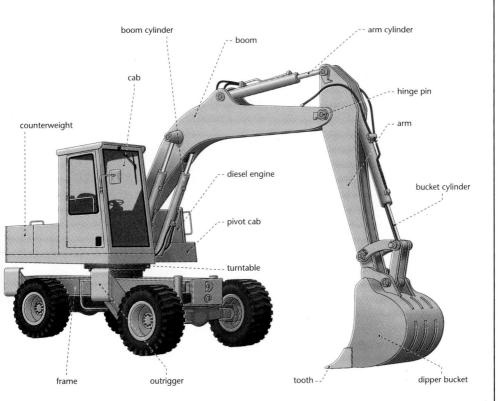

boom cylinder

boom

arm cylinder

cab

hinge pin

counterweight

arm

diesel engine

bucket cylinder

pivot cab

turntable

frame

outrigger

tooth

dipper bucket

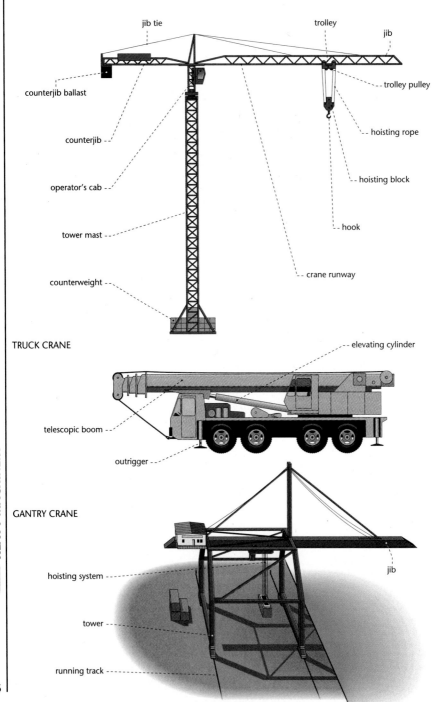

TOWER CRANE

jib tie

trolley

jib

counterjib ballast

trolley pulley

counterjib

hoisting rope

operator's cab

hoisting block

tower mast

hook

counterweight

crane runway

TRUCK CRANE

elevating cylinder

telescopic boom

outrigger

GANTRY CRANE

hoisting system

jib

tower

running track

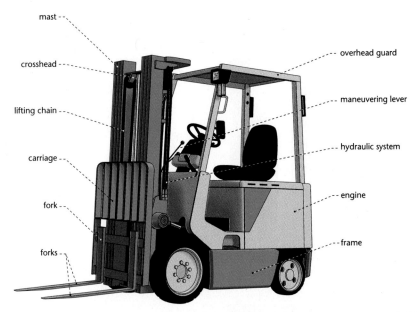

mast
crosshead
lifting chain
carriage
fork
forks

overhead guard
maneuvering lever
hydraulic system
engine
frame

WING PALLET

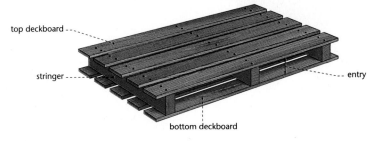

top deckboard
stringer

entry

bottom deckboard

BOX PALLET

double-decked pallet

single-decked pallet

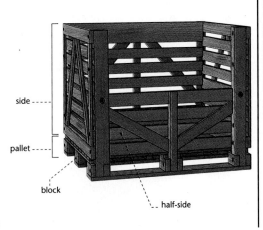

side

pallet

block

half-side

HYDRAULIC PALLET TRUCK

pallet truck

maneuvering lever

steering lever

mast

hydraulic cylinder

hand truck

forks

solid rubber tire

stabilizing shaft

steering axle

frame

roller

platform pallet truck

flatbed pushcart

CONTENTS

STONE AGE WEAPONS 791

WEAPONS IN THE AGE OF THE ROMANS 791

ARMOR 792

BOWS AND CROSSBOW 793

THRUSTING AND CUTTING WEAPONS...794

HARQUEBUS 795

SUBMACHINE GUN..795

AUTOMATIC RIFLE 796

LIGHT MACHINE GUN 796

PISTOL 797

REVOLVER 797

HUNTING WEAPONS 798

SEVENTEENTH CENTURY CANNON 800

MODERN HOWITZER 802

MORTAR 803

HAND GRENADE 804

BAZOOKA 804

RECOILLESS RIFLE 804

TANK 805

SUBMARINE 806

FRIGATE 808

AIRCRAFT CARRIER 810

COMBAT AIRCRAFT...812

MISSILES 814

WEAPONS

STONE AGE WEAPONS

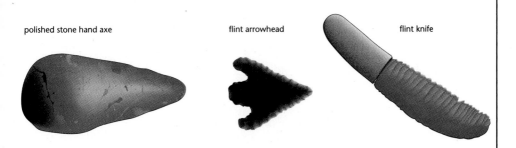

polished stone hand axe

flint arrowhead

flint knife

WEAPONS IN THE AGE OF THE ROMANS

GALLIC WARRIOR

ROMAN LEGIONARY

helmet

breeches

shield

spear

crest

shield

cuirass

gladius

tunic

javelin

sandal

ARMOR

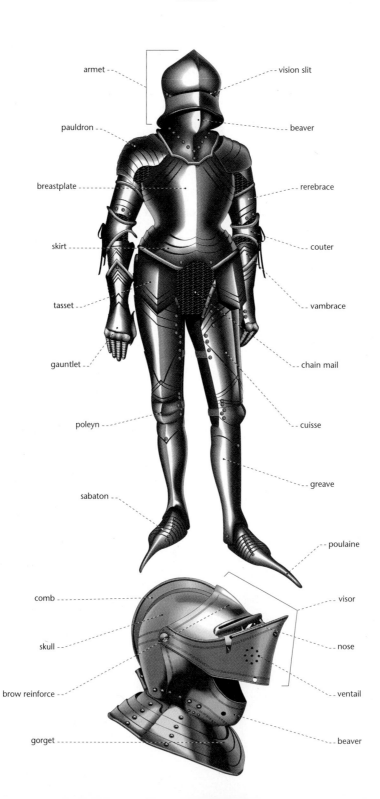

armet — — vision slit

— — beaver

pauldron

breastplate — — rerebrace

skirt — — couter

tasset — — vambrace

gauntlet — — chain mail

— — cuisse

poleyn — — greave

sabaton

— poulaine

ARMET

comb — — visor

skull — — nose

brow reinforce — — ventail

gorget — — beaver

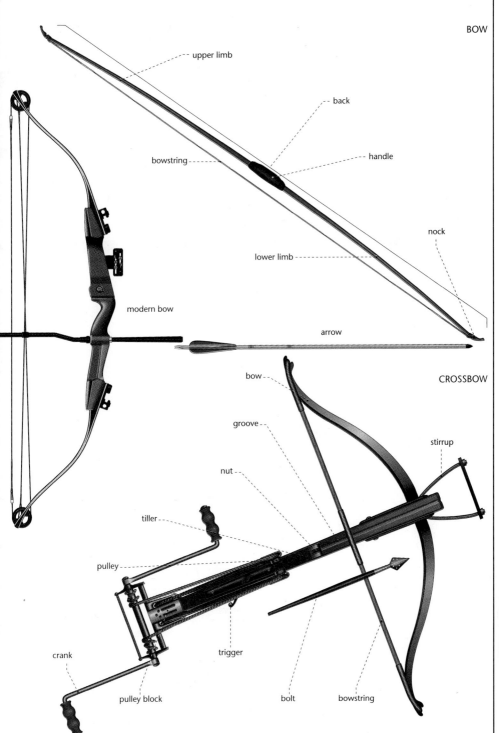

BOW

upper limb

back

handle

bowstring

nock

lower limb

modern bow

arrow

CROSSBOW

bow

groove

stirrup

nut

tiller

pulley

trigger

crank

pulley block

bolt

bowstring

saber

rapier

broadsword

poniard

stiletto

machete

dagger

hilted bayonet

commando knife

integral bayonet

plug bayonet

socket bayonet

HARQUEBUS

ball

ramrod

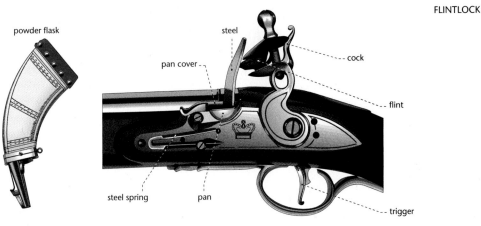

powder flask

steel

pan cover

cock

flint

steel spring

pan

trigger

SUBMACHINE GUN

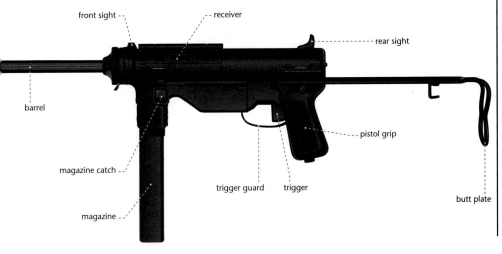

front sight

receiver

rear sight

barrel

pistol grip

magazine catch

trigger guard   trigger

magazine

butt plate

WEAPONS

795

AUTOMATIC RIFLE

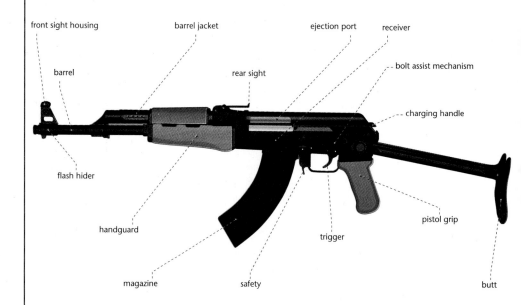

front sight housing

barrel jacket

ejection port

receiver

barrel

bolt assist mechanism

rear sight

charging handle

flash hider

handguard

pistol grip

trigger

magazine

safety

butt

LIGHT MACHINE GUN

flash hider

barrel jacket

rear sight

front sight housing

carrying handle

cover

barrel

gas cylinder

trigger

operating rod

bipod

pistol grip

butt

REVOLVER

hammer

barrel

front sight

muzzle

cylinder

trigger guard

butt

trigger

PISTOL

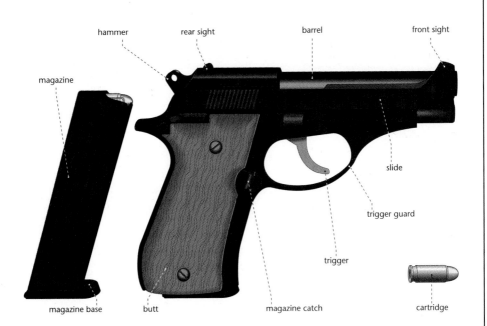

hammer

rear sight

barrel

front sight

magazine

slide

trigger guard

trigger

magazine base

butt

magazine catch

cartridge

CARTRIDGE (RIFLE)

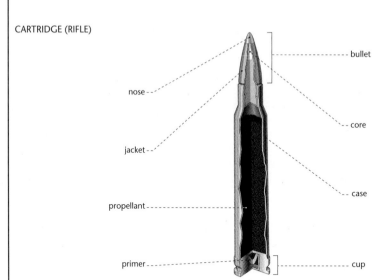

bullet

nose

core

jacket

case

propellant

primer

cup

RIFLE (RIFLED BORE)

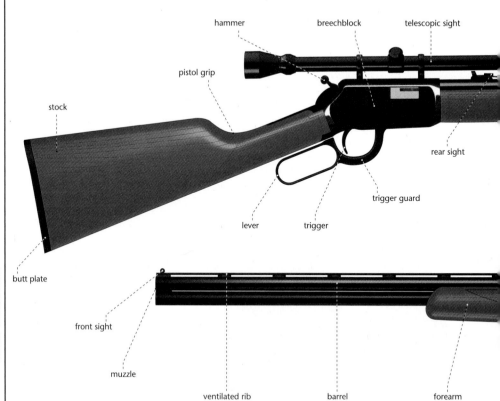

hammer

breechblock

telescopic sight

pistol grip

stock

rear sight

trigger guard

butt plate

lever

trigger

front sight

muzzle

ventilated rib

barrel

forearm

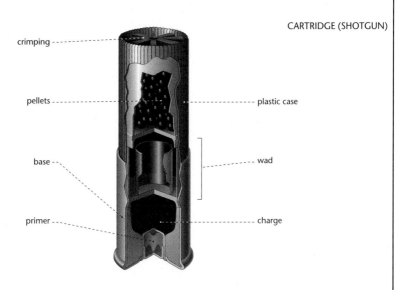

CARTRIDGE (SHOTGUN)

crimping

pellets

plastic case

base

wad

primer

charge

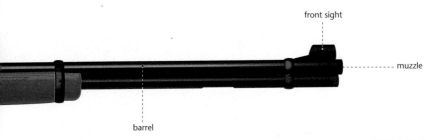

front sight

muzzle

barrel

SHOTGUN (SMOOTH-BORE)

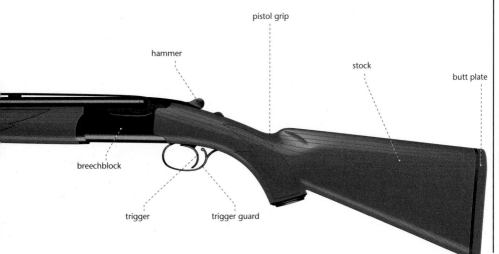

pistol grip

hammer

stock

butt plate

breechblock

trigger

trigger guard

MUZZLE LOADING

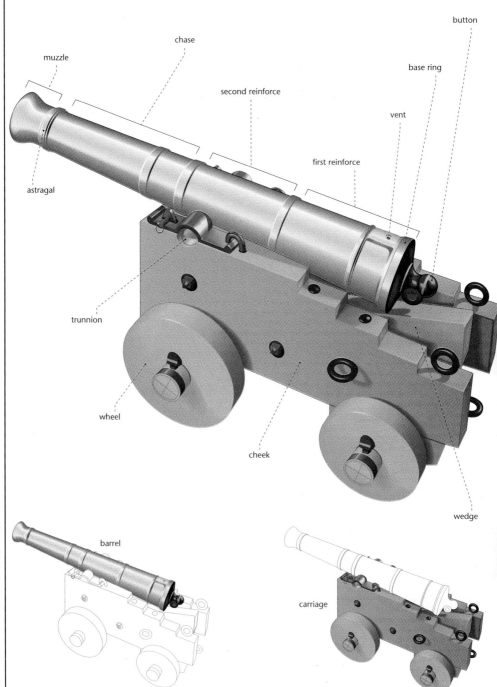

button

chase

muzzle

base ring

second reinforce

vent

first reinforce

astragal

trunnion

wheel

cheek

wedge

barrel

carriage

CROSS SECTION OF A MUZZLE LOADING

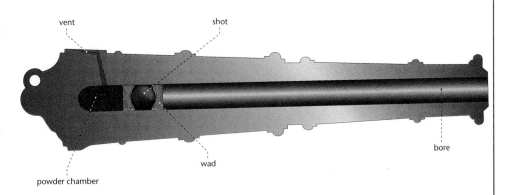

vent

shot

bore

wad

powder chamber

FIRING ACCESSORIES

rammer

linstock

worm

ladle

sponge

PROJECTILES

bar shot

grapeshot

solid shot

hollow shot

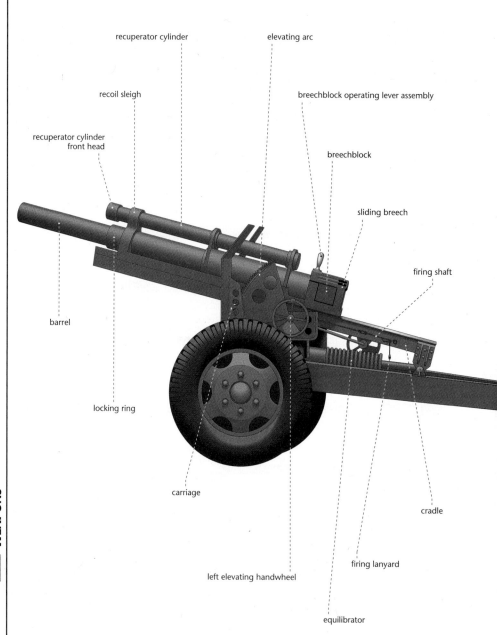

recuperator cylinder

elevating arc

recoil sleigh

breechblock operating lever assembly

recuperator cylinder
front head

breechblock

sliding breech

firing shaft

barrel

locking ring

carriage

cradle

left elevating handwheel

firing lanyard

equilibrator

MORTAR

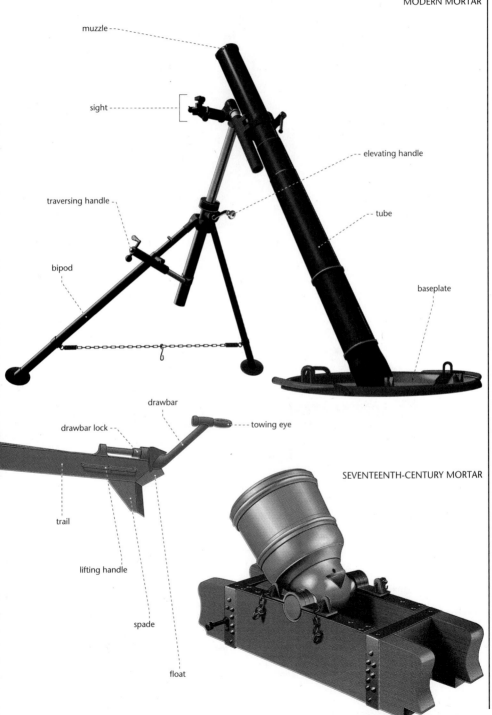

MODERN MORTAR

muzzle

sight

elevating handle

traversing handle

tube

bipod

baseplate

drawbar

drawbar lock

towing eye

trail

SEVENTEENTH-CENTURY MORTAR

lifting handle

spade

float

HAND GRENADE

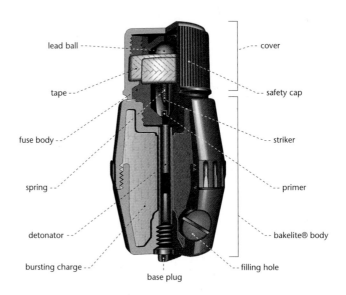

lead ball

tape

fuse body

spring

detonator

bursting charge

base plug

cover

safety cap

striker

primer

bakelite® body

filling hole

BAZOOKA

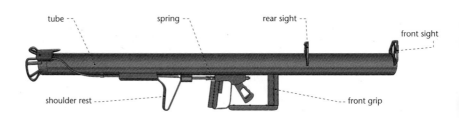

tube

spring

rear sight

front sight

shoulder rest

front grip

RECOILLESS RIFLE

barrel

shoulder pad

firing mechanism

venturi fastening lever

front grip

trigger

cocking lever

anti-tank rocket

venturi

TANK

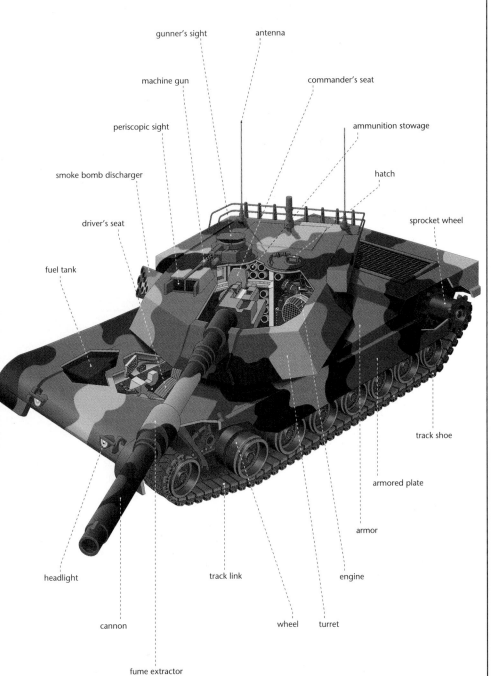

gunner's sight

antenna

machine gun

commander's seat

periscopic sight

ammunition stowage

smoke bomb discharger

hatch

driver's seat

sprocket wheel

fuel tank

headlight

track link

engine

cannon

wheel

turret

fume extractor

track shoe

armored plate

armor

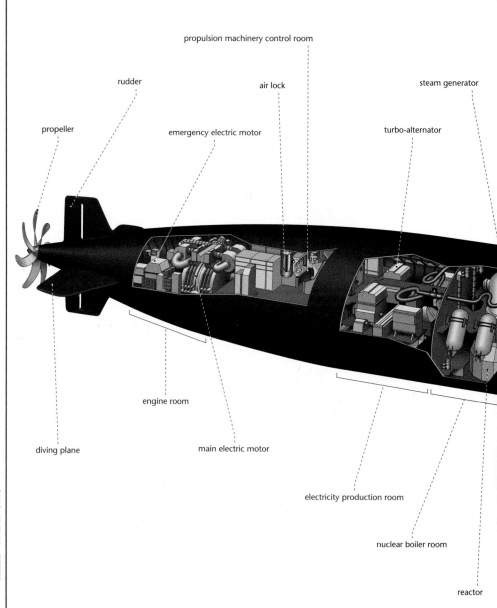

propulsion machinery control room

rudder

air lock

steam generator

propeller

emergency electric motor

turbo-alternator

engine room

diving plane

main electric motor

electricity production room

nuclear boiler room

reactor

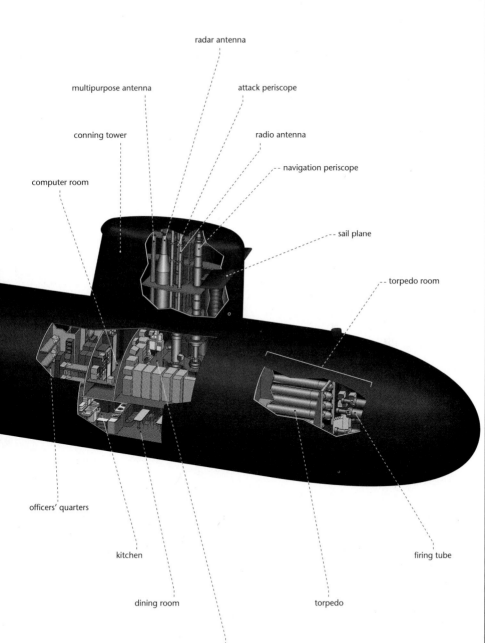

radar antenna

multipurpose antenna

attack periscope

conning tower

radio antenna

computer room

navigation periscope

sail plane

torpedo room

officers' quarters

kitchen

dining room

firing tube

torpedo

operation control room

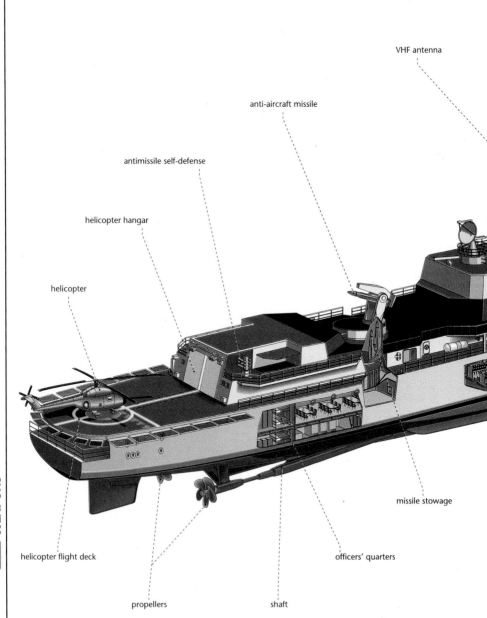

VHF antenna

anti-aircraft missile

antimissile self-defense

helicopter hangar

helicopter

missile stowage

helicopter flight deck

officers' quarters

propellers

shaft

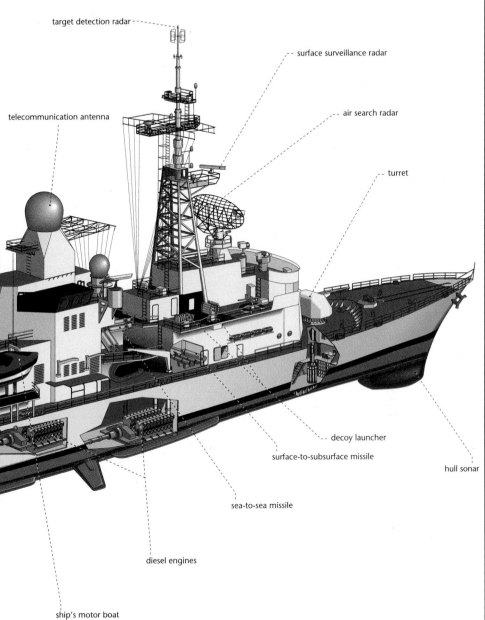

target detection radar

surface surveillance radar

air search radar

telecommunication antenna

turret

decoy launcher

surface-to-subsurface missile

hull sonar

sea-to-sea missile

diesel engines

ship's motor boat

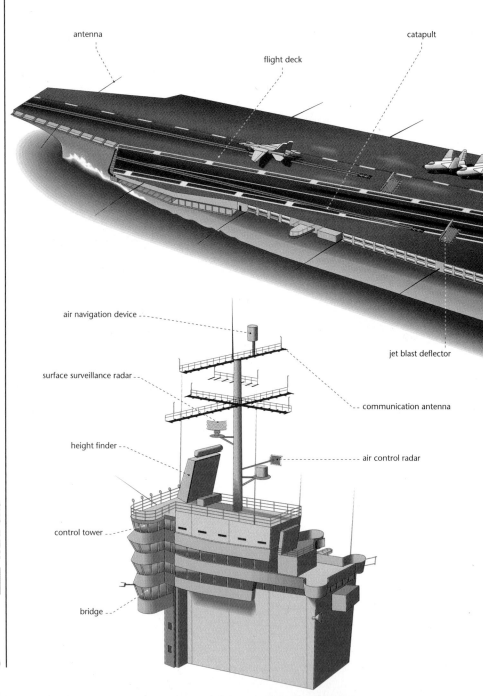

antenna

flight deck

catapult

air navigation device

jet blast deflector

surface surveillance radar

communication antenna

height finder

air control radar

control tower

bridge

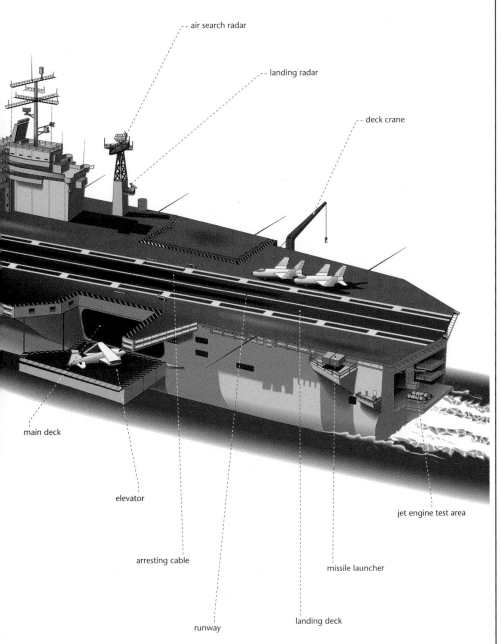

air search radar

landing radar

deck crane

main deck

elevator

jet engine test area

arresting cable

missile launcher

runway

landing deck

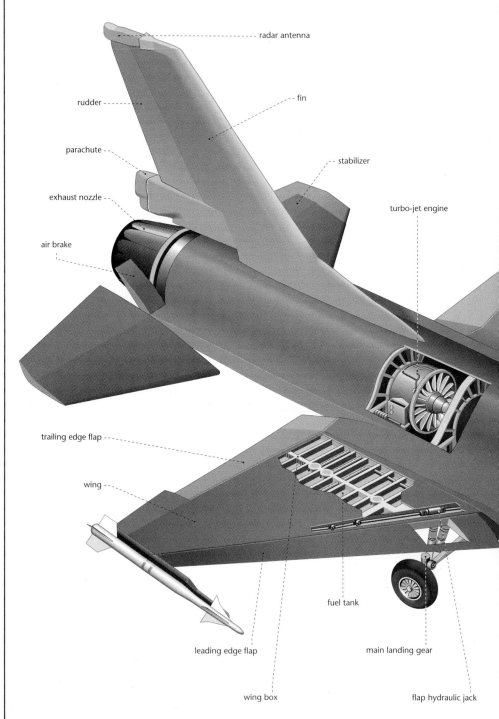

radar antenna

rudder

fin

parachute

stabilizer

exhaust nozzle

turbo-jet engine

air brake

trailing edge flap

wing

fuel tank

leading edge flap

main landing gear

wing box

flap hydraulic jack

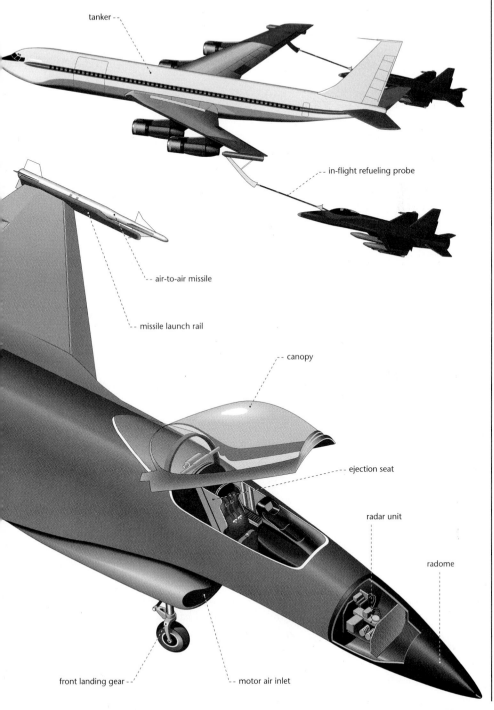

tanker

in-flight refueling probe

air-to-air missile

missile launch rail

canopy

ejection seat

radar unit

radome

front landing gear

motor air inlet

STRUCTURE OF A MISSILE

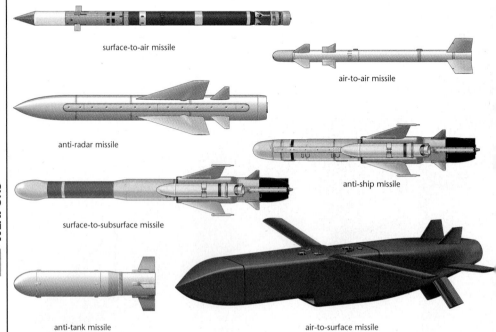

rate gyro

actuator

battery

pilot

warhead

infrared homing head

fixed winglet

rudder

proximity fuse

rocket motor

fin

MAJOR TYPES OF MISSILES

surface-to-air missile

air-to-air missile

anti-radar missile

anti-ship missile

surface-to-subsurface missile

anti-tank missile

air-to-surface missile

CONTENTS

SYMBOLS

PARTS OF A FLAG

finial

emblem

hoist

fly

halyard

toggle

staff

wind sock

streamer

base

square flag

rectangular flag

pennant

double pennant

swallowtail

swallowtail and tongue

burgee

flag with Schwenkel

gonfalon

oriflamme

bunting

fanion

SHIELD DIVISIONS

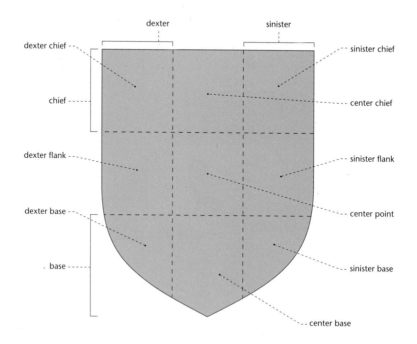

dexter — sinister

dexter chief — — sinister chief

chief — — center chief

— sinister flank

dexter flank — — center point

dexter base — — sinister base

base — — center base

EXAMPLES OF PARTITIONS

per fess

party

per bend

quarterly

EXAMPLES OF ORDINARIES

chief

chevron

pale

cross

fleur-de-lis

crescent

lion passant

eagle

mullet

EXAMPLES OF METALS

argent

or

EXAMPLES OF FURS

ermine

vair

EXAMPLES OF COLORS

azure

gules

vert

purpure

sable

SYMBOLS

SIGNS OF THE ZODIAC

FIRE SIGNS

Aries the Ram (March 21)

Leo the Lion (July 23)

Sagittarius the Archer (November 22)

EARTH SIGNS

Taurus the Bull (April 20)

Virgo the Virgin (August 23)

Capricorn the Goat (December 22)

AIR SIGNS

Libra the Balance (September 23)

Aquarius the Water Bearer (January 20)

Gemini the Twins (May 21)

WATER SIGNS

Cancer the Crab (June 22)

Scorpio the Scorpion (October 24)

Pisces the Fishes (February 19)

SAFETY SYMBOLS

DANGEROUS MATERIALS

corrosive

electrical hazard

explosive

flammable

radioactive

poison

PROTECTION

eye protection

ear protection

head protection

hand protection

feet protection

respiratory system protection

coffee shop

telephone

restaurant

men's rest room

women's rest room

access for physically handicapped

pharmacy

no access for wheelchairs

first aid

hospital

police

taxi transportation

camping (tent)

camping prohibited

camping (trailer)

camping (trailer and tent)

picnics prohibited

picnic area

service station

information

information

currency exchange

lost and found articles

fire extinguisher

MAJOR NORTH AMERICAN ROAD SIGNS

stop at intersection

no entry

yield

one-way traffic

direction to be followed

direction to be followed

direction to be followed

direction to be followed

no U-turn

passing prohibited

two-way traffic

merging traffic

stop at intersection

no entry

yield

one-way traffic

direction to be followed

direction to be followed

direction to be followed

direction to be followed

no U-turn

passing prohibited

two-way traffic

priority intersection

MAJOR NORTH AMERICAN ROAD SIGNS

right bend

double bend

roadway narrows

slippery road

bumps

steep hill

falling rocks

overhead clearance

signal ahead

school zone

pedestrian crossing

road work ahead

right bend

double bend

roadway narrows

slippery road

bumps

steep hill

falling rocks

overhead clearance

signal ahead

school zone

pedestrian crossing

road work ahead

MAJOR NORTH AMERICAN ROAD SIGNS

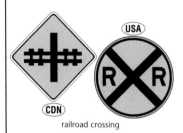

railroad crossing

deer crossing

closed to pedestrians

closed to bicycles

closed to motorcycles

closed to trucks

MAJOR INTERNATIONAL ROAD SIGNS

railroad crossing

deer crossing

closed to pedestrians

closed to bicycles

closed to motorcycles

closed to trucks

FABRIC CARE

WASHING

do not wash

hand wash in lukewarm water

machine wash in lukewarm water at a gentle setting/reduced agitation

machine wash in warm water at a gentle setting/reduced agitation

machine wash in warm water at a normal setting

machine wash in hot water at a normal setting

do not use chlorine bleach

use chlorine bleach as directed

DRYING

hang to dry

dry flat

tumble dry at medium to high temperature

tumble dry at low temperature

drip dry

IRONING

do not iron

iron at low setting

iron at medium setting

iron at high setting

MATHEMATICS

— subtraction	**+** addition	**X** multiplication	**÷** division
= is equal to	**≠** is not equal to	**⇌** is approximately equal to	**⌣** is equivalent to
≡ is identical with	**≢** is not identical with	**±** plus or minus	**Ø** empty set
> is greater than	**⩾** is equal to or greater than	**<** is less than	**⩽** is equal to or less than
∪ union	**∩** intersection	**⊂** is contained in	**%** percent
∈ belongs to	**∉** does not belong to	**√** square root of	**Σ** sum
	∞ infinity	**∫** integral	**!** factorial

GEOMETRY

○ degree	**′** minute	**″** second	**π** pi	**⊥** perpendicular
∠ acute angle	**L** right angle	**⌐** obtuse angle	**‖** is parallel to	**∦** is not parallel to

male

female

birth

blood factor positive

Rh-
blood factor negative

death

negative charge

positive charge

reversible reaction

reaction direction

recycled

recyclable

ampersand

registered trademark

copyright

prescription

pause/still

SYMBOLS

stop

rewind

play

fast forward

DIACRITIC SYMBOLS

acute accent

umlaut

grave accent

circumflex accent

cedilla

tilde

PUNCTUATION MARKS

semicolon

period

comma

ellipses

colon

asterisk

quotation marks
(French)

single quotation marks

quotation marks

dash

( )
parentheses

/
virgule

!
exclamation point

?
question mark

[ ]
square brackets

EXAMPLES OF CURRENCY ABBREVIATIONS

$
dollar

¢
cent

£
pound

¥
yen

F
franc

DM
deutsche mark

Dr
drachma

L
lira

Kr
krone

IS
shekel

ECU
European Currency Unit

Esc
escudo

Pta
peseta

Fl
florin

SYMBOLS

A

a 537.
abacus 166, 167.
abdomen 78, 79, 81, 91, 108, 116, 118.
abdominal aorta 126, 132.
abdominal cavity 127, 128.
abdominal rectus 120.
abdominal segment 78.
ablutions fountain 172, 173.
aboveground pipeline 740.
abruptly pinnate 56.
absorbent cotton 725.
absorbing plate 768.
absorbing surface 772.
abutment 176, 454, 455, 456.
abyssal plain 29.
abyssal plain 29.
acanthus leaf 167, 220.
acceleration lane 452.
accelerator cable 271.
accelerator control 272.
accent mark 539.
accept machine 764.
access for physically handicapped 822.
access gallery 747.
access panel 207.
access road 502.
access shaft 752.
access window 529.
accessory box 568.
accessory gear box 501.
accessory pocket 429.
accessory pouch 684.
accessory shoe 391, 409.
accidentals 538.
accordion 536.
accordion bag 380.
accordion pleat 335.
account book 518.
Ace 695.
acetylene cylinder 306.
acetylene valve 306.
achene 62, 66.
acorn nut 279.
acoustic ceiling 189.
acoustic guitar 546.
acoustic meatus 138, 139.
acromion 123.
acroterion 167, 168.
action lever 541.
action of wind 35.
active tracking 402.
actual temperature 213, 705.
actuator 814.
actuator arm 529.
actuator arm motor 529.
acute accent 832.
acute angle 830.
Adam's apple 116.
adaptor 399.
add in memory 523.
add key 523.
addition 830.
additional production personnel 412.
adductor muscle 92.
adhesive bandage 725.
adhesive disk 85.
adhesive tape 725.
adipose tissue 129, 136.
adjustable antenna 722.
adjustable channel 278.
adjustable clamp 234.
adjustable frame 277.
adjustable lamp 234.
adjustable platen 521.
adjustable seat 460.
adjustable spud wrench 299.
adjustable strap 350.
adjustable waist tab 322.
adjuster 728.
adjusting band 406.
adjusting buckle 645.
adjusting catch 641.
adjusting lever 539.
adjusting screw 278, 282, 306.
adjusting tube 659, 661.
adjustment for horizontal-circle image 713.
adjustment for vertical-circle image 713.
adjustment knob 428.
adjustment pedal 591.
adjustment slide 323.

adjustment wheel 311.
administrative building 752.
advertising panel 474.
advertising sign 477.
adze 587.
adze 681.
aerator 294, 295.
aerial ladder truck 780.
aerodynamic brake 774.
Africa 21.
aft shroud 16.
afterbay 746, 747, 749, 750.
afterfeather 110.
aftermast 478.
agitator 258.
aileron 498, 638.
air 437.
air bladder 89.
air brake 638, 812.
air brake handle 639.
air bulb shutter release 393.
air cap 304.
air chamber 298.
air communications 417.
air compression unit 458.
air compressor 469.
air concentrator 370.
air conditioner 449.
air conditioner compressor 435.
air conditioning 214.
air conditioning unit 415.
air control radar 810.
air data computer 500.
air fan 161.
air filter 210, 272, 469.
air flow 590.
air gap 772.
air hole 385, 389.
air horn 440.
air hose 590, 627, 734.
air hose connection 304.
air inlet 443, 501, 508.
air inlet control 204.
air intake 14, 493.
air leg 734.
air lock 806.
air mattress 687.
air navigation device 810.
air pressure, measure 41.
air pump 453.
air purifier 210.
air scoop 445.
air sealing gland 543.
air search radar 809, 811.
air signs 820.
air space 14, 109.
air start unit 506.
air temperature 38.
air tube 209.
air unit 352.
air valve 304, 590.
air vent 257.
air-cleaner filter 783.
air-inlet grille 370.
air-outlet grille 370.
air-pressure pump 710.
air-supply tube 777.
air-to-air missile 813, 814.
air-to-surface missile 814.
air/fuel mixture 436.
airbrush 590.
airbrush, cross section 590.
aircraft carrier 810.
aircraft maintenance truck 506.
airframe 637.
airlock 14.
airplane 722.
airport 502, 504, 506.
airport 502.
airspeed indicator 639.
aisle 177.
ala 141.
alarm threshold display button 485.
alarm threshold setting 485.
albumen 109.
alcohol bulb 705.
alcohol column 705.
alidade 41, 713.
alidade level 713.
alighting board 82.
alley 614, 618.
almond 63, 66.
alphanumeric keyboard 422, 530.
alpine skier 640.
alpine skiing 640.
Alsace glass 237.
Altar 13.
altazimuth mounting 15.

alteration line 565.
alternator 434, 468.
alternator warning light 431.
altimeter 635, 639.
altitude clamp 720, 721.
altitude fine adjustment 720, 721.
altitude scale 19.
altocumulus 44.
altostratus 44.
alula 110.
aluminum layer 405.
alveolar bone 144.
AM antenna 400.
ambulatory 177.
American betting layout 700.
American corn bread 153.
American football, playing field 604.
american plug 309.
American roulette wheel 700.
American white bread 153.
amethyst 362.
ammunition stowage 805.
ampersand 831.
amphibians 84.
amplification of seismic waves 714.
amplifier 402.
amplifier 714.
amplifier's back 400.
ampulla of fallopian tube 129.
anal fin 87.
anal proleg 78.
analog watch 706.
analytical balance 709.
anchor 483.
anchor 656.
anchor pin 432.
anchor wires 738.
anchor-windlass room 495, 497.
anchorage block 456.
anchors, types 483.
ancient costume, elements 315, 316, 318.
anconeus 121.
andirons 205.
Andromeda 11.
anemometer 41.
Anik-E 418.
animal cell 115.
ankle 116, 118.
ankle boot 357.
ankle length 325.
ankle/wrist weight 665.
anklet 344.
announcer turret 407.
annual ring 59.
annular combustion chamber 501.
annular eclipse 8.
annulet 167.
annullate 90.
anode rod 297.
anorak 353.
ant 77.
Antarctic Circle 3.
Antarctica 21.
antefix 169.
antenna 16, 43, 78, 79, 80, 81, 91, 408, 427, 498, 508, 613, 805, 810.
antennae cleaner 80.
antennule 90.
anterior chamber 140.
anterior end 95.
anterior notch 139.
anterior root 135.
anterior tibial 120.
anterior tibial artery 126.
anther 60.
anti-aircraft missile 808.
anti-friction pad 641.
anti-radar missile 814.
anti-ship missile 814.
anti-skating device 404.
anti-slip shoe 302, 661.
anti-tank missile 814.
anti-tank rocket 804.
anti-torque tail rotor 508.
anti-vibration handle 272.
anticline 737.
anticollision light 498.
antihelix 139.
antimissile self-defense 808.
antireflection coating 768.
antiseptic 725.
antitragus 139.
anus 89, 92, 127, 128, 131.
aorta 125, 130.
aortic valve 125.
aperture 94.

aperture changer 717.
aperture diaphragm 717.
aperture door 16.
aperture scale 396.
aperture/exposure value display 396.
apex 83, 94, 143, 144.
apical foramen 144.
apocrine sweat gland 136.
apogee motor firing 419.
apogee passage 419.
apple 64.
apple 64.
appoggiatura 538.
appointment book 518.
approach 654, 655, 657, 683.
approach ramp 456.
approach wall 492.
apricot 63.
apron 219, 220, 223, 502, 669.
apse 177.
apsidiole 177.
Apus 13.
aquamarine 362.
Aquarius 13.
Aquarius the Water Bearer(January 20) 820.
aquastat 209.
aquatic bird 111.
aqueous humor 140.
Aquila 11.
Ara 13.
arbor 263.
arc welding 305.
arc welding machine 305.
arcade 176.
arch 174.
arch 14, 455.
arch bridge 455.
arch bridges, types 455.
arch dam 750.
arch dam, cross section 750.
arch of aorta 124, 125, 126.
arch of foot artery 126.
archboard 518.
Archer 13.
archer 684.
archery 684.
arches, types 174, 455.
archipelago 51.
architectural styles 166.
architrave 166, 168.
Arctic 20.
Arctic Circle 3, 47.
arctic continental 38.
arctic maritime 38.
Arctic Ocean 21.
area of ice 620.
arena 654.
Arenberg parquet 200.
areola 129.
argent 819.
Aries 11.
Aries the Ram(March 21) 820.
arm 100, 117, 119, 157, 220, 234, 264, 483, 535, 561, 568, 718, 727, 782, 785.
arm cylinder 782, 785.
arm elevator 404.
arm guard 602.
arm lock 668.
arm nut 568.
arm pad 609.
arm position 625.
arm rest 404.
arm slit 331.
arm stump 220.
armchair 220.
armchairs, principal types 220.
armet 792.
armet 792.
armguard 684.
armhole 325.
armoire 225.
armor 792.
armor 805.
armored cord 422.
armored plate 805.
armpit 116, 118.
armrest 428, 429, 727.
armstand 624.
armstand dive 625.
arpeggio 539.
arrector pili muscle 136.
arresting cable 811.
arris 167.
Arrow 11, 793.
arrow 684.
arrow rest 684.
arteries 126.

The terms in **bold type** indicate the title of an illustration.

artichoke 69.
articulated mannequin 592.
articulation 431.
artificial fly 670.
artificial satellite 19.
ascending aorta 124.
ascending colon 131.
ascot tie 324.
ash 386.
ash layer 25.
ashtray 386.
Asia 21.
asparagus 72.
asphalt 745.
asphalt shingle 286.
asphalt still 745.
aspirin 725.
assist grip 429.
assistant timer 626.
asterisk 832.
asteroid belt 4.
asthenosphere 22.
astragal 167, 800.
astronomical observatory 14.
asymmetrical bars 659.
athletic shirt 325.
Atlantic Ocean 20.
atlas 102, 123.
atmosphere 22, 31.
atoll 28.
atrium 170.
attaché case 378.
attached curtain 228.
attack line 613.
attack on human being 35.
attack on nature 35.
attack periscope 807.
attack zone 613.
attacking zone 608.
audio console 407, 412, 415.
audio control room 412, 415.
audio monitor 407, 412, 413, 415.
audio monitoring selector 413.
audio system 430.
audio technician 412, 415.
audio volume unit meters 413.
audio/video preview unit 413.
auditorium 16.
auditory ossicles 138.
auditory ossicles 139.
auger bit 281.
auger bit 270.
auricle, ear 139.
auricle 81, 138.
auriculars 109.
Auriga 11.
Australia 21.
auto answer indicator 420.
auto reverse button 408.
auto/manual range 310.
autofocus on/off switch 397.
automatic dialer index 420.
automatic drip coffee maker 247.
automatic rifle 796.
automatic sorting trays 532.
automatic tank gauge 741.
automatically-controlled door 504.
automobile 425, 426, 428, 430, 432, 434, 438.
automobile car 473.
autopilot controls 500.
autumn 8.
autumn squash 69.
autumnal equinox 8.
auxiliary facilities room 412.
auxiliary handle 280.
auxiliary heating 211.
auxiliary projector 16.
auxiliary tank 441.
auxiliary video switcher 413.
avenue 52.
average key 396.
avocado 68.
awl 688.
awning channel 449.
axial compressor blade 501.
axial rib 94.
axillary artery 126.
axillary bud 57.
axillary nerve 133.
axillary vein 126.
axis 123.
axle 468, 645.
axon 135.
axon hillock 135.
azimuth clamp 720, 721.
azimuth fine adjustment 720, 721.
azure 819.

B

b 537.
baby doll 348.
back 322.
back 101, 106, 108, 117, 119, 223, 239, 240, 241, 242, 277, 288, 386, 727, 793.
back beam 573.
back belt 330.
back binding 633.
back board 577.
back boundary line 618.
back check 541.
back crossbar 645.
back judge 603, 605.
back line 611.
back pad 609, 653.
back pocket 323.
back score line 620.
back strap 653.
back wall 616, 617.
back zone 613.
back-hoe 782.
back-hoe controls 782.
backboard 610.
backcourt 614, 617.
backdrop 188.
backgammon 697.
backguard 255, 258, 259.
backing 579.
backing board 579.
backing hammer 579.
backing plate 432.
backing press 579.
backrest 428, 445.
backstay 479, 644.
backstep 778.
backstretch 651.
backstroke 623.
backstroke start 623.
backstroke turn indicator 621.
backup light 429.
backward 624.
backward bucket 782.
backward bucket cylinder 782.
backward dive 625.
badminton 618.
badminton racket 618.
badminton, court 618.
badminton, net 618.
baffle 216.
bag well 679.
baggage cart 463.
baggage check-in counter 504.
baggage claim area 504.
baggage compartment 458, 508.
baggage conveyor 507.
baggage lockers 463.
baggage racks 492.
baggage room 462.
baggage trailer 507.
bagpipes 536.
baguette cut 363.
bail 599.
bail arm 671.
bail arm opening mechanism 671.
bailey 180.
Bailey bridge 457.
baize 675.
bakelite® body 804.
baking utensils 245.
balaclava 329.
balalaika 535.
balance beam 659.
balance control 402.
balance rail 541.
balcony 189.
balk area 674.
balk line 674.
balk line spot 674.
ball 598, 795.
ball 530, 566, 575, 683.
ball assembly 294.
ball bearing 567.
ball boy 614.
ball of clay 584.
ball peen 275.
ball return 683.
ball stand 683.
ball winder 575.
ball-cock supply valve 293.
ball-peen hammer 275.
ball-type faucet 294.
ballast 466.
ballerina 356.
balloon 634.
balloon 634.
balloon curtain 229.

ballooning 634.
ballpoint pen 389, 515.
ballroom 497.
balustrade 194.
banana 68.
band 404.
band ring 364.
band selector 402.
bandage 669.
banding wheel 584.
bangle 364.
banister 201.
banjo 535.
bank 451, 752.
bank of heliostats 770, 771.
banquette 222.
bar 104, 376, 554, 662, 663, 665, 697.
bar frame 235.
bar line 537.
bar nose 272.
bar shot 801.
bar stool 222.
barb 38, 110, 671.
barbell 663.
barber comb 368.
barbican 180.
baren 582.
bargraph type peak meter 407.
bark 59.
barley 152.
barn 148.
barograph 41.
barometer scales 710.
barometer/thermometer 710.
barometric pressure 38.
barometric tendency 38.
barrack buildings 179.
barred spiral galaxy 9.
barrel 800.
barrel 370, 389, 698, 795, 796, 797, 798, 799, 802, 804.
barrel jacket 796.
barrette 369.
barrier 186.
bartizan 178, 181.
basaltic layer 22.
base 166, 204, 232, 233, 236, 252, 283, 368, 404, 410, 450, 466, 471, 579, 656, 661, 708, 712, 718, 774, 799, 817, 818.
base course 451.
base line 719.
base of splat 220.
base plate 40, 284, 404, 641, 713, 719.
base plug 804.
base ring 800.
base width 756.
baseball 595, 596.
baseball, cross section 596.
baseball, field 597.
baseboard 199, 201, 399.
baseboard register 207.
baseline 614.
basement 190.
basement 197.
basement window 197.
baseplate 87.
basic building materials 286.
basic components 528, 530.
basic source of food 31.
basic weaves 576.
basil 74.
basilic vein 126.
basin 752.
basin side 752.
basin wrench 299.
basket 610, 635.
basket 247, 252, 258, 610, 634, 641, 642.
basket handle 174.
basket handle 635.
basket stitch 567.
basket suspension cables 634.
basket weave pattern 200.
basketball 610.
basketball, court 610.
bass bridge 540.
bass clarinet 556.
bass drum 552, 557.
bass keyboard 536.
bass pickup 547.
bass register 536.
bass tone control 402.
bass trap 412.
bassoon 548.
bassoons 557.
baster 246.
bastion 179.

bat 112, 596, 598.
bat 160, 595, 598.
bateau neck 343.
bath 215.
bathing wrap 349.
bathrobe 348.
bathroom 292.
bathroom 194, 195.
bathroom scale 709.
bathtub 194, 292.
batsman 599.
batten 188, 231, 628, 631, 637.
batten pocket 628, 631.
batter 595.
batter 597.
batter head 552, 553.
batter's helmet 595.
battery 393, 439.
battery 409, 468, 528, 769, 777, 814.
battery box 441.
battery case 439.
battery cover 439.
battery eject switch 409.
battery modules 43.
battery radiator 49.
batting glove 595.
battlement 179, 181.
batwing sleeve 339.
bay 7, 51.
bay antler 105.
bay window 197.
bayonet base 232.
bayonet mount 392.
bazooka 804.
beach 23, 30.
bead 433.
bead wire 433.
beam 105, 156, 659, 708.
beam balance 708.
beam bridge 454.
beam bridges, types 454.
beam diameter reduction 717.
beam gantry 756.
beam reach 629.
bean bag chair 222.
bean sprouts 72.
bearer 543.
bearing pad 765.
beater 156, 250, 572.
beater ejector 250.
beater handtree 572.
beater sley 572.
beaters 250.
beaver 98.
beaver 792.
bed 224, 687.
bed 450, 578, 659.
bed chamber 170.
bed lamp 234.
bedrock 714.
bedroom 194, 195, 685.
beer mug 237.
beet 71.
beginner's course 646.
belfry 175, 176.
bell 549, 551.
bell bottoms 336.
bell brace 549.
bell roof 183.
bell tower 175.
bellow 543.
bellows 399, 536.
bellows strap 536.
belly 101.
belly scale 97.
belongs to 830.
belt 323.
belt 319, 433, 668.
belt drive 492.
belt highway 52.
belt loader 733.
belt loop 319, 323, 688.
bench 222.
bench 475, 663, 733.
bench height 733.
bench seat 428.
bend 376, 671.
bent blade 587.
Berenice's Hair 11.
beret 329.
bergère 220.
bergschrund 26.
Bering Sea 21.
berm 748.
Bermuda sail 482.
Bermuda shorts 336.
berries, major types 62.
berry fruits 62.
berry, section 62.
berth 460.

INDEX

The terms in **bold type** indicate the title of an illustration.

bertha collar 342.
bevel 726.
bevel square 713.
bezel 364.
bezel facet (8) 363.
bias 566.
bias-ply tire 433.
bib 349.
bib 350, 351, 667.
bib necklace 361.
biceps of arm 120.
biceps of thigh 121.
biconcave lens 722.
biconvex lens 722.
bicorne 318.
bicycle 446, 448.
bicycle bag 448.
bicycle, accessories 448.
bidet 292.
bifocal lens 376.
bikini 347.
bikini briefs 325.
bill 108, 483.
bill compartment 379.
bill-file 516.
billfold 379.
billhook 269.
billiard cue 675.
billiard spot 675.
billiards 673.
bills, principal types 111.
bimetallic helix 705.
bimetallic thermometer 705.
binder 159.
binding 328, 642.
bindings 633.
binocular microscope 718.
biology 831.
biomedical monitoring sensor 512.
biosphere, structure 31.
biparous cyme 60.
bipod 796, 803.
bird 108, 110.
Bird of Paradise 13.
bird of prey 111.
bird, morphology 108.
birth 831.
Bishop 696.
bishop sleeve 340.
bit 385, 648, 734, 737.
bits, types 650.
bitter taste 143.
bivalve shell 95.
Black 696, 700, 701.
black ball 673.
black currant 62.
black rye bread 153.
black salsify 71.
Black Sea 21.
black square 696.
black stone 697.
blade 783.
blade 57, 214, 239, 242, 251, 256,
    268, 271, 276, 277, 284, 285, 291,
    304, 309, 369, 374, 562, 564, 607,
    609, 619, 627, 632, 644, 666, 672,
    681, 754, 778, 783, 784.
blade close stop 369.
blade guard 285.
blade height adjustment 285.
blade injector 374.
blade lever 578.
blade lift cylinder 783.
blade lift fan 492.
blade lifting mechanism 784.
blade locking bolt 284.
blade rotation mechanism 784.
blade tilting lock 284.
blade tilting mechanism 284, 285.
blade with two beveled edges 587.
blades, major types 587.
blank 695.
blanket 224.
blanket insulation 287.
blanket sleepers 350.
blast valve 635.
blastodisc 109.
blazer 338.
bleeder valve 208.
blender 250.
blending attachment 250.
blinker 653.
block 542, 656, 787.
block bracket 230.
block cutter 581, 587.
blockboard 288.
blood circulation 124, 126.
blood circulation, schema 124.
blood factor negative 831.
blood factor positive 831.

blood vessel 136.
blood vessels 112.
blouses, types 337.
blow pipe 536.
blower 207, 213, 543, 760.
blower motor 207, 214.
blucher oxford 355.
blue ball 673.
blue beam 410.
blue cap 626.
blue flag 626.
blue line 608.
blue mussel 93.
blueberry 62.
blueprint reading 193, 195.
blusher brush 366.
board 288.
board 288, 631.
board cutter 578.
board insulation 287.
boarding room 505.
boarding step 508.
boarding walkway 503.
boards 608.
boater 328.
bobber 672.
bobbin 570.
bobbin 561, 562, 570, 573.
bobbin case 562.
bobbin lace 570.
bobbin winder 561, 575.
bobby pin 369.
bobeche 236.
bobsled 643.
bobstay 479.
bodies, types 425.
body 426.
body 143, 252, 256, 281, 294, 295,
    445, 449, 453, 542, 546, 549, 645,
    658, 670, 707, 719.
body flap 511.
body guard molding 449.
body of fornix 134.
body of nail 137.
body pad 609.
body shirt 337.
body side molding 427.
body suit 345.
body temperature control unit 512.
body tube 718.
body whorl 94.
body wire 666.
boiler 209.
boiler 208, 771.
boiling-water reactor 763.
bole 59.
bolero 338.
boletus 55.
bolster 224, 239, 242.
bolt 279.
bolt 278, 282, 290, 793.
bolt assist mechanism 796.
bonding jumper 312.
bone folder 577.
boning knife 242.
bonnet 294, 295.
book ends 517.
bookbinding leather 579.
booking hall 462.
boom 628, 782, 785.
boom cylinder 782, 785.
boom truck 506.
boom vang 628.
booster parachute 510.
boot 542, 627, 635, 644, 645, 648.
boot jack 358.
bootee 354.
Bootes 11.
borage 74.
bordeaux glass 237.
border 188, 189.
bore 801.
bottle cart 306.
bottle opener 244, 688.
bottom 633, 640.
bottom bracket axle 448.
bottom cylinder 581.
bottom deck 741.
bottom deckboard 787.
bottom line 621.
bottom of the pool 626.
bottom pocket 675.
bottom rail 202, 225, 231.
bottom ring 753.
bottom road 736.
bottom side rail 470.
bottom-end transverse member 470.
bottom-fold portfolio 378.
bottomboard 543.

boulevard 52, 184.
bound book 577.
bow 544, 793.
bow 328, 497, 628, 631, 793.
bow collar 342.
bow door 493.
bow loading door 494.
bow saw 690.
bow thruster 497.
bow tie 324.
bow window 197.
bowl 682.
bowl 241, 251, 385, 484, 784.
bowl with serving spout 251.
bowler 599.
bowline 691.
bowline on a bight 691.
bowling 683.
bowling ball 683.
bowling crease 599.
bowling lane 683.
bowls and petanque 682.
bows 793.
bowsprit 479.
bowstring 684, 793.
box 156, 189, 204, 209.
box bag 381.
box car 470, 472.
box end wrench 279.
box pallet 787.
box pleat 228.
box spring 224.
boxer 669.
boxer shorts 325.
boxer shorts 353.
boxing 669.
boxing gloves 669.
bra 346.
brace 281.
brace 198, 302, 757.
bracelets 364.
brachial 120.
brachial artery 126.
brachial plexus 133.
brachioradialis 120, 121.
bracket 231.
bracket base 225.
bract 66.
braided rope 692.
brail 480.
brain 88.
brake 664, 727.
brake cable 447.
brake caliper 442.
brake handle 445.
brake lever 447.
brake line 432.
brake lining 432.
brake loop 636.
brake pad 432.
brake pedal 430, 641.
brake shoe 432.
brakelight 429.
brakeman 643.
branch 58.
branch 59, 61, 72, 104, 215, 649, 726.
branch clip 726.
branch duct 206.
branch return pipe 208.
branch supply pipe 208.
branches 59.
branching, plumbing 298.
brandy snifter 237.
brass family 550.
brassiere cup 346.
brattice 181.
brayer 581.
Brazil nut 66.
bread 153.
bread and butter plate 238.
bread guide 252.
bread knife 242.
break line 341.
breaker 30.
breast 129.
breast 108, 116, 118.
breast beam 572.
breast collar 653.
breast dart 320.
breast pocket 320, 324.
breast welt pocket 322.
breastplate 792.
breaststroke 622.
breaststroke kick 622.
breaststroke turn 622.
breather valve 741.
breathing 622.
breathing in 622.
breathing out 622.
breech 549.
breech guard 549.

breechblock 798, 799, 802.
breechblock operating lever assembly
    802.
breeches 315.
breeches 317, 667, 791.
brick 286.
brick wall 199.
bricklayer's hammer 291.
bridge 674.
bridge 52, 230, 376, 491, 544, 546,
    719, 810.
bridge assembly 547.
bridging 198.
bridle 649.
bridle 653.
bridle assembly 486.
bridle tape 541.
briefcase 378.
briefs 346.
briefs 325.
brig 482.
brigantine 482.
brightness control 529.
brilliant cut facets 363.
brilliant full cut 362.
briolette cut 363.
brim 328, 329.
bristle 373, 374.
bristles 304.
broad beans 72.
broad ligament of uterus 129.
broad reach 629.
broad welt side pocket 339.
broad welt side pocket 319, 330.
broad-leaved endive 73.
broadcast satellite
    communication 416.
broadest of back 121.
broadsword 794.
broccoli 69.
brooch 364.
brood chamber 82.
brook 676.
broom 205.
brow brush and lash comb 367.
brow reinforce 792.
brow tine 105.
browband 649.
brown ball 673.
Brunn's membrane 142.
brush 304, 582, 589.
brush 152, 373.
brush and rails 647.
brush and rails 646.
Brussels sprouts 73.
bubble 443.
bucket 754, 782.
bucket cylinder 782, 785.
bucket hinge pin 782.
bucket lever 782.
bucket ring 754.
bucket seat 428.
bucket tooth 782.
bucket wheel excavator 733.
buckle 323, 380, 428, 566, 641.
buckwheat 152.
bud 70.
buffer tank 740.
buffet 227.
bugle 550.
building materials 286, 288.
building sewer 215, 216.
built-in microphone 409.
bulb 72, 104, 232, 233, 310.
bulb dibble 268.
bulb unit 752.
bulb vegetables 70.
bulbil 70.
bulbocavernous muscle 127.
bulk terminal 490.
bulkhead 441.
bulkhead flat car 473.
Bull 11.
bull's-eye 684, 698.
bulldozer 783.
bulldozer 733.
bullet 798.
bullion stitch 571.
bulwark 478.
bumper 260, 426, 440, 441, 464.
bumper guard 617.
bumps 826, 827.
bunch 384.
bunch of grapes 61.
bund wall 741.
bundle 72, 756.
bunker 676.
bunker oil 745.
bunker silo 149.
bunting 817.

The terms in **bold type** indicate the title of an illustration.

bunting bag 349.
buoyage regions 488.
buoyancy compensator 627.
burgee 817.
burgundy glass 237.
burned gases 436.
burner 209, 248, 634, 635, 689.
burner frame 689.
burner gas tube 297.
burner ring 248.
burnisher 582.
burr 105.
bursting charge 804.
bus 190.
bus module 49.
bus shelter 186.
bus stop 186.
busbar 747.
bush 263.
bushing 746, 747, 757.
bustle 316.
butane tank 386.
butt 386, 568, 579, 615, 670, 675, 796, 797.
butt cap 670.
butt end 609.
butt grip 671.
butt guide 671.
butt plate 795, 798, 799.
butt section 670.
butt welding 307.
butt-strap 376.
butte 46.
butter compartment 254.
butter curler 242.
butter dish 238.
butter knife 239.
butterfly 78, 79.
butterfly kick 623.
butterfly stroke 623.
butterfly turn 623.
butterfly, hind leg 78.
buttock 117, 119, 127, 128.
button 232, 324, 326, 530, 536, 666, 800.
button loop 323.
button strap 351.
buttondown collar 324.
buttoned placket 324, 326.
buttonhole 319.
buttress 176, 750.
buttress dam 750.
buttress dam, cross section 750.
by-pass taxiway 502.
bypass duct 501.
bypass feeder 532.

C

c 537.
c clef 537.
C degrees 705.
C-clamp 282.
cab 147, 160, 445, 782, 783, 784, 785.
cabbage lettuce 73.
cabin 496, 508.
cabinet 258, 259, 410.
cable 692.
cable 280, 406, 408, 660, 663, 684, 692.
cable distributor 416.
cable drum compartment 415.
cable guard 684.
cable ripper 311.
cable shutter release 393.
cable sleeve 280.
cable stay anchorage 456.
cable stitch 567.
cable-stayed bridges 456.
cables 414.
cabochon cut 363.
caboose 473.
cabriole leg 220.
cabriolet 220.
Caelum 13.
café curtain 228.
cake mascara 367.
cake pan 245.
cakes 588.
calamus 110.
calandria 759.
calcaneus 103, 123.
calcar 112.
calculator 523.
calculator 379.
calculator dial 396.
calendar pad 518.
calf 151.
calf 117, 119.

caliper 583.
caliper 432.
call director telephone 422.
Callisto 4.
calls indicator 420.
calm 38.
calyx 60, 62, 67, 132.
cam ring 281.
cambium 59.
Camelopardus 11.
camera 414.
camera 16, 412, 414.
camera back 390.
camera body 391.
camera control area 415.
camera control technician 412, 415.
camera control unit 412, 415.
camera pedestal 414.
camera platform 393.
camera platform lock 393.
camera screw 393.
camera viewfinder 414.
camisole 345.
camping 685, 686, 690.
camping (tent) 823.
camping (trailer and tent) 823.
camping (trailer) 823.
camping equipment 688, 690.
camping prohibited 823.
camping tools 690.
camping, accessories 689.
camshaft 434.
can opener 256.
can opener 244, 688.
Canadian football, playing field 604.
canal bed 492.
canal lock 492.
canal lock 490.
Cancer 11.
Cancer the Crab(June 22) 820.
candlepin 683.
cane pen 389.
canes 728.
Canes Venatici 11.
canine 98, 144.
Canis Major 13.
Canis Minor 11.
canister vacuum cleaner 260.
canned failed fuel 764.
cannon 101, 805.
canopy 636.
canopy 375, 636, 685, 785, 813.
canopy release knob 639.
cantaloupe 69.
canteen 690.
cantilever 750.
cantilever bridge 454.
cantilever span 454.
cantle 649.
canvas 669.
canvas 669.
canvas divider 685.
cap 301, 328.
cap 55, 201, 250, 309, 389, 398, 590, 773.
cap iron 277.
cap sleeve 339.
cape 331.
cape 51.
capillary blood vessel 137.
capillary bore 705.
capital 51, 166.
capitulum 60.
caponiere 179.
capped column 37.
capped tee 205.
Capricorn the Goat(December 22) 820.
Capricornus 13.
capstan button 541.
capsule 725.
capsule, section 67.
captain 643.
captain's quarters 497.
captain's seat 500.
capture 697.
car 470.
car 630.
car cleaning yard 465.
car coat 330.
car deck 494.
car repair shop 465.
car wash 453.
carabiner 681.
carabiner 680.
caraco jacket 316.
carafe 247.
carapace 91, 96.
caravan 449.

caraway seeded rye bread 153.
carbon dioxide gas coolant 760.
carbon dioxide reactor 760.
carburetor 442.
card case 379.
card case 379.
card games 695.
card games, symbols 695.
card reader 422.
card support 40.
cardboard 589.
cardigan 326.
cardinal marks 488.
cardoon 72.
Caribbean Sea 20.
caribou 105.
Carina 13.
carnassial 98.
carnivore's jaw 98.
carnivores 31, 33.
carom billiards 673.
carpal pad 106.
carpenter's hammer 275.
carpentry: tools 275, 276, 278, 280, 282, 284.
carpus 102, 122.
carriage 800.
carriage 787, 802.
carriage control dial 569.
carriage handle 568.
carriage return 525.
carriages 568.
carrier 230, 446.
carrier bag 381.
carrot 71.
carry-on bag 382.
carrying handle 796.
cart path 676.
cartography 47, 50, 52.
carton 384.
carton 384.
cartridge 797.
cartridge 291, 295, 389, 404, 527, 730.
cartridge (rifle) 798.
cartridge (shotgun) 799.
cartridge drive 527.
cartridge faucet 295.
cartridge film 395.
cartridge fuse 312.
cartridge stem 295.
cartridge tape recorder 407.
cartwheel hat 329.
carver's bench screw 586.
carving 586.
carving fork 242.
carving knife 242.
case 335, 365, 539, 540, 705, 706, 710, 711, 798.
casement 203.
casement window 203.
cash readout 453.
cashew 66.
casing 201, 213, 214, 271, 702.
casing first string 740.
Caspian Sea 21.
cassette 403.
cassette 408, 526.
cassette compartment 409, 411.
cassette deck 407.
cassette drive 526.
cassette eject switch 409, 411.
cassette film 395.
cassette holder 403.
cassette player 408.
cassette player controls 408.
cassette tape deck 403.
cassette tape deck 400.
Cassiopeia 11.
cast-on stitches 567.
castanets 554.
castanets 556.
caster 260, 553.
castle 180.
castle 180.
casual shoe 356.
cat 107.
cat's head 107.
catalytic converter 439.
catalytic reforming plant 744.
catapult 810.
catch glove 609.
catcher 595.
catcher 541, 595.
catcher's glove 595.
catenary 459.
catering vehicle 507.
caterpillar 78.
cathedral 176.
cathedral 184.
cathedral, plan 177.

catwalk 188.
caudal fin 87.
caudal vertebrae 103.
cauliflower 69.
caulking gun 291.
cave 24.
cave 30.
cavernous body 127.
CD/ROM player 526.
cecum 131.
cedilla 832.
ceiling 205, 616, 617.
ceiling bracket 230.
ceiling collar 205.
ceiling fan 214.
ceiling fitting 236.
ceiling joist 198.
ceiling projector 41.
ceiling register 207.
celeriac 71.
celery 72.
celestial coordinate system 3.
celestial equator 3.
celestial meridian 3.
celestial sphere 3.
celiac trunk 124, 132.
cell 79, 82.
cell body 135.
cell membrane 115.
cell wall 115.
cello 545.
cellos 557.
cellular telephone 417.
Celsius scale 705.
cement screed 200.
cementum 144.
cemetery 52.
cent 832.
Centaur 13.
Centaurus 13.
center 603, 605, 608, 610, 611, 697.
center aisle 460.
center back 601, 612, 613.
center back vent 322.
center base 818.
center chief 818.
center circle 601, 610.
center console 430.
center court 617.
center divider strip 186.
center electrode 439.
center face-off circle 608.
center field 597.
center fielder 597.
center flag 601.
center forward 601, 607, 612, 613.
center half 607.
center hole 404.
center line 607, 608, 610, 612, 618, 619, 620, 666, 682.
center mark 614.
center pocket 674.
center point 818.
center post 225, 427.
center service line 614.
center span 456.
center spot 601, 674.
center strap 614.
center third 611.
center wheel 706, 707.
centerboard 628.
centering 524.
centering control 529.
Central America 20.
central circle 611.
central column 774.
central focusing wheel 719.
central incisor 144.
central nervous system 134.
central pumping station 740.
central screw 579.
centrifugal compressor 501.
centriole 115.
cephalic vein 126.
cephalothorax 90.
Cepheus 11.
cereals, principal types 152.
cerebellum 134.
cerebrum 134.
cervical vertebra (7) 123.
cervical vertebrae 102.
cervix of uterus 128.
Cetus 11, 13.
chain 448, 661, 707.
chain brake 272.
chain drive 156, 158.
chain guide 448.
chain mail 792.
chain of dunes 46.

The terms in **bold type** indicate the title of an illustration.

chain of neurons 135.
chain pipe wrench 299.
chain stay 446.
chain stitch 571.
chain wheel A 448.
chain wheel B 448.
chainsaw 272.
chainsaw chain 272.
chairs, types 223.
chaise longue 223.
chalaza 109.
chalk 675.
Chamaeleon 13.
Chameleon 13.
chamois leather 358.
champagne flute 237.
chandelier 236.
change sign key 523.
channel scan buttons 411.
channel selector controls 411.
chanter 536.
chanterelle 55.
Chantilly parquet 200.
chapel 181.
character correction 525.
charcoal 588.
charge 799.
charge indicator 374.
charges, examples 819.
charging handle 796.
charging light 374.
charging plug 374.
Charioteer 11.
Charleston cymbal 552.
charm bracelet 364.
charms 364.
Charon 5.
chart room 494.
chase 800.
check nut 40.
check valve 216, 306.
check-rail 467.
checkbook 379.
checkbook 379.
checkbook/secretary clutch 379.
cheek 100, 106, 118, 275, 670, 800.
cheek ring 650.
cheek strap 649.
cheese knife 239.
chemical treatment 745.
chemise 181.
chemistry 831.
cherimoya 68.
cherry 63.
chervil 74.
chess 696.
chess notation 696.
chess, men 696.
chess, movements 696.
chessboard 696.
chest 100, 116, 118.
chest expander 665.
chest protector 595, 602, 684.
chesterfield 221.
chestnut 66, 100.
chevet 177.
chevron 818.
chevron stitch 571.
chick 150.
chick peas 72.
chicory 73.
chief 818.
chief 818.
chief timekeeper 621.
chiffonier 226.
children's clothing 349, 350.
chimney 205.
chimney 197, 209.
chimney connection 204.
chimney pot 197.
chimney stack 197.
chin 108, 118.
chin guard 777.
chin protector 443.
chin rest 544.
chin strap 602, 777.
China Sea 21.
Chinese cabbage 73.
Chisel 13.
chisel 581.
chive 70.
chloroplast 115.
chock 681.
chock 680.
choir 177.
choir organ manual 542.
choker 361.
chord 539.
choroid 140.
Christmas tree 740.

Christmas tree 738, 740.
chromatin 115.
chromosphere 6.
chrysalis 78.
chrysalis 82.
chuck 276, 280, 281, 283, 735.
chuck key 281.
chukka 354.
church 185.
chute 736.
cicada 77.
cigar 384.
cigar band 384.
cigarette 384.
cigarette holder 384.
cigarette pack 384.
cigarette papers 384.
ciliary body 140.
ciliate 56.
cine scale 396.
circuit breaker 212, 747.
circuit vent 215.
circular body 535.
circular needle 567.
circular route 52.
circular saw 284.
circular saw blade 284.
circulating pump 208, 772.
circulation pump 763.
circumflex accent 832.
cirque 7.
cirrocumulus 44.
cirrostratus 44.
cirrus 44.
citrus fruit, section 65.
citrus fruits 65.
citrus fruits, major types 65.
citrus juicer 243, 251.
city 51.
city houses 187.
city limit 52.
clam 93.
clam cleat 630.
clam cleat 630.
clamp 309, 370, 575, 578, 642.
clamp binder 519.
clamp lever 370.
clamp spotlight 235.
clarinet 548.
clarinets 556.
clasp 378, 380.
class ring 364.
classic blouse 337.
classification yard 465.
clavicle 122.
claw 78, 80, 90, 91, 97, 106, 107, 108,
112, 275, 364, 579.
claw hammer 275.
claw, extended 107.
claw, retracted 107.
clay core 748.
cleaning brush 374.
cleaning tools 260.
cleanout 296.
clear key 523.
clear sky 39.
clear space 613.
clear-entry key 523.
cleat 630.
cleat 628.
cleated shoe 602.
cleaver 242.
clefs 537.
clew 631.
clew line 481.
click 706, 707.
cliff 7, 23, 27, 30.
climate control 430.
climates of the world 45.
climber 664.
climbing harness 680.
climbing iron 358.
climbing plant 263.
clinical thermometer 705.
clip 515.
clip 230, 389, 711.
clip earrings 361.
clipboard 519.
clippers 369.
cloche 329.
clock 407, 413, 415, 430, 714.
clock operator 610.
clock timer 253, 255.
clog 357.
close hauled 629.
close reach 629.
close-up lens 392.
closed stringer 201.
closed to bicycles 828.

closed to motorcycles 828.
closed to pedestrians 828.
closed to trucks 828.
closeness setting 374.
closet 194, 226.
closure rail 467.
cloth roller 572.
clothing guard 727.
cloud 36.
cloud ceiling, measure 41.
cloud of volcanic ash 25.
clouds 44.
clouds of vertical development 44.
clouds symbols 44.
cloudy sky 39.
clove hitch 691.
cloverleaf 452.
cloverleaf 450.
club 695.
club chair 221.
clubhouse 651, 676.
clubhouse turn 651.
clubs, golf 678.
clump of flowers 263.
clutch bag 381.
clutch housing 444.
clutch lever 272, 442, 444.
clutch pedal 430.
coach car 460.
coach's box 597.
coal mine 733, 734, 736.
coarse adjustment knob 718.
coastal features 30.
coat dress 332.
coat hook 522.
coat rack 522.
coat tree 522.
coats, types 330.
cob 72.
coccyx 122.
cochlea 139.
cochlear nerve 139.
cock 795.
cocking lever 804.
cockle 93.
cockleshell 220.
cockpit 639.
cockpit 628.
cockpit canopy 638.
cockpit ventilation 639.
cocktail cabinet 227.
cocktail glass 237.
coconut 66.
code 524.
coffee makers 247.
coffee mill 256.
coffee mug 238.
coffee pot 688.
coffee shop 822.
coffee spoon 241.
coil 714.
coil spring 231.
coiling 584.
coin chute 702.
coin purse 379.
coin reject slot 702.
coin return bucket 422.
coin slot 422, 702.
colander 243.
cold air 501, 772.
cold air inlet 438.
cold coolant 771.
cold heavy water 761.
cold shed 491.
cold-water circuit 215.
cold-water riser 215.
cold-water supply line 293, 296, 297,
298.
collar 341.
collar 57, 319, 322, 324, 352, 374,
663.
collar bar 364.
collar point 324, 341.
collar stay 324.
collaret 318, 341.
collars, types 341, 342.
collateral 135.
collecting funnel 40.
collecting vessel 40.
collector 753.
collet 283, 393.
colon 832.
color chart 592.
color control 532.
color display 569.
color filter 392.
color selection filter 410.
color spray 590.
color television camera 512.
colored pencils 588.

colors, examples 819.
colter 156, 158.
colter's shaft 156.
Columba 13.
columella 94.
columella fold 94.
column 24, 36, 166, 168, 169, 208,
236, 283, 393, 399, 455, 561, 621,
700, 701.
column crank 393.
column lock 393.
column of mercury 705.
column radiator 208.
coma 9.
Coma Berenices 11.
comb 574.
comb 792.
combat aircraft 812.
combination box and open end
wrench 279.
combination lock 378.
combine harvester 160.
combine harvester 155.
combs 368.
combustion 436, 437, 501.
combustion chamber 434, 438.
comet 9.
comforter 224.
comma 832.
command control dial 391.
command key 530.
command module 509.
commander's seat 805.
commando knife 794.
commercial area 190.
commissure of lips of mouth 142.
common carotid artery 126.
common extensor of fingers 121.
common iliac artery 126, 132.
common iliac vein 132.
common periwinkle 83.
common peroneal nerve 133.
common scientific symbols 830.
common symbols 822.
common whipping 691.
communicating ramus 135.
communication antenna 810.
communication devices 526.
communication module 418.
communication panels 500.
communication set 477.
communication tunnel 510.
communications volume controls 512.
commuter train 464.
compact 366.
compact disk 405.
compact disk 408.
compact disk player 405.
compact disk player 400, 407, 408.
compact disk player controls 408.
compact disk unit 527.
compartment 701.
compass 639.
compass bridge 494, 495, 497.
compass card 484, 719.
compass meridian line 719.
competition ring 646.
competitive course 621.
completion 692.
complex dune 46.
complexus 121.
compluvium 170, 171.
compound bow 684.
compound eye 79, 80, 81.
compound leaves 56.
compressed air reservoir 469.
compressed-air cylinder 627, 777.
compression 436, 437, 501.
compression coupling 296.
compression fitting 300.
compression link 147.
compression/admission 436.
compressor 212, 517.
compressor turbine 438, 501.
computer communication 417.
computer room 807.
computer screen intensity controls 512.
computer table 521.
concave 160.
concave lens 722.
concha 139.
Concorde 19.
concrete base 714.
concrete block 286.
concrete drain 741.
concrete shielding 760, 761, 762, 763.
concrete wall 772.
condensation 35.
condensation of steam into water 767.
condensation pool 763.

INDEX

839

condenser 717, 718, 758, 771.
condenser adjustment knob 718.
condenser backwash inlet 759.
condenser backwash outlet 759.
condenser coil 214.
condenser cooling water inlet 759.
condenser cooling water outlet 759.
condenser fan 214.
condenser height adjustment 718.
condominiums 187.
conductor's podium 556.
cone 24, 58.
configuration of an office automation system 526.
conic projection 50.
conical broach roof 183.
conical buoy 487.
conical buoy 489.
conical washer 293.
conifer 58.
conjunctiva 140.
connecting cable 400, 406, 585.
connecting module 528.
connecting rod 434, 436.
connecting terminal 561.
connection 697.
connection box 412.
connection cable 530.
connection point 757.
connective tissue 137.
connector 300, 312, 406.
conning tower 807.
constellations of the northern hemisphere 10.
constellations of the southern hemisphere 12.
constriction 705.
consumer 417.
consumer number 712.
contact 697.
contact 233.
contact lever 235.
contact printer 398.
container 470.
container 40, 250, 304, 495.
container car 473.
container hold 495.
container ship 494.
container ship 490.
container terminal 491.
container-loading bridge 490.
container/pallet loader 507.
containment building 765, 766.
contest area 668.
contestant 668.
continent 29.
continental climates 45.
continental margin 29.
continental rise 29.
continental shelf 22, 29.
continental slope 22, 29.
continents, configuration 20.
continuity tester 310.
continuous beam 454.
continuous drizzle 39.
continuous rain 39.
continuous snow 39.
contour feather 110.
contrabassoons 556.
contrast control 529, 532.
control bar 637.
control box 297.
control cable 270, 448.
control column 500.
control console 16, 500.
control deck 493, 699.
control key 530.
control keys 421.
control knob 255, 257, 258, 259.
control knobs 531.
control lever 735.
control pad 699.
control panel 257, 532.
control panel 210, 214, 253, 255, 258, 259, 391, 532, 717, 779.
control rod 760, 761, 762, 763.
control room 14, 15, 16, 189, 407, 746, 759.
control room, radio 407.
control room, television 412.
control stand 468.
control stick 508, 639.
control tower 502, 810.
control tower cab 502.
control valve 689.
control visual display 717.
control wheel 500, 778.
convection zone 6.
convector 211.
convenience outlet 310.

convention center 184.
conventional door 202.
converging lenses 722.
convertible 425.
convex lens 722.
conveyor 733, 735.
conveyor belt 504.
cook's knife 242.
cookie cutters 245.
cookie sheet 245.
cooking set 688.
cooking surface 253.
cooking utensils 248.
cooktop 255.
cooktop edge 255.
cool tip 370.
coolant 766.
coolant 771.
coolant inlet 768.
coolant outlet 768.
coolant transfers the heat to the steam generator 766.
coolant: boiling water 763.
coolant: carbon dioxide 760.
coolant: pressurized heavy water 761.
coolant: pressurized water 762.
cooler 690.
cooling 744.
cooling fan 434, 438.
cooling/heating coils 213.
copper plate 582.
copper to plastic 301.
copper to steel 301.
coprocessor 528.
copy output mode 532.
copy quantity 532.
copyright 831.
corbel 180, 181.
corbel piece 204.
cord 231, 256, 260, 268, 271, 310, 578.
cord grip 658.
cord sleeve 283, 305.
cord tieback 229.
cordate 56.
cordless telephone 422.
core 6, 64, 677, 692, 798.
coriander 74.
corinthian order 167.
cork ball 596.
cork tip 618.
corkscrew 688.
corn 72, 152.
corn salad 73.
cornea 140.
corner 577, 669.
corner arc 601.
corner cap 470.
corner cupboard 227.
corner fitting 470.
corner flag 601, 607.
corner pad 669.
corner stool 669.
corner stud 198.
corner tower 180.
cornerpiece 383.
cornet 550, 556.
cornice 166, 168, 196, 202, 225, 229.
corolla 60.
corona 6.
Corona Australis 13.
Corona Borealis 11.
corona radiata 128.
coronet 101.
corpus callosum 134.
correction fluid 515.
correction key 569.
correction paper 515.
corridor connection 461.
corrosive 821.
corselette 347.
corset 346.
cortex 132.
Corvus 13.
corymb 60.
cosmetic tray 382.
costal shield 97.
cot 726.
cotehardie 316.
cottage 187.
cottage curtain 228.
cotter pin 290.
cotton applicators 725.
couched stitches 571.
counter 352.
counter reset button 403.
counterguard 179.

counterjib 786.
counterjib ballast 786.
counterscarp 178.
countersink 281.
counterweight 15, 147, 404, 457, 471, 721, 784, 785, 786.
country 51.
coupler head 471.
coupler head 147, 469.
coupler head 156, 157, 158, 159, 162.
coupler knuckle 471.
coupler knuckle pin 471.
coupler-tilt tablet 542.
coupling bolt 754.
coupling guide device 459.
course, golf 676.
court referee 612.
courtyard 172, 173.
couscous kettle 249.
couter 792.
cover 375.
cover 213, 251, 309, 386, 532, 596, 677, 705, 712, 719, 796, 804.
covered parapet walk 180.
covered way 178.
covering 579.
covering 619.
covering disk 158.
covering grille 208.
covering materials 286.
cow 151.
cow hitch 691.
cowl 426.
cowl neck 342.
Cowper's gland 127.
cowshed 149.
coxa 78, 80.
coxed four 632.
coxed pair 632.
coxless four 632.
coxless pair 632.
Crab 11, 90.
cradle 399, 720, 721, 802.
crak rye bread 153.
crakow 318.
crampon strap 680.
cranberry 62.
Crane 13, 14, 738.
crane runway 786.
cranial nerves 133.
crank 281, 448, 671, 793.
crank handle 583.
crankcase 436.
crankshaft 434, 436.
crash helmet 643.
crater 7, 13, 25, 733.
crawl kick 622.
crawler tractor 783.
crayfish 90.
creamer 238.
crease 323.
credenza 520.
creel 672.
cremaster 78.
crenate 56.
crenel 181.
crenulate margin 95.
crepidoma 166, 168, 169.
crescendo pedal 542.
crescent 819.
crescent wrench 279.
crescentic dune 46.
crest 27, 30, 596, 791.
crest of spillway 746.
crevasse 46.
crevice tool 260.
crew neck 350.
crew neck sweater 326.
crew quarters 494.
crew's locker 461.
cribriform plate of ethmoid 141.
cricket 598.
cricket ball 598.
cricket player 598.
cricket shoe 598.
cricquet, field 599.
crimping 799.
crisper 254.
crisscross curtains 229.
crochet hook 567.
croissant 153.
crook 548.
crook key 548.
crop elevator 160.
cross 818.
cross brace 727.
cross cut 736.
cross handle 701.
cross head 276.

cross rail 223.
cross section of an electron microscope 717.
cross stitches 571.
cross-country ski 642.
cross-country ski 642.
cross-country skier 642.
cross-country skiing 642.
cross-headed tip 276.
cross-tip screwdriver 688.
crossarm 756, 757.
crossbar 446, 535, 574, 578, 626, 637, 657.
crossbeam 572.
crossbow 793.
crossbuck sign 471.
crosshead 787.
crossing 176, 177.
crossing gate mechanism 471.
crossover back straps overalls 351.
crosspiece 219, 572, 728.
crosstree 628.
crosswise grain 566.
crotch 335.
crotch piece 337.
croup 101, 661.
Crow 13.
crown 59, 109, 144, 328, 329, 363, 483, 545, 553, 590, 706.
crown block 737.
crown tine 105.
crownpiece 649.
crude oil 744.
crude-oil pipeline 740.
crus of helix 139.
crushing roll 158.
crustacean 90.
Crux 13.
crystal button 236.
crystal drop 236.
cucumber 69.
cue ball 673.
cuff 315.
cuff 323, 324, 354, 609.
cuff link 339.
cuirass 791.
cuisse 792.
culet 363.
culottes 334.
cultivated mushroom 55.
cultivating soil, steps 154.
cultivator 157.
cultivator 154.
cumulonimbus 44.
cumulus 44.
Cup 13, 798.
cup 238, 688.
cup gasket 730.
cupola 486.
cupule 66.
curb 186.
curb bit 650.
curb bit 649.
curb chain 649, 650.
curb hook 650.
curb rein 649.
curled endive 73.
curled kale 73.
curler 629.
curling 620.
curling brooms 620.
curling brush 370.
curling iron 370.
curling stone 620.
curling, rink 620.
currant 62.
currency abbreviations, examples 832.
currency exchange 823.
current coil 712.
cursor movement keys 530.
curtain 229.
curtain 178, 383, 414.
curtain pole 230.
curtain track 230.
curtain wall 180.
curtains, types 228.
curved jaw 278.
customer's service entrance 757.
customs control 505.
customs house 491.
cut for gemstones 363.
cut-off trench 748, 749.
cuticle nippers 365.
cuticle pusher 365.
cuticle scissors 365.
cuticle trimmer 365.
cutlery basket 257.
cutlery set 688.

The terms in **bold type** indicate the title of an illustration.

cutter 311.
cutter bar 158, 160.
cutter link 272.
cutting blade 250, 256, 578.
cutting cylinder 271.
cutting edge 239, 242, 369, 783, 784.
cutting guide 578.
cutting line 565.
cutting oxygen handle 306.
cutting tip 306.
cutting torch 306.
cutting wire 584.
cyclorama 414.
Cygnus 11.
cylinder 290, 295, 436, 784, 797.
cylinder case 290.
cylinder head cover 435.
cylinder pressure gauge 306.
cylindrical buoy 486.
cylindrical projection 50.
cymbal 552.
cymbals 554.
cymbals 557.
cypress scalelike leaves 58.
cytoplasm 115, 128.

D

d 537.
«D» 674.
dabber 581.
dagger 794.
daggerboard 631.
daggerboard well 631.
dairy 149.
dairy compartment 254.
dairy products 33.
dam 746.
damper 206, 541, 585.
damper lever 541.
damper pedal 540, 555.
damper rail 541.
dandelion 73.
danger 488.
danger area 668.
Danish rye bread 153.
darkness 489.
dart 698.
dart 565.
dart, playing area 698.
dartboard 698.
dash 832.
dashboard 430.
dashboard 442.
data bus 528, 531.
data display 396, 409, 411, 421.
data display illumination button 396.
data hold 310.
data record system 717.
data storage devices 526.
date 63.
dater 516.
dating nail 466.
davit 478.
daymark 486, 487.
daymarks (region B) 489.
dead ball line 606.
dead bolt 289, 290.
dead bowl area 682.
deadly poisonous mushroom 55.
death 831.
decanter 237.
deceleration lane 452.
decimal key 523.
decimal tab 524.
deck 441, 453, 455, 456, 736.
deck arch bridge 455.
deck crane 811.
declination 3.
declination axis 14.
declination setting scale 720, 721.
décolleté bra 346.
decorative braid 349.
decoy launcher 809.
deep fryer 252.
deep peroneal nerve 133.
deep-sea floor 22.
deer antlers 105.
deer crossing 828.
deer family 105.
deer, kinds 105.
defending zone 608.
defense 605.
defense 605.
defense third 611.
deferent duct 127.
deflector 210, 264, 271.
degree 830.
Deimos 4.
delete key 530.

delicious lactarius 55.
delivery 682.
delivery entrance 190.
delivery ramp 184.
Delphinus 11.
delta wing 499.
deltoid 120.
deluge gun 778.
demilune 179.
demitasse 238.
dendrite 135.
dental alveolus 144.
dental care 373.
dental floss 373.
dentate 56.
dentil 166, 167.
dentin 144.
departure time indicator 463.
deployment mechanism 49.
depressed-center flat car 473.
depth adjustment 283.
depth of focus 23.
depth scale 485.
depth stop 283.
depth-adjustment mechanism 277.
depth-of-field preview button 391.
depth-of-field scale 392.
derby 328.
dermis 137.
derrick 737, 738, 740.
descender 681.
descending aorta 124.
descending colon 131.
desert 46.
desert 45.
designed orbit 48.
desired temperature 213, 705.
desk lamp 234.
desk mat 520.
desk tray 517.
desktop video unit 527.
despun section 42.
detachable control 253.
detection of seismic waves 714.
detergent dispenser 257.
detonator 804.
deuterium oxide upgrading 759.
deutsche mark 832.
developer bath 399.
developing baths 399.
developing tank 398.
dew 37.
dew pad 106.
dew shield 721.
dewclaw 106.
dexter 818.
dexter base 818.
dexter chief 818.
dexter flank 818.
diacritic symbols 832.
diagonal 756.
diagonal buttress 177.
diagonal movement 696.
**diagram of weaving, diagram of
principle** 576.
dial 705, 706, 707, 708, 712.
dial-type display 485.
diamond 695.
diamond interchange 451.
diamond mesh metal lath 286.
diamond point 225.
diaper 349.
diaphragm 130, 390, 400, 406.
diastema 98.
dibble 268.
dice 699.
dice cup 697.
die 697.
diesel engine 437.
diesel engine 469, 495, 782, 785.
diesel engine ventilator 468.
diesel engines 809.
diesel lift engine 493.
diesel motor 783.
diesel oil 745.
diesel propulsion engine 492.
diesel shop 464.
diesel-electric locomotive 468.
diffuser 396.
diffuser pin 264.
digestive gland 92.
digestive system 131.
digit 84.
digital audio tape recorder 407.

digital display 310, 709, 710.
digital frequency display 402.
digital nerve 133.
digital pad 106, 107.
digital pulp 137.
digital video effects monitor 413.
digital video special effects 413.
digital watch 706.
digitizing pad 526.
dike 25.
dill 74.
dimmer room 412.
dimmer switch 309.
dimple 677.
dining car 460.
dining room 171, 195, 496, 807.
dining section 460.
dinner fork 240.
dinner knife 239.
dinner plate 238.
dinnerware 238.
diode 769.
dioptric ring 486.
dioxide 33.
dip switch 444.
dipper 592.
dipper bucket 785.
direct home reception 416.
direct-reading rain gauge 40.
direction of Mecca 173.
direction of points 488.
direction to be followed 824, 825.
directional sign 475.
director's chair 220.
disc faucet 295.
discharge bay 764.
discharge line 216.
discharge liner 753.
discus 658.
discus and hammer throw 654.
disgorger 672.
dishwasher 257, 298.
dishwasher 298.
disk 157, 432, 433, 529, 583, 663,
712.
disk brake 432.
disk brake 442.
disk camera 395.
disk compartment 405.
disk compartment control 405.
disk drive 555.
disk drive port 528.
disk motor 529.
disk spacing lever 158.
diskette 526.
diskette drive 526.
disks 251.
display 420, 422, 523, 709.
display cabinet 227, 522.
display setting 420.
disposable camera 394.
disposable fuel cylinder 299, 307.
disposable razor 374.
distal phalanx 107, 122, 123, 137.
distal sesamoid 102.
distance 376.
distance scale 392.
distance traveled 711.
distribution board 757.
distribution box 216.
distribution by cable network 416.
distributor cap 435.
distributor service loop 757.
district 52.
district limit 52.
ditch 451, 682.
diverging lenses 722.
diversion canal 746.
divide key 523.
divider 160, 378.
dividers 519.
dividing breeching 779.
diving 624.
diving glove 624.
diving installations 624.
diving plane 806.
diving tower 624.
diving, entries 624.
diving, flights 624.
diving, starting positions 624.
division 830.
do not iron 829.
do not use chlorine bleach 829.
do not wash 829.
dock 490.
document folder 519.
document handler 532.
document receiving 421.
document-to-be-sent position 421.
does not belong to 830.

dog 106.
dog ear collar 341.
dog's forepaw 106.
dog, morphology 106.
dollar 832.
Dolphin 11.
dome roof 183.
dome shutter 14.
dome tent 686.
domestic appliances 250, 252, 254,
256, 257, 258, 260.
dominoes 695.
door 202, 429.
door 173, 225, 253, 259, 427, 449,
498, 617, 685, 686.
door access 709.
door handle 427.
door lock 427.
door open warning light 431.
door panel 225.
door shelf 254.
door stop 254, 471.
door switch 259.
doorknob 202, 289.
doors, types 202.
Dorado 13.
doric order 167.
dormant volcano 24.
dorsalis pedis artery 126.
dorsum of nose 141.
dot matrix printer 531.
dot matrix printer 527.
double bass 545.
double basses 557.
double bend 826, 827.
double boiler 249.
double curtain rod 230.
double flat 538.
double glazing 772.
double handles 633.
double kitchen sink 215.
double oxer 647.
double over 646.
double pennant 817.
double plate 198.
double pole breaker 312.
double reed 549.
double ring 698.
double scull 632.
double seat 477.
double sharp 538.
double sheet bend 691.
double zero 700.
double zero key 523.
double-blank 695.
double-breasted buttoning 319.
double-breasted jacket 322.
double-decked pallet 787.
double-edge blade 374.
double-edge razor 374.
double-leaf bascule bridge 457.
double-six 695.
double-twist auger bit 281.
doubles pole 614.
doubles service court 618.
doubles sideline 614, 618.
doublet 316.
doublet 695.
doubling die 697.
doubly dentate 56.
dough hook 250.
dousing water tank 759, 766.
dousing water valve 759.
Dove 13.
dovetail 718.
down tube 447.
down wind 629.
downspout 197.
downstream face 749.
downstream shoulder 748.
downstream toe 748.
downtown 184.
dozen (1 to 12) 700, 701.
dozen (13 to 24) 700, 701.
dozen (25 to 36) 700, 701.
drachma 832.
Draco 11.
draft arm 784.
draft hole 209.
draft tube 747, 753, 784.
drafting machine 591.
drafting table 591.
drag 670.
Dragon 11.
dragonfly 77.
drain 215.
drain hose 257, 258, 298.
drain tile 199.
drain valve 297, 741.

INDEX

drainage blanket 748.
drainage layer 748.
draining circuit 215.
draining spoon 244.
draped neck 343.
draped neckline 343.
draped swag 229.
draw drapery 229.
draw hoe 266.
draw tube 718.
drawbar 803.
drawbar lock 803.
drawbridge 180.
drawer 219, 226, 255.
drawers 325.
drawing 586, 588, 590, 592.
drawing, accessories 591, 592.
drawing, equipment 589.
drawstring 320, 381.
drawstring bag 381.
drawstring hood 351.
dredger 246.
dress with bustle 316.
dress with crinoline 318.
dress with panniers 317.
dresser 226.
dresses, types 332.
dressing room 189.
dressmaker's model 564.
drift 736.
drill 280.
drill collar 737.
drill pipe 737.
drill press 283.
drill rod 734.
drill ship 739.
drilling drawworks 737.
drilling rig 737.
drip bowl 255.
drip dry 829.
drip molding 427.
drive belt 258.
drive chain 446.
drive shaft 492, 508.
drive wheel 256, 280.
drive wheels 784.
driver 652, 678.
driver's cab 459, 468.
driver's seat 805.
driveway 193, 196.
driving glove 327.
driving turbine 438.
driving wheel 147, 575.
drone 81.
drone pipe 536.
drop earrings 361.
drop light 310.
drop waist dress 332.
drop-leaf 219.
drum 167, 231, 259, 432, 484, 707, 714.
drum brake 432.
drums 552.
drupelet 62.
dry dock 490.
dry flat 829.
dry fruits 66.
dry gallery 24.
dry point 582.
dry subtropical 45.
dry well 763.
drying 829.
drypoint 583.
dual seat 443.
dual swivel mirror 368.
duck 150.
duckpin 683.
duffel bag 380, 381.
duffle coat 320.
dugout 597.
dumbbell 665.
dump 733, 734.
dump body 785.
dump truck 785.
dune 30.
duo 558.
duodenum 131.
dura mater 134, 135.
dust 34, 35.
dust cover 404.
dust receiver 260.
dust tail 9.
dusting brush 260.
Dutch oven 249.
duty-free shop 505.
dynamic brake 468.
dynamic microphone 406.
dynamics propeller 492.

E

e 537.
Eagle 11.
eagle 819.
ear 107, 112, 116, 223.
ear cushion 406.
ear drum 139.
ear flap 328.
ear loaf 153.
ear plugs 729.
ear protection 729.
ear protection 821.
ear, auricle 139.
ear, parts 138.
earphone 406.
earpiece 376, 726.
earrings 361.
Earth 4, 8.
Earth coordinate system 3.
earth foundation 450.
earth radiation scanner 43.
earth radiation sensor 43.
earth sensor 42, 43, 49.
earth signs 820.
Earth's atmosphere, profile 19.
Earth's crust 22, 23.
Earth's crust, section 22.
Earth, structure 22.
earthquake 23.
easel 398, 591.
East 488.
East cardinal mark 489.
East reflector deployment 419.
Eastern hemisphere 47.
Eastern meridian 47.
eccrine sweat gland 136.
echinus 167.
echo 722.
echo sounder 485.
echo sounder probe 485.
eclipse crossing 419.
eclipse preparation 419.
eclipses, types 8.
ecliptic 3.
ecology 31, 32, 34.
edge 288, 564, 640, 643, 644, 719.
edger 271.
edging 263.
edible crustaceans 90.
edible gastropods 83.
edible mollusks 93.
edible mushrooms 55.
edit/search buttons 409.
effluent 216.
egg 109, 128.
egg 82.
egg beater 245.
egg butt snaffle bit 650.
egg poacher 249.
egg slicer 246.
egg timer 244.
egg tray 254.
eggplant 69.
eggs 84, 89.
Egyptian reed pen 389.
eight 632.
eight cut 362.
eighth note 538.
eighth rest 538.
ejaculatory duct 127.
eject button 403.
ejection port 796.
ejection seat 813.
ejector 784.
elastic 224.
elastic ligament 92, 107.
elastic strainer 685, 686.
elastic support bandage 725.
elastic waistband 321.
elastic webbing 323.
elasticized leg opening 325.
elbow 301.
elbow 100, 106, 112, 117, 119, 206.
elbow pad 602, 609.
elbow, 45° 301.
electric baseboard radiator 210.
electric circuit 233.
electric connection 207, 213.
electric drill 280.
electric dryer 259.
electric foil 666.
electric furnace 207.
electric golf cart 679.
electric guitar 547.
electric kiln 585.
electric motor 209, 268, 271, 438.
electric range 255.
electric razor 374.

electric variometer 639.
electrical box 309.
electrical connection 441.
electrical connection panel 415.
electrical hazard 821.
electrical inlet 585.
electrical payout linkage 702.
electrical power unit 506.
electrical scoring apparatus 666.
electrician's tools 311.
electricity 309, 310, 312, 746, 748, 750, 752, 754, 756.
electricity cable 186.
electricity meter 757.
electricity production 767.
electricity production room 806.
electricity transmission 757.
electricity transmission 767.
electricity transmission network 771.
electricity, tools 310, 311.
electrode 232, 305.
electrode assembly 209.
electrode holder 305.
electrode lead 305.
electron beam 410, 717.
electron beam positioning 717.
electron gun 410, 717.
electron microscope 717.
electron microscope elements 717.
electronic ballast 233.
electronic flash 393.
electronic instruments 555.
electronic piano 555.
electronic scales 709.
electronic typewriter 524.
electronic viewfinder 409.
elevating arc 802.
elevating cylinder 780, 786.
elevating handle 803.
elevation 193.
elevation adjustment 718.
elevator 15, 190, 499, 639, 736, 764, 811.
elevon 511.
ellipses 832.
elliptical galaxy 9.
embankment 450.
embankment dam 748.
embankment dam, cross section 748.
emblem 817.
embrasure 179.
embroidered fabric 571.
embroidery 571.
emerald 362.
emerald cut 362.
emergency brake 477.
emergency electric motor 806.
emergency regulator 627.
emergency support vessel 739.
emergency switch 444.
emery boards 365.
emery pack 563.
empty set 830.
emptying hose 258.
en prison 700, 701.
enamel 144.
enclosure 149.
end bracket 230.
end button 544.
end cap 230, 765.
end door 470.
end grain 288.
end joist 198, 199.
end ladder 470.
end line 604, 610, 613, 619.
end piece 127.
end plate 765.
end stop 230, 630.
end wall 621.
end zone 604.
end-piece 674.
endocarp 63, 64.
endoplasmic reticulum 115.
endpaper 577.
endpiece 376.
energy saving bulb 233.
engagement ring 364.
engine 147, 442, 737, 784, 787, 805.
engine and crew alarm display 500.
engine block 435.
engine fuel valves 500.
engine housing 272.
engine mounting pylon 499.
engine room 496, 806.
engines 510.
engines, types 436.
English billiards 673.
English billiards and snooker 674.

English cane 728.
English horn 548.
English horns 557.
English loaf 153.
enlarger 399.
enlarger timer 399.
enlarging lens 399.
ensiling 155, 162.
ensiling tube 162.
entablature 166, 168, 202.
enter key 530.
entire 56.
entrance 82, 452.
entrance slide 82.
entrance turnstile 474.
entries 624.
entry 625, 787.
envelope 634.
epaulet 319.
epaulet sleeve 340.
épée 666.
épéeist 667.
epicalyx 62.
epicenter 23.
epicondyle 123.
epidermis 136.
epiglottis 130, 142, 143.
epitrochlea 123.
equal key 523.
equalizing buckle 231.
equator 3, 47.
equilateral 174.
equilibrator 802.
equipment compartment 458.
equipment lock 764.
equipment rack 412, 415.
equipment section 16.
Equuleus 11.
erase button 420.
eraser 515.
eraser holder 515.
erecting lenses 718.
Eridanus 13.
ermine 819.
escalator 189, 190, 474.
escape wheel 706, 707.
escapement mechanism 539.
escudo 832.
escutcheon 95, 289, 295, 296.
esophagus 88, 92, 97, 130, 131, 142.
espadrille 357.
espresso coffee maker 247.
etching press 581.
Eurasia 21.
Europa 4.
Europe 21.
European Currency Unit 832.
European plug 309.
Eustachian tube 139, 141.
Eutelsat II 418.
euthynteria 166, 168.
evaporation 34, 35.
evaporator blower 214.
evaporator coils 214.
even 700, 701.
evening glove 327.
examples of instrumental groups 558.
exclamation point 832.
excretory opening 83.
executive desk 520.
executive length 325.
exercise wear 353.
exhalation valve 730.
exhaust 436, 437, 501.
exhaust duct 501.
exhaust gas admission 438.
exhaust guide vanes 501.
exhaust manifold 435, 437, 438, 439.
exhaust nozzle 812.
exhaust pipe 438, 439, 443, 444, 508, 783.
exhaust port 436, 735.
exhaust stack 147, 440, 784.
exhaust system 439.
exhaust tube 232.
exhaust valve 435, 436, 438.
exit 452.
exit cone 82.
exit taxiway 505.
exit turnstile 474.
exocarp 62, 63, 64.
exosphere 19.
expandable file pouch 378.
expanding file 517.
expansion bolt 276.
expansion chamber 485, 705.
expansion connector 528.
expansion diaphragm 485.
expansion space 466.

INDEX

The terms in **bold type** indicate the title of an illustration.

expansion tank 208, 772.
expert drivers course 646.
explosion 436.
explosive 821.
export pipeline 738.
exposure adjustment knob 391.
exposure meter 396.
exposure mode 391.
exposure value 396.
exposure-time scale 396.
extended character 530.
extended claw 107.
extension 219.
extension ladder 302.
extension pipe 260.
extension table 219.
exterior dome shell 14.
exterior door 202.
exterior gauge 578.
exterior of a house 196.
exterior pocket 378, 382.
exterior sign 474.
external ear 138.
external fuel tank 510.
external gills 84.
external jugular vein 126.
external oblique 120, 121.
external tooth lock washer 278.
extrados 174.
eye 140.
eye 83, 90, 96, 97, 107, 118, 275, 562, 563, 573, 649, 671, 681.
eye guard 777.
eye makeup 367.
eye protection 729.
eye protection 821.
eye ring 109.
eyeball 140.
eyeball 84.
eyebrow 140.
eyebrow pencil 367.
eyebrow stripe 109.
eyebrow tweezers 365.
eyeglasses 376.
eyeglasses case 379.
eyeglasses parts 376.
eyeglasses, major types 377.
eyelash 140.
eyelash curler 367.
eyelashes 107.
eyelet 230, 353, 354, 381, 569, 644.
eyelet tab 354.
eyelid 97.
eyepiece 390, 396, 409, 718, 719, 720, 721.
eyepiece holder 721.
eyeshadow 367.
eyestalk 83.

F

f 537.
f clef 537.
F degrees 705.
F-1 engine 509.
fabric care 829.
fabric guide 256.
fabric structure 566.
façade 175.
face 116, 119, 275, 277, 579, 619, 677, 733, 736.
face mask 602, 609, 643.
face shield 308.
face side 288.
face-off circle 608.
face-off spot 608.
facepiece 730.
faceplate 289, 290.
facial makeup 366.
facial nerve 139.
facsimile machine 421.
facsimile machine 417.
factorial 830.
faculae 6.
Fahrenheit scale 705.
failed fuel bay 764.
failed fuel canning 764.
fairing 442.
fairlead 630.
fairway 676.
fall 341.
fall front 226.
falling rocks 826, 827.
fallopian tube 128.
fallopian tubes 128.
fallout 35.
fallow 148.
false rib (3) 123.
false tuck 349.
family tent 685.

fan 162, 209, 212, 259, 501, 528.
fan belt 434.
fan brush 366, 589.
fan cable stays 456.
fan control 214.
fan heater 211.
fan housing 370.
fan motor 214.
fan thermostat 438.
fan trellis 263.
fan's tube 162.
fang 96.
fanion 817.
fantail 773.
far turn 651.
farm animals 150.
farm pollution 32.
farmhouse 148.
farmhouse bread 153.
farmstead 148.
farmyard 148.
fascia 166.
fast data entry control 555.
fast forward 831.
fast forward 411.
fast forward button 411.
fast operation 405.
fast-forward button 403, 408, 420.
fastener binder 519.
fasteners 566.
fastening device 230.
fastening system 661.
faucet 292.
fault 23.
feather crown 618.
feather stitch 571.
feathering 684.
feed dog 562.
feed lever 283.
feed pin 531.
feed table 162.
feed tube 251.
feeder header 759.
feeder output tray 532.
feeding tube 160.
feedwater 760, 761, 762, 763.
feet protection 730.
feet protection 821.
feet, principal types 111.
feet-first entry 624.
felt 581.
felt hat 328, 329.
felt tip pen 588.
female 831.
female cone 58.
female ferrule 670.
female genital organs 128, 129.
femoral artery 126.
femoral nerve 133.
femoral vein 126.
femur 78, 80, 103, 122.
fence 148.
fencer 667.
fencing 666.
fencing shoe 667.
fencing weapons 666.
fencing, parts of the weapon 666.
fencing, piste 666.
fencing, positions 667.
fencing, target areas 667.
fender 426, 440, 446.
fennel 72.
ferrule 304, 375, 675, 678.
ferry 494.
ferryboat 491.
fertilizers 32.
fertilizing soil 154, 156.
fetlock 101.
fetlock joint 101.
fettling knife 585.
fiber 692.
fibula 102, 122, 315.
field hockey 607.
field judge 605.
field lens 718.
field lens adjustment 718.
fielder's glove 596.
fielders 599.
15 yards line 606.
fifth 537.
5th metacarpal 112.
fifth wheel 440.
fifty-yard line 604.
figure skate 644.
figure ski 633.
figure skiing handle 633.
figure-eight knot 691.
filament 6, 60, 232.
filament support 233.
file 277.

file 688.
file guides 518.
filing box 517.
fill opening 256.
filler 384.
filler cap 271, 438, 440.
filler rod 307.
filler tube 293.
fillet 166, 167.
filleting knife 242.
filling hole 804.
filling inlet 741.
film 390.
film advance mode 391.
film cartridge chamber 390.
film disk 395.
film drying cabinet 398.
film guide rail 390.
film guide roller 390.
film leader 395.
film leader indicator 390.
film pack 395.
film recorder 527.
film rewind knob 391.
film rewind system 390.
film speed 391, 396.
film sprocket 390.
films 395.
filter 207, 252, 255, 385, 772.
filter cover 730.
filter tip 384.
fin 210, 499, 508, 627, 633, 812, 814.
fin-mounted tail unit 498.
finderscope 720, 721.
fine adjustment knob 718.
fine bookbinding 577, 578.
fine data entry control 555.
fine guidance system 16.
finely threaded screw 711.
finger 137.
finger 596.
finger board 535, 544, 547.
finger button 550.
finger flange 726.
fingernail 137.
finial 817.
finish 646.
finish line 654.
finishing 586.
finishing line 651.
finishing post 654.
fir needles 58.
fire engine 778, 780.
fire extinguisher 823.
fire hose 778.
fire hydrant 186.
fire hydrant wrench 779.
fire irons 205.
fire pot 204, 209.
fire prevention 777.
fire signs 820.
firebrick 204.
firebrick back 204.
fireman 777.
fireman's hatchet 781.
fireplace 204.
fireplace 195.
fireproof and waterproof garment 777.
firestopping 198.
firing 585.
firing accessories 801.
firing chamber 585.
firing lanyard 802.
firing mechanism 804.
firing shaft 802.
firing tube 807.
firmer chisel 587.
firn 26.
first aid 822.
first aid equipment 726.
first aid kit 725.
first aid manual 725.
first base 597.
first baseman 597.
first classification track 465.
first dorsal fin 86.
first floor 194.
first floor 197.
first focal room 15.
first molar 144.
first officer's seat 500.
first premolar 144.
first quarter 6.
first reinforce 800.
first space 610.
first stage 509.
first valve slide 550.
first violins 556.
first-class cabin 498.
fish 86, 88.

fish fork 240.
fish knife 239.
fish platter 238.
fish poacher 248.
fish scaler 688.
fish wire 311.
fish, anatomy 88.
fish, morphology 86.
fishbone stitch 571.
fisherman's knot 691.
Fishes 11.
fisheye lens 392.
fishhook 671.
fishhook 670.
fishing 670, 672.
fishing garment 672.
fishing vest 672.
fishplate 466.
fishplate bolt 466.
fission of uranium fuel 766.
fitness equipment 663, 664.
fitted sheet 224.
fitting 778.
fittings 301.
fittings 383.
5 m platform 624.
5 yards line 606.
five-number bet 700.
fivepin 683.
fixative 592.
fixed arch 455.
fixed base 282.
fixed blade 578.
fixed bridges 454, 456.
fixed distance marking 505.
fixed jaw 279, 282.
fixed platform 739.
fixed weight 539.
fixed winglet 814.
fixed-roof tank 741.
fixing bath 399.
fixture drain 215.
flag 606.
flag shapes 817.
flag with Schwenkel 817.
flag, parts 817.
flagstone 263.
flail mower 158.
flail mower 154.
flame adjustment wheel 386.
flame spreader tip 307.
flammable 821.
flank 101, 108, 179, 579.
flank forward 606.
flanker 605.
flanking tower 180.
flap 322, 380, 649.
flap hydraulic jack 812.
flap lever 500.
flap pocket 339.
flap pocket 320, 322.
flare 6, 738.
flare joint 300.
flare nut wrench 279.
flash hider 796.
flash lamp 393.
flashcube 393.
flashing 205.
flashing light 471.
flashtube 393.
flat 538.
flat brush 589.
flat car 473.
flat end pin 231.
flat head 276.
flat mirror 14, 720.
flat part 567.
flat roof 182.
flat sheet 224.
flat shuttle 573.
flat stitches 571.
flat tip 276.
flat washer 278.
flat-back brush 368.
flat-bed 561.
flat-plate solar collector 768.
flatbed 441.
flatbed pushcart 788.
flesh 62, 63, 64.
fleshy fruits 62, 65.
fleshy leaf 70.
fleur-de-lis 819.
flews 106.
flexible hose 260, 735.
flexible hose connection 735.
flexible rubber hose 298.
flexible skirt 493.
flexible tube 726.
flies 188.
flight 625, 698.

The terms in **bold type** indicate the title of an illustration.

flight bag 637.
flight deck 500.
flight deck 498, 508, 510, 810.
flight information board 505.
flight instruments 635.
flight management computer 500.
flight of stairs 201.
flights 624.
flint 307, 795.
flint arrowhead 791.
flint knife 791.
flintlock 795.
flip turn 622, 623.
float 216, 485, 803.
float ball 293.
float clamp 216.
floater 626.
floating bridge 457.
floating crane 490.
floating head 374.
floating rib 122.
floating roof 741.
floating sleeve 316.
floating-roof tank 741.
floodlight 414.
floodlight on pantograph 414.
floor 205, 616, 617, 773.
floor brush 260.
floor drain 215.
floor joist 198, 199.
floor lamp 236.
floor tile 286.
floorboard 200.
floppy disk 529.
floppy disk drive 528.
florin 832.
flotation section 486.
flow 493.
flow bean 740.
flow tube 768.
flower 57.
flower bed 263.
flower bud 57.
flower, inflorescences 60.
flower, structure 60.
flowering 61.
flue 297, 542.
flue hat 297.
flue pipe 542.
fluid adjustment screw 304.
fluid cup 590.
fluke 483.
fluorescent tube 232.
fluorescent tube 233.
flush 695.
flush bushing 301.
flush handle 293.
flute 166, 167, 281, 548.
fluted land 281.
fluted pole 230.
fluted shaft 431.
fluteroni 587.
flutes 556.
Fly 13, 77, 323, 325, 350, 817.
fly agaric 55.
fly front closing 330, 351.
fly line 670.
fly reel 670.
fly rod 670.
flying buttress 175, 176.
Flying Fish 13.
flying jib 481.
flyleaf 179.
flywheel 435, 581, 584, 664.
FM antenna 400.
foam 30.
foam cushion 729.
foam insulation 287.
foam pad 687.
foam-rubber insulation 287.
focal plane shutter 390.
focus 23.
focus mode selector 391.
focus setting ring 392.
focusing knob 720, 721.
focusing lenses 717.
focusing magnifier 399.
focusing ring 719.
focusing screen 390.
fodder corn 149.
fog 37, 39.
fog light 429, 440.
foible 666.
foil 666.
foil warning line 666.
foilist 667.
fold 315.
fold line 565.
foldaway ladder 303.
folder 518.

folding chair 223.
folding cot 687.
folding door 202.
folding door 194.
folding grill 690.
folding nail file 365.
folding ramp 494.
folding shovel 690.
foliage 59.
follicle 67.
follicle, section 67.
follow-through 682.
fondue fork 240.
fondue pot 248.
fondue set 248.
food chain 31.
food pollution 32.
food processor 251.
foot 83, 112, 116, 117, 118, 119, 225, 350, 542, 545, 553, 579, 631, 670, 671.
foot control 561.
foot cushion 675.
foot fault judge 614.
foot hole 542.
foot pocket 627.
foot score line 620.
foot strap 631.
foot support 664.
football 602, 604.
football player 602.
footboard 224, 445.
footbridge 180, 464, 475.
footing 198, 199.
footless tights 353.
footlights 188.
footrest 584, 727.
footrope 478.
footstool 222.
footstrap 336, 664.
forage blower 162.
forage blower 155.
forage harvester 162.
forage harvester 155.
foramen cecum 143.
forced hot-water system 208.
forced warm-air system 206.
fore edge 577.
fore royal sail 481.
fore-royal mast 479.
fore-topgallant mast 479.
fore-topmast 479.
forearm 106, 117, 119, 798.
forearm crutch 728.
forearm support 728.
forecastle 495, 497.
forecourt 614.
forehead 109, 116.
foreleg 79, 80.
foreleg, honeybee 80.
forelimb 84.
forelock 100.
foremast 479.
foresail 481.
forest 27.
forestay 628.
forewing 79, 81.
fork 240.
fork 105, 447, 688, 707, 721, 787.
fork pocket 470.
forked tongue 96.
forklift truck 787.
forks 787, 788.
forks, principal types 240.
formeret 177.
forming 692.
Fornax 13.
forte 666.
fortified wall 172.
forward 624.
forward dive 625.
forward slide change 397.
forward swing 682.
forward/reverse 272.
foul line 597, 683.
foundation 198, 199, 750.
foundation blockage 750.
foundation of dam 748.
foundation of tower 456.
foundation slip 345.
foundations 199.
fountain pen 389, 515.
four blade beater 250.
four-door sedan 425.
four-four time 537.
four-masted bark 478, 480.
4 m line 626.
four-of-a-kind 695.
four-stroke-cycle engine 436.
four-toed hoof 99.

fourchette 327.
fourth 537.
4th metacarpal 112.
fourth wheel 706.
fovea 140.
foyer 189.
fractionating tower 744.
fraise 318.
frame 198, 572.
frame 82, 156, 157, 159, 204, 225, 272, 282, 302, 319, 323, 378, 382, 383, 443, 484, 536, 554, 583, 595, 615, 645, 659, 660, 685, 711, 726, 768, 769, 773, 785, 787, 788.
frame push 783.
frame stile 225.
frame, embroidery 571.
frames 376.
framing square 275.
franc 832.
Francis turbine 754.
free margin 117.
free throw lane 610.
free throw line 610, 612.
freeway 184, 452.
freewheel 448.
freezer bucket 251.
freezer compartment 254.
freezer door 254.
freezing rain 39.
freight car 464.
freight cars, types 472.
freight expedition 505.
freight hold 499.
freight reception 505.
freight station 464.
French betting layout 701.
French bread 153.
French cuff 339.
French cut 363.
French horn 551.
French horns 557.
French knot stitch 571.
French loaf 153.
French roulette wheel 701.
French window 203.
fresco 170.
fret 546, 547, 701.
friction strip 307, 386.
frieze 166, 168, 225.
frigate 808.
fringe 318.
fringe trimming 229.
frock coat 317.
frog 84.
frog 104, 156, 320, 467, 544.
frog, life cycle 84.
frog-adjustment screw 277.
front 322, 324.
front apron 324.
front axle 784.
front beam 708.
front binding 633.
front board 577.
front brake 447.
front brake lever 444.
front crawl stroke 622.
front crossbar 645.
front derailleur 446, 448.
front fender 442.
front flap 386.
front foil 495.
front footrest 443, 444.
front grip 804.
front knob 277, 281.
front landing gear 813.
front leg 223.
front lights 189.
front pocket 381.
front point 680.
front runner 643.
front sight 795, 797, 798, 799, 804.
front sight housing 796.
front tip 256.
front top pocket 323.
front view 147.
front wall 616, 617.
front wheel 147, 727, 784.
front-end loader 782.
frontal 120.
frontal bone 122.
frontal sinus 141.
frontcourt 617.
fronts 39.
frontwall 441.
frost 37.
fruit branch 61.
fruit tree 149.
fruit vegetables 69.
fruit-picking ladder 303.

fruition 61.
frying pan 249, 688.
fuel 766.
fuel 761.
fuel bundle 765.
fuel bundle 765.
fuel control 501.
fuel handling sequence 764.
fuel indicator 431.
fuel injector 437.
fuel lines 635.
fuel oil 744.
fuel pellet 765.
fuel tank 272, 440, 442, 468, 508, 805, 812.
fuel tank door 427.
fuel transfer pipe 509.
fuel: enriched uranium 762, 763.
fuel: natural uranium 760, 761.
fueling machine 759, 760, 761, 764.
fulcrum 624.
full and by 629.
full back 606.
full cheek snaffle bit 650.
full deployment 419.
full face mask 777.
full house 695.
full moon 7.
full-load adjustment screw 712.
fullback 603, 605.
fumarole 24.
fume extractor 805.
function button 699.
function display 555.
function key 530.
function keys 421, 422, 709.
function selector 214, 402.
function selectors 420.
funiculus 62, 67.
funnel 243.
funnel 410, 496.
fur 107.
furlong chute 651.
Furnace 13, 206, 770.
furs, examples 819.
fuse 757, 769.
fuse body 804.
fuse box 312.
fuse cutout 757.
fuse holder 757.
fuse puller 311.
fuselage 499, 639.
fuselage mounted tail unit 498.
fuses 312.

G

g 537.
g clef 537.
gable roof 182.
gable stud 198.
gable vent 197.
gaff 478.
gaff sail 482.
gaff sail boom 478.
gaff topsail 480.
gain control 485.
gaits, horse 101.
galaxy 9.
galaxy, classification 9.
gall bladder 97.
gallbladder 131.
gallery 175, 189, 486, 773.
galley 498.
Gallic warrior 791.
gallop 101.
game cartridge 699.
game of darts 698.
gantry crane 786.
gantry crane 746, 747.
Ganymede 4.
gap 671.
garage 196.
garbage disposal sink 296.
garbage disposal unit 296.
garden 171.
garden hose 265.
garden line 268.
garden sorrel 73.
gardening equipment 264, 266, 268, 270, 272.
gardening tools 264, 266, 268, 270, 272.
garlic 70.
garlic press 243.
garment bag 382.
garment fabric 565.
garment strap 383.
garment, fishing 672.

INDEX

garnet 362.
garrison cap 328.
garter 347.
garter belt 347.
garter stitch 567.
gas 34, 35, 232, 737, 744.
gas burner 297.
gas cock 297.
gas cylinder 796.
gas lift module 738.
gas lighter 386.
gas main 186.
gas pedal 430.
gas tail 9.
gas tank cap 444.
gas water-heater tank 297.
gasket 257, 300.
gaskin 101.
gasoline 744, 745.
gasoline engine 434.
gasoline pump 453.
gasoline pump 453.
gasoline pump hose 453.
gastrocnemius 120, 121.
gastropod 83.
gate 647.
gate 462, 490, 646, 681, 747, 752.
gate arm 471.
gate arm lamp 471.
gate arm support 471.
gate operating ring 753.
gate-leg 219.
gate-leg table 219.
gather 337.
gather skirt 335.
gathering 577.
gauge 578.
gauntlet 308, 327.
gauntlet 327, 792.
gauze bandage 662.
gauze roller bandage 725.
gear 575.
gear housing 671.
gear shift 444.
gearbox 495, 583.
gearshift lever 430, 443.
gelatin capsule 725.
Gemini 11.
Gemini the Twins(May 21) 820.
generator 753.
generator 446, 758.
generator unit 753.
generator unit 747.
genital opening 83.
geometry 830.
geostationary orbit 43.
geostationary satellite 42.
germ 152.
German rye bread 153.
geyser 25.
gill 55.
gill filament 87.
gill raker 87.
gills 87.
gills 88, 92.
gimbal ring 485.
Giraffe 11.
girder 14, 198.
girdle 346, 363.
girth 649, 651.
girth strap 649.
glacial cirque 26.
glacier 26.
glacier tongue 26.
glacis 178.
gladius 791.
glans penis 127.
glass 768, 769.
glass case 709.
glass cover 254.
glass curtain 228.
glass dome 484.
glass lens 376.
glass slide 718.
glass sphere 40.
glass-fronted display cabinet 227.
glass-lined tank 297.
glassed roof 190, 195, 462.
glassware 237.
glider 638.
gliding 638.
globe 689.
glottis 96, 142.
glove 512, 598, 609, 635, 642, 643, 667.
glove compartment 430.
glove finger 327.
gloves 327.
glue 200.
glue stick 515.

gluteal nerve 133.
gnomon 706.
go 697.
go, board 697.
goal 601, 604, 606, 607, 608, 612, 626.
goal area 601, 612.
goal area line 612.
goal attack 611.
goal circle 611.
goal crease 608.
goal defense 611.
goal judge 608, 626.
goal line 604, 606, 607, 608, 612, 626.
goal line referee 612.
goal shooter 611.
goal third 611.
goalkeeper 609.
goalkeeper 601, 607, 608, 611, 612, 626.
goalkeeper's pad 609.
goalkeeper's stick 609.
goalpost 604, 611.
Goat 13.
goat 150.
gob hat 329.
goggles 308.
goggles 635.
golf 676, 678.
golf bag 679.
golf ball 677.
golf ball, cross-section 677.
gate-leg table 219.
golf cart 679.
golf clubs 678.
golf clubs, types 677.
golf course 676.
golf glove 679.
golf shoe 679.
golf, iron 678.
golf, wood 678.
Golgi apparatus 115.
gondola car 473.
gonfalon 817.
gong 554.
gong 557.
goose 150.
goose-neck 201.
gooseberry 62.
gooseneck 784.
gored skirt 334.
gorge 24.
gorget 792.
gothic cathedral 175, 176.
gouge 587.
gour 24.
grab handle 440, 449, 461, 779.
grade slope 193.
grader 784.
graduated arc 484.
graduated dial 719.
graduated scale 708, 709, 710.
grafting knife 269.
grain 288.
grain auger 161.
grain elevator 161.
grain of wheat, section 152.
grain pan 161.
grain tank 160.
grain terminal 490.
grain tube 158.
grandfather clock 707.
grandstand 651.
granitic layer 22.
granivorous bird 111.
granny knot 691.
granulation 1.
grape 61, 62.
grape 61, 62.
grape leaf 61.
grape leaf 73.
grapefruit 65.
grapefruit knife 242.
grapeshot 801.
graphic equalizer 400.
grapnel 483.
grassbox 271.
grasshopper 77.
grater 243.
grating, utensils for 243.
grave accent 832.
gravel 199, 216.
gravity band 483.
gravity dam 749.
gravity dam, cross section 749.
gravy boat 238.
gray matter 135.
grease well 253.
greases 745.
great adductor 121.
Great Bear 11.

Great Dog 13.
great organ manual 542.
great saphenous vein 126.
great scallop 93.
greater alar cartilage 141.
greater covert 110.
greater pectoral 120.
greater trochanter 123.
greatest gluteal 121.
greave 792.
Greek bread 153.
Greek temple 168.
Greek temple, plan 169.
green 682.
green ball 673.
green beam 410.
green bean 69.
green cabbage 73.
green peas 72.
green russula 55.
green walnut 66.
greenhouse 149.
Greenland Sea 20.
grid 188, 410.
grid system 47.
griddle 253.
grille 168, 214, 426, 438, 536.
grinding, utensils for 243.
grip 632, 665, 677, 684.
grip handle 277.
grips, tennis table 619.
grips, types 619.
groin 116, 118.
groove 578.
groove 562, 598, 641, 678, 793.
ground 312, 741.
ground air conditioner 506.
ground airport equipment 506.
ground bond 312.
ground clamp 305.
ground connection 312, 400.
ground electrode 439.
ground fault circuit interrupter 312.
ground moraine 26.
ground sill 178.
ground surface 733.
ground wire 312, 757.
ground-wire peak 756.
ground/neutral bus bar 312.
grounded receptacle 216.
grounding prong 309.
grow sleepers 350.
growth line 83, 95.
Grus 13.
guard 201, 242, 310, 666.
guard rail 254.
guardhouse 178, 180.
guava 68.
guide 670.
guide bar 272.
guide handle 283.
guide mark 612.
guide roller 403.
guiding and current bar 476.
guiding tower 457.
guillotine trimmer 398.
gules 819.
gulf 51.
gum 142, 144.
gun 291.
gun body 304.
gun flap 319.
gunner's sight 805.
gusset 378, 380.
gusset pocket 339.
gusset pocket 338.
Gutenberg discontinuity 22.
gutta 167.
gutter 105, 197, 683.
guy cable 660.
guy line 685.
guy wire 774.
guyot 28.
gymnasium 496.
gymnastics 659, 660.
gypsum tile 286.

H

H 38.
hack 620.
hackle 670.
hacksaw 277, 299.
hail 37.
hail shower 39.
hair 117, 119, 136, 544.
hair bulb 136.
hair clip 369.
hair dryer 370.
hair follicle 136.

hair roller 369.
hair roller pin 369.
hair shaft 136.
hairbrushes 368.
haircutting scissors 369.
hairdressing 368, 370.
hairpin 369.
hairspring 706.
hairstyling implements 369.
half barb 38.
half cell 636.
half court line 616.
half handle 242.
half indexing 525.
half note 538.
half rest 538.
half-distance line 626.
half-glasses 377.
half-mask respirator 730.
half-side 787.
half-slip 345.
half-through arch bridge 455.
halfback 605.
halfway line 601, 606.
hall 189.
hall 194, 496.
hallway 194.
halyard 480, 817.
ham knife 242.
hammer 311.
hammer 540, 541, 658, 797, 798, 799.
hammer ax 681.
hammer ax 680.
hammer butt 541.
hammer drill 734.
hammer felt 541.
hammer head 681.
hammer rail 540, 541.
hammer shank 541.
hand 137.
hand 117, 119.
hand blender 250.
hand brake gear housing 470.
hand brake wheel 470.
hand brake winding lever 470.
hand drill 280.
hand fork 268.
hand grenade 804.
hand grip 670.
hand lamp 777.
hand mixer 250.
hand mower 271.
hand protection 821.
hand protector 268.
hand shield 308.
hand truck 788.
hand vacuum cleaner 260.
hand vice 582.
hand warmer pocket 330.
hand warmer pouch 339.
hand wash in lukewarm water 829.
hand wheel 561.
hand-warmer pocket 321.
hand-wheel 579.
handbags 380.
handball 612.
handball, court 612.
handgrip 442, 728.
handgrips 665.
handguard 796.
handhold 652.
handicap spot 697.
handle 633.
handle 204, 224, 239, 240, 241, 250, 251, 252, 253, 254, 255, 256, 260, 265, 270, 271, 272, 275, 276, 277, 278, 279, 281, 282, 284, 291, 294, 295, 304, 306, 310, 370, 373, 374, 375, 378, 380, 382, 383, 408, 544, 563, 564, 570, 573, 579, 596, 598, 607, 615, 619, 620, 640, 643, 658, 666, 670, 671, 679, 688, 727, 735, 793.
handlebar 272, 664.
handlebars 415, 447.
handrail 201, 477.
handsaw 277.
handset 420, 422.
handset cord 420.
hang glider 637.
hang gliding 637.
hang point 637.
hang to dry 829.
hang-up ring 370.
hanger 397.
hanger bracket 727.
hanger loop 326.
hanging basket 263.
hanging file 518.

The terms in **bold type** indicate the title of an illustration.

hanging glacier 26.
hanging pendant 236.
hanging sleeve 316.
hanging stile 202, 203, 225.
hank 630.
harbor 490.
hard disk drive 529.
hard disk drive 526, 528.
hard palate 141, 142.
hard shell clam 93.
hard top gondola 472.
hardboard 289.
hardwood base 635.
Hare 13.
harmonica 536.
harness 573, 627, 635, 636, 637, 645.
harness racing 652.
harnesses 572.
harp 545.
harp cable stays 456.
harps 556.
harquebus 795.
harvesting 155, 159, 160, 162.
hasp 383.
hastate 56.
hatband 328.
hatch 510, 805.
hatchback 425.
hatchet 690.
hatching 576.
haulage road 733.
hawk 291.
hay baler 159.
hay baler 155.
hayloft 148.
hazelnut 66.
hazelnut, section 66.
head 112.
head 9, 72, 78, 79, 80, 83, 117, 119,
  124, 127, 275, 276, 279, 283, 373,
  374, 384, 386, 466, 544, 546, 547,
  554, 561, 567, 570, 579, 615, 658,
  670, 677, 681.
head cover 679.
head cushion 674.
head harness 730.
head linesman 603.
head number 653.
head of femur 123.
head of frame 203.
head of humerus 123.
head pole 653.
head protection 729.
head protection 821.
head roller 577.
head tube 306, 447.
head, bat 112.
head, bird 109.
headband 406, 408, 577, 615, 642,
  729, 730.
headbay 746.
headboard 224.
headcap 577.
header 161.
header 198, 202.
headframe 736.
headgear 328.
headings, types 229.
headlamp 447.
headland 30.
headlight 147, 426, 440, 442, 444,
  445, 459, 469, 805.
headlight/turn signal 430.
headlights 429.
headphone jack 402, 408, 555.
headphone plug 408.
headphones 406.
headphones 408.
headpin 683.
headrail 231.
headrest 428.
headwind 629.
hearing 138.
heart 125, 695.
heart 88, 92, 97, 130.
heartwood 59.
heat control 209.
heat deflecting disc 232.
heat exchanger 209, 760, 772.
heat production 766.
heat pump 212.
heat ready indicator 370.
heat selector switch 370.
heat shield 510.
heat transport pump 759.
heater 689.
heating 204, 206, 208, 210, 212.
heating coil 635.
heating duct 259.

heating element 207, 209, 257, 259,
  305, 585.
heating grille 477.
heating oil 745.
heating, forced hot-water system
  208.
heating, forced warm-air system
  206.
heating, registers 207.
heating/air conditioning equipment
  494.
heaving line knot 691.
heavy drifting snow low 39.
heavy duty boot 355.
heavy gasoline 744.
heavy machinery 785.
heavy thunderstorm 39.
heavy vehicles 782, 784.
heavy-water reactor 761.
heddle rod 574.
heddles 573.
heddles 572, 574.
hedge 263.
hedge shears 269.
hedge trimmer 268.
heel 104, 117, 119, 156, 242, 277,
  325, 352, 354, 544, 546, 596, 609,
  644, 678.
heel grip 354.
heel loop 727.
heel piece 633, 640.
heel rest 250, 256.
heel stop 645.
heel-piece 641.
heeled shoe 318.
heelplate 642, 643.
height adjustment 157, 159, 659,
  661, 664.
height adjustment scale 284.
height adjustment screw 641.
height control 399.
height finder 810.
height of the dive 625.
height scale 399.
helicopter 508.
helicopter 808.
helicopter flight deck 808.
helicopter hangar 808.
helipad 738.
helium sphere 509.
helix 139.
helm roof 183.
helmet 777.
helmet 512, 602, 609, 635, 636, 680,
  777, 791.
helmet lamp 680.
helmet ring 512.
hem 231.
hemispheres 47.
hemlath 773.
hemline 565.
hen 150.
hen house 148.
hennin 318.
hepad 42.
hepatic vein 124.
heraldry 817, 818.
herbivore's jaw 98.
herbivores 31, 33.
herbs 74.
Hercules 11.
Herdsman 11.
herringbone parquet 200.
herringbone pattern 200.
herringbone stitch 571.
Hertzian wave transmission 416.
hex nut 439.
hexagon bushing 301.
hidden pocket 379.
high (19 to 36) 700, 701.
high beam 429.
high beam indicator light 431.
high beam warning indicator 445.
high card 695.
high clouds 44.
high focal plane buoy 487.
high jump 657.
high jump 654.
high pressure center 38.
high warp loom 574.
high-back overalls 350.
high-pressure steam inlet 758.
high-rise apartment 187.
high-rise apartment 185.
high-speed exit taxiway 502.
high-speed train 458.
high-voltage tester 310.
highball glass 237.
highland climates 45.
highland climates 45.
highlight key 396.

highlighter pen 515.
highway 52, 452.
highway crossing 471.
highway crossing bell 471.
highway number 52.
hill 27, 770.
hilted bayonet 794.
hind leg 79, 81.
hind leg, butterfly 78.
hind leg, honeybee 81.
hind limb 84, 85.
hind toe 108, 111.
hind wing 79, 81.
hinge 202, 203, 225, 253, 257, 378,
  382, 404, 429, 585, 641, 719.
hinge pin 785.
hinge tooth 95.
hinged door 195.
hinged presser foot 561, 562.
hip 117, 119.
hip pad 602.
hip roof 182.
hip-and-valley roof 183.
hitch pin 540.
hitting area 596.
hive 82.
hive 149.
hive body 82.
hobble 652.
hobble hanger 652.
hobo bag 380.
hock 101, 106.
hockey ball 607.
hockey skate 644.
hockey, playing field 607.
hoe 267.
hoe-fork 266.
hog score line 620.
hoist 188, 817.
hoist room 735.
hoisting block 786.
hoisting ring 483.
hoisting rope 302, 786.
hoisting system 786.
holdback 229.
holding 668.
holding area marking 504.
holding timekeeper 668.
holds, judo 668.
hole 583, 676.
hollow barrel 726.
hollow shot 801.
home plate 597.
home-plate umpire 597.
homestretch 651.
honey cell 82.
honeybee 80, 82.
honeybee, foreleg 80.
honeybee, hind leg 81.
honeybee, middle leg 80.
honeycomb 82.
honeycomb section 82.
hood 204, 260, 320, 349, 426, 440,
  627, 680.
hooded sweat shirt 352.
hoof 104.
hoof 101.
hoof, plantar surface 104.
hoofs, types 99.
hook 267.
hook 203, 230, 310, 562, 566, 567,
  568, 644, 674, 709, 711, 726, 786.
hook and eyes 566.
hook ladder 303.
hook ladder 781.
hooker 606.
hoop 571.
hoop earrings 361.
hopper 158, 162.
hopper car 472.
hopper ore car 472.
horizon mirror 484.
horizon shade 484.
horizontal bar 660.
horizontal clamp 713.
horizontal control 529.
horizontal end handhold 470.
horizontal member 756.
horizontal motion lock 393.
horizontal movement 696.
horizontal pivoting window 203.
horizontal seismograph 714.
horizontal stabilizer 499, 508, 639.
horizontal-axis wind turbine 774.
horn 364.
horn 400, 444, 468, 779.
horns 83.
horns of giraffe 99.
horns of mouflon 99.
horns of rhinoceros 99.
horns, major types 99.

horny beak 97.
hors d'oeuvre dish 238.
horse 98, 100, 102, 104.
horse 661.
horse racing 651.
horse, gaits 101.
horse, morphology 100.
horse, skeleton 102.
horseradish 71.
horseshoe 104, 174, 364.
horseshoe 104.
horseshoe mount 14.
hose 344.
hose 306, 347, 780.
hose connector 264.
hose nozzle 265.
hose trolley 265.
hospital 822.
hot air 501.
hot bus bar 312.
hot coolant 771.
hot line connector 757.
hot pepper 69.
hot-air outflow 207.
hot-air outlet 204.
hot-air register 206.
hot-shoe contact 391.
hot-water circuit 215.
hot-water heater 215.
hot-water outlet 208, 297.
hot-water riser 215.
hot-water supply line 296, 298.
hotel 185.
hotel reservation desk 504.
houppelande 317.
hour angle gear 14.
hour hand 707.
house 193, 620.
house drain 298.
house dress 333.
house, exterior 196.
house, foundations 199.
house, frame 198.
house, structure 198.
housing 233, 280, 305, 310, 374,
  403, 406, 422, 485, 486.
hovercraft 492.
hub 447, 727, 754, 774.
hub cover 754.
Hubble space telescope 16.
Hubble's classification 9.
huckleberry 62.
hull 67, 628.
hull column 738.
hull sonar 809.
human body 116, 118.
human denture 144.
humerus 102, 122.
humid - long summer 45.
humid - short summer 45.
humid subtropical 45.
humidifier 210.
humidity 210.
humidity, measure 41.
hump 465.
hump lead 465.
hump office 465.
Hunter 11, 13.
hunting cap 328.
Hunting Dogs 11.
hunting weapons 798.
hurdle 656.
hurricane 39.
hurricane lamp 690.
husk 66.
husk 72.
hut 165.
Hydra 11, 13.
hydrant intake 778, 779.
hydraulic coupler 147.
hydraulic cylinder 147, 788.
hydraulic hose 156, 157, 158.
hydraulic jack 449.
hydraulic pallet truck 788.
hydraulic resistance 664.
hydraulic shovel 785.
hydraulic system 787.
hydroelectric complex 746.
**hydroelectric power station,
  cross section** 747.
hydrofoil boat 495.
hydrologic cycle 34.
hydrometer 439.
hydrosphere 31.
hydrostatic pad 14.
Hydrus 11, 13.
hygrograph 41.
hygrometer 210.
hypha 55.
hyssop 74.

The terms in **bold type** indicate the title of an illustration.

I

ice 34.
ice ax 681.
ice ax 680.
ice cream freezer 251.
ice cream scoop 246.
ice cube tray 254.
ice dispenser 453.
ice hockey 608.
ice hockey player 609.
ice hockey, rink 608.
ice piton 680.
ice screw 680.
icing syringe 245.
identification bracelet 364.
identification tag 383.
idler wheel 445.
igloo 165.
igneous rocks 23.
ignition box 501.
ignition key 271.
ignition switch 430, 444, 445.
ignition transformer 209.
ileum 131.
iliohypogastric nerve 133.
ilioinguinal nerve 133.
ilium 122.
illumination mirror 713.
imagesetter 527.
imperial roof 183.
impervious rock 737.
impluvium 170, 171.
impost 174.
impulse sprinkler 264.
in goal 606.
in-flight refueling 813.
in-flight refueling probe 813.
inactive dyke 752.
inbound line 604.
incandescent lamp 232.
incandescent lamp 486, 769.
incised figure 580.
incisor 98.
incisors 144.
incoming message cassette 420.
incus 138.
indent 524.
index arm 484.
index card cabinet 517.
index card drawer 517.
index cards 517.
index finger 137.
index hole 529.
index mirror 484.
index shade 484.
Indian 13.
Indian chapati bread 153.
Indian fig 68.
Indian naan bread 153.
Indian Ocean 21.
indicator 710.
indicator board 462, 654.
indicator lights 531.
indicator needle 396.
indicators 405, 410.
indoor shutters 231.
indoor unit 213.
Indus 13.
industrial communications 417.
industrial pollution 32, 33.
inert gas 232, 233.
inferior cymbal 552.
inferior dental arch 142.
inferior mesenteric artery 132.
inferior nasal concha 141.
inferior umbilicus 110.
inferior vena cava 124, 125, 126, 132.
infield 597.
infiltration 34.
infinity 830.
inflated carrying tire 476, 477.
inflated guiding tire 476, 477.
inflator 687.
inflator 627.
inflator valve 627.
inflator-deflator 687.
inflorescences, types 60.
inflorescent vegetables 69.
information 823.
information console 627.
information counter 504.
information processing 722.
infrared homing head 814.
infrared sounder 43.
infraspinous 121.
infundibulum of fallopian tube 129.
inhalation valve 730.

injection/explosion 437.
injector 434.
ink 581, 588.
ink 389, 581.
inked surface 580.
inking slab 581.
inlaid parquet 200.
inlet hose 399.
inlet valve 434, 436.
inner boot 641, 645.
inner circle 620.
inner core 22.
inner door shell 429.
inner edge 104.
inner hearth 204.
inner jib 481.
inner lining 433.
inner lip 94.
inner stators 501.
inner table 697.
inner tent 685, 686.
inner toe 108.
input devices 526.
input monitors 413.
input selector 402.
input terminal 310.
insectivores 31.
insectivorous bird 111.
insects 77.
inset pocket 339.
inside 241.
inside knob 290.
inside left 601.
inside linebacker 603.
inside right 601.
inside-leg snap-fastening 350.
insole 358.
inspection plug 216.
instep 325.
instrument pallet 511.
instrument panel 431.
instrument panel 430.
instrument platform 43.
instrument shelter 41.
instrument unit 509.
insulated blade 310.
insulated handle 310, 311.
insulating materials 287.
insulating sheet 528.
insulating sleeve 309.
insulation 209, 297, 768.
insulation layers 512.
insulator 439, 757.
intaglio printing 580.
intaglio printing process 582.
intaglio printing process, equipment 582.
intake 436, 437.
intake manifold 434, 437.
intake port 436.
integral 830.
integral bayonet 794.
Intelsat VII 418.
interchangeable end assembly 14.
interchangeable studs 600.
interchanges, major types 450.
intercom microphone 413.
intercom station 413.
intercooler 438.
intercostal nerve 133.
interfacing 565.
interfemoral membrane 112.
interior dome shell 14.
interior door handle 429.
interior door lock button 429.
interior pocket 383.
interlining 565.
interlock 576.
intermediate booster station 740.
intermittent drizzle 39.
intermittent rain 39.
intermittent snow 39.
internal boundary 51.
internal ear 138.
internal filum terminale 134.
internal iliac artery 124, 126, 132.
internal iliac vein 124.
internal jugular vein 126.
internal tooth lock washer 278.
international boundary 51.
international road signs 825, 827, 828.
international weather symbols 39.
internode 57.
interrupted projection 50.
intersection 830.
intertragic notch 139.
interval 489.

intervals 537.
intestine 88, 92, 97, 124.
intrados 174.
intrusive rocks 23.
invert 476.
inverted pleat 228, 335.
inward dive 625.
Io 4.
Ionic order 166.
iris 140.
Irish bread 153.
iron 677.
iron at high setting 829.
iron at low setting 829.
iron at medium setting 829.
iron curtain 188.
iron, golf 678.
ironing 829.
irregular crystal 37.
irregular galaxy 9.
is approximately equal to 830.
is contained in 830.
is equal to 830.
is equal to or greater than 830.
is equal to or less than 830.
is equivalent to 830.
is greater than 830.
is identical with 830.
is less than 830.
is not equal to 830.
is not identical with 830.
is not parallel to 830.
is parallel to 830.
isba 165.
ischium 123.
island 51, 452.
isobar 37.
isolated danger mark 489.
isoseismal line 23.
isthmus 51.
isthmus of fallopian tube 129.
isthmus of fauces 142.
ivory ball 701.

J

J-2 engine 509.
jabot 342.
jack 682, 695.
jack 400, 541, 682.
jack field 407.
jack spring 541.
jack-up platform 739.
jacket 321, 331.
jacket 331, 529, 667, 668, 798.
jackets 338.
jackleg drill 734.
jackpot box 702.
jackpot feed 702.
jalousie 203.
jamb 202, 204.
Japan plum 64.
Japanese persimmon 68.
javelin 361, 362, 364.
javelin throw 654.
javelins 658.
jaw 276, 280, 281, 311, 365.
jaw, carnivore's 98.
jaw, herbivore's 98.
jaw, rodent's 98.
jaws, types 98.
jazz band 558.
jeans 336.
jejunum 131.
jersey 602.
Jerusalem artichoke 71.
jet blast deflector 810.
jet engine test area 811.
jet fuel 745.
jet refueler 506.
jet tip 373.
Jew's harp 536.
jewel 706.
jewel cap 485.
jewelry 361, 362, 364.
Jewish hallah 153.
jib 628, 786.
jib tie 786.
jibsheet 628.
jigger topgallant staysail 480.
jigger topmast staysail 480.
jingle 554.
jockey 651.
jockey rollers 448.
jodhpur 648.
joint 389, 577, 670, 675.
joint filler 291.
jointed mouth 650.
jointed mouth bit 650.

joist 200.
Joker 695.
journal box 468.
joystick 526.
judge 666, 668, 669.
judge's stand 651.
judo 668.
judo suit 668.
juice sac 65.
juicer 251.
jump rope 665.
jump ski 633.
jumper 333.
jumpsuit 336, 349, 351.
junction box 471.
Jupiter 4.
justaucorps 315.

K

K-frame 756.
Kaplan turbine 754.
keel 637.
keep 181.
keeper ring 670.
kelly 737.
kernel 72.
kerosene 744, 745.
kerosene tank 509.
ketch 482.
kettle 252.
kettledrum 553.
key 290, 536, 539, 540, 541, 543, 549.
key case 379.
key finger button 549.
key guard 549.
key lever 549.
key lock 378.
key signature 538.
keybed 540.
keyboard 530.
keyboard 422, 526, 527, 540, 555, 683.
keyboard instruments 540.
keyboard port 528.
keystone 174, 177.
keyway 290.
kick pleat 335.
kickstand 443.
kidney 89, 97, 124.
kilt 335.
kimono 348.
kimono sleeve 340.
King 695.
King 11, 696.
king post 199, 637.
King's side 696.
kingpin 441.
kiosk 453, 475.
kitchen 171, 195, 460, 807.
kitchen knife 242.
kitchen knives, types 242.
kitchen scale 244.
kitchen timer 244.
kitchen utensils 242, 244, 246.
kitchenette 195.
kiwi 68.
knapsack 680.
knee 100, 106, 116, 118.
knee boot 653.
knee boot suspender 653.
knee pad 595, 602, 609.
knee roll 649.
knee sock 642.
knee-high sock 344.
knickers 336.
knife 239, 581, 587, 690.
knife 688.
knife pleat 335.
knife pleat 323.
knife-blade cartridge fuse 312.
Knight 695.
knit cap 329.
knit shirt 326.
knitting 567.
knitting machine 568.
knitting measure 567.
knitting needles 567.
knives, principal types 239.
knob 219, 596.
knob handle 284.
knockout 312.
knot 576.
knot stitches 571.
knots 691, 692.
knurled bolt 304.
kohlrabi 71.
krone 832.
kumquat 65.

L

L 38.
label 404.
label holder 517.
label maker 516.
labial palp 79, 81, 92.
labium majus 128, 129.
labium minus 128, 129.
laboratory 15.
laccolith 25.
lace 596, 644, 669.
lace carriage 568.
Lacerta 11.
lacing 645.
lacrimal duct 140.
lactiferous duct 129.
ladder 449, 487, 493, 741, 785.
ladder and hose strap 777.
ladder pipe nozzle 781.
ladder scaffold 303.
ladders 302.
ladle 801.
ladle 244.
Lady chapel 177.
Lady in the chair 11.
ladybug 77.
lagging 741.
lagoon 30.
lake 7, 27, 51.
lam 572.
lamb 150.
laminboard 288.
lamp 718.
lamp base 486.
lamp socket 309.
lamphouse elevation control 399.
lamphouse head 399.
lanceolate 56.
lancet 174.
land 281.
landing 194, 201, 736.
landing area 655, 657.
landing deck 811.
landing gear lever 500.
landing light 508.
landing net 672.
landing radar 811.
landing window 508.
lane 683.
lane 621, 655.
lane line 656.
lane number 621.
lane rope 621.
lane timekeeper 621.
language display button 422.
languid 542.
lantern 689.
lantern 263, 486.
lantern pane 486.
lapel 322, 341.
lapiaz 24.
lapis lazuli 362.
larch 58.
large blade 688.
large intestine 131.
large wheel 727.
larger round 121.
larva 82.
larynx 130, 142.
laser beam 405.
laser printer 527.
last quarter 7.
latch 253, 257, 383, 568, 681.
latch bolt 289, 290.
latch lever 562.
latch needle 568.
latch needle 569.
lateen sail 482.
lateral bar 663.
lateral condyle of femur 123.
lateral cutaneous nerve of thigh 133.
lateral filing cabinet 520.
lateral great 120, 121.
lateral groove 104.
lateral incisor 144.
lateral line 87, 620.
lateral mark 489.
lateral moraine 27.
lateral rectus muscle 140.
lateral semicircular canal 139.
lateral-adjustment lever 277.
lath 231.
lath tilt device 231.
latitude 3.
latitude scale 40.
latrines 171.
launch escape system 509.
launcher/satellite separation 419.

launching into orbit 419.
launching orbit 48.
laundry room 194.
lava flow 25.
lava layer 25.
lavatory 195.
lavatory truck 506.
lawn 193, 263.
lawn aerator 266.
lawn edger 266.
lawn rake 267.
leach field 216.
lead 620.
lead ball 804.
lead pencil 389.
lead screw 281.
lead-in wire 232.
leader 672.
leading edge 341, 499, 636, 638.
leading edge flap 812.
leading edge tube 637.
leaf 56.
leaf 57, 72.
leaf axil 56.
leaf margin 56.
leaf node 57.
leaf vegetables 73.
leakproof cap 689.
lean-to roof 182.
leash rod 574.
leather end 323.
leather goods 378.
leather sheath 690.
leather sheath 632.
leather skin 598.
leaves, types 56.
leaves, types of 58.
ledger 198.
ledger line 537.
leech 631.
leek 70.
left atrium 124, 125.
left back 601, 607, 612, 613.
left center 606.
left channel 401.
left cornerback 603, 605.
left defense 608.
left defensive end 603, 605.
left defensive tackle 603, 605.
left elevating handwheel 802.
left field 597.
left fielder 597.
left forward 610, 613.
left guard 603, 605, 610.
left half 601, 607.
left halfback 603.
left inner 607.
left kidney 132.
left lung 124, 130.
left outside linebacker 605.
left pulmonary vein 125.
left safety 603.
left safety back 605.
left service court 614, 616.
left tackle 603, 605.
left valve, shell 95.
left ventricle 124, 125.
left wing 606, 607, 608.
left winger 612.
leg 97, 117, 119, 156, 219, 224, 270,
    325, 553, 619, 659, 671.
leg curl bar 663.
leg extension bar 663.
leg position 625.
leg-of-mutton sleeve 340.
leg-warmer 353.
legging 680.
legume, section 67.
lemon 65.
length post 651.
lengthwise grain 565, 566.
lens 140, 390, 392.
lens accessories 392.
lens aperture scale 392.
lens cap 392.
lens hood 392, 409, 484.
lens mount 390.
lens release button 391.
lens system 719.
lenses 392, 722.
lenticular galaxy 9.
lentils 72.
Leo 11.
Leo Minor 11.
Leo the Lion(July 23) 820.
leotard 353.
Lepus 13.
lesser covert 110.
Lion 11.
lion 98.
lion passant 819.
lip 100, 107.

leucoplast 115.
level 736.
level crossing 464.
leveling foot 257, 258, 259.
leveling head 713.
leveling head level 713.
leveling head locking knob 713.
leveling screw 40, 709, 713.
leveling-adjustment foot 397.
lever 252, 278, 295, 296, 365, 453,
    583, 702, 798.
lever corkscrew 244.
lever cover 295.
levigator 583.
Libra 13.
Libra the Balance(September 23)
    820.
license plate light 429.
lid 247, 248, 251, 252, 253, 256, 258,
    398, 585.
lid brace 585.
lierne 177.
life buoy 495.
life raft 492.
life support system 512.
life support system controls 512.
lifeboat 478, 494, 496, 738.
lift 478.
lift arm 782.
lift bridge 457.
lift chain 293.
lift cord 231.
lift cord lock 231.
lift span 457.
lift-arm cylinder 782.
lift-fan air inlet 493.
lifting chain 787.
lifting handle 803.
lifting hook 737.
lifting lever 147.
lifting link 147.
ligament 95.
ligature 548.
light 477, 486, 487, 489, 720, 721.
light bar 779.
light machine gun 796.
light sensor 390.
light shield 16.
light signal 539.
light-load adjustment screw 712.
light-reading scale 396.
lightbox 398.
lighted mirror 368.
lighthouse 486.
lighthouse 491.
lighthouse lantern 486.
lighting 368, 500.
lighting board 412.
lighting board operator 412.
lighting cable 449.
lighting grid 414.
lighting grid access 412.
lighting technician 412.
lighting/camera control area 412.
lightning 36.
lightning arrester 747, 757.
lightning rod 197.
lights 232, 234, 236, 429.
limb 59, 684.
limb top 718.
limousine 425.
limpet 83.
line 537, 700, 701.
line gauge 671.
line hook 492.
line judge 603, 605.
line map 474.
line of scrimmage 603, 605.
linear 56.
lineman's pliers 311.
linen 224.
linen 460.
linen chest 226.
lines of latitude 47.
lines of longitude 47.
linesman 601, 605, 608, 613, 614,
    618.
lingual papillae 143.
lingual tonsil 143.
lining 322, 324, 352, 354, 378, 565,
    644.
linseed oil 592.
linstock 801.
lint filter 258.
lint trap 259.
lintel 175, 204.
Lion 11.
lion 98.
lion passant 819.
lip 100, 107.

lip makeup 366.
lip strap ring 650.
lipbrush 366.
lipid droplet 115.
lipliner 366.
lipstick 366.
liqueur glass 237.
liquid compass 484.
liquid compass, cross section 485.
liquid cooling and ventilation garment
    512.
liquid eyeliner 367.
liquid foundation 366.
liquid hydrogen tank 509.
liquid mascara 367.
liquid nitrogen tank 717.
liquid oxygen tank 509.
liquid oxygen tank baffle 509.
liquid-crystal display 706.
liquid/gas separator 439.
lira 832.
listen button 420.
lists 181.
litchi 68.
litho crayon 583.
litho pencil 583.
lithographic press 583.
lithographic printing 580.
lithographic stone 583.
lithographic tusche 583.
lithography 583.
lithography, equipment 583.
lithosphere 31.
Little Bear 11.
Little Dog 11.
little finger 137.
little finger hook 551.
Little Horse 11.
Little Lion 11.
liver 88, 97, 124, 131.
Liverpool bit 650.
livestock car 472.
living room 195, 685.
Lizard 11.
load support 635.
loading area 764.
loading bunker 734.
loading dock 190.
loading door 204.
loafer 355.
lobate 56.
lobate toe 111.
lobby 190, 504.
lobe 111.
lobster 90.
lobule 139.
local station 416.
location of the statue 169.
lock 289, 290.
lock 202, 225, 289, 380, 383, 429,
    448, 752.
lock dial 530.
lock emptying system 492.
lock filling and emptying opening 493.
lock filling and emptying system 492.
lock filling intake 493.
lock filling opening 493.
lock forward 606.
lock nut 40, 711.
lock rail 202.
lock ring 397.
lock switch 396.
lock washer 278.
lock-chamber 493.
locked groove 404.
locker 522.
locket 361.
locking button 260.
locking device 260, 302.
locking lever 471.
locking pliers 278.
locking ring 276, 802.
locknut 296.
locomotive track 465.
log 288.
log carrier 205.
log chute 746.
log tongs 205.
log, section 288.
loin 101, 117, 119.
long adductor 120.
long and short stitch 571.
long extensor of toes 120.
long jump take-off board 655.
long palmar 120.
long peroneal 120.
long radial extensor of wrist 121.
long residue 744.
long service line 618.

INDEX

The terms in **bold type** indicate the title of an illustration.

long-range jet 498.
longitude 3.
longitudinal dunes 46.
loop 324, 452.
loop stitches 571.
loophole 181.
loose curtain 228.
loose fill insulation 287.
loose powder 366.
loose powder brush 366.
lopping shears 269.
lore 109.
lorgnette 377.
lost and found articles 823.
loudspeaker 779.
loudspeakers 400.
lounge 496.
louver 214.
louver-board 175.
louvered window 203.
lovage 74.
love seat 221.
low (1 to 18) 700, 701.
low bar 659.
low beam 429.
low clouds 44.
low fuel warning light 431.
low pressure center 38.
low warp loom 572.
low-pressure steam 758.
low-tension distribution line 757.
lower blade guard 284.
lower bowl 247.
lower cheek 650.
lower chord 455.
lower eyelid 84, 107, 140.
lower fore topgallant sail 481.
lower fore topsail 481.
lower gate 492.
lower gill arch 87.
lower girdle facet (16) 363.
lower guard retracting lever 284.
lower lateral lobe 61.
lower lateral sinus 61.
lower level 493.
lower limb 793.
lower lip 142, 542.
lower lobe 130.
lower mandible 109.
lower mantle 22.
lower mast 478.
lower shell 641.
lower sphere clamp 40.
lower support screw 40.
lubber's line 485.
lubricants plànt 745.
lubricating oils 745.
lubricating system 469.
lubricator 735.
Luer-Lock tip 726.
luff 631.
lug 432, 553.
luge 643.
luggage 382.
luggage carrier 382.
luggage elastic 382.
luggage rack 445, 449, 461.
lumbar pad 602.
lumbar plexus 133.
lumbar vertebra 135.
lumbar vertebra (5) 123.
lumbar vertebrae 103.
lunar eclipse 8.
lunar features 7.
lunar module 509.
lung 97.
lunula 137.
lunule 95.
Lynx 11.
Lyra 11.
Lyre 11.
lyre 535.
lysosome 115.

M

macaroni 587.
machete 794.
machicolation 181.
machicolation 180.
machine gun 805.
machine hall 746, 747.
**machine wash in hot water at a
    normal setting** 829.
**machine wash in lukewarm water
    at a gentle setting/reduced
    agitation** 829.
**machine wash in warm water at a
    gentle setting/reduced
    agitation** 829.

**machine wash in warm water at a
    normal setting** 829.
machinery shed 148.
macro set button 409.
magazine 795, 796, 797.
magazine base 797.
magazine catch 795, 797.
magma 25, 28.
magma chamber 25.
magnet 563.
magnet 406, 485, 714.
magnetic compass 719.
magnetic damping system 708.
magnetic field 410.
magnetic gasket 254.
magnetic lid holder 256.
magnetic needle 719.
magnetic suspension 712.
magnetometer 42.
magnifier 688.
main breaker 312.
main carriage 568.
main circuit vent 215.
main cleanout 215.
main deck 811.
main duct 206.
main electric motor 806.
main engines 511.
main entrance 190, 194.
main fan 792.
main handle 280.
main inlet 741.
main landing gear 499, 812.
main lanes 452.
main leg 756.
main lever 590.
main line 464.
main lower topgallant sail 481.
main lower topsail 481.
main mirror 720.
main parachute 635.
main power cable 312.
main preview monitor 413.
main reflex mirror 390.
main return pipe 208.
main royal sail 481.
main sail 481.
main scope tube 718.
main section 700, 701.
main sewer 186.
main stalk 61.
main stand 443.
main steam header 759.
main steam pipes 759.
main supply pipe 208.
main switch 757.
main transformer 458.
main tube 720, 721.
main upper topgallant sail 481.
main upper topsail 481.
main vent 25.
main wheel 707.
mainmast 479.
mainsail 628.
mainsheet 628.
maintenance 453.
maintenance area 415.
maintenance hangar 503.
maintenance shop 734.
major amphibians 85.
major inner reaping throw 668.
major outer reaping throw 668.
makeup 366.
malar region 109.
male 831.
male cone 58.
male ferrule 670.
male genital organs 127.
male urethra 127.
mallet 275, 581, 586.
mallet 552.
mallets 553.
malleus 138.
mammary gland 129.
mandarin 63.
mandarin collar 342.
mandible 78, 80, 81, 86, 102, 122.
mandolin 535.
mane 100.
maneuvering bar 162.
maneuvering engine 511.
maneuvering lever 787, 788.
mango 63.
manhole 186, 741.
manicure 365.
manicure set 365.
manicuring implements 365.
manifold 738.
manned maneuvering unit 512.
manometer 741.

manrope 457.
mansard roof 183.
mantel 204.
mantel shelf 204.
mantle edge 92.
manual 543.
manual focusing knob 397.
manual release 641.
manual/automatic mode 585.
manually-operated switch 467.
manuals 542.
manure spreader 156.
manure spreader 154.
manway 736.
map projections 50.
Marconi cutter 482.
margin 57.
margin control 525.
margin release 527.
marginal shield 96.
marine 45.
marine diesel 745.
maritime buoyage system 488.
maritime communications 417.
maritime signals 486.
maritime transport 735.
marker 389, 515.
marker 683.
marker light 440, 441.
marker pen 588.
marking dot 565.
marks by night, rhythm 489.
Mars 4.
mars light 781.
martingale 666.
mascara brush 367.
mask 595, 627, 667.
mason's trowel 291.
masonry 291.
mass 714.
masseter 120.
mast 464, 471, 508, 628, 631, 787,
    788.
mast foot 631.
mast sleeve 631.
master bedroom 194.
master carrier 230.
master cord 645.
master gate valve 740.
masthead 479, 631.
masthead light 495.
masting 478.
mat 668.
mat 682.
matchbook 386.
matchbox 386.
matchstick 386.
material handling 786, 788.
mathematics 830.
matinee-length necklace 361.
mattress 687.
mattress 224, 726.
mattress cover 224.
maulstick 591.
maxilla 81, 86, 90, 122, 141.
maxillary bone 144.
maxillipeds 90.
maximum thermometer 41.
meadow 149.
measure of air pressure 41.
measure of angles 713.
measure of cloud ceiling 41.
measure of distance 711.
measure of humidity 41.
measure of length 711.
measure of pressure 710.
measure of rainfall 40.
measure of seismic waves 714.
measure of snowfall 41.
measure of sunshine 40.
measure of temperature 41, 705.
measure of thickness 711.
measure of time 706.
measure of weight 708.
measure of wind direction 41.
measure of wind strength 41.
measuring button 396.
measuring cups 244.
measuring spoons 244.
measuring tube 40.
measuring, utensils 244.
meat 33.
meat grinder 243.
meat keeper 254.
meat thermometer 244.
mechanical connectors 300.
mechanical pencil 389, 515.
mechanical shovel 733.
mechanical stage 718.
mechanical stage control 718.

mechanical variometer 639.
mechanical watch 706.
mechanics 453.
medial condyle of femur 123.
medial great 120.
medial moraine 26.
medial rectus muscle 140.
median 452.
median groove 104.
median lingual sulcus 143.
median nerve 133.
median strip 184.
Mediterranean Sea 21.
Mediterranean subtropical 45.
medium 666.
medium format SLR (6 x 6) 395.
medium tension distribution line 757.
medulla 132.
medulla oblongata 134.
Meissner's corpuscle 136.
melody strings 535.
meltwater 27.
memo pad 518.
memory button 402, 420.
memory cancel 396, 523.
memory key 396, 405.
memory recall 523.
memory recall key 396.
men 697.
men's bag 380.
men's clothing 319, 320, 322, 324.
men's rest room 822.
Mercury 4, 232.
mercury barometer 41.
mercury bulb 705.
merging traffic 824.
méridienne 221.
merlon 181.
mesa 46.
mesh 619.
mesocarp 62, 63, 64, 65.
mesosphere 19.
mesothorax 78.
message display 532.
metacarpus 102, 107, 122.
metal A 307.
metal arm 264.
metal B 307.
metal counterhoop 553.
metal frame 540.
metal head 658.
metal rail 517.
metal rod 554.
metal structure 463.
metallic contact grid 768.
metallic plastron 667.
metals 33.
metals, examples 819.
metamorphic rocks 23.
metatarsus 80, 103, 122.
metathorax 78.
meteorology 38.
**meteorology, measuring
    instruments** 40.
meteorology, station model 38.
metronome 539.
mezzanine 195, 474.
mezzanine floor 194.
mezzanine stairs 195.
Michigan snowshoe 645.
micrometer caliper 711.
micrometer screw 484, 713.
microphone 407, 414, 420, 639.
microphone boom 412, 414.
microphone boom tripod 414.
microprocessor 528.
microwave dish 415.
microwave oven 253.
microwave scanner 43.
microwave transmitter 415.
mid-calf length 325.
mid-ocean ridge 28.
middle clouds 44.
middle covert 110.
middle ear 138.
middle finger 137.
middle jib 481.
middle leg 79, 80.
middle leg, honeybee 80.
middle linebacker 603, 605.
middle lobe 130.
middle nasal concha 141.
middle panel 202.
middle phalanx 107, 122, 123, 137.
middle piece 127.
middle primary covert 110.
middle sole 352.
middle toe 108.
middle torus 167.

INDEX

The terms in bold type indicate the title of an illustration.

middy 337.
midrange 16, 400.
midrange pickup 547.
midrib 56, 67.
midriff band 346.
Mihrab 173.
Mihrab dome 173.
military communications 417.
milk bread 153.
Milky Way 11.
millet 152.
minaret 172, 173.
Minbar 173.
miners' changing-room 735.
mini shirtdress 337.
mini-floppy disk 529.
minimum thermometer 41.
minivan 425.
mint 74.
minute 830.
minute hand 706, 707.
mirror 292, 382, 442, 444.
missile launch rail 813.
missile launcher 811.
missile stowage 808.
missile, structure 814.
missiles 814.
missiles, major types 814.
mist 37, 39.
miter gate recess 493.
miter gauge 285.
miter gauge slot 285.
mitochondrion 115.
mitral valve 125.
mitt 327.
mitten 308, 327.
mitten 680.
mixing bowl 250.
mixing bowls 245.
mixing chamber 306.
mizzen royal brace 480.
mizzen royal staysail 480.
mizzen sail 480.
mizzen topgallant staysail 480.
mizzen topmast staysail 480.
mizzenmast 478.
moat 178, 181.
mobile drawer unit 521.
mobile filing unit 521.
mobile passenger stairs 507.
mobile unit 415.
mobile unit 416.
moccasin 355.
mock pocket 330.
mode 525.
mode selector 402.
mode selectors 408.
modem 526.
modem port 528.
moderator 766.
moderator tank 761.
moderator: graphite 760.
moderator: heavy water 761.
moderator: natural water 762, 763.
modern bow 793.
modern howitzer 802.
modern mortar 803.
modesty panel 521.
modillion 167.
modulation wheel 555.
Mohorovicic discontinuity 22.
moist surface 580.
moistener 516.
moisture in the air 34.
molar 98.
molar, cross section 144.
molars 144.
moldboard 156.
molded insulation 287.
molding 199.
mollusk 92.
monitor roof 182.
monitor wall 412, 413, 415.
monocle 377.
mons pubis 128.
monster 605.
monument 52.
Moon 4, 8.
Moon dial 707.
Moon's orbit 8.
Moon, phases 6.
moons 4.
mooring chain 486.
moose 105.
mordent 538.
morel 55.
mortar 243, 803.
mortise 385.
mortise lock 290.

mosaic 171.
mosque 172.
mosque, plan 173.
moss stitch 567.
motor 161, 214, 257, 258, 259, 270, 271, 272, 283, 284.
motor air inlet 813.
motor car 476, 477.
motor end plate 134.
motor home 449.
motor neuron 135.
motor root 135.
motor truck 459.
motor unit 250, 251, 256, 260, 373, 458.
motorcycle 442, 444.
motorcycle dashboard 445.
motorcycle, dashboard 445.
motorized earth auger 270.
mount frame binder 397.
mountain 27.
mountain mass 51.
mountain range 7, 23, 51.
mountain slope 27.
mountain torrent 27.
mountaineer 680.
mountaineering 680.
mountaineering boot 680.
mountaineering shovel 680.
mountaineering, equipment 681.
mounting 666.
mounting bracket 684.
mounting foot 393.
mounting plate 233.
mounting point 501.
mouse 530.
mouse 526, 527.
mouth 142.
mouth 83, 84, 92, 118, 542, 650.
mouthparts 81.
mouthpiece 548, 550, 627, 669.
mouthpiece receiver 550.
mouthpipe 550.
movable bridges 457.
movable jaw 279, 282.
movable maxillary 96.
movie theater 496.
moving coil 406.
mowing 154, 158.
Mt Everest 19.
mud flap 427, 440, 441.
mud injection hose 737.
mud pit 737.
mud pump 737.
mudguard 147.
muff 381.
muffin pan 245.
muffler 439.
muffler felt 540.
muffler pedal 540.
mule 355.
mullet 819.
multi-ply plywood 288.
multi-purpose ladder 303.
multimeter 310.
multiple exposure mode 391.
multiple use key 523.
multiple-span beam bridge 454.
multiplication 830.
multiply key 523.
multipurpose antenna 807.
multipurpose tool 311.
multipurpose vehicle 425.
mummy 687.
muntin 202, 203.
Musca 13.
muscle fiber 134.
muscle scar 95.
muscle segment 89.
muscles 120.
museum 185.
mushroom 55.
mushroom anchor 483.
mushroom, structure 55.
music rest 539.
music stand 539.
music stand 542, 555.
musical accessories 539.
musical advisers 412.
musical notation 537, 538.
muskmelon 69.
mustard 67.
mute 551.
mutule 167.
muzzle 100, 106, 107, 797, 798, 799, 800, 803.
muzzle loading 800.
muzzle loading, cross section 801.
mycelium 55.
myelin sheath 135.

N

nacelle 774.
nacreous cloud 19.
nail 275.
nail 104.
nail bed 137.
nail cleaner 365.
nail clippers 365.
nail file 365.
nail hole 104.
nail matrix 137.
nail nick 688.
nail scissors 365.
nail shaper 365.
nail whitener pencil 365.
naked strangle 668.
name plate 280, 712.
nameplate 364.
naos 169.
nape 108, 117, 119.
naris 141.
nasal bone 141.
nasal cavity 130.
nasal fossae 141.
nasopharynx 141.
national broadcasting network 416.
national park 52.
natural 538.
natural arch 30.
natural sponge 367.
nave 177.
navel 116, 118.
navette cut 363.
navigation devices 484.
navigation display 500.
navigation light 493, 499.
navigation periscope 807.
Neapolitan coffee maker 247.
neck 97, 100, 117, 118, 119, 127, 144, 240, 241, 410, 544, 545, 546, 547, 579, 661, 678.
neck end 324.
neck guard 777.
neck of femur 123.
neck strap 279.
neckhole 325.
necklaces 361.
necklines 343.
neckroll 224.
necks 343.
neckstrap eyelet 390.
necktie 324.
nectarine 63.
needle 562, 632.
needle 36, 561, 562, 563, 590, 726.
needle assembly 590.
needle bar 562.
needle bed 568.
needle bed 568.
needle bed groove 568.
needle clamp 562.
needle clamp screw 562.
needle hub 726.
needle plate 561.
needle position selector 561.
needle threader 563.
needle tool 585.
needle-nose pliers 311.
negative 399.
negative carrier 399.
negative carrier 399.
negative charge 831.
negative contact 768, 769.
negative meniscus 722.
negative plate 439.
negative plate strap 439.
negative region 768.
negative terminal 439.
negligee 348.
neon lamp 310.
neon tester 310.
Neptune 5.
nerve 136.
nerve fiber 136.
nerve termination 136.
nervous system 133, 134.
nest of tables 219.
Net 13, 610, 612, 613, 614, 618, 619, 626.
net 613, 614, 618.
net band 614.
net judge 614.
net stocking 344.
net support 619.
netball 611.
netball, court 611.
network communication 527.
network port 528.
neural spine 89.

neurons 135.
neutral conductor 757.
neutral indicator 445.
neutral service wire 312.
neutral wire 312.
neutral zone 603, 605, 608.
new crescent 6.
new fuel storage room 764.
new moon 6.
newel post 201.
next call 422.
nib 389.
nictitating membrane 107.
nightgown 348.
nightwear 348.
nimbostratus 44.
nipple 301.
nipple 116, 118, 129.
no access for wheelchairs 822.
no entry 824, 825.
no U-turn 824, 825.
no. 3 iron 678.
no. 3 wood 678.
no. 4 iron 678.
no. 5 iron 678.
no. 5 wood 678.
no. 6 iron 678.
no. 7 iron 678.
no. 8 forward 606.
no. 8 iron 678.
no. 9 iron 678.
nock 684, 793.
nocking point 684.
noctilucent cloud 19.
node 756.
node of Ranvier 135.
non-add/subtotal 523.
North 488.
North America 20.
North American road signs 824, 826, 828.
North celestial pole 3.
North Pole 3.
North Sea 21.
North Star 11.
Northeast 488.
Northern Crown 11.
Northern hemisphere 3, 47.
Northwest 488.
nose 141.
nose 100, 118, 498, 637, 638, 792, 798.
nose cone 501.
nose landing gear 498.
nose leaf 112.
nose leather 107.
nose of the quarter 352, 354.
nose pad 376.
noseband 649.
nosing 201.
nostril 84, 86, 96, 100, 109.
notch 322, 341, 565, 656, 674, 708.
notched double-edged thinning scissors 369.
notched edge 369.
notched lapel 319, 320.
notched single-edged thinning scissors 369.
note symbols 538.
nozzle 209, 264, 291, 304, 509, 510, 590, 778.
nuchal shield 97.
nuclear boiler room 806.
nuclear energy 758, 760, 762, 764, 766.
nuclear envelope 115.
nuclear fuel handling sequence 764.
nuclear generating station 758.
nuclear reactor 765.
nuclear whorl 94.
nucleolus 115, 128.
nucleus 9, 115, 128, 135.
number 656, 701.
number key 423, 523.
number of decimals 523.
number of tracks sign 471.
number three 620.
number two 620.
numbering machine 516.
numeric keyboard 422, 709.
numeric keypad 530.
nut 279.
nut 278, 279, 290, 300, 466, 544, 546, 547, 793.
nutcracker 243.
nuts 66.
nuts, major types 66.
nylon rumba tights 349.
nylon yarn 271.

The terms in **bold type** indicate the title of an illustration.

O

o-ring 294, 295.
oar 664.
oarlock 632.
oars, types 632.
oasis 46.
oats 152.
object balls 673.
objective 718.
objective lens 391, 392, 396, 397, 405, 718, 719, 721.
oboe 548.
oboes 557.
obscured sky 39.
observation deck 505.
observation window 510.
observatory 14.
obstacles 647.
obturator nerve 133.
obtuse angle 830.
occipital 121.
occipital bone 123.
occluded front 39.
ocean 7, 35, 51.
ocean floor 28.
ocean, topography 28.
Oceania 21.
oche 698.
octave 537, 667.
octave mechanism 548.
odd 700, 701.
odd pinnate 56.
odometer 431.
offense 603.
offense 605.
office 453, 462.
office building 190.
office building 185, 491.
office furniture 520, 522.
office tower 184, 190.
officers' quarters 807, 808.
officials' bench 608.
offset 301.
offshore drilling 739.
offshore well 740.
ogee 174.
ogee roof 182.
oil 737, 738, 740, 744.
oil 737.
oil burner 209.
oil drain plug 434.
oil paint 588.
oil pan 272, 434.
oil pan gasket 434.
oil pastel 588.
oil pressure warning indicator 445.
oil processing area 738.
oil pump 209.
oil supply inlet 209.
oil supply line 209.
oil terminal 491.
oil warning light 431.
oil-filled heater 211.
oil/gas separator 738.
oiler 734.
oilstone 582.
okra 69.
old crescent 7.
old-fashioned glass 237.
olecranon 102, 123.
olfactory bulb 88, 142.
olfactory membrane 142.
olfactory nerve 88, 142.
olive 63.
on guard line 666.
on the wind 629.
on-air warning light 407.
on-deck circle 597.
on-off button 256.
on-off indicator 370.
on-off switch 234, 247, 260, 305, 368, 370, 373, 374, 485.
on/off 408.
on/off light 420.
on/off switch 391, 397, 406.
on/off/volume 408.
on/play button 420.
1 m springboard 624.
one pair 695.
one way head 276.
one-arm shoulder throw 668.
one-bar shoe 356.
one-person tent 686.
one-piece coverall 635.
one-piece suit 643.
1/10th second hand 706.
120-volt circuit 312.
one-toe hoof 99.

one-way traffic 824, 825.
opal 362.
open end wrench 279.
open stringer 201.
open strings 535.
open-air terrace 497.
open-face spinning reel 671.
open-pit mine 733.
opening 327.
opening, utensils 244.
opera glasses 377.
opera-length necklace 361.
operating cord 230.
operating dam 752.
operating floor 752.
operating rod 796.
operation control room 807.
operation keys 422.
operator's cab 786.
operculum 84, 86.
Ophiuchus 11, 13.
opisthodomos 169.
opposite prompt side 189.
optic chiasm 134.
optic nerve 140.
optical disk 527.
optical disk drive 527.
optical scanner 526.
optical sight 713.
or 819.
oral cavity 130, 131.
oral hygiene center 373.
oral irrigator 373.
orange 65.
orange 65.
orbicular of eye 120.
orbiculate 56.
orbit of the satellites 43.
orbits of the planets 4.
orchard 149.
orchestra pit 188.
orchestra seats 188.
order 175.
ordinaries, examples 818.
ordinary die 699.
ore 733.
ore pass 736.
oregano 74.
organ 542.
organ console 542.
organ, mechanism 543.
organ, production of sound 543.
Oriental couching stitch 571.
oriflamme 817.
original overlay 532.
Orion 11, 13.
ornamental tree 148, 263.
ornaments 538.
ortho-cane 728.
oscillating sprinkler 264.
otolith 88.
ottoman 222.
outbound track 465.
outdoor condensing unit 212.
outdoor light 196.
outdoor unit 212.
outer boundary line 616.
outer circle 620.
outer core 22.
outer edge 104.
outer jacket 297.
outer jib 481.
outer lip 94.
outer shell 309.
outer stators 501.
outer table 697.
outer toe 108.
outgoing announcement cassette 420.
outlet 309.
outlet 449.
outlet grille 211.
outlet hose 399.
output devices 527.
output jack 547.
output monitor 413, 415.
outrigger 632, 780, 785, 786.
outside counter 354.
outside knob 290.
outside left 601.
outside linebacker 603.
outside mirror 426.
outside mirror control 429.
outside right 601.
outside ticket pocket 322.
outsole 353, 355.
outwash plain 27.
oval cut 363.
oval head 276.
ovary 60, 128, 129.
ovate 56.

oven 255.
oven control knob 255.
over-blouse 337.
overalls 336.
overburden 733.
overcast sky 39.
overcheck 653.
overcoat 320, 331.
overdrapery 229.
overflow 215, 292.
overflow pipe 297.
overflow protection switch 257.
overflow tube 293, 399.
overhand knot 691.
overhead clearance 826, 827.
overhead connection 757.
overhead frame 784.
overhead ground wire 756.
overhead guard 787.
overhead switch panel 500.
overlap carrier 230.
overlay flooring 200.
overpass 452, 454.
ovule 60.
ox 151.
oxer 646.
oxford shoe 354.
oxyacetylene welding 306.
oxygen cylinder 306.
oxygen feeding control 639.
oxygen feeding knob 639.
oxygen pressure actuator 512.
oxygen valve 306.
oyster 92.
oyster 93.
oyster fork 240.
oyster knife 242.
oyster mushroom 55.
ozone 19.

P

pace 101.
Pacific Ocean 20.
Pacinian corpuscle 136.
packing 294.
packing nut 294.
packing retainer ring 294.
pad 598.
pad arm 376.
pad plate 376.
padding 635.
paddock 651.
pagoda sleeve 340.
paint roller 304.
painted line 452.
Painter's Easel 13.
painting 588, 590, 592.
painting knife 589.
painting upkeep 304.
painting, accessories 591, 592.
painting, equipment 589.
pajamas 348.
palatine tonsil 143.
palatoglossal arch 142.
pale 818.
palette with dipper 592.
palette with hollows 592.
paling fence 263.
pallet 543, 707, 787.
pallet spring 543.
pallet truck 788.
pallial line 95.
pallial sinus 95.
palm 105, 137, 327, 483, 596.
palm grove 46.
palmar pad 106.
palmate 56.
palmette 220.
pan 708, 709, 795.
pan cover 795.
pan hook 708.
panama 328.
pancake pan 249.
pancreas 131.
pane 203.
panel 589.
panel 589.
panel 202, 229, 323, 346, 634, 649, 736, 756.
panoramic head 393.
panoramic window 190, 460.
panpipe 536.
pantograph 458.
pantry 195.
pants 323.
pants 353, 595, 602, 609, 680.
pants, types 336.
panty corselette 347.
panty girdle 346.
panty hose 344.

papaya 68.
paper 589.
paper 384, 580.
paper advance setting 531.
paper bail 524, 531.
paper bail release lever 525.
paper bail roller 531.
paper catcher 521.
paper clamp 531.
paper clips 515.
paper fasteners 515.
paper feed channel 521.
paper feed key 523.
paper guide 421, 531.
paper in reserve 532.
paper punch 516.
paper release lever 525.
paper support 525.
paper tray 521.
paper trays 532.
papilla 136, 140.
papillary muscle 125.
parabolic antenna 415.
parabolic dune 46.
parabolic mirror 770.
parabolic reflector 15.
parachute 812.
parachute valve 634.
parade ground 178.
paraffins 745.
paragliding 636.
paragliding pilot 636.
parallel 47.
parallel bars 661.
parapet 454.
parapet walk 181.
parcels office 462.
parentheses 832.
parietal bone 123.
parietal pleura 130.
paring knife 242.
park 52, 184.
parka 321.
parka 680.
parking 190, 193, 464.
parking area 503.
parking brake lever 430.
parking lot 185, 491, 504.
parsley 74.
parsnip 71.
parterre 189.
partial eclipse 8.
particle board 289.
partition 520.
partition 66.
partitions, examples 818.
partlow chart 441.
party 818.
pass 27.
passenger cabin 493, 494, 495, 499.
passenger car 477.
passenger car 458, 476.
passenger liner 496.
passenger platform 462.
passenger station 462.
passenger station 184, 464.
passenger terminal 504.
passenger terminal 491, 503.
passenger train 462.
passenger transfer vehicle 507.
passenger transfer vehicle 505.
passing lane 452.
passing prohibited 824, 825.
passport case 379.
passport control 505.
pasta maker 243.
pastern 101.
pastry bag and nozzles 245.
pastry brush 245.
pastry cutting wheel 245.
patch pocket 339.
patch pocket 320, 322, 350.
patella 103, 122.
patera 220.
path 263.
patio 193, 263.
patio door 195.
pattern 565, 586.
pattern 570.
pattern start key 569.
pauldron 792.
pause 539.
pause button 403.
pause/still 411, 831.
pavilion 8.
pavilion facet (8) 363.
pavilion roof 183.
Pavo 13.
pawl 281.
Pawn 696.

pay phone 422.
payload 509.
payload bay 510.
payload bay door 510.
payload module 49.
payout tray 702.
payout trigger 702.
pea 67.
pea jacket 330.
peach 63.
peach 63.
Peacock 13.
peak 27, 328, 329, 729.
peak level meter 403.
peaked lapel 322.
peanut 66.
pear 64.
pear-shaped body 535.
pear-shaped cut 363.
pearl 105.
pearls 105.
pecan nut 66.
pecten 81.
pectoral deck 663.
pectoral fin 86.
pectoral limb 124.
pedal 446, 448, 545, 552, 553, 656, 664.
pedal key 542.
pedal keyboard 542.
pedal pushers 336.
pedal rod 540.
pedestal 453, 545.
pedestal-type sump pump 216.
pedestrian crossing 826, 827.
pedestrian crossing 186.
pedicel 60, 61, 62, 63, 64.
pedicle 105.
pediment 166, 168, 707.
pedometer 711.
peeled veneer 288.
peeler 242.
peep hole 471.
peg 225, 385, 544, 546, 571, 575.
peg box 544.
Pegasus 11.
pelerine 330.
pellets 799.
peltate 55.
Pelton runner 754.
pelvic fin 86.
pelvic limb 124.
pelvis 103.
pen 714.
pen blade 688.
pen holder 379.
pen holder 378.
penalty arc 601.
penalty area 601.
penalty area marking 601.
penalty bench 608.
penalty line 612.
penalty spot 601.
pencil 389, 515.
pencil 765.
pencil pleat heading 229.
pencil point tip 299, 307.
pencil sharpener 515, 516.
pendant 361.
pendulum 707.
pendulum bar 539.
pendulum rod 707.
penholder grip 619.
peninsula 51.
penis 116, 127.
pennant 817.
pennant 38.
penstock 746, 747, 752.
pentaprism 390.
penumbra shadow 8.
peplos 315.
pepper shaker 238.
per bend 818.
per fess 818.
percent 830.
percent key 523.
perching bird 111.
percolator 247.
percussion bar 780.
percussion instruments 552, 554.
perforated hardboard 289.
perforated pipe 216.
perforated toe cap 355.
perforation 327, 395.
pergola 263.
pericardium 130.
pericarp 65, 66.
period 832.
period 489.
periodontal ligament 144.

periople 104.
peripheral device port 528.
peripheral joint 750.
peripheral nervous system 133.
periscopic sight 805.
peristyle 168, 169, 171.
peritoneum 127, 128.
permanent pasture 148.
peroxide 725.
perpendicular 830.
perpetual snows 27.
perron 196.
Perseus 11.
personal communications 417.
personal computer 526.
personal computer (view from above) 528.
personal radio cassette player 408.
peseta 832.
pesticides 32.
pestle 243.
petal 60.
petanque bowl 682.
Peter Pan collar 341.
petiolar sinus 61.
petiole 56.
petrochemical industry 744.
petrochemicals 745.
phalanx prima 103.
phalanx secunda 103.
phalanx tertia 103.
pharmacy 822.
pharynx 130, 131.
phase conductor 757.
phases of the Moon 6.
philtrum 141.
phloem 59.
Phobos 4.
Phoenix 13.
phosphorescent coating 232.
photocopier 532.
photocopy control 532.
photoelectric cell 393.
photographic accessories 393.
photographic chamber 717.
photographic picture 397.
photography 390, 392, 394, 396, 398.
photosphere 6.
photovoltaic panel 486, 487.
physical map 51.
physician 669.
pi 830.
piano 556.
piccolo 548, 557.
pick 267.
pick 385, 681.
pickguard 547.
pickling onion 70.
pickup cylinder 159, 162.
pickup reel 158, 160.
pickup selector 547.
pickup truck 425.
picnic area 823.
picnics prohibited 823.
Pictor 13.
picture tube 410.
pie pan 245.
piedmont glacier 27.
pier 739.
pier 174, 175, 454, 455.
pierce lever 256.
pierced earrings 361.
pig 151.
piggyback car 473.
pigsty 149.
pike pole 780.
pike position 624.
pile dwelling 165.
pillar 176, 545, 714, 736.
pillar buoy 487.
pillar buoy 489.
pillbox hat 329.
pillion footrest 443, 444.
pillow 570.
pillow 224, 570.
pillow protector 224.
pillowcase 224.
pilot 459, 469, 637, 814.
pilot gas tube 297.
pin 232, 233, 563, 683, 780.
pin base 232.
pin block 540.
pin cushion 563.
pince-nez 377.
pinch 251.
pinch pleat 228.
pine needles 58.
pine nut 66.

pine seed 58.
pineal body 134.
pineapple 68.
pinion 280, 707.
pink ball 673.
pinking shears 564.
pinnacle 176, 181.
pinnatifid 56.
pinocytotic vesicle 115.
pins 364.
pins, types 683.
pip 62, 64, 65, 695.
pipe 385.
pipe 260, 543.
pipe A 300.
pipe B 300.
pipe cleaners 385.
pipe coupling 301.
pipe diffusers 501.
pipe rack 385.
pipe section 205.
pipe threader 299.
pipe tools 385.
pipe wrench 299.
pipe, cross section 385.
pipe-wrapping insulation 287.
pipeline 740.
pipework 543.
Pisces 11.
Pisces the Fishes(February 19) 820.
Piscis Austrinus 13.
pistachio nut 66.
piste 666.
pistil 60.
pistol 797.
pistol grip 795, 796, 798, 799.
pistol grip handle 280, 305.
pistol nozzle 264.
piston 432, 435, 436, 438.
piston lever 291.
piston release 291.
piston skirt 434.
pit 96, 405, 683.
pita bread 153.
pitch 599.
pitch 599.
pitch scale 524.
pitch wheel 555.
pitched roof 182.
pitcher 597.
pitcher's mound 597.
pitcher's plate 597.
pitchfork comb 368.
pitching 748.
pitching wedge 678.
pith 59.
pithead 734.
pithead 736.
piton 681.
piton-carrier 680.
pituitary gland 134.
pivot 311, 369, 374, 484, 485, 539, 564, 590, 719.
pivot cab 785.
placard board 471.
placing judge 621.
plain 51.
plain gypsum lath 286.
plain pole 230.
plain weave 576.
plan reading, elevation 193.
plane 277.
plane figure 580.
plane projection 50.
planetarium 16.
planetarium 184.
planetarium projector 16.
planets 4.
planets, orbits 4.
plano-concave lens 722.
plano-convex lens 722.
plant cell 115.
plant, structure 57.
plantar 121.
plantar interosseous 120.
plantar pad 107.
plantar surface of the hoof 104.
planting 154, 158.
planting box 657.
plasmodesma 115.
plaster bat 584.
plastic case 799.
plastic insulator 312.
plastic pants 349.
plastic-laminated particle board 289.
plastron 96.
plate 688.
plate 253, 393.

plate crystal 36.
plate grid 439.
plateau 27, 51.
platen 524, 531, 579.
platen knob 531.
platform 302, 457, 475, 504, 621, 709.
platform edge 462, 475.
platform entrance 463.
platform ladder 302.
platform number 462.
platform pallet truck 788.
platform shelter 464.
platter 238.
platter 404.
play 831.
play 411.
play button 403, 408, 411.
play/pause 405.
player 626.
player's number 602.
player's stick 609.
players' bench 604, 608, 610, 612, 613.
playing area 496.
playing surface 619.
playing window 403.
pleasure garden 263.
pleasure garden 193.
pleated heading 229.
pleats, types 228, 335.
plectrum 535.
plenum 206, 207.
pleural cavity 130.
plexus of nerves 144.
plinth 707.
plotter 527.
plow anchor 483.
plowing soil 154, 156.
plug 280, 400, 401, 406, 485.
plug adapter 374.
plug bayonet 794.
plug fuse 312.
plum 63.
plumber's snake 299.
plumbing 292, 294, 296, 298, 299, 300.
plumbing system 215.
plumbing tools 299.
plunger 247, 299.
plunger 726.
plungerhead 159.
plunging neckline 343.
plus or minus 830.
plus/equals key 523.
Pluto 5.
ply 288.
pneumatic armlet 710.
pneumatic hammer 735.
pocket 378, 673, 679, 683.
pocket calculator 523.
pocket camera 395.
pocket handkerchief 322.
pockets, types 339.
podium 190.
podium 190.
point 240, 242, 389, 544, 562, 567, 644, 671, 684, 697, 698.
point of interest 52.
point wire 467.
pointed tab end 324, 339.
pointer 213, 705, 708, 709, 710.
poison 821.
poisonous mushroom 55.
poker 205.
poker die 699.
poker, standard hands 695.
polar axis 14.
polar climates 45.
polar ice cap 45.
polar lights 19.
polar maritime 38.
polar orbit 43.
polar tundra 45.
polar-orbiting satellite 43.
Polaris 11.
polarizing filter 392.
Polaroid® Land camera 394.
pole 657.
pole 230, 479.
pole grip 642.
pole shaft 642.
pole tip 643.
pole vault 657.
pole vault 655.
poleyn 792.
police 822.
polished stone hand axe 791.
political map 51.
pollen basket 81.

pollen brush 80, 81.
pollen cell 82.
pollen packer 81.
pollution, atmospheric 34.
pollution, food 32.
polo collar 342.
polo dress 333.
polo shirt 337.
polo shirt 615.
polojama 351.
pome fleshy fruits 64.
pome fruit, section 64.
pome fruits, major types 64.
pomegranate 68.
pommel 649, 661, 666.
pommel horse 661.
poncho 331.
pond 263.
poniard 794.
pons Varolii 134.
pontoon 457, 738.
pool 673.
pool 772.
poop 478.
pop-up tent 686.
popping crease 599.
poppy 67.
porch 172, 177.
porch dome 172, 173.
pore 67, 115, 136.
Porro prism 719.
port 650, 764.
port glass 237.
port hand 488, 489, 497.
**portable CD radio cassette
  recorder** 408.
portable cellular telephone 422.
portable fire extinguisher 780.
portable shower head 292.
portable sound systems 408.
portal 175.
portal bridge 455.
portal frame 455.
portal vein 124, 126.
porthole 496.
position light 459, 508.
position marker 546, 547.
position of the ligament 95.
positive charge 831.
positive contact 768, 769.
positive meniscus 722.
positive plate 439.
positive plate strap 439.
positive region 768.
positive terminal 439.
positive/negative junction 768.
post 572, 613, 618, 626, 773.
post and plank 647.
post and plank 646.
post and rail 647.
post binder 519.
post lantern 235.
post mill 773.
posterior chamber 140.
posterior cutaneous nerve of thigh 133.
posterior end 95.
posterior root 135.
posterior rugae 117, 119.
posterior semicircular canal 139.
postern 179, 181.
potable water truck 506.
potato 71.
potato masher 244.
potential coil 712.
pothole 24.
pottery 584.
pottery, tools 584, 585.
pouch 380.
pouch of Douglas 128.
poulaine 792.
poultry shears 246.
pound 832.
powder blusher 366.
powder chamber 801.
powder flask 795.
powder puff 366.
power button 402, 405, 410, 411.
power car 459.
power cord 374.
power indicator 529.
power mower 271.
power plant, cross section 752.
power plug 408.
power station 752.
power supply cord 370.
power switch 509, 555.
power switch machine 467.
power takeoff 147.
power train 448.
power turbines 501.

power zoom button 409.
power-off/slide-select bar 397.
power-on button 420.
power-on light 420.
power-takeoff shaft 156, 159, 162.
power/light switch 561.
powerhouse 746.
practice green 676.
prairie 51.
prayer hall 172, 173.
precious stones 362.
precipitation 34, 35.
precipitation area 38.
precipitations 36.
preferred channel 489.
premaxilla 86.
premolar 98.
premolars 144.
prepuce 127.
prescription 831.
present state of weather 38.
present weather 39.
preset buttons 411.
preset tuning button 402.
president 666.
press bar 663.
press bed 581, 583.
press chamber 159.
press wheel 158.
pressed area 405.
pressed powder 366.
presser bar 562.
presser foot 562.
pressing 579.
pressing board 579.
pressure bar 540.
pressure change 38.
pressure control 373.
pressure control valve 710.
pressure cooker 248.
pressure demand regulator 777.
pressure dial 561.
pressure gauge 627, 710, 740.
pressure plate 390.
pressure regulator 306.
pressure regulator 248, 306, 689.
pressure relief valve 209.
pressure screw 581, 583.
pressure tube 765.
pressure vessel 762.
pressure-relief valve 297.
pressurized-water reactor 762.
pressurizer 761.
prestressed concrete 286.
preview monitor 415.
preview monitors 413.
price per gallon/liter 453.
pricker 570.
primaries 110.
primary consumers 31.
primary covert 110.
primary flight display 500.
primary mirror 14, 16.
primary root 57.
prime 667.
prime focus 14.
prime focus observing capsule 14.
prime meridian 47.
primer 798, 799, 804.
princess dress 332.
princess seaming 345.
principal rafter 199.
print drying rack 399.
print head 531.
print head drive 531.
print washer 399.
printed circuit 528.
printed image 580.
printer 417, 523.
printer port 528.
printer table 521.
printing 580.
printing calculator 523.
printing of messages 421.
printing unit 524.
printout 709.
priority intersection 825.
prism binoculars 719.
private broadcasting network 416.
probe 310.
probe receptacle 253.
proboscis 79.
procedure checklist 512.
producer 412, 415.
producer turret 407.
product code 709.
production adviser 412.
production control room 413.
production control room 412, 415.

production desk 413.
**production of electricity from
  nuclear energy** 766.
**production of electricity from
  solar energy** 771.
production of electricity, steps
  755.
production platform 738.
production platform 740.
production video switcher 413.
production/export riser system 738.
program selector 555.
progressive wave 30.
projectiles 801.
projection dome 16.
projection screen 397.
proleg 78.
promenade deck 496.
prominence 6.
prompt box 188.
prompt side 189.
pronaos 168, 169.
prop forward 606.
propane gas cylinder 449.
propellant 798.
propellant level gauge 512.
propeller 160, 495, 496, 806.
propeller duct 492.
propeller shaft 495.
propellers 808.
property line 193.
propulsion machinery control room
  806.
propulsion module 418.
proscenium 188.
prostate 127.
protect tab 529.
protection layer 512.
protective cup 602, 609.
protective equipment 602.
protective girdle 609.
protective helmet 443.
protective helmet 448.
protective surround 698.
protective window 410.
prothorax 78.
protoneuron 135.
protractor 713.
province 51.
proximal phalanx 107, 122, 123.
proximal sesamoid 102.
proximity fuse 814.
pruning knife 269.
pruning saw 269.
pruning shears 269.
psychrometer 41.
pubis 116, 118.
public building 52.
public garden 190.
puck 608.
puff sleeve 340.
pull bail 397.
pull rod 467.
pull strap 383.
pulley 230, 302, 434, 793.
pulley block 793.
pulley safety guard 283.
pulling ring 726.
pullman case 383.
pulmonary artery 126, 130.
pulmonary opening 83.
pulmonary trunk 125.
pulmonary valve 125.
pulmonary vein 126.
pulp 65, 144.
pulp chamber 144.
pulverizing soil 154, 157.
pulvino 750.
pumice correcting pencil 583.
pump 356.
pump 257, 258, 689, 761, 762, 771.
pump island 453.
pump motor 216.
pump nozzle 453.
pump suction head 216.
pumper 778.
pumpernickel bread 153.
pumping station 740.
pumpkin 69.
punch 586.
punch hole 323, 353, 355.
punctuation marks 832.
pup tent 686.
pupil 107, 140.
Puppis 13.
purfling 544, 546.
purge valve 627.
purple border 315.
purpure 819.
purse 379.

push button 250, 257, 375.
push buttons 420, 422.
push rim 727.
push-button 290, 389, 397.
push-button telephone 422.
push-up bra 347.
push-up stand 664.
pusher 251.
putter 677.
putter 678.
putting green 676.
pygal shield 96.
pylon 756.
pylon body 756.
pylon foot 756.
pylon top 756.
pylon window 756.
pyloric cecum 88.
pyramid spot 674.
pyrometric cone 585.
Pyxis 13.

Q

Qibla wall 173.
quad cane 728.
quarte 667.
quarter 104, 352, 354.
quarter note 538.
quarter rest 538.
quarter window 427.
quarter-deck 496.
quarterback 603, 605.
quarterly 818.
quartet 558.
quartz metronome 539.
quay 490.
quay ramp 490.
quayside crane 490.
quayside railway 491.
Queen 695.
Queen 695.
queen cell 82.
queen excluder 82.
Queen's side 696.
queen, honeybee 81.
question mark 832.
quiche plate 245.
quick release system 393.
quill 385.
quill 281, 283.
quill brush 368.
quince 64.
quinte 667.
quintet 558.
quiver 684.
quotation marks 832.
quotation marks (French) 832.

R

raceme 60.
rachis 110.
rack 674.
rack 248, 252, 255, 257, 656.
rackboard 543.
rackboard support 543.
racquetball 617.
racquetball racket 617.
racquetball, court 617.
radar 722.
radar 493, 494, 495, 497.
radar antenna 48, 807, 812.
radar reflector 487.
radar unit 813.
Radarsat satellite 49.
radial nerve 133.
radial passenger loading area 503.
radial ply 433.
radial thruster 42.
radial tire 433.
radiant heater 211.
radiation zone 6.
radiator 438.
radiator 16, 208, 469.
radiator grille 440.
radiator hose 438.
radiator panel 510.
radicle 57, 59.
radio 639.
radio antenna 494, 495, 497, 807.
radio mast 738.
radio telescope 15.
radio wave 15.
radioactive 821.
radiometer 42, 43.
radish 71.
radius 102, 112, 122.
radome 813.
rafter 198.

raglan 330.
raglan sleeve 340.
raglan sleeve 319, 330, 350.
rail 225, 466, 568, 627, 675.
rail joint 466.
rail section 466.
rail track 735.
railroad 184.
railroad crossing 828.
railroad line 52.
railroad station 464.
railroad station 52.
railroad track 466.
railway shuttle service 504.
rain 36.
rain cap 205.
rain gauge recorder 40.
rain shower 39.
rainbow 36.
raincoat 319.
raindrop 36.
rainfall, measure 40.
rainfly 685, 686.
raining, utensils for 243.
raised band 577.
raised figure 580.
rake 159, 267.
rake 155.
rake bar 159.
rake comb 368.
Ram 11.
ramekin 238.
rammer 801.
ramp 168, 452, 733.
rampart 178, 180.
ramrod 795.
random access memory (RAM)
    module 528.
range hood 255.
rangefinder 394.
rapier 794.
rasp 587.
raspberry, section 62.
ratchet 276, 281, 573, 670.
ratchet box end wrench 279.
ratchet knob 711.
ratchet wheel 573, 706, 707.
rate gyro 814.
rattle 97.
rattlesnake 97.
razor clam 93.
razors 374.
reaction direction 831.
reaction engine assembly 43.
reactor 759, 764, 766, 806.
reactor building 759, 765.
reactor building airlock 758.
reactor core 760, 762, 763.
reactor tank 763.
reactor vessel 765.
read-only memory (ROM) module
    528.
read/write head 529.
reading 376.
reading mirror 512.
reading start 405.
reamer 251.
rear apron 324.
rear beam 708.
rear brake 446.
rear brake pedal 444.
rear bumper 445.
rear derailleur 446, 448.
rear foil 495.
rear leg 223.
rear light 446.
rear limit line 666.
rear runner 643.
rear seat 428.
rear shock absorber 443.
rear sight 795, 796, 797, 798, 804.
rear view 147.
rearview mirror 430.
récamier 221.
receiver 15, 420, 614, 616, 618, 795,
    796.
receiver volume control 420.
receiving line 617.
receiving station 722.
receiving yard 465.
receptacle 60, 62.
receptacle analyzer 310.
reception bay 764.
reception hall 172, 173.
recharging base 260.
reclining back 726.
recoil sleigh 802.
recoilless rifle 804.
record 404.
record 411.

record announcement button 420.
record button 403, 411.
record control 402.
record muting button 403
record player 404.
record player 400.
recorder 621.
recording level control 403.
recording tape 403.
recording unit 40.
rectangular 687.
rectangular flag 817.
rectum 127, 128, 131.
recuperator cylinder 802.
recuperator cylinder front head 802.
recyclable 831.
recycled 831.
Red 697, 700, 701.
red ball 673.
red balls 673.
red beam 410.
red flag 626, 668.
red ocher pencil 583.
red safelight filter 399.
Red Sea 21.
reduce/enlarge 532.
reducing coupling 301.
redundant bracing 756.
reed 548, 572.
reed hooks 573.
reed pipe 542.
reeds 549.
reef band 480.
reef point 480.
reel 265, 398, 666, 702.
reel plate 702.
reel seat 670, 671.
referee 601, 603, 605, 606, 608, 610,
    613, 621, 626, 668, 669.
refill 389.
refill tube 293.
refinery 740.
refinery products 744.
reflecting surface 770.
reflecting telescope 720.
reflecting telescope, cross section
    720.
reflective stripe 730, 777.
reflector 310, 441, 445, 446.
reflex camera, cross section 390.
refracting telescope 721.
**refracting telescope, cross
    section** 721.
refractory brick 585.
refrigerant tank 212.
refrigerant tubing 213.
refrigeration unit 441.
refrigerator 254.
refrigerator car 472.
refrigerator compartment 254.
register 712.
registered trademark 831.
registers, types 207.
regulating button 541.
regulating valve 208.
regulator first stage 627.
regulator second stage 627.
rehearsing room 188.
reheater 758.
rein 651.
rein ring 650.
reinforced concrete 286.
reinforced toe 730.
release lever 278.
release setting screw 641.
release treadle 573.
relief printing 580.
relief printing process 581.
**relief printing process,
    equipment** 581.
relocation 525.
remote command antenna 49.
remote control 411.
remote control 397.
remote control sensor 405, 410.
remote control terminal 391.
remote detection satellite 48.
remote-control arm 510.
remote-controlled switch 467.
removable-bottomed pan 245.
renal artery 126, 132.
renal hilus 132.
renal papilla 132.
renal pelvis 132.
renal vein 126, 132.
reniform 56.
repeat keys 405.
repeat mark 537.
reptile 96.

rerebrace 792.
reserve parachute 635.
reservoir 247, 543, 746, 747, 748,
    749, 750.
reservoir-nib pen 589.
reset 532.
reset button 297, 411, 706, 711.
reset key 421.
resin surface 405.
resistance adjustment 664.
resonator 406, 542, 554.
respirator 730.
respiratory system 130.
respiratory system protection
    730.
respiratory system protection 821.
rest area 52.
rest symbols 538.
restaurant 822.
restaurant 185, 190, 494.
restricted area 610.
restricting circle 610.
retainer 735.
retaining ring 295.
retarding magnet 712.
reticle 718.
Reticulum 13.
retina 140.
retractable handle 378.
retractable step 449.
retracted claw 107.
retrenchment 178.
retriever 613.
return 521.
return air 206, 207.
return crease 599.
return key 530.
return spring 432.
reverse dive 625.
reverse slide change 397.
reverse stitch button 561.
reversible reaction 831.
reversing device 212.
revolver 797.
revolving cylinder 570.
revolving nosepiece 718.
revolving sprinkler 264.
rewind 831.
rewind 411.
rewind button 403, 408, 411, 420.
rhubarb 61.
rhythm selector 555.
rib 72, 97, 102, 129, 375, 544, 546,
    729, 785.
rib pad 602.
rib stitch 567.
ribbing 326, 350, 670.
ribbing plow 156.
ribbing plow 154.
ribbon cartridge 531.
ribosome 115.
ribs 584.
ribs 122.
rice 152.
rider 648.
ridge 27.
ridge beam 199.
riding 646, 648.
riding cap 648, 651.
riding crop 648, 651.
riding glove 648.
riding jacket 648.
riffler 587.
rifle (rifled bore) 798.
rift 28.
rigging 478.
rigging wire 637.
right angle 830.
right ascension 3.
right ascension setting scale 720, 721.
right atrium 124, 125.
right back 601, 607, 612.
right bend 826, 827.
right bronchus 130.
right center 606.
right channel 401.
right cornerback 603, 605.
right defense 608.
right defensive end 603, 605.
right defensive tackle 603, 605.
right field 597.
right fielder 597.
right forward 610, 613.
right guard 603, 605, 610.
right half 601, 607.
right halfback 603.
right inner 607.
right kidney 132.
right lung 124, 130.

right outside linebacker 605.
right pulmonary vein 125.
right safety 603.
right safety back 605.
right service court 614, 616.
right tackle 603, 605.
right ventricle 124, 125.
right wing 606, 607, 608.
right winger 612.
rigs, types 482.
rim 147, 376, 433, 442, 447, 610,
    658.
rim flange 433.
rim soup bowl 238.
rinceau 220.
rind 65.
ring 669.
ring 55, 230, 290, 375, 434, 483, 551,
    566, 660, 681, 706, 709, 754.
ring binder 519.
ring gate 753.
ring nut 300.
ring post 669.
ring step 669.
ringhandle 369.
ringing volume control 420.
rings 364, 660.
ringside 669.
rink 608, 620.
rink 620, 682.
rink corner 608.
rinse-aid dispenser 257.
rip fence 284, 285.
rip fence guide 285.
rip fence lock 285.
rip fence rule 285.
rip fence slot 285.
ripeness 61.
ripening 61.
ripper 783.
ripper cylinder 783.
ripper tip 783.
ripper tooth 783.
rise 201.
riser 201, 636.
river 51, 52.
River Eridanus 13.
river estuary 30, 51.
rivet 242, 278.
road 52.
road communications 417.
road map 52.
road number 52.
road signs 824, 826, 828.
road system 450, 452.
road transport 491.
road work ahead 826, 827.
road, cross section 450.
roadway 186, 450.
roadway narrows 826, 827.
roasting pans 248.
Roberval's balance 708.
rock 30.
rock basin 26.
rock garden 263.
rock step 26.
rocker arm 435.
rocket 509.
rocket motor 814.
rocking chair 221, 223.
rocking tool 582.
rocky desert 46.
rod 214, 539, 573.
rodent's jaw 98.
roll 341.
roll film 395.
roll-up blind 231.
roller 270.
roller 230, 231, 369, 530, 583, 788.
roller board and arms 543.
roller cover 304.
roller frame 304.
roller shade 231.
roller skate 645.
rolling ladder 303.
rolling pin 245.
romaine lettuce 73.
Roman house 170.
Roman legionary 791.
Roman metal pen 389.
roman shade 231.
Romanian couching stitch 571.
rompers 351.
roof 82, 171, 197, 205, 427, 470,
    733.
roof pole 686.
roof truss 199.
roof vent 196, 215, 449.
roofs 182.
Rook 696.

room 736.
room air conditioner 214.
room thermostat 213, 705.
rooster 150.
root 70, 143, 144, 240.
root canal 144.
root cap 57.
root hairs 57.
root of nail 137.
root of nose 141.
root rib 498.
root system 57, 61.
root vegetables 71.
rope 361.
rope 669, 680, 692.
rope ladder 303.
rose 265, 289, 290, 546.
rose cut 363.
rose window 175.
rosemary 74.
rosette 167.
rostrum 90.
rotary engine 437.
rotary file 516.
rotary hoe 157.
rotary system 737.
rotary table 737.
rotating auger 160, 162.
rotating dome 14.
rotating dome truck 14.
rotating drum 714.
rotating track 15.
rotating wheel 701.
rotor 161, 290, 437, 753, 773, 774.
rotor blade 508.
rotor head 508.
rotor hub 508.
rotunda 190.
rotunda roof 183.
rough 676.
roughing out 586.
roulette 582.
roulette table 700.
round brush 368.
round end pin 231.
round eye 566.
round head 276.
round ligament of uterus 129.
round neck 343.
round pronator 120.
router 283.
routing cardboard 471.
row 373.
row counter 568.
row number display 569.
rower 664.
rowing (one oar) 632.
rowing and sculling 632.
rowing boats 632.
royal agaric 55.
royal antler 105.
royal flush 695.
rub rail 441.
rubber 355.
rubber boot 777.
rubber bulb 726.
rubber gasket 296.
rubber mat 404.
rubber snaffle bit 650.
rubber stamp 516.
rubber thread 677.
rubber tip 302, 728.
rubber wall 433.
rubbing alcohol 725.
rubbing strip 433.
ruby 362.
ruching 349.
rudder 492, 496, 499, 511, 628, 639, 806, 812, 814.
rudder pedal 639.
Ruffini's corpuscule 136.
ruffle 228, 317.
ruffled rumba pants 349.
ruffled skirt 334.
rug and floor brush 260.
rugby 606.
rugby ball 606.
rugby, field 606.
ruler 578, 591, 688.
rump 109.
run 201, 599.
rung 302.
runner 643, 697, 753.
runner blade 752, 753, 754.
running 654.
running bowline 691.
running rail 476.
running shoe 352.
running surface 466.

running track 786.
runway 504.
runway 476, 811.
runway center line markings 504.
runway designation marking 504.
runway side stripe markings 504.
runway threshold markings 505.
runway touchdown zone marking 505.
Russian pumpernickel 153.
rutabaga 71.
rye 152.

S

S-band antenna 43.
S-band high gain antenna 42.
S-band omnidirectional antenna 42.
sabaton 792.
saber 794.
saber 666.
saber and épée warning line 666.
sable 819.
sabreur 667.
sacral plexus 133.
sacral vertebrae 103.
sacrum 122, 123.
saddle 649.
saddle 397, 636, 648, 651, 661.
saddle pad 648.
saddlecloth 648, 651.
safari jacket 338.
safe water mark 489.
safelight 398.
safest water 488.
safety 796.
safety area 668.
safety binding 641.
safety boot 730.
safety cage 654.
safety cap 729.
safety cap 804.
safety chain 449.
safety earmuff 729.
safety glasses 729.
safety goggles 729.
safety handle 271.
safety line 475.
safety match 386.
safety pad 659.
safety pin 566.
safety rail 302, 468.
safety scissors 365.
safety suit connection 512.
safety symbols 821.
safety tank 761.
safety tether 512.
safety thermostat 259.
safety thong 617.
safety valve 248, 766.
safety vest 730.
sage 74.
Sagitta 11.
Sagittarius 13.
Sagittarius the Archer(November 22) 820.
sail 631, 637, 773.
sail cloth 773.
sail panel 628.
sail plane 807.
sailbar 773.
sailboard 631.
sailboat 628.
sailing 628, 630.
sailing, points 629.
sailor collar 342.
sails 480.
sails, types 482.
salad bowl 238.
salad dish 238.
salad fork 240.
salad plate 238.
salad spinner 243.
salamander 85.
salient angle 178.
saline lake 46.
salivary glands 131.
salsify 71.
salt marsh 30.
salt shaker 238.
salt taste 143.
sample 567.
sand 748.
sand bar 30.
sand island 30.
sand shoe 441.
sand wedge 678.
sandal 356, 357.
sandal 791.
sandbox 469.
sandstorm or dust storm 39.

sandy desert 46.
saphenous nerve 133.
sapphire 362.
sapwood 59.
sarong 334.
sartorius 120.
sash frame 203.
sash window 203.
satchel bag 380.
satellite 416.
satin weave 576.
Saturn 5.
saucepan 249, 688.
sauté pan 249.
savory 74.
sawing-in 578.
sawtooth roof 182.
saxhorn 551.
saxophone 548.
saxophone 548.
scale 537.
scale 87, 96, 97, 111, 705, 711, 719, 726.
scale leaf 70.
Scales 13.
scallion 70.
scallop 93.
scalper 653.
scampi 91.
Scandinavian crak bread 153.
scapula 102, 122, 123.
scapular 110.
scarp 178.
scatter cushion 224.
scattered sky 39.
scenery lift 188.
scenery storage 188.
scenic route 52.
schedules 463.
school zone 826, 827.
schooner 482.
sciatic nerve 133.
scientific air lock 511.
scientific instruments 16, 511.
scissors 564, 688, 725.
scissors crossing 464.
scissors cut 362.
scissors-glasses 377.
sclera 140.
scoop 385.
score-console 683.
scoreboard 698.
scorer 610, 613, 666, 668.
scoring light 666.
Scorpio the Scorpion(October 24) 820.
Scorpion 13.
Scorpius 13.
scotia 166, 167.
scraper 304, 582, 784.
scraper 583.
scraper bar holder 583.
screen 161, 374, 397, 410, 747.
screen case 397.
screen print 350.
screen window 685.
screw 276.
screw 544.
screw base 232.
screw earrings 361.
screw locking nut 670, 671.
screwdriver 276.
screwdriver 688.
screwsleeve 681.
scrimmage 603.
scrimmage in Canadian football 605.
script assistant 412.
scroll 544.
scroll case 747.
scroll foot 220.
scrotum 116, 127.
scrum half 606.
scuba diver 627.
scuba diving 627.
scuffle hoe 266.
sculling (two oars) 632.
sculling boats 632.
scythe 267.
sea 7, 51, 752.
sea anchor 483.
sea bag 381.
sea level 22, 28.
sea side 752.
sea-level pressure 38.
sea-to-sea missile 809.
seal 295.
sealed cell 82.
sealing ring 741.

seam 327, 384, 598.
seam allowance 565.
seam gauge 563.
seam line 565.
seam pocket 339.
seam pocket 330.
seaming 322.
seamount 29.
search-and-rescue antennas 43.
seasons of the year 8.
seat 220, 223, 292, 293, 428, 445, 446, 584, 639, 649, 652, 664, 727.
seat belt 428.
seat cover 293.
seat post 446.
seat stay 446.
seat tube 446.
seat-belt warning light 431.
seats 222.
second 830.
second 537, 669.
second base 597.
second baseman 597.
second classification track 465.
second dorsal fin 86.
second floor 194.
second floor 196.
second focal room 15.
second hand 706.
2nd metacarpal 112.
second molar 144.
second premolar 144.
second reinforce 800.
second space 610.
second stage 509.
second valve slide 550.
second violins 556.
secondaries 110.
secondary channel 489.
secondary consumers 31.
secondary inlet 741.
secondary mirror 16, 390.
secondary reflector 15.
secondary road 52.
secondary root 57.
seconde 667.
secretarial desk 521.
secretary 226.
secretary 612, 626.
section of a bulb 70.
security casing 271.
security check 504.
security trigger 272.
sedimentary rocks 23.
seed 62, 63, 64, 65, 66, 67.
seed coat 63, 152.
seed drill 158.
seed drill 154.
seed leaf 57.
seed vegetables 72.
seeder 268.
segment 65.
segment score number 698.
seismic wave 23.
seismogram 714.
selector switch 310.
self-adhesive labels 518.
self-contained breathing apparatus 777.
self-inflating mattress 687.
self-timer indicator 391.
selvage 566.
semaphore 464.
semi-circle 610.
semi-detached cottage 187.
semi-fisheye lens 392.
semi-mummy 687.
semi-submersible platform 739.
semicircular arch 174.
semicolon 832.
semimembranous 121.
seminal vesicle 127.
semiprecious stones 362.
semitendinous 121.
semitrailer 441.
semitrailer 440.
sense organs 136, 138, 140, 141.
sense receptor 134.
senses of smell 142.
senses of taste 142.
sensor probe 253.
sensory impulse 135.
sensory neuron 134.
sensory root 135.
sent document recovery 421.
sepal 60, 62, 64.
separator 439, 758.
separator steam release 758.
septal cartilage of nose 141.

septic tank 216.
septime 667.
septum 67, 141.
septum pellucidum 134.
sequencer control 555.
serac 26.
Serpens 11, 13.
Serpent 11, 13.
Serpent Bearer 11, 13.
server 613, 614, 616, 618.
service area 52, 503, 613.
service box 616, 617, 757.
service box line 617.
service building 764.
service judge 614, 618.
service line 614, 616, 617.
service main 186.
service module 418, 509.
service road 502.
service room 172, 173.
service station 453, 823.
service zone 617.
serving cart 219.
sesame seeded pita 153.
set 525.
set of utensils 244.
set-in sleeve 324, 326.
setting 364.
setting indicator 641.
setup 683.
setup 683.
7.5 m platform 624.
seventeenth century cannon 800.
seventeenth-century mortar 803.
seventh 537.
sew-through buttons 566.
sewer 186.
sewing 561, 562, 564, 566, 578.
sewing frame 578.
sewing machine 561.
sewing, accessories 563, 564.
sewn-in floor 685, 686.
Sextans 13.
Sextant 13.
sextant 484.
sextet 558.
shackle 630.
shade 234, 236.
shade cloth 231.
shadow 706.
shadow key 396.
shadow roll 651.
shady arcades 172, 173.
shaft 38, 166, 575, 584, 609, 615, 632, 652, 658, 674, 675, 677, 681, 684, 698, 705, 753, 808.
shaft head 734.
shaft holder 653.
shake-hands grip 619.
shallot 70, 542.
shallow root 59.
sham 224.
shank 275, 276, 281, 369, 375, 385, 483, 562, 563, 564, 567, 568, 671.
shank button 566.
shank protector 783.
shapka 328.
share 156.
sharp 538.
sharpening steel 242.
shaving brush 374.
shaving mug 374.
shawl collar 341.
sheath 690.
sheath 56, 101, 106, 688, 692.
sheath dress 332.
sheath of Schwann 135.
sheath skirt 334.
sheathing 198, 199.
shed 193, 263.
shed stick 574.
sheep 150.
sheep shelter 149.
sheepshank 691.
sheepskin jacket 321.
sheer curtain 229.
sheet 480, 577.
sheet bend 691.
sheet film 395.
sheet lead 630.
sheet of paper 714.
shekel 832.
shelf 226, 254, 302.
shelf channel 254.
shell 96.
shell 66, 83, 92, 109, 383, 553, 643, 741.
shell membrane 109.
shell, valve 95.
shield 426, 791.

shield divisions 818.
shift key 524, 530.
shift lock key 524, 530.
shifter 447, 448.
shin boot 648, 652.
shin guard 595, 600.
shin pad 609.
shingle 286.
ship's anchor 483.
Ship's Compass 13.
Ship's Keel 13.
ship's motor boat 809.
Ship's Sails 13.
Ship's Stern 13.
shirred heading 229.
shirt 324, 349.
shirt 656.
shirt collar 341.
shirt sleeve 340.
shirttail 324, 337.
shirtwaist dress 333.
shock absorber 445.
shoe 397.
shoe polish 358.
shoe polisher 358.
shoe rack 358.
shoe, parts 353.
shoebrush 358.
shoehorn 358.
shoelace 352, 354.
shoes 354, 356, 358.
shoes, accessories 358.
shoes, major types 354, 355, 356.
shoeshine kit 358.
shoetree 358.
shoot 57, 59.
shooting adjustment keys 409.
shooting star 19.
shop 170.
shopping bag 381.
shore 30.
short extensor of toes 120.
short glove 327.
short line 616, 617.
short palmar 120.
short peroneal 121.
short radial extensor of wrist 121.
short service line 618.
short sleeve 318.
short sock 344.
short splice 692.
shorts 336.
shorts 351, 600, 656.
shortstop 597.
shot 658, 801.
shot put 655.
shotgun (smooth-bore) 799.
shoulder 100, 106, 116, 118, 279, 451, 545, 615, 670.
shoulder bag 380.
shoulder belt 428.
shoulder blade 117, 119.
shoulder bolt 279.
shoulder pad 602, 609, 804.
shoulder rest 804.
shoulder strap 346, 375, 380, 382, 679.
shovel 205, 266.
shovel 640, 642.
shower 194.
shower and tub fixture 215.
shower head 292.
shower stall 292.
shrimp 90.
shroud 479, 628.
shutoff switch 216.
shutoff valve 215, 293, 296, 298.
shutter 203, 529, 772.
shutter release button 391.
shutter speed setting 396.
shutting stile 202.
shuttle 573.
shuttle 510.
shuttlecock 618.
sickle 269.
side 239, 479, 787.
side back vent 322.
side chair 223.
side chapel 176.
side door 477.
side footboard 469.
side handle 280.
side handrail 477.
side judge 605.
side ladder 470.
side lane 452.
side line 619.
side mirror 368.
side panel 319.
side post 199.

side rail 302, 441.
side span 456.
side vent 25, 449.
side wall 104, 470, 492, 616, 617, 621.
side wall line 616.
side-marker light 429.
side-tilt lock 393.
sideline 604, 607, 610, 611, 612, 613.
sidewalk 186.
sidewall 441.
sieve 161.
sifter 245.
sight 140.
sight 684, 719, 803.
sighting line 719.
sighting mirror 719.
sigmoid colon 131.
signal ahead 826, 827.
signal background plate 471.
signal gantry 464.
signal lamp 247, 252, 255, 256, 257, 585.
signature 577.
signet ring 364.
signs of the zodiac 820.
silencer 735.
silique, section 67.
silk 72.
sill 24, 199.
sill of frame 203.
sill plate 198, 199.
sill step 470.
silos 490.
silverware 239, 240.
sima 161.
simple eye 78, 80, 81.
simple leaves 56.
simple-span beam bridge 454.
single curtain rod 230.
single pole breaker 312.
single quotation marks 832.
single reed 549.
single scull 632.
single seat 477.
single twist 281.
single zero 700, 701.
single-breasted jacket 322.
single-burner camp stove 689.
single-decked pallet 787.
single-family home 187.
single-handle kitchen faucet 296.
single-leaf bascule bridge 457.
single-lens reflex (SLR) camera 391.
single-lens reflex camera 394.
singles pole 614.
singles service court 618.
singles sideline 614, 618.
sinister 818.
sinister base 818.
sinister chief 818.
sinister flank 818.
sink 215, 292, 296.
sinker 486, 672.
sinkhole 24.
sinus 315.
siphon 24.
siphonal canal 94.
site plan 193.
sitting room 195.
sixte 667.
sixteenth note 538.
sixteenth rest 538.
sixth 537.
sixty-fourth note 538.
sixty-fourth rest 538.
skate 609.
skate guard 644.
skating 644.
skeg 631.
skeleton 122.
skeleton, horse 102.
ski 445, 641.
ski boot 640, 641.
ski boot 640.
ski glove 640.
ski goggles 640.
ski hat 640, 642.
ski pants 336.
ski pole 640, 642.
ski stop 640, 641.
ski suit 640, 642.
ski tip 642.
skid 508.
skimmer 244.
skin 136.
skin 62, 63, 64, 84, 134.
skin surface 137.
skip 620, 736.

skirt 331, 615, 649, 792.
skirt finger 493.
skirt marker 564.
skirts, types 334.
skull 88, 102, 116, 134, 792.
skullcap 328.
sky coverage 39.
sky diver 635.
sky diving 635.
skylight 194, 197.
skyscraper 185.
slab 288.
slab building 584.
slalom ski 633.
slat 571.
sled 264, 643.
sleeper-cab 440.
sleepers 350.
sleeping bags 687.
sleeping car 460.
sleeping compartment 460.
sleet 37, 39.
sleeve 318, 322, 667.
sleeve strap 319.
sleeve strap loop 319.
sleeveless jersey 662.
sleeves, types 339, 340.
slender 121.
slide 257, 397, 566, 797.
slide chair 467.
slide plate 561, 562.
slide projector 397.
slide tray 397.
slide-bar 568.
slider 543.
sliding block 476.
sliding breech 802.
sliding channel 470.
sliding cheek bit 650.
sliding cover 484.
sliding door 202.
sliding door 292.
sliding folding door 202.
sliding folding window 203.
sliding lever 428.
sliding rail 428, 630.
sliding seat 664.
sliding sunroof 427.
sliding weight 539, 708.
sliding window 203.
slight drifting snow low 39.
slightly covered sky 39.
sling back shoe 356.
slip 345.
slip joint 278.
slip joint pliers 278.
slip-stitched seam 324.
slippery road 826, 827.
slit 576.
slope 451.
sloped turret 183.
sloping cornice 168.
slot 188, 240, 252, 276, 379, 578.
slot machine 702.
slotback 605.
slow-burning stove 204.
slow-motion 411.
slower traffic 452.
sludge 216.
small decanter 237.
small hand cultivator 268.
small intestine 131.
smaller round 121.
smell 141.
smock 337.
smoke 39.
smoke baffle 204.
smoke bomb discharger 805.
smoking accessories 384, 386.
smoking candle 582.
smoking-apparatus 582.
snaffle bit 650.
snaffle bit 649.
snaffle rein 649.
snaffle strap 649.
snail 83.
snail dish 246.
snail tongs 246.
snap 566, 672.
snap fastener 321, 327.
snap shackle 630.
snap-fastening front 350.
snap-fastening tab 321.
snap-fastening waist 350.
snare 553.
snare drum 553.
snare drum 552, 557.
snare head 553.
snare strainer 553.
snelled fishhook 672.

INDEX

856

snooker 673.
snorkel 627.
snout 84.
snow 34.
snow crystals, classification 36.
snow gauge 41.
snow guard 445.
snow pellet 37.
snow shower 39.
snowfall, measure 41.
snowmobile 445.
snowshoe 645.
snowsuit 351.
soap dish 292.
soccer 600.
soccer ball 600.
soccer player 600.
soccer shoe 600.
soccer, playing field 601.
sock 344.
sock 602, 615.
socket 309, 401, 566.
socket bayonet 794.
socket head 276.
socks 325.
sofa 221.
soft palate 141, 142.
soft pastel 588.
soft pedal 540, 555.
soft ray 87.
soft shell clam 93.
soft-drink dispenser 453.
soil 750.
solar array 42, 48, 418.
solar array deployment 419.
solar array drive 42.
solar cell 768.
solar cell 523, 769.
solar cell panel 769.
solar cells 42.
solar collector 772.
solar eclipse 8.
solar energy 768, 770, 772.
solar furnace 770.
solar house 772.
solar panel 16.
solar radiation 768, 769, 770, 771, 772.
solar ray reflected 770, 771.
solar reflectors 418.
solar shield 512.
solar system 4.
solar-cell system 769.
solder 307.
soldering 305, 306, 308.
soldering gun 305.
soldering iron 305.
soldering torch 307.
soldering torch 299.
sole 104, 325, 641, 644, 678.
soleplate 256.
soleus 120.
solid body 547.
solid rubber tire 788.
solid shot 801.
solid-rocket booster 510.
solitaire ring 364.
solvent extraction unit 744.
sorghum 152.
sound alarm 485.
sound digitizing processor 528.
sound hole 544.
sound receiver 726.
sound reproducing system 400, 402, 404.
sound reproducing system, components 400.
sound signal 539.
soundboard 535, 540, 544, 545, 546.
soundbox 545.
soup bowl 238.
soup spoon 241.
soup tureen 238.
sour taste 143.
sources of pollution 34.
South 488.
South America 20.
South cardinal mark 489.
South celestial pole 3.
South Pole 3.
Southeast 488.
Southern Cross 13.
Southern Crown 13.
Southern Fish 13.
Southern hemisphere 3, 47.
Southern Triangle 13.
Southwest 488.
southwester 329.
sow 151.
soybeans 72.

space 537.
space bar 525, 530.
space probe 19.
space shuttle 510.
space shuttle at takeoff 510.
space shuttle in orbit 510.
spacelab 511.
spacer 727, 765.
spacesuit 512.
spade 266, 632, 695.
spade 803.
spading fork 266.
spadix 60.
spaghetti tongs 246.
spandrel 174.
spanker 480.
spar 498.
spar buoy 489.
spark 436.
spark plug 439.
spark plug 271, 435, 437.
spark plug body 439.
spark plug cable 435.
spark plug gap 439.
spark plug gasket 439.
spark plug terminal 439.
sparkling wine glass 237.
spatial dendrite 36.
spatula 589.
spatula 244, 581.
spatulate 56.
speaker 408, 420, 500.
speaker cover 400.
speaker selector 402.
spear 72, 791.
speargun 627.
special mark 489.
specimen chamber 717.
specimen positioning control 717.
spectrometer 717.
speed control 250, 271.
speed controller 561.
speed course 646.
speed selector 251, 404.
speed selector switch 370.
speed skate 644.
speedbrake lever 500.
speedometer 431, 445, 664.
spelling corrector 524.
spencer 338.
spent fuel discharge bay 758.
spent fuel port 764.
spent fuel storage bay 758, 764, 765.
spermatic cord 127.
spermatozoon 127.
sphenoidal sinus 141.
sphere support 40.
sphincter muscle of anus 131.
spicules 6.
spider 77.
spider 77.
spike 60, 466, 656, 680, 681.
spiked shoe 595.
spillway 746.
spillway chute 746.
spillway gate 746.
spinach 73.
spinal cord 89, 134, 135.
spinal ganglion 135.
spinal nerve 135.
spindle 223, 251, 290, 294, 404, 707, 711, 712.
spine 577.
spine of scapula 123.
spine of the book 579.
spinner 672.
spinning rod 671.
spinous process 135.
spiny lobster 91.
spiny ray 86.
spiracle 78, 79.
spiral 276, 404.
spiral arm 9.
spiral beater 250.
spiral binder 519.
spiral case 753.
spiral galaxy 9.
spiral rib 94.
spiral screwdriver 276.
spiral staircase 194.
spiral-in groove 404.
spire 94, 175.
spirit level 291.
spit 30.
splash plate 741.
splat 220.
splay 175.
spleen 88, 124.
splenius muscle of head 121.
spline 439.

splints 725.
split bet 700, 701.
split end 603, 605.
split link 672.
spoiler 442, 498.
spoke 447.
spoked wheel 652.
sponge 801.
sponge-tipped applicator 367.
sponges 367.
spool 570, 670, 671.
spool pin 561.
spool rack 575.
spoon 241.
spoon 688.
spoon blade 587.
spoons, principal types 241.
spores 55.
sports car 425.
sportswear 352.
spot 235.
spot white ball 673.
spotlight 414, 777, 778, 780.
spotmeter 396.
spout 162, 247, 252, 294, 295.
spout assembly 296.
spray 256.
spray button 256.
spray arm 257.
spray control 256.
spray head 296.
spray hose 292, 296.
spray nozzle 264.
spray nozzle 741.
spray paint gun 304.
sprayer 264.
spread collar 324.
spreader 270.
spreader 375.
spreader adjustment screw 304.
spring 8, 234, 258, 278, 290, 294, 389, 469, 659, 804.
spring balance 709.
spring binder 519.
spring housing 230.
spring linkage 702.
spring wing 276.
spring-metal insulation 287.
springboard 659.
springer 174.
sprinkler hose 265.
sprinklers 766.
sprocket 445.
sprocket wheel 783, 805.
spur 27, 80, 281, 552, 648.
squall 39.
square 184, 577.
square bet 700, 701.
square flag 817.
square head plug 301.
square knot 691.
square movement 696.
square neck 343.
square root key 523.
square root of 830.
square sail 482.
square trowel 291.
square-headed tip 276.
squash 616.
squash ball 616.
squash racket 616.
squash, court 616.
stabilizer 636, 684, 812.
stabilizer fin 496.
stabilizing fin 509.
stabilizing shaft 788.
stable 651.
stack 30, 494.
stacking chairs 223.
stadium 185.
staff 537.
staff 817.
stage 189.
stage 188, 717, 718.
stage clip 718.
stage curtain 188, 189.
stained glass 175.
stairs 201.
stairs 194, 474, 741.
stairwell 194.
stake 263, 685, 686.
stake loop 685, 686.
stake pocket 441.
stalactite 24.
stalagmite 24.
stalk 62, 63, 64, 72.
stalk vegetables 72.
stamen 60, 64.
stamp 384.

stamp pad 516.
stamp rack 516.
stanchion 644.
stand 651.
stand 236, 248, 250, 341, 370, 382, 552, 586, 714.
stand-off half 606.
stand-up collar 342.
standard A 539.
standard lens 392.
standardbred pacer 652.
standby airspeed indicator 500.
standby altimeter 500.
standby attitude indicator 500.
standing press 579.
standpipe 298.
stapes 138.
staple remover 515.
stapler 515.
staples 515.
star anise 67.
star diagonal 721.
star facet (8) 363.
star tracker 16.
starboard hand 488, 489, 497.
starch 152.
starch granule 115.
start 532.
start and finish 646.
start button 706.
start key 421.
start line 655, 656.
start switch 259.
start wall 621.
start-up key 530.
starter 271, 272, 621.
starter handle 272.
starting bar (backstroke) 621.
starting block 621, 656.
starting block 621.
starting cable 270.
starting dive 622.
starting position 625.
starting step 201.
state 51.
station circle 38.
station entrance 474.
station name 474.
station platform 464.
station wagon 425.
stationary bicycle 664.
stationary bowl 701.
stationary front 39.
stationery 515, 516, 518.
stationery cabinet 522.
stator 290, 753.
stay 479.
stay ring 753.
stay vane blade 753.
stays 456.
staysail-stay 479.
steak knife 239.
steam generator 759, 761, 762, 771, 806.
steam generator room cooler 759.
steam iron 256.
steam outlet 760, 761, 762, 763.
steam pressure drives turbine 767.
steam release pipes 759.
steel 286.
steel 346, 795.
steel bar 660.
steel belted radial tire 433.
steel pen 389.
steel safety wheel 476.
steel spring 795.
steel to plastic 301.
steelyard 708.
steep hill 826, 827.
steeplechase 655.
steeplechase hurdle 656.
steering axle 788.
steering cylinder 784.
steering lever 788.
steering wheel 147, 430.
stellar crystal 36.
stem 55, 57, 70, 232, 247, 385, 447, 479, 705.
stem bulb 497.
stem faucet 294.
stem holder 294.
stem washer 294.
step 147, 302, 440.
step chair 222.
step cut 363.
step groove 201.
step setting 711.
step stool 302.
stepladder 302.
stepladders 302.

The terms in **bold type** indicate the title of an illustration.

steppe 45.
steps 773.
stereo camera 395.
stereo control 408.
stereo phase monitor 413.
sterile pad 725.
stern 496, 631.
sternocleidomastoid 120.
sternum 102, 122.
stethoscope 726.
steward's desk 461.
stick 375, 607.
stick 544.
stick eraser 515.
stick umbrella 375.
stickpin 364.
sticks 553.
stifle 101.
stigma 60, 66.
stile 223.
stile groove of sash 203.
stile tongue of sash 203.
stiletto 794.
still cameras 394, 395.
still video camera 395.
still video film disk 395.
still water level 30.
stilt 585.
stilted 174.
stimulator tip 373.
stinger 81.
stipule 56.
stirrup 793.
stirrup iron 648.
stirrup leather 649.
stirrup sock 595.
stitch 352, 355.
stitch control buttons 569.
stitch length regulator 561.
stitch pattern memory 569.
stitch patterns 567.
stitch selector 561.
stitch width selector 561.
stitches 596.
stitches, embroidery 571.
stitching 327.
stock 483, 536, 773, 798, 799.
stock pot 249.
stocked anchor 483.
stocking 344.
stocking 667.
stocking cap 329.
stocking stitch 567.
stockless anchor 483.
stomach 88, 92, 97, 124, 131.
stomach throw 668.
stomacker 317.
stone 286.
stone 63, 364.
Stone Age weapons 791.
stone fleshy fruits 63.
stone fruit, section 63.
stone fruits, major types 63.
stoner 246.
stop 831.
stop 106, 411, 532, 566, 570, 632.
stop at intersection 824, 825.
stop bath 399.
stop button 272, 403, 411, 420, 706.
stop knob 542, 543.
stop rod 543.
stop watch 407.
stop/clear key 405.
stopwatch 706.
storage compartment 397, 440, 449, 778, 780.
storage door 254.
storage furniture 225, 226.
storage space 461.
storage tank 744, 772.
storage tray 591, 764.
storm collar 205.
storm sewer 186.
stormy sky 36.
stove oil 745.
straight 695.
straight bet 700, 701.
straight blade 587.
straight eye 566.
straight flush 695.
straight jaw 278.
straight ladder 303.
straight muscle of thigh 120.
straight position 624.
straight razor 374.
straight skirt 334.
straight wing 499.
straight-up ribbed top 325.
straight: post and rail 646.

strainer 243.
strainer 251, 685.
strainer body 296.
strainer coupling 296.
straining, utensils for 243.
strait 51.
strand 692.
strap 365, 596, 660, 662, 706, 777.
strap wrench 299.
strapless brassiere 346.
stratocumulus 44.
stratosphere 19.
stratum basale 136.
stratum corneum 136.
stratum granulosum 136.
stratum lucidum 136.
stratum spinosum 136.
stratus 44.
straw spreader 161.
strawberry, section 62.
streamer 817.
street 52, 184, 190.
street bet 700, 701.
street light 185, 186.
street, cross section 186.
stretcher 219, 726.
strike plate 290.
striker 307.
striker 804.
striker wheel 386.
striking circle 607.
string 541, 544, 545.
stringed instruments 544, 546.
stringer 787.
stringing 615.
strings 540.
strip flooring with alternate joints 200.
strip light 235.
strip mine 733.
stroke judge 621.
strokes, types 622.
strongbox 702.
structure of the Sun 6.
strut 199, 495, 553, 774.
stud 198, 353.
studio 407.
studio floor 412.
studio, radio 407.
studio, television 412, 414.
studs 598.
stummel 385.
stump 59.
stump 598, 599.
style 60, 62, 63, 64, 67.
styling brush 370.
stylobate 166, 168.
stylus 389.
stylus cartridge 404.
sub-base 40.
subarctic climates 45.
subarctic climates 45.
subbase 451.
subclavian artery 126.
subclavian vein 126.
subcutaneous tissue 137.
subfloor 198, 199, 200.
subgrade 451.
sublimation 34.
submachine gun 795.
submarine 806.
submarine canyon 29.
submarine pipeline 740.
subsidiary track 464.
substation 752.
substitute corridor 612.
substructure 737.
subterranean stream 24.
subtract from memory 523.
subtract key 523.
subtraction 830.
subtraction 830.
subtropical climates 45.
suburban commuter railroad 464.
suburbs 52.
subway 474, 476.
subway 190.
subway map 475, 477.
subway station 474.
subway train 476.
subway train 474.
sucker 61.
suction hose 778.
sudoriferous duct 136.
sugar bowl 238.
suit 331.
sulcus terminalis 143.
sulky 652.
sum 830.
sumie 589.
summer 8.

summer solstice 8.
summer squash 69.
summit 27.
sump 216, 736.
Sun 6.
Sun 4, 8.
Sun mode position 419.
sun sensor 42, 43, 49.
sun visor 430, 449.
Sun, structure of 6.
sundae spoon 241.
sundeck 497.
sundial 706.
sundress 332.
sunglasses 377.
sunshade 42.
sunshine recorder 40.
sunshine, measure 40.
sunspot 6.
super 82.
superficial peroneal nerve 133.
superior cymbal 552.
superior dental arch 142.
superior mesenteric artery 126, 132.
superior mesenteric vein 126.
superior nasal concha 141.
superior semicircular canal 139.
superior umbilicus 110.
superior vena cava 124, 125, 126, 130.
superstructure 486.
supply duct 213.
supply line 215.
supply point 757.
supply tube 296.
support 40, 223, 230, 232, 574, 720.
support leg 156, 441, 449.
support leg crank 441.
support structure 15, 48.
supports 589.
suprarenal gland 132.
sural nerve 133.
surcingle 653.
surface cold front 39.
surface course 450.
surface element 255.
surface insulation 510.
surface of the water 624.
surface runoff 32, 34.
surface scum 216.
surface surveillance radar 809, 810.
surface warm front 39.
surface-piercing foils 495.
surface-to-air missile 814.
surface-to-subsurface missile 809, 814.
surroyal antler 105.
suspended span 454.
suspender 456.
suspender clip 323.
suspenders 323.
suspension 477.
suspension arm 258.
suspension band 729.
suspension bridge 456.
suspension cable 456.
suspension insulator string 756.
suspension lines 636.
suspension spring 707.
suspension truck 458.
suspensory ligament 140.
suture 67, 94.
swagger stick 375.
swallow hole 24.
swallowtail 817.
swallowtail and tongue 817.
Swan 11.
sweat pants 352.
sweat shirt 352.
sweater 326.
sweaters 326, 338.
sweeping hip throw 668.
sweeping score line 620.
sweet bay 74.
sweet peas 72.
sweet pepper 69.
sweet potato 71.
sweet taste 143.
sweetheart neckline 343.
swell organ manual 542.
swell pedals 542.
swept-back wing 499.
swift 575.
swimmerets 91.
swimming 621, 622.
swimming pool 496, 621, 626.
swimming trunks 353.
swimsuit 353.
swing bridge 457.
Swiss army knife 688.
Swiss chard 72.

switch 309.
switch 254, 280, 283, 285, 464.
switch lock 280.
switch plate 309.
switch point 467.
switch rod 467.
switch signal 467.
switch stand 467.
switch tower 464.
swivel 658, 672, 737.
swivel base 282.
swivel cord 370.
swivel head 282.
swivel lock 282.
swivel wall lamp 234.
swivel-tilter armchair 520.
Swordfish 13.
symbol 702.
symbols, dangerous materials 821.
symbols, protection 821.
sympathetic ganglion 135.
symphony orchestra 556.
symphysis pubis 127, 128.
synapse 135.
synthesizer 555.
synthetic sponge 367.
syringe 726.
syringe for irrigation 726.
system buttons 555.
systems display 500.

T

T-shirt dress 351.
T-strap shoe 356.
T-tail unit 498.
tab 518.
tab 319, 375, 378, 379, 566, 649.
tab key 530.
tab setting 525.
table 219, 674.
table 283, 285, 363, 578.
table cut 363.
table extension 285.
table lamp 236.
table mixer 250.
table saw 285.
table tennis 619.
table tennis ball 619.
table tennis paddle 619.
table, tennis 619.
table-locking clamp 283.
tables, types of 219.
tablespoon 241.
tablet 725.
tablinum 170.
tabulator 524.
tachometer 431, 445.
tack 631.
tackle box 672.
tadpole 84.
tag 352, 354.
tail 91, 96, 97, 101, 106, 107, 112, 127, 499, 579, 633, 638, 641, 642, 643, 645, 670.
tail assembly 499.
tail boom 508.
tail comb 368.
tail edge 577.
tail feather 109.
tail of helix 139.
tail pipe 439.
tail pipe extension 439.
tail pole 773.
tail shapes, types 498.
tail skid 508.
tail-out groove 404.
tailing auger 161.
taillight 147, 429, 441, 443, 444.
taillights 429.
tailored collar 341.
tailored collar 330.
tailored sleeve 340.
tailpiece 296, 544.
tailrace 747.
take-up handle 572.
take-up reel 403.
take-up spool 390.
talon 111.
talus 123.
tambourine 554.
tamper 385.
tandem disk harrow 157.
tandem disk harrow 154.
tandem tractor trailer 440.
tang 239, 242, 291.
tank 805.
tank 216, 398, 399, 689, 780.
tank ball 293.

INDEX

The terms in **bold type** indicate the title of an illustration.

tank car 472.
tank farm 740.
tank gauge float 741.
tank lid 293.
tank sprayer 265.
tank top 351, 353.
tanker 491, 813.
tanks 511.
tap connector 265.
tape 566, 571, 607, 613, 711, 804.
tape counter 403.
tape dispenser 516.
tape lock 711.
tape measure 563, 711.
tape selector 403.
tape-guide 403.
tapered wing 499.
tapestry bobbin 574.
tapestry bobbin 574.
taproot 59.
tar paper 286.
target 684.
target area 770.
target areas 667.
target detection radar 809.
tarlatan 582.
tarragon 74.
tarsus 78, 80, 103, 108, 122.
tassel 229, 231.
tasset 792.
taste sensations 143.
Taurus 11.
Taurus the Bull(April 20) 820.
taxi transportation 822.
taxiway 502.
taxiway line 503.
tea ball 246.
team bench 626.
team shirt 595, 600.
teapot 238.
tear-off calendar 518.
teaser comb 368.
teaspoon 241.
technical equipment compartment 415.
technical identification band 405.
technical producer 412, 415.
technical producer monitor 413.
technical specifications 433.
tedding 155, 159.
teddy 345.
tee 301.
tee 298, 620, 677.
teeing ground 676.
teeth 144.
teeth 566.
tele-converter 392.
telecommunication antenna 494, 497, 809.
telecommunication satellites 418.
telecommunication satellites, examples 418.
telecommunication terminal 422.
telecommunications by satellite 417.
telecommunications by telephone network 417.
telephone 822.
telephone 413.
telephone answering machine 420.
telephone cable 186.
telephone index 516.
telephone index 420.
telephone network 417.
telephone set 420.
telephone set 415, 417.
telephone, communication 420, 422.
telephones, types 422.
telephoto lens 392.
teleport 417.
teleprompter 414.
telescope 14.
telescope 14, 42, 484, 713.
telescope base 14.
telescopic boom 780, 786.
telescopic corridor 503.
telescopic front fork 442.
telescopic leg 726.
telescopic sight 718.
telescopic sight 798.
telescopic umbrella 375.
telescoping leg 393.
telescoping uncoupling rod 470.
television 410, 412, 414.
television set 410.
television set 401.
telex 421.

telex 417.
telltale 616, 628.
telson 91.
temperate climates 45.
temperature 210.
temperature control 213, 252, 256, 297.
temperature control knob 585.
temperature indicator 431.
temperature of dew point 38.
temperature scale 19.
temperature scales 710.
temperature selector 253, 258, 259.
temperature set point knob 705.
temperature, measure 41.
template 738.
temple 573.
temple 116, 376, 578.
tempo control 555.
tempo scale 539.
temporal bone 122.
10 m platform 624.
10 yards line 606.
tenaille 179.
tendon 91.
tendon guard 644.
tendril 61.
tennis 614.
tennis ball 615.
tennis player 615.
tennis racket 615.
tennis shoe 355.
tennis shoe 615.
tennis, court 614.
tennis, net 614.
tenon saw 578.
tenor drum 553.
tenpin 683.
tensiometer 710.
tension adjustment 671.
tension block 562, 569.
tension block 561.
tension dial 562, 568, 569.
tension disk 562, 569.
tension guide 569.
tension pulley wheel 230.
tension rod 553.
tension screw 552.
tension spring 431, 562, 569, 665.
tensor of fascia lata 120.
tentacle 83.
tents, major types 686.
tepee 165.
terminal 255, 309, 312, 421, 740, 757.
terminal arborization 135.
terminal box 769.
terminal bronchiole 130.
terminal bud 57.
terminal filament 134.
terminal lobe 61.
terminal moraine 27.
terminal tackles 672.
terreplein 179.
terrestrial sphere 3.
tertial 110.
tertiary consumers 31.
test pattern 414.
testicle 127.
text 524.
text display 524.
theater 188.
theodolite 713.
theodolite 41.
thermal barrier 42.
thermal louver 43.
thermocouple 297.
thermocouple tube 297.
thermometer 705.
thermometer 627, 635, 741.
thermos 690.
thermosphere 19.
thermostat 210, 214, 252, 297.
thermostat control 254.
thigh 101, 106, 108, 117, 119, 127, 128.
thigh pad 602.
thigh-boot 357.
thigh-high stocking 344.
thimble 563.
thimble 711.
thinning razor 369.
third 537.
third base 597.
third baseman 597.
third finger 137.
3rd metacarpal 112.
third stage 509.
third valve slide 551.
third wheel 706, 707.
35 mm still camera 512.

thirty-second note 538.
thirty-second rest 538.
thong 357.
thoracic legs 90.
thoracic vertebra (12) 123.
thoracic vertebrae 102.
thorax 78, 79, 80, 116, 118.
thread 276, 294.
thread guide 561, 562.
thread take-up lever 561.
thread trimmer 562.
threaded cap 301.
threaded rod 279.
three-four time 537.
three-hinged arch 455.
three-of-a-kind 695.
3 m platform 624.
3 m springboard 624.
three-quarter coat 321.
three-quarter sleeve 339.
three-toed hoof 99.
threshing area 161.
threshold 202.
throat 108, 282, 483, 615, 671.
throat latch 649.
throat protector 595, 609.
throttle valve 735.
throttles 500.
through arch bridge 455.
throwing circle 654, 655.
throwings 658.
thrust 455.
thrust bearing 753.
thrust device 389.
thrust tube 389.
thruster 49, 512.
thrusting and cutting weapons 794.
thumb 112, 137, 327, 596.
thumb hook 550.
thumb piston 542.
thumb rest 549, 726.
thumb tacks 515.
thumbscrew 279.
thunderstorm 39.
thyme 74.
tibia 78, 80, 103, 112, 122.
tibial nerve 133.
ticket collector 463.
ticket collector's booth 474.
ticket control 463.
ticket counter 504.
tidal power plant 752.
tie 375, 466, 539.
tie bar 364.
tie beam 198.
tie closure 375.
tie plate 466.
tie rod 553.
tieback 228.
tiepin 364.
tierce 667.
tierceron 177.
tight end 603, 605.
tightener 661.
tightening band 40.
tilde 832.
tile 286.
tile 169, 170, 511.
tiller 272.
tiller 628, 793.
tilt tube 231.
tilt-back head 250.
timber 168, 170.
time signatures 537.
timed outlet 255.
timekeeper 610, 612, 626, 666, 668, 669.
timer 398.
timer 252, 585, 664.
timing belt 434.
timpani 557.
tine 157, 240, 272.
tip 57, 72, 239, 241, 275, 276, 284, 291, 305, 306, 323, 375, 633, 637, 640, 645, 658, 670, 675.
tip cleaners 307.
tip of nose 141.
tip protector 726.
tip section 670.
tip-ring 670, 671.
tipping lever 727.
tire 433.
tire 440, 447.
tire pump 446.
tire valve 447.
tissue holder 292.
Titan 5.
toad 85.
toaster 252.

tobacco 384.
tobacco hole 385.
tobacco pouch 385.
toe 104, 106, 111, 116, 118, 277, 325, 678.
toe binding 642.
toe box 644.
toe clip 104, 446, 448.
toe guard 730.
toe guard 595.
toe hole 645.
toe pick 644.
toe piece 633, 640.
toe piston 542.
toe strap 633.
toe-piece 641.
toenail scissors 365.
toeplate 642.
toga 315.
toggle 817.
toggle bolt 276.
toggle fastening 320.
toggles 650.
toilet 293.
toilet 215, 292, 461.
toilet bowl 293.
toilet tank 292.
tom-tom 552.
tomato 69.
tombolo 30.
tone arm 404.
tone control 547.
tone leader generator 407.
tongs 246.
tongue 81, 88, 131, 142, 323, 352, 354, 536, 542, 566, 641, 644.
tongue sheath 96.
tongue, dorsum 143.
tonsil 142.
tool 735.
tool holder 283.
tool shelf 302.
tool tether 512.
tooth 96, 158, 159, 160, 162, 268, 277, 284, 369, 785.
toothbrush 373.
toothbrush 373.
toothbrush shaft 373.
toothbrush well 373.
toothed jaw 278.
toothpaste 373.
top 59, 219, 302, 478.
top bar 659.
top coat 331.
top cylinder 581.
top deck 741.
top deckboard 787.
top edge 577.
top hat 328.
top ladder 781.
top lift 354.
top of dam 746, 748, 749, 752.
top plate 525.
top pocket 675.
top rail 202, 223, 225.
top rail of sash 203.
top road 736.
top stitched pleat 335.
top stitching 323, 350.
top-end transverse member 470.
topaz 362.
topmark 486, 488.
topping 670.
topping lift 478.
toque 329.
torpedo 807.
torpedo room 807.
torque converter 258.
torus 166, 167.
total 709.
total eclipse 8.
tote bag 380, 382.
tote board 651.
Toucan 13.
touch 136.
touch judge 606.
touch line 601.
touchline 606.
touring boot 642.
tourmaline 362.
tow bar 506.
tow bar 158, 159, 162, 449, 633.
tow line 633.
tow release knob 639.

The terms in **bold type** indicate the title of an illustration.

tow tractor 506, 507.
towel bar 292.
tower 176, 456, 486, 770, 771, 773, 774, 786.
tower crane 786.
tower ladder 781.
tower mast 786.
tower silo 149.
towing eye 803.
towing hitch 147, 449.
town houses 187.
trachea 130.
tracing wheel 563.
track 476, 651.
track 230, 445, 463, 474, 783.
track and field athletics 654, 656, 658.
track idler 783.
track lighting 235.
track link 805.
track number 405.
track roller frame 783.
track search keys 405.
track shoe 656, 805.
trackball 526.
tracker 543.
tractor 147.
tractor engine 784.
trade building 185.
trade name 384.
traditional houses 165.
traditional musical instruments 535, 536.
traffic circle 52, 450.
traffic island 184.
traffic lane 452.
traffic light 186.
tragus 112, 139.
trail 803.
trailer 449.
trailing edge 498, 636, 637, 638.
trailing edge flap 498, 812.
trainer 669.
training set 351.
training suit 352.
training wall 746.
trampoline 659.
transceiving dish 418.
transcription of seismic waves 714.
transducer 485.
transept 177.
transept spire 176.
transfer canal 764.
transfer dispensing machine 475.
transfer of heat to water 766.
transfer port 436.
transfer ramp 452.
transfer scale 396.
transform fault 28.
transformer 235, 747, 757, 758, 771.
transit shed 490.
transition fittings 301.
translation wave 30.
transmission 258.
transmission cable 485.
transmission dish 418.
transmission of the electrical current 714.
transmission/reception of messages 421.
transmitted pulse 722.
transmitter 420.
transmitting station 722.
transparency slide 397.
transpiration 35.
transporter bridge 457.
transverse colon 131.
transverse dunes 46.
transverse process 135.
trap 301.
trap 215, 293, 296.
trap coupling 296.
trapeze dress 332.
trapezius 120, 121.
traveler 630.
traveler 628.
traveling block 737.
traveling crane 747.
traverse arch 177.
traverse rod 230.
traversing handle 803.
tray 210, 226, 270, 304, 383.
tread 201, 433, 649.
tread bar 147.
tread design 433.
treadle 572.
treadle cord 572.
treatment plant 735.
treble 646.

treble bridge 540.
treble fishhook 672.
treble keyboard 536.
treble pickup 547.
treble register 536.
treble tone control 402.
tree 59.
tree 649.
tree frog 85.
tree pruner 269.
tree, structure 59.
tree, trunk 59.
trees 676.
trefoil 174.
trefoil 175.
trench 28, 733.
trench coat 319.
Triangle 11, 556.
triangle 554.
triangular bandage 725.
triangular body 535.
triangular fossa 139.
Triangulum 11.
Triangulum Australe 13.
triceps bar 663.
triceps of arm 121.
tricorne 318.
tricuspid valve 125.
trifoliolate 58.
trifoliolate leaf 58.
trigger 268, 304, 780, 793, 795, 796, 797, 798, 799, 804.
trigger guard 795, 797, 798, 799.
trigger switch 284.
triglyph 167.
trill 538.
trim 383.
trim panel 429.
trim ring 255.
trimmer 374.
trimming 578.
trimming 379.
trimming tool 563.
trio 558.
trip lever 264, 293.
trip odometer 431.
triple bars 647.
triple bars 646.
triple jump take-off board 654.
triple jump take-off line 654.
triple ring 698.
triple tail unit 498.
tripod 393.
tripod 397, 415, 539, 721.
tripod accessories shelf 721.
tripod stand 552.
tripod tail support 507.
Triton 5.
trochanter 78, 80.
trolley 457, 786.
trolley crank 265.
trolley pulley 786.
Trombe wall 772.
Trombe wall 772.
trombone 550.
trombones 556.
tropic of Cancer 3, 47.
tropic of Capricorn 3, 47.
tropical climates 45.
tropical fruits 68.
tropical fruits, major types 68.
tropical maritime 38.
tropical rain forest 45.
tropical savanna 45.
tropical storm 39.
troposphere 19.
trot 101.
trough 30, 38.
trousers 668.
trowel 268.
truck 476.
truck 468, 645.
truck crane 786.
truck frame 468.
truck tractor 440.
truck tractor 440.
truck trailer 440.
trucking 440.
truffle 55.
trumpet 550.
trumpet 550.
trumpet interchange 451.
trumpets 556.
trunk 383.
trunk 59, 61, 117, 119, 427.
trunk hose 316.
trunk, cross section 59.
trunks 662.
trunnion 800.
trussed arch 455.
tub 257, 258, 263.

tub platform 292.
tub rim 258.
tuba 551, 557.
tube 588.
tube 397, 710, 803, 804.
tube cutter 299.
tube end 300.
tube flaring tool 299.
tube retention clip 233.
tuber vegetables 71.
tubing 740.
tubing head 740.
tubing valve 740.
tubular bells 554.
tubular bells 556.
tubular element 255.
tubular heater 744.
tubular ice screw 681.
tubular lock 290.
tubular member 738.
tubular structure 487.
Tucana 13.
tuck 384.
tuck position 624.
Tudor 174.
tumble dry at low temperature 829.
tumble dry at medium to high temperature 829.
tuner 402.
tuner 400, 408.
tungsten filament 233.
tungsten-halogen lamp 233.
tunic 337.
tunic 791.
tunic dress 333.
tuning control 402, 408.
tuning controls 410.
tuning dial 408.
tuning fork 539.
tuning gauge 553.
tuning mode 402.
tuning peg 545, 547.
tuning pin 540.
tuning slide 551.
tuning wire 542.
tunnel 474.
turban 329.
turbine 753.
turbine 758.
turbine building 758.
turbine headcover 753.
turbine runner 752.
turbine shaft turns generator 767.
turbine stop valve 758.
turbine-compressor shaft 501.
turbo-alternator 771, 806.
turbo-compressor engine 438.
turbo-jet engine 812.
turbofan engine 501.
turbojet engine 499.
turkey 150.
turn 538.
turn and slip indicator 639.
turn and slip knob 639.
turn signal 429, 441, 442, 443, 444.
turn signal indicator 431, 445.
turnbuckle 630.
turnbuckle 669.
turner 244.
turning 584.
turning handle 280.
turning judge 621.
turning wall 621, 622.
turning wheel 584.
turnip 71.
turntable 404.
turntable 250, 400, 407, 457, 784, 785.
turntable mounting 780.
turpentine 592.
turquoise 362.
turret 180, 805, 809.
turret cap 718.
turtle 97.
turtle neck 642.
turtleneck 326, 342.
turtleneck 338.
tusks of elephant 99.
tusks of walrus 99.
tusks of wart hog 99.
tusks, major types 99.
TV mode 411.
TV power button 411.
TV/video button 411.
tweeter 16, 400.
tweezers 725.
25 ring 698.
25 yards line 606, 607.
twig 57, 59.

twill weave 576.
twin skis 633.
twin-lens reflex camera 394.
twin-set 338.
Twins 11.
twist bar 665.
twist dive 625.
twist drill 281.
twist grip throttle 444.
twisted rope 692.
two columns split bet 700.
two dozens split bet 701.
240-volt circuit 312.
240-volt feeder cable 312.
2 m line 626.
two pairs 695.
two-burner camp stove 689.
two-door sedan 425.
two-hand clean and jerk 662.
two-hand snatch 662.
two-hinged arch 455.
two-person tent 685.
two-sided copies 532.
two-stroke-cycle engine 436.
two-toed hoof 99.
two-two time 537.
two-way collar 319.
two-way traffic 824, 825.
tympanum 84, 97, 166, 168, 175.
type of fuel 453.
type of high cloud 38.
type of low cloud 38.
type of middle cloud 38.
type of the air mass 38.
types of heads 276.
types of passenger cars 460.
typist's chair 521.

U

U-bend 301.
U-shaped gouge 581.
UHF antenna 42.
ulna 102, 122.
ulnar extensor of wrist 121.
ulnar flexor of wrist 120, 121.
ulnar nerve 133.
ultraviolet spectrometer 43.
umbel 60.
umbo 95.
umbra shadow 8.
umbrella 375.
umbrella pine 58.
umbrella ring 679.
umbrella stand 375.
umlaut 832.
umpire 599, 603, 605, 611, 613, 614, 618.
under tail covert 109.
underarm crutch 728.
underarm portfolio 378.
underarm rest 728.
underground flow 32, 35.
underground mine 736.
underground passage 464.
underground stem 70.
underlining 565.
underlying fabrics 565.
underpass 454.
undershirt 595.
underwater camera 394.
underwear 325, 345, 346.
underwiring 347.
union 830.
union 300.
union nut 300.
union suit 325.
uniparous cyme 60.
unison 537.
unit price 709.
univalve shell 94.
universal step 507.
unleavened bread 153.
unloading tube 161.
uphaul 631.
upholstery nozzle 260.
upper 641.
upper blade guard 284.
upper bowl 247.
upper cheek 650.
upper chord 455.
upper cold front 39.
upper cuff 641.
upper deck 498.
upper edge 619.
upper eyelid 84, 107, 140.
upper fore topgallant sail 481.
upper fore topsail 481.
upper gate 493.
upper gill arch 87.

INDEX

upper girdle facet (16) 363.
upper laboratory 15.
upper lateral lobe 61.
upper lateral sinus 61.
upper level 493.
upper limb 793.
upper lip 81, 142, 542.
upper lobe 130.
upper mandible 109.
upper mantle 22.
upper shell 641, 645.
upper sphere clamp 40.
upper strap 641.
upper support screw 40.
upper tail covert 109.
upper warm front 39.
upperboard 543.
upperworks 630.
upright 573, 574, 578, 579, 657, 659, 660, 661, 728.
upright piano 540.
upright piano action 541.
upstage 188, 189.
upstream blanket 748.
upstream face 749.
upstream shoulder 748.
upstream toe 748.
Uranus 5.
urban map 52.
ureter 132.
urethra 128, 129, 132.
urinary bladder 89, 127, 128, 132.
urinary meatus 127.
urinary system 132.
urogenital aperture 89.
uropod 91.
Ursa Major 11.
Ursa Minor 11.
use chlorine bleach as directed 829.
utensils, set 244.
uterovesical pouch 128.
uterus 128, 129.
utility case 382.
utility liquids 592.
uvula 141, 142.

V

V-neck 322, 326.
V-neck cardigan 326.
V-neck cardigan 338.
V-shaped gouge 581.
V-shaped neck 322.
vacuole 115.
vacuum chamber 710, 717.
vacuum coffee maker 247.
vacuum diaphragm 435.
vacuum distillation 744.
vacuum manifold 717.
vacuum system console 717.
vagina 128, 129.
vair 819.
valance 224, 228.
valley 27.
valve 67, 95, 550.
valve casing 550.
valve seat 294.
valve seat shaft 293.
valve seat wrench 299.
valve spring 434.
vambrace 792.
vamp 353, 355.
vane 110, 259.
vanity cabinet 292.
vanity mirror 430.
vanity case 382.
vaporizer 210.
vaporizing grille 210.
variable geometry wing 499.
variable spacer 525.
variation keys 569.
variometer 635.
various dry fruits 67.
varnish 592.
varnish-roller 582.
Vauban fortification 178.
vault 177.
vaulting horse 659.
VCR controls 411.
VCR mode 411.
VCR power button 411.
vector/waveform monitor 413.
vegetable bowl 238.
vegetable brush 246.
vegetable garden 148, 193.
vegetable sponge 367.
vegetable steamer 249.
vegetables 69, 70, 71, 72, 73.
vegetables 33.

veil 670.
vein 56.
veins 126.
Vela 13.
Velcro® closure 349.
velum 80.
velvet-band choker 361.
Venetian blind 231.
venom canal 96.
venom gland 96.
venom-conducting tube 96.
venomous snake's head 96.
vent 214, 340, 800, 801.
vent brush 368.
vent door 441.
vent hole 304.
ventail 792.
ventilated rib 798.
ventilating circuit 215.
ventilating fan 469.
ventilating grille 260.
ventilation 772.
ventilation hood 486.
ventilator 477.
ventral aorta 88.
ventricular septum 125.
venturi 804.
venturi fastening lever 804.
Venus 4.
vermiform appendix 131.
vernal equinox 3, 8.
vernier 708.
vernier scale 484.
Versailles parquet 200.
vert 819.
vertebral body 135.
vertebral column 89, 122, 134.
vertebral shield 97.
vertical control 529.
vertical cord lift 256.
vertical frame 574.
vertical movement 696.
vertical pivoting window 203.
vertical pocket 316.
vertical pupil 96.
vertical shaft 736.
vertical side band 613.
vertical stabilizer 639.
vertical-axis wind turbine 774.
very cloudy sky 39.
vest 315, 322, 338.
vestibular nerve 139.
vestibule 139, 170, 461.
vestibule door 461.
VHF antenna 808.
viaduct 454.
vial 725.
vibrating mudscreen 737.
vibrato arm 547.
video camera 409.
video camera 526.
video cassette recorder 526.
video connection panel 415.
video entertainment system 699.
video monitor 529.
video monitor 526, 527.
video monitoring selector 413.
video port 528.
video switcher technician 412, 415.
videocassette recorder 411.
videocassette recorder 401.
videotape operation controls 409.
Vienna bread 153.
view camera 394.
viewfinder 399.
viewfinder adjustment keys 409.
vine shoot 61.
vine stock 61.
vine, maturing steps 61.
vinyl grip sole 350.
vinyl insulation 287.
viola 545.
violas 545.
violin 544.
violin 545.
violin family 545.
Virgin 11, 13.
Virgo 11, 13.
Virgo the Virgin(August 23) 820.
virgule 832.
vise 282.
vision slit 792.
visor 443, 471, 642, 730, 792.
visor hinge 443.
visual display 699.
visual display unit 421, 422.
visual transmission 717.
visualization of seismic waves 714.
vitelline membrane 109.
vitreous body 140.

vocal cord 130.
voice edit buttons 555.
voice selector 555.
Volans 13.
volcanic bombs 25.
volcanic island 28.
volcano 25.
volcano 23.
volcano during eruption 25.
volleyball 613.
volleyball, court 613.
volleyball, net 613.
voltage increase 767.
voltage tester 310.
volume control 402, 408, 411, 420, 422, 547, 555.
volume readout 453.
volume unit meters 407.
volute 166, 167, 220.
volva 55.
voussoir 174.
vulva 118, 128.

W

wad 799, 801.
waders 672.
wading bird 111.
waferboard 288.
waffle iron 253.
wagon 162.
wagon tent 686.
waist 117, 119, 354, 544, 756.
waistband 320, 323, 325.
waistband extension 323.
waistcoat 317.
walk 101.
walk-in 195.
walker 728.
walking aids 728.
walking leg 78.
walking stick 375.
walking stick 728.
wall 647.
wall 7, 65, 104, 646, 685.
wall and rails 647.
wall and rails 646.
wall bracket 230.
wall fitting 234.
wall lantern 235.
wall register 207.
wall stack section 206.
wall stud 199.
wall tent 686.
wallet 379.
wallet 523.
walnut 66.
walnut, section 66.
waning gibbous 7.
wapiti 105.
wardrobe 226.
wardrobe 195.
warhead 814.
warm air 772.
warm air outlet 438.
warm-air baffle 204.
warming plate 247.
warning device 777.
warning lights 431.
warning plate 280.
warning track 597.
warp 573, 574.
warp roller 573.
warp thread 576.
warping frame 575.
warty skin 85.
wash tower 257.
washer 258, 298.
washer 215, 294, 298.
washer nozzle 426.
washers 278.
washing 829.
wasp-waisted corset 347.
Wassily chair 221.
waste pipe 293.
waste stack 215.
waste tee 298.
Water Bearer 13.
water bottle 447.
water bottle clip 447.
water carrier 690.
water cools the used steam 767.
water goblet 237.
water hazard 676.
water hose 257, 734.
water inlet 295.
water intake 747.
water is pumped back into the steam generator 767.
water jump 647.

water jump 646.
water key 551.
water level 210, 247.
water main 772.
water meter 215.
water pitcher 238.
water polo 626.
water polo ball 626.
water polo, goal 626.
water polo, playing area 626.
water pressure gauge 778.
water separator 734.
water service pipe 215.
water signs 820.
water skiing 633.
water skiing handles, types 633.
water skiing skis, types 633.
Water Snake 11, 13.
water table 24.
water tank 210, 373, 469.
water tower 465.
water turns into steam 766.
water-heater tank 772.
water-level selector 258.
water-level tube 256.
water/alcohol 485.
watercolor and gouache 588.
watercress 73.
waterfall 27.
watering can 265.
waterline 487.
watermelon 69.
waterproof pants 349.
watt-hour meter 712.
watt-hour meter, mechanism 712.
wave 30.
wave base 30.
wave clip 369.
wave guide 415.
wave height 30.
wave length 30.
wave wall 748.
wax seal 293.
waxing gibbous 6.
weapons in the age of the Romans 791.
weather map 38.
weather radar 498.
weather satellite 42.
weatherboard 202, 203.
weaving 572, 574, 576.
weaving pattern brush 568.
weaving pattern lever 568.
weaving, accessories 573, 575.
web 84, 111, 466, 596.
webbed foot 84.
webbed toe 111.
webbing 428, 571, 634.
wedding ring 364.
wedge 542, 800.
wedge iron 277.
wedge lever 277.
weeder 268.
weeding hoe 266.
weekender 383.
weft 573, 574.
weft thread 576.
weighing platform 709.
weight 658, 665, 707, 708, 709.
weight belt 627.
weight stack exercise unit 663.
weight-driven clock mechanism 707.
weightlifter 662.
weightlifting 662.
weightlifting belt 662.
weightlifting shoe 662.
weights 663.
weld bead 307.
welding 305, 306, 308.
welding curtain 308.
welding torch 306.
welding torch 306, 307.
well flow line 738.
welt 322, 355.
welt pocket 339.
welt pocket 322, 326.
West 488.
West cardinal mark 489.
West Coast mirror 440.
Western hemisphere 47.
Western meridian 47.
wet suit 627.
wet well 763.
Whale 11, 13.
whale boat 482.
wheat 152.
wheat, grain 152.
wheel 433.

wheel 270, 383, 427, 440, 563, 583, 645, 684, 800, 805.
wheel chock 506.
wheel cover 427.
wheel cylinder 432.
wheel head 584.
wheel loader 782.
wheel tractor 782.
wheelbarrow 270.
wheelchair 727.
wheelchair 461.
whelk 83.
whipping 678.
whisk 245.
whiskers 107.
whistle 252.
White 696, 697.
white balance sensor 409.
white cabbage 73.
white cap 626.
white cue ball 673.
white flag 626.
white light 488.
white line 104.
white matter 135.
white spot ball 673.
white square 696.
white stone 697.
white tape 618, 619.
white wine glass 237.
white-tailed deer 105.
whole note 538.
whole rest 538.
whole wheat bread 153.
wholemeal bread 153.
whorl 83, 94.
wicker basket 635.
wicket 599.
wicket 599.
wicket gate 753.
wicketkeeper 599.
wide-angle lens 392.
wigwam 165.
willow 598.
winch 630.
wind 38.
wind 629.
wind abeam 629.
wind arrow 38.
wind chest 543.
wind chest table 543.
wind deflector 440.
wind direction 38.
wind direction and speed 38.
wind direction, measure 41.

wind duct 543.
wind energy 773, 774.
wind guard 634.
wind indicator 628.
wind instruments 548, 550.
wind sock 817.
wind speed 38.
wind strength, measure 41.
wind supply 543.
wind trunk 543.
wind vane 41.
windbag 536.
windbreaker 320.
winder 706.
winding adjustment 718.
winding mechanism 231, 707.
winding shaft 736.
winding tower 735.
windmill 773.
window 203.
window 194, 195, 253, 255, 379, 399, 427, 429, 477, 498, 631.
window accessories 228, 230.
window canopy 685.
window regulator handle 429.
window sill 198.
window tab 518.
windows 379.
windows, types 203.
windscreen 14, 406.
windshaft 773.
windshield 426, 440, 442, 445, 498, 500.
windshield wiper 431.
windshield wiper 426.
windshield wiper blade 431.
wine waiter corkscrew 244.
wing 316.
wing 78, 108, 499, 511, 637, 670, 812.
wing attack 611.
wing box 812.
wing covert 108.
wing defense 611.
wing membrane 112.
wing nut 279.
wing pallet 787.
wing rib 498.
wing shapes, types 499.
wing slat 499.
wing tip 638.
wing vein 79.
wing, bird 110.
Winged Horse 11.
winglet 499.

wings 112, 189, 638.
wings, bat 112.
winning line 702.
winter 8.
winter solstice 8.
winze 736.
wiper 431.
wiper arm 431.
wiper switch 430.
wire 641, 658, 714.
wire beater 250.
wire brush 553.
wire cutter 311.
wire sling 681.
wire stripper 311.
wire support 689.
wisdom tooth 144.
wishbone boom 631.
withers 100, 106.
wok 248.
wok set 248.
women's clothing 330, 332, 334, 336, 338, 340, 342, 344, 346, 348.
women's rest room 822.
wood 288, 677.
wood carving 586.
wood chip car 472.
wood chisel 275.
wood engraving 581.
wood flooring 200.
wood flooring 199.
wood flooring arrangements 200.
wood flooring on cement screed 200.
wood flooring on wooden structure 200.
wood ray 59.
wood, golf 678.
wood-based materials 288, 289.
woodbox 204.
woodcut 581.
wooden bar 661.
wooden modeling tools 585.
woods 52.
woodwind family 548.
woofer 16, 400.
word correction 525.
work lead 305.
worker, honeybee 80.
worker, honeybee 81.
working area 16.
working pressure gauge 306.
worm 801.
worm 575.
wraparound dress 333.

wraparound skirt 334.
wrapover top 337.
wrapper 384.
wrist 106, 112, 117, 119, 137.
wrist sling 681.
wrist strap 640, 642.
wrist-length glove 327.
wristband 602, 615.
write protect notch 529.
writing brush 389.
writing case 378.
writing instruments 389.

X

X-band antenna 49.
xylophone 554.
xylophone 556.

Y

Y-branch 301.
Y-tube 726.
yard 465.
yard 478.
yard line 604.
yarn 692.
yarn ball 596.
yarn clip 569.
yarn rod 569.
yarn feeder 569.
yarn tension unit 569.
yellow ball 673.
yellow onion 70.
yen 832.
yield 824, 825.
yoke 230, 320, 324, 337.
yoke skirt 334.
yolk 109.
yurt 165.

Z

zenith 16.
zenith S-band antenna 49.
zest 65.
zester 242.
zipper 566.
zipper 321, 350, 365, 382, 685.
zipper line 565.
zither 535.
zona pellucida 128.
zoom lens 392.
zoom lens 409, 414.
zucchini 69.
zygomatic bone 122.

The terms in **bold type** indicate the title of an illustration.